The Greenwood
Encyclopedia of Daily Life

1 THE ANCIENT WORLD

The Greenwood Encyclopedia of Daily Life

A Tour through History from Ancient Times to the Present

Joyce E. Salisbury
GENERAL EDITOR

Gregory S. Aldrete
VOLUME EDITOR

GREENWOOD PRESS
Westport, Connecticut • London

Library of Congress Cataloging-in-Publication Data

The Greenwood encyclopedia of daily life : a tour through history from ancient times to the
    present / Joyce E. Salisbury, general editor.
        p. cm.
        Includes bibliographical references and index.
        Contents: v. 1. The ancient world / Gregory S. Aldrete, volume editor; v. 2. The medieval
    world / Joyce E. Salisbury, volume editor; v. 3. 15th and 16th centuries / Lawrence Morris,
    volume editor; v. 4. 17th and 18th centuries / Peter Seelig, volume editor; v. 5. 19th
    century / Andrew E. Kersten, volume editor; v. 6. The modern world / Andrew E. Kersten,
    volume editor.
        ISBN 0–313–32541–3 (set: alk. paper) — ISBN 0–313–32542–1 (v. 1: alk. paper)
    — ISBN 0–313–32543–X (v. 2: alk. paper) — ISBN 0–313–32544–8 (v. 3: alk. paper)
    — ISBN 0–313–32545–6 (v. 4: alk. paper) — ISBN 0–313–32546–4 (v. 5: alk. paper)
    — ISBN 0–313–32547–2 (v. 6: alk. paper)
        1. Manners and customs—History—Encyclopedias. I. Salisbury, Joyce E.
    GT31.G74   2004
    390—dc21   2003054724

British Library Cataloguing in Publication Data is available.

An online version of *The Greenwood Encyclopedia of Daily Life* is available from
Greenwood Press, an imprint of Greenwood Publishing Group, Inc. at:
http://dailylife.greenwood.com (ISBN 0–313–01311–X).

Library of Congress Catalog Card Number: 2003054724
ISBN: 0–313–32541–3 (set)
        0–313–32542–1 (vol. 1)
        0–313–32543–X (vol. 2)
        0–313–32544–8 (vol. 3)
        0–313–32545–6 (vol. 4)
        0–313–32546–4 (vol. 5)
        0–313–32547–2 (vol. 6)

First published in 2004

Greenwood Press, 88 Post Road West, Westport, CT 06881
An imprint of Greenwood Publishing Group, Inc.
www.greenwood.com

Printed in the United States of America

The paper used in this book complies with the
Permanent Paper Standard issued by the National
Information Standards Organization (Z39.48–1984).

10   9   8   7   6   5   4   3   2   1

Everyday life consists of the little things one hardly notices in time and space. . . . Through the details, a society stands revealed. The ways people eat, dress, or lodge at the different levels of that society are never a matter of indifference.

~Fernand Braudel, *The Structures of Everyday Life*
(New York: Harper and Row, 1979), 29.

CONTENTS

Contents

TOUR GUIDE: A PREFACE FOR USERS

What did people, from the most ancient times to the most recent, eat, wear, and use? What did they hope, invent, and sing? What did they love, fear, or hate? These are the kinds of questions that anyone interested in history has to ask. We spend our lives preoccupied with food, shelter, families, neighbors, work, and play. Our activities rarely make the headlines. But it is by looking at people's everyday lives that we can truly understand history and how people lived. *The Greenwood Encyclopedia of Daily Life* brings into focus the vast majority of human beings whose existence is neglected by the standard reference works. Here you will meet the anonymous men and women of the past going about their everyday tasks and in the process creating the world that we know.

Organization and Content

The Greenwood Encyclopedia of Daily Life is designed for general readers without a background in the subject. Articles are accessible, engaging, and filled with information yet short enough to be read at one sitting. Each volume provides a general historical introduction and a chronology to give background to the articles. This is a reference work for the 21st century. Rather than taking a mechanical alphabetical approach, the encyclopedia tries something rather more elegant: it arranges material thematically, cascading from broad surveys down to narrower slices of information. Users are guided through this enormous amount of information not just by running heads on every page but also by "concept compasses" that appear in the margins: these are adapted from "concept mapping," a technique borrowed from online research methods. Readers can focus on a subject in depth, study it comparatively through time or across the globe, or find it synthesized in a way that provides an overarching viewpoint that draws connections among related areas—and they can do so in any order they choose. School curricula have been organizing research materials in this fashion for some time, so this encyclopedia will fit neatly into a modern pedagogical framework. We believe that this approach breaks new ground in the structuring of reference material. Here's how it works.

Level 1. The six volumes of the encyclopedia are, naturally, arranged by time period: the ancient world, the medieval world, 15th and 16th centuries, 17th and 18th centuries, the 19th century, and the modern world.

Level 2. Within each volume, information is arranged in seven broad categories, as shown in this concept compass:

DAILY LIFE

DOMESTIC LIFE

ECONOMIC LIFE

INTELLECTUAL LIFE

MATERIAL LIFE

POLITICAL LIFE

RECREATIONAL LIFE

RELIGIOUS LIFE

Level 3. Each of the introductory essays is followed by shorter articles on components of the subject. For example, "Material Life" includes sections on everything from the food we eat to the clothes we wear to the homes in which we live. Once again, each category is mapped conceptually so that readers can see the full range of items that make up "Material Life" and choose which ones they want to explore at any time. Each volume has slightly different categories at this level to reflect the period under discussion. For example, "eunuchs" appear under "Domestic Life" in volume 2 because they served a central role in many cultures at that time, but they disappear in subsequent volumes as they no longer served an important role in some households. Here is one example of the arrangement of the concepts at this level (drawn from the "Domestic Life" section of volume 1):

DOMESTIC LIFE

FAMILY LIFE

WOMEN

MARRIAGE

CHILDREN

SEXUALITY

Level 4. These conceptual categories are further subdivided into articles focusing on a variety of representative cultures around the world. For example, here users can read about "Children" in Egypt, Greece, medieval Europe, and 16th-century Latin America. Here is an example of a concept compass representing the entry on money in Ancient India:

ECONOMIC LIFE
|
MONEY
|
Mesopotamia

Egypt

Greece

Rome

India

The articles at each level can stand alone, but they all also offer integrated information. For example, readers interested in food in ancient Rome can focus right in on that information. If curious, they can look at the next conceptual level and learn how Roman food compares with that of other cultures at the same time, or they can see how food fits into material life in general by looking at the highest conceptual level. Readers may also decide to compare ancient Roman food with menus in Italy during the Renaissance; they need only follow the same process in another volume. Readers can begin at any of the levels and follow their interests in all directions: knowledge is linked conceptually in these volumes, as it is in life. The idea is to make it easy and fun to travel through time and across cultures.

This organization offers a number of advantages. Many reference works provide disparate bits of information, leaving it to the reader to make connections among them. More advanced reference tools assume that readers already have the details and include articles only on larger conceptual issues. *The Greenwood Encyclopedia of Daily Life* assumes no previous knowledge but recognizes that readers at all stages benefit from integrated analysis. The concept-mapping organization allows users to see both the details of the trees and the overall shape of the forest. To make finding information even easier, a cumulative subject index to the entire encyclopedia appears at the end of each volume. With the help of detailed running heads, concept compasses, and an index, anyone taking this "Tour through History" will find it almost impossible to get lost.

This encyclopedia is the work of many contributors. With the help of advisory boards, specialists in daily life around the world wrote the detailed articles in the "level 4" concept category. Many of these experts have published books in Greenwood's award-winning "Daily Life through History" series, and their contributions were crafted from those books. Each volume's editor wrote all of the many higher-level conceptual articles that draw connections across the topics, thus providing a consistent voice and analysis throughout the volume.

Coverage

The chronological coverage of this encyclopedia is consistent with the traditional organization of history as it is taught: the six volumes each take on one of the standard periods. But in reality, history is messy, and any strictly chronological organization has flaws. Some societies span centuries with little change, whereas others change rapidly (usually because of cross-cultural interactions). We have addressed these questions of change and continuity in two ways. Sometimes, we introduce cultures in one volume, such as the Australian Aborigines in volume 1, and then we do not mention them again until they were transformed by colonial contact in volume 4. In these entries, readers are led by cross-references to follow the story of the Australian indigenous peoples from one volume to another. At other times, cultures have experienced enough change for us to introduce many new entries. For example, volume 5, devoted to the 19th century, includes many entries on Muslim lands. But some aspects of the 19th-century Muslim world (e.g., education) had long remained largely unchanged, and in these instances readers are led by cross-references to entries in earlier volumes. This network of cross-references highlights connections and introduces users to the complexities of change and continuity that form the pattern of the social fabric.

We also depart from the chronological constraints of each volume when describing cultures that left few written records. Borrowing from anthropological methods, we sometimes (cautiously) use evidence from later periods to fill in our understanding of earlier lives. For example, colonial observers have at times informed our description of earlier indigenous cultures in many parts of the world.

The geographic scope of this encyclopedia reflects the relatively recent recognition that culture has always operated in a global context. In the Stone Age, bloodstone from Rhum, an inaccessible island off the stormy coast of Scotland, was traded throughout Europe. Domesticated plants and animals from Mesopotamia spread to Africa through Nubia in the third millennium B.C.E., and throughout the ancient world the trade between China and the Mediterranean was an essential part of life. Global history is woven throughout these volumes.

We do not attempt to document every one of the thousands of societies that have arisen throughout history and around the world. Our aim—to provide a general reference source on everyday life—has led to a careful focus on the most studied and representative cultures of each period. For example, ancient India is introduced in volume 1 and then reappears in the complexities of a global society in volumes 5 and 6. Nubia, the path from Egypt to sub-Saharan Africa, is introduced in volume 1, but the range of African cultures is addressed in depth in volume 4 and again in volume 6. Muslim cultures are introduced in volume 2 with the birth of the Prophet, reappearing in volume 3 with the invigorated society of the Turks and then again in volumes 5 and 6 with modern Muslim states. This approach draws from archaeological methods: we are taking deep samples of cultures at various points in time. The overall picture derived from these samples offers a global perspective that is rich and comprehensive. We have covered every area of the world from Australia and the South Pacific to Viking Scandinavia, from indigenous cultures to colonial ones, from age-old Chinese civilization to the modern United States.

Another issue is that of diversity within some dizzyingly complex regions. Africa, China, Polynesia, and India, for example, all contain many cultures and peoples whose daily life is strikingly diverse. Rather than attempt exhaustiveness, we indicate the range of diversity within each entry itself. For instance, the many entries on Africa in volume 4 recognize that each society—Yoruba, Swahili, Shona, and all the others—is unique, and each entry focuses on the cultures that best represent trends in the region as a whole.

The United States is yet another complex region. It grew from its inception with a mingling of European, Native American, African, and other cultural groups. Instead of treating each individually, we combine them all within the entries on the United States. For example, as volume 4 discusses Colonial New England, it weaves a description of Native American life within the entries showing the full range of social interaction between native peoples and colonists. This organization recognizes the reality that all these groups grew together to become the United States.

Features

This work has been designed by educators, and pedagogical tools help readers get the most out of the material. In addition to the reader-friendly organization already described, we have added the following special features:

- *Concept compasses*. Each section of each volume contains a concept compass that visually details the contents of that section. Readers are immediately able to see what topics are covered and can decide which ones they want to explore.
- *Illustrations*. The illustrations drawn from primary sources are in themselves historical evidence and are not mere ornament. Each shows some aspect of daily life discussed in the text, and the captions tell what the picture illuminates and what readers can see in it.
- *Maps*. Maps give readers the necessary geographic orientation for the text. They have been chosen to reinforce the global perspective of the encyclopedia, and readers are consistently offered the view of the parts of the world under discussion.
- *Chronologies*. In addition to geography, students can quickly lose track of the chronology of events. Each volume offers a list of the major events of the periods and of the cultures covered in the volumes. These chronologies serve as a quick reference that supplements the historical introduction.
- *Snapshots*. The fascinating details of the past engage our curiosity. Each volume is scattered with boxed features that highlight such evidence of past life as a recipe, a song, a prayer, an anecdote, or a statistic. These bits of information enhance the main entries; readers can begin with the snapshot and move to more in-depth knowledge or end with the details that are often designed to bring a smile or a shocked insight.
- *Cross-references*. Traditional brief references point readers to related entries in other volumes, highlighting the changes in daily life over time. Other "See" references replace entries and show readers where to find the information they seek within the volume.
- *Primary documents*. The encyclopedia entries are written to engage readers, but nothing brings the past to life like a primary source. Each volume offers a selection of documents that illustrate the kinds of information that historians use to re-create daily life. Sources range widely, from the unforgettable description of Vikings blowing their noses in a water basin before they wash their faces in it to a ration book issued by the United States government during World War II.

- *Bibliography.* Most entries are followed by a section called "For More Information." These sections include recommended readings, as one might expect in a bibliographic attachment, but they often provide much more. For this media age, the authors recommend Web sites, films, educational videos, and other resources.
- *Index.* Even in the 21st century, a comprehensive index is essential. Concept compasses lead readers from one topic to the next, but an index draws connections among more disparate entries: for example, the history of the use of wine or cotton can be traced across many volumes and cultures. A cumulative index appears in each volume to allow fast and easy navigation.

The Greenwood Encyclopedia of Daily Life: A Tour through History from Ancient Times to the Present has been a labor of love. At the end of the day, we hope that readers will be informed and entertained. But we also hope that they will come to a renewed appreciation of an often-spoken but seldom-felt reality: at the most basic level all humans, across time and space, share concerns, pleasures, and aspirations, but the ways these are expressed are infinite in their range. The six volumes of this encyclopedia reveal both the deep similarities and the fascinating differences among people all over the world. We can participate in our global village more intelligently the more we understand each other's lives. We have also learned that people are shown at their best (and sometimes their worst) in the day-to-day activities that reveal our humanity. We hope readers enjoy taking this tour of people's lives as much as we have enjoyed presenting it.

~*Joyce E. Salisbury*

Acknowledgments

I would like to thank the editorial staff at Greenwood Press, whose useful comments and prompt replies made the editing process both productive and enjoyable. Joyce E. Salisbury, the editor of this series, was a model of efficiency and a pleasure to collaborate with. Finally, my deepest thanks and appreciation are due to my wife, Alicia, who made invaluable contributions to this project at every stage, from research to writing to editing.

~*Gregory S. Aldrete*

1

HISTORICAL OVERVIEW

Ancient Mesopotamian History

The flat landscape of central Mesopotamia, the land between the Tigris and Euphrates Rivers, allowed the growth of large political empires because there were few geographic boundaries to inhibit conquerors. Although subject to dangerous floods, this land was also highly fertile, and by the late Neolithic period it was being intensely farmed. The resultant concentration of population and agricultural surpluses naturally led to the establishment of the earliest cities and labor specialization. By about 3200 B.C.E., the city of Uruk had a substantial population, and some sort of centralized government was forming.

Out of this background, Sumerian civilization (ca. 3100–2350 B.C.E.) emerged in southern Mesopotamia. The Sumerians had sizable city-states, built large temples, and developed the first known writing. Scribes pressed sticks into clay tablets to produce at first symbols for objects called pictograms and later a more complex system of signs called cuneiform. Officials used cylinder seals with carvings that were rolled onto clay tablets as a way to "sign" documents. The classic temple form that developed was a step pyramid shape called a ziggurat, which would remain in use in Mesopotamia for thousands of years.

About 2300 B.C.E., a man named Sargon from the city of Akkad became the first great Mesopotamian conqueror when he united the entire region under his rule by military force and established the Akkadian Dynasty (2350–2193 B.C.E.). After the fall of the Akkadians, several hundred years of confusion followed, with various city-states rising to prominence and then falling to rivals.

By 1900 B.C.E, the city of Babylon had emerged as one of the largest and most powerful cities, and it became especially significant under the rule of King Hammurabi (1792–1750 B.C.E.). Hammurabi established Babylon as a seat of power and is perhaps best known today for the law code that bears his name. Although harsh in its punishments and unequal in its justice, this earliest known law code represents an important step forward for civilization because it offered a way to mediate disputes

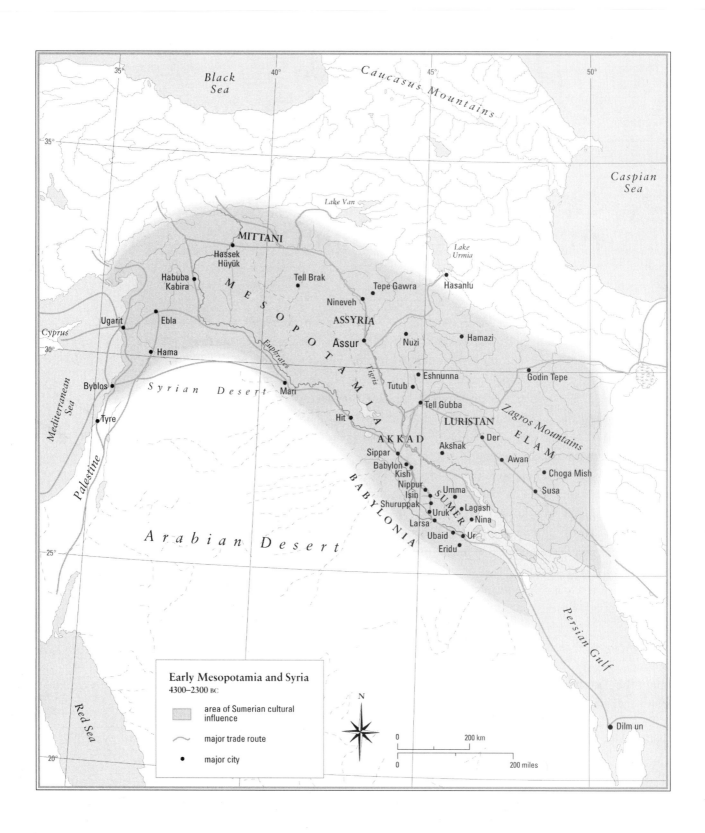

Early Mesopotamia and Syria
4300–2300 BC

- area of Sumerian cultural influence
- major trade route
- • major city

Black Sea

Caucasus Mountains

Caspian Sea

Lake Van

MITTANI

Hassek
Hüyük

Habuba
Kabira

Tell Brak

Tepe Gawra

Lake Urmia

Hasanlu

Nineveh

ASSYRIA

Ugarit

Ebla

Cyprus

Assur

Nuzi

Hamazi

Mediterranean Sea

Hama

Eshnunna

Godin Tepe

Byblos

Syrian Desert

Mari

Tutub

Tell Gubba

Zagros Mountains

Tyre

Hit

LURISTAN

ELAM

Palestine

AKKAD

Akshak

Der

Awan

Sippar

Babylon

Kish

Choga Mish

Nippur

Umma

Susa

Isin

SUMER

Lagash

Shuruppak

Uruk

Nina

BABYLONIA

Larsa

Ubaid

Ur

Eridu

Arabian Desert

Red Sea

N

Persian Gulf

Dilm un

0   200 km

0   200 miles

Euphrates

Tigris

MESOPOTAMIA

and provide the stability and protections necessary if large numbers of people were to live together in urban centers. Another important civilization was developing around this time in northern Mesopotamia—the Assyrians, based around the city-state of Assur.

Throughout the second millennium B.C.E., the Babylonians, Assyrians, and others, such as the Elamites, Hittites, and Kassites, vied for control in Mesopotamia. Historians have divided this politically turbulent time into various eras, such as the Old (1900–1595 B.C.E.) and Middle (1595–1000 B.C.E.) Babylonian periods, or the Old (1900–1750 B.C.E.) and Middle (1300–1100 B.C.E.) Assyrian periods, but the truly dominant Mesopotamian empires did not clearly emerge until the first millennium B.C.E.

About 1000 B.C.E., the highly militarized Assyrians began a series of successful campaigns that would eventually lead to the establishment of the Assyrian Empire. Ruthless military campaigns were followed by massive deportations of conquered peoples. A sequence of energetic warrior-kings such as Assurnasirpal II, who also founded a new capital city of Nimrud, led the Assyrian armies to victories over their enemies. Assyria's supremacy is reflected in the many stone carvings depicting Assyrian monarchs mounted in war chariots hunting down lions. Ultimately, Assyria extended its domination as far as Egypt, and yet another spectacular new capital was constructed at Ninevah. By the end of the seventh century B.C.E., however, Assyria's foes had multiplied, and revolutions and civil war led to the collapse of the empire in 612 B.C.E.

Meanwhile, Babylon had also been reemerging as a force, and the Neo-Babylonian Empire (1000–539 B.C.E.) witnessed some great cultural and architectural achievements, including the investigations of Chaldean astronomers and the construction of the famous walls and gardens of Babylon.

In 538 B.C.E., the Persian Empire arose and swiftly supplanted the previous Mesopotamian empires. Persia grew and expanded until it became the most powerful ancient civilization of its time, stretching far beyond the bounds of Mesopotamia, from the coast of Asia Minor in the east nearly to India in the west. Persia, including Mesopotamia, was eventually conquered by Alexander the Great in 331 B.C.E.

~Gregory S. Aldrete

Ancient Egyptian History

Egyptian culture and history are heavily influenced by the country's unique geography. Egypt is bordered on three sides by blisteringly hot, nearly uninhabitable desert and on the fourth by the Mediterranean Sea. The Nile River flows northward into the sea and with great predictability floods every year, leaving behind rich, fertile soil. Thus Egypt was fortunate to have abundant agricultural potential as well as natural barriers against invasion.

The history of Egypt as a country really begins about 3000 B.C.E., when a man named Narmer managed, for the first time, to unite both the upper and lower regions of Egypt. He thus became the first pharaoh and according to legend, also established the capital city of Memphis at the juncture between the two halves of the land. About this time, the key Egyptian concepts concerning the pharaoh as a god and the belief in resurrection after death began to develop. Toward the end of this Early Dynastic period (ca. 3150–2686 B.C.E.), the first step pyramid was constructed for the pharaoh Zoser.

With the initiation of the great pyramid-building era, the Old Kingdom (2686–2181 B.C.E.) got under way. This was the time when the huge pyramids of Giza were erected, and in general it was a very prosperous time for Egypt, when the country was peaceful and productive. The land seemed blessed by the gods, and during this time, many great art works and construction projects were created. Eventually, however, the power of the central government gradually eroded, local officials amassed privileges and authority, and the land finally fell into a state of anarchy. This period, known as the First Intermediate period (2181–2041 B.C.E.), lasted until another strong military leader emerged to unite the upper and lower regions together once again and reestablish central authority.

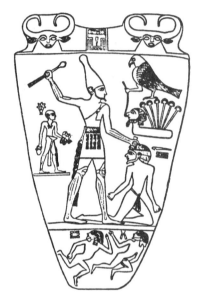 

The Narmer Palette. Narmer, the first man to unite Upper and Lower Egypt, is shown with upraised mace about to strike a kneeling captive.

On the surface, the subsequent Middle Kingdom (2040–1782 B.C.E.) closely resembled the Old Kingdom. The land was united and at peace, and the pharaohs once again began constructing giant pyramids. There was, however, an undercurrent of unease that tainted the placid surface of the Middle Kingdom. The country had fallen apart once, and so everyone was aware it might happen again. This attitude can be seen in the letters of advice that survive, written by a pharaoh to his son, cautioning against trusting anyone. The pyramids of this time offer another apt metaphor; they were still covered with fine stone on the exterior, but unlike the solid-rock pyramids of the Old Kingdom, those of the Middle Kingdom had cores of mud brick.

The collapse of the Middle Kingdom was precipitated by the appearance for the first time of foreign invaders from the Mediterranean, a mysterious people called the Hyksos, who conquered Lower Egypt. The Second Intermediate period (1782–1570 B.C.E.) followed and eventually ended when, for a third time, a powerful warrior united the country and drove out the invaders.

The subsequent New Kingdom (1570–1070 B.C.E.) was an era characterized by Egypt becoming an imperial power and conquering lands beyond its traditional borders. These expeditions also brought great wealth back to Egypt, and the phar-

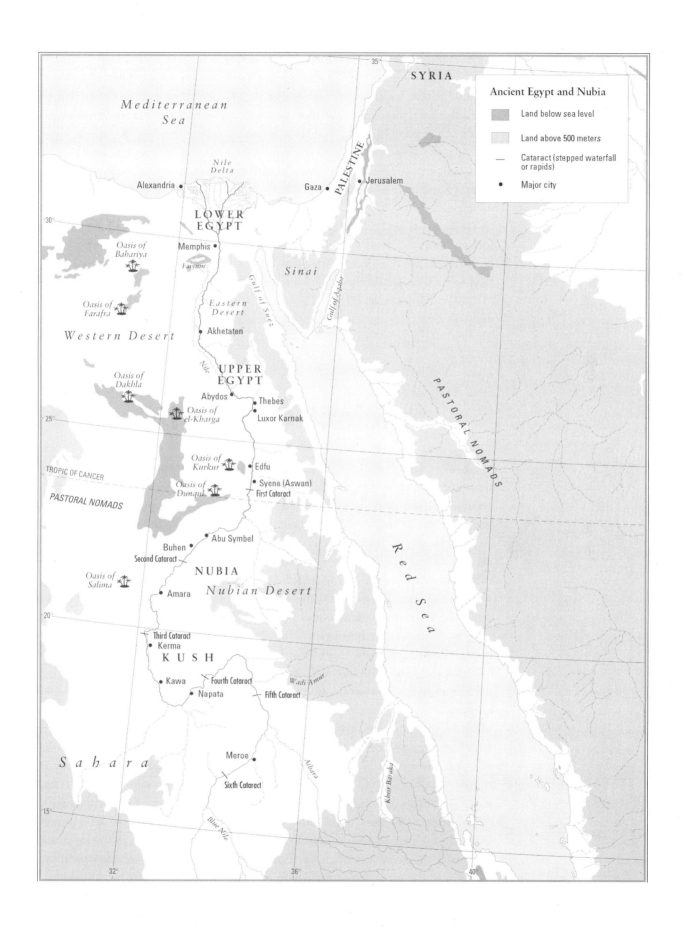

Ancient Egypt and Nubia

Land below sea level

Land above 500 meters

Cataract (stepped waterfall or rapids)

Major city

SYRIA

Mediterranean Sea

Nile Delta

Alexandria

Gaza   Jerusalem

PALESTINE

LOWER EGYPT

Oasis of Bahariya

Memphis

Fayum

Sinai

Gulf of Suez

Gulf of Aqaba

Oasis of Farafra

Eastern Desert

Western Desert

Akhetaten

Nile

UPPER EGYPT

Oasis of Dakhla

Abydos   Thebes

Oasis of el-Kharga

Luxor Karnak

TROPIC OF CANCER

Oasis of Kurkur

Edfu

PASTORAL NOMADS

Oasis of Dunqul

Syene (Aswan)
First Cataract

Abu Symbel

Buhen

Second Cataract

PASTORAL NOMADS

Red Sea

Oasis of Salima

NUBIA

Nubian Desert

Amara

Third Cataract

Kerma

KUSH

Kawa   Fourth Cataract   Wadi Amur

Napata   Fifth Cataract

Sahara

Meroe

Atbara

Sixth Cataract

Khor Baraka

Blue Nile

aohs of the New Kingdom amassed great stores of gold and other treasures. The New Kingdom also marked a change in the way pharaohs were buried since all the pyramid tombs had been looted during the Intermediate periods. In an attempt to avoid this fate, pharaohs now adopted a strategy of hiding their tombs underground. Many of the pharaohs best known today ruled during the New Kingdom, including Akhenaton, who attempted to institute a monotheistic religion, Ramses the Great, who built many elaborate temples, and Tutankhamen, who, although an insignificant pharaoh, is the only one whose tomb escaped looting in the subsequent centuries.

The Late period (1069–332 B.C.E.) was one of general decline and frequent foreign domination. It ended with the conquest of Egypt by the Macedonian general, Alexander the Great. After the death of Alexander, one of his generals seized Egypt and established the Ptolemaic dynasty of kings, which endured until the last of the Ptolemies, Cleopatra, allied herself with the losing side in a Roman civil war and Egypt was taken over by the Romans in 30 B.C.E.

~*Gregory S. Aldrete*

Ancient Greek History

Classical Greek civilization traced itself back to a dimly remembered older culture that existed on the mainland of Greece roughly from 1600 to 1100 B.C.E. This civilization is known as the Mycenaens after one of the larger cities. The later epic poems of Homer are set in Mycenaen times and tell the story of a united expedition against the city of Troy on the coast of Asia Minor. Mycenaen civilization collapsed about 1100 B.C.E. for reasons that remain ambiguous, and Greece entered a period called the Dark Ages, during which populations declined, trade diminished, cities were abandoned, and even writing was forgotten. After several hundred years, these trends reversed dramatically, and by the end of the eighth century B.C.E., populations were rapidly increasing, writing was rediscovered, the Homeric poems were written down, and even the Olympic games had been established.

The geography of Greece is extremely mountainous, which encouraged the development of numerous small independent city-states rather than a single monolithic government. Although politically separate, the Greek city-states shared similar culture. In the next centuries, these states began minting coins, established pan-Greek religious sanctuaries such as the Delphic Oracle, and developed a new and brutally effective style of warfare based on the heavy infantryman, the hoplite. The growing population strained available resources, and the Greek city-states solved this problem by sending out groups of citizens to found new overseas colonies. The Era of Colonization (ca. 700–600 B.C.E.) saw the Greeks establish colonies all around the Mediterranean basin, from the Black Sea region to the southern coast of modern France. The notable exception to this policy was the city of Sparta, which solved its land problem by conquering and enslaving the neighboring Messenians. This event ended up warping Spartan society as it refashioned its entire social system with the obsessive goal of producing the best and toughest hoplites to keep the Messenians dominated.

During the period from approximately 600 B.C.E. to 490 B.C.E., known as the Archaic period, the Greek cities (except Sparta) continued to develop and often went through a stage when they were ruled by tyrants. The largest city-state was Athens, and after expelling its tyrants, the Athenians began to experiment with democratic forms of government. Two reformers, Solon in 594 B.C.E. and Cleisthenes in 507 B.C.E., helped shape the emerging form of Athenian democracy.

The Classical period (490–323 B.C.E.) began with a pivotal event in 490 B.C.E. when Persia, the unchallenged superpower of the time, invaded Greece. Against

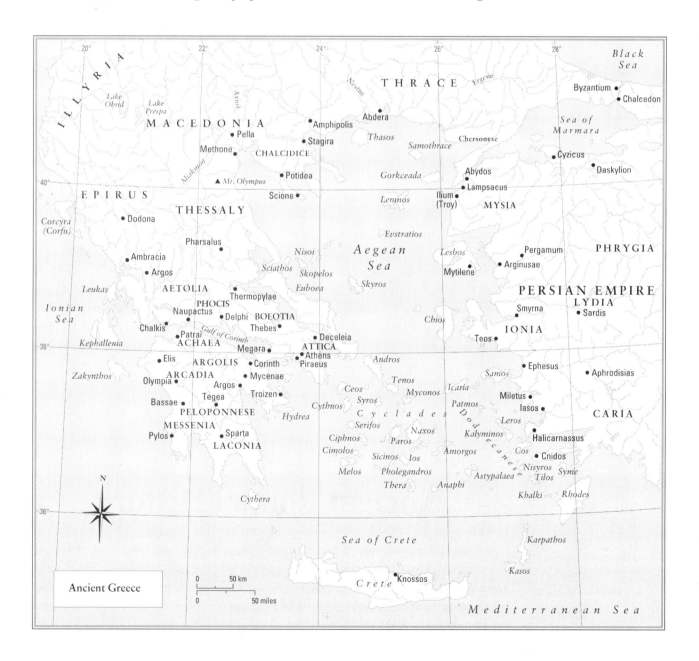

Ancient Greece

all expectations, the heavily outnumbered Greeks stopped the Persian advance at the battle of Marathon. In 480 B.C.E., an even larger Persian invasion was again defeated with equally stunning victories at Salamis and Platea. The Greeks emerged from these experiences with a new sense of their own potential.

Athens, which had played a leading role in resisting Persia, became the dominant city-state and gradually asserted political hegemony over many of the other Greeks, establishing an Athenian Empire. During this period, Athenian democracy achieved its most radical form, and with heavy Athenian patronage of the arts, many of the finest achievements in Greek architecture, sculpture, and theater were produced.

Resentment at Athenian dominance led to the creation of an opposing coalition of states centered around Sparta. After several decades of a kind of cold war atmosphere of hostility, war broke out in 431 B.C.E. between the Athenian Empire and the Spartan-led Peloponnesian league. The resultant Peloponnesian War was destructive to both sides and ended with Athens's defeat in 404 B.C.E.

For the next half century, various Greek city-states vied without great success to dominate the Greek world. Meanwhile, to the north of Greece in the kingdom of Macedonia, the energetic king, Philip II, was forging a powerful new military force. In 338 B.C.E., he swept into Greece, and although the Greek city-states banded together to oppose him, they were decisively defeated at the battle of Chaeronea. Shortly afterward, Philip was assassinated, but his teenage son, Alexander, took his place. Alexander was both a military commander of genius and a fervent admirer of Greek culture, and he determined to lead an expedition against Persia, ostensibly as revenge for the Persian invasions of Greece. In 15 years of brilliant campaigning, Alexander conquered the entire Persian Empire and even penetrated into northern India.

With Alexander's premature death in 323 B.C.E., the Hellenistic era (323–30 B.C.E.) began, during which Alexander's generals and their successors fought a seemingly endless series of wars over the pieces of Alexander's now-fragmented empire. This period came to an end with the arrival on the scene of a new dominant military force, the Romans, who by 30 B.C.E. had brought the Greek world firmly under their control.

~Gregory S. Aldrete

Ancient Roman History

Roman history falls into three distinct periods, designated by the form of government in use during each time: the Monarchy, the Republic, and the Empire. According to Roman tradition, the city of Rome was founded in 753 B.C.E. by Romulus and Remus, twin offspring of the god Mars. Romulus promptly murdered his brother to become the first king of Rome. For most of the subsequent Monarchy

(753–509 B.C.E.), Rome was simply one of hundreds of small city-states in Italy, often under the control of more powerful neighbors such as the Etruscans. In 509 B.C.E., there was a revolution, the last Etruscan king was expelled from Rome, and the Roman Republic (509–31 B.C.E.) was established.

Over the next several hundred years, Rome began a gradual process of military expansion into the rest of Italy. This was a time of nearly constant warfare, and although the Romans were not superior to their enemies in technology or tactics, they practiced a unique policy in treating conquered cities. Rather than destroying them and enslaving the populace, the Romans granted full or, more commonly, partial citizenship to the captured people and demanded in return that they contribute troops to the Roman army. This gave Rome enormous manpower reserves on which to draw; many future wars would be won by a combination of determination and manpower. Over this same time period, the Roman constitution developed, with a system of annually elected magistrates, a legal code, and a kind of balance of powers among different organs of the state.

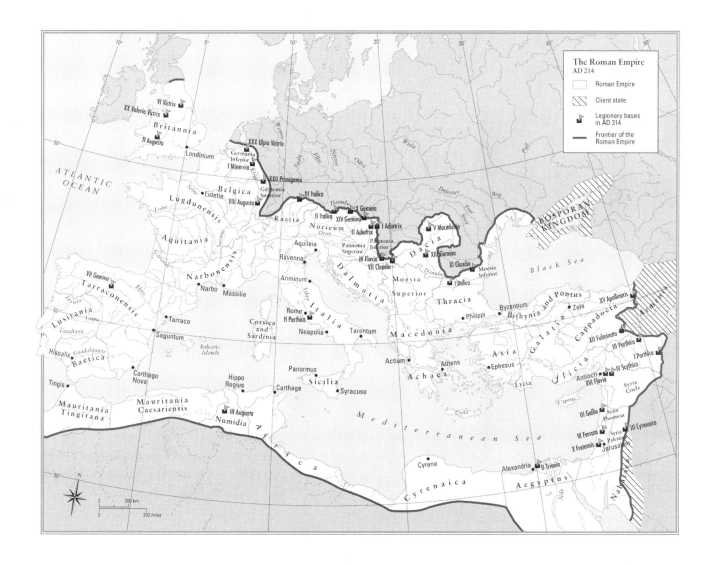

By the middle of the third century B.C.E., Roman consolidation of Italy was largely complete, and Rome soon became embroiled, whether by accident or design, in a series of wars with overseas enemies. The most significant of these were the Punic Wars, fought against another young expanding empire in the western Mediterranean, the North African city of Carthage. In the Second Punic War (218–201 B.C.E.), Rome was brought to the verge of defeat by the brilliant Carthaginian general Hannibal, who with his army successfully crossed the supposedly impassable Alps and inflicted three crushing defeats on the Romans in battles in which more than 100,000 Romans were killed. Most of the Italians stayed loyal to Rome, however, and drawing on their manpower reserves, the Romans eventually outlasted Hannibal and won the war.

After passing through the crucible of the Second Punic War, Rome's armies were highly professionalized and in the next couple of hundred years conquered nearly the entire Mediterranean basin, including the rich, highly cultured world of the Greek east. No longer did Rome share citizenship so freely, but these overseas areas were organized as tax-paying provinces. Rome's very overseas success, however, began to create internal tensions as individual generals began to amass too much power and prestige, poor Romans lost their farms and fell into debt, the old Italian allies and half-citizens became resentful, and a government system developed to rule a city was strained by having to manage an empire.

These tensions exploded during the Late Republic (133–31 B.C.E.), when a sequence of bloody civil wars wracked the Roman world and a succession of ever-more-daring strong men made bids to dominate the state. This process culminated in the civil war between Julius Caesar and Pompey the Great. Following his victory, Caesar established himself as dictator for life. His kinglike behavior soon led to his assassination by the senate on the ides of March, 44 B.C.E., and his death touched off a final round of civil wars that ultimately were won by Caesar's adopted son, Octavian, in 31 B.C.E.

Octavian, who was remarkably adept at what today would be termed image making and political propaganda, established himself as the dominant figure at Rome. Now called Augustus, he became emperor and ushered in the final era of Roman history, the Roman Empire. Despite occasional eccentric or insane emperors, such as Nero, for the next 200 years, the Roman Empire enjoyed relative stability and prosperity.

In the third century C.E., barbarian invasions, economic crises, and political instability led to a time of crisis, and complete collapse was only narrowly averted. In 312 C.E., Constantine became the first emperor to convert to Christianity, and soon after, the empire split permanently into eastern and western halves. The western half staggered along for another century or so but eventually fragmented into numerous barbarian kingdoms. The Eastern (Byzantine) Roman Empire, with its capital at Constantinople, continued to exist for many centuries, finally falling to the Ottoman Turks in 1453.

Marble portrait bust of Julius Caesar. Caesar's generalship won him domination over the Roman state, but his arrogant behavior resulted in his assassination. © The Art Archive/Museo della Civilta Romana Rome/Dagli Orti.

~Gregory S. Aldrete

Ancient Indian History

The Indian subcontinent comprises an area roughly equivalent in size to Europe, bounded by the Indian Ocean to the south and high mountain ranges, including the Himalayas, to the north. The northern plain features the great river systems of the Ganges and the Indus Rivers, and it was along the Indus River that the earliest civilization in India emerged about the middle of the third millennium B.C.E. This so-called Indus Valley civilization (2500–1500 B.C.E.) remains somewhat mysterious because its writing has not been deciphered. Its people did leave evidence of the impressive size and sophistication of their civilization through the ruins of the enormous cities they constructed, such as Harappa and Mohenjo-Daro, with estimated ancient populations in the tens of thousands. The Indus Valley civilization was based on intensive agriculture, which supported large urban centers.

About 1500 B.C.E., a group of Indo-Europeans called the Aryans began to migrate into India from the north, bringing with them the Sanskrit language. The Aryans gradually displaced or assimilated with the indigenous Dravidian peoples. In the religion of the Aryans, the Brahmins (priests) sang hymns to the gods to accompany sacrifices. A collection of 1,028 such hymns, known as the *Rig Veda*, was eventually written down and constitutes the oldest piece of Indo-European literature to survive until the present. The material culture of the Vedic/Aryan era (1500–500 B.C.E.) was less urban than that of the Indus Valley civilization. Over time, a strict class structure developed, and the power of the Brahmans and the importance of ritual itself increased, as reflected in a series of texts called the *Brahmanas*.

The late Vedic or Brahmanic era ended with a dramatic religious and cultural challenge to the existing system. The Upanishad thinkers posited a new emphasis in religion that shifted away from ritual and toward the self's attainment of knowledge. This included a concept of existence as a repeating cycle of life and death in which the morality of one's actions carry over from one life to the next. In addition to the challenges posed by the Upanishads, two new religions appeared about the fifth century B.C.E., building on these concepts and further emphasizing asceticism, monasticism, and nonviolence. Vardhamana Mahavira established Jainism, and Siddhartha Gautama, later known as the Buddha, founded Buddhism.

In 326 B.C.E., the Macedonian king, Alexander the Great, appeared in northern India and defeated the local rulers. His further conquests in India were forestalled, however, when his weary army mutinied and demanded to return to the Mediterranean. Shortly afterward, a new Indian power arose when Chandragupta Maurya united northern India by military force and founded the Mauryan Dynasty (321–ca. 185 B.C.E.). He and his descendants forged an empire that encompassed nearly the whole of India. The most famous of these rulers, Asoka, was horrified by the brutality of the first campaign he directed, which caused him to convert to Buddhism, espouse nonviolence, and become a vegetarian.

The next several hundred years were politically confused, with various foreign powers, among them, Greek, Bactrian, and Kushan, establishing brief hegemonies.

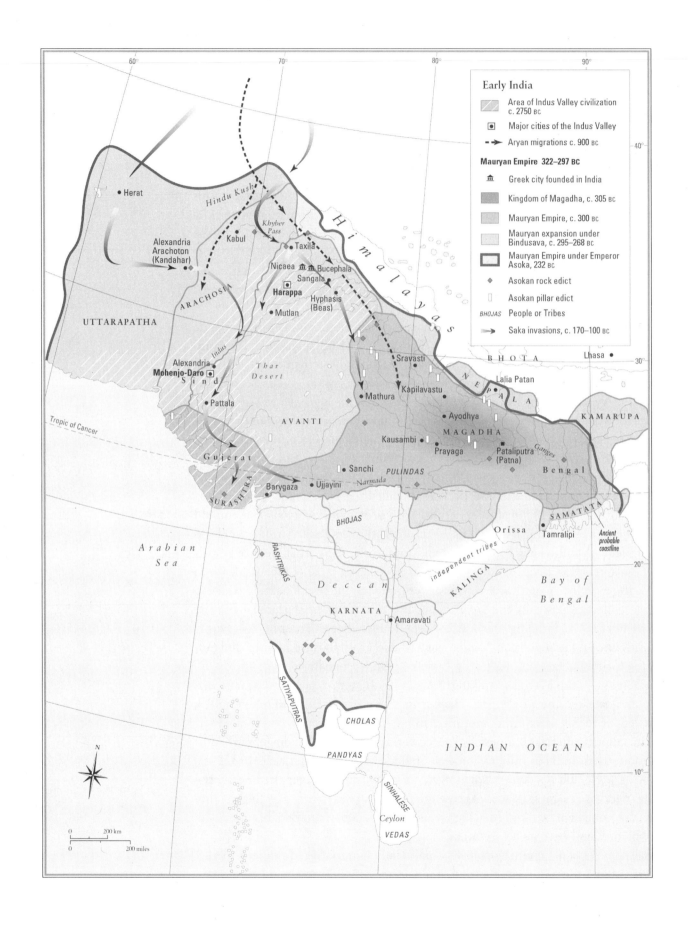

Early India

	Area of Indus Valley civilization c. 2750 BC
	Major cities of the Indus Valley
	Aryan migrations c. 900 BC

Mauryan Empire 322–297 BC

🏛	Greek city founded in India
	Kingdom of Magadha, c. 305 BC
	Mauryan Empire, c. 300 BC
	Mauryan expansion under Bindusava, c. 295–268 BC
	Mauryan Empire under Emperor Asoka, 232 BC
	Asokan rock edict
	Asokan pillar edict
BHOJAS	People or Tribes
	Saka invasions, c. 170–100 BC

Herat

Hindu Kush

Khyber Pass

Alexandria Arachoton (Kandahar)

Kabul

Taxila

ARACHOSIA

Nicaea 🏛 🏛 Bucephala

Sangala

Harappa

Hyphasis (Beas)

Mutlan

UTTARAPATHA

Indus

Thar Desert

Alexandria
Mohenjo-Daro

S i n d

Pattala

AVANTI

Sravasti

Mathura

Kapilavastu

H i m a l a y a s

B H O T A

Lhasa

N E P A L A

Lalia Patan

KAMARUPA

Ayodhya

MAGADHA

Kausambi

Prayaga

Pataliputra (Patna)

Ganges

Bengal

Tropic of Cancer

Gujerat

SURASHTRA

Barygaza

Ujjayini

Sanchi

PULINDAS

Narmada

SAMATATA

Arabian Sea

RASHTRIKAS

BHOJAS

Orissa

Tamralipi

Ancient probable coastline

independent tribes

D e c c a n

KALINGA

Bay of Bengal

KARNATA

Amaravati

SATIYAPUTRAS

CHOLAS

PANDYAS

SINHALESE

Ceylon

VEDAS

I N D I A N   O C E A N

N

0   200 km

0   200 miles

Important cultural developments included the evolution of Hinduism, which incorporated elements of Vedic religion. In literature, the Sanskrit epic masterpieces, the *Mahabharata* and the *Ramayana*, were written down. The *Mahabharata* tells the story of a titanic struggle between two factions, while the *Ramayana* recounts the journeys of Prince Rama. Both epics can be read on an allegorical level, and the human and the divine interact and intermingle. Other Hindu poems, the *Puranas*, also record mythology and legends. Ultimately, the Indian dynasty of the Guptas (320–550 C.E.) established itself and succeeded in once again uniting India.

~Gregory S. Aldrete

Ancient Nubian History

The region of Africa centered around the upper Nile basin and stretching from the first cataract of the river to beyond the fifth, as early as the Neolithic period was one of the sites of cultivation of crops and use of pottery (see map on p. 5). The culture of the so-called A-Group Nubians flourished here between 3700 and 2800 B.C.E. in Lower Nubia between the first and second cataracts of the Nile. Archaeological excavations of cemetery sites of the A-Group Nubians reveal carefully interred burials. This region had frequent interaction with Egyptian civilization to the north, and the Egyptians ultimately seem to have seized control of the area and forced the A-Group Nubians from their homelands.

After a gap during which the archaeological record is sparse, two new Nubian groups emerged, the C-Group culture (2300–1600 B.C.E.) and, further south, the kingdom of Kerma (2500–1500 B.C.E.). The C-Group Nubians employed more sophisticated architectural techniques, such as unbaked bricks and burial mounds, than previous groups. The kingdom of Kerma (also known as Kush) proved to be a powerful and long-lasting civilization. Based in the capital city of Kerma, these Nubians erected large urban centers that included temples covered with wall paintings and other decoration. Kerma also served as a bustling trade entrepôt through which goods such as gold, ivory, and precious stones moved.

The Pyramids of Meroe. These structures demonstrate the strong influence of Egyptian culture on this Nubian civilization. © The Art Archive/The Art Archive.

Throughout Nubian history, there was constant communication, as well as conflict, with Egyptian civilization to the north. During times when Egyptian civilization was strong, it tended to dominate or conquer Nubia, but when Egyptian power waned, the southern kingdoms thrived. Thus the kingdom of Kerma reached its peak during the Second Intermediate period of Egyptian history (ca. 1600 B.C.E.), when centralized government collapsed. But when the expansionist Egyptian New Kingdom was firmly established, it conquered most of Nubia.

About 1000 B.C.E., when the New Kingdom grew weaker, a revived Nubian kingdom known as the Napatan Empire, after its capital city located near the fourth-cataract, emerged and united Upper and Lower Nubia. The culture of the Napatan Empire was heavily influenced by Egypt and emulated Egyptian customs; its people wore Egyptian-style clothes, used Egyptian titles, and even mummified their kings in pyramids. Egypt of this time was so weak that it was conquered by the Napatans, who briefly ruled it as the 25th Dynasty of Pharaohs (750–650 B.C.E.), until expelled from Egypt by the Assyrians.

The growing power of first the Assyrians and later the Persians in coastal Egypt caused the Nubian kingdom to turn inward and to reestablish itself at the city of Meroe farther south up the Nile from Napata. The subsequent Meroitic Empire consolidated control over a broad area of northeastern Africa. It was a relatively stable and quite prosperous kingdom with advanced iron-smelting techniques, fine pottery, large urban centers, and widely flung trade contacts. This incarnation of Nubian/Kushite culture flourished until at least the fourth century C.E.

~*Gregory S. Aldrete*

Australian Aboriginal History

The culture of the Australian Aborigines constitutes perhaps the oldest continuous civilization in history. Excavations at sites such as Lake Mungo in New South Wales and Kakadu National Park suggest that the continent was already inhabited perhaps as early as 50,000 years ago by the Aboriginal peoples of Australia. Originally, the more resource-rich coastal areas were the primary areas inhabited, but by at least 10,000 years ago, people had spread to all the regions and ecosystems of Australia, including the deserts of the center.

These people lived in small hunter-gatherer bands and practiced a nomadic lifestyle, sometimes moving over extraordinarily large territories in pursuit of seasonal foods. The Aborigines did not produce large amounts of material culture. There were no urban centers, and even manufactured goods were limited to a small assortment of basic hand tools crafted of stone or wood. Technology remained relatively unchanging for thousands of years. There were, however, widespread trade networks among different bands and regions. Despite the apparently rudimentary level of technology, the Aboriginal lifestyle was wonderfully well suited to survival in the often apparently inhospitable environment. The Aborigines made clever use of scarce natural resources, and by practicing nomadism, they avoided depleting the resources in any one area. By the time

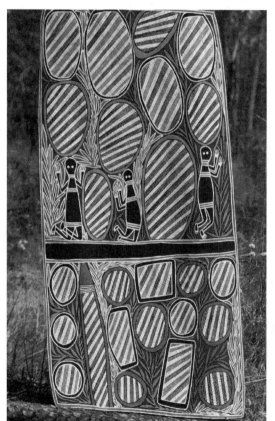

Aboriginal painting of Dreamtime mythology. This painting, done on bark, depicts episodes concerning the birth of the human race. © Penny Tweedie/ CORBIS.

of contact with European settlers in the eighteenth century, the Aborigines' successful adaptation to their environment supported a healthy population numbering perhaps in the hundreds of thousands.

The minimalist approach of the Aborigines to their material culture did not extend to their intellectual and spiritual life. Complex rituals played an important role in daily life, and the Aborigines developed a rich heritage of storytelling and spiritual beliefs, including the unique Aboriginal notion of the Dreamtime. These beliefs were also expressed through distinctive art. By the time of contact with outsiders, several hundred Aboriginal languages were spoken by dozens of clan groups.

~*Gregory S. Aldrete*

Chronology of the Ancient World

ca. 50,000? B.C.E.	Aborigines arrive in Australia
ca. 10,000 B.C.E.	Aborigines inhabit all parts of Australia
ca. 4000–3150 B.C.E.	Predynastic period in Egypt
ca. 4000–3100 B.C.E.	Uruk period in Mesopotamia
3700–2200 B.C.E.	A-Group culture in Nubia
ca. 3150–2686 B.C.E.	Early Dynastic period in Egypt; Narmer, first Egyptian pharaoh, unites Upper and Lower Egypt
ca. 3100–2350 B.C.E.	Sumerian civilization; writing invented
ca. 2686–2181 B.C.E.	Old Kingdom in Egypt; pyramids of Giza built
2500–1500 B.C.E.	Indus Valley civilization in India; cities of Harappa and Mohenjo-Daro
2500–1500 B.C.E.	Kingdom of Kerma in Nubia
2350–2193 B.C.E.	Akkadian (Sargonic) Kingdom; ziggurat step pyramids built
2300–1600 B.C.E.	C-Group culture in Nubia
2181–2041 B.C.E.	First Intermediate period in Egypt
2040–1782 B.C.E.	Middle Kingdom in Egypt
1900–1750 B.C.E.	Old Assyrian period; chariot warfare developed
1900–1595 B.C.E.	Old Babylonian period; Hammurabi's code of law issued
1782–1570 B.C.E.	Second Intermediate period in Egypt; Hyksos invade and conquer Lower Egypt
ca. 1600–1100 B.C.E.	Mycenaen period in Greece
1595–1000 B.C.E.	Middle Babylonian period
1570–1070 B.C.E.	New Kingdom in Egypt; reigns of Akhenaton, Tutankhamen, and Ramses the Great; pharaohs buried underground in Valley of the Kings
ca. 1500 B.C.E.	Aryans arrive in India, introduce Sanskrit language

1500–500 B.C.E.	Vedic culture in India
1300–1100 B.C.E.	Middle Assyrian period
ca. 1200 B.C.E.	Destruction of Troy; according to legend, Aeneas escapes Troy, flees to Italy, and founds the Roman people
ca. 1100–c. 750 B.C.E.	Greek Dark Ages
1069–332 B.C.E.	Late period in Egypt; period marked by foreign domination of Egypt
1000–612 B.C.E.	Neo-Assyrian period; height of Assyrian power
1000–ca. 600 B.C.E.	Napatan Empire in Nubia
1000–539 B.C.E.	Neo-Babylonian period; Chaldean astronomy flourishes; reign of King Nebuchadnezzar of Babylon
ca. 800–750 B.C.E.	Writing rediscovered in Greece; Homeric myths transcribed
ca. 780–650 B.C.E.	25th Dynasty of Nubian Pharaohs rule Egypt
776 B.C.E.	First Olympic Games held in Greece
753 B.C.E.	Traditional date for foundation of city of Rome by Romulus
753–509 B.C.E.	Rome ruled by kings
ca. 700–ca. 600 B.C.E.	Greek Era of Colonization; Sparta conquers Messenia
ca. 600 B.C.E.	First coins minted in Lydia, a kingdom in Asia Minor
538–331 B.C.E.	Persian (Achaemenid) Empire dominant
509 B.C.E.	Expulsion of last king of Rome, Tarquinius Superbus; foundation of Roman Republic
507 B.C.E.	Cleisthenes' political reforms at Athens
ca. 500 B.C.E.–ca. 330 C.E.	Meroitic Empire in Nubia
fifth century B.C.E.	Buddhism and Jainism founded in India
490 B.C.E.	First Persian invasion of Greece defeated at Marathon
480 B.C.E.	Second Persian invasion of Greece defeated at Salamis
ca. 450 B.C.E.	Roman law code known as the Twelve Tables established
ca. 450–429 B.C.E.	Age of Pericles at Athens; creation of Athenian Empire and building program on Acropolis
431–404 B.C.E.	Peloponnesian War between Athens and Sparta and their allies; Athens defeated
399 B.C.E.	Trial and death of Socrates at Athens
338 B.C.E.	Battle of Chaeronea; Philip II of Macedon conquers Greece
336–323 B.C.E.	Reign of Alexander the Great of Macedon; Alexander conquers Persian Empire, Egypt, northern India
323–30 B.C.E.	Hellenistic era of Greek history; Ptolemaic era of Egyptian history
321 B.C.E.–ca. 185 C.E.	Mauryan Dynasty in India; edicts of King Asoka
264 B.C.E.	Roman conquest of Italy completed
218–201 B.C.E.	Second Punic War; Rome suffers several disastrous defeats at hands of Carthaginian general Hannibal; Rome eventually defeats Carthage under generalship of Scipio Africanus
146 B.C.E.	Rome destroys Carthage and Corinth; Rome's conquest of Greece completed

91–88 B.C.E.	Social War of Rome against allies
59–50 B.C.E.	Julius Caesar fights Gallic Wars
49 B.C.E.	Julius Caesar crosses the Rubicon River and marches on Rome, thereby initiating civil war with Pompeii
44 B.C.E.	Assassination of Julius Caesar
31 B.C.E.	Octavian (future emperor Augustus) defeats Mark Antony and Cleopatra at Battle of Actium and becomes sole ruler of Rome
27 B.C.E.	Beginning of Roman Empire; Augustus first emperor, 27 B.C.E.–14 C.E.
14–37 C.E.	Reign of Tiberius; Christ crucified ca. 30 C.E.
37–41 C.E.	Reign of mad emperor Caligula
41–54 C.E.	Reign of Claudius; Britain invaded in 43 C.E.
54–68 C.E.	Reign of Nero; Great Fire of Rome in 64 C.E.
70 C.E.	Vespasian establishes Flavian Dynasty of Emperors
79 C.E.	Pompeii and Herculaneum buried by eruption of Mount Vesuvius
96–180 C.E.	"Five Good Emperors" rule Rome (Nerva, Trajan, Hadrian, Antoninus Pius, Marcus Aurelius)
180–284 C.E.	Time of political instability; rapid turnover of Roman emperors
212 C.E.	Emperor Caracalla extends Roman citizenship
284–305 C.E.	Reign of Diocletian; military and economic reforms restore empire
312–337 C.E.	Reign of Constantine; first Christian emperor, eastern capital established at Constantinople
320–550 C.E.	Gupta Dynasty in India
395 C.E.	Christianity made official state religion of Roman Empire
410 C.E.	Rome sacked by Visigoths under Alaric
476 C.E.	Romulus Augustulus, last Roman emperor of Western Empire deposed by barbarians; Eastern (Byzantine) Empire continues
518–527 C.E.	Reign of Justinian, in the Eastern (Byzantine) Empire; Digest of Roman Law assembled
1453 C.E.	Constantinople conquered by Ottoman Turks; end of Eastern (Byzantine) Roman Empire

HISTORICAL OVERVIEW: WEB SITES

http://www.museum.upenn.edu/Greek_World/Index.html
http://www.perseus.tufts.edu/cgi-bin/ptext?doc=Perseus:text:1999.04.0009
http://dalton.org/groups/rome/Rmap.html
http://www.usfca.edu/westciv/Mesochro.html
http://www.mnsu.edu/emuseum/prehistory/egypt/history/history.html

2

DOMESTIC LIFE

DOMESTIC LIFE
|
FAMILY LIFE
WOMEN
MARRIAGE
CHILDREN
SEXUALITY

The center of daily life is the home and, more important, the people who inhabit our domestic space. Domestic life can be defined as the humans who share our private spaces, as distinct from our friends and acquaintances with whom we interact in the public worlds of work, politics, and sometimes recreation. However, even this definition of domestic life is a little slippery because it includes family members within our private sphere even if they live in separate homes and join us on the holidays and for celebrations that mark our domestic life. Over time, the definitions of those who are our intimates have changed. Who are the people who might share our domestic life?

The first ties are a married couple with their children. But even these relationships defy clear definition. Throughout history, children have often depended on the kindness of strangers to raise them, whether they were orphaned or fostered or fed by wet nurses. All these people shared the domestic intimacy of home life. In addition, households included others outside the nuclear family, from relatives to servants to slaves. In ancient Rome, the head of the family (the *paterfamilias*) was responsible for family, relatives, slaves, and freed slaves, and he also cared for clients who put themselves in his charge. Families might also include unmarried partners or even roommates who combined living space out of convenience or necessity, or concubines who shared the private life of rulers. The relationships that make up domestic life are impossible to define perfectly, but (like art) we recognize them when we see them.

A study of domestic life not only involves the people who create a private sphere but also encompasses the roles they play—including at times the emotional functions they fill. Fathers of nineteenth-century families were to be distant and angry, while mothers were to be accessible and nurturing. Mothers in ancient Rome, by contrast, were stern disciplinarians and teachers of values, while nursemaids handled the nurturing. Here in the domestic life, societies define the roles of men, women, children, and everyone else who shares this space. It is here that we learn early on who we are and how we are to act and feel.

The idea of home life as a separate realm from the public sphere already existed in the ancient world. Indeed, our word *domestic* is derived from the Latin word for house, *domus*. These different realms of human activity were often pictured as being demarcated spatially, not just figuratively. The home was a feminized space, where women raised children and tended to the physical needs of the family, whereas the public world was masculine. In contrast, women were often confined to the home. For a Greek wife to venture out in public was seen as immoral, and she often spent her entire life relegated to the women's section of the house, first in her father's home and then in her husband's. The Greek goddess Hestia, whose role was to tend the hearth, is the one divinity who functioned primarily as a symbol, who had no love affairs and no adventures outside Olympus; her role reflects that of the good wife, who was not talked about because she stayed inside and literally kept the home fires burning. The women venturing outside freely were primarily prostitutes, slaves running errands, or lower-class women who could not afford slaves. Ironically, in some ancient civilizations, slaves might move about more freely than respectable women because they could leave the house and go out into the city and the marketplace, as they had no reputation to risk.

The roles and emotional bonds between husband and wife, parent and child took many forms. Whereas many mothers' roles focused on comfort and nurturing, Spartan mothers would harshly instruct their sons who were departing for war to return either with their shields or on them, meaning that they would rather see their sons dead than learn that they had shirked their duty in battle. In Greece and Rome, a man's closest emotional bonds were often with his male friends rather than his wife, who was simply seen as an agent for producing children.

Nevertheless, the basic form of most ancient families was a husband, wife, children, and servants in a shared dwelling, and it was within, and with reference to, this domestic world that a large part of a person's identity and roles in society became established.

~Joyce E. Salisbury and Gregory S. Aldrete

FOR MORE INFORMATION

Saggs, H. W. *Civilization before Greece and Rome.* New Haven, Conn.: Yale University Press, 1989. Reprint, New Haven, Conn.: Yale University Press, 1991.

Veyne, P., ed. *A History of Private Life.* 2 vols. Cambridge, Mass.: Harvard University Press, 1987.

DOMESTIC LIFE

FAMILY LIFE

Mesopotamia

Egypt

Greece

Rome

Australian Aboriginals

Family Life

The unit of husband, wife, and children living in their own residence, which is the conventional basic unit of the family today, was also the composition of the standard ancient family. In these cultures, it was not unusual to find various relatives also forming a part of the household, although this was usually because, for one reason or another, they had either not yet established their own household or it had been broken up. Thus an unmarried or divorced sister or a widowed mother would be a common addition to the basic family unit. One other type of person found living with ancient families, especially wealthier ones, was the household slave. The household of Sin-ishmeni of Babylon cited in the following entry for "Mesopotamia" was typical, consisting as it did of himself, his wife, a daughter, two sons, a slave woman, and her son.

All these cultures also tended to place great importance on the extended family. What clan someone belonged to could hold considerable significance, and clan membership not only served to give individuals a sense of identity but, in an era with only rudimentary forms of welfare, also provided a network of support and assistance in times of difficulty or trouble. The members of a *genos,* or kin group, in ancient Greece were not only related to one another but frequently comprised the members of a religious group maintaining a particular cult site, or acted in concert politically.

The importance attached to clan membership can be traced in the naming customs of the ancient world. In a number of cultures, sons were named after their fathers, but perhaps no one was more concerned with labeling people by family than the Romans. Each Roman male was given at least three names, which identified not only his kin group but even the sub-branch of the family to which he belonged. The daughters within a family were simply named by being given a feminized form of the family name. Family mattered greatly to these people—it determined their place in society and their relationship to the community.

One final common theme in ancient families was the power and prestige accorded to the male head of the household. The Mesopotamian patriarch and the Roman *paterfamilias* both wielded nearly total life-and-death control over the members of their families. At least in formal legal terms, the status of women in the ancient world was almost always significantly inferior to that of men.

~Gregory S. Aldrete

MESOPOTAMIA

The term *nuclear family* refers to a married couple and their children. In ancient Mesopotamia, the nuclear family was called a "house," and a man was expected "to build a house." To achieve this goal, he married one woman. If she was unable to bear children, he could take a second wife or a concubine, or the couple could decide to adopt children. On average, from two to four children survived early childhood; the initial number of children born remains unknown. In ancient Mesopotamia, the extended household might include unmarried sisters, widowed mothers, and under-age brothers; it was called "the house of the father." These family members referred to each other as "brother" or "my [own] flesh and blood."

In the ancient Near East, the family was patriarchal. The father was head of the family and wielded authority over his wife and children. The Laws of Hammurabi (§195) reflected the cultural attitudes of the time, stating, "If a son strikes his father, they shall cut off his hand." The father was head of the family until he died, and his rule was law. In case of debt, the father could offer slaves as well as any member

Mesopotamian terra-cotta plaque showing an affectionately embracing couple. Note the elaborate hairstyles of both man and woman. © Copyright The British Museum.

of his family to his creditor to satisfy his obligation. The father had the right but not the obligation to redeem them. If he died and left unmarried children, the eldest son became head of the family and administrator of the estate. If the children were young, their mother might be given the authority of "fatherhood."

Men were identified by their father's name. Therefore, having a son and heir was of great significance for the family; a son could support his parents in their old age and perform the proper rites after their death. In the first millennium B.C.E., free citizens were identified by their given name, followed by their father's name and that of an ancestor who lived centuries ago; that is, X, the son of Y, the descendant of Z. Slaves were not given a family name. Sons and daughters lived in their father's home until they left to establish their own household or to marry into another. An excerpt from a distribution list (rations as payment for services) portrayed family life in Kish, a northern Babylonian city:

30 liters—Ishtar-gamelat, his wife
20 liters—Ahassunu, his daughter
20 liters—Ikuppi-Adad, his son
15 liters—Shamash-andulli, his son
House of Ishme-Adad

30 liters—Humusi, his wife
20 liters—Ibbi-Adad, his son
20 liters—Tabni-Ishtar, his daughter
15 liters—Rabi-sillashu, his son
20 liters—Munawwirtum, his slave-woman
10 liters—Ad-mat-ili, her son
House of Sin-ishmeni (cited in Donbaz and Yoffee, 58–59)

An Assyrian census list from the first millennium B.C.E. records the farmers and their holdings in the district of Haran. The census also lists the names of the family members, for example:

Adad-duri, farmer
Nashukh-dilini, his adolescent son
1 woman; total 3
30 units of land, 15 cultivated thereof
1 orchard
1 cow
Total of the estate Arrizu in the administrative district of Haran (cited in Saggs, 137)

This census list in its entirety shows that the Assyrian villager was usually monogamous. Some of the sons at home were reported to be adolescents, and some of the daughters "of marriageable age." According to this census list, there were 1.43 children per family; however, this statistic indicates families too small even to maintain the population and may have excluded some circumstances. For example, daughters may have left to set up their own households. Adult sons could have departed for military duty or other state service (Nemet-Nejat, 126–28).

FOR MORE INFORMATION

Contenau, G. *Everyday Life in Babylon and Assyria.* Translated by K. R. Maxwell-Hyslop and A. R. Maxwell-Hyslop. New York: St. Martin's Press, 1954.

Donbaz, V., and N. Yoffee. *Old Babylonian Texts from Kish Conserved in the Istanbul Archaeological Museums.* Bibliotheca Mesopotamica 17. Malibu, Calif.: Undena Publications, 1986.

Nemet-Nejat, K. R. *Daily Life in Ancient Mesopotamia.* Westport, Conn.: Greenwood Press, 1998.

Saggs, H. W. F. *Civilization before Greece and Rome.* New Haven, Conn.: Yale University Press, 1989. Reprint, New Haven, Conn.: Yale University Press, 1991.

Stol, M. "Private Life in Ancient Mesopotamia." In *Civilizations of the Ancient Near East,* ed. J. Sasson. Vol. 1. New York: Scribner's, 1995.

EGYPT

DOMESTIC LIFE
|
FAMILY LIFE
|
Mesopotamia
Egypt
Greece
Rome
Australian Aboriginals

The primary family unit in ancient Egypt was a household composed of husband, wife, and their children. This household might be expanded to include other relatives, especially unmarried or widowed women. The acquisition of property and a house meant that it was time for a man to get married and establish his own independent household—ideally, by the age of 20, so that he could have children while still a young man. Whereas arranged marriages were common among the royal family, the average person seemingly had more freedom to choose. Moving in together and establishing a joint household served as the sign that a couple had become husband and wife; there was no formal marriage ceremony. The woman would simply leave her father's house, taking all her possessions and her dowry to her husband's house. (Some scholars hypothesize that an impressive procession marked her transfer from one household to the other.) A wife was referred to as "mistress of the house," suggesting the importance of her role in her husband's household, of which he was the "head."

Husband and wife possessed the same legal rights and jointly owned property within the marriage, although married women were permitted to retain ownership of their own property even after marriage, which was rare in the ancient world. This sense of a joint existence continued after death, when they would share the same tomb and appear in tomb paintings performing religious rituals side by side. Wills divided a couple's property among their children. The existence of medical papyri containing prescriptions for contraception has been interpreted by some scholars as showing Egyptian couples' awareness of scarceness of viable land for farming and the subsequent need to limit family size. Others suggest that large families were not uncommon.

Whereas marriages in many ancient societies were viewed primarily as economic arrangements or means for the procreation of legitimate heirs, the ideal of marriage in ancient Egypt also included notions of mutual respect and love. Ancient Egyptian wisdom texts advise men to love and care for their wives, provide them with food and clothing, and strive to make them happy. During the New Kingdom, love poems were written that describe the feelings of the enamored man or woman and the attractiveness of the beloved. Some of these poems suggest that such love might lead to marriage. Depictions of families in Egyptian art communicate a feeling of affection, harmony, and intimacy uniting the family group. Husbands and wives are often shown holding hands or sitting side by side with their arms linked or encircling one another's shoulders. Children are portrayed gathered around their parents, who sometimes make gestures of affection.

These happy family portraits reflect the value placed on children. If a wife was infertile, this was a great cause for sadness; in such a case, a female slave could instead produce legal heirs to the household in the wife's place. Childbirth was a dangerous process for both mother and infant; death during or soon after giving birth was common, and many babies did not survive their first year. High death rates also meant that remarriage of widows and widowers, often still relatively young, was not unusual. There are records of people marrying even three or four times.

When the head of the household died, his eldest son was responsible for burying his father and making sure that he received (and continued to receive) the proper rites. The family was supposed to bring food offerings to the father's tomb regularly.

Divorce was allowed in ancient Egyptian society. Like marriage, it was conducted in a simple and direct manner. The woman would take her belongings and return to her parents' house; this symbolized that the marriage was over. If a husband divorced his wife, he was required to pay her compensation, and she was able to keep her own property. Many causes could be cited for divorce, from falling in love with another to what would today be called irreconcilable differences.

In the area of marriage, the pharaoh was not an example to be followed; marital practices for the pharaoh were quite different from those of his subjects. Whereas bigamy and polygamy were quite uncommon among the general population, pharaohs frequently had multiple wives. Also, the marriage of brother and sister (in imitation of the union of the gods Isis and Osiris) was customary in the royal family but practically nonexistent among commoners (until much later, during Greco-Roman times). Interestingly, however, *brother* and *sister* were used as terms of endearment between lovers in the love poems that survive from the New Kingdom, and husbands addressed their spouses as "sister" rather than "wife."

~*Gregory S. Aldrete*

FOR MORE INFORMATION

Brier, B., and H. Hobbs. *Daily Life of the Ancient Egyptians*. Westport, Conn.: Greenwood Press, 1999.

David, R. *Handbook to Life in Ancient Egypt*. New York: Facts on File, 1998.

Montet, P. *Everyday Life in Egypt in the Days of Ramesses the Great*. Translated by A. R. Maxwell-Hyslop and M. Drower. Reprint, Philadelphia: University of Pennsylvania Press, 1981.

GREECE

DOMESTIC LIFE
|
FAMILY LIFE
|
Mesopotamia

Egypt

Greece

Rome

Australian Aboriginals

The basic social unit throughout the Greek world was the family, although there was no word exactly equivalent to the term *family*. The nearest equivalent is *oikos* (or *oikia*), which more accurately translates as "household." An *oikos* denoted all those living under the same roof: the master and mistress, their children and other dependents, and all their household slaves. It also included the estate and all its livestock. The head of the *oikos* was the oldest male, who was also in charge of the religious practices that were conducted in the home.

The next largest unit was the *genos* (plural, *genê*), a word best translated as "noble kin group." Members of the same *genos* traced their descent from a common ancestor, who in many cases was either mythical or divine. We know of the existence of about 60 Athenian *genê*; the most prominent of these was the Alkmaionidai, to which both Cleisthenes and Pericles belonged. All of Athens's most venerable cults were administered by *genê*, and the election to their priesthoods remained hereditary throughout history. The priesthoods of both Athena Polias (of the city) and Poseidon Erechtheus, the two principal state cults, were restricted to a small *genos* known as the Eteoboutadai. Precisely what *gennêtai* (members of the same *genos*) did in common apart from worship is not known. Until the reforms of Cleisthenes at the end of the sixth century B.C.E., *genê* effectively controlled the political process. Even after the democratic reforms carried out about 462 B.C.E., they still continued to wield considerable influence.

Whereas only aristocrats belonged to a *genos*, all Athenians were members of a phratry. *Phratry*, from which our word *fraternal* is derived, means "brotherhood." Until Cleisthenes' reforms, membership in a phratry was the basis of Athenian citizenship. The blood ties between *phrateres* (members of the same phratry) are likely to have been much looser than those that bound together members of the same *genos*. *Phrateres* gathered together to perform religious ceremonies. They were also under an obligation to afford protection to one another. In particular, if one of their members was murdered, they were required to seek legal redress on the victim's behalf. The Athenian population was divided into at least 30 phratries. Phratries are first mentioned in Homer and may be of Mycenaean origin. They also existed in Sparta, Argos, Delphi, Syracuse, and on the island of Chios.

A baby boy was admitted into his phratry in the first year of his life at a festival known as the Apatouria. Admission was contingent upon a vote of all the members of the phratry, who were required to substantiate the father's claim that his child was the legitimate offspring of Athenian parents. The boy was later reintroduced to his phratry at the age of 14. The ceremony of induction, which included a sacrifice, was accompanied by a ritual cutting of the candidate's hair, an action that symbolically marked the end of his growing years. It is not known whether girls were also admitted to phratries, nor is it known what procedure was used to determine whether a girl was the legitimate offspring of Athenian parents.

The Greeks regarded the care of the elderly, which they called *gêroboskia*, as a sacred duty, the responsibility for which rested exclusively with the offspring. Greek law laid down severe penalties for those who did not discharge their obligations. In Delphi, for instance, those who failed to look after their parents were liable to be put in irons and thrown into prison. In Athens, those who neglected either their parents or their grandparents were fined and partially deprived of their citizen rights. There were no public facilities for the aged—the very idea of an old people's home would have been utterly alien to the Greeks.

In Athens, it was customary for a childless man to adopt a male heir of adult years to whom he would leave the entirety of his estate. In return, the adopted son would look after the man in old age, give him a proper burial, and pay regular visits to his tomb. The adopted son would lose all legal connection with the family into which he had been born, including the right to inherit. In this way, if he had an heir himself, he would prevent his adoptive father's household from dying out. To a limited degree, this arrangement may have served to redistribute wealth; presumably, the majority of adopted sons would not have relinquished their entitlement to inherit from their natal homes without the expectation of an improvement in their financial prospects. Adoption was as much a practical as a sentimental arrangement into which both parties entered with a firm calculation of their own advantage (Garland, 43–44).

FOR MORE INFORMATION

Garland, R. *Daily Life of the Ancient Greeks*. Westport, Conn.: Greenwood Press, 1998.
Lacey, W. K. *The Family in Ancient Greece*. London: Thames and Hudson, 1968.
Pomeroy, S. *Families in Classical and Hellenistic Greece*. Oxford: Oxford University Press, 1997.

DOMESTIC LIFE
|
FAMILY LIFE
|
Mesopotamia

Egypt

Greece

Rome

Australian Aboriginals

ROME

Rome was a male-dominated society that accorded the male head of a family, the *paterfamilias* (father of the family), enormous respect and power. He wielded *pater potestas*, "paternal power," over all the members of his extended family, including adults, children, and slaves, and this power gave him nearly unlimited authority to control the lives of his family. In the most extreme example, a *paterfamilias* could even put to death his own children, an action that was viewed as being within his proper rights. In addition, he arranged marriages for his children and he could command them to divorce, he could sell members of his family into slavery, and he could order a newborn baby to be abandoned. Naturally, he exercised complete control over lesser familial matters as well. The father's role within the family was one of authority and decision making.

Women did not have equivalent legal status with men, but Roman mothers were still expected to be strong figures within the household and to play an important role in supervising the children's upbringing and education and maintaining the smooth day-to-day running of the household. Above all, the Roman wife was expected to be self-effacing and to provide strong support for, but not any challenge to, the *paterfamilias*.

It is difficult to discern from the extant sources the emotional bonds that existed within Roman families. In the idealized portraits presented in literature, the mother and father appear rather stern and remote figures, but sometimes glimpses emerge of warmer, more intimate relationships, such as in a letter written by the orator Cicero in which he expresses deep grief over the death of a daughter (*Letter to Atticus* 12.46).

What family someone belonged to mattered greatly in Roman society, and at certain periods in Roman history it could even determine a person's legal rights. It is thus no surprise that Roman names were not randomly chosen but instead revealed a great deal about a person and his family. Most Roman men possessed a tripartite name. The three components were labeled *praenomen, nomen,* and *cognomen.*

The *praenomen,* equivalent to a modern first name and chosen by the parents shortly after a son's birth, was limited to only about 16 possibilities: Aulus, Appius, Gaius, Gnaeus, Decimus, Lucius, Marcus, Manius, Numerius, Pulius, Quintus, Servius, Sextus, Spurius, Titus, and Tiberius.

The second name, the *nomen,* was the name of a person's *gens,* or family. It was the most important section of one's name because it told who one's ancestors were. The nomen also determined whether one was a patrician or a plebeian.

The last name, called the *cognomen,* was a personal name that identified the particular branch of a family. These names were often hereditary, although not always. They often referred to a physical characteristic or an action of some famous member of the family. One famous cognomen was Ahenobarbus, meaning "red beard." Others included Strabo "cross-eyed," Verrucosus "warty," and Clodius "gimpy." Gaius Julius Caesar's *cognomen* in Latin means "hairy," which was ironic since Caesar himself was balding.

When it came to naming women, the only thing that the Romans viewed as important was their clan or family. Therefore, all daughters were named by giving them the female form of the *nomen.* The daughter of Gaius Julius Caesar, for example, would be named Julia. What happened if he had a second daughter? The Roman solution was to call the older one Julia Maior (Julia the elder) and the younger one Julia Menor (Julia the younger). If a man had even more daughters, he simply began to assign them numbers, starting with Julia Tertia (Julia the third), and so on. In reality, many women probably used nicknames to avoid confusion.

Slaves also received only one name, which was chosen for them by their owner. Sometimes these names seem to have been given with a touch of irony; one popular slave name, for example, was Felix, meaning "Lucky." When a male slave was freed, he took the *praenomen* and *nomen* of his ex-master and then added his slave name as *cognomen.* For example, the famous orator Marcus Tullius Cicero had a slave named Tiro who acted as his personal secretary. Eventually, Cicero freed his faithful servant, who then went by the name Marcus Tullius Tiro. Thus, even when freed, slaves could not fully escape their former masters.

~*Gregory S. Aldrete*

FOR MORE INFORMATION

Bradley, K. R. *Discovering the Roman Family.* New York: Oxford University Press, 1991.
Dixon, S. *The Roman Family.* Baltimore, Md.: Johns Hopkins University Press, 1992.

DOMESTIC LIFE
|
FAMILY LIFE
|
Mesopotamia

Egypt

Greece

Rome

Australian Aboriginals

AUSTRALIAN ABORIGINALS

Every Aboriginal person was born into a complex set of memberships in different groups depending on such factors as place of birth and kinship relationships. When they reached marriageable age (much younger for women than for men), a set of rules restricted the possible number of people they could marry, and a suitable spouse was selected for them. After marriage, the couple might live for a period of time with the wife's family but then would generally move to live in the area where the husband's family was located. It was uncommon for any nuclear family to live by itself. Usually, several families related through male kinship lines would live and work together.

Men could have more than one wife at a time, and people could remarry after the death of a partner. Marriages usually involved reciprocal arrangements, whereby a group that had obtained a wife for one of its men would be expected to provide a wife at some later time for a man from the other group. The suitability of marriage between two people was determined by their kinship. Everyone in a group had relationships to everyone else, determined by which generation they belonged to and who their parents' relatives were. The details of these relationships varied in different regions, but usually, sets of people with a particular kinship relation had generic titles such as uncle, grandmother, cousin, mother's brother, granddaughter, and so on. People belonging to certain of these categories were ideally suited to marry a particular person, whereas the same person would be forbidden to marry people in other categories of relationship.

Such rules were aimed at preventing incest within relatively small groups, but they also meant that relationships existed between all members of a group. In an important sense, everyone who was a member of the same social category as you was part of your extended family. If a person was unknown to you, he or she could be included in your web of relationships and given a title by asking a few questions establishing what relationships he or she had with other people and how he or she fitted into the kinship classification system. These relationships could be essential in hard times, when kin lent support to one another in difficult circumstances. Even in everyday life, your relationships to the other members of a group determined where you built your house within a camp, how food was shared, whom you could or could not speak to, and which teams of people were responsible for the organization of parts of ceremonies. Furthermore, marriages between members of different groups extended these relationships over wide areas.

Although the actual parents had primary responsibility for very young children, all members of a group took part in rearing children. A child would have many uncles, aunts, cousins, and grandparents, some of whom were related by "blood," others by kinship, but all of whom accepted responsibility for the child. Similarly, education was a group responsibility—a boy would be taught to hunt by all of his uncles, and a girl would be taught about medicinal plants by all of her aunts. Children acquired skills that would be important in ceremonies by, for example, learning children's versions of songs. Just as education was important to equip children to live in a difficult and often harsh environment, the context of that education also mattered. Aboriginal kinship structures were perhaps some of the most complex of any familial relationships in the world. This complexity meant that everyone had a place within a large family that helped to nurture and support each individual Aboriginal person.

To read about marriage and the roles of men and women in the early British colony in Australia, see the Colonial Australia entries in the sections "Marriage" and "Men and Women" in the "Domestic Life" chapter of volume 4 of this series, *Seventeenth and Eighteenth Centuries*.

~David Horton

FOR MORE INFORMATION

Berndt, R., and C. Berndt. *The World of the First Australians*. Canberra: Aboriginal Studies Press, 1988.

Hamilton, A. *Nature and Nurture: Aboriginal Child Rearing in North-Central Arnhem Land*. Canberra: Australian Institute of Aboriginal Studies, 1981.

Horton, D., ed. *The Encyclopedia of Aboriginal Australia*. Canberra: Aboriginal Studies Press, 2001.

Mulvaney, J., and J. Kamminga. *Prehistory of Australia*. Sydney, New South Wales: Allen and Unwin, 1999.

Women

DOMESTIC LIFE

|

WOMEN

|

Mesopotamia

Egypt

Greece

Rome

India

Although almost all women in the ancient world did not have formal legal equality with men, they sometimes found roles for themselves in which they could nonetheless exercise influence over their families and even society. The degree of legal recognition accorded to women varied considerably. Women in ancient Egypt could own property and were recognized as legal entities separate from male members of their family. Even in fairly restrictive societies, some women were allowed to exercise a fair amount of independence when there was not a male relative available, as in the case of widowed women in Mesopotamia.

The dominant attitude toward women, however, can be summarized in a remark by a Greek statesman, "A woman's greatest glory is not to be talked about by men, whether for good or ill" (Thucydides, *The Peloponnesian War* 2.45.3). The ideal of womanhood, at least in many men's eyes, was to be unheard and unseen. This attitude was perhaps taken to its extreme among upper-class Greek women, who were expected to almost never set foot outside the house except when they got married and when they were buried. The house was the stereotypical realm of women, who not infrequently had separate quarters from their husbands within the household, as in many Roman houses. The main duty of women was seen as producing children to continue the family line. The traditional occupation of women throughout the ancient world was weaving and producing textile products for use by their families.

Because surviving ancient sources were written overwhelmingly by men from the wealthiest sectors of society, it can be difficult to discern how realistic or typical the attitudes expressed therein are in regard to the reality of ordinary women's lives. Even harder to tell is what ancient women actually thought and felt about their roles and status. Probably, many poor women by necessity had to work for a living and therefore did not lead lives of seclusion and isolation. Some women clearly obtained education and skills, such as the female scribes attested in ancient Mesopotamia and the Roman women identified as the owners of small businesses.

Finally, no matter what women's legal status, there were obviously many dynamic women who got their way or even exercised power through their influence over their husbands or sons.

~Gregory S. Aldrete

DOMESTIC LIFE

|

WOMEN

|

Mesopotamia

Egypt

Greece

Rome

India

MESOPOTAMIA

In Mesopotamia, women's social status was similar to men's. But women were never the legal equals of men. The position of women was generally higher in the early Sumerian city-state because of the importance of goddesses in the Sumerian religion. Later, in Mesopotamia, when Sargon (2334–2279 B.C.E.), the Akkadian king, rose to power, the Akkadians took part in Sumerian religious observances. To ensure religious legitimacy, Sargon was the first king in a long line of monarchs to appoint his daughter, Enkheduanna, as high priestess of the moon god, Nanna, at Ur. Enkheduanna was a highly accomplished poet.

The kings of the Ur III Dynasty (2112–2004 B.C.E.) were praised in the songs of their royal women. Female scribes have been identified as the authors of lullabies for the crown prince, long songs to the king, and even laments. Although scribes were usually men, there were female scribes in Old Babylonian Sippar and Mari. Some were even the daughters of scribes. At Sippar, female scribes worked at the cloister, which also functioned as an economic institution of that city. These female scribes recorded the transactions of the members of the cloister. From Mari, we know the names of at least 10 female scribes. Nine of them were slaves; they received small rations, indicating the low regard in which they were held. Slaves with scribal skills were sometimes given to princesses as part of their dowries.

Only one fragment of an Old Babylonian vocabulary text lists female scribes as scholars. There were female counterparts to diviners, physicians, performers, and artists. But once again, their activities were eclipsed by males in the same jobs.

In the second millennium B.C.E., free women at Nuzi, a Mesopotamian provincial town, played an active role in the economy and in the courts. Although women were not always allowed to participate in the economic spheres, once they participated, they took part in the same range of business transactions as men, ensuring their legal equality with men. Women could acquire land by purchase, inheritance, and royal grant. The real estate ranged in size from simple rural structures to complex urban structures to extensive agricultural estates. In one instance, a free woman owned land in at least six towns. Women sued and were sued regarding the title and ownership of land. The inclusion of free women at Nuzi in real estate transactions was particularly important because ownership of property at Nuzi was the path to power and wealth.

Women had less control in commercial life despite their legal parity with men. A woman could take part in business with her husband's permission. Women also became involved in economic activities when men were not available. That is, a widow, particularly one responsible for minor children, could inherit, become head of the surviving family, and administer the family estate. Although loans could be given interest free, women usually charged interest when they lent silver.

Women had little control over the management of either real estate or slaves. A woman's dowry became part of the estate of her in-laws and was managed by the head of the house, that is, the father or the eldest son. Therefore, women used loans as an opportunity for financial gain. Women from wealthy families received additional sums of silver or precious metal as part of their dowry; they then made a profit for themselves on this capital by separate investments.

In a hymn, the goddess Gula (the patron goddess of doctors and healing) described the stages of a woman's life: "I am a daughter, I am a bride, I am a spouse, I am a housekeeper" (cited in Stol, 486). In other words, women were never completely independent from men in the roles they played in their lifetime.

Relief from Mesopotamia of a wealthy woman spinning yarn while her servant fans her. Note the ornate decoration of their clothes and the furniture. Photo RMN–P. Bernard.

In ancient Mesopotamia, the most important role of a woman in marriage was to bear children, particularly sons, who were preferred as heirs. Women who bore no children were in a difficult position. When the husband predeceased his wife and left no will, the widow was permitted to continue to live in his house and to be supported by his children. However, if she had children with a previous husband, the children of her second marriage could return the widow to the children of her first marriage. The Middle Assyrian law code allowed widows the freedom to cohabit with a man without a marriage contract; however, after two years, the widow would legally become a wife despite the lack of a marriage contract. At Assur, a long tablet of Middle Assyrian laws has 59 clauses concerned with matters related to women.

Few references have been found to women outside the patrilinear household. Widows and orphans were protected by the charity of a righteous ruler. Prostitution was an option, and prostitutes were found in public places in the city—the tavern, the harbor, or under the city wall. Prostitutes dressed to attract business, wearing a special type of leather jacket. They were forbidden by law to wear a veil outdoors, as respectable married women did. An Assyrian text describes a prostitute having to untie her undergarment to prepare herself for clients. The prostitute was often pictured as leaning out of a window. Female servers in taverns were also a part of city life, but whether these women were considered "respectable" remains unclear (Nemet-Nejat, 150–53).

FOR MORE INFORMATION

Nemet-Nejat, K. R. *Daily Life in Ancient Mesopotamia.* Westport, Conn.: Greenwood Press, 1998.

Stol, M. "Private Life in Ancient Mesopotamia." In *Civilizations of the Ancient Near East,* ed. J. Sasson. Vol. 1. New York: Scribner's, 1995.

DOMESTIC LIFE

WOMEN

Mesopotamia

Egypt

Greece

Rome

India

EGYPT

Unlike many other ancient societies, Egypt granted women legal rights equal to those of men. Under Egyptian law, women could own property, enter into contractual agreements, and even be prosecuted and suffer punishment for crimes just as men were. The unusual degree of freedom and rights afforded women in ancient Egypt compared with the rest of the ancient world may have helped to inspire the Greek historian Herodotus's description of Egyptian society as exactly reversing the "usual" customs. According the Herodotus, Egyptian men stayed at home and weaved while their wives went to the marketplace to trade, thus switching the typical gendered behaviors at that time, where women stayed inside and sewed while only men ventured into public to do business. Whether this portrayal is true, it reveals that Egypt was perceived as being different from other societies in terms of women's roles and treatment.

Despite their equality with men in certain respects, women were more limited in terms of occupation, since work was usually divided according to gender. Contrary to Herodotus's description, women tended to work primarily in the home, while men pursued careers outside domestic confines in the public sphere: men ran the farm, fished the Nile, fought in wars, held government jobs, and apprenticed as craftsmen and artisans. Men alone trained to be scribes and temple priests (although in exceptional cases, royal or socially high ranking women might learn to write in a class separate from the male students). However, the title that a woman acquired upon marriage, "mistress of the house," suggests some degree of status. Competently managing the household was crucial to a family's well-being. Out of necessity, women had to gain valuable skills required for the running of a home, such as making clothing and pots, grinding grain, cooking meals, baking bread, and brewing beer. Because children were valued, the role of motherhood also elicited respect; statues of nursing mothers survive, and wives were often included alongside their husbands in paintings and sculptures, sometimes with their children as well. When a man was a farmer, his wife helped with the agricultural duties; after men dug the furrows, women carried baskets of seed through them, sowing as they went, and harvest required the labor of the entire family.

Paintings of female musicians, dancers, and acrobats indicate that women worked as entertainers, although it is unclear whether these were free women pursuing a career or slaves. Less-privileged women might have worked as servants in the households of the wealthy. It has also been suggested that women played a significant role in the hugely important industry of linen manufacturing. Some women were recorded among those bearing the title "overseer of the house of weavers," a managerial role invested with responsibility and authority. Women also served as professional mourners, hired and paid to provide public displays of intense grief; their loud weeping, tearing of their clothes and hair, and beating and befouling their bodies were standard rituals at funerals. The greater the number of mourners, the higher the prestige and status of the deceased, and the more glorious the send-off to the afterlife.

Finally, women in the royal family were often able to exert considerable power and influence. Although pharaohs could have multiple wives and concubines, one wife functioned as the royal consort and frequently was represented in art alongside her husband, conducting official business or rituals. Instances are recorded of women ruling as regent in the place of sons not yet old enough, as well as of royal women corresponding with high-ranking foreign officials. One woman, Hatshepsut, even reigned alone as pharaoh; reliefs depict her wearing the fake beard worn by male pharaohs strapped around her chin and fighting in battles against Egypt's enemies.

~Gregory S. Aldrete

FOR MORE INFORMATION

Tyldesley, J. *Daughters of Isis: Women of Ancient Egypt.* New York: Penguin Books, 1984.
Watterson, B. *Women in Ancient Egypt.* New York: St. Martin's Press, 1991.

GREECE

DOMESTIC LIFE
|
WOMEN
|
Mesopotamia

Egypt

Greece

Rome

India

At the opening of Homer's *Odyssey*, Odysseus's son Telemachus delivers this stern rebuke to his mother, Penelope, who, understandably pained by allusions to her missing husband, has just asked the bard Phemios to choose a theme other than that of the Greeks' homecoming from Troy:

Go inside the house, and do your own work, the loom and the distaff, and bid your handmaidens be about their work also. But discussion is the concern of men, of all men, but of me most of all. (lines 1.356–59)

Telemachus's reprimand summarizes perfectly the bipolarity of Greek society, which was both patrilineal and patriarchal. Women, although necessary for propagation, served few other useful functions. They were to be subdued and secluded, controlled and confined. Greek society was sexist and chauvinistic; there is more than enough evidence to support this view. And yet the picture is not quite so simple and straightforward as all that, for there are indications that Greek men did not have it entirely their own way.

Despite Telemachus's claim about the dominant role of men in Homeric society, his father, Odysseus, constantly finds himself in a position of weakness and inferiority vis-à-vis women. As in the real world, so in the world of the poem; female power takes many guises: beauty, intelligence, cunning, resourcefulness, wisdom, and charm. The women whom Odysseus encounters exercise their power in ways that are usually indirect, sometimes magical, and often dangerous. They possess access to privileged information. They control hidden forces that can assist or impede him on his way. They counterfeit and deceive. And they can kill.

The power that wives wield is aptly symbolized by the different fates of Odysseus and his commander in chief. Whereas Odysseus is blessed in the possession of a wife, Penelope, who remains faithful to him for 20 years and has the skill to ward off no fewer than 108 suitors, Agamemnon is murdered on his return from the Trojan War by his wife Clytemnestra, who had taken a lover in his absence. The question, however, remains: To what extent does this picture of women's power in early Greece mirror reality, and to what extent does it constitute a fantasy on the part of the poet?

In the funeral speech delivered over the Athenian dead in the first year of the Peloponnesian War, Pericles states, "Women's greatest glory is not to be talked about by men, either for good or ill" (Thucydides, *The Peloponnesian War* 2.45.2). Likewise, in Euripides' *Trojan Women*, Andromache, the wife of Hector, declares, "There is one prime source of scandal for a woman—when she won't stay at home" (line 648f.). Patronizing though such statements may appear from our perspective, they also reveal an overriding concern on the part of Greek husbands concerning their wives' fidelity. One Greek records that he gave his wife the following advice soon after they were married:

You must stay indoors and send out the slaves whose work is outside. Those who remain and do chores inside the house are under your charge. You are to inspect everything that enters it and distribute what is needed, taking care not to be extravagant. . . . When the slaves bring in wool, you must see that it is used for those who need cloaks. You must take care of the grain-store and make sure that the grain is edible. One of your less pleasant tasks is to find out whenever one of the slaves becomes sick and see that they are properly looked after. (Xenophon, *Household Management* 7.35–37)

As this passage indicates, the mistress of the house was in charge of the domestic arrangements and was held accountable if anything went amiss. In addition to running the home, a wife was expected to contribute to its economy by plying the distaff and working the loom. Spinning and weaving were regarded as essential accomplishments in a woman, not least because most garments were made in the home.

Men spent most of the day outside the home, shopping, conversing, deliberating, attending the assembly or the law courts, and visiting in other public places. On the few occasions that respectable women went out of doors, by contrast, they were invariably accompanied by their slaves or female acquaintances.

Athenian women had no political rights. Legally, too, their position was one of inferiority. A law quoted by the fourth-century B.C.E. orator Isaios decreed, "No child or woman shall have the power to make any contract above the value of a *medimnos* of barley" (10.10). (A *medimnos* was sufficient to sustain a family in food for about a week.) They were not permitted to buy or sell land, and although they were entitled to acquire property through dowry, inheritance, or gift, it was managed for them by their legal guardian (i.e., their father, male next of kin, or husband). Women thus remained perpetually under the control of one man or another, whatever their age or status.

The wives and daughters of the poor, as well as many spinsters and widows, could not lead lives of seclusion and would therefore have been frequently seen in the streets. The orator Demosthenes reports that one of the effects of the poverty that afflicted Athens after its defeat in the Peloponnesian War was that many women had to go out to work, typically as wet nurses, weavers, and grape pickers (57.45). In Aristophanes' *Thesmophoriazousai*, a widow with five children describes how she earns a precarious living by weaving chaplets (lines 446–49).

To offer any final assessment regarding the condition and status of women in the Greek world is impossible. Because we possess no testimony by the women themselves, all we have to go on are statements made by men about women. Furthermore, our ability to make an objective judgment is complicated by contemporary assumptions about the role and status of women in our own society—assumptions, moreover, that continue to be in a state of flux. Certain unpalatable facts are not in dispute, however. For instance, a girl's chances of survival were poorer than those of a boy from birth on, her life expectancy was shorter than that of a male, her opportunities for acquiring an education were virtually nonexistent, the law regarded her as a minor whatever her years, and should she choose to abandon her traditional role as mother and housekeeper, virtually the only profession available to her was prostitution.

At the same time, some evidence suggests that men did not invariably have the upper hand. Just to give a humorous example, Socrates' wife, Xanthippe, is said to have doused the philosopher in water on one occasion and to have stripped him of his cloak in public on another (Diogenes Laertios, *Lives of Famous Philosophers* 2.36–37). Relationships between the sexes were no doubt complex, as they have been throughout history. As Andromache observed, "I offered my husband a silent tongue and gentle looks. I knew when to have my way and when to let him have his" (Euripides, *Trojan Women* 655f.). Even so, we should probably not attach too much credence to a remark ascribed by Plutarch to the Athenian politician Themistocles, who claimed that his son was the most powerful person in Greece on the grounds that the Athenians commanded the Greeks; he, Themistocles, commanded the Athenians; his wife commanded him; and his son commanded his wife (*Life of Themistocles* 18.5) (Garland, 47–48, 52–57).

FOR MORE INFORMATION

Cantarella, E. *Pandora's Daughters: The Role and Status of Women in Greek and Roman Antiquity.* Translated by M. Fant. Baltimore, Md.: Johns Hopkins University Press, 1987.
Garland, R. *Daily Life of the Ancient Greeks.* Westport, Conn.: Greenwood Press, 1998.
Just, R. *Women in Athenian Law and Life.* London: n.p., 1981.

ROME

Roman women in poor families often had to work hard, whether on the farm or in a business, just like the men in the family. Thus for most women, their day-to-

day lives were not much different from men's, although legally they were accorded inferior status. Women did not possess Roman citizenship, could not vote in elections or run for political office, and were not permitted to take part in the speech making and debates that characterized Rome's lively public life.

Upper-class girls were raised in the household, rarely venturing outside the house itself. The chief figure in their lives was their mother, who supervised whatever education they received. In terms of reading, writing, and literature, the education that these girls obtained varied enormously from house to house. There are a few famous examples of highly educated women, but excessive knowledge or intellectual ability was regarded with suspicion and disfavor. The main focus of a girl's education was to learn how to spin thread and weave clothing. Eventually, she would be married to a man selected by her father, often chosen for economic or political reasons.

Once married, the woman became subject to her husband, who gained all the powers over her that her father had once exercised. In legal terms, she was treated like her husband's daughter; her property became his, and he even had the right to kill her if given sufficient provocation, such as discovering her committing adultery. (A husband, by contrast, could freely cheat on his wife without fear of blame or reprisal.) It was a woman's responsibility to run her husband's household, which entailed supervising the slaves and overseeing the education of their young children. Spinning wool, weaving cloth, and sewing were seen as important skills for the woman to possess, regardless of whether her husband could afford to buy cloth or the slaves to make it. Even an emperor, Augustus, required that his wife and daughter spin, weave, and produce the clothes for his household. While other abilities and talents in a woman were praised on occasion, suspicion was sometimes aroused by women who were considered excessively intelligent or accomplished. Cleverness could lead to improper behavior. In early Rome, even a talent for singing and dancing was viewed as an incitement to vice.

Generally speaking, a woman was supposed to spend most of her time within the confines of the household. When upper-class women did venture out of the house— to visit the marketplace, the baths, temples, or women friends—they often were transported in curtained litters carried by slaves, both to avoid the filth in the streets and to stay concealed and unseen in public. Women were supposed to be modest and chaste. A Roman matron's clothing was intended to cover her completely, and statues frequently depict women making a gesture to indicate their *pudicitia*, or modesty. Fidelity to one's husband was crucial. The historian Livy's story about the heroic woman, Lucretia, is revealing; Lucretia wins a contest as best of wives because she is at home sewing late into the night rather than visiting and gossiping with friends, and when she is raped, she commits suicide because she has betrayed her husband, albeit against her will. Although her husband and father tell her she is blameless, she feels disgraced and fears that her ruined reputation will sully her family's good name. Roman girls were instructed to view Lucretia as a role model, and self-sacrifice as a virtue. Cornelia, the mother of the Gracchi, was also lauded as a heroic woman; she bore 12 children who all died before her, but she stifled her grief and endured her losses bravely. The Republican ideal of womanhood called for frugality, industriousness, restraint, piety, self-effacement, obedience to one's husband, and the ability to control one's emotions and maintain a stoical demeanor. It was wrong for a woman to be avaricious, ambitious, ostentatious or self-promoting.

However, there was a certain degree of divergence between the ideal behavior of wives and the reality. Women did commit adultery and divorce their husbands to marry others. Particularly during the empire, some women obtained a degree of legal independence. Some women married or related to powerful men could even have an impact on politics and government and exercise power, such as Marc Antony's wife, Fulvia. Women who dared to assume masculine roles were derided, as when Valerius Maximus describes a small number of women advocates as being unwomanly and monstrous (*Memorable Deeds and Sayings* 8.3). Under the empire, many writers decried the growing decadence and immorality of contemporary society and praised the days of early Rome, when men and women had still been virtuous. Sumptuary laws were passed to regulate the clothing and jewelry of wealthy women. Satirists lampooned women for enhancing their appearance through excessive makeup, hair dyes, and wigs, all of which were seen as suggesting dishonesty and falseness of character. Augustus promulgated laws meant to promote the institution of marriage and procreation, which he thought were on the decline. The supposed deterioration of women's virtue was considered an indicator that something was wrong with society as a whole.

Comparatively little is known about the lives of lower-class women who had to work outside the home to help support their families or themselves. They may have worked as vendors in the marketplace or learned a trade, such as cloth making or perfume manufacture. The medical profession was one of the few open to women; there is record of a number of female doctors, although women more commonly served as midwives and as wet nurses in wealthy families.

While women could not act onstage in theatrical productions, they could perform in mimes and pantomimes, although this imparted a shady reputation. A bad reputation also plagued women who worked at *tabernae* (taverns) as tavern keepers, waitresses, barmaids, and cooks; they were considered to be practically on the level of prostitutes—another career open to poor women. Contact with the public sphere, in whatever capacity, seems to have compromised a woman's reputation.

~Gregory S. Aldrete

FOR MORE INFORMATION

Cantarella, E. *Pandora's Daughters: The Role and Status of Women in Greek and Roman Antiquity.* Translated by M. Fant. Baltimore, Md.: Johns Hopkins University Press, 1987.

Fantham, E., H. P. Foley, N. B. Kampen, S. B. Pomeroy, and H. A. Shapiro. *Women in the Classical World.* New York: Oxford University Press, 1994.

Lefkowitz, M., and M. Fant. *Women's Life in Greece and Rome.* Baltimore, Md.: Johns Hopkins University Press, 1982.

INDIA

Little is known about domestic life during the Indus Valley civilization (2500–1500 B.C.E.), primarily because the texts, written in proto-Dravidian script, have never been deciphered.

DOMESTIC LIFE
|
WOMEN
|
Mesopotamia

Egypt

Greece

Rome

India

We do know that the Indus Valley civilization was not clearly patriarchal, nor was it clearly matriarchal. Gender roles, and human sexuality in general, seem to have been integrated into everyday life, and even into religious iconography. Female powers of fertility were clearly celebrated, as is evidenced by terra-cotta figurines that accentuate the female breasts, as well as the curves of the waist and legs. Graves of priestesses have also been found. Strong evidence exists of goddess worship within the home, but animals were also revered, and they are usually depicted as male in gender. Residential and commercial areas of Indus towns were arranged on a grid pattern, and there is evidence of extensive public works systems. This suggests a well-ordered domestic life, integrated fully into the wider community. There is evidence of the accumulation of wealth, with enough to furnish most households even with children's toys and jewelry. Marriage seems to have been a relatively equal arrangement between men and women. By the time of the *Brahmanas*, written about the eighth century B.C.E., the status of women was in gradual decline.

At the dawn of the Vedic era, the status of women was relatively equal to that of men, but the Vedic concern for the purity of ritual sacrifice marginalized women, especially during menstruation. The worship of goddesses, dominant in the Indus Valley civilization, gave way to reverence for male deities. In the earliest of the Vedic texts, the *Rig Veda*, the authors offer prayers asking the gods for sons and grandsons over daughters and granddaughters. Throughout the *Atharva Veda*, prayers are offered to grant the birth of daughters elsewhere in favor of granting the birth of a son within one's own family. The *Aitereya Brahmana* notes that the daughter is a source of misery and that the son is the savior of the family.

These trends continued into the Epic and Puranic period, which dates from about 500 B.C.E. into the first millennium C.E., although the negative attitudes toward females were moderated somewhat. The Laws of Manu, for instance, command kindness toward daughters. In this era, women generally filled one of three roles: daughter, wife, or as a *sati*. The word *sati* (literally, "faithful wife") refers both to a goddess and to the practice of self-immolation on the husband's funeral pyre. In the Epic and Puranic period, women were taught that their husbands were to be treated as gods, but this also meant that women were themselves identified with goddesses, like Sati, the faithful wife of the god Shiva. Self-immolation, rarely practiced, was the final act of devotion to a husband and a way for a wife to ensure her status as a goddess.

Another example of the faithful wife comes from the *Ramayana*. In this epic, the god Vishnu is born on earth as Rama and wins his faithful wife, Sita. Sita's fidelity, however, comes into question when she is abducted by a demon-king. She is required to prove herself in a trial by fire. Women's sexuality by this time was generally seen as dangerous, unless controlled by their husbands. One final example of this comes from the *Brahmavaivarta Purana*, where Parvati, another of Shiva's wives, builds up tremendous power merely from spending years controlling her own sexuality. These trends in ancient Indian domestic life have provided the framework for family life and marital life throughout the history of Hindu India.

To read about women in nineteenth-century India, see the India entry in the section titled "Women" in the "Domestic Life" chapter of volume 5 of this series,

Nineteenth Century; for twentieth-century India, see the India entry in the "Domestic Life" chapter of volume 6.

~*Eric Rothgery*

FOR MORE INFORMATION

Auboyer, J. *Daily Life in Ancient India*. London: Phoenix Press, 1965.

Basham, A. L. *The Wonder That Was India*. London: Sidgwick and Jackson, 1967.

Meyer, J. *Sexual Life in Ancient India*. Columbia, Mo: South Asia Books, 1989.

Marriage

DOMESTIC LIFE

| MARRIAGE |

Mesopotamia

Egypt

Greece

Rome

The existence of elaborate marriage ceremonies in nearly all cultures suggests a strong human impulse to demarcate important life-changing events with rituals that symbolically indicate the altered status of the individuals involved. Couples in Mesopotamia, Egypt, Greece, and Rome all took part in elaborate wedding rituals before a gathering of family and friends. Many elements of ancient marriage ceremonies would still be familiar to modern brides and grooms, including the wearing of a veil by the bride, the exchange of vows, the giving of gifts, and even the custom of showering the newlyweds with small food items (nuts in Greece and Rome).

It is important to note that whereas wedding ceremonies today are religious rituals, ancient weddings were mainly secular events, although they usually included some prayers and sacrifices. In fact, the ceremony itself was often more of a social event than the legally binding force that created the marriage. In Rome and Mesopotamia, to be legally married, all a couple had to do was verbally state their intent. The union of the two people was rarely romantically motivated; it was more often representative of an economic or political union between the families involved. The dowry, a usually substantial sum of money or valuables that accompanied the bride, was an intrinsic part of ancient wedding agreements. Weddings were most typically arranged by fathers for their children through written contracts that were far more influenced by level-headed business sense than by romantic fancies.

The goal of marriage was to produce children, and the rituals of marriage usually emphasized this purpose. The marriage ceremonies also tended to stress the transition of the woman from her father's family and house to those of her new husband. Thus ceremonies in both Greece and Rome included a lively procession from one house to the other, and in Rome the groom even symbolically abducted his new wife from her old family by wrenching her from the grasp of her mother.

Procedures for dissolving marriages through some form of divorce also existed in all of these cultures. Then as now, one of the main focal points of divorce law was how the property owned by the couple was to be divided up. Women often received the blame for divorce or disproportionately suffered the consequences. In Babylon, a woman could be tortured or put to death for even expressing desire for a divorce.

In Egypt, on the other hand, divorced women could count on receiving alimony from their ex-husbands.

~*Gregory S. Aldrete*

DOMESTIC LIFE
|
MARRIAGE
|
Mesopotamia

Egypt

Greece

Rome

MESOPOTAMIA

Reconstructing marital relationships in the ancient Near East has proved a difficult task. Generally, marriage was monogamous, even among the gods. Happy marriages flourished in ancient times; a Sumerian proverb mentions a husband boasting that his wife had borne eight sons and was still ready to make love. Like people the world over and throughout time, ancient Mesopotamians fell deeply in love. Texts refer to ensuing depression in the case of rejection. To remedy this situation, the man or woman prayed to a god or used a magic spell. Some magic rituals came with a guarantee, promising that if the man performed it, "this woman will speak to you whenever you meet her, she will be powerless to resist and you can make love to her." In the case of lovers' quarrels, the man might also resort to charms or spells with similar claims: "With this charm she will not sleep alone; she will be loved" (cited in Saggs, 146).

The law codes addressed various aspects of marriage. Legal documents were drawn to define property rights—a kind of ancient prenuptial agreement. A unique document from Ur recorded the expenses, gifts, and payments incurred by the father of the bride over a four-month period during the negotiations over the marriage of his daughter.

Customs varied over time and place, but the process of marriage included at least four stages: (1) the engagement, (2) payments by the families of both the bride (dowry) and the groom (bride-price), (3) the bride's move to her father-in-law's house, and (4) sexual intercourse.

The legal definition of marriage is found in the Laws of Eshnunna §§27–28, in which marriage included a contract as well as a feast: If a man marries the daughter of another man without the consent of her father and mother, and moreover does not conclude the wedding feast and contract for her father and her mother, even if she lives in his house for a full year, she is not a wife. If he concludes a wedding feast and a contract for her father and her mother, and he marries her, she is indeed his wife; the day she is caught lying with another man (literally, "in the lap of another man"), she shall die, she will not live.

The contract described in the Laws of Eshnunna was between the two families, commonly represented by the fathers. For the groom's family, the contract concerned payment of the bride-price, which was a considerable sum of silver in the Old Babylonian period. The bride-price was an act of good faith, ensuring the groom's right to the bride.

Both the bride-price and the dowry could be paid in installments until the first child was born, at which time the balance of both payments was due. The marriage was then legally finalized, and the mother assumed the legal rights of a "wife."

The bride-price was equal in value to the dowry provided by the bride's family. The dowry consisted of household utensils, silver rings (a form of ancient coinage), slaves, and even fields. In addition to these items, the dowry in later periods included other household goods such as furniture, textiles, and jewelry. The bride brought her dowry with her. A husband could use his wife's property and manage it with his own assets.

In Old Babylonian times, the dowry was often itemized. A document was drawn to specify that the bride's father "sent it and her into the house of A, her father-in-law, for B, his son" (Postgate, 103). The document concluded with the payment to be made by the groom's family in the event of divorce. If the groom died or had a change of heart, his father could insist that the bride be given to one of the groom's brothers if one were available and of age. That is, the bride married into her husband's family—she did not marry an individual.

The marriage contract was also an oral agreement, probably accompanied by formal or symbolic actions and marriage vows. The words recited at marriage can be reconstructed from the spoken formula of divorce, namely, "You are not my husband" and "You are not my wife"—that is, an annulment of words cited in a wedding described in a magical text: "I will fill your lap with silver and gold: You are my wife, I am your husband" (cited in Greengus, 516).

Not much is known about the wedding ceremonies. Among wealthy families, the wedding party lasted several days or even weeks. The groom and his family customarily gave gifts to the bride and her family at the wedding celebration. These gifts included food for the wedding feast and the prenuptial celebrations leading up to it. Also, gifts of clothing, jewelry, and other valuables could be added. During the wedding celebration, the bride was covered with a veil that the groom removed. Once married, women were not veiled in Babylonia. Legal texts imply that married women were veiled in Assyria.

The next step in the marriage process varied. Because girls often married young, as teenagers, the young bride might either continue to live in her father's house or move to her father-in-law's house. Assyrian texts speak of brides who were "four half cubits high" (about three feet). Under these circumstances, consummation occurred later. The groom was usually 10 years older than his bride.

Even if the bride continued to reside in her parental home, the groom could visit his father-in-law's home to consummate the marriage. This event was accompanied by traditional ceremonies. The bridegroom might be accompanied by a male companion, and both would reside in the father-in-law's house for a period of time. Marriage was euphemistically alluded to as "calling at the house of the in-law." A bed, included in dowry lists, was used to consummate the marriage. There are extant terra-cotta models (some of which include a couple in the throes of passion), and royal hymns spoke of beds used for making love.

The virginity of the bride was a matter of concern. The "best men" of the bride were a group of "friends" who protected her against dangers and were responsible for her chastity. After the wedding night, they displayed "the bloody sheet." When virginity was disputed, the courts called on expert female witnesses to offer testimony. A letter from Mari describes the situation of a betrothed girl: "The 'wife' of

Sin-iddinam declared as follows: Before Sin-iddinam took me, I had agreed with [the wish of] father and son. When Sin-iddinam had departed from his house, the son of Asqudum sent me the message 'I want to take you.' He kissed my lips, he touched my vagina—his penis did not enter my vagina. Thus I said, 'I will not sin against Sin-iddinam' " (cited in Stol, 489–90). In an earlier trial in Nippur, a man denied physical penetration using the same words. Obviously, penetration was the criterion to establish whether a woman—virgin, betrothed, married, or slave—was raped or seduced, to determine culpability.

With rare exceptions, a man could not have more than one formally recognized wife at a time. Both Babylonian law codes and court proceedings indicate that only under exceptional circumstances was a man permitted to have more than one wife at the same time. For example, the Laws of Hammurabi (§148) allowed the husband to take a second wife when his first wife was incapacitated by illness; however, he could not divorce his first wife, whom he was obliged to support until her death.

Divorce usually was initiated by the husband. He could divorce his wife, but he had to return her property and sometimes pay a fine. The divorce was accompanied by the symbolic act of cutting the hem of the wife's robe—the reverse of knotting the original bride-payment in her robe.

Social stigma was attached to divorce; therefore, it was not undertaken without grave cause, such as adultery by the wife or a childless marriage. Many Old Babylonian marriage contracts forbade the wife to divorce her husband, often by threatening her with penalties customary for adultery: drowning in the river, being pushed from a tower, or impalement. The wife could even be sold into slavery. Also, at various times in ancient Mesopotamia, a woman who expressed the desire to divorce could be thrown out of her husband's home, penniless and naked. The conditions of the divorce were influenced by whether the wife had sons. If the woman had no sons, the husband's family did not care if she returned to her father's house or went elsewhere. However, some agreements and Assyrian and Babylonian marriage contracts permitted either the husband or the wife to divorce; each was fined the same amount in silver. This arrangement contrasted markedly with the inferior position of women under Middle Assyrian law. It seems that the status and independence of specific women gave them equal rights in the marriage; possibly these women were independent widows or the daughters of rich families.

Because marriage was treated as a bond between families, its purpose was to secure sons to perpetuate the male line. But an infertile marriage did not result in an automatic divorce. Both law and custom allowed a barren wife to supply a slave girl as her surrogate to bear children, who were legally considered the wife's children. Another arrangement permitted the childless wife to adopt a second woman as her sister and permit that woman to marry her husband. The exact same principles of law were applied to a priestess, who was permitted to marry but not to have sexual relations with her husband; she, too, could provide a surrogate to bear sons.

In Assyria, if a woman's husband abandoned her, did not support her, or left no sons who could support her, she could take another husband after five years. Her first husband could not reclaim her. If a woman did not wait for the five-year period to elapse, but went to live with a man and bore him children, her husband could return and take her children on his return. In addition, if the first husband was absent for reasons beyond his control, such as being captured, he could reclaim his wife after the five-year period. He then had to provide the second husband with a replacement (Nemet-Nejat, 132–36, 140–41).

FOR MORE INFORMATION

Greengus, S. "The Old Babylonian Marriage Contract." *Journal of the American Oriental Society* 89 (1969).

Nemet-Nejat, K. R. *Daily Life in Ancient Mesopotamia.* Westport, Conn.: Greenwood Press, 1998.

Postgate, J. N. *Early Mesopotamia: Society and Economy at the Dawn of History.* New York: Routledge, 1992.

Saggs, H. W. F. *The Might That Was Assyria.* London: Sidgwick and Jackson, 1984.

Stol, M. "Private Life in Ancient Mesopotamia." In *Civilizations of the Ancient Near East,* ed. J. Sasson. Vol. 1. New York: Scribner's, 1995.

EGYPT

DOMESTIC LIFE
|
MARRIAGE
|
Mesopotamia
Egypt
Greece
Rome

Whether rich or poor, any free person in Egypt had the right to the joys of marriage. Marriage was not a religious matter in Egypt—no ceremony involving a priest took place—but simply a social convention that required an agreement, which is to say a contract, negotiated by the suitor and the family of his prospective wife. The agreement involved an exchange of objects of value on both sides. The suitor offered a sum called the "virginity gift," when appropriate, to compensate the bride for what she would lose, indicating that in ancient times virginity was prized in female brides. The gift did not apply in the case of second marriages, of course, but a "gift to the bride" would be made even in that case. In return, the family of the bride-to-be offered a "gift to become a wife." In many cases, these two gifts were never delivered because the pair soon merged households. However, in the event of divorce, either party could later sue for the agreed gift. A third sum, called the "alimentation," consisted of a periodic subsidy from the bride's family to compensate for the additional expense of a second person in the household, and it was given with stipulations of how the wife must be treated in return. The remainder of the contract consisted of a kind of ancient prenuptial agreement, specifying what property belonged to the woman and what belonged to the man, as well as stating who would inherit what on the death of either party.

In some cases, a written contract was executed before witnesses; in others, only a verbal agreement took place. Either satisfied the official requirement for marriage, although, human nature being what it is, a party to celebrate the happy event generally followed. The new husband and wife presided at this affair, rather than being the guests of either set of parents.

After recovering from the merriment, the couple began married life with the presumption that their union would last until death. Of course, life did not always work out so well; divorces, although not common, did occur. Because no religion or state had joined the pair, no authorization was required for their separation. All that severing involved was living apart. Yet, given marriage's contractual obligations, divorce for most couples involved a legal declaration of the dissolution of the marriage, which freed them to marry again. The original marriage contract also contained stipulations about gifts and other matters. If a husband initiated a divorce, he forfeited the entire gift to the bride or in some cases, an amount double that gift. If the wife instituted a divorce, she returned half of the gift to the groom. Regardless of who began the proceedings, the husband was obliged to continue paying the wife's alimentary money, providing full financial support until she married again. Not without its modern counterparts, this clause certainly held some marriages together that otherwise would have dissolved. Other contracted sums were generally assigned to the children (Brier and Hobbs, 71–72).

FOR MORE INFORMATION

Allam, S. *Some Pages from . . . Everyday Life in Ancient Egypt.* Cairo: Prism Books, 1985.

Brier, B., and H. Hobbs. *Daily Life of the Ancient Egyptians.* Westport, Conn.: Greenwood Press, 1999.

Tyldesley, J. *Daughters of Isis: Women of Ancient Egypt.* New York: Penguin Books, 1984.

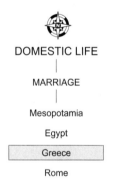

DOMESTIC LIFE
|
MARRIAGE
|
Mesopotamia

Egypt

Greece

Rome

GREECE

Although we have no documentary evidence regarding age at marriage in Greece, literary sources suggest that girls in their early to mid-teens typically married men who were old enough to be their fathers. Hesiod, in *Works and Days*, recommends that a man should be "not much less than in his thirtieth year" and a girl "in her fifth year past puberty" (lines 695–99). Hesiod's view, though that of a peasant farmer, was by no means unique. Solon was of the opinion that the right time for a man to marry was between the ages of 27 and 34. Similarly, Plato claimed that a man was at his peak for marriage at age 30. Some brides would have been even younger than the age recommended by Hesiod, particularly those who came from wealthy families, as we know from a law code from Gortyn on Crete, which decreed that heiresses should be married when they are 12 or older.

Arranged marriages were the norm in Greek society, although a mature suitor would negotiate on his own behalf with his future bride's parents. Wealth and status, rather than emotional attachment, were the principal criteria for choosing a wife. Mercenary and cynical though this system may seem to us, one must bear in mind that there were very few opportunities for the creation of wealth in ancient Greece. A marriage alliance was thus primarily an opportunity both to produce offspring and to increase the family's finances. A girl would almost invariably have been provided with a dowry, since without one she risked ending her life "unwed and barren" (Sophocles, *Oedipus the King* line 1502). Dowries varied considerably in size. The aristocratic politician Alcibiades received the huge sum of 10 talents when he married the sister of Kallias, one of the wealthiest men of his day. Because the function of the dowry was to provide maintenance for the wife, legal restraints were imposed on its use. In the event of divorce, for instance, the husband was required to return it intact to his wife's father or legal guardian. If for any reason he was unable to produce the entire sum, he was required to pay interest on it. The wife's personal possessions were also returned to her family. The orator Isaios informs us that when Menecles divorced his wife, he returned not only the dowry but also her jewelry and clothing. The clear purpose of this law was to ensure that a divorced woman did not become financially destitute.

Athenian law also imposed strict regulations on the marriage of a daughter whose father died leaving no male heir behind. (Athenians were required by law to leave the bulk of their estates to their sons.) Such a woman was known as an *epiklêros*, which literally means "attached to the *klêros,* or estate." The estate in question did not actually belong to her but merely accompanied her when she married. Because it was the duty of the nearest male relative to claim an *epiklêros* as his wife, an *epiklêros* might, and presumably occasionally did, marry her own uncle. So strictly was the law upheld that in some cases, existing marriages were dissolved to comply with it. Its purpose was to keep property within the family and thus prevent the amalgamation of several *oikoi,* or households. For much the same reason, marriages were often contracted between relatives, especially among the wealthy.

Marriage created a much more violent disruption in the life of a woman than it did in the life of a man. The bride not only was removed from her family at an age when she was scarcely past playing with her dolls but also had to take on a number of onerous duties, chief of which was to produce an heir for her husband as soon as possible.

The most popular time for getting married was in the winter month of Gamelion, which actually means "the time of wedding." The ceremony began with a sacrifice to the gods of marriage, Zeus and Hera, to whom the bride dedicated a lock of her hair. She then dedicated her childhood possessions to the virgin goddess Artemis.

On the day of the wedding, an Athenian bride took a ritual bath in water. This was poured from a special vase known as a *loutrophoros,* which means "a carrier of *loutra* (sacred water)." This bath prepared her for her new life. It was followed by a feast held at the house of the bride's father. Here, the bride, who was veiled, sat apart from all the men, including the bridegroom. Beside her sat an older woman called a *nympheutria,* who guided her through the ceremony. Little cakes covered in sesame seeds were served to the guests. These were believed to make women fertile. Toward evening, the bridegroom led his bride, still veiled, from her father's house in a wagon drawn by mules or oxen. The bride sat in the middle with the groom on one side and the best man, or *paranymphos,* on the other. A torchlight procession preceded the wedding party along the route, and wedding hymns were sung to the accompaniment of the flute and lyre. On arrival at the bridegroom's house, the couple was showered with nuts and dried figs by other members of the household. They now entered the bridal chamber, and the bride removed her veil. The door to the bridal chamber was closed, and a hymn called an *epithalamion* was sung outside. Its macabre purpose, according to a late source, was to cover the cries of the bride as she underwent the violence of penetration. A Greek wedding was a private ceremony, which did not require the services of a state official or priest.

The first and overriding duty of a Greek wife was to provide her husband with offspring, preferably male offspring, to ensure that his household did not die out. In the absence of any reliable method of birth control, there would be little opportunity for respite between pregnancies. In addition to the pressure that came from the husband and the husband's family, there would also have been pressure from society at large, since every Greek community expected its citizens to beget legitimate children to keep the population at parity. Because of the high level of infant mortality, it is estimated that each married couple would have had to produce four or five children to achieve even this modest target. The obligation to become pregnant was further reinforced by medical theory, which taught that abstinence from sex was injurious to health. A text ascribed to Hippocrates, the legendary founder of Greek medicine, states:

Women who have intercourse are healthier than those who abstain. For the womb is moistened by intercourse and ceases to be dry, whereas when it is drier than it should be it contracts violently and this contraction causes pain to the body. (*Seed* 4)

Giving birth was an extremely risky undertaking partly because the standards of hygiene were deplorably low and partly because women often became pregnant while still pubescent. Miscarriages were extremely common, as were the deaths of women in labor. Echoing no doubt the judgment of many Greek women, Medea in Euripides' play of that name sums up the perils of childbirth: "I would rather stand in battle-line three times than give birth once" (line 250f.).

The failure to become pregnant was typically regarded with grave suspicion or interpreted as a biological problem from which the woman was suffering. Conversely, once a woman had provided her husband with a male heir, her standing and respect within the household increased considerably. One Athenian husband who discovered his wife in bed with her lover and slew the latter on the spot justified his action to the jury by stating that after the arrival of his firstborn, he had bestowed upon his wife complete control of his estate in the belief that "the two of us had now achieved a condition of complete intimacy" (Lysias 1.6). Given the importance of producing offspring, it is hardly surprising that concern about fertility and pregnancy features prominently among the miraculous cures that are inscribed on stones in the healing sanctuary of Aesculapius at Epidaurus in the northeast Peloponnese. One inscription, for instance, states: "Agamede from Chios. She slept in the sanctuary to have children and saw a dream. A snake seemed to lie on her belly and as a result five children were born."

> ### 📷 *Snapshot*
>
> **A Greek Divorce Document**
>
> Soulis, gravedigger, to Senpais, daughter of Psais and Tees, gravedigger, greetings. Because it has come about as the result of some evil spirit that we are estranged from one another in respect to our common life, I, the said Soulis, hereby admit before sending her away that I have received all the objects given to her by me . . . and that she is free to depart and marry whomever she wishes.
>
> I, the said Senpais, acknowledge that I have received from the said Soulis all that was given to him by way of dowry. (as cited in Garland, 55)

A wife seeking a divorce would most commonly be represented in the courts by her next of kin. If she sought to represent herself, the law afforded her no protection from further abuse, as we learn from an anecdote told by Plutarch about Hipparete, Alcibiades' wife, who became so distressed by her husband's philandering that she went to live with her brother. When she lodged a complaint against her husband in the courts, however, Alcibiades "seized hold of her and dragged her back home through the Agora, with no-one daring to stop him or rescue her" (*Life of Alcibiades* 8.2–4). If a divorce was granted, no formalities were required other than the return of the dowry to the wife's *oikos*. The husband, too, was free to claim back whatever he had contributed.

Because of the large age difference between men and women at marriage, many wives became widows by the time they reached their late 20s or early 30s. Young widows were expected to remarry, whereas older widows probably enjoyed considerable freedom. In view of the fact that the dowry which a wife brought with her had to be returned to her natal household (i.e., to the head of the family into which she was born) in the event of her husband's death, widows, like divorcees, were guaranteed some degree of economic security.

Athenians could also enter into a less formal and less binding arrangement with a partner of the opposite sex known as a *pallakê*, close to the modern equivalent of a common-law wife. Such unions were made primarily with foreigners, prostitutes, and women who had no dowries. The prostitute Aspasia, virtually the only woman in fifth century B.C.E. Athens who is known to us other than by name, was the *pallakê* of Pericles. A *pallakê* was placed under the authority of the man with whom she lived in much the same way as a legitimate wife. There were, however, two important differences: such a union did not involve the transfer of a dowry, and the offspring were not regarded as citizens and so had no claim on the man's *oikos*. In the last decade of the Peloponnesian War, however, this regulation was suspended because of the shortage of Athenian manpower. Citizens were therefore permitted to have a legitimate wife as well as a *pallakê* (Garland, 48–52, 55–56).

FOR MORE INFORMATION

Demand, N. *Birth, Death, and Motherhood in Classical Greece*. Baltimore, Md.: Johns Hopkins University Press, 1994.

Garland, R. *Daily Life of the Ancient Greeks*. Westport, Conn.: Greenwood Press, 1998.

Hunt, A. and C. Edgar, trans. *Select Papyri* 1, no. 8 in Loeb Classical Library. Cambridge, Mass.: Harvard University Press, 1932.

ROME

Roman girls would have led sheltered lives, and many may have hardly ventured outside their home until their marriage. Boys were considered to be ready for marriage at the age of 14, whereas girls were considered to be ready for marriage at 12, and a woman who was not married by 20 was considered a deviant. The emperor

DOMESTIC LIFE
|
MARRIAGE
|
Mesopotamia

Egypt

Greece

Rome

Augustus formalized this tradition by passing a law that heavily penalized any woman over the age of 20 and any man over the age of 25 who were not married.

The Romans allowed marriages between closer family members than modern society would. It was permissible for first cousins to marry, and from the early empire on, even uncles could marry their nieces. Roman law did not recognize a marriage with a foreigner, a slave, or a freedman. Also, up until 217 C.E., soldiers were not allowed to marry. It was, of course, common for a soldier to form long-lasting relationships with a woman and for the two to live together and consider themselves a couple. However, their union was not formally recognized by law. The two great drawbacks to this system were that the women were not subject to inheritance laws and any children they had were considered illegitimate.

At least among the aristocracy, nearly all marriages were arranged by the parents. The *paterfamilias* (male head of the family) would negotiate with his counterpart in the other family to arrange the marriage. Even if somehow two people met, fell in love, and wished to marry, they still needed the permission of the *paterfamilias;* lacking such permission, a marriage could not occur. There were only two ways to get married without the express permission of a *paterfamilias*. The first was if the *paterfamilias* was judged to be insane. The second was if he had been captured in war and had been a prisoner for at least three years.

Marriages were not love matches but rather were seen as political tools and as a way to cement an alliance between two families or political factions. It was extremely common for politicians to marry, divorce, and remarry as their political allegiances shifted or to contract marriages among their children. The desire to use children as political pawns led to children being engaged at very young ages, sometimes even as babies. In an attempt to curb this practice, a law was passed stating that to be engaged, the two people had to be at least seven years old.

To symbolize the engagement, the man (or boy) placed an iron ring on the middle finger of the left hand of his fiancée. The reason for this was that while conducting dissection of human bodies, Roman doctors believed that they discovered a nerve that ran directly from this finger to the heart. To make a marriage legally binding was simple. The only requirement was a public statement of intent. Marriage was viewed as a religious duty whose goal was to produce children to ensure that the family gods would continue to be worshiped.

There were two basic types of Roman marriages, and during the Republic almost all were of the first type, known as a *manus* marriage. *Manus* means "hand" in Latin, and this marriage received its name from the fact that the woman was regarded as a piece of property that passed from the hand of the father to that of the husband. In this type of marriage, the woman had no rights, and any property she had was under the control of her husband. She herself was considered the equivalent of a daughter to her husband, and he had all the powers of life and death that a father held over a daughter. There were two subcategories of the *manus* marriage. The first is called *coemptio*. In this type of marriage, the groom symbolically gave money to the bride's father and lit-

Statue perhaps depicting a Roman marriage. One tradition at the marriage feast was for the bride and groom to sit on chairs over which was stretched a single sheepskin. Reproduced from the collections of the Library of Congress.

erally bought her. Another type was called *usus*. In this type of marriage, the man and woman simply began to live together, and on the day after they had lived together continuously for one year, the woman passed into the control of her husband in a *manus* marriage. Some women who did not wish to lose their independence made sure that each year they spent three consecutive nights away from their husband and because of this, never came under his control.

The second main type of marriage was rare in the Republic but became quite common under the empire. It is known as a free marriage, and in it the woman retained all her own property, was not under the control of her husband, and if they separated, could take anything with her that she owned.

Just as today, there were many rituals associated with the marriage ceremony. First, the bride dedicated her childhood toys to the house gods, symbolizing that she was making the transition from child to woman. While she had been a child, she usually would have worn her hair in a ponytail, but on her wedding day, her hair was parted into six strands that were then tied together on top of her head in a complex fashion, forming a cone shape. It was traditional that her hair be parted using a bent iron spearhead, and the best spearhead of all was one that had been used to kill a gladiator. Gladiators were sometimes seen as symbols of virility, so perhaps this custom was viewed as a way to ensure a fertile union. The bride then donned a veil of transparent fabric that was bright orange or red in color, which her shoes matched. Her tunic was white, and she placed a wreath of marjoram on her head.

Before a gathering of friends and relatives, various sacrifices were performed, and the woman declared to her husband, "I am now of your family," at which point their hands were joined. A feast followed, at which the new bride and groom sat side by side in two chairs over which was stretched a single sheepskin. At the feast, it was customary for the guests to shout "Feliciter!" which means happiness or good luck. Toward the end of the evening, the bride was placed in the arms of her mother, and then the groom came and tore her out of her mother's grasp.

All this occurred at the bride's house, and now the bride, groom, and guests marched to the bride's new home, the home of her husband. As they went through the streets in a torch-lit procession, the guests threw nuts and shouted "Talassio," a traditional Roman wedding acclamation, and they also often sang obscene songs. When they reached the groom's house, the couple threw one of the torches, which was a special torch known as the wedding torch, into the crowd of guests; whoever caught it was supposed to enjoy long life. The bride then rubbed oil and fat on the door posts, and her new husband picked her up and carried her over the threshold. Once inside, she symbolically touched fire and water indicating that she was now the guardian of the hearth. In the entry hall was placed a miniature marriage bed intended for the spirits of the bride and groom. After the fire and water ceremony, the new couple went off to their marriage bed.

None of this elaborate ceremony was necessary to make a marriage legal. It was the statement of intent that actually made a marriage legal, but performing some or all of these rituals was common practice.

Usually, the wife's family had to provide some kind of dowry, which among very rich families could easily amount to one million sesterces, equivalent to the minimum wealth qualification for a senator. Whatever the sum, dowries were usually paid in three annual installments.

The main duty of the wife was to produce children, and because many women married before they were physically mature, not surprisingly, many young wives died of complications in childbirth. One of the main sources of information on Roman women is their tombstones. Many of these record the sad stories of girls who were married at 12 or 13, gave birth five or six times, and died in childbirth before they reached the age of 20. These tombstones are also the best guide to what Roman men considered the ideal qualities of a wife. Some of the most common positive attributes used by husbands to describe their deceased wives include chaste, obedient, friendly, old-fashioned, frugal, content to stay at home, pious, dressed simply, good at spinning thread, and good at weaving cloth.

Conversely, one way that men were praised on their tombstones was to say that they treated their wife kindly, with the implication that such kindness was not necessary and was unusual. If in a *manus* marriage, the husband could beat his wife with impunity—and was expected to do so if she misbehaved. In one famous instance, a man beat his wife to death because she took a drink of wine; all his friends and family approved because her action was a clear sign of immorality. In the Republic, regardless of the type of marriage, a husband could kill his wife if she was caught committing adultery. Augustus stopped this but still allowed husbands to kill their wives if they were found in the house committing adultery with someone of lower status. A father could kill his daughter if he caught her committing adultery as long as he killed, or at least tried to kill, her lover at the same time.

Divorce was as easy as marriage. All a couple had to do was declare that they were getting divorced, and they were. Augustus passed another law that declared that if a woman was between the ages of 20 and 50 and got divorced, she had to marry again within six months; if her husband had died, she was granted longer for mourning but still had to get remarried within one year.

~Gregory S. Aldrete

FOR MORE INFORMATION

Treggiari, S. *Roman Marriage*. Oxford: Oxford University Press, 1991.

DOMESTIC LIFE
|
CHILDREN
|
Mesopotamia

Egypt

Greece

Rome

Australian Aboriginals

Children

If it is difficult to reconstruct the opinions of women in the ancient world because of a lack of written sources authored by them, such a gap in knowledge is even more acute when it comes to understanding the lives of children and the experience of childhood.

Some of the best clues to the lives of children come from archaeology, which has unearthed large numbers of ancient toys. Children in all ages and cultures, it seems, have enjoyed play. One of the most universal types of toys, excavated from sites in

Mesopotamia, Egypt, Greece, and the Roman world, are dolls. These range from crude clay figures to complex wooden dolls with articulated joints. Boys in the ancient world obviously enjoyed war toys, such as the miniature bows and arrows found in Mesopotamia or the model chariots from Egypt. Other toys attested from the ancient world include such familiar items as board games, spinning tops, and jump ropes.

Childhood was not all fun and games, however. Many children from an early age had to contribute their labor to the family farm or business, and only a lucky few received any education. An even more alarming aspect of childhood in the ancient world was the slender odds of surviving to reach adulthood. As a result of childhood diseases and poor nutrition and sanitation, probably a good third of successfully born children died before attaining puberty. The *bulla*, a bag containing magic protective charms and worn around the neck by Roman children, was one attempt to safeguard children from the hazards of childhood. Further decreasing the odds of survival was the widespread custom of abandoning unwanted babies.

These high mortality figures have led some to speculate that parents could not afford to form strong emotional attachments to their children, but it is clear from surviving documents that many parents did grieve deeply when their children died.

~*Gregory S. Aldrete*

MESOPOTAMIA

DOMESTIC LIFE

CHILDREN

Mesopotamia

Egypt

Greece

Rome

Australian Aboriginals

Prenatal care involved the use of amulets, herbal potions, rituals, and incantations. Amulets were objects believed to have magical and protective power, bringing luck or averting evil. To produce the necessary magical effect, amulets were worn by a person or placed at a specific location. Death in childbirth and infant mortality were imminent dangers. Many texts refer to Lamashtu (alias Daughter of Anu), the female demon who threatened the life of both mother and child. A woman in labor wore an image of the demon Pazuzu or his head to counteract the evil of Lamashtu for herself, her unborn children, and her newborn child. Lamashtu also caused miscarriage and crib death. This female demon was known to slip into the house of a pregnant woman and touch the woman's stomach seven times to kill the baby. Lamashtu also kidnapped the child from the wet nurse. Pazuzu was depicted with a canine face, extraordinarily bulging eyes, a scaly body, a snake-headed penis, talons, and sometimes wings. Metal or stone plaques against Lamashtu were engraved with an image of Lamashtu on one side and an incantation against the female demon on the other. Rows of demons and divine symbols were also engraved on these plaques. Lamashtu was depicted as having a lion's head, donkey's teeth, naked breasts, a hairy body, stained hands, long fingers and fingernails, and bird talons. She clutched snakes in her hands, while a piglet and puppy suckled at her breasts (Black and Green, 147–48).

Texts describe prescriptions for making a barren woman conceive and for giving birth easily: "Total: 21 stones to help a barren woman to become pregnant; you string them on a linen thread and put them around her neck" (cited in Biggs, 1917).

If a woman became sick during pregnancy, the prescribed treatment involved plants mixed over a fire to which oil and beer were added. Woolen material was saturated with this mixture and then placed in the woman's vagina twice daily. The treatment was supplemented by anointing and bandaging.

To help a woman in labor, she was given the bark of a tree to chew. Her stomach was massaged with ointment, or a rolling-pin of magic wood was rolled over her. Midwives or female relatives could be present at the birth.

> *To help a woman in labor, she was given the bark of a tree to chew.*

Medical texts often describe "female problems" related to pregnancy and childbirth. There were numerous prescriptions for a physician to treat a woman with complications after childbirth. One text provides a prescription to abort a fetus.

Lullabies, originating from incantations, were sung to stop babies from crying so that the gods would remain undisturbed. The ancient Mesopotamians believed that human "noise" enraged the gods and provoked them to do evil.

Soon after birth, the baby was given a name. Akkadian proper names were unique in the Semitic world because many of them reflected the family's feelings about the newborn, such as "My god has had mercy on me" or "Sin has heard my prayer." The name of King Sennacherib means "the god Sin has replaced a brother," indicating that even the royal family was affected by infant mortality. Children were also named for their grandfathers. Names could be changed when adults assumed administrative positions; at that time they often took a name praising their king's divine status.

A newborn baby was at risk if the mother failed to produce milk. The rich could hire a wet nurse, but the poor faced certain death of the child. Children were nursed for two or three years. Nursing also served as a means of birth control because women are relatively infertile while nursing.

The infant slept in a basket. As the baby grew, the mother or nurse wore a sling to carry the infant around. The birth of boys was considered a blessing. Abandoning infants was probably more common for daughters than sons.

We know little about how children were raised. The emotional bonds between children and their parents were very strong. Numerous terra-cotta figurines, mostly miniatures, portray a naked woman carrying a child on her arm. Many of the gods were referred to as either father or mother. Parents sold their children only in times of dire circumstances. Babylonian and Assyrian lists describe the life cycle as follows: a child at the breast, a weaned child, a child, an adolescent, an adult, and an elderly person.

Both action and nonaction toys from Mesopotamia have been found. Some, like today's toy guns, were miniaturized weapons of the time; these included slingshots, bows and arrows, and boomerangs or throw sticks. Other action toys and games included the spinning top, rattles, jump ropes (sometimes called "the game of Ishtar"), puck and mallet, hoop, balls (seals are shown with jugglers and balls), and the buzz or button (a disk or piece of pottery with holes for strings). Nonaction toys were used by children to play "house" or "grown-up." For their role-playing, children used miniature furniture such as tables, beds, stools, dolls, and a variety of small-sized animals. Model vehicles clearly mirrored the time with miniature carts, wagons, chariots, and ships for children.

Children were usually adopted when there was no male heir. The simplest form of adoption was that of a newborn, abandoned right after birth "to the dog" while still "in (its) water and blood" (cited in Stol, 491). Older children were adopted by reimbursing their parents for the expenses of feeding and raising them. These transactions were recorded as if they were sales. Adults could become part of another family by their own will, called "arrogation." Even slaves could be freed and adopted as sons. The reason for adoption and arrogation was to have a son to care for his parents in their old age. The adoptive parents agreed that the child would be their heir, regardless of how many natural children were born to them after the adoption.

In a letter between a son and his biological mother, the young man complains, "Though you bore me, and his mother adopted him, you do not love me as (much) as his mother loves him." From this letter, we can conclude that the parties to an adoption could have emotional bonds as well as economic ones. Adopted children were responsible for providing financial and physical security for adoptive parents in their old age. When the parents died, the adopted heirs were obligated to bury and mourn their parents.

Each city followed different customs concerning inheritance. Generally, the eldest son was favored in the following ways: (1) he might receive two shares instead of one; (2) he might be allocated an extra agreed-upon proportion of the total estate, at least 10 percent; and (3) he might be allowed to choose his share, while the others drew lots. The estate was physically divided after the father's death so that the married brothers would be able to set up independent households.

Although the eldest son often received a larger share of the inheritance, often real estate was kept intact to conserve the revenue. In ancient Sumer, the custom was to leave the estate undivided; all became the property of the eldest son, who was the designated heir and leader of the family. The eldest son was then obligated to support all of his siblings.

Usually, the eldest son inherited certain entitlements. For example, at Nippur, the heir received temple offices, and he usually had first claim on the family residence. In later periods, all of the brothers divided the estate equally, but the eldest son received an additional share. In Old Babylonian times, documents described in detail how property rights remained within the nuclear family. When the head of the household died, the brothers divided the estate. Family members could remain in the house after the father's death, but the actual division of the rooms might be postponed until much later, sometimes until the grandchildren divided the house among their families.

If the house was large enough to accommodate the brothers separately, it was divided. Mesopotamian inheritance laws often resulted in subdividing a single home into many smaller units. Mud brick was used to block old doorways, and new doorways were cut where necessary. When a house was inherited (or sold), the rooms were counted and their area measured. Beams and doors were considered a valuable part of the house; specific doors have been listed in sale or inheritance texts.

The custom of giving a preferred share to the eldest son was prevalent in southern Babylonia; elsewhere, the brothers divided equally. Many house-sale documents from Old Babylonian times were merely "paper transactions" to provide compensation for the transfer of ownership of very small parts of the family home that could not in practice be occupied.

According to the patrilinear system, property was divided among sons or the surviving male line. The children of a dead brother also inherited. Nasty uncles were sometimes libelous in casting slurs on the paternity of a baby born posthumously. In the following case, a boy's uncles questioned his paternity once he was old enough to lay claim to his inheritance:

Ninurta-ra'im-zerim, the son of Enlil-bani, approached the (court) and faced the court officials and judges of Nippur, (and testified): "When I was still in the womb of Sin-na'id, my mother, Enlil-bani my father, the son of Ahi-shagish, died. Before (my mother) gave birth Khabannatum, my paternal grandmother, informed Luga, the herdsman, and Sin-gamil, the judge, (and) she sent a midwife and (the midwife) delivered me. When I grew up, in 20th year of Samsu-iluna . . . (his uncles attempt to question his paternity). . . . "The court officials and the judges investigated the case. They read the earlier tablet with the oath. They questioned their witnesses, and discussed their testimony. . . . The witnesses who knew the paternity of Ninurta-ra'im-zerim, affirmed (it) by oath and they (the judges) ordered the case brought back to the assembly.
(Witnesses testified:) "Until she (Sin-nada) gave birth, they (the mother-in-law, the herdsman, the midwife and the judge) looked after her. We know that Ninurta-ra'im-zerim is the offspring of Enlil-bani." (cited in Leichty, 349–56)

Such procedures suggest that the birth of important people was witnessed. There were also tablets with baby footprints, indicating their paternity, and the seal of the witness.

The hereditary system functioned in another way. Usually, a son learned his father's trade or profession by observing and helping at an early age. He was able to take over his father's position in due time, as a scribe, an artisan, and so on. Current research has shown that the Old Babylonian buildings where the school texts were discovered were actually private houses. The schoolmaster lived there with his family and taught his sons his art at home. Some scribal families can be traced through several generations. Children were also apprenticed to craftsmen; apprenticeship contracts stipulate the responsibilities of both parties. An artisan would take a boy (often a slave) into his house and teach him his profession: for example, cook, carpenter, singer, or seal cutter (Nemet-Nejat, 128–32, 147–48, 166–67).

FOR MORE INFORMATION

Biggs, R. D. "Medicine, Surgery, and Public Health in Ancient Mesopotamia." In *Civilizations of the Ancient Near East*, ed. J. Sasson. Vol. 3. New York: Scribner's, 1995.

Black, J., and A. Green. *Gods, Demons, and Symbols of Ancient Mesopotamia: An Illustrated Dictionary*. Austin: University of Texas Press, 1992.

Leichty, E. "Feet of Clay." In *Sjöberg Festschrift*. Occasional Publications of the Samuel Noah Kramer Fund, vol. 11. Philadelphia: University Museum, 1989.

Nemet-Nejat, K. R. *Daily Life in Ancient Mesopotamia*. Westport, Conn.: Greenwood Press, 1998.

Postgate, J. N. *Early Mesopotamia: Society and Economy at the Dawn of History*. New York: Routledge, 1992.

Stol, M. "Private Life in Ancient Mesopotamia." In *Civilizations of the Ancient Near East*, ed. J. Sasson. Vol. 1. New York: Scribner's, 1995.

EGYPT

Although few details are known about childhood in ancient Egypt, one clue to children's activities is provided by the toys that archaeologists have uncovered. Children have always played with dolls, and Egyptian children were no exception. Some of these beloved playthings were stuffed with cloth; others were carved from ivory or wood. One unusual type was made from a carved piece of wood, thick or even bulbous at the bottom, decreasing to a tiny top, with shoulders and arms barely indicated. Because of their shape, excavators call them paddle-dolls. They are often found with bead-hair covering the "head." More familiar were dolls accurately carved from wood and sometimes with movable arms. Models in wood or clay of cats, dogs, donkeys, mongooses, hedgehogs, and pigs show Egyptian children's love of animals. War toys, such as a two-inch-high painted wood chariot and miniature weapons, existed as well. For babies, there were rattles—either simple pottery bulbs with handles or more engaging models of animals with pebbles inside—which soothed infants as they do today. Puppets and tops have also been found.

Mechanical toys, operated by strings, have also been found. One catlike wood animal has a mouth that opens and closes with the pull of a string. A toy crocodile performs the same motions. Another toy consists of a man bent over an inclined board while holding something in his hands—either rubbing clothes on a washboard or kneading bread. Whatever the object, he moves it up and down the board whenever a string is pulled. A "dancing dwarves" toy consists of three dwarves in a line who spin when activated by a string (Brier and Hobbs, 96).

Tomb paintings depict boys and girls playing ball games and leapfrog, while boys are also shown fishing, wrestling, running, and shooting at targets. A game called "whiptops and tipcats" involved hitting a wooden peg, the "cat," into the air using a stick; the goal was to keep it up in the air, and the one who could propel it the farthest distance was the winner.

Egyptian children seem to have been regarded affectionately by their parents and are often depicted in art as being part of a loving family. Paintings represent children accompanying their fathers during their daily activities, whether they are nobles engaged in hunting and fishing

Drawing of an Egyptian woman giving birth, attended by two goddesses. Her seated posture was the preferred one for birthing.

or farmers and shepherds working in the fields; however, the disproportionately small size of the children in relation to their fathers indicates his greater status. The Greek geographer Strabo expressed surprise when recording that Egyptian parents raised all their children, since custom in ancient Greece and Rome permitted fathers to abandon unwanted infants. As in many cultures, a son was especially desirable (perhaps partially because of the custom that the eldest son was responsible for his father's proper burial and funeral rites). Although infant mortality rates were high and many did not survive the first few months of life, the discovery of mummies and burials of babies and young children show care and concern for the child's fate in the afterlife.

Children went naked until puberty, when they assumed gender-specific clothing. Hairstyle also differentiated children from adults; a side lock of hair was symbolic of childhood. It is thought that children remained under their mother's supervision until about the age of four, during which time she was responsible for their education. A girl's education then typically stopped, and she would prepare for the roles of wife and mother, while her brothers continued to be educated either in village schools or specialized academies where one trained to be a scribe, a priest, or a civil servant. Sons tended to follow their fathers into the same trade, craft, or profession. Tutors taught noble and royal children separately, although children of lowly origin sometimes managed to receive education and embark upon a more prestigious profession. Because there were no family surnames, inscriptions often specify "the son of" or "the daughter of" along with the father's name after an individual's given name.

~*Gregory S. Aldrete*

FOR MORE INFORMATION

Brier, B., and H. Hobbs. *Daily Life of the Ancient Egyptians*. Westport, Conn.: Greenwood Press, 1999.

David, R. *Handbook to Life in Ancient Egypt*. New York: Facts on File, 1998.

Montet, P. *Everyday Life in Egypt in the Days of Ramesses the Great*. Reprint, Philadelphia: University of Pennsylvania Press, 1981.

DOMESTIC LIFE
|
CHILDREN
|
Mesopotamia

Egypt

Greece

Rome

Australian Aboriginals

GREECE

In the absence of hospitals, most births took place in the home or out of doors. Male physicians were present only when there were fears for the mother's life. Medical texts indicate that the presence of male physicians would have caused embarrassment and shame to women in labor. The most important assistant was the *maia*, or midwife, who combined medical expertise with proficiency in ritual.

Birth and religion were in fact inseparably bound together. Women in labor were placed under the protection of Eileithyia, or "She who comes." The goddess was so named because her arrival was believed to enable birth to take place. Artemis, herself a virgin who rigorously shunned sexual intercourse, was also prominent in the birthing ritual. It was necessary to appease the goddess's anger by invoking her in prayer before delivery and by dedicating clothing in her shrine afterward. Perhaps as an indication that the house was polluted by birth, an olive branch was hung on the front door when a boy was born, and a tuft of wool in the case of a girl. The walls were smeared with pitch to prevent the pollution from seeping into the community.

On the fifth day after birth, the newborn baby was officially introduced into the home and placed under the protection of the household deities. The ceremony, which was called the Amphidromia or "running around," was so named because the child's father would run around the domestic hearth holding his infant in his arms to consecrate it to Hestia, goddess of the hearth. Relatives would bring gifts for the newborn, including charms for protection against bad luck or the evil eye. Probably on the 10th day after birth, the child would officially be given his or her name. The majority of firstborn boys were named after their grandfather, as is still the custom in Greece to this day.

In all periods, it was customary for the well-to-do to secure the services of a wet nurse to breast-feed their infants. The following contract from Hellenistic Egypt, dated to 13 B.C.E., lays down terms of hire:

Didyma agrees to nurse and suckle outside at her own home in the city with her own milk that is to be pure and unsullied for a period of sixteen months . . . the foundling slave girl . . . that Isidora has given to her. She is to receive from the said Isidora as pay for the milk and the nursing ten silver drachmas and half a litre of oil every month. (*Select Papyri* 1, no. 16 in Loeb Classical Library)

Although most nurses were slaves, a few were impoverished freeborn women. Soranus in *Gynaecology* (2.19.1) recommended that the ideal nurse should be "self-controlled, sympathetic, well-tempered, Greek, and tidy." Servile or free, many won the confidence and gratitude of their masters and mistresses, as is indicated by the fact that they often retained a position of trust in the household even in old age. The following humorous sepulchral inscription testifies eloquently to the enduring bond that existed between a nurse and her former charge:

Mikkos looked after Phrygian Aischre [the name means something like "Commoner"] all her life, even in old age. When she died he set up this monument for future generations to see. Thus the old woman departed from this life, having received due recompense for her breasts.

Despite the keen desire for children, inevitably some pregnancies were unwanted. One solution was to undergo an abortion. Those who resorted to this measure were primarily unmarried girls, prostitutes, and slaves. Although the Hippocratic Oath contained a prohibition against giving a pessary to cause an abortion, it is unclear whether the ban was a result of ethical or medical considerations. Abortion would have been extremely dangerous, not least because of the risk of infection. Soranus recommended the procedure only if a woman's life was in danger. There were also legal objections. An Athenian law quoted by Lysias made it a criminal offense for a pregnant woman whose husband had died to undergo an abortion, on the grounds that the unborn child could have survived to claim its father's estate. Most objections were based on the fear of the polluting effect of an aborted fetus. A sacred law from the sanctuary of Artemis in Cyrene, for instance, decreed that "if a woman has a miscarriage or abortion when the foetus is fully formed the household is polluted as if by death [i.e., heavily], whereas if it is not fully formed, the household is polluted as if by childbirth [i.e., lightly]." Not until the third century C.E., however, was a law introduced that established an outright ban on abortion as a crime against the rights of the parents.

Although the Greeks had certain reservations about terminating an unwanted pregnancy, they showed little concern for the rights, as we would phrase it, of the newborn child. They did not, however, go so far as to kill unwanted babies, for the simple reason that to do so would cause pollution and involve the murderer in blood guilt. Instead, the unwanted infant was carried outside the city and abandoned to its fate. In Sparta, the abandonment of handicapped and sickly infants was required by law. Plutarch informs us that the father of a newborn child had to present his offspring for inspection before the council of Spartan elders. If it was strong, the council ordered him to raise it, but if it was not, the father was ordered to expose it at the foot of Mount Taygetos "in the belief that the life which nature had not provided with health and strength was of no use either to itself or to the state" (*Life of Lykourgos* 16.1–2).

Girls were abandoned more frequently than boys, partly because their usefulness in the home was more limited than that of boys and partly because they had to be provided with a substantial dowry to attract a suitable husband. For this reason, families with more than two daughters were probably somewhat rare. In a lost work, Posidippus, a comic writer of the third century B.C.E., puts the following revealing remark into the mouth of one of his characters: "If you have a son you bring him up, even if you're poor, but if you have a daughter, you abandon her, even if you're rich." The same preference for a son is poignantly revealed in a letter written on a papyrus from Hellenistic Egypt. The writer, a soldier who was billeted in Alexandria, informs his pregnant wife that if she gives birth to a boy, she should raise him, but if to a girl, she should expose her. Evidently, the mother's feelings were regarded as irrelevant. Other groups that were at risk of being exposed included the deformed and those who were the product of rape or incest.

Some estimates actually put the level of female exposure in Athens at as high as 10 percent. However, almost everything that we know about the practice derives from literary sources. Infertility was a serious problem in the Greek world, and many childless couples would have been only too happy to act as the foster parents of an unwanted child.

In the fourth year of its life, an Athenian child was brought to the Anthesteria, or Flower Festival, which took place in early spring. Here, it was presented with a wreath to wear on its head, a small jug known as a *chous*, and a small cart. This was also when the child experienced its first taste of wine. Because wine was the gift of Dionysos and the drinking of wine was invariably accompanied by religious ritual, the Anthesteria functioned as a kind of rite of passage, marking an important transitional moment in a child's life.

Athenians felt particular tenderness toward children who died before attending their first Anthesteria. A *chous* was placed beside them in the grave, evidently to compensate them for the fact that they had not received one in life. In the graves of even younger children, feeding bottles have been found. In some cases, the black glaze around the spout has worn away, indicating that the bottle had been used before the baby died. Infant mortality—deaths during the first year of life—was extremely high in Greece, perhaps accounting for more than a quarter of all live births. Diarrheal diseases resulting from a lack of clean drinking water and the absence of a satisfactory waste disposal system—the two main killers in the developing world today—were major causes.

Drawing of baby's feeding bottle from Greece. The inscription reads, "Drink, don't drop." Created by Robert Garland.

Many funerary monuments commemorate the deaths of small children. One bears an inscription that informs us that the deceased, whose name was Philostratos, bore the nickname Little Chatterbox, and that he was "a source of joy" to his parents "before the spirit of death bore him away." Another shows a pudgy child of about three stretching out his hands in the direction of a bird that his sister is holding. The inscription on the gravestone states that the monument was erected in honor of Mnesagora and her little brother Nikochares, "whom the doom of death snatched away," perhaps as the result of a joint accident or an illness to which they both succumbed.

Most toys were made in the home. There is archaeological evidence for miniature horses on wheels, boats, spinning tops, and rattles. Dolls with movable limbs were also very popular. In the following passage from Aristophanes' *Clouds*, Strepsiades, a doting father, tells how his precocious son used to construct his own toys:

Oh he's clever all right. When he was only knee-high to a grasshopper, he made houses out of clay and wooden boats and chariots from bits of leather, and he carved pomegranates into the shape of little frogs. You just can't imagine how bright he was! (lines 877–81)

A favorite game, especially among girls, was knucklebones, in which knucklebones are tossed and an attempt is made to catch them on the back of the hand, without dropping any. If any are dropped, the player must attempt to pick them up without dropping those already in her hands. Another popular game, which resembled checkers, was played on a board with black and white squares. The best throw was three sixes, which was proverbial for good luck. Ball games were extremely popular, despite the fact that it was impossible to manufacture a truly spherical ball. Children would blow up a pig's bladder and try to make it rounder by heating it in the ashes of a fire. Some ancient ball games are still in vogue today. In one, a player was selected to throw the ball and the others had to drop out one by one as they were hit. Boys at puberty and girls at marriage customarily dedicated their toys to the gods.

Both boys and girls spent a great deal of time in the company of their mothers and slaves. Fathers, who were absent much of the time, played only a minor role in the rearing of their children, until they reached puberty. In Sparta, where men spent most of their time communally with their peers, the matricentral tendency of the home was especially pronounced. Spartan mothers had a reputation for putting extreme moral pressure upon their sons. One is said to have remarked to her son as she handed him his shield before he departed for war that he should return, "Either with this or on this" (Plutarch, *Moral Sayings* 241f.), meaning that he should not disgrace himself by throwing away his shield in flight.

Although the mother was the primary figure in a child's growing years, the one with authority was the father or legal guardian. This authority was formidable and entitled him, for instance, to enslave his daughter if he caught her in an act of illicit sexual intercourse.

Despite the fact that the Greek family was a much stronger unit than today's family unit, it was by no means spared all the ills that afflict contemporary society. Although we do not hear about the children of broken homes, many must have grown up in acute poverty. Paradoxically, however, juvenile delinquency seems to have been more common among the well-to-do than among the poor. A detailed description is preserved in a speech by Demosthenes, which was written on behalf of a young man called Ariston around the middle of the fourth century B.C.E. Ariston claims to have been the victim of an unprovoked attack while walking home late one night through the Agora. He subsequently indicted the father of his chief assailant, a man called Konon, who played a leading part in the assault. Unfortunately, we do not have the speech for the defense, so it is impossible to determine what part Ariston himself might have played in stirring things up. What is evident, however, is that rivalry among privileged youths featured prominently in a society that encouraged a high degree of competitiveness among all social groups (Garland, 57–64).

FOR MORE INFORMATION

Garland, R. *Daily Life of the Ancient Greeks.* Westport, Conn.: Greenwood Press, 1998.

Golden, M. *Children and Childhood in Classical Athens.* Baltimore, Md.: Johns Hopkins University Press, 1990.

Hunt, A. and C. Edgar, trans. *Select Papyri* 1, no. 16 in Loeb Classical Library. Cambridge, Mass.: Harvard University Press, 1932.

DOMESTIC LIFE

|

CHILDREN

|

Mesopotamia

Egypt

Greece

Rome

Australian Aboriginals

ROME

When a child was born, it was placed on the floor in front of the father. If it was a male and he wanted to acknowledge it as his son, he would pick it up. This action meant that he agreed to accept it as his own son and to raise it. If it was a girl, he would not pick it up but would just instruct one of the women, either his wife or a slave, to feed it. If, for whatever reason, he did not want it, he would leave it on the floor, and the child would be taken outside and abandoned.

Romans thought that to produce strong children and soldiers, it was important not to be too nice to babies. Thus they were always bathed in cold water, and all throughout childhood they were forbidden to take warm baths for fear it would make them soft. For the first several months of life, the baby was tightly wrapped in cloth so it could not move, with its arms and legs tied to sticks so they could not be bent. Eventually, they freed the right arm but not the left in an attempt to make sure the baby would grow up right-handed since left-handedness was regarded as unlucky. The only time they were released was for their cold bath, at which time the nurse would also knead the baby's head to try to form it into a pleasant round shape.

Often a man would instruct his wife to breast-feed not only her own children but the slave children as well, with the idea that when the master and the slaves grew up, the slaves would be unusually loyal because they had all been raised on the same milk.

A Roman boy was known as a *puer*, and the symbol of his childhood was his clothing, which was called the *toga praetexta*, a toga with a purple stripe along the edge. Roman children were usually given a little leather bag filled with magical amulets called the *bulla*, which was worn at all times around his neck. The Romans believed that children were vulnerable to evil influences, and this measure was intended to protect the child while it passed through its vulnerable state. In further efforts to toughen them up, boys were forbidden to eat lying down, which was the mark of an adult, and were also not allowed to get much sleep because it was believed that too much sleep decreased intelligence and stunted growth.

Until the age of six or seven, the child was raised in the family. All the children, both free and slave, grew up together and played together. This resulted in the common phenomenon that when grown up, personal slaves would be loyal to and fond of their master, since they were, after all, old childhood playmates.

~*Gregory S. Aldrete*

FOR MORE INFORMATION

Eyben, E. *Restless Youth in Ancient Rome*. London: Routledge, 1991.

Wiedemann, T. *Adults and Children in the Roman Empire*. New Haven, Conn.: Yale University Press, 1989.

AUSTRALIAN ABORIGINALS

Childhood in Aboriginal Australia was a special time, and children were seen as being separate from adults until they had been through initiation and had become full members of society. Childhood also involved responsibilities, however. As soon as they were able, children were expected to contribute to the welfare of the group by helping their mothers collect food. In addition, childhood was an "apprenticeship" in a much larger sense than it is in modern society. Children were required to learn all the skills needed to make a living, as well as the complex rules and philosophy on which their society was based. In most areas of Australia, survival entailed hard work for much of the year, and children were obligated neither to interfere with nor to be a distraction from this work.

There was, nevertheless, time for games, play, and laughter. One of the classic games for Aboriginal children (as for children in many parts of the world) was a kind of "cat's cradle," in which long pieces of string were looped around hands and fingers and knotted to form various patterns. All of the objects used in games in

Aboriginal Australia were made from natural materials, and these games also served to educate the young in useful practices and to train their bodies in needed skills. Young boys, for example, had toy spears and boomerangs, which were scaled-down versions of the real thing.

Like children everywhere, Aboriginal children swam, raced, jumped, and threw. With small spears, boys pretended to be warriors, and with baby dolls, girls practiced being mothers. Games involving hiding objects trained them in observation and memory. Children dropped leaves into the hot air rising from a campfire, and yelling with delight, ran to see where they landed. Skins were rolled into a ball and kicked around by excited groups of children, and pigments used to make rock paintings were smeared on the fingers. Children's versions of adult songs were memorized. Children, struggling to stay awake in the flickering firelight of the evening, listened to stories and watched round-eyed while a monster was mimed or an ancient battle recalled, or they looked up with awe as the storyteller pointed to the stars and talked of the Dreamtime.

~*David Horton*

FOR MORE INFORMATION

Berndt, R., and C. Berndt. *The World of the First Australians*. Canberra: Aboriginal Studies Press, 1988.

Haagen, C. *Bush Toys: Aboriginal Children at Play*. Canberra: Aboriginal Studies Press, 1994.

Miller, M. "Changes in the Games and Pastimes of Australian Aborigines." Master's thesis, University of California, Santa Barbara, 1983.

DOMESTIC LIFE
|
SEXUALITY
|
Mesopotamia

Greece

Rome

Sexuality

When considering sexuality in antiquity, one has to keep in mind that this was a pre-Christian world. Much of the way in which topics such as sexual practices, nudity, and homosexuality are viewed today is inescapably colored by Christian moralizing, but these same topics to the ancients were, on the whole, free of religiously motivated stigmas. Further, it is even debatable whether many ancient societies, such as Greece and Rome, even conceived of people as belonging to a rigid sexual orientation in the way that today people are often identified as being heterosexual or homosexual. In these cultures, men, at least, were at various times expected to sometimes desire to perform sexual acts with members of both sexes. On the other hand, some societies frowned heavily on same-sex intercourse, such as Assyria, where a man who had sex with another man would be castrated as punishment.

Prostitution was widespread and usually legal. Most often, governments were concerned with regulating prostitutes not out of moral disapproval but rather to be sure they collected appropriate taxes. There were specialized houses of prostitution, as have been excavated at Pompeii, but clearly, many ordinary inns or taverns could offer their patrons the sexual services of one of the staff. A curious aspect of prostitution in Greece was that of high-class prostitutes known as *hetairai*. They were among the few women to be well educated because they were expected to be able to converse intelligently with their lovers. These women also were able to lead independent and public lives. One ready outlet for sexual tensions in a household was the already-unfortunate slave, who was regarded as fair game for the males in the family.

Sex was not usually seen as a shameful activity, as attested by the ubiquitous and graphic depictions of sexual activities found on material objects. Erotic art was common in Mesopotamia, and paintings and clay plaques with scenes that today would be regarded as pornographic have been found in houses, temples, and tombs. Graphic depictions of sex are the subject of some of the finest Greek vase paintings, and in front of many Greek homes was a herm, a pillar sporting an erect male penis. In Rome, adults and children would routinely wear a clay or bronze sculpture of a phallus on a rope around their necks as a kind of good luck charm, and scenes of sexual intercourse were a common subject found decorating ordinary household olive oil lamps.

Perhaps nothing better summarizes the more relaxed attitude of much of the ancient world toward sex and nudity than the fact that athletes competed naked, even at the Olympics.

~*Gregory S. Aldrete*

MESOPOTAMIA

DOMESTIC LIFE

SEXUALITY

Mesopotamia

Greece

Rome

Assyrian laws detailed which classes of women must and must not be veiled. A married woman had to be veiled in public, but prostitutes were strictly forbidden from this practice. Should a prostitute be veiled, she would be severely punished by being caned 50 times and having pitch poured over her head.

Both Mesopotamia and Syria demonstrated interest in erotic art. There are handmade or molded clay figurines of naked women, as well as cylinder seals and terracotta or pierced metal plaques depicting various positions for sexual intercourse. Erotic art was found in temples, tombs, and houses and may have reflected a genre somewhere between official and popular art. The art from the Amarna period (fourteenth century B.C.E.) is rather graphic in depicting sexual intimacy and sensual pleasure. Cylinder seals with erotic scenes are not very common. Plaques illustrate a variety of subjects: squatting women spreading their legs apart with their hands; couples standing facing each other, with the woman guiding the man by holding his member with her hand; and couples having intercourse from behind. The omens also speak of anal intercourse between a man and his wife, that is, a man "keeps saying to his wife: 'Bring your backside' " (Saggs, 144). However, the most common position for sexual intercourse was what is commonly known today as the missionary position. Another position described was the woman on top of the man, perhaps alluded to in the Amorite saying, "You be the man, let me be the woman" (cited in Lambert, 226–27, 230).

Anal intercourse may have been used as a means of contraception. The priestesses were said to have had anal intercourse to avoid pregnancy. Contraception was used, particularly by certain priestesses, "who by skillful ways keep their wombs intact," possibly by herbs or charms. Nevertheless, accidents happened, and unwanted babies were left in the street to die or to be eaten by a dog. Occasionally, we learn of a passerby grabbing a child from a dog's mouth.

Some plaques depicted a woman leaning against a mud-brick tower, perhaps the town walls, where prostitutes usually lived and worked. In some tavern scenes, one or more persons were shown drinking from vases or cups. The taverns, run by ale-wives, were houses of pleasure where men drank, listened to music, and had intercourse with prostitutes. The walls of the taproom were decorated with clay plaques of naked women or other erotic scenes. Ishtar, the goddess of love, was the patron of taverns.

There were also love lyrics and love charms, which are abundant for some periods and nonexistent for others. Love lyrics between humans were formulated as a dialogue, often accompanied by a musical instrument. The poems are narrative, with a beginning, a middle, and an end. The songs are characterized by passionate love and sexual desire for the beloved. Themes related to marriage, such as the bridal sheets laid out on a marriage bed, pervade the poetry. The beauty of the bride is described by her natural attributes as well as her jewelry. The love stories occur at sunset or later, in the streets, squares, and homes. The poems incorporate all the senses: touch, smell, sight, taste, and hearing. The metaphors used, the apple tree and the pillar of alabaster, which may rise in a garden or stone, refer to the male and female sexual organs, respectively. Incantations praise the qualities of the genitals but demonstrate little interest in breasts.

Texts speak of women menstruating for six days as "hit by the weapon" (cited in Stol, 490). During this time, women were considered unclean and released from work. A man who touched a menstruating woman was also regarded as unclean for six days.

Men sometimes suffered from sexual dysfunctions such as impotence and premature ejaculation. To help reverse impotence, a group of rituals was performed and various medicinal preparations, including ointments and aphrodisiacs, were used. Although alluded to, no treatment for premature ejaculation was mentioned; perhaps the ancients believed that time and practice would eventually provide a cure.

Male homosexuality was described from the third millennium B.C.E. onward in Mesopotamia. Texts refer to sodomy between men as well as between men and boys. The Babylonians did not condemn this practice. But male prostitutes were either despised or considered laughable. Homosexual acts were never clearly depicted in visual art, with the possible exception of cylinder seals in which the gender of the protagonists is questionable. However, the Assyrians did not follow the Babylonian policy of "live-and-let-live" in regard to homosexual practices. During the Middle Assyrian period (ca. 1300–1100 B.C.E.), homosexuality was severely punished. According to the Middle Assyrian laws, "If a man sodomizes his comrade and they prove the charges against him and find him guilty, they shall sodomize him and they shall turn him into a eunuch [that is, castrate him]" (cited in Roth, 160).

Lesbianism was seldom mentioned. The women of ancient Mesopotamia seemed much more interested in taking male lovers. The Laws of Hammurabi describe a wife who took a lover, whom she encouraged to murder her husband so that the lovers would be free to marry. In this case, the wife was punished by being impaled. If the cuckolded husband caught the lovers, he could bring them up on charges before either the king or judges. If the couple was found guilty, Middle Assyrian law provided for several courses of punishment: "If the woman's husband kills his wife, then he shall also kill the man; if he cuts off his wife's nose, he shall turn the man into a eunuch and they shall lacerate his entire face; but if [the husband wishes to release] his wife, he shall [release] the man" (cited in Roth, 158).

Eunuchs ("those not having a beard") were quite common, but a man who became a eunuch as a punishment was exceptional. Eunuchs served at court, and many of them became high officials—an administrative practice that continued up to the nineteenth century C.E. in the Turkish and Persian empires. However, not all Assyrian courtiers were eunuchs, a point emphasized by a list of courtiers that included both eunuchs and noneunuchs. In Assyria, as elsewhere, a small proportion of males failed to develop normally and became natural eunuchs; many of them were possibly male prostitutes.

Incest was also addressed in the law codes. In the Laws of Hammurabi (§§155–56), if a father-in-law had sex with his son's bride-to-be, the law demanded a fine of half a mina of silver, and the girl could return to her family home with her dowry and marry someone else. However, if his son had consummated the marriage and incest was committed, the father was sentenced to drowning. Other forms of incest were treated in the law codes, namely, cases of a man with his sister, his niece, his daughter, his mother-in-law, or his mother after his father's death. The last offense was considered particularly loathsome, and the punishment was to burn the mother and son. In Assyria, a man could raise a concubine to the status of wife. The Middle Assyrian laws explained the procedure: "If a man intends to veil his concubine, he shall have five or six of his comrades, and he shall veil her in their presence, he shall declare 'She is my wife.' She is (then) his wife."

> *To help reverse impotence, a group of rituals was performed.*

The concubine was permitted to wear the veil only when she accompanied the legal wife outdoors. Her status remained secondary, and in the event that the legal wife bore sons, the children of the concubine could not inherit. The concubine was chosen from among the slaves and was still expected to perform her duties for the legal wife, such as carrying her chair when she went to the temple and assisting her in her toiletries.

The Mesopotamians recognized that sex had a religious component. There were religious prostitutes—male, female, and neuter—associated with some temples. Reference to temple sexual activity was more common for Babylonia than for Assyria. Although male prostitutes were often eunuchs, this was not always the case. Certain priests in the cult of Ishtar were homosexuals; they were also accomplished in dancing and cross-dressing. The ancient Mesopotamians' problem with homosexuals and prostitutes stemmed from the fact that they did not have children (prostitutes appear to have had an understanding of birth control) (Nemet-Nejat, 136–40).

FOR MORE INFORMATION

Lambert, W. G. *Babylonian Wisdom Literature*. Oxford: Clarendon Press, 1960.
Nemet-Nejat, K. R. *Daily Life in Ancient Mesopotamia*. Westport, Conn.: Greenwood Press, 1998.
Roth, M. *Law Collections from Mesopotamia and Asia Minor*. Atlanta, Ga.: Scholars Press, 1995.
Saggs, H. W. F. *The Might That Was Assyria*. London: Sidgwick and Jackson, 1984.
Stol, M. "Private Life in Ancient Mesopotamia." In *Civilizations of the Ancient Near East*, ed. J. Sasson. Vol. 1. New York: Scribner's, 1995.

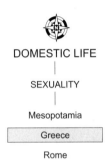

DOMESTIC LIFE
|
SEXUALITY
|
Mesopotamia

Greece

Rome

GREECE

The function of marital sex in Greece was procreation. So important was procreation that in Sparta, it was acceptable for a husband to lend out his wife to another man for the purpose of making her pregnant. In addition, most adult males, both married and unmarried, engaged in sex with prostitutes or slaves. Given the extreme emphasis that was placed on women's virginity and fidelity, it would have required much ingenuity and not a little luck to conduct a sexual liaison with a well-bred woman. For this reason, the image of a Don Juan is alien to Greek culture. In myth, even the Trojan prince Paris, the most notorious of all philanderers, remained faithful to the woman he seduced. The exception is Alcibiades, who was much admired by men and women, and who numbered among his conquests a Spartan queen.

It is sometimes suggested that the Greeks were more liberated in sexual matters than people are today. The truth simply is that they were different. They were remarkably unabashed about the depiction of male genitals in art, images of which, both erect and unerect, were ubiquitous. Anal and oral intercourse between men and women appear frequently in depictions on vases. Statues of naked youths in the guise of Apollo served as funerary markers. Herms, stone pillars with carved heads and penises, marked the boundaries of properties. Giant penises were borne aloft by Athenian virgins in Dionysiac processions. In the performance of comic plays, actors wore oversize penises made out of padding to draw attention to their sexual organs.

Artistic representations are one thing. Reality is another. In everyday life, the Greeks may well have been prudish. Although males appeared naked before other males in the gymnasium and in competitive athletics, women were not allowed to approach the sanctuary of Olympian Zeus during the Olympic Games, evidently to prevent them from spying on the naked bodies of male athletes. In certain Spartan rituals, however, girls were encouraged to appear naked before Spartan youths in what appears to have been a kind of civic-sponsored incentive to marriage.

The famous myth of Pandora ("All-gifted"), told by Hesiod in *Theogony*, defines women as "a beautiful evil" that men cannot resist, evidently because of their sexual appetites and vulnerability to female charms. These characteristics are made comic sport of in Aristophanes' masterpiece *Lysistrata,* which presupposes that an international sex strike by women will bring about peace, by reducing all the combatants to another kind of impotence. The popular notion that men were slaves to their sexual appetites was balanced by the medical belief that women needed to have sexual intercourse for their physical and mental well-being.

The Greeks did not identify themselves as either homosexual or heterosexual. They did not, as we do, perceive sexual orientation in terms of a life choice. A homosexual union between males was acceptable especially when asymmetrical, that is to say, when it involved a younger boy and an older man. Often these relationships had a pedagogical as well as a sexual dimension. Such associations provided the basis of aristocratic education in the Archaic period and were institutionalized by the symposium. Plato's *Symposium* elevates homosexual above heterosexual love but probably provides a somewhat unbalanced picture of Athenian sexual mores at the turn of the fourth century B.C.E.

Any Athenian who practiced homosexuality exclusively was likely to become a target of abuse, as we see from contemptuous references in Aristophanic comedy. The most famous homoerotic relationship is that of Achilles and Patroclus in the *Iliad,* although Homer overtly avoids suggesting that it has a sexual basis.

Virtually the only profession available to freeborn women in the Greek world was that of prostitute. It is important to bear in mind, however, that the English word conjures up a very limited picture of the range of services that women performed under this general title. As the Greek word *hetaira,* which means "female companion," suggests, they charged for their companionship rather than their sexual favors. The ideal *hetaira* was gifted, charming, and intellectually accomplished. *Hetairai* were the only women permitted to attend private gatherings known as *symposia.* The *hetaira* Aspasia was so respected that Socrates and his friends would call on her to elicit her opinions on political and philosophical matters. Such was her influence over Pericles that the latter's decision to lead an expedition against the island of Samos is said to have been taken on her advice (Plutarch, *Life of Pericles* 24.1–3). In addition, many brothels existed in Athens, largely staffed by slaves. In fact, the state acted as pimp by farming out the right to collect taxes from prostitution to enterprising individuals, in the same way, say, that it farmed out the right to collect harbor dues.

Greek drinking cup depicting Zeus, the king of the gods, seducing the boy Ganymede. Zeus was extremely promiscuous and had affairs with numerous mortal women as well. © The Art Archive/ Archaeological Museum Spina Ferrara/Dagli Orti (A).

Male prostitution, although regarded with severe disfavor, was an ineradicable feature of Greek society. Athenians over the age of 18 who entered the profession were debarred from holding any executive or religious office and from addressing the assembly or council, although the law stopped short of depriving them of their citizenship. If a boy under the age of 18 engaged in prostitution, his father or legal guardian was liable for prosecution. The boy in question was also released from the obligation to support his father in old age, as the law otherwise enjoined on him (Aischines 1.13–20). Intercourse between slaves and their masters and mistresses probably was commonplace.

Adultery was punished more severely than rape because rape was regarded as "merely" an act of violence; adultery, however, required the transfer of a woman's affections and made it difficult to determine whether her offspring were legitimate. Whereas rapists were required to pay recompense to the husband, convicted adulterists faced the death penalty. If a husband discovered his wife in bed with her lover, he was permitted to take the lover's life with impunity. The husband of an adulterous woman was required by law to divorce her. If he failed to do so, he could be deprived of his citizenship. Adulterous women were not permitted to attend religious rites conducted by the citizen body. If they attempted to do so, the public was free to do to them any form of physical violence short of killing them.

Pornography, a made-up word of Greek root that literally means a writer about or painter of whores or *pornai*, seems not to have been regarded as a corrupting influence. Occasionally, it even attained the status of high art. One of the most striking depictions of women undergoing sexual abuse is the battle between the Lapiths and Centaurs depicted on the west pediment of the temple of Zeus at Olympia. To the right of the figure of Apollo, who stands in the center of the composition, we see the centaur Eurytion intent on raping the bride Deidameia. To the left of Apollo, another centaur is about to kick in the groin a Lapith woman who is scratching his cheek.

Naked bathing women appear on the interior of red-figure cups of the late sixth and early fifth century B.C.E. The bather was revealed as the (male) drinker drained the cup. Pornographic literature existed in the Hellenistic period but seems to have been limited to sex manuals enumerating the positions of heterosexual intercourse. There was no genre devoted to sexual fantasy, although fantasy is not absent from the Hellenistic Greek novel. A prime example is Longus's *Daphnis and Chloe*, which carries strong undertones of sexual violence (Garland, 56, 112–14).

FOR MORE INFORMATION

Dover, K. J. *Greek Homosexuality*. London: Duckworth, 1978.
Garland, R. *Daily Life of the Ancient Greeks*. Westport, Conn.: Greenwood Press, 1998.
Halperin, D. M., J. J. Winkler, and F. I. Zeitlin. *Before Sexuality: The Construction of Erotic Experience in the Greek World*. Princeton, N.J.: Princeton University Press, 1990.

DOMESTIC LIFE
|
SEXUALITY
|
Mesopotamia

Greece

Rome

ROME

In the old Roman Republic, the Romans took a stern attitude toward sex, or this is at least the impression they tried to give in idealizing literature. Public manifestations of emotion were frowned upon. For example, a distinguished senator who was running for the consulship was not only kicked out of the race but actually expelled from the senate itself for immorality simply because he was seen giving his wife a kiss in public. A person was considered immoral if he had sex in the daytime because sex was only supposed to be done at night and secretly. Using a lamp to provide light at night also labeled you as an unhealthy, immoral person. And any woman who took off all of her clothing while having sex was plainly debauched and immoral. Women were supposed to keep on as much clothing as possible.

These attitudes began to change after the introduction of Greek culture, and by the late Republic and early empire, Romans had become much more open about sexuality and seemingly much more adventurous as well. This more open attitude did not extend to marriage, however. Husbands and wives were obligated to produce children, but there often seems not to have been much affection between them. Marriage was seen as a social and a political relationship, not a romantic one. Some of this lack of affection no doubt stemmed from the fact that most Roman men and women did not themselves choose their spouses and that often there was a vast age difference between the two. Married couples did not share a bed; instead, both husband and wife had their own suite of rooms and their own servants in different parts of the house. This remoteness seems to have led to a certain degree of resentment on the part of Roman wives. An example of this occurred when there was a rash of aristocratic deaths at Rome. Upon investigation, it was discovered that many wives were poisoning their husbands. Some of the women claimed that they had been trying to give their husbands aphrodisiacs to make them fall in love with them and that the aphrodisiacs unfortunately turned out to be toxic. Whether this was their motivation or whether they simply were getting revenge on their unfaithful husbands, 170 women were convicted of poisoning.

Oddly enough, it was sometimes seen as dishonorable if a husband was deeply in love with his wife. The Roman general Pompey was in love with his wife and enjoyed spending time with her. He and his young wife would spend hours walking together in the gardens and watching the peasants work on their country farms. As a result, Pompey was widely ridiculed. Some even ascribed his defeat at the hands of Julius Caesar to the fact that Caesar spent his time plotting and raising armies whereas Pompey dallied away the hours with his wife.

Despite the lack of affection between husband and wife, a lot of sex was going on in Roman households. All slaves were regarded as fair game by the free members of the household, and it was not uncommon for a master and other members of his family to be simultaneously sleeping with several generations of their slaves. This was not regarded as shameful, at least for the males.

The entire Roman concept of sexuality was very different from our modern one. Romans did not categorize people into homosexual and heterosexual, and in fact there are not really words in Latin that correspond to modern definitions of homosexual or heterosexual. Romans could and did have sex with men, women, and children, and it was regarded as the normal state that one would have relations both with people of one's own sex and of the opposite one. In the same way that the Romans did not even have our modern category of sexual orientation, they were not that concerned with the types of sexual acts that people practiced. There were verbs to describe the different sexual acts; the three main ones were for what we would now term vaginal sex, oral sex, and anal sex. Again, it was expected that a Roman might practice all of these.

Roman attitudes toward sexuality is currently a much-debated topic among scholars. Some contend that there was one classification that the Romans were obsessed with. What mattered to them was not the act or the gender of their partner, but the role they played. In Roman society, passivity or submission was equivalent to inferiority, and to be active was to be superior. What the Romans were obsessed with was penetration. If they were the penetrator, they were superior, and there was nothing shameful about what they were doing. Who or what they penetrated did not matter nearly as much as the fact that they were the active partner. On the other hand, being penetrated implied that they were like a woman and thus, in the Romans' view, that they were inferior, submissive, and bad. Other scholars argue that more important to the Romans was the degree to which one exerted control over his or her desires and practiced moderation.

One of the greatest insults for a Roman man was to be called effeminate, but this was not necessarily a comment on his demeanor. Julius Caesar had an extremely active sex life, but there was always additional suspicion attached to him because it was suspected that he played the inferior role at times (Suetonius, *Julius Caesar*, 49–52). According to a popular Roman witticism, Caesar was "every woman's man and every man's woman" (Suetonius, *Julius Caesar*, 52). The first half means that he was promiscuous, and the second half was insulting because it implies his inferiority.

With Roman men seeking relationships outside of marriage and with most women being married, by necessity there was a great deal of adultery going on in Rome. Our best source for these affairs comes from Roman poets, and two in particular.

The first of these is the poet Catullus. He lived during the late Republic at the time of civil wars, and although the topic of his poetry was love, his troubled attitude toward it reflects the turmoil of the times in which he lived. Catullus fell in love with a married woman named Clodia. His most famous poems record the course of his affair, ranging from celebrations of passion and the euphoria produced by love to bitter and angry poems recording his hatred of her when she rejects him. Because she was married, he could not refer to her by her real name, so his poetry is addressed to a woman he calls Lesbia. Catullus's poetry captures the extremes of emotion produced by love—happiness, jealousy, and hatred—as exemplified by the beginning line of one of his poems, "I hate you and

Wall painting from Pompeii of a couple having sex. The woman retains the wrapping around her breasts as a sign of modesty. © Mimmo Jodice/ CORBIS.

I love you" (poem 85). Catullus's intense emotion, particularly when he was ultimately rejected, perhaps wore him out, and his lifestyle also caused him to become bankrupt. He died at the age of 33, leaving behind a small but powerful body of work.

The next poet of love lived during the empire. His name was Publius Ovidius Naso, or Ovid. Ovid's *Art of Love* is essentially a practical manual of advice on how to seduce women. To Ovid, love was a game whose goal was seduction, and he offers tips on how to win this game. He describes places where one can go in Rome to pick up women, such as the law courts and the colonnades where many likely women could be found. He offers a considerable amount of practical and modern-sounding advice for hopeful lovers, such as to wear clean, well-fitting clothes, to comb your hair neatly, to wash your hands, to trim your nostril hair, and to avoid bad breath and body odor. He also comments that a tan looks nice (1.510–20).

Morality was unimportant to Ovid, so he recommends that no matter what the truth, men should shower the women they are wooing with flattery and praise and compliment them constantly on their physical appearance (1.620). He advises the man to be persistent and not give up when a woman rejects him, since often the man can wear down her defenses (1.470–85). He suggests that getting her drunk can hurry things along and that another good strategy is to cry; if real tears are not forthcoming, he suggests inducing them artificially (1.229–33, 1.660). In seducing a woman, Ovid says that the man should become friends with the woman's maid and her servants because this will help enormously in sending secret love letters to her and in sneaking into her house (1.352–55). His solution for mending a lover's quarrel is to try to get the woman into bed (2.663).

Ovid further recommends taking a woman to the circus to watch chariot races as a good date. He tells the lover to find out what horse she is cheering for and then, no matter what his own preference is, to cheer loudly for her favorite. The man should buy her a cushion to sit on and prevent the people sitting behind her from poking her in the back with their knees. The crowded benches on which the audience sat can also give opportunities to press up against her, and the dust thrown up into the air by the chariots allows an excuse to fondle her while pretending to brush dirt off her clothes (1.135–62).

The emperor Augustus was very concerned with public morality and consequently was quite offended by Ovid's *Art of Love*, so much so that he banished Ovid and sent him to live in exile north of the Black Sea. For someone who thrived on the sophisticated urban culture of the city of Rome, this amounted to torture, and Ovid spent the rest of his life writing bad poetry praising Augustus in the hope that Augustus would allow him to return to Rome. Unfortunately for Ovid, Augustus never forgave him, and Ovid died alone and miserable far from the city that he loved.

The attitude of the Romans toward Ovid and people like him is hard to determine. Roman literature is filled with moralizing against adultery, yet it is clear that many people practiced it. With all this sexual activity going on, contraception was obviously a concern. The Romans did have the idea of using sheep's intestines as a condom, and this was probably at least somewhat effective. The most common types of contraception were magic potions and charms. A Roman encyclopedia records one that was thought to be highly effective. Women were instructed to find a certain species of large hairy spider. It was believed that if the head of the spider was cut open, one would find two small worms, and if a woman wore these worms on her body, it would prevent pregnancy. This contraceptive was thought to be effective for one year, after which she would have to find another spider (Pliny the Elder, *Natural History* 29.27.85).

Rome had its share of prostitutes. The term for a prostitute was *meretrix*. Prostitution was legal in Rome, and all prostitutes were supposed to register themselves with an aedile (urban magistrate), who would collect taxes from them. The tax was computed on a daily basis and was supposed to be equal to the amount she received from one client. Some prostitutes would roam the streets of the city—one good place to find them was around the Circus Maximus—but most were based in brothels.

It is known that in the third century C.E., Rome had 45 brothels. By law, a brothel could not open before 3:00 P.M. Many of these brothels have been excavated, particularly at Pompeii. They consisted of many little rooms, each one with a stone bed on which was placed a mattress. The walls were decorated with graphic and obscene paintings. In addition, many inns and hotels would provide prostitutes for their guests, and this was regarded as a normal service. One hotel bill lists the charges run up by a guest, including his room, meals, hay for his mule, and the price of a girl (*C.I.L.* 9.2689).

Finally, Roman culture had a great deal of what we would classify today as pornography, although the Romans did not see it as such. Many Roman lamps and bowls were decorated with graphic erotic scenes. The number of these that survive indicates that they were mass-market items used in everyday life by average Romans. There was a healthy market in erotic artwork, and many private homes contained sexually explicit paintings and mosaics. The Romans were a superstitious people and wore many charms to ward off evil. The most common of these was cast in the shape of an erect male organ.

~*Gregory S. Aldrete*

FOR MORE INFORMATION

Hallett, J., and M. Skinner, eds. *Roman Sexualities*. Princeton, N.J.: Princeton University Press, 1997.

DOMESTIC LIFE: WEB SITES

http://emuseum.mnsu.edu/prehistory/egypt/index.shtml
http://www.fordham.edu/halsall/source/cjc-marriage.html
http://www.fordham.edu/halsall/women/womensbook.html
http://www.stoa.org/diotima/
http://www.uwgb.edu/sophia/

3

ECONOMIC LIFE

People work. The basic principle of economic life is that men and women must work to provide for themselves. Of course, throughout history it has always been the case that some have to work harder than others, but this does not violate the basic importance of work; it only reveals the complexities of economic life, which includes everything from the production of income to trade to its unequal distribution throughout society.

At the basic level, people work on the land to produce their food and the other items they need. However, even at this simplest level, people trade goods among themselves. Thus, economic life moves from the work that we do to the exchange of the products of our labor. This diversification contributes to increasing variety in society, as some work on the land, living in villages and farms, while others move to urban areas that grow ever larger throughout history. The patterns of farm, village, and urban life exist all over the world and help define the lives of the people who work within them.

Commerce, or the exchange of goods, is as central to human economic life as the production of goods. From the beginning of town life in Mesopotamia, the excitement generated within shops lining a street is palpable in the sources. Merchants hawking their wares and shoppers looking for the exotic as well as the ordinary form a core of human life. Merchants (and merchandise) have always ranged far beyond local markets as people moved their goods across large areas. Even during the prehistoric late Stone Age, domestic animals native to the Middle East moved down the Nile valley to sub-Saharan Africa, and plants native to the Euphrates valley moved as far east as China. Our global marketplace is only the logical extension of the constant movement of people and things that goes on as people engage in their economic life.

All societies have been in part defined by people at work. They have built societies with divisions of labor, of city and country, and of class, as some people grow richer than others. To study daily life through history is in large part to understand people at work.

The history of the ancient world encompasses the very beginnings of many aspects of economic life, including specialized craftsmen, long-distance trade, and even money itself. The first small towns arose in Mesopotamia and quickly became little economic centers where goods and services were bought and exchanged, and wealth was collected and redistributed by commerce and taxation. Specialized workers began to be able to make a living by producing one type of product. Merchants appeared who acted as middlemen for the buying and selling of goods, and some of them next began to travel from town to town, establishing trade routes. Because of limitations of technology, transportation was difficult, expensive, slow, and dangerous, but nevertheless, when there was sufficient motivation, the ancients could, and did, move people and goods impressive distances. From these humble beginnings, commerce and trade grew, so that by the second century C.E., Aelius Aristides, a Greek living under the Roman Empire, could describe the city of Rome as "a kind of common marketplace of the world," where "whatever is grown and manufactured by every people from every land is found at all times and in great quantity . . . all the arts and crafts that exist, or have ever existed, and all the things that are produced or grown from the earth" (*In Praise of Rome* 11, 13).

The word *economy* is derived from the Greek word *oikonomia*, which means the management of the household, and the basic unit of the economy was the individual family. Although the root word for economy derives from the ancient world, economic theory is a relatively recent development, and the languages of the ancient world did not have much vocabulary to describe or analyze more sophisticated economic phenomenon, such as budgets or trade imbalances, in a way that would be recognizable to economists today. Some scholars believe that this, together with the lack of any surviving explicit discussion of economy or markets, means that the ancients did not think "rationally" about economic subjects at all. Whether there was a well-developed theory underlying the ancient economy, in practical terms, there was obviously a great deal of buying and selling that went on in the ancient world.

~*Joyce E. Salisbury and Gregory S. Aldrete*

FOR MORE INFORMATION

Braudel, F. *The Wheels of Commerce.* New York: Harper and Row, 1979.

Finley, M. *The Ancient Economy.* 2nd ed. Berkeley: University of California Press, 1985.

Polanyi, K., C. Arensberg, and H. Pearson, eds. *Trade and Market in the Early Empires.* Chicago, Ill.: Gateway, 1957.

Wallerstein, I. M. *Historical Capitalism.* London: Verso, 1983.

ECONOMIC LIFE
|
RURAL LIFE
& AGRICULTURE
|
Mesopotamia

Egypt

Greece

Rome

India

Nubia

Rural Life and Agriculture

Unlike modern Western societies where most of the populace live in and around cities, the vast majority of people in the ancient world lived in the countryside on farms. This was a basic fact of life in most of the ancient world (and is really true of the entire preindustrial world), no matter what civilization or culture. Probably

85 to 95 percent of all people who lived in the ancient world were born on the family farm, grew up on the farm, tilled the soil for a lifetime, likely never traveled more than 15 miles from their home, and died on the farm. As with all farmers, the dominant forces that governed their lives were the change of the seasons, the forces of nature, and the life cycles of the crops they cultivated. Whether the language they spoke was Greek or Latin, whether they owed allegiance to a pharaoh or to a king, was usually far less significant than the never-ending and universal agricultural cycle imposed by nature of seeding, planting, fertilizing, weeding, and harvesting. The truly typical inhabitant of the ancient world was not a king, philosopher, artist, soldier, or even a merchant but was instead a simple farmer, whose lifestyle and experiences would have been instantly familiar to most other ancient people over a time period of thousands of years and spanning dozens of cultures.

The three great necessities for farming are plentiful sun, good soil, and abundant water, and while in the Mediterranean basin the first is universal and the second fairly common, the third is rarer. It is no surprise that the earliest intensive organized farming developed along the banks of rivers that routinely flooded, bringing water to the neighboring fields. The Tigris and the Euphrates, the rivers that demarcate Mesopotamia (literally, "the land between the rivers"), were prone to frequent floods that although often destructive, nevertheless served to irrigate and reinvigorate the neighboring soil. The inhabitable portions of Egypt and Nubia consisted of the slender strip, sometimes only a few hundreds of yards wide but thousands of miles long, that bordered the Nile as it snaked its way from the depths of Africa to the coast of the Mediterranean. More regularly than any other river, the waters of the Nile rose at the same time each year to flood the nearby fields and deposit the nutrient-laden soil that was the basis of Egypt's rich agriculture. Much of the best and most sophisticated technology of the ancient world focused around the collection and distribution of water, from the elaborate canals of the ancient Near East to the monumental aqueducts of Rome.

Rural life and agriculture were life in its totality for most of the ancient world, and the fact that nearly the entire population devoted itself to this one activity is reflective of how narrow the margins of survival were. Simply to survive, most people had to be farmers. It was the tiny surplus produced by intensive farming, however—probably amounting to no more than 10 percent of the crop in a perfect year—that made it possible for a small number of people not to be tied to the farm but instead to live in cities, and there to produce nearly all of what we now regard as civilization.

~*Gregory S. Aldrete*

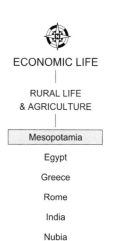

ECONOMIC LIFE
|
RURAL LIFE
& AGRICULTURE
|
Mesopotamia

Egypt

Greece

Rome

India

Nubia

MESOPOTAMIA

Mesopotamia was home to some of the oldest farming communities. By approximately 6000 B.C.E., most staple crops known from later texts were already cultivated, the basic herd animals had been domesticated, and irrigation systems were well established, at least in northern Babylonia. The availability of profitable cereals (such as barley and wheat), irrigation, and plow agriculture were all factors that contributed to the development of large-scale farming. Despite its desertlike climate, Mesopotamia became the richest agricultural area in the ancient world. The plants grown for food in ancient Mesopotamia provided about 90 percent of the diet; the remaining 10 percent of the food supply came from domesticated animals and their products—meat, milk, cheese, and eggs.

Mesopotamians survived by trade, storage, and war.

Barley was the most common agricultural product and was also used as a means of exchange, with an accepted value, much like silver. In fact, wages were mostly paid in barley. Trade in grain and dates, among other goods, became the staple articles of commerce.

Because of the uncertainty of the food supply as a result of blight, locusts, or lack of rain, Mesopotamians survived by trade, storage, and war. Law codes and legal documents constantly refer to crop loss through flooding. Swarms of locusts also presented a major threat to crops. However, the Assyrians caught and ate the locusts, which they considered a luxury food. The kings received letters from provincial administrators and astrological reports about the potential disaster from locusts.

Barley and emmer wheat were harvested with sickles made with flint teeth set in a wooden or bone handle. After the harvest, grain was carefully stored in granaries near the fields or transported, wherever possible, on the waterways. The silos were depicted as high and cylindrical, a shape that has remained unchanged to the present day. Some had a ladder attached to enable the grain carriers to climb up and empty their sacks into the top. The amount of grain was measured by volume, not weight. The silos rested on a latticed wooden foundation, which provided protection against damp ground and rodent attacks.

The vegetables most frequently mentioned were onions, garlic, leeks, turnips, lettuce, and cucumbers. Vegetables needed more frequent attention and were cultivated in separate plots, usually under the canopy provided by plantations of date palms interplanted with lower fruit trees such as apples and pomegranates. Numerous spicy and aromatic seeds such as cress, mustard, cumin, and coriander were part of the Mesopotamian diet; others remain unidentified. Linseed was the only oil seed cultivated before 6000 B.C.E. The plant was used mainly to produce a fine oil, which quickly became a staple food of the Mesopotamian diet. Olive trees grew only in the foothills, and olive oil was manufactured locally.

The date palm was first cultivated in Lower Mesopotamia. Its position was unique because every part of the date palm could be used. Dates, which had high nutritional value, were sometimes used as a sweetener; they could be preserved and stored. The palm sprout provided a celery-like vegetable, and an alcoholic beverage was made from the fruit. There were separate male and female plants. The Sumerians practiced artificial fertilization of the female palm. Lexical texts enumerate 150 words for various palms and their different parts. The date and the pomegranate were the most common fruits, although apples, figs, pears, and a type of plum were also known.

Animal husbandry began in the Neolithic period. The animals used by the early inhabitants of the ancient Near East were wild, managed, or domesticated. Remains of wild mammals and birds have been discovered at various sites; such animals may have been traded between regions or eaten during difficult economic times. Dependence on wild herd animals such as the gazelle, deer, and onagers declined. Managed but not domesticated species were protected or tamed; these included fish raised in ponds, bees, and game. The animals with the temperament to be domesticated were common and widely distributed. Many species were domesticated after complex societies emerged. Throughout the history of the ancient Near East, domestic animals provided meat, dairy products, leather, wool, or hair. Pastoralists viewed animals as capital on the hoof, whereas hunters viewed animals as game to be redistributed.

Sheep were the most important animal economically and numerically; they were domesticated the longest and were present from the Mediterranean to the Indus Valley. These animals were more important for their milk products and their wool than for their meat, which was used for offerings, taking omens, gifts for weddings, and presents to gain access to the king. A specialist called the "animal fattener" gradually increased the rations of sheep, mostly males, to improve the flavor or fat content of the meat. Sheep adapted well to any agricultural environment. Where there was plenty of water and hence, plant growth, they could be herded. In cases of little rainfall and an arid climate, they could be moved in search of plant growth.

Sheep and goats, known as "small cattle," were also kept in large flocks that belonged to the state, the temple, or private owners. When flocks were of considerable size, each animal was branded with its owner's mark. Flocks belonging to the temples were marked with the symbol of the god to whom they belonged, for example, a spade for Marduk and a star for Ishtar. If animals were not tended by a family member, they were given to shepherds, who subcontracted the actual herding to "shepherd boys."

Sheep were often herded together with goats. Goat hair was used for weaving carpets and containers. Flocks were often isolated by herdsmen to protect against the spread of disease and, perhaps, theft. As societies became more complex, animals no longer roamed to find grazing. Both isolation and segregation resulted in a reduction of the gene pool. Local animal populations showed distinctive characteristics.

Sheep were plucked until the middle of the second millennium B.C.E.; that is to say, the wool was pulled or combed out at the time of molt. Later, shearing became the usual practice. A contract was drawn up with the herdsman at the spring shearing, when the wool was weighed and the lambing season was finished.

Cows, ewes, and goats were important to the milk industry. Animal products included meat, yogurt, cheese, and ghee. Milk, which spoiled rapidly in hot climates, was not popular as a drink; rather, it was used in making medicines. Animals also provided wool and leather hides.

Animal husbandry developed along with inventions in agriculture. The shift to plow farming in the fifth millennium B.C.E. required animal traction and favored an increase of cattle. Cattle were seldom sacrificed except in ceremonies of state. Cattle were primarily important as draft animals, preparing the land before sowing and seeding.

In early periods, the ox was the only draft animal, but by the end of the fourth millennium B.C.E., the onager was used to pull wheeled vehicles. The Sumerians of the Early Dynastic period used domestic asses that they crossbred with wild onagers ("donkey of the steppes") to produce a sterile offspring, uniting the donkey's docility with the onager's speed and strength. This hybrid did not survive the second millennium B.C.E. with the arrival of the horse, which was crossed with the donkey to produce mules. The donkey was the traditional beast of burden and retained that distinction even after the introduction of the horse. Donkeys were used to haul plows and carts; Assyrian merchants in Anatolia used caravans of donkeys.

The horse was called "donkey of the mountain," indicating its origins in mountainous regions. In the second millennium B.C.E., horses were used for drawing fighting chariots and in the first millennium B.C.E. for the cavalry. They were also used in ritual offerings and for ritual acts in making treaties.

Camels were not widely known in Mesopotamia until the first millennium B.C.E. and were used mostly by nomadic Arab tribes. They were called "the donkey of the sea" or "the donkey of the south," indicating their origins.

The dog was one of the earliest domestic animals and served primarily to protect herds and dwellings against enemies. To date, we have been able to distinguish only two main breeds of dog: large greyhounds, which were used primarily in hunting, and a very strong breed of dog (on the order of Danes and mastiffs) suitable for herding.

Honey collected from wild bees was rare and expensive. The use of bees for honey and beeswax probably first began with hunting for honey in the wild hives of the Paleolithic period and evolved into full apiculture by the third millennium B.C.E. Beeswax was used for various purposes, including medicines and surfaces on writing boards.

Agricultural land was best classified by its water supply, which regulated farming, the types of crops, the amount and dependability of yields, and the total area of land cultivated. Mesopotamia had two kinds of agriculture: dry farming in the north (Assyria) and irrigation farming in the south (Babylonia and Sumer).

Dry farming relied only on natural rainfall and was practiced in northern Mesopotamia. Large-scale irrigation with complex canal systems, supplemented by natural rainfall, was used in southern Mesopotamia. Barley and other cereal crops such as emmer and wheat were grown in dry farming areas. Fallow land or crop rotation was vital to the productivity of grain lands. Dry farming was characterized by extensive farming methods and a fairly mixed rural economy; a high proportion of poor and failed grain harvests could be endured.

Irrigation was necessary for crops because the salinity of the soil was a problem early on. Water was channeled to the fields from the major watercourses through branch canals and feeders, which often ran along the tops of artificial dikes. The width of the primary watercourses could be 120 meters or more; the branch canals were as narrow as 1 to 1.5 meters in width and .5 to 2.25 meters in depth, with a length just under two kilometers. Construction and maintenance of canal systems were considered an important duty (as well as an act of piety) to be executed by Mesopotamian kings, but cleaning and dredging accumulated silt in other canals was under the jurisdiction of the local authorities. The rivers and canals provided drinking water for people and animals, irrigated vegetation, and created a cool, green world along their banks.

The costs of farming included seed, plows, tools, and draft animals, which were expensive because oxen needed good food to work. The laborers also had to be fed, either in rations or by a residual share of the crop. Major irrigation works were usually performed during slack seasons.

Large territories supported the households and administrations of the royal family and high-ranking state officials. Minor- and middle-ranking officials, as well as military personnel, held relatively small plots, which ensured a comfortable living. Low revenue assessments were usually offered to favored officials. Prosperous small landholders formed a significant part of the population. The extended family worked together to take advantage of joint cultivation. The equal division of agricultural land through successive generations could create fragmentation that was further complicated by alternating fallow lands and access to water.

Agricultural workers or tenants on the estates often became dependent upon the landlords. With a chronic shortage of manpower, an indebted farmer's downward spiral could be hastened. Old Babylonian loans record that the borrower was committed to work a specific number of days on the creditor's fields. Thus the rich ensured that their crops were harvested at the optimum time so that their economic success would surely increase. At the threshing floor, when the year's harvest was ready for storage, the crop was usually divided, with one-third going to the landlord and two-thirds to the tenant.

Camels were not widely known in Mesopotamia until the first millennium B.C.E.

The most striking organizational characteristic of Mesopotamian society in all periods was its economic division into the haves and have-nots, into those who held land and those who depended on the landholders. Private, literary, and legal documents (including Hammurabi's Law Code) portray a society in which individual rights again became an issue. A considerable portion of the populace was now legally free, attached to neither palace nor temple. The private sector of the economy—based on ownership of agricultural land and use of hired labor or slaves—flourished in Amorite-dominated Babylonia, similar to the situation under the Amorites' Semitic predecessors, the Akkadians.

Nomads were shepherds who migrated with their herds through areas not suited for cultivation. Early nomads in the Near East were never more than one day's travel from a water hole. Nomadic groups also had bases to which they returned periodically. For example, both the Amorites and Aramaeans used Jebel Bishri as their headquarters, between the Euphrates and the main oasis of Tadmor (Palmyra).

Nomads belonged to social groups larger than the family, such as the tribe or clan. The political organization of nomads varied from small, decentralized "egalitarian" groups to large, hierarchical "chiefdoms." Many nomadic tribes or clans farmed and raised animals on the outskirts of settlements. These tribes have been termed semi-nomads or transhumants. Today, we use the term *bedouin*, borrowed from Arabic, to refer only to camel-nomads, who cross the desert by dromedary, an animal whose capabilities are superior to those of the ass.

Nomads did not leave written records; even archaeological remains are meager relative to those of the sedentary or settled people. Despite the progress of archaeologists in their field methods and scientific techniques, we have only a bare outline of nomadic life in ancient times.

The traditional view of scholars on nomadic-sedentary relations in the Near East stresses their mutual antagonism. This opinion was influenced by ancient Near Eastern textual sources, written by scribes who lived in the city: the authors stress the uncivilized behavior of nomadic groups and their potential danger to sedentary society. The nomadic way of life may have served as an alternative when farming was no longer feasible.

In time, each nomadic group was absorbed into other populations or became sedentary. Traditionally, this process was viewed in terms of successive stages in which the tribes transformed from nomadic barbarism to settled life. Passing through social strata, some nomads eventually became princes or kings and, as "town-dwellers," founded dynasties.

Near Eastern agriculture was always a risky business, at the mercy of severe environmental or climatic difficulties, greedy governmental authorities, and crop damage in times of war (Nemet-Nejat, 112–15, 245–58, 263).

FOR MORE INFORMATION

Civil, M. *The Farmer's Instructions: A Sumerian Agricultural Manual.* Aula-Orientalis-Supplementa 5. Barcelona: Editorial AUSA, 1994.

Hesse, B. "Animal Husbandry and Human Diet in the Ancient Near East." In *Civilizations of the Ancient Near East*, ed. J. Sasson. Vol. 1. New York: Scribner's, 1995.

Hunt, R. C. "Hydraulic Management in Southern Mesopotamia in Sumerian Times." *Bulletin on Sumerian Agriculture* 4 (1988).

Nemet-Nejat, K. R. *Daily Life in Ancient Mesopotamia.* Westport, Conn.: Greenwood Press, 1998.

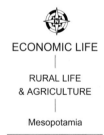

ECONOMIC LIFE
|
RURAL LIFE
& AGRICULTURE
|
Mesopotamia

Egypt

Greece

Rome

India

Nubia

EGYPT

Farmers, the vast majority of the population in Egypt, repeated the same pattern year after year, but with greater regularity than elsewhere in the world where rainstorms, snow, or temperature swings made agriculture less predictable. Each time the Nile receded, Egyptian farmers returned to the fields to plow after having spent the previous month readying their tools. Plowing was relatively easy in the still-moist ground. If a farmer had cattle, two would pull while he leaned his weight on the plow to ensure deep furrows and a son guided the team in a straight line; otherwise, the farmer would enlist two men to take the place of the cattle. After the furrows were dug, the farmer followed with a mattock to break up the large clumps of dirt lifted by the plow. Then it was time for the women to scatter the seeds from their wicker baskets, slung by a cord over their shoulders, into the furrows. Later, encouraged by strewn grass or straw, a herd of sheep would be driven onto the land to bury the seeds with their hooves, allowing them to germinate hidden from hungry birds and rodents.

Next came a season of nurture to ensure bountiful crops. Dirt dikes and canals needed continual repair to guarantee a constant water flow to every young shoot. Farmers alternated work in their fields with regular stints at the Nile, raising bucket after bucket of river water up the bank to spill into the system of canals used by neighboring farms. The *shadoof,* a cantilevered pole, made this work easier than walking every bucket up the bank, but no less monotonous. When not participating in his community water chore, a farmer had weeds to clear, rats to fend off, and birds to shoo—a reason the family cat often accompanied his master to work.

Three months later, as soon as the grain ripened, local officials appeared to measure the field to set taxes. Only then did the whole family arrive to harvest the crop before it spoiled or was eaten by animals. Some cut the grain heads with a short sickle held in one hand while the other hand held the grain steady; others gathered the loose heads into piles, tied them with lengths of straw, and then loaded them on donkeys for transport to the local threshing area. The long wheat stems were left standing in the field for later harvesting as straw for the livestock.

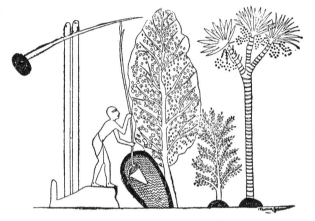

Drawing of a *shadoof,* the invaluable mechanism used to raise water from the Nile and its canals and irrigate fields.

At the threshing area, the whole community assembled to separate usable seeds from unusable stems and chaff. First, oxen were driven round and round to break the seeds free while the men turned the mixture over to ensure every seed received a hoof. Afterward, the same pitchforks carried the straw away, leaving only the finer grain and its hulls (chaff) on the threshing floor. Using wooden scoops, the men lifted this mixture above their heads, letting it spill back to the floor so the wind could blow the lighter chaff away. In the end, only the seeds remained, which were then distributed to each family in proportion to its production. As the year closed, a short new year's hiatus signaled that it was time, once again, to start repairing the tools—and to begin another year just like the one before.

Tens of thousands of cattle, goats, and sheep were the responsibility of herdsmen who roamed the plains of Egypt caring for their charges, while other herdsmen settled on farm estates with smaller herds. Both carried long staves to enforce their commands, although the real affection they felt for their herds is illustrated by the names they bestowed on their animals, for example, "Beauty," "Golden," and "Brilliant."

A herdsman lived with his herd, guiding them to fresh grazing areas, defending them against hyena and crocodile predators, and carrying the sick and injured on his back. When a cow gave birth, he was at her side, cooing affectionately and, when necessary, easing the calf from her womb; when a stream had to be forded, he shouldered those calves too small to walk safely across. Just as today, cattle were rounded up, lassoed, and branded; of course, in Egypt, what was burned on the cattle's right shoulder was a hieroglyphic sign.

Egyptians called their delta *Mehit*—papyrus marsh. Although sufficient dry land existed in this area to allow tens of thousands of cattle to graze, almost a third of it remained under water throughout the year, providing work and shelter for an unusual group of people. Marshmen hunted, fished, or gathered papyrus and in consideration of their moist work conditions, wore either no clothing at all or tied a simple wrap of cloth around the waist and then between their legs.

Marshmen, who also caught fish by spearing them in the shallow delta waters and trapped birds in large nets in the same marshes, enjoyed a degree of unsupervised independence unusual in highly structured Egypt (Brier and Hobbs, 77–82, 87, 89).

FOR MORE INFORMATION

Bender, B. *Farming in Prehistory*. London: John Baker, 1975.

Brier, B., and H. Hobbs. *Daily Life of the Ancient Egyptians*. Westport, Conn.: Greenwood Press, 1999.

Butzer, K. W. *Early Hydraulic Civilization in Egypt: A Study in Cultural Ecology*. Chicago, Ill.: University of Chicago Press, 1976.

ECONOMIC LIFE

RURAL LIFE
& AGRICULTURE

Mesopotamia

Egypt

Greece

Rome

India

Nubia

GREECE

Because of the importance attached to land ownership, the most respected occupation in Greece was farming. Even in the late fifth century B.C.E., at least half the population of Athens was still engaged in agriculture. The overwhelming majority were smallholders, who owned no more than two or three acres of land. Only a small minority were wealthy landowners, whose estates occupied several hundred acres. We learn most about farming from Hesiod, whose *Works and Days* provides a vivid account of the agricultural year. As the poet emphasizes, it was an extremely hard occupation even at the best of times, owing to the poor quality of the soil. The fact that land had to be left fallow for a year after each season's cultivation so as not to exhaust its goodness made agriculture even more laborious.

From the fifth century B.C.E. onward, crops were rotated and manure was used. As a general rule, the cultivation of olives and grapes, along with animal husbandry, was more profitable than that of wheat and vegetables. To economize on space, vines, planted in rows, were interspersed with vegetables and fruit trees. Grains, such as wheat, were the main staples of Greek diets. Plowing took place twice a year, in spring and in autumn. Wooden plows, sometimes tipped with iron, were pulled by teams of oxen. Behind them walked the farmer (or one of his slaves), breaking up the clods with a hoe and covering the seeds with earth. In the harvest season, in May, all available hands gathered in the ripe grain. The grain was threshed on a stone threshing floor by driving oxen around in a circle to separate the wheat from the chaff. Each procedure was accompanied by religious ceremonies to ensure the favor of the gods. Few small farms were entirely self-sufficient. Most farmers had to travel to market to exchange their produce. In the Hellenistic period, Egypt became the most intensively cultivated region in the Greek world (Garland, 153).

Although the majority of inhabitants of ancient Greece were farmers working small family plots, the geography of Greece itself made producing enough food difficult. Greece is an extremely mountainous country, and flat land is usually only found in small valleys between the mountains. With approximately 80 percent of the country covered by hills or mountains, good flat farmland was at a premium. Greek farmers became adept at maximizing the use of this space through intercultivation and by identifying food that could be grown on hillsides.

The fact that olive trees grow readily on hillsides is one reason olives assumed such an important place not only in ancient Greek diets but in Greek culture generally. Even today, many hillsides in Greece are covered with gray-green olive trees planted so as to take advantage of these otherwise difficult-to-use spaces. Olive trees can be established by cuttings or grafting and once planted, can live for centuries. Nonetheless, they are slow-growing trees, and planting an olive tree grove was a long-term investment. Olive oil was used for a wide range of purposes in addition to cooking. Among many other uses, olive oil was burned in lamps to provide light, and it was the basis of perfumes and soaps. The olives were harvested by hand and then milled to separate the pit from the rest of the olive. Once the pits were removed, the olives were pressed to extract their oil. Greek olive presses varied in technological complexity. A simple press might consist of a wooden beam with one end attached to the floor while the other end was pulled down against the olives by weights or pulleys. More sophisticated presses (but also expensive and prone to breaking) employed a screw mechanism to lower the beam and press the olives. Grapevines could similarly be planted on hillsides, and the wine made from grapes also formed a staple of the Greek diet.

Again, to take advantage of as much of the rugged terrain as possible, the main animals raised by the Greeks for food were goats rather than cattle, which need flatter pastures for grazing. Herders shepherded flocks of goats up and down the steep mountains. Milk and milk products such as cheese were also obtained from goats rather than from cows. Other animals commonly raised on Greek farms included sheep, from which wool was obtained, and pigs. Greek farmers also practiced beekeeping; honey was the only readily available sweetener, and clusters of carefully tended hives often dotted the hillsides of ancient Greek farms.

~Gregory S. Aldrete

FOR MORE INFORMATION

Adkins, L., and R. Adkins. *Handbook to Life in Ancient Greece*. Oxford: Oxford University Press, 1997.

Garland, R. *Daily Life of the Ancient Greeks*. Westport, Conn.: Greenwood Press, 1998.

White, K. D. *Country Life in Classical Times*. London: Elek Books, 1977.

ROME

The Roman word for farmer is *agricola*. It is made up of two other words, *ager*, which means "field," and the verb *colere*, which means "to cultivate." Thus an *agricola* is literally "one who cultivates the field." From these terms comes our modern English word *agriculture*.

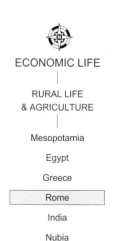

ECONOMIC LIFE

RURAL LIFE
& AGRICULTURE

Mesopotamia

Egypt

Greece

Rome

India

Nubia

During the Republic, farms tended to be fairly small. The average farm was typically as much land as one family could manage. Archaeological evidence suggests that farms may have averaged about four acres. Roman farmers had a saying that one cannot trust anyone whose farm is larger than 12 *iugera* (7 acres). They were suspicious of anyone who farmed more than he needed because this indicated that he must be greedy and therefore also dishonest. Cincinnatus, the ideal Roman citizen-hero, had a farm of about three acres.

In the Late Republic when rich men began buying up all the land and putting together huge estates, the Romans passed legislation that stipulated that it was illegal for any one person to own more than 500 *iugera* of land. In practice, this law was plainly ignored or people found loopholes to circumvent it, but it is an interesting indication of how suspicious Romans were of large landholders.

The core of Roman agriculture was what is known as the Mediterranean triad: wheat, olives, and wine. The cultivation of wheat was a multistep process. Many Romans seem to have used a two-field system, which meant that each year they only planted on half their land while letting the other half rest to recover nutrients and moisture. Next, the farmer prepared the land he was going to farm, which meant plowing. Each field had to be plowed between three and six times before it would be properly ready. This was extremely hard work. In addition, oxen, which pulled the plows, were quite expensive. Often, a village would share one team of oxen, which often were the most valuable things in the village. After plowing, the farmer mixed manure, often by hand, into the soil. It is estimated that it took a family six days working dawn to dusk to properly manure a single acre of soil. The next step was the actual sowing of the seeds. Romans just scattered the seed around by hand so they ended up wasting a lot. Modern sow-to-reap ratios are very high, on the order of 1:50 or so, but Romans farmers may have had to sow on the order of 1:4. Thus one-quarter of each crop had to be saved to produce the next one. Once seeds were sown, the soil had to be worked over with hoes and weeded by hand. Finally came harvest time. The farmers would walk through the wheat fields with a sickle and cut off the wheat stalks. The work was by no means finished, however. The wheat stalks were then threshed to separate the grain from the straw. On the threshing floor, farmers would beat the wheat with flails or sometimes even have cows trample on it. Threshing was followed by winnowing, in which the wheat was tossed into the air to separate out the heavier grain from the chaff.

If all these stages went well and the crop was not destroyed by rain, flood, cold, or vermin or stolen by thieves, then the farmer at last ended up with some wheat. The amount was probably barely enough to feed the family for the year, and in a perfect year, the surplus might amount to 5 to 10 percent. This was a world literally always on the brink of starvation. The routine of Roman farming varied little and demanded much hard work, and the rhythms of the cultivation process governed life for the vast majority of people in the Roman world.

Other cereal crops included barley and millet. Ancient sources seem to have regarded these as less desirable for human consumption. They were mostly used as feed for animals, and in the army it was a common punishment to have to eat barley instead of wheat. Despite all this, many poor people probably depended on barley for subsistence.

Another important crop was olives. The olive is the definitive plant of the Mediterranean. It is also the most restricted by environmental factors. Olives were of course eaten as food, but olive oil was used for many other purposes, including cooking (instead of butter), as a light source (in olive oil burning lamps), as a kind of soap (after bathing, Romans would rub olive oil over their bodies and then scrape it off), and as the basis for all sorts of perfumes (modern perfumes have an alcohol base). Olives were truly central to the Mediterranean lifestyle.

Olives were harvested in the fall. Olive trees were precious resources; trees could take five to ten years to even start producing olives, but they could live hundreds of years. The trees are biennial, producing a crop every other year. The olives had to be carefully picked by hand because they are quite tender and bruise easily. After harvesting, olives could be transformed into olive oil by putting the olives in a press. The yield from this process was one-quarter to one-third the original weight of the olives as oil.

Grapes were cultivated to be converted into wine. The main labor in grape growing was pruning, grafting, and harvesting. This work could be done by the elderly and by children, leaving the able-bodied adults free for more demanding activities, such as wheat farming. Wine was made by pressing the grapes and then allowing the juice to ferment.

The main animals that were raised were sheep and goats. From these were also obtained milk and cheese. Cattle herding was relatively rare around the shores of the Mediterranean. Beekeeping was important because honey was the only sweetener widely available to the Romans.

~Gregory S. Aldrete

FOR MORE INFORMATION

White, K. D. *Roman Farming*. Ithaca, N.Y.: Cornell University Press, 1970.

INDIA

The village community was the most basic focus of economic life in traditional India. Villages were typically rural and agricultural. The most common crops produced were wheat, barley, millet, rice, beans, and lentils. Sugar cane and cotton were other widespread crops, and a variety of spices—cardamom, ginger, cinnamon, and black pepper—were grown in the south of India. Bananas and mangoes were the most common fruit harvested.

Cattle were employed for plowing the fields. From cows came milk and curds, as well as *ghee*, made from melted butter with the fat skimmed off. In ancient India, the cow was revered, and although slaughter of cows was forbidden in later times, in the era of the vegetarian emperor Asoka, cow slaughter was still permitted, although this practice may have ceased after Asoka embraced Buddhism.

ECONOMIC LIFE
|
RURAL LIFE
& AGRICULTURE
|
Mesopotamia

Egypt

Greece

Rome

India

Nubia

At the level of the village, economic distribution of labor relied on the *jajmani* system. Within the caste system, various *jati* were specialized for different kinds of labor: carpentry, weaving, tailoring, and so on. Craftsmanship was the cornerstone of the economy. Goods produced, as well as crops, were distributed in a natural economy whereby each worker produced with regard to the good of the whole community. The same held for crops: food was collected and distributed by the head of the community, and shares were distributed to each family in the community.

~*Matthew Bingley*

FOR MORE INFORMATION

Auboyer, J. *Daily Life in Ancient India*. London: Phoenix Press, 1965.
Basham, A. L. *The Wonder That Was India*. London: Sidgwick and Jackson, 1967.
Kenoyer, J. M. *Ancient Cities of the Indus Valley Civilization*. New York: Oxford University Press, 1998.

ECONOMIC LIFE
|
RURAL LIFE
& AGRICULTURE
|
Mesopotamia

Egypt

Greece

Rome

India

Nubia

NUBIA

In the period before about 10,000 B.C.E., the Nubians relied on the Nile River as a source of life, hunting animals that came there for water and catching the fish and perhaps also the fowl of its waters and marshes, respectively. They gathered edible plants and lived in temporary shelters, most probably constructed from the hides of hunted animals or from gathered reeds or grasses.

The subsequent development of Nubian agriculture may be regarded as part of the Neolithic Revolution in general, during which time individuals developed a sedentary lifestyle that gradually replaced their earlier hunter-gatherer societies. About 5500 B.C.E., the Nubians appear to have domesticated oxen, sheep, goats, and dogs. Because these animals do not seem to have been indigenous to the homelands of the Nubians, scholars suggest that there may have been social intercourse with individuals from the Sahara to the north that may have resulted in their introduction. Regardless, Nubians in the vicinity of Khartoum appear to have pioneered the animal husbandry of cattle, whose importance as an index of both wealth and social status was to dominate subsequent Nubian culture.

Evidence for the development of agriculture is more difficult to interpret. It is clear that during the sixth millennium B.C.E., the climate of the northeastern quadrant of Africa grew progressively drier, but whether this was a catalyst for the later development of agriculture is moot. Equally problematic is the equivocal nature of millet, a grain often found in some of the earliest pottery created on the African continent, dated to the fifth millennium B.C.E. Because of the close similarity of the morphological characteristics of cultivated and wild millet, botanists cannot determine with any degree of certainty whether this millet was gathered in the wild or intentionally grown.

The data recovered from the trash heaps of the site of Kadero, about 20 kilometers north of Khartoum, portray the gradual agricultural transformation of Nubia during this period. Bones of both wild and domesticated animals, particularly sheep and goats, suggest that hunting and animal husbandry coexisted with fishing. Fragments suggested to be millstones argue for the presence of edible plants, but whether these included domesticated millet is unclear.

Nevertheless, the farming techniques pioneered by these early Nubians are fundamentally African and may have had an impact on the emerging agricultural practices of contemporary Egyptians. In Egypt, as in other African river basin cultures, seed was sown in October after the flood waters of the rivers, including the Nile, had subsided. This differs from the agricultural practices of other contemporary cultures of the ancient Near East, in which seed was planted in the fall before the arrival of the winter rains. The types of crops planted by the Nubians, particularly indigenous African cereals such as sorghum, were initially not suitable for cultivation in Egypt proper because of their differing ecological requirements.

It is clear that the Nubians were cultivating barley by the middle of the fifth millennium B.C.E. Archaeological excavations have revealed countless grinding stones at many Nubian sites, which suggest an ever-expanding agricultural basis. With the passage of time, the number of stone blades for insertion into wooden handles for use as sickles also increased.

By the time of the Kerma culture (about 2500–1500 B.C.E.), the Nubians had developed extensive agricultural and animal husbandry practices. The discovery of what appear to be entire herds of either sheep or goats in tombs, as well as quantities of choice cuts of meat and innumerable bowls and jars presumably containing stores of (plant-based) foodstuffs, bears eloquent testimony to the abundance of their crops and the fecundity of their flocks. Cattle continued to serve as an index of both status and wealth.

With the acculturation to Egyptian norms by the Nubians during the course of the New Kingdom, there seems to have been an intersection of agricultural and animal husbandry practices, although the types of crops grown depended on local ecological conditions. These were often passed over in silence because the preserved records stress the ancient interest in Nubia's natural resources, such as ebony, ivory, myrrh, the ostrich and other exotic beasts and their body parts.

Indeed, it has been suggested that as late as the Kingdom of Meroe, the types of animals domesticated and the crops cultivated by the Nubians would not have differed significantly from those of the earlier periods. There is, however, evidence for the introduction of new crops. These include the grape and perhaps wine production during the 25th Dynasty in Nubia proper, as well as the subsequent cultivation of sesame and cotton in the later Meroitic period. There is also evidence for royal gardens in which palm trees were planted, if we can trust the Classical sources, and a royal inscription of King Harsiyotef, who claims to have planted six palm trees each in royal gardens associated with the sanctuaries of Amun of Napata and Amun of Meroe.

How extensively the Nubians relied on irrigation is difficult to gauge. In regions such as Meroe and its surrounding areas, with large annual summer rainfalls, the Nubians apparently harnessed the channeling of water through natural wadis to help irrigate their crops. Doubt has been cast on the use of *hafir*—large, circular catchment basins with raised earthen walls—in which rain water is collected and stored. Because of their habitual location in proximity to settlements, the capacity of these *hafirs* would seem to satisfy the domestic needs of the inhabitants with little surplus for the demands of agriculture. The *saqia,* or water wheel, was not widespread until the post-Meroitic period.

~*Robert S. Bianchi*

FOR MORE INFORMATION

Adams, W. *Nubia: Corridor to Africa.* Princeton, N.J.: Princeton University Press, 1977.

O'Connor, D. *Ancient Nubia: Egypt's Rival in Africa.* Philadelphia: University of Pennsylvania, 1993.

Trigger, B. *Nubia under the Pharaohs.* Boulder, Colo.: Westview Press, 1976.

Welsby, D. A. *The Kingdom of Kush: The Napatan and Meroitic Empires.* London: British Museum Press, 1996.

ECONOMIC LIFE

| URBAN LIFE |

Mesopotamia

Egypt

Greece

Rome

Urban Life

Whereas the vast majority of people in the ancient world (probably around 90 percent) were farmers, much of the remainder lived in cities, and it was there that they produced and defined the nature of ancient civilizations. Simply put, civilization itself is an urban phenomenon. Government, philosophy, religion, law, art, buildings, trade, literature: all of these things are generated in cities. Therefore, although a very small number of people in the ancient world actually lived in cities, a disproportionately large amount of the events and ideas that we tend to study and remember happened and were produced in an urban environment. It is revealing that while humans existed for thousands of years prior to the start of the civilizations discussed in this volume, it was not until people began to gather in urban conglomerations larger than small farm villages that we begin to speak of them as being civilizations. The first place that these urban centers began to emerge was in Mesopotamia, where the application of intensive agriculture produced a critical mass of surplus food, which was the necessary precursor to cities. From these beginnings, the phenomenon of urbanization spread, and with it, the development of distinct political and cultural entities.

The ancient world gave rise not only to the first cities but to the largest as well, at least up until very recently. At its height, Rome's population achieved the staggering size of one million inhabitants, and a number of other cities such as Alexandria in Egypt boasted populations measured in the hundreds of thousands. Cities such as these and others, including Athens, Thebes, Babylon, Meroe, and Antioch, were the great urban centers of the ancient world, but it was the network of smaller cities that often gave cohesion and identity to civilizations. The Roman Empire, for example, while conventionally filled in on maps as a solid mass of red or blue, might more accurately be portrayed as a series of dots denoting cities, with blank countryside in between. This is because it was mostly in the cities that Roman culture could be found; it was there that people spoke Latin and that one would encounter Roman magistrates, buildings, and law. Out in the countryside, many provincials had their own ancestral languages, customs, and leaders, so that the Roman Empire was really a system of nodelike cities embodying Roman culture connected to one another by a web of roads, leaving the interstitial spaces largely untouched.

Something about cities in the ancient world seemed to generate new ideas and to spur innovation. Law codes may have developed from the need to find a way for people to live in large, densely packed groups without descending into chaos. Great art and literature frequently flourished as the result of patronage from rulers who wished to glorify their capitals and commemorate their deeds. Cities and civilization are inseparable, and the history of one is really the history of the other.

~*Gregory S. Aldrete*

MESOPOTAMIA

ECONOMIC LIFE
|
URBAN LIFE
|
Mesopotamia

Egypt

Greece

Rome

The cities of Mesopotamia were sizable (100 acres or more) and well populated. They functioned as political, even imperial, capitals, trade centers, and principal shrines of a region.

The average Sumerian city—and most probably, later cities—included three parts. First, the city itself referred to the walled area, which included the temple or temples, the palace with residences for royal officials, and the houses of the citizens. Second, the "suburb," called the "outer city" in Sumerian, consisted of houses, farms, cattle folds, fields, and gardens, all furnishing the city with food and raw materials. We do not know how the "outer city" extended or whether it was protected by secondary walls or by fortified outposts, the latter known from the Neo-Babylonian period. Third, the wharf section functioned not only as a wharf but also as the center of commercial activity. The wharf had administrative independence and separate legal status for the citizens transacting business there. Foreign traders had stores here, and their needs were met by the tavern keeper of the wharf.

The standard of living for a typical city was only slightly above subsistence level. The city enjoyed real prosperity only when its king was victorious and brought back from his campaigns booty, tribute from subject cities, and gifts from intimidated neighbors. The spoils of war were added to the wealth of the ruler and redistributed among the military hierarchy and the bureaucracy, thereby raising the city's standard of living. The temples grew rich and were elaborately decorated; temple personnel were allotted grants in land. Decorating the palace and temple drew traders, who brought typical imports (e.g., metals, timber, and precious stones) as well as luxury items (e.g., certain spices, perfumes, wines, finery, and rare animals). Only a few Babylonian cities prospered for more than one or two short periods, and most not at all. Affluence was soon replaced by a wretched existence, with people living among ruins, the sanctuaries dilapidated, and the city walls disintegrating. The citizens were debt-ridden under the authority of greedy administrators. The inhabitants soon fell prey to invading enemies and raids of people living in the open country.

Once a city was destroyed, the remaining inhabitants continued to live in the ruins, preserving the city's name through the millennia.

The shapes of cities varied. Usually, the wall of a Mesopotamian city was constructed either in wide curves or in rectangular, often symmetrical designs. Other shapes were found, such as ovals (Ur and Uruk), triangles (Der), diamonds (late Babylon), rectangles (Sippar), trapezoids (Nineveh), and squares (Dur-Sharrukin and Nimrud). In Zinjirli in northern Syria (second millennium B.C.E.), the outer wall was almost a perfect circle, with 100 wall towers; it enclosed a circular inner city, with a palace, a temple, barracks, and other structures. Often, round cities were built after the collapse of the Babylonian and Seleucid empires. There is even a map of Nippur drawn on clay; it is the only Mesopotamian city map found to date, and it is true to scale.

Southern cities were similar to northern cities along the Euphrates in their dependence on agriculture. But as northern settlements were transformed from villages to cities in the third and second millennia B.C.E., the small mounds of the early settlements were used as raised platforms on which to build their temples and palaces on a high citadel, sometimes separated from the rest of the city by their own fortifications. Whether the Assyrians occupied an old settlement or founded a new one, they separated parts of the city by elevation, whereas the southern cities used the maze of waterways for this purpose.

In the south, the city was the primary settlement pattern, situated along canals; the rural population inhabited more temporary sites that shifted as the waterways changed course. In the north, permanent villages, some dating back to the Neolithic period, were distributed regularly across the fertile land.

Urban centers often grew because of their temples, which served the religious needs of the people, and also because of their administrative and economic functions.

Once a city was destroyed, the remaining inhabitants continued to live in the ruins.

By the beginning of the fourth millennium B.C.E., the cities operated as hubs for negotiating among different groups inhabiting Mesopotamia, such as the herders of the desert, the fishermen of the marshes, and the farmers of the plains. Later, the cities became centers of communication and trade between Mesopotamians and the people of far-off mountain areas, which provided materials Mesopotamia lacked, such as stone, metal, and wood.

By 3500 B.C.E., in cities like Uruk, the temple organized Mesopotamian society. The temple was built on a raised platform and could be seen for miles around. The temple generated writing, government, a judicial system, fine art, architecture, and so on. For the first 500 years of Mesopotamian history, the temples alone controlled most facets of society and the economy.

By approximately 2800 B.C.E., territorial disputes erupted in the south. Monumental fortifications were built to maintain security and define boundaries between rural and urban areas. But these wars required leadership, and so another major urban institution emerged—the palace. Mesopotamian cities now had two centers of power: the palace, which controlled the political and military arena, and the temple, which regulated the economy and religious life. Monumental fortifications were built to maintain security and to define boundaries between rural and urban areas.

In the third and early second millennia B.C.E., some Assyrian villages became centers of political power and expanded, often abruptly, into cities. Temples were built on the mounds of the old settlement, and new fortifications were constructed to enclose a larger, lower town. At some northern sites, the citadel mound was located at the edge of the new city, next to the city wall.

Excavations at the city of Mashkan-shapir have provided the best picture to date of the layout of a southern Mesopotamian city. In the nineteenth and eighteenth centuries B.C.E., Mashkan-shapir was the second capital of the kingdom of Larsa, as well as an important trade center. The city was suddenly abandoned about 1720 B.C.E. and was never reoccupied in any significant way. The main roads of Mashkan-shapir ran either parallel to canals or at right angles to them, with bridges or ferries to link neighborhoods. The residential areas were connected by a network of streets, and most homes were entered through narrow alleyways and culs-de-sac. The layout of the narrow streets was like a maze. The street surfaces were uneven, in part a result of the constant rebuilding of homes on previous foundations that were never leveled, and in part because garbage was dumped onto the streets. Dogs and other scavenging animals ate some rubbish, but the rest was dried by the sun and walked on. At Mashkan-shapir, all residential areas included artisans; some areas even provided evidence of craft specialization, such as the production of pottery, copper-bronze smelting, and lapidary work.

Archaeology and texts have provided no evidence of either a central marketplace or a commercial quarter in Mesopotamian cities. Textual references to wine shops around squares have still not explained the role of these stores in the distribution of goods. Some small buildings in residential areas have been identified as shops, but the archaeological evidence is shaky. Furthermore, the texts rarely mention shops. Perhaps the agricultural products and crafts were traded near the centers of production or importation, such as workshops, city gates, and wharves. The establishment of markets was a late development, stimulated by the extraordinary size of the cities, which led to the creation of supply markets. Thus, the markets served to link those who lived inside the city to those who lived outside.

Most archaeologists have calculated populations based on 200 persons per hectare (1 hectare = 2.5 acres) in southern irrigated areas. The resulting figure correlates with textual information. That is, the populations of major cities in southern Mesopotamia ranged from 10,000 to nearly 100,000 people. Such estimates should be regarded as maximum populations of cities in their heyday. The archaeological evidence, however, has suggested that the population density in the south was approximately 100 persons per hectare, similar to rural villages of today in southwestern Asia. The population of the cities changed as their political fortunes changed. Unfortunately, calculating the population of northern cities has been more difficult because large residential areas have rarely been excavated.

The main institutions of each city were the temple and the palace. The main temple was always located in the highest part of the city but not necessarily in the center. Ziggurats were often built near the temple. The other urban institution, the palace, was not as easy for archaeologists to find because it was not built on a platform like the temple.

During times of political centralization, capitals were governed by kings, and cities were ruled by governors. Power lay with three groups: the temple, the king, and senior members of ancient or wealthy families.

Mesopotamian cities, both large and small, were divided as well as united by streets and canals. City streets were not paved until the Assyrian period of the first millennium B.C.E. Sennacherib enlarged Nineveh's squares, pulled down buildings to let light into alleys and narrow streets, and straightened and widened various streets to create a main ceremonial avenue. Both inside and outside the city, major roads probably ran parallel to the canals and rivers, much like today. Other main streets were laid at right angles, demarcating blocks of approximately one hectare. Coincidentally, both the average size of a small Mesopotamian village and the size of a residential area were one hectare.

All major Mesopotamian cities were enclosed by fortifications, which separated the city itself from its surroundings. Walls were usually built at the edge of the settlement mound so that later they could be extended to include nonsettled areas. Walls served both symbolic and practical purposes. Rulers celebrated building a new wall, and when a city was conquered, standard military practice was to demolish its fortifications.

The sources of drinking water in Mesopotamia were the Twin Rivers and their canals; for many cities, these remained the main sources of water down through the first millennium B.C.E. But some palaces, especially in Assyria, obtained their water supply from deep wells, safe from pollution. For the most part, large cities were built near water supplies. Smaller cities survived if they had many springs, wells, aqueducts, or cisterns.

Pure water was especially important in the ancient Near East. At the Hittite court, water for the king had to be strained; records note that the king one time found a hair in his water jug and ordered the guilty water carrier put to death. Mesopotamian texts also refer to the risk of death from drinking contaminated water. For the Assyrians, cleanliness was essential, particularly for ritual purposes.

The health of a community was directly connected to its ability to eliminate human waste without contaminating its water supply. As early as the third millennium B.C.E., royal palaces and even the homes of the rich had indoor lavatories. Usually, the lavatories were placed against outside walls, with a seat over a terracotta drainage pipe. Human waste was often carried to a distant river through a complex system of drains and sewers beneath the streets. Of course, lavatories were a luxury most could not afford. Archaeological excavations have demonstrated that the homes of ordinary workers and peasants had no lavatories, not even communal bathrooms. Instead, the poor would defecate outside in orchards, in fields within city walls, and in surrounding fields.

Garbage was usually thrown into the streets and empty lots with layers of ash, perhaps indicating incineration. There was no municipal rubbish collection. Animal teeth and bones at Mesopotamian sites show that both pigs and dogs were found in all parts of the city; they probably played a role in the disposal of garbage. Scavenging pigs and dogs roamed around Babylonian cities, and among the Hittites these scavengers even wandered inside the palace of the king. These animals were only prohibited from crossing the threshold of the place where the food for the king or the god was prepared. In time, the scavenging pigs were eaten (except by people such as the Israelites, for whom the pig was taboo). However, if this meat was not thoroughly cooked, the flesh transmitted dangerous *Trichinella* worms. Rodents also thrived in the constant presence of garbage, with rats carrying fleas, an agent of the bubonic plague (Nemet-Nejat, 107–11).

FOR MORE INFORMATION

Nemet-Nejat, K. R. *Daily Life in Ancient Mesopotamia*. Westport, Conn.: Greenwood Press, 1998.

Saggs, H. W. F. *Civilization before Greece and Rome*. New Haven, Conn.: Yale University Press, 1989. Reprint, New Haven, Conn.: Yale University Press, 1991.

EGYPT

ECONOMIC LIFE
|
URBAN LIFE
|
Mesopotamia

Egypt

Greece

Rome

Egypt featured a large number of small towns that served as administrative and economic centers for their region. Each nome (district) usually had a main city or town. Impromptu and sometimes transitory workers' towns sprang up near the sites of major construction projects such as pyramids or temples. The largest permanent cities, especially Thebes and Memphis, owed their existence to the presence or the activities of the pharaohs.

Some of the largest and most impressive urban areas consisted mostly of the residences of the rulers and their attendant courts. Kings lived in style with hosts of retainers. Unlike modern countries with royal heads of state, Egypt did not maintain a national palace into which succeeding rulers moved. Although palaces covered acres of land, they too were constructed of adobe to last only a generation or so, allowing the next pharaoh to build a new one to his own specifications. Each ruler constructed not just one new residence but several for the different places in which he needed to reside—the capitals of Thebes and Memphis at the very least. Unhappily, none of these grand palaces has survived, so what we know of them is based on tomb pictures and on the few floors and crumbling walls that make up the remains of the two best-preserved examples. These belonged to a father and his son, Amenhotep III and the heretical pharaoh Akhenaton, and were built during the 18th Dynasty, the apex of Egypt's wealth and power.

Akhenaton's palace may well have been the grandest ever constructed in Egypt. A 100-foot-wide thoroughfare, the Royal Road, divided the palace proper from the royal residences, joined by a bridge over the road. This bridging of structures was an innovation in Egypt, perhaps modified from Assyrian buildings that also spanned thoroughfares. On the east side of the road lay the formal palace, called the House of Rejoicing of the Aten, including the state reception rooms, some government offices and servants' quarters; on the west stood the residence area for the pharaoh, his immediate family, and personal retainers.

The private residence of the king on the west side ran for 100 yards beside the Royal Road and stretched back for at least 150 yards more. Servants' quarters (or perhaps residences for royal guards) were discretely on the right before entering a square garden, 150 feet per side, that occupied the northern side of the compound. South of the garden lay the private apartments of the royal family inside their own walled structure. Its three areas consisted of personal servants' quarters filling the west half, a separate structure in its southeastern corner of six rooms plus bathroom, presumably for the six daughters of the king, and the pharaoh's private rooms. Separated from the children's area by a court and a wall, a large columned hall divided the king's suite of two rooms on one side, with a bathroom and latrine, from an open area with an altar on the other side. Additional courtyards and rooms for family recreation filled the middle part of these private apartments. The rest of the compound, its easternmost third, consisted of magazines for storing food and an artificial pond in the northeastern corner 40 feet in diameter. A family of eight could live most comfortably in this 145,000-square-foot home.

Across the bridge on the other side of the Royal Road stood the formal state palace of the pharaoh, a huge structure that stretched for at least 700, and possibly 1,000, feet along the Royal Road and ran back from it for at least 600 feet more. It comprised several distinct areas: a palace, a festival hall, servants' quarters, and vast suites of rooms, often considered harems, lining the Royal Road.

The only entrance from the road led into a pair of back-to-back courtyards, dividing what early excavators considered the harem into two roughly equal parts. The northern half centered around a sunken garden with a pond, flanked both east and west by rows of 15 rooms. North and south of the sunken garden stretched more halls and still more rooms. One hall in the north section contained a floor painted with sublime scenes of a fish-filled pool surrounded by marsh grasses and fowl. At least 50 rooms in the southern half bordered four large courtyards, making this structure seem far too large for harem purposes, especially for a king with only two known wives in addition to his queen, Nefertiti. An absence of bathrooms confirms the point. More likely this vast complex of suites, north and south, consisted of offices for various high- and middle-grade government officials. If so, they worked in grand surroundings, although some labored in mere cubicles.

Deeper into the compound, behind the "harem" lining the Royal Road, lay servants' quarters to the north and the palace proper to the south. The servants' quarters, which covered an area of at least 300 square feet, consisted of roomy suites composed of a bedroom, bath, and living room bordering a courtyard. Although never completely excavated, such servants' suites probably numbered 50 or more.

The state palace, south of the servants' quarters and west of the harem, consisted simply of eight grand courtyards and one august hall. Uncharacteristic of Egyptian palaces, this part was constructed of stone. One hall, the farthest north, which ran the entire 500-foot length of the building, incorporated a magnificent dais on the long wall, 45 feet by 30 feet, with a roof supported by 12 massive columns fronted by a ramp for access. Over-life-size statues of the king and queen lined the three innermost sides. Presumably, this space was used for huge gatherings to hear the king speak from the dais. A door behind the dais led through a long transverse hall of columns, where representations of trussed ducks hung on the column sides and carved foliage decorated their tops, above a floor of pure alabaster. This hall opened into a central courtyard with ramps from the three other sides for chariots to ride into any of seven additional courtyards. Each courtyard averaged 100 square feet, but only the central one contained carved stelae—two dozen of them—with scenes of the royal family at worship. Porticos flanked the eastern companion of the central courtyard, leading to the Window of Appearances, where the pharaoh and his family would present themselves to citizens below and distribute gold rewards for special service.

A family of eight could live most comfortably in this 145,000-square-foot home.

South from the state palace stood another, separate, square structure, 300 feet on each side. In this huge hall, square pillars supported a ceiling brightly painted to look like vines against a yellow background; its walls were tiled in plant patterns in accordance with the nature religion of Akhenaton. At the far end of this hall, two narrow rooms bordered a sunken area. This structure may have served as the coronation hall for Smenkhkare, who briefly succeeded Akhenaton before Tutankhamen.

Although some functions of the many parts of Akhenaton's palace are not understood today, enough remains to impress with its size and grandeur. The two massive compounds combined accommodations for servants, probably government offices, private rooms for the king and his family and awesome spaces for public events.

Although not quite as large as the palace of his son, Amenhotep III's palace at Malkata across the river from Thebes is more easily understood (Badawy, 47–54). Inside a 1,000-by-1,500-foot compound, lined with passageways for patrolling guards, lay a variety of separate structures. The pharaoh's apartments faced the river behind gardens that ran the length of the south face of the enclosure. Interior walls of these living quarters were painted with ornamental designs, together with scenes of hunting, flora, fauna, ladies of the court, and the pharaoh. Beside it stood the harem, a separate building one-fourth the size of the king's quarters, with a separate structure behind both serving as the royal kitchen. Also along the south face, next to the palace, stood a building to house the palace guard. In the center of the compound, on the east side of the palace proper, another separate structure held offices, as well as housing for servants and the workmen who maintained the compound. This building was 600 feet long by about 150 feet wide. Entrance to the whole compound, for all but the highest personages, was through the northwest corner where the official rooms—the grand audience hall, throne room, and so on—were situated. Behind these, trailing south, a hall of columns 150 feet long and lined with offices for high officials led to the private apartments of the pharaoh. Far to the rear of the enclosure (north) stood a grand festival hall, 500 feet square, where the anniversaries of Amenhotep's coronation were celebrated. Just outside lay an artificial lake, two miles around, for private outings on the royal barge.

After this 18th Dynasty magnificence, palaces changed. By the 20th Dynasty, the palace of Ramses III at Medinet Habu, although probably not his main residence, was no larger than the accommodations Amenhotep III provided for his royal guards. Ramses' palace was surrounded by truly massive defensive walls, suggesting that this pharaoh feared powerful enemies. Egypt's fortunes had begun to decline.

Extensive buildings must have existed to accommodate the thousands of government officials who managed the country, but such utilitarian structures were not the sort of thing anyone preserved. One of the few examples whose plan could be reconstructed from residual remains was the office of the main tax collector in Akhenaton's city of Akhetaten. It consisted of a rectangular walled structure 120 by 190 feet, which included special provisions for storing and protecting grain and animals, the forms in which taxes were paid. For security, a gatekeeper lived beside the two entrances to serve as a watchman. A large area beyond the entrance was walled to hold horses and donkeys; another was divided into magazines for storing tons of grain. After being accepted and recorded here, the animals and grain would have been shipped to larger facilities for permanent storage. The family lived in a typical large house toward the rear of the compound, and their servants resided in separate quarters along the back enclosure wall. Fully half of the area inside the compound remained open to facilitate the comings and goings of taxpayers with their goods.

This example of a "home office" was not typical of government buildings, which generally consisted of walls surrounding smaller cubicles where government functionaries labored—the records office in Akhenaton's city of Akhetaten consisted of a rectangle almost 300 feet long by 50 feet wide, inside of which over 40 rooms averaged 10 feet by 20 feet. Workers commuted to these offices from their homes (Brier and Hobbs, 147–53).

FOR MORE INFORMATION

Badawy, A. *History of Egyptian Architecture*. Berkeley, Calif.: University of California Press, 1968.

Brier, B., and H. Hobbs. *Daily Life of the Ancient Egyptians*. Westport, Conn.: Greenwood Press, 1999.

Kemp, B. J. "The Early Development of Towns in Egypt." *Antiquity* 51 (1977).

Kemp, B. J., and S. Garfi. *A Survey of the Ancient City of El-Amarna*. London: Egypt Exploration Society, 1993.

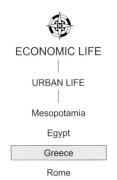

ECONOMIC LIFE

URBAN LIFE

Mesopotamia

Egypt

Greece

Rome

GREECE

Divided from one another by a landscape comprised of mountains, valleys, and expanses of the Aegean Sea, Greek cities were initially left to develop as individual entities rather than forming a united Greece (or Hellas, as they called it). Instead, each Greek polis, or city-state, had its own government, history, traditions, and even coinage (although all Greeks were bound together by a common language and by their willingness to unite against an external enemy, as during the Persian Wars). Despite their differences, Greek city-states usually exhibited similar structures and uses of public space.

Many of the older Greek cities grew around an acropolis, a high point (hill or cliff) that could function as a defensible fortress during sieges. The city would cluster on the slopes of the hill. The acropolis frequently acquired a sense of religious as well as military significance, and temples were often constructed near what was considered sacred ground. In addition to high ground, proximity to water was another geographical feature that often led to city building, since a harbor and access to the Aegean Sea would expedite trade and travel. Another important area in the Greek city was a large open space near the center of town called the agora, which roughly translates as "marketplace." Its functions, however, extended beyond commercial ones; the agora was also a center for political activity, religious observances, and social interaction. Temples, monuments, and public buildings usually surrounded it. A characteristic Greek structure, the stoa—an open colonnade formed by putting a roof over two rows of columns—acted as an all-purpose space that could accommodate market stalls, shrines, and even school lessons; any teacher or philosopher could set up shop in a stoa (specific school buildings did not exist at this time). The acropolis and agora functioned as a sort of double city center, often near one another. But over time, importance shifted from the former to the latter.

Some other crucial structures in Greek cities included the theater, often constructed on a natural slope, to house dramatic performances and public assemblies; the gymnasium, an athletic training field whose main focus was a track for running (the stadium), but which often included dressing rooms and areas for specialized training, such as boxing, discus throwing, and the long jump; and temples for public worship of the gods.

City streets in older cities were usually narrow, winding, and spread in a random fashion. Although homes of the rich sometimes had a private water supply, most city inhabitants had to rely on public cisterns, fountains, and wells, at which they lined up with buckets to collect water and haul it (sometimes a long distance) home. Adequate sanitation, fire fighting, and a police force were lacking. Imposing city walls provided protection from outside invaders. The gymnasium, which required a lot of space, often lay on the outskirts of town. Private tombs lined the main thoroughfare leading out of town, outside the walls, since burial was not allowed within the city limits.

As city-states began to establish colonies overseas to ease the too rapidly expanding growth in population, it was possible to practice more deliberate town planning as new cities were founded. Although the rectangular grid system of urban planning had existed as long ago as archaic times, Hippodamus of Miletus (born ca. 500 B.C.E.) gained fame finding innovative ways to help Greek cities better conform to the "gridiron" plan. This sort of city plan became extremely popular in the Hellenistic period and remained an influential model under Roman rule. Newly founded colonies boasted wider, more logically arranged streets.

~Gregory S. Aldrete

FOR MORE INFORMATION

Lawrence, A. W. *Greek Architecture*. 5th ed. Revised by R. A. Tomlinson. New Haven, Conn.: Yale University Press, 1996.

Wycherley, R. E. *How the Greeks Built Cities*. 2nd ed. London: Macmillan, 1978.

ROME

Roman civilization was an intensely urban culture. Wherever the Romans went, they established towns that became focal points of Roman administrative control and centers from which Roman culture was disseminated. Many towns in Italy and in the provinces were established by granting land to Roman soldiers upon their retirement from the army. Others grew up around or began as Roman army camps. Often these incorporated the gridlike arrangement of streets standard to military camps. The Romans developed a hierarchy of status for cities, just as there was for people. At the top were cities that received the designation of *colonia*, or colonies. Originally, these were what they sounded like—colonies of Roman citizens or retired veterans. By the time of the empire, the term *colony* became simply a designation of status, and all the inhabitants of colonies would have Roman citizenship and the city itself would enjoy a certain degree of autonomy from the local governor. Next were *municipia*. Although *municipia* were not as prestigious as *colonia*, most inhabitants of *municipia* would still have possessed Roman citizenship. The remaining ordinary cities were called *civitates*. Roman cities featured a number of distinctive architectural features. Chief among these was a general-purpose open space in the center of town known as the forum, around which usually clustered important government buildings and temples. Most Roman towns of any size or pretensions would also construct baths, gymnasiums, a theater, an amphitheater, and perhaps a circus. Local aristocrats in the provinces who wished to rise in status would sometimes pay for the construction of such cultural centers in their hometown. Whether in Spain or Gaul, North Africa or Judea, Roman cities tended to look similar because they all constructed the same types of buildings that unmistakably identified them as Roman cities.

Two images of urban life dominate the primary sources. On the one hand, cities (and especially Rome itself) were seen as the focal point of opportunity, wealth, and luxury, consisting of magnificent public works and ceremonial buildings. On the other hand, the city was viewed as corrupt, decadent, and dangerous, with rampant poverty and disease. Both these images have validity. The magnificent and impressive buildings and monuments that made up the capital city are discussed in the entry on Rome in the following section, "The Great Cities." The focus here is on some of the less attractive aspects of urban life. Most of the examples discussed are drawn from Rome, but many of these problems were common to any sizable city in the ancient world.

Much of the city of Rome was built on top of what were originally swamps, and when the Tiber flooded, as it often did, these areas were submerged under water. These floods caused great havoc to both the city and its inhabitants. Many buildings were undermined or weakened by the waters, causing spectacular collapses. The floods also caused the sewers to back up, spreading filth and disease. Finally, the floods spoiled the food stored in the warehouses. Therefore, every flood was inevitably followed by a famine. These floods were often so severe that boats were necessary to travel through the flooded streets of the city. On one occasion during the reign of Augustus, the flooding was so severe that the streets were navigable by boat for seven days.

Probably the greatest hazard faced by city dwellers was the threat of fire. Everyone had to cook over open flames, and olive oil lamps were easy to knock over. Not surprisingly, fires were extremely frequent. In addition, because of the narrowness of the streets, the widespread use of wood as a building material, and the lack of effective fire-fighting techniques, once started, fires could spread easily and cause enormous destruction. The impression given by ancient sources is that not a night went by without a serious fire somewhere in Rome, and larger fires that destroyed entire neighborhoods seem to have occurred roughly every other year. The great fire of 64 C.E. raged for six days, and devastated 10 out of Rome's 14 districts. In an attempt to combat this menace, Augustus set up a brigade of 7,000 watchmen who would patrol the city at night carrying buckets and attempt to extinguish any fires that started before they could spread (Suetonius, *Augustus* 30.1).

 Snapshot

Graffiti Written on the Walls of Pompeii

Aufidius was here. (*Corpus Inscriptionum Latinarum* 4.6702)

Marcus loves Spendusa. (*Corpus Inscriptionum Latinarum* 4.7086)

Serena hates Isidore. (*Corpus Inscriptionum Latinarum* 4.3117)

Elect Gaius Cuspius Pansa to the aedileship! All the goldsmiths support his election. (*Inscriptiones Latinae Selectae* 6419c)

The chicken venders urge you to vote for Epidius and Suettius as duovirs. (*Corpus Inscriptionum Latinarum* 4.7473)

Crescens the *retiarius* (a type of gladiator) is admired by all the young women. (*Inscriptiones Latinae Selectae* 5142d)

I have had sex with many girls here. (*Corpus Inscriptionum Latinarum* 4.2175)

Food shortage was another hazard faced by urban dwellers. The diet for the average inhabitant of Rome centered around two staples: grain, consumed in the form of bread or gruel, and olives, usually in the form of olive oil. Because of Rome's enormous size, local resources were nowhere near enough to support the city's populace, and food had to be imported on a gigantic scale from all over the Mediterranean, particularly Egypt, North Africa, Sicily, and Spain. How large these imports were is suggested by one of the hills of modern Rome, called Monte Testaccio; it is not a natural feature at all but is in fact an artificial mountain composed entirely of the shattered remains of 50 million North African and Spanish olive oil containers. Despite imperial involvement in the food supply, famine and the threat of famine were a constant worry. In the first century of the empire, there were no less than 20 incidents when food shortages were so severe that they resulted in riots in the city.

From its combination of overcrowding and lack of adequate sanitation, Rome would appear by modern standards to have been an unbelievably disgusting place to live. The normal course of events produced enormous numbers of dead bodies, many of which were not properly disposed of. Great numbers of the truly impoverished, along with Rome's large population of homeless and beggars, simply lay where they dropped or were thrown in the Tiber or into open pits just outside the city. Some of these pits have been excavated, revealing that human and animal corpses were indiscriminately tossed onto these heaps, along with garbage and excrement. Over half the human skeletons show signs of having been gnawed by animals, indicating that the corpses were not buried at all but instead lay decomposing in the open air. Two literary anecdotes vividly illustrate this. The poet Martial describes the gruesome death of one beggar whose last moments are spent trying to fend off the dogs and vultures that have gathered to feed on him (Martial, *Epigrams* 10.5). Suetonius mentions an incident in which a stray dog ran into the room where the emperor Vespasian was dining and deposited a human hand beneath the table (Suetonious, *Vespasian* 5.4). Thus, even the emperor was not immune to the presence of corpses, body parts, and scavengers that permeated Rome.

Model of Rome built by Gismondi. It illustrates the density and size of structures in the city. The Circus Maximus is visible in the bottom left, and the Colosseum is at the right. The Art Archive/Museo della Civilta Romana Rome/Dagli Orti.

Although Rome possessed some sewers, their purpose was more to provide drainage than to actually carry away waste. Most of Rome's garbage and sewage literally ended up in the streets. Roman law offers an insight into sanitation and living conditions through the numerous cases that survive of people seeking damages for being struck by objects thrown from windows (*Digest of Roman Law* 9.3.1). Some of the items thrown included animal carcasses, bones, broken pots, garbage, and one of the most common items, human excrement. Most people emptied their chamberpots by simply dumping them out the window. Rome's animals certainly contributed to the general filth, and its streets probably more closely resembled open sewers than roadways. It is no surprise that Rome's wealthy preferred to travel about the city in perfumed litters carried by slaves rather than wade on foot through the muck themselves. The smell, particularly on a summer's day, would have been overwhelming.

Life in the city would have assaulted one's senses not only of sight and smell but of hearing as well. The Stoic philosopher Seneca, whose apartment was above a public bath, vividly describes the annoying sounds that emanated from below, including the grunting of weight lifters, noisy athletes yelling at one another, people who liked to sing while bathing, and merchants hawking snack foods (Seneca, *Moral Epistles* 56). Nor did night offer any relief from the noise; in an effort to reduce congestion in the streets, it was decreed that all supply wagons had to bring in their goods at night, thus filling the night with the noisy rumble of carts on stone roads, the braying of pack animals, and the shouts of drivers.

Living in a large city offered variety of experiences, excitement, and the opportunity to enjoy luxurious public amenities, but there was a darker side to this existence as well.

~*Gregory S. Aldrete*

FOR MORE INFORMATION

Stambaugh, J. E. *The Ancient Roman City*. Baltimore, Md.: Johns Hopkins University Press, 1988.

The Great Cities

Certain cities achieved greater prominence and size than their contemporaries. Usually, this was a result of their status as the capital city of a great empire. This was certainly the case with Babylon in Mesopotamia, which was one of the first great urban centers and the center of the Babylonian Empire. Athens similarly achieved its peak during the fifth century B.C.E. at the height of the Athenian Empire, when much of the income from the Delian League was diverted from mutual defense to construction projects at Athens. Under the capable and determined leadership of Pericles, Athens underwent a cultural boom, during which such enduring monuments as the Parthenon atop the Acropolis were erected. Rome, which had already grown to enormous size by the end of the late Republic, began to acquire many of its grand buildings and monuments under the first emperor, Augustus. This emperor once claimed that when he inherited Rome, it was an ugly city of brick, but he left it a city of shining marble. There is considerable truth to this boast.

The glories of these great cities are well documented, but there are other characteristics that they shared besides impressive monuments. Any time large numbers of people are packed into a small space to live and work, there are attendant problems, and the types of urban problems found in ancient cities would be very familiar to any inhabitant of a large city today. Urban dwellers then and now have to contend with violent crime and robbery, noise, fire, high rents and unscrupulous landlords, unsanitary conditions, and problems of waste disposal. Although the degree of some of these problems might differ between the ancient world and today, the basic benefits and hazards of living in a big city remain remarkably timeless.

~Gregory S. Aldrete

BABYLON

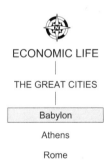

According to the Greek historian Herodotus, Nebuchadnezzar enhanced the ancient capital of Babylon with his building and renovation projects. The topography of the ancient capital described in detail by Herodotus matches well with archaeological excavations of the city. The remarkable sights included the ziggurat, the famous Hanging Gardens (one of the Seven Wonders of the Ancient World), and the museum next to Nebuchadnezzar's new palace. Babylon was more or less square, covering approximately 1,000 hectares, and bisected by the Euphrates River. The Euphrates itself could be crossed by a bridge that rested on five piers.

The city walls of Babylon can be traced. According to Herodotus, the outer wall extended more than eight kilometers and had enough space on top for a four-horse chariot to turn around. The most-detailed and best-preserved gate was dedicated to Ishtar; its 36-foot-high walls are still standing. The walls were constructed of deep-blue-glazed bricks with molded figures of bulls and dragons in yellow and white.

Nebuchadnezzar's Southern Palace had five courtyards surrounded by offices, royal apartments, and reception rooms. In a corner of the palace, archaeologists found an underground crypt. There, a three-shafted well in one of the cellars appeared to have been some kind of hydraulic lifting system, perhaps the water source of the Hanging Gardens of Babylon. Farther south, the Processional Way came to the main temple complex, the dwelling place of the god Marduk. Here stood the ziggurat, the famous Tower of Babel. Today, only 300 square feet of its foundations remain. Nearby was Esagila, Marduk's main temple, with a golden statue of Marduk, restored by Nebuchadnezzar II.

Before Desert Shield and Desert Storm, Saddam Hussein had plans to restore the city of Babylon. In the tradition of Mesopotamian kings, he planned to put his name in one of the bricks. From September 22 through October 6, 1994, Hussein hosted a celebration billed as "From Nebuchadnezzar to Saddam Hussein: Babylon Invokes Its Glories on the Path of Jihad and Glorious Development." A poster featured his profile superimposed on that of Nebuchadnezzar II at the top and the famous glazed bricks with lion friezes and a turreted gate at the bottom (Nemet-Nejat, 106–7).

FOR MORE INFORMATION

Nemet-Nejat, K. R. *Daily Life in Ancient Mesopotamia*. Westport, Conn.: Greenwood Press, 1998.
Oates, J. *Babylon*. Rev. ed. London: Thames and Hudson, 1986.

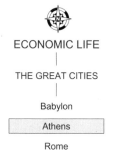

ECONOMIC LIFE

THE GREAT CITIES

Babylon

Athens

Rome

ATHENS

Like any other Greek polis, the Athenian city-state was a combination of urban center, or *asty*, and countryside, or *chôra*. Ancient Athens is today best known for the magnificent buildings erected on the Acropolis. This is a small, artificially leveled hilltop no more than 300 meters by 200 meters that was the home of Athens' patron goddess, Athena, and other major state gods. Here stands the monumental gateway known as the Propylaia, the Parthenon or temple of Athena Parthenos, and the Erechtheion or temple of Poseidon-Erechtheus, all justly renowned as the crowning achievements of Classical architecture. These monuments should not, however, so overwhelm us that we lose sight of the image of Athens as a city—a city, moreover, that possessed many of the same problems as any modern urban development, as well as others that were peculiar to the ancient world.

Despite the grandeur of its civic buildings, in many respects Athens resembled a country town rather than a city. Most of the amenities that one takes for granted today were virtually nonexistent. Only a few major roads were paved. The majority of private dwellings were modest in scale and appearance. There was only a very rudimentary and highly inefficient method of waste disposal. There were no public toilets. There was no street lighting. There was no fire brigade. There were no hospitals. The police force, such as it was, consisted of publicly owned slaves, whose job primarily was to keep the peace, not to detect or to prevent crime. Water was brought to the city from distant springs by means of terra-cotta pipelines that fed public fountains. With one or two notable exceptions, the majority of fountain houses were simple reservoirs cut into the living rock.

It was the duty of municipal law enforcement officers known as *astynomoi* to determine that certain minimum standards of hygiene and safety were upheld. Their tasks included ensuring that dung collectors did not deposit dung within a radius of 10 stades (approximately half a mile) of the circuit wall, that buildings did not encroach upon the streets, and that the bodies of those who expired upon the public highways were collected for burial. The checking of such abuses, particularly the proper disposal of dung, must have been an uphill battle; disease was an ever-present hazard, especially during the summer months.

From 479 B.C.E. onward, and possibly earlier, the limits of Athens's growth were defined by a circuit wall built on top of a stone socle with mud brick in its upper courses. This wall, hurriedly constructed after the defeat of the Persians, was pierced by at least 17 gates. Through these gates passed roads connecting the city with the outlying districts of Attica-Acharnai to the north, Eleusis to the west, and Piraeus to the south. The most famous of these gates was the Dipylon, or Double Gate, so named because it consisted of an entrance at each end of a long corridor that was designed to entrap the invader. Outside the Dipylon lay the Kerameikos or Potters' Quarter, where the most impressive grave monuments have been discovered. Reconstructed according to its Classical plan, the Kerameikos is today a tranquil oasis of peace amid the bustle of modern Athens. In the Eridanos brook that ambles through it, frogs frolic playfully as they did in antiquity.

The road from the Dipylon Gate joined the Panathenaic Way, one of the few paved roads in Athens. This was the route taken by the Panathenaia or All-Athenian Festival, held annually in honor of Athena. As it wound its way up to the Acropolis, the Panathenaic procession passed through the Agora, a flat, open space roughly rectangular in shape and lined on all four sides with administrative buildings.

The Agora, which has no real equivalent in the modern world, occupied a central position in the life of the community until the destruction of Athens in 267 C.E. by a barbarian people known as the Herulians. It was the civic, commercial, administrative, social, and political heart of the city. The Altar of the Twelve Gods in the northwest corner of the Agora marked the spot where all roads converged and from which measurements to other parts of Attica were taken. Temporary stalls selling agricultural produce and manufactured goods were also set up here. In addition, the Agora provided the setting for most trials. Its unique flavor is conveyed in a fragment from a lost play by the comic dramatist Euboulos, who lists the following items for sale (quoted in Athenais, *Professors at Dinner* 14.640b): figs, issuers of summonses to attend the law courts, grapes, turnips, pears, apples, witnesses, roses, medlars, haggis, honeycombs, chickpeas, lawsuits, bee stings, curds, myrtle berries, ballot boxes, bluebells, lamb, water clocks, laws, and indictments.

Amply provided with colonnaded walkways or stoas, of which the reconstructed Stoa of Attalos on the east side is the finest example, the Agora was also a place for Athenians to engage in their favorite pastime—lively and animated discussion. Here at the end of the fifth century B.C.E., the philosopher Socrates was invariably to be found. Here, too, a century later gathered the Stoics, philosophers who took their name from the Painted Stoa, remains of which have recently been identified in the northwest corner of the Agora. The Agora was also a place to pass the time of day, as suggested by the verb *agorazein,* which came to mean to "loaf about." Groups of Athenians, as well as foreigners, had their favorite meeting places. As the speaker in a law-court oration by Lysias states (*The Peloponnesian War* 24.20), "Each of you is in the habit of frequenting some place, a perfumer's shop, a barber's shop, a cobbler's and so forth." The Dekeleians, for instance, gathered at the barber's shop beside the Herms, whereas the Plataians could be found at the cheese market on the last day of the month.

One of the most popular spots was the monument to the Eponymous Heroes, which stood in the southwest corner of the Agora close to the law courts. This monument honored the heroes who gave their names to the 10 Athenian tribes that were created by Cleisthenes. Its base served as a public notice board that provided news about military conscription, forthcoming trials, agendas for public meetings, proposed legislation, and other public matters. Other important secular buildings located in the Agora include the public mint, the Bouleutêrion or council house, the Metrôön or public record office, and the Tholos. This last was a circular building that served as the living quarters for the 50 members of the council who were permanently on duty day and night to deal with emergencies. Despite its importance, the Agora possessed only very rudimentary civic amenities. Storm water and sewage were disposed of by means of a stone channel that modern archaeologists have rather grandiosely named the Great Drain.

The Acropolis, which means "high part of the city," dominates the countryside of Attica for miles around. In early times it functioned as a palace, a sanctuary, and a fortress. Its massive surrounding wall dates to the late thirteenth century B.C.E. The Acropolis continued to be used for defensive purposes until the 460s B.C.E., when a new wall was built to encompass a larger area. All its temples were destroyed by the Persians in 479 B.C.E., and little trace of them survives today apart from a few fragments of architectural sculpture. For 40 years, the Acropolis remained in its ruined condition as testimony to Persian barbarity, until 447 B.C.E., when an ambitious building program was instigated on the initiative of Pericles, financed by the surplus tribute paid by Athens's allies.

The Acropolis of Athens with the buildings constructed during the Periclean age. The temple on the left is the Parthenon, dedicated to the patron goddess of the city, Athena. © Erwin C. Nielson/Painet Inc.

As one enters the Acropolis through the Propylaia or Monumental Gateway today, one finds oneself facing the diminutive Erechtheion on the left and the massive Parthenon on the right. The Parthenon stands starkly isolated at the highest point of the rock, surrounded by a wasteland of broken marble. Yet the Acropolis played host to many other temples, of which virtually no trace has survived. To appreciate the effect that it would have presented in antiquity, one must imagine a forest of dedicatory statues, jockeying for position like insistent petitioners.

Before the beginning of the sixth century B.C.E., Athens possessed few public buildings. Nor, so far as we know, was any part of the city specifically laid aside for civic activity. About the beginning of the sixth century B.C.E., however, the city began to expand dramatically, albeit in a haphazard fashion and without reference to any functional master plan or guiding architectural principle. By the next century, its population had grown to such an extent that it could no longer gather in the Agora for public meetings. The *ekklêsia*, or assembly, was therefore moved to a hill overlooking the Agora, called the Pnyx. The Theater of Dionysos, located on the south slope of the Acropolis, was also enlarged at this date. To the west, the Odeion of Pericles was built—a vast, roofed building capable of accommodating an audience of 5,000. Much later, in 169 C.E., the Theater of Herodes Atticus was constructed, and the entire southern slope of the Acropolis became a vast cultural center, rather like the Kennedy Center in Washington, D.C., or the South Bank Arts Complex in London.

Although fifth-century B.C.E. Athens was an urban entity, its growth and development did not bring about an exodus from the countryside. Even at the outbreak of the Peloponnesian War, most of the population still resided outside Athens, as Thucydides tells us (*The Peloponnesian War* 2.16.1). It is difficult to gauge the extent to which those living in the countryside were incorporated into the life of the city. Although most Athenian citizens would have needed to travel to Athens at least once or twice a year for official business, it is highly improbable that many of them would have done so on a regular basis, even though the distance to Athens from the farthest demes was only 30 miles.

Athens would have struck the modern eye as a curious amalgam of public magnificence and private squalor. It was a city to be admired for the breathtaking beauty of its public buildings, for which there was hardly any equal in the entire Greek world. In regard to its housing and public amenities, however, it was inferior to many of its contemporaries. It may strike one as remarkable that the Athenians, who adorned their city with some of the most splendid buildings ever constructed, were prepared to tolerate such discomfort in private. It says everything about the difference in mentality between them and us that no one ever suggested that their priorities should be reversed (Garland, 23–30).

FOR MORE INFORMATION

Camp, J. *The Athenian Agora*. London: Thames and Hudson, 1986.

Connolly, P., and H. Dodge. *The Ancient City*. Oxford: Oxford University Press, 1998.

Garland, R. *Daily Life of the Ancient Greeks*. Westport, Conn.: Greenwood Press, 1998.

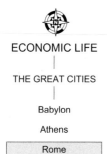

ROME

Among cities, Rome was an exception because of its enormous population. It was at least twice as large as any other city in the ancient world. By the late first century B.C.E., the population of Rome was about one million and probably stayed close to that level for the next couple of centuries. A measure of how remarkable this size was can be sensed by considering that no other city in the Western Hemisphere reached that size for another 2,000 years until London hit one million in the nineteenth century.

Some of the negative aspects of living in a Roman city have been noted in the section on urban life, so this section will concentrate on the grand buildings and monuments that formed the physical city. These structures can be organized into five categories based on different aspects of the city of Rome: Rome the political center, Rome the home of the emperor, Rome the religious center, Rome the entertainment center, and the practical infrastructure of Rome.

Rome was the political capital of the Roman Empire, and many buildings in the city reflected this role. Most Roman towns were centered around the forum, an open space in the center of town. During the Republic, Rome's forum had been the center of legislative and judicial activity, and despite the new political realities of the empire, the forum continued to be an important space. The senate house where the senate usually met was located here, as was the rostrum or speaker's platform, from which many orations were given.

As time went on, the physical city of Rome itself began more and more to symbolize Rome's conquest of the Mediterranean world through its actual structures. One example of this is the many triumphal arches that sprang up in the early empire. The emperors Augustus, Tiberius, Claudius, Nero, Titus, Domitian, Marcus Aurelius, Constantine, Septimius Severus, and others all erected triumphal arches celebrating military victories. These arches served as permanent reminders of Rome's conquests, particularly because they were usually decorated with carvings depicting Romans slaughtering foreigners and carrying off exotic booty.

Similar in purpose were the columns that some emperors erected to celebrate military triumphs. These columns were completely covered with a series of carved panels that spiraled upward and could be read like a cartoon, telling the story of a campaign from the departure of the army to its triumphant return to Rome. The most famous of these is Trajan's Column, depicting the invasion of Dacia. The city could also be considered a giant trophy case for the display of captured objects; its public spaces were decorated with items stolen from all over the Mediterranean during Roman campaigns. The Temples of Mars the Avenger and Jupiter Optimus Maximus were both literally stuffed to overflowing with captured enemy flags, standards, armor, and other military trophies. The rostrum derived its name from the fact that it was decorated with dozens of ships' rams acquired in Rome's naval victories. The streets, gardens, baths, and houses of Rome were decorated with works of art seized during Rome's campaigns, particularly in the Greek east.

Finally, the very stones that made up the great public buildings of Rome were themselves reminders of Rome's status as conqueror of the known world. Rome imported colored marbles and decorative stones at great expense and effort from all over the Mediterranean. The buildings that made up the city were themselves literally composed of booty from the conquered territories.

Rome was also the religious capital of the Roman Empire and in fulfillment of this role, contained a vast number of temples and sacred sites. The emperor Augustus in his autobiography claims to have renovated no less than 82 temples, which suggests how abundant these were in Rome. Most temples were the standard rectangular shape with colonnades and a triangular pediment, although some varied from this form. One of the most important temples in Rome was the Temple of Jupiter Optimus Maximus, literally, "Jupiter the Best and the Greatest," located on top of the Capitoline Hill. This magnificent temple had gold-plated doors and a gilded roof; an idea of the splendor of its decoration is suggested by the fact that the gilding alone cost nearly 300 million sesterces (equivalent to the annual pay for 300,000 Roman soldiers).

Rome was the official residence of the emperor, and he emphatically left his mark on the city and its buildings. The most obvious structure that resulted from his presence was the imperial palace. Augustus had lived in a modest house on the Palatine Hill, but by the time of Domitian, the emperor's palace had bloated to an enormous size, displacing all other residences and ultimately covering the entire hilltop. The ground floor alone of Domitian's palace covered 120,000 square feet, and this does not include numerous auxiliary buildings, servants' quarters, and a private race course almost 500 feet long. Nero took advantage of the great fire of 64 c.e. to construct a gigantic and bizarre palace for himself known as the Golden House of Nero. The complex covered 300 acres in the center of Rome and included an artificial lake, a mile-long colonnade, a dining room with a revolving roof, sliding ceiling panels that could open to shower the diners with flowers and perfume, and, in front of the complex, a 120-foot-high colossal nude bronze statue of Nero himself.

Rome also possessed many buildings dedicated to the entertainment of its populace. The most famous of these is certainly the Colosseum (correctly called the Flavian Amphitheatre), the site of gladiatorial games and beast hunts. On one occasion, Trajan gave games lasting 123 days, during which 11,000 animals were slaughtered. The largest entertainment complex in Rome was not the Colosseum, however, but the Circus Maximus, where the chariot races were held. This structure was over a third of a mile long and could seat well over 200,000 spectators. Rome also possessed numerous theaters, where plays, mime shows, and other theatrical events were held. Finally, there were the luxurious Roman baths, which were not merely places to bathe but were also centers of social life, and that included athletic fields, art displays, and food vendors.

In addition to its magnificent decorative buildings, Rome also possessed more practical structures, which were often just as impressive simply because of their scale. Rome's bridges, walls, and roads are justly famous, and in fact, many of them are still standing and in use today. To supply the city with water, Rome ultimately had a vast system of nine aqueducts delivering three million cubic feet of water per day to the city's baths and 600 public fountains. Lining the banks of the Tiber was a network of docks and warehouses where the food for the city was unloaded and stored. These warehouses were enormous feats of engineering. For example, one grain warehouse that has been excavated had 140 storage rooms covering 225,000 square feet. Finally, to drain the city and dispose of at least some of the waste produced by the city, Rome had an elaborate sewer system that emptied into the Tiber.

~Gregory S. Aldrete

FOR MORE INFORMATION

Coulston, J., and H. Dodge. *Ancient Rome*. Oxford: Oxford University School of Archaeology, 2000.

Stambaugh, J. E. *The Ancient Roman City*. Baltimore, Md.: Johns Hopkins University Press, 1988.

ECONOMIC LIFE
|
SLAVERY
|
Mesopotamia

Egypt

Greece

Rome

Slavery

Slavery is a status in which one human being is owned by another and is viewed as a piece of property rather than as a person. A famous Roman definition of slaves was "articulate property," that is, a piece of property that possessed the ability to speak. The modern view of slavery in the ancient world is often seen through the prisms of modern Christianity and Marxism. Each imposes value judgments upon the institution, and these value judgments tend to distort our investigation of slavery's place in ancient society. Modern Christianity deplores slavery as barbaric and inhumane. Marxist historians identify slaves with the subjected European proletariat of the nineteenth century. Friedrich Engels even went so far as to allege that the moral and political collapse of the ancient world was chiefly caused by slavery. Additionally, modern notions of slavery are often intertwined with concepts of racism, in which one group views another as unequal or even subhuman.

In most instances in the ancient world, however, slavery was truly an economic status, unrelated to the race or culture of the persons involved. Free citizens in Mesopotamia, Egypt, Greece, and Rome could all find themselves stripped of citizenship and reduced to the state of being slaves by falling into debt that they could not repay. Capture in warfare, however, was by far the most common way that people became enslaved. Ancient slavery encompassed a wide range of experiences, from the skilled and respected clerk slaves of Greece to the frequently beaten chain-gang agricultural slaves of some large Roman farms. In some societies, slaves held skilled positions, while the most undesirable jobs were performed by free laborers who worked for daily wages.

In some ancient societies, slaves formed a substantial percentage of the workforce, and much scholarly ink has been spilled debating how much of the economies and the achievements of these civilizations depended on and were made possible by slave labor. Although neither the Christian nor the Marxist viewpoint does full justice to the complexities and realities of slavery in the ancient world, it is clear that slavery, no matter how benevolent the form, always has the potential for abuse and degradation.

~*Gregory S. Aldrete*

MESOPOTAMIA

The first slaves captured by Mesopotamia were men and women seized in raids on the mountains, so that the ideograms for "slave" and "slave girl" were composed of the signs for "man" or "woman" plus the sign for "mountain." Initially, because the economy could not accommodate captives, they were killed. Later, the kings saved captives and organized them into gangs serving as laborers or soldiers; the king could still kill them because he "owned" them. The slaves worked with conscripted laborers, and some hired workers to construct roads, dig canals, build military fortifications, erect temples, till the crown lands, and work in palace factories. State slaves lived in special barracks; their names, ages, and lands of origin were recorded. Temple slaves were drafted from both prisoners of war and the offerings of private citizens. Preclassical societies, however, were never economically dependent upon slave labor. These societies began increasingly to use slaves as domestics, as military conquests brought in more prisoners of war.

In the third millennium B.C.E., citizens went into debt slavery because they could not repay loans to the aristocracy. Penniless men and women sold themselves or their children into slavery or were seized by creditors. By the eighteenth century B.C.E., debt slavery was well established, with five of Hammurabi's laws regulating aspects of it. In fact, in the Old Babylonian period, Mesopotamian kings would issue, at the beginning of their reigns, a reform edict of "righteousness" or "justice," which included economic measures such as freeing citizens from debt slavery. In later times, children were often given to temples to save their lives in times of famine. In first-millennium B.C.E. Babylonia, these temple slaves represented a significant economic class that was able to rise to important positions within the temple administration.

Babylonian merchants sold foreign slaves: Subarians from the north were much in demand. The cuneiform texts show that slaves were frequently bought and sold, sometimes with an implied warranty; that is, if a slave suffered an epileptic attack within 100 days of purchase, the seller was obligated to take back the slave.

During the Old Babylonian period, the average price for a slave was approximately 20 shekels of silver, but sometimes as much as 90. The average wage paid to hired laborers was 10 shekels a year. Therefore, landowners preferred to hire seasonal laborers because it was cheaper than owning slaves for agricultural work.

Slaves became the property of their owner. A slave who tried to escape was severely punished. Runaway slaves were rare, and according to one text, on the foreheads of captured runaways would be marked, "A runaway—seize him!" A slave was often distinguished by a characteristic lock of hair, although others wore tags or fetters. The authorities were responsible for capturing runaway slaves and returning them to their masters. The theft of slaves was punished severely, with special laws applied to palace slaves.

Private slaves were relatively uncommon and were employed largely in domestic service. Slaves born in the house had special status. In the Old Babylonian period, they were often adopted to care for their adoptive parents in their old age. Upon the death of their "parents," the slaves gained their freedom. Slaves had certain legal rights: they could take part in business, borrow money, and buy their freedom. If a slave, either male or female, married a free person, the children they had together would be free.

Household slaves were usually female, but male slaves could also reside with the family. Sometimes as many as 10 male and 10 female slaves resided in a single household. The children of slaves belonged to their owners. When large estates were divided, the slaves were included in the division of property and could be sold.

Slave owners encouraged slaves to marry one another to increase the owners' wealth. The children of such marriages belonged to the master, who was free to sell them individually. But separating members of a family was rather uncommon.

A slave could, upon the master's consent, marry a free woman. Even if she brought no dowry with her, both she and her children remained free. If she brought a dowry and invested it with her enslaved husband, who later died or abandoned her, the widow's dowry was returned to her, but only half the profits—the other half belonged to her husband's master.

Female slaves could be considered concubines, whether supplied by a barren wife as a surrogate or owned by the husband. If, as a concubine, the slave bore her owner children, she still remained a slave and could be sold. After her owner's death, both she and her children were given their freedom.

If a female slave was purchased by a married woman to act both as her servant and as her husband's concubine, the slave was still the sole property of the wife. The law codes provided, but did not require, that the children of this union could inherit from the paternal estate (Nemet-Nejat, 117–18, 126).

FOR MORE INFORMATION

Nemet-Nejat, K. R. *Daily Life in Ancient Mesopotamia.* Westport, Conn.: Greenwood Press, 1998.

ECONOMIC LIFE
|
SLAVERY
|
Mesopotamia

Egypt

Greece

Rome

EGYPT

Slavery did not exist in the early days of Egyptian civilization. (The pyramids were not built by slave labor, as shown in film epics, but by free workers, usually local peasants.) Slaves originally consisted only of foreigners captured in war and increased in number during the New Kingdom as Egypt accelerated successful campaigns to foreign lands. Conquered nations included slaves among the tribute they sent. Because the caste was hereditary, its population grew as slaves taken in battle gave birth to children in Egypt. Extant lists of households include the names of a family's slaves that shared their living space. The government, the royal family, temples, and individuals who could afford it all used slaves.

Apparently, free Egyptians could also descend to this class because of debts or perhaps as legal punishment. Members of the slave class, who could be bought, sold, and rented to others, formed the very bottom of the social scale. However, slaves still possessed some legal rights. They could own property and land (which their children could inherit) and do with it what they liked. Male slaves could marry free women. Slaves could actually hire their own servants if they managed to accumulate enough wealth. But if slaves did occasionally manage to establish a comfortable life for themselves, their movements were nonetheless always controlled by their owners. Indeed, if apprehended, runaway slaves were returned to their owners, and slaves were not immune from cruel masters and beatings.

The pharaoh before Ramses conducted an extensive military campaign into Canaan, including the upper valley of Galilee, returning with many prisoners. He began constructing a city in the delta, which his son finished and named Pa Ramses. By traditional Egyptian practice, slaves would have been employed on such a large project, likely including those captured in Canaan. Such major construction projects, which would have used Egyptian peasants as laborers during the Old Kingdom, were now built largely by slaves and prisoners of war. That Hebrews were enslaved by Egypt and forced to work constructing cities, including the one called "Rameses" in the Bible, is entirely consistent with the Exodus story (Brier and Hobbs, 73).

FOR MORE INFORMATION

Bakir, A. *Slavery in Pharaonic Egypt.* Cairo: French Institute of Archaeology, 1952.

Brier, B., and H. Hobbs. *Daily Life of the Ancient Egyptians.* Westport, Conn.: Greenwood Press, 1999.

David, R. *Handbook to Life in Ancient Egypt.* New York: Facts on File, 1998.

GREECE

The vast majority of Greeks, from Homer to Aristotle, regarded slavery as an indisputable fact of life. Its existence at the heart of the Classical world is thus a source of considerable disquiet to those who admire Greek culture for its supposedly enlightened humanism. It is important to appreciate, however, that slavery was not an absolute condition but one that admitted many different statuses. It included at one end of the scale chattel slaves, those who in Aristotle's telling phrase had the same status as "an animate or ensouled piece of property" (*Politics* 1253b 33), and at the other end those who lived independently and remitted a part of their income to their masters.

The origins of slavery in Greece are not precisely understood, but the institution was certainly in existence by the end of the eighth century b.c.e. In the world evoked by the Homeric poems, most slaves were obtained by piracy, kidnapping, or warfare. Odysseus's swineherd Eumaios, for instance, is captured and sold into slavery as a child. Enslavement was the fate that awaited female members of the royal household when Troy was taken. It would also have been the fate of women and children in

ECONOMIC LIFE

SLAVERY

Mesopotamia

Egypt

Greece

Rome

historical times when a besieged city fell. In seventh-century B.C.E. Greece, slavery appears to have been widespread even among the poorest section of society. Hesiod, in *Works and Days* (line 405f.), is of the opinion that an ox and a bought woman formed an essential part of a small farmer's holding.

Slaves were particularly numerous in Athens and may well have outnumbered those in any other Greek community. Thucydides (*The Peloponnesian War* 7.27.5) claims that "more than 20,000," most of them manual workers, absconded to Dekeleia in northern Attica when it was occupied by the Spartans in 413 B.C.E. All other evidence is anecdotal. In Classical times, the possession of at least one slave was regarded as a necessity. In a lawsuit written by Lysias, the speaker states, "I have a trade but I don't earn much. I find it difficult making ends meet and I can't save enough money to buy a slave to do the work for me" (24.6). It is a mark of his meanness that Theophrastus's "Tight-Fisted Man" refuses to buy his wife a slave girl and instead hires one from the women's market (*Characters* 22.10). The majority of well-to-do Athenians probably owned 2 or 3 slaves, whereas the wealthy possessed between 10 and 20. A few, however, owned a great many more. Nicias, one of the richest men in Athens in the late fifth century B.C.E., owned 1,000 slaves, whom he leased out to fellow citizens at the rate of one obol per slave per day (Xenophon, *Revenues* 4.14). The only surviving slave census relates to Athens in the late fourth century B.C.E. The total, which is put at 400,000, exceeds all bounds of credibility.

Athenian slaves were imported from a wide variety of regions, including Thrace, Scythia, Illyria, Colchis, Syria, Caria, and Lydia. Such diversity was probably fairly typical. The purchase price of a slave varied according to his or her skills and looks. Obviously, an educated slave who could read and write fetched considerably more than one who was only good for menial duties. Likewise, a pretty young girl cost much more than an older woman. Slaves with management skills were extremely expensive. A slave in good health probably cost the equivalent of half a year's salary.

Domestic slaves served in practically every capacity, including that of washerwoman, cook, porter, cleaner, tutor, escort, messenger, nurse, and companion. Whether slaves were also employed in large numbers as agricultural laborers is unclear.

On becoming a member of an Athenian household, a slave underwent an initiation ceremony similar to that which a bride underwent on first entering her new home. This was intended to place the slave under the protection of Hestia, the goddess of the hearth. The poems of Homer suggest that close ties arose between master and slave. When, for instance, Odysseus reveals himself to his faithful slaves Eumaios and Philoitios on his return to Ithaca after 20 years, they throw their arms around him and kiss him (*Odyssey* 21.222–25). Scenes of mistress and maid figure prominently on Athenian grave monuments, testimony to the fact that the two spent much time together in the *gynaikeion*, or women's quarters. In Classical Athens, slaves were occasionally buried in family plots beside their masters and mistresses.

Overall, the treatment of slaves varied greatly from one household to the next. Although Athenian slaves were protected by the law against violent abuse, in practice it was virtually impossible for them to lodge a complaint against their masters because they could not represent themselves in court. Starvation and flogging were regular punishments for bad behavior. A runaway slave was branded with a hot iron upon capture. If a slave was required to be a witness in a lawsuit, his or her testimony could be accepted only under torture.

The most privileged Athenian slaves were owned by the state. They included the notaries, jury clerks, coin testers, and executioner. In addition, a large number of publicly owned slaves toiled as road menders. As building accounts make clear, slaves sometimes worked alongside Athenian citizens on building projects. Athens's force of Scythian archers, who kept the peace, was also the property of the state.

Because Athenian citizens refused to satisfy the demand for wage labor in the second half of the fifth century B.C.E., the conditions and opportunities for a limited number of slaves improved dramatically. Such slaves, who paid a commission to their owners, were described as "living separately" (*chôris oikountes*). They included the managers of shops and factories, bankers, captains of trading vessels, bailiffs, and artisans. One was a certain Pasion, who rose to be one of the wealthiest men in Athens. Pasion, who worked as a banker, was eventually granted Athenian citizenship because he gave generously to the state at a time of crisis. Overall, however, the Athenians were reluctant to free their slaves, even when they had served their owners dutifully all their life.

> *A runaway slave was branded with a hot iron upon capture.*

The most dangerous and exhausting work performed by Athenian slaves was in the silver mines of Lavrion in southeast Attica. Inscriptions reveal that the vast majority of industrial slaves were barbarians. Xenophon (*Memorabilia* 2.5.2) informs us that the price of slaves who served in this capacity could be as low as 50 drachmas. Work in the mines continued uninterruptedly for 24 hours a day. From the discovery of miners' lamps containing oil, it has been estimated that shifts were 10 hours in length.

Although it had its critics, the institution of slavery was never seriously challenged in the ancient world. Even philosophers such as the Cynics and Stoics, who professed to believe in the brotherhood of mankind, were muted in their opposition. In the *Politics*, Aristotle goes so far as to justify slavery as part of the order of existence, although he makes a distinction between what he calls slaves by nature, those born in captivity, and slaves by law, those captured in war. Aristotle proposed this distinction in response to those who regarded the very existence of slavery as "contrary to nature" (1253b–1255b).

With the exception of Spartan agriculture and Athenian silver mining, there is little evidence to suggest that the Greeks depended on slavery for what Marxists call their means of production. Overall, therefore, it remains questionable whether the achievements of Greek civilization were made possible by slavery (Garland, 69–73).

FOR MORE INFORMATION

Fisher, N. R. E. *Slavery in Classical Greece*. Bristol, England: Bristol Classical Press and Focus Publishing, 1993.

Garlan, Y. *Slavery in Ancient Greece.* Translated by J. Lloyd. Ithaca, N.Y.: Cornell University Press, 1982.

Garland, R. *Daily Life of the Ancient Greeks.* Westport, Conn.: Greenwood Press, 1998.

ECONOMIC LIFE
|
SLAVERY
|
Mesopotamia

Egypt

Greece

Rome

ROME

Today when we consider slavery, we tend to think of the form of slavery practiced in the American South, but Roman slavery was a very different institution for a number of reasons. The first and by far the biggest difference is that Roman slavery was not racial slavery. There was absolutely no correlation between race and slavery. Slaves were any and all races, genders, cultures, and ages. A second major difference was that the line between slave and free was not rigid. It was a permeable boundary through which people passed in large numbers in both directions. A great many slaves were eventually freed, and perhaps even greater numbers of free people became slaves.

The most common source of slaves in the Roman world was military conquest. Whenever a Roman army took the field, it was inevitably followed by a train of slave dealers. The soldiers would catch people and sell them on the spot to the slave dealers, who in turn would send the slaves to one of the great slave markets such as the strategically located island of Rhodes, whose markets could process tens of thousands of slaves each day. The number of slaves generated by Rome's wars was truly astounding. Rome's destruction of Carthage in the Third Punic War glutted the slave markets with a quarter of a million new slaves at once. In the course of Julius Caesar's campaigns in Gaul, his legions sold over a million people into slavery. Other sources of slaves included children born of slaves and free people who became slaves as the result of legal action, most commonly when they fell into debt and were unable to pay it off. Sometimes abandoned children were picked up by slave dealers and raised as slaves. Finally, desperate free people could actually voluntarily sell members of their family, or even themselves, into slavery.

An unskilled adult male slave might sell for around 2,000 sesterces; skilled slaves could sell for considerably more. Slaves could either be bought outright, which was most common, or could be rented—from dealers who ran "rent-a-slave" businesses—for a certain time period ranging from a few hours to an entire year.

Under law, slaves were regarded as property just like any other object owned by their master. Thus when a slave ran away, the actual crime he was committing in the Romans' eyes was theft because he had stolen himself from his master. Varro famously offered a classification of types of property one might find on a farm. To him, all objects were tools used by the farmer, and there were three types of tools: "dumb tools" were things like wagons or baskets; animals, such

---

📷 *Snapshot*

Inscriptions from Collars Placed around the Necks of Two Roman Slaves

I am a runaway slave. Seize me. When you return me to Zoninus, my owner, you will get a gold coin as reward. (*Corpus Inscriptionum Latinarum* 15.7194)

I am Asellus, a slave belonging to Praeiectus, who is an official of the State Grain Supply. I have left my job. Seize me, because I have run away. Turn me in at the barbershop next to the temple of Flora. (*Corpus Inscriptionum Latinarum* 15.7172)

as oxen, he termed "semi-articulate tools"; and finally, there were the "articulate tools," slaves (Varro, *On Agriculture* 1.17.1).

The lifestyle of Roman slaves could vary enormously, and there was a significant distinction between rural and urban slaves. Rural slaves were unskilled farm workers, and their lives were often very harsh. Frequently, they were chained together or had their feet chained and spent their time doing heavy manual labor in the fields under the eyes of cruel overseers. At night, they were locked up in a jail-like enclosure known as the *ergastulum*. This type of slave was rarely freed by his master and had little to look forward to in life. Cato the Elder wrote down his advice for managing rural slaves, which includes the callous suggestion that if a slave became too sick or too old to work, he be sold so that the owner didn't have to waste any food on him (Cato, *On Agriculture* 2.7).

Urban slavery encompassed a much wider range of experiences. Some of these slaves, particularly family ones raised together with the master's children, were the confidantes and even friends of their masters and could receive an education, have their own families, and live nearly as well as the free members of the family. Many skilled professions, such as teacher, carpenter, doctor, and clerk, were often filled by slaves who enjoyed, at least to some degree, the high standard of living and the respect due to one with their talents. The imperial bureaucracy included huge numbers of slaves as clerks and accountants, and public services such as the groups who maintained the aqueducts were composed of slaves as well.

Many of these slaves had the hope that they might actually buy their freedom from their masters through an odd Roman institution known as the *peculium*. A *peculium* was a fund of money that the slave was allowed to build up, and once it reached the slave's own value, the slave could give it to his master and literally buy his own way out of slavery. The *peculium* was viewed by the Romans as an incentive for slaves to work harder. Thus a master might tell a slave who was a teacher that he could keep 5 percent of all the tuition money that he generated or tell a slave who worked as a salesman that he could keep 5 percent of the profit from the sales he generated. With this incentive, presumably the slave would work harder and thus generate more money for his master. Romans usually calculated that it would take a particularly industrious slave approximately seven years to build up his *peculium* to the level where he could buy his freedom.

Many urban slaves were also freed outright by their masters. The act of freeing a slave was known as *manumission*. Manumission most commonly occurred either posthumously in a will or when a man became a *paterfamilias* and freed his childhood slave friends. So many Romans were freeing slaves in their wills that Augustus actually passed a law prohibiting anyone from freeing more than 100 slaves in a will. When a slave was freed, he was presented with a floppy cone-shaped red hat, which was known as the liberty cap and which he was supposed to wear to demonstrate his new status.

Because of the sheer numbers of slaves in Roman society, Romans were extremely fearful—almost paranoid—that their slaves would turn against them. The most obvious example of this is seen in a law that stated that if a slave killed his master, then all the slaves owned by that person would be put to death. The harshness with which Romans punished their children and themselves for misbehavior was extended to their slaves, who were whipped, beaten, and tortured for the slightest error.

Once at a dinner party at which Augustus was present, one of the slaves serving the meal dropped and broke a glass. The master ordered that the slave should be thrown into a pool of man-eating lampreys. Augustus intervened to save the slave, but the incident is representative of the sort of punishment meted out for even trivial offenses (Seneca, *On Anger* 3.40). Even normally humane slave owners would abuse their slaves in moments of anger, illustrating again how slaves were regarded as property more than as humans. Augustus once had both the legs of a slave who had annoyed him broken, and when another slave ate one of the emperor's fighting quails, Augustus had the slave nailed alive to the mast of a ship (Suetonius, *Augustus* 67.2; Plutarch, *Sayings of the Romans* 207B). The culture-loving and enlightened Emperor Hadrian in a moment of annoyance stabbed one of his slaves in the eye with a stylus (Galen 5.17–18).

Urban slaves who misbehaved were threatened with being sent to the country to work on a farm. Slaves were often branded to mark them as slaves, and many times the branding was done on the face so that the slave could not hide the marks with clothing. Some masters outfitted their slaves with iron collars from which were hung tags inscribed with messages such as, "If you find this slave, he has run away. Please return him to his owner at the following address." These are exactly the same as modern dog tags in both purpose and appearance. When slaves were summoned as witnesses in law cases, the only way their testimony was considered valid was if they had been tortured.

Despite this cruelty, some masters treated their slaves with great kindness. Pliny the Younger, who owned 4,116 slaves, was very concerned for the health of his slaves and bragged that he did not place chains on his agricultural slaves (Pliny the Younger, *Letters* 8.16 and 3.19). Once, when a favorite slave contracted tuberculosis, Pliny sent him on a luxurious cruise up the Nile River in Egypt to recuperate (Pliny the Younger, *Letters* 5.19).

Romans were always fearful that their slaves would band together against them. An indication of the depths of their fear can be seen by the fact that despite their obsession with public pronouncements and indications of status, a proposal that all slaves should be made to wear some distinguishing item of clothing was rejected on the grounds that if the slaves were able to recognize one another, they would realize how vast their numbers really were and be incited to rebellion.

During the Republic, there were indeed a number of times when groups of slaves rose in rebellion against their masters. The most famous of these slave revolts was led by a man named Spartacus. He was a Thracian who had served as an auxiliary in the Roman army. Later falling into slavery, he was sent to the gladiator school at Capua. In 73 B.C.E., he led his fellow gladiators in slaughtering their overseers and then pillaging the countryside. He collected a huge army of 90,000 slaves, barbarians, and discontented people. He defeated three Roman armies and two consuls as he marched up Italy. His army successfully reached the Alps, at which point Spartacus urged his followers to disband and escape back to their homes in the north. His army had developed a taste for plundering, however, and refused, so Spartacus led them back down into Italy. Eventually, he was cornered near the heel of Italy by three Roman armies. Spartacus negotiated with several pirate fleets to transport his army away, but at the last moment they deserted him, and Spartacus and most of his followers were killed in a battle. The 6,000 who were captured were crucified on the Appian Way, so that for hundreds of miles along the main road there was a constant row of crucified slaves serving as a warning to any others who might revolt, and indeed, after this, there were no other major revolts.

During the Roman Empire, laws were gradually changed to ensure more humane treatment for slaves, and once Christianity became a dominant force, slaves were endowed with more rights and received better treatment. Roman slavery was a curious mixture of brutality and kindness, oppression and hope. The most famous stories are of the lucky slaves who obtained their freedom and went on to success. At the time of his death, one ex-slave owned 7,200 oxen, had a net worth of 60 million sesterces, and himself owned 4,000 slaves. Such stories, however, represent the exception. Perhaps the more typical attitude of a slave can be summed up in the words of a slave in a Roman play by Plautus: "Being a slave, you have to suffer many injustices. It's a hard burden to bear" (Plautus, *Amphitryon* 174–75).

~*Gregory S. Aldrete*

FOR MORE INFORMATION

Bradley, K. R. *Slavery and Society at Rome*. Cambridge, England: Cambridge University Press, 1994.

Finley, M. I. *Ancient Slavery and Modern Ideology*. London: Chatto and Windus, 1980.

Hopkins, K. *Conquerors and Slaves: Sociological Studies in Roman History I*. Cambridge, England: Cambridge University Press, 1978.

INDIA

By about 1000 B.C.E., Indian society had become strictly stratified into different social classes, called *castes*. These castes included priests, warriors, cultivators, and landless peasants. A few centuries later, Indians added the category of "untouchables," people who performed tasks that were considered polluting, such as butchering meat. Although not legally enslaved like other groups in the ancient world, the untouchables surely saw themselves as enslaved by their status. See the section "Social Structure" in chapter 6 of the present volume for further discussion of the caste system in India. Also, see volume 6 of this series, the chapter titled "Economic Life," under the section "Class and Caste Experience," for the endurance of this system.

Work

Those who were not farmers in the ancient world still had to find some form of employment to survive, and in villages and cities, a class of specialists emerged who concentrated on one craft or skill. Initially, these craftsmen worked mostly with raw

ECONOMIC LIFE
|
WORK
|
Mesopotamia

Egypt

Greece

Rome

materials such as clay, cloth, wood, and metal to produce manufactured goods such as pots, clothes, and tools. Most urban centers of village size and larger would have had at least a local blacksmith and a carpenter. Ceramic workers in the ancient world sometimes produced not just practical items but also pots that today are regarded as works of art. The fine black and red figure paintings on Greek pottery are both magnificent artistic creations and one of our best guides to the clothes and appearance of ancient Greeks themselves.

Most skilled professions were male dominated, but one type of work that was often regarded as the domain of women was the work associated with the production of cloth and clothing. Although there were some large-scale producers of cloth, such work was often the main duty of women within each family. Spinning thread and using a loom were the stereotypical skills of a woman, and her ability to perform these tasks was often regarded as a measure of her worth. When the Greek hero Agamemnon describes the duties and attributes of a recently acquired young slave girl, the features he highlights are first, her physical attractiveness and second, her skill with the loom (Homer, *Iliad* 1.30, 1.114–15).

Skilled craftsmen in the ancient world often handed down their knowledge within families from father to son, or took on apprentices. In larger cities, the craftsmen would sometimes organize themselves into professional organizations or guilds. The *collegia* of ancient Rome are one example; these groups were not merely professional organizations but often served as the center of social life as well, with regular meetings and parties. The membership rolls and club rules of many of these organizations survive and can be extraordinarily detailed documents, specifying items down to the exact number of sardines that each member was to be given to munch on at club banquets.

Ancient workers held a surprisingly large number of different jobs. This is partly because, with no factories churning out huge numbers of identical goods, every item was handcrafted, and this encouraged extreme specialization. The 200-plus different jobs attested in inscriptions from the city of Rome, ranging from jeweler to dock worker, represented greater variety than nearly any other civilization up until very recent times.

One aspect of ancient employment that may seem odd to a modern audience but that actually makes rational economic sense is that often the more skilled jobs were held by slaves and that menial, arduous, or dangerous jobs were filled by free wage laborers. For a craftsman, teaching his slaves a skill was a form of investment in his property because this would increase both the income they generated and their intrinsic value. If he spent the same effort training a free employee, on the other hand, not only would he not get as much of the income, but the person could leave at any time, and the craftsman's time and effort would have been wasted.

Another attitude that is markedly different from modern Western notions of work is the disdain that the Greeks and Romans shared for what we would consider gainful employment. Rather than seeing dignity in work, both cultures regarded having to labor for another person, and especially having to earn a salary, as morally degrading. Nevertheless, the number of people who had the luxury of not having to work was small, and for most inhabitants of the ancient world who were not farmers, employment of some sort was a necessity.

~Gregory S. Aldrete

MESOPOTAMIA

ECONOMIC LIFE

|

WORK

|

Mesopotamia

Egypt

Greece

Rome

Sumerian and Akkadian had a word meaning "specialist," which included specific artisans, artists, and scholars—that is, people with specialized learning or skills. Knowledge of crafts was learned by oral teaching, apprenticeship, and writing, in the case of scribes. Crafts were often taught within families or clans. Apprenticeship was long, as much as eight years for a house builder and four for a seal cutter. Sometimes, the craftsmen were slaves, but only wealthy families could afford to have their slaves trained.

Throughout the history of Mesopotamia, the importance of the private and institutional sectors varied. The temples and the palaces were the principal patrons of the crafts. There were craftsmen employed as part of the workforce of the great institutions, but independent workers were also hired as needed.

The status of free artisans varied throughout history. Unlike slaves, who received only rations, artisans received payment. In the Old Babylonian period, their compensation was regulated by the Laws of Hammurabi, which listed payment for textile workers, leather workers, reed workers, and others. The same craftsman could make both ordinary objects and works of art. Metalworkers and jewelers sometimes worked with more than one kind of metal.

The activities of the private sector remain undocumented. We do not know whether crafts were organized as guilds outside of the temple or palace. Some crafts had a patron deity, such as the brick god Kulla, who may have held the group together through common worship. Trades passed from father to son, so that a family connection tended to concentrate members of the same craft in one part of a city. Some crafts, such as textile work, could be done at home. Texts mention craft quarters named after trades, such as the wards of goldsmiths, bleachers, and potters, a craft quarter at Mari, the street of the bakers in Jerusalem (Jeremiah 37:21), and the "gate of the foundry workers" at Assur.

In the Old Babylonian period, "guilds" of brewers, smiths, and other trades were organized under an administrator, as part of the palace or temple organization. Important craftsmen, such as brewers, smiths, and weavers, achieved some kind of independence within and among the organizations. The overseers of these artisans achieved social status and power, and they were well compensated. But the supervisor of the musicians was much poorer because he had little to sell or hire. Guilds, as known from medieval times, could not function as independent bodies because of the difficulty of acquiring raw materials.

Beginning with the early Neo-Babylonian period, the names of professions became family names (similar to the present-day Smith, Weaver, Miller, etc.), suggesting that craftsmen enjoyed status in the preceding period. Most were scribes, but there were also carpenters, metalworkers, and goldsmiths. Their ancestors' names could be traced back to the Kassite period. Texts also refer to the "city" of the tanners and the "city" of the metalworkers, that is, special quarters to which certain crafts were limited or in which they were concentrated for convenience.

Wood, regardless of quality, was used for building bridges, wagons, ships, and occasionally, houses. The Babylonian lexical lists of wood objects were longer than those for objects made from copper, clay, or leather. Because wood survived only in the desert, often as carbonized remains, our knowledge of woodworking must be drawn almost entirely from the numerous ancient texts, which survive in abundance for all of Mesopotamia and northern Syria. The range of skill for woodworking required trained craftsmen.

We do not know if carpenters were asked to build simple, single-story homes or parts of them such as the roof, the door frame, or the doors. Little is known about their tools. Carpenters were certainly employed for building temples and palaces, which involved all kinds of cypress, cedar, beech, and other imported woods. The great tree trunks from Syria and other forested regions were floated downriver on rafts and used to make palace doors.

The most common craft was pottery made from clay. Utensils included pots, drinking vessels, plates, and bowls; their shapes are still found today. The potter also made large jars for storing goods, ovens, and even coffins (in the latter, he competed with the carpenter and basket maker). Some pottery was formed by hand and manufactured by punching a central hole into a lump of clay and adding pieces of clay as pellets, slabs, or coils. Some vessels were pressed in a mold, and others were shaped on a slow wheel (ca. 4500 B.C.E.) or on a fast wheel (ca. 2000 B.C.E.) to create thin-walled vessels with spouts, handles, covers, and even reliefs. We do not know what these potter's wheels looked like and how they functioned. There is no Akkadian word for "potter's wheel." The potter's wheel was instrumental in mass-producing large quantities of pottery to supply the needs of the major cities. Containers of fired clay were needed as offerings to the gods and kings and to store oil, wine, grain, and so on.

Potters may have specialized in particular types of pottery. Painted ware as well as enameled and glazed ceramic ware appeared, primarily in Assyria, with old motifs revised. The development of glazed pottery came during the Neo-Assyrian and Neo-Babylonian periods, suggesting craft communication with glass and metal workers. Inscribed pottery was widespread throughout the history of Mesopotamia, ranging in size from small vessels to ones holding up to 250 liters. Whether pottery was made by men or by women assisted by children remains uncertain. Women may have decorated pots, but men may have worked with apprentices on a full-time basis. Because manufacture and decoration were characteristic of different regions and periods, pottery has been used for dating. Pottery has also provided information as to trading activities and cultural influences.

Most miniature sculptures were made from clay. Terra-cottas were rarely made individually; usually, clay forms were used to produce them, and then they were fired. For three-dimensional figures, two forms were needed. Terra-cotta figurines were often painted and in later periods, overlaid with colorful glazes.

The most famous and costly dye of antiquity was a purple extracted from a gland in sea mollusks.

Mud and clay were necessary for the monumental building projects for which hundreds of thousands of bricks were used. After the mud was prepared, it was put into a wooden form and removed after each brick had dried. After sun drying, some bricks were baked in small ovens and then smoothed and polished. Thousands of workers were recruited for making bricks and building monuments. Supervisors made certain that a given number of bricks was stamped and inscribed. Later in Assyria and Nebuchadnezzar's Babylon, brick reliefs were created from embossed, often colorfully glazed bricks. The glazed brick walls of the Ishtar Gate and Processional Way at Babylon were made of blue, turquoise, green, yellow, white, and black glazed bricks, providing evidence of ceramic mass production. The glazing substance was frequently artificial lapis lazuli. Asphalt was used to cover bricks used in foundation walls and courts.

According to cuneiform records, glass was produced in Sumerian times, but it has not been found at sites predating 1500 B.C.E. Spinning and weaving of flax and wool were predominantly women's work. Weavers, following a period of apprenticeship, specialized in particular types of work, such as weaving linen or colored textiles. Female weavers were frequently mentioned. Many kinds of materials were woven, both coarse and fine, and with colors and bleaches. Both male and female washers, called fullers, were considered skilled workers.

Textiles were produced on looms. The first, and probably earliest, was a ground loom, with stakes in the ground to keep the warps stretched tightly and the loom secured. The ground loom was favored by nomads because of its portability and ease of assembly. The second basic loom was the warp-weighted loom, which has been documented in the ancient Near East by the presence of ceramic weights and by illustrations on seals and in paintings. Numbers of large beads with a single hole may be identified as drop spindles used for spinning, and those with a circular groove may have served as bobbins for weaving tapestries. Among grave goods have been found slim bone knives used by carpet weavers.

Color in ancient textiles was produced from natural dyestuffs derived from animal, plant, or mineral matter. The Syrians and Phoenicians produced purple cloth from purple snails found only off the Phoenician coast. The most famous and costly dye of antiquity was a purple extracted from a gland in sea mollusks. Other natural colors such as red, yellow, blue, and black have all been described.

Sack maker and rug tyer were textile professions. The production of rugs and tapestries was well attested at Old Babylonian Mari and Nuzi, although the technique of tying carpets was probably developed later, after 1500 B.C.E. Rugs provided warmth and decoration on a wall or floor and could be used in both nomadic and sedentary environments. There is little material evidence for the presence of carpets before the eighth century B.C.E.

Reeds were especially important in treeless areas; they grew in abundance along waterways and in the marshes and thickets. They were used for making baskets of all kinds, the shafts of arrows, spears, fences, doors, reed furniture, mats, boat building, and shelters for humans and animals in the countryside. In the construction of public works, such as ziggurats, layers of reed mats were laid at intervals between the layers of bricks. Reed mats were used for roofs; their carbonized remains are still frequently preserved.

The leather worker provided sandals, boots, and other types of shoes. Leather was particularly important in military equipment. Leather straps and insets were needed mainly for helmets, shields, and armor, which also were made in part from bronze or iron. In the first millennium B.C.E., quivers were made from leather. Leather was even used for war chariots and bridles.

In the Bronze Age, the metalworker was a specialist whose products helped to transform society by their effect on agriculture, warfare, and transportation. The metals known and used in the ancient Near East were copper, tin, bronze (an artificial alloy of copper and tin), gold, silver, electrum (a natural alloy of gold and silver), lead, iron, and steel (an artificial alloy of iron and carbon). Metals such as arsenic and zinc were usually used as materials alloyed with copper to produce arsenical copper and brass, respectively. Only copper, lead, and silver-bearing ores were mined prior to about 1000 B.C.E. The Iron Age began about 1200 B.C.E., although miscellaneous pieces of iron have been found in archaeological contexts as far back as the fifth millennium B.C.E. Once serious ironwork began, the technology soon followed. The early history of iron metallurgy has been traditionally viewed as a monopoly on the secrets of working with iron. The Hittites used iron metallurgy in their military successes, particularly against the Egyptians at the battle of Qadesh in Syria (ca. 1275 B.C.E.). When the Hittite Empire collapsed at the end of the Bronze Age, control over the use of iron and iron technology fell to the Philistines. Iron became the metal of choice for the common man (Nemet-Nejat, 282–303).

FOR MORE INFORMATION

Mathews, D. "Artists and Artisans in Ancient Western Asia." In *Civilizations of the Ancient Near East,* ed. J. Sasson. Vol. 1. New York: Scribner's, 1995.

Nemet-Nejat, K. R. *Daily Life in Ancient Mesopotamia.* Westport, Conn.: Greenwood Press, 1998.

Powell, M. A., ed. *Labor in the Ancient Near East.* New Haven, Conn.: American Oriental Society, 1987.

ECONOMIC LIFE
|
WORK
|
Mesopotamia

Egypt

Greece

Rome

EGYPT

Egyptians lived in an economic environment completely different from ours. Money did not exist, the idea of a workweek had no meaning, and the concept of leisure time was unknown to most of the population. Surprisingly, however different the context and specifics might have been, work and play in Egypt's ancient culture closely resembled that of modern societies—at least until the nineteenth century, when machines took over the world.

Those who worked at jobs less controlled by nature followed rhythms set by their masters or by supply-and-demand principles. Government workers were allowed to rest every 10th day. Craftspeople worked according to demand. Those who made objects, either utilitarian or artistic, earned no great status in Egyptian society, however wonderful their creations might seem to us today. Lists of offerings to various temples refer to furniture and statues in the same citations as grain, beer, and cattle.

In addition to painstaking labor, knowledge of materials was essential for each craft. No directions on papyri explained how to make things because that information was transferred from master to apprentice as part of an oral tradition. In this way, knowledge of a craft was passed—usually by father to son—from generation to generation.

Craftsmen enjoyed little independence. The jeweler needed metal and stones for his creations, and the carpenter needed various woods; however, gold, silver, and semiprecious stones, along with most desired woods, were all royal monopolies. To obtain the supplies they needed, most craftsmen worked for estates that manufactured an array of goods, a temple, or if fortunate, the royal workshop—larger organizations that could secure the raw materials required. Although the estate carpenter could obtain his chisel from the estate smithy more easily than he could on his own, he was also subject to rigid supervision and told what to produce. A goldsmith, for example, was given raw ore only after it had been carefully weighed; the completed gold object was weighed again to ensure that no precious metal had been stolen during the process. Under the vigilant eye of an overseer, a covey of scribes recorded every object and judged its suitability. The wonder is that lovely objects were produced in such abundance, for innovation and aesthetics had little place in this bureaucratic process.

At least the arrangement gave the craftsman security—regular pay in the form of food, drink, and in most cases, shelter. Because leaving one employer to find work with another was almost impossible, craftsmen depended on the good will of their patron. The bounty of their reward varied with the patron's generosity, whether he was a nobleman, a chief priest, or the pharaoh. Fortunately for the craftsman, patrons believed that the treatment of their workers would be known to the gods and affect their own reception in the next world: in messages meant for divine eyes, tomb after tomb records how generously owners dealt with underlings.

By all odds, the worst occupations in Egypt were those of the quarry and mine worker. The labor was so exhausting and the conditions were so dusty, dank, and dangerous that mine stints were sometimes used as jail sentences for serious crimes.

Until sandstone (which can bear greater stress) came into vogue in the New Kingdom, limestone was the material of choice for large construction projects. Quarries for both these soft stones were plentiful in Egypt, but freeing the blocks of either material involved dusty, dirty work using copper or bronze chisels and picks that, blow upon blow, chipped away the stone. Work proceeded from the top layer down because swinging a pick downward was less fatiguing than swinging upward. Luckier workers toiled in open pits; the less fortunate worked underground. For a subterranean stoneworker, extracting the first blocks required crawling in spaces just large enough to wriggle through. His body covered in stone dust, he labored in a dark and eerie world peopled by shadows made by his flickering oil lamp, constantly at risk of being crushed by rocks or falling prey to endemic lung disease.

Egyptian pottery adequately served its purpose, but it never achieved the quality of Egyptian sculpture, painting, and architecture. Bowls could convey charm, however, as in the case of small predynastic "footed" ones, which rested on two tiny human legs and feet. The most interesting pottery also dates back to such early times. To produce two-color pots, the potter oxidized iron impurities in the clay by firing it to a red color, while the top of the pot lay buried under the fire's ashes to carbonize black. The finished product, which could be as thin as an eighth of an inch for a pot over a foot tall, exhibits a distinct shine that came not from a glaze, which Egyptians never discovered, but from being burnished with a smooth stone before firing.

Something like a potter's wheel was invented during the Old Kingdom, if not before. A heavy circular stone rested on a pivot for turning by hand or foot, at a level lower than our modern version. It spun more slowly but produced round vessels of consistent thickness. The kiln was also an early invention. In the Egyptian version, a tall, conical brick structure held a fire at the bottom while a shelf supported the unfired clay above the ashes. In this simple way, pots were produced—for cooking, storing and carrying—during all ancient Egypt's history. Because they were utilitarian objects, their makers seldom paid much attention to their beauty.

When artisans turned their attention to ceramic amulets, however, they invested more imagination and care and produced thousands of images—from the tiny to a foot in height—depicting gods, the magical eye of Horus (for health), the *djed* pillar (of stability), the sacred scarab beetle (for long life), and even images of servants, called *ushabtis*, which people took to their tombs to work for them during the afterlife. These figures, generally colored a rich sky blue, aqua, or green, were molded not from clay but from a material of Egyptian invention. Called Egyptian faience, it consisted of a core produced from finely ground quartz coated with a glasslike glaze. This Egyptian invention, which consisted of a solution of natron and quartz dust, could be shaped by hand or pressed into a clay mold that, when fired, solidified into a solid mass harder than soft stone. The glaze consisted of natron mixed in solution with malachite or another oxide of copper. The solution, which was washed over the object to be glazed and then heated to fuse with the silicon of the quartz, produced a blue or green glass that was literally bound to the object. The coloring agent could instead be mixed in with the quartz powder and fired, causing it to rise to the surface as a self-glaze.

In addition to making delicate figures by the thousands, Egyptians used their faience to manufacture small bowls and dishes of rich blue. They even learned, by changing the oxide, to produce red and yellow versions and to create objects in two and three colors. One early experiment produced the first glazed tiles in history. A room in a second tomb of Zoser, called the Southern Burial, was found lined with rows of lovely green-blue tiles, about three inches long by an inch-and-a-half wide. A method to fix them to a wall was lacking, however. The tiles were attached by string through a hole in the back of each.

Egyptian glaze not only shone like glass, it actually was glass, so Egyptians must be counted among the very first glass producers. Some pure glass may have been manufactured as early as predynastic times, but evidence that the process was understood and intentional remains unclear. By the time of the New Kingdom, glass had become an industry that turned out thousands of excellent inlays, beads, vases, bowls, and amulets. Strangely, production had declined by the 20th Dynasty, two dynasties later, and disappeared entirely during the Late period, not to be resurrected until many centuries later by the Ptolemies.

Egyptian carpentry dates from predynastic times when coffins were constructed of lap-joined planks held together at the corners with lashing tied through holes. By the First Dynasty, construction had become more sophisticated, resulting in admirable work. Even at this early time, carpenters had mastered the craft of producing flat pieces of wood, then cutting and joining them into a well-built box. Predynastic tombs contained boxes with inlaid panels and mortise-and-tenon joints for the rails and stiles, mitered corners and inlays of ivory strips, and even faience plaques attached by tree resin to a gesso base. Splendidly carved bull's feet with sinews and fetlock accurately depicted in ivory for use as the feet of beds or chairs serve today as museum exhibits.

Chairs tended to have low seats, less than 10 inches above the ground.

Carpenters had gotten off to a precocious start, barely hampered by the absence of glue and of nails. Glue, made from boiling down the bones and cartilage of animals, did not come into use as an adhesive until about the Fifth Dynasty. By the Fourth Dynasty, boxes with barrel or gabled lids, others with cavetto cornices and some with curved sides, show that shaping presented no problem. Sloping lids rising to a curved peak attained the height of complexity in the Sixth Dynasty. Rope handles tied through side holes aided carrying, or in the case of larger boxes, copper loops on the box bottom secured carrying poles that slid out when not needed. Lids were locked by a string tied to a knob on the front, the top, or both.

In addition to boxes in many styles and designs, carpenters produced wooden beds and small tables that stood on three or four legs. Chairs tended to have low seats, less than 10 inches above the ground, and almost-straight backs, often intricately cut out. Some examples have been found of folding stools with leather seats that collapsed for transport to the battlefield or the hunt.

Although carpenters did not have the best woods at their disposal, available material proved adequate when supplemented by imports. Egypt grew no tall trees for tall ship masts, large coffins, and towering temple doors. For these uses, tall cedar from Lebanon or cypress trees were imported. Tough, elastic ash was imported from Syria for use in bows and chariots. Beautiful, hard dark ebony, whose name derives from the ancient Egyptian word *hbny*, was imported from tropical Africa and Punt (Somalia) for the solid furniture of the rich and for inlays and veneers for those on a budget. From Palestine (Israel) came elm for strong chariot axles and supports; yew from Persia was imported for coffins. Egypt was not, however, without its own lumber. Acacia grew tall enough for shorter ship masts and boat planking. Date palm trunks provided roof beams, although its fibrous wood made it inappropriate for furniture. Sycamore, which served many uses, from boxes to coffins, proved to be one of the most useful native woods. The shorter tamarisk tree provided wood for boxes and some coffins, though much pieced together.

Wood from willow trees became knife handles and parts of some boxes (Brier and Hobbs, 82, 84–87, 190–93).

FOR MORE INFORMATION

Brier, B., and H. Hobbs. *Daily Life of the Ancient Egyptians*. Westport, Conn.: Greenwood Press, 1999.

Lucas, A., and J. R. Harris. *Ancient Egyptian Materials and Industries*. London: E. Arnold, 1989.

Petrie, F. *Arts and Crafts of Ancient Egypt*. London: T.N. Foulis, 1909.

ECONOMIC LIFE

|

WORK

|

Mesopotamia

Egypt

Greece

Rome

GREECE

The Greeks regarded the condition of working for someone else as worse than that of being a slave; slaves at least enjoyed some security. Temporary employees, in addition to being laid off at a moment's notice, had to endure the indignity of taking orders from a fellow citizen. Inimical though employment was, however, it is likely to have been fairly widespread. In Athens, those who wished to hire themselves out as wage laborers gathered each day on a hill overlooking the Agora. The most acceptable type of employment was as an employee of the state because this did not entail subjection to a fellow citizen. In the second half of the fifth century B.C.E., the livelihoods of an increasing number of Athenians were made possible by the imperial tribute. Even when Athens had lost its empire, the state continued to be a major employer. Although Aristotle's claim that state pay supported "over twenty thousand men" in the fourth century B.C.E. is an exaggeration (*Constitution of Athens* 24.3), there can be little doubt that it enabled the poor to participate in democracy.

Most of the revenue received from the empire went to pay the rowers of Athens's fleet. Sailors' rate of pay reflected Athens's changing economic fortunes. When its naval expedition was dispatched to Sicily in 415 B.C.E., the pay stood at one drachma per day. At the end of the Peloponnesian War, when Athens's reserves were well-nigh exhausted, that figure was cut by half. Unlike hoplites, whose service was intermittent, rowers were a full-time professional body. Since Athens generally maintained at least 100 ships on active service during the fifth and fourth centuries B.C.E., the fleet must have provided employment for some 20,000 men. Because the rowers were mostly drawn from the poorest class of citizens, the growth in Athenian naval power coincided with a growth in the political importance of the lowest social group, known as the *thêtes*. Maintaining the fleet in a seaworthy condition required the services of a large and highly specialized workforce of joiners, fitters, rope makers, painters, and sailcloth makers. Many of these were probably also rowers, who worked in these capacities when the fleet was laid up.

Because the size of its tribute exceeded the cost of maintaining its fleet, Athens could also support other programs that paid the wages of state employees. The most costly was the Periclean building program, instituted in 447 B.C.E. The building accounts for the Erechtheion indicate that citizens, slaves, and metics worked alongside one another on this project. Skilled workers, like rowers, were paid one drachma per day.

The allied tribute also funded Athens's jury service, which consisted of a pool of 6,000 citizens. The pay of jurors amounted to only two obols per day in court, which was increased to three obols after about 425 B.C.E. Since most jurors were elderly, this served as a kind of old-age pension. Although being a state employee was decidedly preferable to being in the employ of another citizen, any Athenian who had to work for his living was regarded as socially inferior to those whose livelihood and leisure were guaranteed by landed wealth.

Lacking any notion of job satisfaction, the Greeks were not much in favor of hard work. Nor were they burdened with anything comparable to the Protestant work ethic. Aristotle was of the opinion that leisure was the precondition of civilized life, and no doubt the majority of Greeks would have agreed. Just as they did not believe in the virtues of work for work's sake, so, too, they hardly had any notion of the concept of wasting time. Loafing was thus an essential part of every citizen's life who could afford it. It was by loafing in the Agora each day that Athenians learned the latest gossip, exchanged ideas about the burning political issues of the day, and discussed informally the proposals that were tabled for the next meeting of the assembly. Athenians also used their time in the Agora to make their daily purchases, since respectable women were expected to stay at home (Garland, 154–56).

FOR MORE INFORMATION

Burford, A. *Craftsmen in Greek and Roman Society*. London: Thames and Hudson, 1972.
Garland, R. *Daily Life of the Ancient Greeks*. Westport, Conn.: Greenwood Press, 1998.
Glotz, G. *Ancient Greece at Work*. Translated by M. R. Dobie. New York: W.W. Norton, 1927.

ROME

ECONOMIC LIFE
|
WORK
|
Mesopotamia

Egypt

Greece

Rome

Employment for 80 to 90 percent of the people in Rome simply meant being a farmer out in the countryside. The remaining population who were not in the army mostly lived in cities. For them, there was a variety of ways to earn a living.

The upper-class Romans, who wrote all the surviving sources, had very definite ideas about work and employment. For them, how one earned an income had strong moral overtones. In fact, they believed that most forms of employment were degrading and that truly civilized people should not work at all. This is quite an extreme way of viewing employment; nearly everything we would consider a form of work was considered to be morally degrading by aristocratic Romans. Earning a salary, buying or selling goods, manufacturing goods—all of these were considered vulgar, and an aristocrat could not dirty himself with them. Thus to the upper-class Romans, only those people who were so rich that they did not have to do anything to earn a living were considered fully human and civilized.

The things that aristocrats did that we would consider jobs—such as serving as lawyers in a law case or being elected to a magistracy such as praetor or consul—

were not considered jobs because they received no pay. Politics or the law were truly the preserve of rich men because they entailed spending a lot of money but receiving no money in return. In keeping with the Republican ideology of virtue exemplified by Cincinnatus, the only profession that did not degrade someone was being a farmer. Rich men were expected to gain and maintain their wealth primarily by owning land. By the empire, of course, aristocrats did not do any actual farming themselves and in fact spent almost all their time in Rome rather than on their estates. They lived off the

> *One of the most unappealing jobs was the alipilus, whose task was to pluck out underarm hair.*

labor of hundreds or thousands of slaves who did the actual farming on the estates. The sources are full of expressions of contempt for anyone who made a living by working or through commerce. This was the Romans' ideology, but in reality, the picture is more complex. Many rich Romans gained and maintained their fortunes through means other than farming. Some were moneylenders who charged up to 60 percent annual interest on a loan. Some were in essence factory owners who had shops that produced goods such as lamps, bricks for building, or plates and containers made out of clay.

A few aristocrats got very creative in the ways they amassed wealth. The best example of these was a man named Crassus, who lived in the late Republic. Crassus became the richest man in Rome through a clever strategy. He would prowl the streets of Rome at night with a huge band of his slaves carrying buckets and axes. As soon as one of the frequent fires broke out, Crassus and his slaves would rush to the spot, where Crassus would offer to buy the burning building from its owner. He would usually offer between one-quarter and one-third of its real value. The poor owner, faced with the choice of one-quarter of the value or losing everything when it burnt down usually sold it to Crassus. As soon as the document was signed, Crassus would order his well-trained gang of fire-fighting slaves into action, and they would put out the fire. In this way, Crassus ended up owning much of Rome, which he acquired literally at fire-sale prices.

Whereas the upper classes could afford to be choosy about employment, the vast majority of people in cities had to work. The working classes can be divided into two basic groups: those whose profession required some sort of training, talent, skill, or capital, and those who were unskilled and sold their labor for wages. One of the ironies of Rome is that most poor citizens fell into the second category, the unskilled wage laborer. The skilled workers were often slaves and ex-slaves. In inscriptions on tombstones, about two-thirds of those who are identified as some sort of skilled worker were freedmen. More than 200 different jobs are mentioned on tombstones from the city of Rome. Many of the jobs listed at Rome were specialty jobs manufacturing luxury items, such as the *plumarii*, who apparently made a living exclusively doing embroidery using feathers, or the *fabri ocularii*, whose full-time employment was to manufacture the eyes for statues. There were six or seven different makers of footwear, including those who made only boots, those who made only women's shoes, and those who wove sandals. Another large category consisted of people who provided specialized services to the rich. These included one whose full-time job was to memorize the names of a patron's clients. Perhaps one of the most unappealing service specialties was the *alipilus,* whose job was to pluck out underarm hair.

Although aristocrats regarded work and moneymaking with scorn, many freedmen seem to have taken great pride in their work. This can be seen most clearly on their tombstones, which often include a sculptural relief showing the deceased practicing whatever profession the owner had followed. Even if they didn't have a picture, tombstones would often include symbols that indicated the job he had held. For example, a butcher would have a selection of knives and cleavers on his tombstone. Sometimes, freedmen would get quite creative with their funeral monuments. One man named Eurisaces, who owned a shop that baked bread, had his tomb carved in the shape of a giant bread oven, on the sides of which were carved pictures of the baker overseeing his workers grinding grain, kneading dough, and baking it. Another well-known tomb belongs to a man who owned a construction company; his monument mostly consists of a carving of a building crane used to erect structures. This attitude can also be seen in the decoration found in the houses of some of these people, such as one at Pompeii who had set into the floor of his house the phrase "Profit is happiness."

In addition to tombstones, we know about Roman jobs from the professional associations formed by people who practiced the same profession. These trade associations were called *collegia,* and often the members of a *collegia* would put up a monument commemorating their accomplishments. The *collegia* also seemed to play a role in politics, and much of the graffiti on Roman walls consists of *collegia* urging people to vote for a certain politician.

Many Romans owned small shops where they sold goods. One interesting type of small business was the *popinae,* a kind of Roman combination of bar and fast-food restaurant. *Popinae* were small rooms usually located at the intersections of major streets. Across the front was a counter with two or three large clay pots set into it. Underneath the pots were places where small fires could be built to keep the pots warm. Probably these pots contained an assortment of gruel, fish stew, and garum, and pedestrians passing by could purchase a ladleful of whatever quick food they wanted.

The lowest form of employment was the unskilled workers, who had nothing to offer except their labor. They would hire themselves out for a salary to perform various menial jobs. Such wage labor was considered the most degrading because the Romans considered this to be the equivalent of becoming someone's slave. These wage laborers were called *mercenarii.* This is obviously the root of our word *mercenary.* Today, wage labor is usually calculated on an hourly basis, but in ancient Rome, the standard unit of labor for a *mercenarius* was one day's work. A day's worth of work was known as an *operae,* and contracts would specify a certain number of days' labor that the *mercenarius* was selling to his employer. The most common type of day labor job was simply to carry things around. In particular, a sizable percentage of the free inhabitants of Rome would have found employment in two fields, the supply of food and other commodities to Rome, and the construction industry. Especially in the early empire, the emperors built lavishly, and these projects would have employed thousands of people simply in digging the foundations and carrying away the dirt. A single construction project of the emperor Claudius employed 30,000 men for 11 years as diggers (Suetonius, *Claudius* 20.2–3).

~*Gregory S. Aldrete*

FOR MORE INFORMATION

Garnsey, P. D. A., ed. *Non-Slave Labour in the Graeco-Roman World*. Cambridge, England: Cambridge Philological Society, 1980.

Loane, H. J. *Industry and Commerce of the City of Rome, 50 B.C.–200 A.D.* Baltimore, Md.: Arno Press, 1938.

ECONOMIC LIFE

MONEY

Mesopotamia

Egypt

Greece

Rome

India

Money

The earliest civilizations did not have actual money; instead, goods were exchanged for one another in a barter system. This may be a perfectly workable system for a simple local economy, but as soon as there develops a wide range of goods and services that have to be assigned relative values or the need to engage in more complex economic functions such as credit, lending, and interest, money becomes essential. The earliest societies, such as Mesopotamia and Egypt, did not quite develop full-fledged coinage but for convenience would convert the value of commodities into weights of a precious metal, usually silver. From here it was only a short step to begin minting bits of metal with standardized values assigned to them, which were the first coins. Nowadays money is made of relatively worthless material such as paper and derives its value from being backed by a reliable government that guarantees its value. In the ancient world, money was made of precious metals whose intrinsic worth by weight was equivalent to its assigned value.

The first true coins were minted in Asia Minor in the seventh century B.C.E., and in the next century, there was an explosion of different types and denominations of coinage as nearly every city in the Greek world began issuing its own coins. The Greeks were avid long-distance traders, which may have contributed to their being the first to really make use of money in the modern sense. Each city would stamp its coin with a symbol representing the city, and these Greek coins are not only useful economic tokens but intricate and beautiful works of art as well. Certain cities acquired reputations for minting coins that were particularly uniform in weight and pure of metal; these coins became readily accepted for financial transactions around the Mediterranean in much the same way that dollars today are eagerly accepted as payment in many different countries. Probably the best examples of such a coinage were the universally accepted silver "owls" of Athens, which were so called because they were stamped on one side with an owl, the bird associated with the patron goddess of the city, Athena.

The Romans continued the Greek practice of coinage, and because they were in the habit of minting coins with portraits of their emperors on one side, these coins have become one of the most reliable guides to what these rulers looked like. By the second century B.C.E., the use of inscribed coinage had spread to India. Although the invention of money constituted a great step forward in the development of a complex economy, the ancient world was not free of the problems associated with currency, and there were numerous instances of counterfeiting, inflation, and debasement of the coinage.

~Gregory S. Aldrete

MESOPOTAMIA

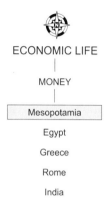

Ur III balance sheets used silver as a unit of accounting. All incoming goods were assigned values in silver by weight, which were totaled, thus providing a capital sum at the merchant's disposal—a sum for which he was responsible as well. Likewise, items bought were valued in silver; thus the merchant's account could be balanced. Was silver then used as currency or as an accounting practice for merchants? During the Old Babylonian period, payments for real estate, slaves, goods, and services were rarely paid in silver, although their prices were quoted according to a silver standard. Since Old Babylonian legal documents did not specify the quality and fineness of the silver used in payment, silver probably did not change hands in the transaction. However, in the Neo-Babylonian period, the legal texts had a rich vocabulary for describing the quality of silver given or expected. Silver was imported and taxed (in silver itself) since the Ur III period. In the Old Babylonian period, the palace controlled the circulation of silver. Accumulations of silver as treasure were restricted to the palace and the temple.

Currency has four different functions: (1) as a standard of value, (2) as a medium of exchange, (3) as a means of payment, and (4) as a means for accumulating wealth. Each has a role distinct from the others; that is, there is general-purpose money, which serves all four functions, and special-purpose money, which serves one function only. The use of silver was still a long way from coinage, which was invented in Lydia (now western Turkey). The earliest Lydian coins date to about 650 B.C.E. Greek coins were not found before 575 B.C.E. and did not become popular until 550 B.C.E. Lydian coins found so far were made of electrum, a natural alloy of gold and silver. Coinage may have begun as a way of guaranteeing and certifying the weights of metal. The administrators who first issued such coins probably were, in effect, certifying that they would repurchase the coins at the same value.

In the annals of Sennacherib, small copper "coins" were already in use in Mesopotamia at this time: "I built clay molds, poured bronze into each and made their figures perfect as in the casting of half-shekel pieces" (cited in Oates, 187). A puzzling reference by Sennacherib in 694 B.C.E. to casting bronze colossi "like the casting of half shekels" probably refers to craftsmen handling large amounts of bronze as skillfully as if no more than half a shekel of metal was involved; however, coined money was not used until the very end of the Assyrian Empire. The decisive moment was the first occasion when business was transacted in terms of small silver ingots stamped with some device such as the "head of Ishtar" or the "head of Shamash" (Oppenheim, 87). In 493 B.C.E., Darius I issued an edict introducing silver coinage, *darics*, into the Persian Empire, including Babylonia. In the Seleucid period, the value of silver coins depended on their weight and the ruler under whom they were struck. With the circulation of coinage, private banking thrived in Babylonia. From the late sixth century B.C.E. onward, there were several dynastic banking houses, such as the Egibi family in Babylon and the Murashu family in Nippur, who amassed huge fortunes through usurious rates of interest.

Societies that used metal as currency presented it in a specific form. In Mesopotamia, silver was weighed, but some texts from the Old Akkadian period through the Old Babylonian period refer to the casting of precious metals into rings as a means of storing metal. The Ur III texts about casting show that the ring did not always contain the full weight of the silver that was supposed to go into it, but such objects were weighed when they were exchanged anyway. Ur III tablets indicate that silver "rings" (in the shape of a spiral coil) of uniform weight were used by the administration. Rings varied from 1 to 10 shekels, with the majority being 5 shekels. The rings were manufactured with one to five coils. The ring as a kind of money appeared in the Old Babylonian period, but later texts no longer recorded the use of rings as currency. Silver was measured in traditional units of weight: the mina, about 500 grams, and its subdivision, the shekel (1 mina = 60 shekels), and the talent (1 talent = 60 minas). Silver was used in the form of sheets stamped to guarantee the alloy, but also in the form of "blocks," shavings, or pieces of jewelry, rings, and bracelets.

In the early second millennium B.C.E., silver was the preferred currency, but barley was used as well. Other commodities, including metals such as copper, tin, bronze, and gold, available from the periphery of Mesopotamia, were all used as moneys in the sense that they at least functioned as a means of payment, with an established fixed ratio. Silver was used as a standard of accounting, although gold served this purpose later, in the Amarna age. Standardized ingots have been found at archaeological sites. Because of their heavy size and rarity, both the ingots and rings were probably not used as a means of exchange, although all the other functions of currency might apply. Silver and other metals were weighed on a scale to determine the amount, and if smaller amounts were needed, the metal block or wire was broken into smaller pieces that were then weighed. The Akkadian word for silver means "the broken thing." Other terms in Akkadian refer to broken bits of silver, and the process of breaking metals and weighing each item was widely attested before and after coinage was introduced. The most commonly found quality of silver was called "alloyed one-eighth." Silver metal was used to pay taxes, to purchase valuable property (real estate and slaves), and in certain financial operations. Texts have noted that workers were given rations of bread and beer in addition to a small amount of copper, which could be used to purchase other goods.

The actual process of weighing remains uncertain. No complete balance has been found intact, although we do have actual series of weights. Authorities who issued coins distrusted their value and required that the coins be weighed. Coins have been found that have shown signs of tampering—that is, coin users had a tendency to shave bits from the coins. Counterfeiting was a problem as well.

The Third Dynasty of Ur provided the best evidence for the type of work, the number of working days, food rations, and wages. Wages were different from rations. Wages were calculated on a daily basis, and rations on a monthly basis. From the Ur III period on, the daily wage of a worker was 10 liters (about 2.5 gallons) of barley, a standard that appeared in school books and continued to be valid for two thousand years. However, actual hiring contracts showed that most people earned less than 10 liters per day. Rations for male workers included two liters of bread and two liters of beer—bare subsistence level if a family was supported from these rations. Workers also received two kilograms of wool per year, barely enough to make one garment. On special occasions, such as the new year, workers might receive extra rations of barley, meat, and oil. Middle or higher officials had a subsistence field of approximately 6 to 36 hectares (15 to 90 acres). The disappearance or flight of workers was not uncommon.

Once in debt, people easily became impoverished as a result of usurious rates of interest, usually 20 percent for silver and 12 percent for grain. Additional amounts reflected penalties for late payments. When the borrower could no longer pay these usurious rates, he had to repay his debt by working for his creditor (Nemet-Nejat, 264–65, 267–69).

FOR MORE INFORMATION

Nemet-Nejat, K. R. *Daily Life in Ancient Mesopotamia*. Westport, Conn.: Greenwood Press, 1998.

Oates, J. *Babylon*. Rev. ed. London: Thames and Hudson, 1986.

Oppenheim, A. L. *Ancient Mesopotamia: Portrait of a Dead Civilization*. Rev. ed. by Erica Reiner. Chicago, Ill.: University of Chicago Press, 1977.

Snell, D. C. "Methods of Exchange and Coinage in Ancient Western Asia." In *Civilizations of the Ancient Near East*, ed. J. Sasson. Vol. 3. New York: Scribner's, 1995.

EGYPT

ECONOMIC LIFE

|

MONEY

|

Mesopotamia

Egypt

Greece

Rome

India

Egyptians worked for food and goods rather than for money, which was unknown until the Ptolemies introduced it during Egypt's final days. Since for most of Egypt's long history no currency existed for exchanging commodities at set values, essential goods were generally manufactured by the user or members of his immediate family: pots, for example, were produced by women in their homes. Commodities, such as bronze plow blades, that could not be made in the average home were secured not by purchase from a store but by barter, which could be a complex procedure involving intricate negotiations. The man who made the plow blade might have enough food, pots, and clothing from other barters, so something he desired would have to be bartered from a third party—a kilt exchanged for a stool, for example, and then the stool for a plow blade. An ancient record of one such transaction documents the trade of an ox for one fine tunic and two ordinary ones, plus 10 sacks of grain and some necklace beads. Needless to say, such acquisitions occurred less frequently than today and only when motivated by strong need.

In an attempt to introduce order to exchanges, items were conventionally valued at amounts of copper or, for more precious objects, silver. The main measure was a weight called a *deben*, which could be divided into 10 *qites*. Exchange values varied over time, but by the Late period, when 10 copper debens equaled 1 of silver, 95 grams of silver per silver deben had become standard. These standards allowed Egyptians to assign a relative value to commodities. As a rough measure, a bushel of grain equaled one deben of copper. A small farm (perhaps an acre by modern measure) could be purchased for two or three debens of silver, which approximated the cost of an ox as well. A slave cost a little more. A pot of honey, an Egyptian treat, was valued at one qite of silver. Because the average Egyptian owned no silver at all and little copper, such valuations served more to indicate which exchanges were fair than to effect a transfer. These standards enabled a farmer to appraise his neighbor's land as being worth about one ox, or between 20 and 30 bushels of grain (Brier and Hobbs, 75–76).

FOR MORE INFORMATION

Brier, B., and H. Hobbs. *Daily Life of the Ancient Egyptians*. Westport, Conn.: Greenwood Press, 1999.

Montet, P. *Everyday Life in Egypt during the Days of Ramesses the Great*. Translated by A. R. Maxwell-Hyslop and M. Drower. Reprint, Philadelphia: University of Pennsylvania Press, 1981.

Trigger, B., B. J. Kemp, D. O'Connor, and A. B. Lloyd. *Ancient Egypt: A Social History*. New York: Cambridge University Press, 1983.

ECONOMIC LIFE

|

MONEY

|

Mesopotamia

Egypt

Greece

Rome

India

GREECE

Coinage first appeared in western Anatolia (modern Turkey) about 600 B.C.E. Legend also connects the origins of coinage with this region through Midas, the legendary king of Phrygia whose touch turned everything to gold. Prior to the invention of coinage, most transactions were conducted in kind. At the beginning of Homer's *Odyssey*, Athena in the guise of Mentes declares that she has a cargo of iron which she is going to exchange for bronze (1.182–84). This was no doubt how many exchanges continued to take place throughout antiquity.

The first kingdom to mint coins was Lydia, whose king's name, Croesus, has become a byword for wealth ("as rich as Croesus"). The earliest productions were made of electrum, an alloy of gold and silver found in the waters of the river Paktolos near the Lydian capital of Sardis. Later, the Lydians struck coins of pure gold and silver. Coinage was introduced to the Greek mainland in the first half of the sixth century B.C.E. The leader was the island of Aigina, which began minting silver coins circa 570 B.C.E. Aiginetan coins were stamped with a sea tortoise, the island's emblem, on the obverse (i.e., principal face of a coin). In time, all cities identified their coins by stamping them with an emblem. Corinthian coins are identified by the figure of Pegasus, the winged horse, whereas Athenian coins bear an owl, the symbol of Athena. In all, some 1,500 mints have been identified. A notable absentee is Sparta, which used iron spits known as obols as currency. These ranged from 12 to 18 inches in length. This cumbersome system seems to have been intentionally designed to discourage the flow of trade across its borders. Not until the third century B.C.E. did Sparta begin to mint coins. Arguably the most beautiful coins were minted by Syracuse and Akragas, two Sicilian cities. Their die cutters took such pride in their work that they even signed the dies.

Athens first began minting its famous owls during the Peisistratid tyranny. These coins were so named because they bore the image of an owl, the symbol of wisdom, on the reverse. On the obverse, they bore the helmeted head of the goddess Athena. Beside the head of Athena were written the letters ATHE, an abbreviation for the name of the city. The principal units of Athenian currency were the following:

6 obols = 1 drachma
100 drachmas = 1 mina
60 minas = 1 talent

Silver tetradrachma of Athens imprinted with owl logo. The owl was associated with the goddess Athena. Athenian coins were trusted for the purity of their silver. © The Art Archive/Jan Vinchon Numismatist Paris/Dagli Orti.

One drachma was the equivalent of a day's pay in the second half of the fifth century B.C.E. The commonest unit was the tetradrachm, or four-drachma piece.

To cope with the increasing complexity of financial transactions, money changers, known as *trapezitai*, set up tables in public places and operated a system based on letters of credit that anticipated the use of checks. In the Hellenistic period, Egypt developed a centralized banking system with numerous local branches and a head bank in Alexandria. In the same period, coins bearing the heads of rulers became common. Particularly noteworthy are those issued by Alexander the Great to pay his soldiers. These depict the king in the guise of Hercules wearing the skin of the Nemean lion. On the obverse, Zeus is seated on his throne. The coins of Alexander performed an important propagandist function. By illustrating the king's claim to be the descendant of Hercules, the son of Zeus, they reinforced the view that the Macedonians were genuine Greeks (Garland, 144–45).

FOR MORE INFORMATION

Garland, R. *Daily Life of the Ancient Greeks*. Westport, Conn.: Greenwood Press, 1998.
Jenkins, G. K. *Ancient Greek Coins*. 2nd rev. ed. London: Seaby, 1990.

ROME

At various times, the Romans used many different coin denominations, and the relative values of these denominations also changed over time. Three of the most

ECONOMIC LIFE
|
MONEY
|
Mesopotamia

Egypt

Greece

Rome

India

common coins were the silver denarius, the bronze sesterce, and the bronze as. Much rarer was the gold aureus. The following is a list of equivalents for these coins:

1 aureus = 25 denarii
1 denarius = 4 sesterces
1 sesterce = 4 asses

Sometimes very large sums were expressed using the Greek denomination of a talent. One talent was equivalent to approximately 6,000 denarii.

When writing about the Roman world, most historians express numbers in terms of sesterces, which they abbreviate as HS. It is difficult to meaningfully translate Roman amounts of money into comparable modern sums, but the annual salary of a Roman legionary was 900 HS, and the minimum wealth qualification to be a Roman senator was 1 million HS.

During the Republic, there were no standard designs for coins, although human beings were not supposed to be depicted on the coin. In the empire, most coins were minted with the head of the emperor in profile on one side, with his titles written around the head, and propagandistic symbols and slogans decorating the other side.

Because of the obvious space limitations, the Romans made great use of abbreviations on their coinage. Some of the most common abbreviations and slogans are listed here:

S C (SENATUS CONSULTUM) = By order of the senate
IMP (IMPERATOR) = Emperor
COS (CONSUL) = Has been elected consul
TRIB POT or **TR P** (TRIBUNICIA POTESTAS) = Holder of Tribunician power
F (FILIUS) = Son of
DIVI = divine
AUG (AUGUSTUS)
CAES (CAESAR)
PIUS = pious
PONT MAX (PONTIFEX MAXIMUS) = Chief priest
P P (PATER PATRIAE) = Father of the country
S P Q R (SENATUS POPULUSQUE ROMANUS) = The senate and people of Rome
-ICUS (added onto a geographical place) = Conqueror of that place

Sometimes Roman numerals appear on coins. These were used if someone had held an office more than once. For example, the inscription "COS II" on a coin means that the person had been elected to the consulship twice. These same abbreviations are often used in inscriptions carved in stone.

The Romans often did not put spaces between words or abbreviations, which can make coins or inscriptions hard to read. For example, a typical coin might have the following inscription:

IMPDIVIAUGNEROPONTMAXCOSIVPARTHICUS

This inscription can then be divided up as follows:

IMP DIVI AUG NERO PONT MAX COS IV PARTHICUS

Translated, this inscription means something like, "The emperor, the divine Augustus Nero, chief priest, elected consul four times, conqueror of Parthia."

~*Gregory S. Aldrete*

FOR MORE INFORMATION

Crawford, M. *Coinage and Money under the Roman Republic*. Berkeley: University of California Press, 1954.

Duncan-Jones, R. *Money and Government in the Roman Empire*. Cambridge, England: Cambridge University Press, 1994.

INDIA

Currency was introduced into Indian economies in the middle of the first millennium B.C.E. In the sixth century B.C.E., the first coins were minted in silver and bronze, although they were not inscribed. Inscribed coins came into circulation in the second century B.C.E., and gold coins were seen around this time as well. Occasionally, coins in other metals, such as copper, nickel, lead, and various alloys, were minted. Among the rural poor, cowry shells were often used as currency.

Many states did not mint or issue coins but instead used the coins of other states. It was not uncommon for coins foreign to India to be found in circulation, especially in northwestern India. For example, the Athenian drachma was in circulation before Alexander invaded the region. Other foreign coins in circulation were Achaemenid, Seleucid, Parthian, Sassanian, and Islamic. Roman coins were in circulation both in the northwest and in south India, arriving through sea trade.

Various texts enumerate the rules for money lending and usury. Manu's laws stipulated acceptable rates of interest based on distinctions of class, with lower rates for higher classes. For Brahmans, money was to be lent at 24 percent per annum; for Ksatriyas, 36 percent; for Vaisyas, 48 percent; and for Sudras, 60 percent per annum. Kautilya's *Arthasastra* mandated even steeper acceptable rates of interest, but the scale depended more on the nature of the venture in question. For normal commerce, the rate was to be 5 percent per month; to finance overland trade through forested regions the rate was to be 10 percent per month; and sea trade was to be 20 percent per month. These high rates of interest may reflect both the potential profitability in trade ventures and the risk inherent in trade from both natural calamities and thieves. Debtors who could not repay loans were imprisoned or forced to work off the debt, and occasionally they were sold into slavery.

Lending was often done through trade guilds—there were 18 guilds of artisans in ancient India. Some coins were issued by the guilds of merchants and goldsmiths with the permission of the ruler. The state might also lend money to local communities to finance public works projects, such as cultivating wilderness land or building irrigation systems. In this context, it is noteworthy that traditionally, many lay followers of the Jain religion were involved in banking. This is largely because strict adherence to the doctrine of *ahimsa*, nonviolence, precluded occupations such as farming that might harm living things.

ECONOMIC LIFE

|

MONEY

|

Mesopotamia

Egypt

Greece

Rome

India

Taxation on land was often fixed by the state, from one-sixth up to a quarter or even a third of all harvested crops. Numerous remissions from taxes were available, such as for newly cultivated land. Annual taxes in cash could also be assessed for various things; potters' wheels, weavers' looms, and oil presses are common examples. In southern India, household taxes were frequently imposed. In places where the natural economy prevailed over the monetary one, craftsmen were often expected to devote a day or two per month for the production of goods for the state. Those exempt from taxes were typically Brahmans, women, children, students, ascetics, and places of worship.

Taxation helped finance the army and maintain the state. In reality, taxation could be a crushing burden, especially on poorer, rural communities. Moreover, corruption was rampant at times, despite admonitions in the literature to treat taxation as a bee treats the flower whence it gets honey: that is, to profit, but not to harm the source of its prosperity. Sometimes it was of more benefit to the state to seek resources outside of itself, through warfare.

~Matthew Bingley

FOR MORE INFORMATION

Auboyer, J. *Daily Life in Ancient India*. London: Phoenix Press, 1965.
Basham, A. L. *The Wonder That Was India*. London: Sidgwick and Jackson, 1967.
Kenoyer, J. M. *Ancient Cities of the Indus Valley Civilization*. New York: Oxford University Press, 1998.

ECONOMIC LIFE
|
TRADE
|
Mesopotamia

Egypt

Greece

Rome

India

Nubia

Australian Aboriginals

Trade

The overwhelming majority of foodstuffs grown and goods produced in the ancient world were consumed or used very close to their site of production. Most items were sold by the growers or manufacturers themselves in their own neighborhoods or villages. The local marketplace was the center of most trade and transactions, and whatever goods were regionally available formed the entirety of most people's economic world.

While small regional markets did a lively trade in local commodities, true long-distance trade was a daunting proposition. Transporting anything in large quantities over land was both expensive and hazardous. Bulky cargo could be transported much easier by water, and it is no coincidence that most major cities grew up along the coast or on navigable rivers. However, seafaring technology was rudimentary, there was no effective way to predict storms at sea, and piracy was rampant, so there either had to be very strong motivation or very high profit margins to justify shipping goods across the sea.

Despite these hazards, there was a surprising amount of long-distance trade in the ancient world. While often dangerous to traverse, well-established trade routes existed in all these civilizations. Trade routes criss-crossed Australia and connected

Europe, Asia, and Africa. An important motivation for long-distance trade was the market for luxury goods. Although most people were poor, rulers, their courts, and the wealthy elites had a taste for exotic dyes, spices, cloths, and decorative items and created enough of a market to justify trade in these types of items. Even the earliest civilizations of Mesopotamia conducted a trade in luxury goods with distant regions like India, and these trade links remained established throughout the history of the ancient world. Trade played a particularly important role in the history of Nubia, which served as a gateway through which the luxury goods of Africa, such as ivory, reached the Mediterranean civilizations. Being the only people to travel regularly between such distant lands, traders sometimes doubled as diplomats or ambassadors, as was the case with the great Assyrian merchant families.

One specialized type of long-distance trade dealt not in luxuries but rather in the bulk transportation of basic items. Huge cities such as Athens and Rome were too large to be supported by local agriculture, and this led to large-scale industries collecting and transporting basic foodstuffs to these cities. Athens had a large fleet of grain freighters that kept the city fed, largely with grain grown around the Black Sea region, and Rome possessed an even larger supply infrastructure bringing grain and other foods from Egypt, North Africa, and Spain to the capital city. The journey of the annual grain fleet from Egypt was an important event at Rome, greeted with celebration when the ships were sighted on schedule, or trepidation and riots if they were late. These supply industries are special cases because they were not a free-market creation but rather were industries in which the state often took a direct and active role. Strictly speaking, some do not consider them real trade in a pure economic sense, but they are significant if for no other reason than the gigantic scale of their operation.

~*Gregory S. Aldrete*

MESOPOTAMIA

Trade refers to the exchange of all kinds of goods locally, between cities, and with other lands. Information about trade in Mesopotamia comes from business contracts, manifests of goods, trade letters, and references to trade of every kind in literary texts and official inscriptions. Objects from great distances have been excavated at various sites as well.

Industrial goods and goods produced by serfs or workshops in the temple or palace provided the means of exchange so that metal, stone, lumber, spices, and perfumes could be imported. Trade took place between foreign cities, trading outposts, and barbarian tribes who lacked the status, political power, and necessary initiative to take part in trade relations based on treaties. Foreign trade took place along the Persian Gulf and the Euphrates route into the Mediterranean littoral. Trade helped to raise the standard of living in Mesopotamia and spread the influence of Mesopotamian civilization.

Most needs of daily life were available locally: cereals, date palms, wild and domesticated animals for sustenance; animal hides, fur, or fleece for the manufacture

ECONOMIC LIFE

TRADE

Mesopotamia

Egypt

Greece

Rome

India

Nubia

Australian Aboriginals

of clothing; clay for producing pottery; soil and water for brick making; and basic woods and stone for construction were found throughout western Asia and North Africa.

Luxury items were important for maintaining the prestige and position of the royal palaces and temples. Because of the expense and risk involved in obtaining these rare materials, their acquisition remained almost exclusively the business of kings and queens, powerful governors, and wealthy temple estates.

Over the centuries, both raw materials and finished products came to Mesopotamia from various areas, such as lapis lazuli from the Badakhshan Province in Afghanistan, reaching Mesopotamia and Egypt through a complicated network of overland routes. But many commodities arrived by sea from East Africa, the Arabian peninsula, Iran, and the Indian subcontinent.

Under Sargon the Great (2334–2279 B.C.E.), the first major empire arose with its capital at Agade. Sargon first conquered all of what is now southern Iraq and then followed the old trade routes up the Euphrates to gain control of two major commercial centers, Mari on the middle Euphrates and Ebla in northern Syria, both cities that were important because of their strategic position on trade routes. Mari documents record the distribution of wine, the drink of the rich. Ebla was the center of metal trade in the third millennium B.C.E.

Sargon and his successors also pushed forward along the eastward trade routes in their expansionist efforts as far east as Elam (today, southwest Iran). Military coercion increased the flow of goods to the imperial center from areas firmly under control. But merchants not under Sargon's rule engaged in limited trade.

In the late second millennium B.C.E., the government tightly regulated international trade. A Hittite king (ca. thirteenth century B.C.E.) recorded the conditions under which merchants from Anatolia were permitted to trade inside Ugarit, a vassal kingdom in northern Syria. Complaints had been lodged that merchants were being given trade rights that posed a threat to the livelihood of the citizens of Ugarit. The Hittite overlord ruled that the merchants could operate in Ugarit during the summer but not during the winter. Furthermore, Anatolian merchants were not allowed to acquire rights of residence or even to buy houses or land there.

International trade continued in the Assyrian Empire, most often in the form of tribute such as ivory tusks, which arrived in Assyria at the end of the eighth century B.C.E., after Syrian elephants had become extinct and before Assyria controlled Egypt. At the end of the eighth century B.C.E., the Assyrians began to play a major role east of the Zagros and may have received all their lapis lazuli as tribute from tribes in what is now western Iran, who had received it by trade from farther east. A document recorded the receipt of 730 horses from merchants—clear evidence of trade, not tribute, because horses were important for military use.

Old Assyrian merchant colonies have been well documented in letters, accounts, and legal documents found at sites in Anatolia. These tablets have provided us with most of our information about Asia Minor at the beginning of the second millennium B.C.E. To date, no tablets have been found at Assur, their trade center. The merchants acted as middlemen in the export of textiles from Assur and the distribution of copper and tin within Asia Minor—a practical commercial venture because the animals could only carry a given weight. Each donkey carried a load of about 90 kilograms of textiles and tin, in addition to loose tin for expenses and taxes on the trip. When the merchants left Assur, they paid a tax of 1/120 of the value of the goods to the limmu official (an Assyrian official who gave his name to a year in the king's rule). To enter Kanesh, 2/65 of the value was paid to the local ruler. The cities and territories through which the caravans passed also received customs fees and duties at fixed rates. Occasional reports mention attacks on caravans.

The Assyrians lived outside the walled city of Kanesh in their own quarter, called the *karum,* originally meaning "quay" or "wharf," where canal traffic was unloaded and business transacted; later, *karum* referred to the association of merchants, a kind of trade board, and was applied in the heart of Anatolia where there was no river or harbor. A thousand-kilometer journey took approximately two months, including days of rest.

Standardized weight from Mesopotamia shaped in the form of a duck. This was a 10 mina weight, which is equivalent to about 14 pounds. © Yale Babylonian Collection, Yale University, New Haven.

Assyrian trade was run by family firms. The head of the family lived in Assur, and a junior member of the family would be the resident agent in the *karum* at Kanesh. The family capitalized these ventures, but sometimes partnerships were formed to raise the necessary capital. Although Kanesh was the trade center, there were nine other merchant colonies in Anatolia. These settlements were self-governing, but under the aegis of local princes to whom they paid taxes.

The traders were royal envoys as well, bringing valuable gifts from one ruler to the next. Treaties guaranteed their safety and limited their private entrepreneurial activities. The risks were great, and merchants were often attacked or murdered.

Temples and private persons advanced silver for commercial trade ventures. The merchants would repay the loan in commodities. The lender of the silver would expect to benefit by a favorable price for the commodities at the time of repayment, or by the payment of interest, or both.

The stability of the Persian period led to the accumulation of wealth from the revenues of lands, houses, and slaves; this revenue was invested in financial and commercial operations recorded in numerous cuneiform contracts, usually found in private archives.

Private archives show that a large sector of the population was involved in financial and commercial operations, which were often restricted to where the lenders lived. Commerce was based on a silver standard, whether for borrowing within the family or between neighbors. Some transactions put businessmen within the realm of political power or international commerce. Two archives show a wider range of transactions: those of the Egibi family, which operated throughout Babylonia and sometimes even in Iran, and that of the Murashu family of Nippur in central Babylonia, which dominated that entire region. The field of international commerce was dominated by non-Babylonian merchants.

Commercial and financial operations were modeled on promissory notes. In this type of document, the object of the transaction (precious metal or agricultural produce) was listed, then the names of the lender and the borrower; the duration of the loan; methods of reimbursement, establishing the interest to be collected; and collateral to be held by the lender. The contract ended with a list of witnesses, the scribe, the place, and the date. When the borrower repaid his debt, the promissory-note tablet was returned to him by the creditor and usually broken to mark cancellation of the debt. If the creditor kept the tablet, he provided the debtor with a quitclaim or certificate of payment.

In general, contracts were drafted according to a formal model, from which the scribes could adapt the contracts to fit a variety of situations because of their knowledge of the terminology of "commercial law." Some promissory notes included a clause specifying the purpose of the transaction, "for a commercial expedition." In these capital ventures, two to five people pooled their resources to invest a certain amount of capital, depending on their respective assets. The capital was turned over to an entrepreneur to carry out commercial transactions and make a profit that would be divided pro rata, according to the initial individual investments, or according to a fixed sum paid in advance plus a bonus from surplus profits. The same format was followed in drawing up partnership contracts for commercial purposes (Nemet-Nejat, 265–67, 269–71, 279–82).

FOR MORE INFORMATION

Nemet-Nejat, K. R. *Daily Life in Ancient Mesopotamia*. Westport, Conn.: Greenwood Press, 1998.

Postgate, J. N. *Early Mesopotamia: Society and Economy at the Dawn of History*. New York: Routledge, 1992.

ECONOMIC LIFE

TRADE

Mesopotamia

Egypt

Greece

Rome

India

Nubia

Australian Aboriginals

EGYPT

A portion of the populace in Egypt earned their living as independent business-people, working on their own by bartering for needed materials without the intervention of a patron. Because the number of such independent workers is difficult to estimate—no census was taken in Egypt, and this group would not be included in lists of temple or estate employees—we can only refer to scenes depicting what look like modern Middle Eastern marketplaces filled with single individuals offering various goods for sale. It may be that every village of some size contained a number of independent workers selling in a central location. Still, given that wealthy patrons were supplied by their own workshops and that nonwealthy clients had little disposable surplus to barter, living must have been precarious for such people. It is even probable that the majority of those shown in market scenes, rather than being individual businesspeople, had been sent by large estates to dispose of surpluses.

International trade was also under government control, and all brokers of commerce between countries were state employees. (Travel outside the borders of Egypt was all but unheard of for ordinary citizens.) The reason for the monopoly was that supplies of certain foreign commodities, such as copper, tin, and tall timber, was so necessary to the Egyptian economy that their acquisition could not be left to private initiative. Moreover, the greater the government control of foreign trade, the more it could be used, backed by the might of the Egyptian army, as an instrument of politics to favor friendly foreign governments and punish others (Brier and Hobbs, 86).

FOR MORE INFORMATION

Brier, B., and H. Hobbs. *Daily Life of the Ancient Egyptians*. Westport, Conn.: Greenwood Press, 1999.

Trigger, B., B. J. Kemp, D. O'Connor, and A. B. Lloyd. *Ancient Egypt: A Social History*. Cambridge, England: Cambridge University Press, 1983.

GREECE

ECONOMIC LIFE
|
TRADE
|
Mesopotamia

Egypt

Greece

Rome

India

Nubia

Australian Aboriginals

The Greeks did not have a concept of economics in the modern sense of the word. There is no evidence to suggest that their behavior was determined by economic considerations of the kind that influence modern nation-states. More fundamentally, they did not regard the economy as an autonomous category over which the state might exercise control. There was no such thing as a budget. Except in extreme circumstances, it is doubtful whether they had any way of determining what we would call today the health of their economy.

So far as there was anything resembling economic policy, it was generally limited to the supply of necessities. Clearly, prices fluctuated according to the law of supply and demand, and clearly as well, these fluctuations affected the standard of living. The Peloponnesian War had a profound effect on wealthy and poor Athenians alike, as a result of the devastation of the countryside by the enemy and the heavy burden of taxation. Similarly, at the end of the Social War in 355 B.C.E., Athens was practically bankrupt. Its need to recoup its losses is evident in the subsequent reluctance of its citizens to engage in hostilities. Because Greeks, unlike ourselves, had no expectation that their standard of living would increase over the course of their lifetime, they were doubtless more accepting of this eventuality than we would be.

From the middle of the fifth century B.C.E. onward, Athens was dependent on imported grain, most of which came from the Black Sea area, particularly the Bosphorus. Other major sources of supply included Egypt, Libya, Cyprus, Sicily, and Italy. This dependency was a leading factor in Athens's decision to develop the Piraeus, which became the foremost commercial port in the eastern Mediterranean. So vital was grain to Athens's survival that the demos made it a capital offense to ship it to ports other than the Piraeus. It was also illegal to extend a maritime loan other than to a merchant who agreed to convey grain to the Piraeus. In the high season, a minimum of six grain ships had to dock at the port each day to meet Athens's huge requirement.

Athens also had to import virtually all shipbuilding supplies. These included timber, sailcloth, and ruddle, which was used for the painting of triremes. The chief supplier of timber was Macedon, supplemented by Thrace and southern Italy. Athens also imported slaves, particularly from Thrace, the Black Sea region, and Asia Minor. In the fourth century B.C.E., Athens needed to import approximately 6,000 slaves per annum to maintain its force at full strength. Other imports included tin, iron, and copper.

Athens's essential imports were not the only ones. Pericles boasted with justification that "all the produce of every land comes to Athens" (Thucydides, *The Peloponnesian War* 2.38). An impressive list of the exotic commodities for sale in Athenian markets is provided by a comic writer called Hermippos in a play dated circa 420 B.C.E. It includes silphion (a plant used in medicine or as a condiment) and ox hides from Cyrene in Libya; mackerel and salt fish from the Hellespont; pork and cheese from Syracuse; sailcloth, rigging, and papyrus from Egypt; cypress wood from Crete; ivory from Libya; raisins and dried figs from Rhodes; pears and apples from Euboia; slaves from Phrygia; mercenaries from Arcadia; tattooed and untattooed slaves from Pagasai; acorns and almonds from Paphlagonia; dates and wheat flour from Phoenicia; and finally, rugs and cushions from Carthage.

The most valuable Athenian export was silver. Other exports included olives, olive oil, wine, marble, and honey. The only manufactured goods that were exported were pottery and armor. Athens was fortunate in possessing rich deposits of silver. The mines were located at Lavrion in southeast Attica. Mining concessions were auctioned off annually by state officials to private individuals. They were purchased by both indigent and wealthy lessees. Each successful bidder was free to extract as much silver from his concession as he could for the duration of his lease. The monies accruing to the Athenian state from silver mines were considerable. A strike made in 483 B.C.E. yielded a revenue of 100 talents. On the recommendation of Themistocles, this sum was devoted to the building of a fleet of 100 triremes, or warships. When mining activity reached its peak in the middle of the fourth century B.C.E., production stood at about 1,000 talents per year. Mining was very much subject to external pressures, and in time of war it was sometimes suspended altogether.

Although the Athenians were incapable of planning an economic strategy, they did possess a public exchequer. In Thucydides Pericles informs them on the eve of the outbreak of the Peloponnesian War that the state possessed 6,000 talents of coined silver, stored for safekeeping on the Acropolis (*The Peloponnesian War* 2.13.3–6). In addition, the gold that covered the statue of Athena Parthenos was worth 40 talents. This, he suggests, could be melted down and used in the war effort, so long as it was replaced afterward. It became commonplace in the following century to plunder temple treasures to finance war efforts. Those that suffered the most included the sanctuaries at Delphi and Olympia.

The acquisition of a maritime empire greatly increased Athens's wealth. Although ostensibly the tribute exacted from the allies financed their fleet, the Athenians were in no doubt that they were the beneficiaries of an imperialist enterprise. This is evident from their custom of parading their tribute in the theater of Dionysos at the City Dionysia. In Aristophanes' *Knights*, a character called Demos, who is an unflattering personification of the Athenian people, dotes idiotically on a diet of tribute, flattery, gifts, feasts, and festivals.

Lower- and middle-income Athenians did not pay taxes. Only the wealthy were required to make a contribution to the state. The first instance of direct taxation occurred during the Peloponnesian War, when the state exacted a special levy called an *eisphora*, or "contribution," to meet the cost of soldiers' pay. In the fourth century B.C.E., the 300 wealthiest citizens were required to pay an annual *eisphora*. Wealthy Athenians were also required to subsidize important and costly public programs called liturgies. Those selected to be *gymnasiarchs* had to bear the cost of maintaining a public gymnasium, whereas *chorêgoi* had to pay all the expenses involved in training the chorus for a tragic or comic production. The largest group of all, the trierarchs, had the burden of equipping and maintaining a trireme. No fixed sum of money was laid down for any of these duties because it was confidently expected that *gymnasiarchs*, *chorêgoi*, and trierarchs would compete with one another for the reputation of financing the best gymnasium, the best production, or the best trireme. It is unclear how Athenians in this supertax bracket were identified. As a safeguard against abuse, however, any Athenian who was called on to perform a liturgy and who believed that he had been wrongly identified had the right to issue a challenge to any other Athenian whom he considered to be wealthier than himself. The person so challenged was then under an obligation either to undertake the liturgy himself or to swap properties with the person who had challenged him.

Greeks tended to be either wealthy or poor. There is little evidence for the existence of a middle class. Inevitably, we hear most about the wealthy. The aristocrat Alcibiades led a life of decadence, frittering away his fortune on the training of expensive race horses. As today, there was a sort of lurid interest in his antics on the part of his fellow citizens. Most Athenians, however, lived lives of bare subsistence.

Lower- and middle-income Athenians did not pay taxes.

Most manufacturing enterprises were extremely small. The largest Athenian *ergastêrion* or workshop of which we have a record belonged to Cephalus, a metic who employed 120 slaves in his shield factory. The father of Demosthenes employed over 50 slaves in his knife factory. The majority of enterprises were probably much smaller. It is estimated that Athens's entire force of potters in the fifth century B.C.E. numbered no more than 500, most of whom worked in groups of about six.

Specific cities specialized in the production of specific products. Athens was noted for its painted pottery, Corinth for metalwork, and Megara for cloaks. Most citizens whose livelihood derived from manufactured goods were content to leave their businesses in the hands of trusted slaves, rather than devote the time and energy to expanding them themselves. Many more products were produced in the home than is the case today. Spinning, weaving, and baking were done almost exclusively by women.

The evidence for retailing is very meager. Most establishments took the form of temporary booths set up in the marketplace on specific days each month, since the retailer was in many cases the producer or manufacturer. Only a few permanent establishments have come to light. A notable example is a shoe shop in the Athenian Agora, which was identified by the discovery of leather thongs for sandals and boots, bone eyelets, and hobnails among its ruins. Although Athens and the Piraeus were the principal markets for the exchange of imported goods, each deme possessed its own agora.

With so much surplus wealth in the Athenian economy in the second half of the fifth century as a result of the empire, one might expect that the standard of living would have risen. Archaeological evidence, however, suggests no such thing. As previously noted, the residential quarters of Athens were extremely modest. Evidently, the attainment of private wealth was not seen as a necessary goal. If it had been, the Athenians would not have spent 2,000 talents on one of the most ambitious building programs ever conceived. In sum, although a few wealthy citizens became more wealthy, most of the poor tended to remain poor. What Athens's increased wealth did provide, however, was the means whereby a majority of its citizens could combine leisure with frugality (Garland, 143–49).

FOR MORE INFORMATION

Garland, R. *Daily Life of the Ancient Greeks*. Westport, Conn.: Greenwood Press, 1998.
Hasebroek, J. *Trade and Politics in Ancient Greece*. London: G. Bell, 1933.
Hopper, R. J. *Trade and Industry in Ancient Greece*. London: Thames and Hudson, 1979.

ECONOMIC LIFE

|

TRADE

|

Mesopotamia

Egypt

Greece

Rome

India

Nubia

Australian Aboriginals

ROME

One of the most lucrative businesses in Rome, in which one could make fantastic profits, was the long-distance trade of luxury goods transported by ship. A single shipload of spices, fabrics, or dyes from the East could make one a millionaire overnight. Building a merchant ship and buying its cargo required substantial capital up front, and it was also an extremely risky investment. The seas swarmed with pirates, and because there was no way to predict the weather, many ships were lost in storms at sea. These dangers were so common that perhaps only two out of every three ships made it back from a voyage.

The only people to have the capital necessary to outfit and equip such a ship and to be able to survive the loss if it did not return were the very wealthy. The huge profits possible tempted many aristocrats into backing such expeditions. This sort of activity was dangerously close, in the Romans' eyes, to engaging in vulgar commerce, and the Senate became concerned that too many aristocrats were debasing themselves with merchant ships. This led to a law called the *Lex Claudia*, which was passed in the first century c.e. This law made it illegal for a senator or the son of a senator to own a large merchant ship. To get around this law, aristocrats took advantage of the patron-client system. For example, an aristocrat might free one of his slaves and then provide him with the capital to outfit a ship. Thus the freedman would technically be the owner, but the profits would be funneled back to the patron. Thus Roman aristocrats maintained an ideology in which they were all idle and did not dirty their hands with commerce, while at the same time they were getting rich off of commercial activity.

Keeping Rome's enormous population fed created a substantial industry dedicated to the collection and shipping of food to the city. Much of the surplus food grown in the empire, and especially

Mosaic of a ship from Rome's port of Ostia. Contents such as wine or olive oil were unloaded at Ostia and transferred to riverboats, which carried them upriver to Rome. © The Art Archive/Dagli Orti.

in Egypt, Sicily, southern Spain, and Gaul, was gathered up and sent to feed the capital city.

It is estimated that each person in ancient Rome probably consumed 237 kilograms of wheat, 20 liters of olive oil, and 100 liters of wine per year. Multiplied by a million inhabitants, this resulted in 237,000 tons of wheat and 120,000 tons of oil and wine. Because liquids were transported in large clay pots, this meant adding another 70,000 tons for the weight of the containers. The result means that more than 400,000 tons of food had to be imported each year to feed the city of Rome. Nearly all of this was shipped by sea and arrived at the port of Ostia located at the mouth of the Tiber River. Rome is situated about 25 miles upriver from Ostia. When you factor in all the other items brought to Rome in large quantity, such as timber, stone, wild animals, luxury goods, oil for use in heating, cooking, and in the baths, and all the other things consumed by the city, it becomes apparent that there was a huge shipping and transportation industry serving Rome's needs.

At Ostia, there is a large square in the middle of the city where dozens of small rooms surround a colonnade. In front of all of these rooms are mosaics, and this is thought to be the site where all the shipping companies had their offices. This is called the Piazza of the Corporations. The different mosaics indicate what that shipping company imported. Some mosaics show sheaves of grain; others show jars of wine. There are a number that show animals such as elephants and camels, and these are perhaps the offices of the companies that supplied the amphitheater with the animals used in beast hunts. The importation of wild beasts from Africa was a big business, and the Romans had specialized animal-carrying ships to bring in all the beasts demanded by the games.

Long-distance trade thrived during the Roman Empire, and Rome even had trade links dealing in very expensive commodities such as rare spices to far-off empires, including India.

~*Gregory S. Aldrete*

FOR MORE INFORMATION

Charlesworth, M. P. *Trade-Routes and Commerce of the Roman Empire*. 2nd ed. Chicago, Ill.: Ares Publishers, 1974.

D'Arms, J. *Commerce and Social Standing in Ancient Rome*. Boston, Mass.: Harvard University Press, 1981.

Garnsey, P., K. Hopkins, and C. R. Whittaker, eds. *Trade in the Ancient Economy*. Berkeley: University of California Press, 1983.

ECONOMIC LIFE
|
TRADE
|
Mesopotamia

Egypt

Greece

Rome

India

Nubia

Australian Aboriginals

INDIA

A variety of goods with exquisite workmanship was produced in India. Spices were highly valued outside of India, as were perfumes, jewelry, and textiles. Fine, semitransparent silks and muslins made their way as far abroad as the Roman Empire. Indian iron was also valued highly for its purity and hardness.

Trade routes permitted overland caravans to transport these goods. From Ujjayini in north-central India, a route went south and then east to Kanci and into Tamil Nadu in the south. In the north, trade routes passed from Delhi through the Panjab to Taksasila, and from there into Central Asia. Roads were frequently poorly maintained, largely because of the harsh nature of the Indian climate, especially the annual monsoon rains. Rivers provided important arteries for trade throughout India as well. By sea, ancient travelers had contact with Sri Lanka, certainly, as well as Malaysia and Indonesia to the east. To the west, it is possible that Indian sailors had visited ports in the Middle East and the eastern coast of Africa; more likely, ships from ports in these regions made their way to India for Indian goods.

Despite the emphasis on rural life in India, larger economic organizations did exist. In towns and cities were guilds in various professions. Guilds frequently had their own administration, meting out justice to members in the form of expulsion. This would effectively prevent a person from working and from earning a living. Guilds also had a social function, taking care of orphans and widows of members and making donations to religious institutions. In an interesting twist on the theme of professional life, some places also had guilds of thieves.

While the guilds frequently functioned as a corporate body within their spheres of specialization, large businesses owned by individual entrepreneurs were relatively rare. More common were warehouses and factories, owned or at least supported by the state, for mass production of important goods such as those that would be needed to equip armies.

~Matthew Bingley

FOR MORE INFORMATION

Allchin, B., and R. Allchin. *The Rise of Civilization in India and Pakistan.* Cambridge, England: Cambridge University Press, 1982.

Auboyer, J. *Daily Life in Ancient India.* London: Phoenix Press, 1965.

Basham, A. L. *The Wonder That Was India.* London: Sidgwick and Jackson, 1967.

Kenoyer, J. M. *Ancient Cities of the Indus Valley Civilization.* New York: Oxford University Press, 1998.

NUBIA

ECONOMIC LIFE

TRADE

Mesopotamia

Egypt

Greece

Rome

India

Nubia

Australian Aboriginals

The history of Nubia is inextricably linked to trade because the Nubian lands served as conduits through which the luxury goods of Africa were funneled into Egypt for wider distribution. At times, the Nubians controlled the trade routes and the products passing through their hands, while at other times the Egyptians established trading stations and military fortifications with a view toward gaining more independent control of those routes and the products passing over them. As a result, the products of Africa were bartered by the Nubians for Egyptian products, articles, or other goods not readily available in Nubia. Barter was the standard practice; currency as a medium of exchange in the modern sense was rare and is attested only in the very late periods. Conversely, these same African commodities might have arrived in Egypt as tribute, borne by Nubians when their lands were under the hegemony of pharaoh.

The mechanisms of this pattern for either barter or tribute can be studied by examining Egypto-Nubian mercantile relationships in the epochs between the Neolithic period and the close of the Nubian A-Group culture (ca. 10,000–2800 B.C.E.). As early as the Neolithic period, the Nubians, as seen from their grave goods, were buried with articles made of, among other materials, ivory, shells of marine creatures indigenous to the Red Sea, and minerals that came from mountain ranges ringing the narrow valley of the Nile River. The presence of these luxury materials in elite Nubian graves is the clearest indication that the Nubians, even at this remote period in their history, were not only aware of the richness of Africa's natural resources but also had developed mechanisms for their procurement and manufacture into finished products. In time, these products were brought to the attention of their Egyptian neighbors to the north. As the elite oligarchies of Nubians of the A-Group culture initially consolidated their positions of power and authority, they gradually gained control over the trade routes and enjoyed a peaceful exchange of goods with

Egypt. In the end, the Egyptians sought to control these same trade routes and achieved their objective via a series of military conquests that contributed to the collapse of the A-Group culture of the Nubians. The subsequent history of Egypto-Nubian relationships is dominated by this pendulum of control, swinging at times in favor of the Egyptians and at other times in favor of the Nubians.

The official records of the Egyptians of the Old Kingdom (ca. 2613–2160 B.C.E.) contain references to Egyptian mercantile activity in Nubia. Pharaoh Sneferu of the Fourth Dynasty launched a military campaign that resulted in the capture of 7,000 Nubian prisoners, and Harkuf, an expedition leader, brought back a live pigmy to the delight of Pharaoh Pepy II of the Sixth Dynasty. During this period, the Egyptians pioneered the establishment of multipurpose settlements in Nubian territory to further Egyptian mercantile, mining, security, and other interests.

As the Egyptian pharaohs of the 12th Dynasty secured their positions, they turned their attention to Nubia and fostered the erection of enormous fortresses, often on the sites of their earlier Old Kingdom settlements.

Egyptian control of Nubia collapsed with the close of the Middle Kingdom for reasons linked to the gradual unification of Nubia by the rulers of the Kerma culture (ca. 2500–1500 B.C.E.). The archaeological record suggests that the Egyptian Middle Kingdom fortresses were attacked, stormed, and captured by the Nubians of the Kerma culture, who, in the end, established themselves as the exclusive rulers from the second to the fourth cataracts of the Nile River. Excavations at Kerma, and particularly of a massive mud-brick structure termed the Western *defuffa*, are instructive. This *defuffa* served as a temple complex replete with store rooms in which commodities for trade were kept and both native and imported materials were crafted as finished products. A study of this evidence suggests that the mercantile interests of the Nubians extended to the Syria-Palestine coastal regions and may have included contact with the emerging cultures on the islands of the Aegean and mainland Greece.

The rise of the Egyptian New Kingdom in the sixteenth century B.C.E. witnessed a series of military campaigns by the Egyptians against the Nubians and the concomitant fall of the kingdom of Kerma. For the next millennium, Egyptian interests and presence in Nubia became progressively stronger until the material culture of Nubia's elite became indistinguishable from that of contemporary Egyptian aristocrats. This period was punctuated by a series of punitive military campaigns waged against various Nubian enclaves to ensure the Egypto-Nubian status quo by which the riches of Africa came to Egypt as tribute. Numerous scenes from tombs and temples of New Kingdom Egypt record the bearing of elephant tusks, gold, skins of exotic animals, simians, giraffes, big cats, long-horned cattle, and the like. Many of these products were also obtained by the Egyptians from Punt, the location of which remains problematic but which may have been located at the horn of Africa in the vicinity of the modern nation-state of Somalia.

During the course of the early first millennium B.C.E., the Nubians again consolidated their realm and, during the reign of the Nubian pharaoh Piankhy of the 25th Dynasty (ca. 747–716 B.C.E.), established undisputed control over Egypt, thus ensuring Nubian control of the products of Africa and their ultimate distribution.

The collapse of the Nubian 25th Dynasty as a result of Assyrian invasions reestablished Egyptians as pharaohs, but their attention was focused first on the Near East, and then on the emerging powers of Macedonian Greece and Rome. Occasionally, military campaigns of a punitive nature, on the model of those waged during the New Kingdom, are attested, but by and large a condominium was established whereby the Nubians continued to serve as independent middlemen bartering African goods in exchange for other commodities with the Egyptians. Confirmation of the peaceful coexistence between the two regions comes from the observation that Nectanebo II of the 30th Dynasty sought a safe haven in Nubia when he fled in the wake of the Persian invasion of his realm. Later, Macedonian Greek pharaohs of Egypt during the Ptolemaic period often collaborated with their Nubian counterparts on the erection and decoration of Egyptian, pharaonic style temples in Lower Nubia. Scholars are still divided in their opinion about whether the Nubians were complicit in the revolt led by the Upper Egyptian city of Thebes in the second half of the Ptolemaic period.

The annexation of Egypt by the Roman emperor Augustus in the late first century B.C.E., following his defeat of Cleopatra VII and her suicide, established the frontier at Aswan and reaffirmed the agreement between Rome and the Nubian kingdom of Meroe. Classical sources record at least one expedition, launched during the reign of the Roman emperor Nero, to find the source of the Nile. Such an expedition could scarcely have been possible without the full support and resources of the Meroites. Articles of purely Classical manufacture and origin have been excavated at Meroitic sites, and the baths at Meroe were even appointed with sculptures approximating Classical norms. As late as the early fourth century C.E., elite members of the Nubian Meroites were still gifting Roman emperors with the riches of Africa.

Disjunctions within the Roman Empire proper, assaults on Meroitic settlements by wandering tribes identified as the Blemmyes, and the ultimate decision of the Roman emperor Diocletian in 298 to withdraw military protection accelerated the fall of the Meroitic Kingdom.

~*Robert S. Bianchi*

FOR MORE INFORMATION

Adams, W. *Nubia: Corridor to Africa*. Princeton, N.J.: Princeton University Press, 1977.

O'Connor, D. *Ancient Nubia: Egypt's Rival in Africa*. Philadelphia: University of Pennsylvania, 1993.

Trigger, B. *Nubia under the Pharaohs*. Boulder, Colo.: Westview Press, 1976.

Welsby, Derek A. *The Kingdom of Kush: The Napatan and Meroitic Empires*. London: British Museum Press, 1996.

AUSTRALIAN ABORIGINALS

Australian Aboriginals engaged in trade every day. These exchanges might be as simple as hunters within a small group swapping the results of one man's successful

ECONOMIC LIFE

|

TRADE

|

Mesopotamia

Egypt

Greece

Rome

India

Nubia

Australian Aboriginals

hunt one day for the results of someone else's successful hunt another day, or as complex as the trade that saw valuable items, both natural and manufactured, carried on heads across the north of Australia or even across the whole continent from north to south. Canoes rowed down both sides of Cape York from New Guinea and the Torres Strait, and ships arrived from Indonesia with trade goods for northern Australia in return for fishing rights. Trade also occurred at great ceremonial meetings, to which people traveled hundreds of kilometers and at which a wide range of goods, including food and weapons, were exchanged. Through such meetings, materials such as high-quality stone and ochre were distributed many hundreds of kilometers from the mines where they were quarried.

The variety and uneven distribution of resources in Australia probably encouraged trading from earliest times. Tasmania would originally have been part of trading routes into Victoria, but with the rising of seas at the end of the Ice Age, it was separated from the mainland. From that time (about 10,000 years ago) onward, Tasmania had its own system of trade within the island. Among the many goods known to have been traded were skins, ochre, drugs (native tobaccos and pituri), "blanks" (roughly quarried pieces of stone for making axe or spear heads), spear shafts, and pearl and other valued shells, either decorated or undecorated.

The lack of pack animals and wheeled vehicles in Australia meant that all trade, except that which used canoes in Cape York, involved people carrying goods over long distances. In the case of the great trade routes, however, individual people would not have traversed the entire distance from northern to southern Australia; rather, goods would have been traded along a chain from group to group. Given the harshness and unpredictability of the Australian climate in much of the center of the continent, trading over long distances could only be accomplished where people had an encyclopedic knowledge of water resources. This knowledge was maintained in songs and stories of the travels of ancestors, as well as in paintings. There were well-worn tracks across Aboriginal Australia, where innumerable pairs of feet had followed the trade routes for thousands of years. Travel across the territory of neighboring groups and beyond involved obtaining permission in formal ceremonies and probably also a sharing of roles in the trading process.

In addition to the value of the actual goods that trade contributed to the economies of participating groups, trade in ideas, technology, and artistic methods occurred. Perhaps religious concepts and the stories of the Dreamtime ancestors, as well as news of conditions and unusual (or usual) events in other regions, were as important as the goods themselves. Also significant was the exchange of genes when people from different groups married and the development of continentwide chains of interconnectedness through such marriages and through the reciprocity of the trading cycles.

In a country as difficult for hunter-gatherers as Australia, the ability to rely on other groups in hard times was of vital importance, as was the rapid diffusion of useful inventions across Australia. Such movements of people, goods, and ideas served to maintain the Aboriginality of the whole of Australia, so that while the diversity of people from different regions was important, maintaining a recognizable common social and cultural heritage across Australia was also a significant and valuable outcome of trade.

~David Horton

FOR MORE INFORMATION

Berndt, R., and C. Berndt. *The World of the First Australians*. Canberra: Aboriginal Studies Press, 1988.

McBryde, I. "Kulin Greenstone Quarries: The Social Contexts of Production and Distribution for the Mt. William Site." *World Archaeology* 16 (1984): 267–85.

McCarthy, F. "Trade in Aboriginal Australia." *Oceania* 9 (1939): 405–38; 10 (1939): 80–104; 10 (1939): 171–95.

Mulvaney, D. J., and P. White. *Australians to 1788*. Broadway, New South Wales: Fairfax, Syme, and Weldon, 1987.

Travel and Transportation

ECONOMIC LIFE
|
TRAVEL
& TRANSPORTATION
|
Mesopotamia

Egypt

Greece

Rome

Australian Aboriginals

Transportation is one of the areas in which there have been dramatic technological improvements since the ancient world. In an era when one can fly from one side of the globe to another in a matter of hours, or communicate instantaneously between any two points, it is difficult to imagine a world in which most people probably never ventured more than a few miles from their place of birth, or in which simply sending a message and receiving a reply might require the greater part of a year.

Travel by land occurred mostly on foot and was a slow process in which 20 miles per day was probably an exceptionally rapid pace. Goods could be transported by pack animal or wagon and would have moved even more slowly. There are examples of powerful centralized empires, such as the Assyrians, establishing comparatively swift messenger services for particularly important official mail, but such organizations and their rates of travel were very much the exception rather than the rule. Because of the high expense of land transport, it was profitable to transport only the most valuable goods for long distances.

Some ancient civilizations made valiant attempts to facilitate land transport. The Roman system of roads that connected the capital with the provinces was an impressive feat of engineering constructed with the best available techniques. Major Roman roads such as the famous Appian Way had deep foundations, careful grading, and smooth paving and were built so well that many remained in use up until modern times. No matter how fine the road, however, nothing could be done to substantially alter the limitations inherent in the basic equation of transportation speed and cost.

Travel and transportation by water were much more efficient than land transport in terms of expense and the weight and bulk of cargoes that could be moved long distances. Water-borne transport played a vital role in the development of civilizations, and it is no coincidence that nearly all major cities were located on the coast or on navigable rivers. From the Tigris and the Euphrates to the Nile and the Tiber, rivers were the highways of the ancient world. Again, however, nautical technology imposed severe limitations. Ships could not sail very close into the wind and so were at the mercy of favorable prevailing wind patterns, or else they had to rely on labor-intensive and expensive rowing. Navigational tools were minimal, so most ships never left sight of land except on the most well-established trade routes. Ships were highly vulnerable to storms, and because there was no real means of forecasting them, during stormy seasons such as the winter, all ship traffic in the Mediterranean Sea essentially came to a halt.

Finally, the countryside and the seas were usually infested with bandits and pirates, so that merchants and travelers risked their lives whenever they ventured away from home. Given the many limitations upon and hazards of ancient travel, perhaps the most surprising fact is that so much travel actually went on. Although most people may not have traveled very far, in all civilizations a substantial minority braved the uncertainties and difficulties of travel to conduct business, or simply to see what lay over the horizon.

~*Gregory S. Aldrete*

ECONOMIC LIFE
|
TRAVEL
& TRANSPORTATION
|
Mesopotamia

Egypt

Greece

Rome

Australian Aboriginals

MESOPOTAMIA

In ancient Mesopotamia, the most efficient way of transporting goods was by water, since most places in Mesopotamia could be reached by the Tigris and the Euphrates Rivers and through their network of rivers and canals. Ships sailed down the Persian Gulf and on the Mediterranean, and the Phoenicians may even have circumnavigated Africa. Local regions developed their own types of river craft, but seagoing ships were influenced by the fleets of the Levantine coast and, perhaps, the Aegean. When water transportation was not possible, human porters and draft animals such as donkeys and mules were used.

Wheeled vehicles were known in the ancient Near East from approximately 3500 B.C.E. However, the muddy conditions of the alluvial plains made sledges more practical. In the Royal Cemetery of Ur, a sledge was drawn by a pair of cattle in Queen Puabi's tomb. Sledges transported heavy loads such as the enormous stone winged-bull colossi of Assyrian palaces. The colossi, which weighed as much as 20 tons, were also moved on rollers using poles as levers, as depicted on a bas-relief. Local trips were usually made in carts with solid wooden wheels, which are still used in the Near East today.

The roads of the ancient Near East were generally unpaved, but they had to be staked out, leveled, and—in the case of those intended for wheeled transport—kept in good repair by the local authorities. The well-traveled connections had to be kept passable during the rainy season, at least for the movement of troops. Small rivulets and shallow rivers were bridged whenever possible, and larger rivers were crossed at fords or on ferryboats. The Assyrians even built pontoon bridges. Wooden bridges over raging streams and gorges had to be rebuilt constantly because of frequent destruction by floods; these bridges were supplemented by those of lighter construction meant only for pedestrians and pack animals. According to the texts, permanent bridges were built across the Euphrates in some Babylonian cities early in the second millennium B.C.E. Stone bridges were built in Babylon and Nineveh after 700 B.C.E.

There were a few great roads between important centers, but they were not roads in the modern sense—usually only tracks caused by traffic. For example, in the desert, the firmness of the soil was used to create roads, but elsewhere tracks twisted and turned to circumvent obstacles such as marshes. When the original surface had completely deteriorated through wear and tear, a new path was usually created next to the old one. In the mountains, building roads meant cutting through obstacles and shoring up other parts whenever possible. The earliest roads were probably built by the Urartians circa 800 B.C.E.

Itineraries from royal archives, such as the map of Nippur and, perhaps, the world map, or *mappa mundi,* were usually for military use. Texts refer to the same routes used for centuries for transportation of goods, the movement of troops, and the journeys of merchants or diplomatic envoys, who were often the same person. The Akkadian term for these agents conveys the wide range of activities they undertook; the Akkadian word could be translated "messenger," "envoy," "ambassador," "diplomat," "deputy," and even "merchant," depending on circumstances and contexts. Messengers and diplomats traveled by a variety of means: running on foot, on wagons or chariots pulled by asses, donkeys, or horses, and on riverboats.

Syro-Palestinian routes were longitudinal or transverse, varying in length and playing a major role in international trade because of their location between Anatolia to the north, Upper Mesopotamia to the east, Babylonia to the southeast, Arabia to the south, Egypt to the southwest, and the islands and coasts of the Mediterranean Sea to the west. Syria also imported raw materials and other goods from neighboring regions and exported its own products—timber, wool, olive oil, wine, dyed textiles, and artistic artifacts. The Neo-Assyrian Empire (ninth–seventh centuries B.C.E.) did little to improve the roads it inherited in conquered territories. A few roads were even discontinued. But the Assyrian Empire made one major change: the central government took over the management of the roads. Government maintenance brought about speedy messenger service to and from the capital and the rapid movement of troops against enemies within and without. The roads were kept in good repair, and exact information as to the terrain and distances was essential. The principal roads were called "royal roads." Official letters and legal documents refer to stations built along the royal roads, used as resting places for troops and civilian travelers and as way stations in delivering royal mail. A royal correspondent wrote, "People at the road stations pass my letters to each other and bring them to the king, my lord." A regular postal service was provided by mounted couriers, with relays at every road station. The roads were also measured with great precision, not only in "double hours" but in smaller measures from 360 meters down to 6 meters. That is, the distances on the royal roads were based on actual measurements using surveyor's cords of standard lengths. Highways were well defined and sufficiently permanent to be named as boundaries of fields in documents of land sales. Such roads were referred to as "the royal highway," or more precisely as "the royal highway to such-and-such a place," or "the highway which goes from . . . to

. . ."; the names of towns were listed at each end of that section. These were clearly recognized as permanent highways, maintained by the state.

The Assyrians began to acquire and breed numerous camels in their efforts to control the Syrian and northwestern Arabian deserts and to profit from the caravan trade from Arabia. In this way, they penetrated deep into Arabia despite difficult and poorly marked desert trails. Kings Sargon II and Sennacherib had those segments of royal roads closest to their respective capitals, Dur-Sharrukin and Nineveh, paved with stone slabs and supplied with roadside stelae as milestones. The roads were paved for a short distance outside of the cities and then quickly degenerated into a track and finally disappeared completely. This practice was subsequently discontinued until the Romans applied it, on a far greater scale, to their own imperial road network. Travel in summer was usually undertaken at night. For security purposes, merchants usually formed joint caravans. In mountains and deserts, guides and armed escorts were hired. The track taken by a road depended on the locations of water, food supplies, mountain passes, river fords, and ferries. The rise of a new political center deflected some roads at the height of their power. In Babylonia and Assyria, the unit of road distance was called the "double hour," referring to the distance traveled in two hours' time. The double hour was based on the cubit, which was of several different sizes.

Goods could be carried on wagons drawn by oxen, on light carts drawn by donkeys, or by pack donkeys. In Babylonia, with its far-reaching network of navigable rivers and canals, wagons were used for short hauls such as transporting grain to local granaries. Farther north, in Upper Mesopotamia, and in Syria, roads were more important. Texts refer to two-wheeled, four-wheeled, and three-wheeled wagons (perhaps the third wheel was a spare). Wagons were used for loads too bulky and heavy to be carried on the back of a donkey. The ability to carry such heavy and unwieldy loads as logs of cedar, pine, and cypress over great distances on uneven terrain implied the maintenance of ancient wagon roads. As for building mountain roads for carrying lumber, even greater engineering skill was required.

Roads suitable for wagons were few. Long-distance traffic was usually conducted by donkeys carrying packs. Donkey caravans could follow the most primitive paths and the narrowest mountain trails. The length of a daily stage of a caravan was between 25 and 30 kilometers. The load of an individual donkey, as attested by Old Assyrian texts, varied from 130 minas (65 kilograms) to 150 minas (75 kilograms) (Hallo, 57–88).

The roads were paved for a short distance outside of the cities and then quickly degenerated.

The main form of transportation continued to be the caravan, first with asses and then, after 1100 B.C.E., with camels. The animals traveled single file over difficult terrain, and even the donkey drivers carried some of the goods. The goods were transported over great distances, and the caravan provided protection from occasional bandits and from wild animals. Caravans also helped control costs. Few words have been found for "caravan" in the ancient Near East; the Sumerian and Akkadian word meant "highway," "street," or "journey." The caravans were associated with particular routes, which continued to remain in approximately the same places for millennia. The mountains held few viable passes, and sufficient watering places were rarely found in the steppes. However, for camel caravans, watering stops could be spaced farther apart.

River traffic in Mesopotamia was always heavy. Cuneiform tablets from the Old Babylonian period record the transportation of grain, cattle, fish, milk, vegetables, oil, fruit, wool, stone, bricks, leather, and people over the network of canals, for which clay "canal maps" have been found. Despite the importance of the Persian Gulf trade, there is little evidence concerning how their ships actually looked. Ships were referred to as the "large ship," "short ship," "wide cargo ship," and so on. Crude depictions on seals found on the island of Failaka, near the delta, have provided us with little information other than that open-water vessels also sailed in the Persian Gulf in the Old Babylonian period.

The great inland lakes, mostly in northwestern Iran and Armenia, were particularly important for shipping. Even the seas were navigated in the ancient Near East, but mostly from coastal cities. In Babylonia, river shipping ended in Ur. From there, goods were packed on vessels that were able to navigate the bays and lagoons as far as the islands of Failaka and Bahrain. Shipping in the Persian Gulf was controlled by the Elamites, who traveled to the coast of Oman and the mouth of the Indus. The route around the Arabian peninsula and into the Red Sea was navigated circa 3000 B.C.E. Some major trade centers retained their importance for long periods of time.

Because of the state of the roads, traders transported large cargoes by water routes whenever possible, especially for long-distance trade. Lengthy journeys were undertaken in the Red Sea, Indian Ocean, and Persian Gulf in the third, second, and first millennia B.C.E. Maritime technology for such voyages already existed by the third and second millennia. Rudders were used to steer lighter ships and boats along the current, but heavy transport vessels and rafts were pushed with poles. In the Neo-Babylonian period, a great oar at the stern took the place of the rudder. Sailboats were not suitable, and therefore were uncommon, for use on the Tigris and Euphrates Rivers because the winds blew in the same direction as the currents. Water craft were sometimes towed; according to cuneiform tablets, 16 or 17 days were needed to tow a barge upstream 137 kilometers between Lagash and Nippur, about four times as long as needed to cover the same distance downstream. The texts recording cargoes imply that boats of small capacity were used. As far back as the Third Dynasty of Ur, boats on the canals carried from about 55 to 155 bushels of grain.

Sumerian texts describe boat building. The boatwright constructed the shell of his vessel first, without any interior framework. The technical vocabulary was extensive, but we have not been able to identify the terms as yet. Boat building was a large operation, and very large boats were constructed from wood in special shipyards. These boats were probably used for long sea voyages to places such as Melukkha and Dilmun. During the Neo-Assyrian period, large wooden barges were depicted as being towed from riverbanks. A series of barges or boats were shown serving as the pontoons for floating bridges.

Shipwrecks were recorded in the Persian Gulf, probably along the western shores, which were shallow and full of dangerous reefs and shoals. The dangers of these commercial ventures were so great that businessmen would not enter into full partnerships with merchants. Seafarers sometimes gave silver models of their ships to their gods in gratitude for their safe return. A merchant ship similar to one depicted in a fourteenth-century Egyptian tomb was found off Ulu Burun, Turkey. The cargo was so diverse that the ship's origin is impossible to determine. The ship was traveling the well-known counterclockwise route—from Phoenicia to Egypt by way of southern Crete. No navigation instruments were used other than sounding rods and lines. On the shipwreck at Ulu Burun, there was an inventory of silver, tin, copper, and cobalt-blue glass ingots, as well as ivory, ebony logs, aromatics, and edibles such as oils, nuts, spices, and fruits for the crew.

During the first millennium B.C.E., the history of ships and shipping in the Levant belonged to Canaanite and later, Phoenician ships. Assyrian kings depended on Phoenician sailors and shipwrights.

Two types of boats, the coracle and the *kelek*, were characteristic of Mesopotamia and have survived in identical form today. The coracle was a type of round basket, similar to those laborers used for carrying earth and bricks on top of their heads. It was called *quppu*, "round basket," in Akkadian and *quffa* in Arabic. The basket was made of plaited rushes; it was flat-bottomed, covered with skins, caulked, and not very deep. The boat was navigated by two to four men with oars. When loaded, the cargoes and gunwale cleared the water by only a few inches. The coracle sailors could cross fast-flowing rivers like the Tigris, and they traveled up and down the river carrying goods as well. The raft, called in Akkadian *kalakku* and in Arabic *kelek*, was made of the strongest reeds that grew in the marshes or, preferably, of the best wood the builder could find locally. Its buoyancy was increased by attaching inflated goatskins below its surface. The loaded rafts floated down the river with the current, with the sailors using poles to propel and steer them until they reached their destination. These rafts were particularly useful in parts of the rivers with rapids

and shallows because, despite the loss of some skins, the rafts still kept afloat. When the *kelek* reached its destination, the cargo was unloaded, the boat dismantled, the wood sold, and the goatskins deflated and loaded on donkeys to form a caravan to travel north.

Models and reliefs of canoes show that they were propelled both by paddling and by punting (moving the canoe by means of a pole pushed against the bottom). They, too, resembled modern Mesopotamian marsh canoes and were probably constructed of wood. Most people had to cross the network of canals, which were

Relief showing various forms of Mesopotamian watercraft. Four men row a coracle, while on the right another man catches a fish while seated atop an inflated goatskin. © Copyright The British Museum.

often too wide and too deep to ford. In such cases, people used reed floats or inflated goatskins. The goatskins were made from the skin of an animal from which the head and hoofs had been cut, thus retaining its natural shape. At first, the neck and three legs of the hide were tied tightly, enabling the swimmer to blow from time to time into the open fourth leg to keep the float buoyant. After 700 B.C.E. larger skins were used with all four legs tightly tied. Once it was inflated, the people of ancient Mesopotamia could hold it, placing it under their chests, to cross without fear of drowning. Under Shamshi-Adad of Assyria, such skins were part of a soldier's issue.

The three most important of the successive capitals of Assyria, namely, Assur, Nimrud, and Nineveh, were built alongside the Tigris, which provided a method of transportation between both ends of the central part of the Assyrian kingdom. At Nimrud, a great quay wall has been traced for about 240 yards for access to the ziggurat and the palace complex. The quay way was constructed of large stone blocks rising approximately 33 feet above bedrock and set 21 feet deep below the riverbank. King Sennacherib also built a similar quay along Nineveh; in fact, one of his 15 city gates was named "the Quay Gate." Sennacherib describes using river transportation to bring heavy cargoes such as limestone colossi to Nineveh. The quays also provided national revenue, with users being charged harbor dues (Nemet-Nejat, 271–79).

FOR MORE INFORMATION

Casson, L. *Ships and Seamanship in the Ancient World.* Princeton, N.J.: Princeton University Press, 1971.

Hallo, W. W. "The Road to Emar." *Journal of Cuneiform Studies* 18 (1964): 57–88.

Littauer, M. A. *Wheeled Vehicles and Ridden Animals in the Ancient Near East.* Leiden: Brill, 1979.

Nemet-Nejat, K. R. *Daily Life in Ancient Mesopotamia.* Westport, Conn.: Greenwood Press, 1998.

EGYPT

The inhabited section of Egypt was the corridor along the Nile River, and the river itself served not only as a source of water but as a transportation conduit. Egypt was fortunate to have this natural equivalent of a superhighway running along its length. Boats plied busily up and down the river, transporting people and goods.

The crudest riverine crafts were simple raftlike boats. They were made by gathering bundles of papyrus reeds and then tying them together. Such a design could be used for a one-person craft or scaled up to small ship size. Depictions of these boats in art show them being propelled by oars or, in the shallows, by long poles that were pushed against the river bottom. Reed boats were probably the standard boats used by common people and by fishermen patrolling the marshlands.

More elaborate boats were constructed out of wood. These generally larger craft came in a variety of shapes depending on their purpose. Long, narrow ships propelled by banks of oars were employed by important officials to carry them swiftly along

ECONOMIC LIFE

TRAVEL
& TRANSPORTATION

Mesopotamia

Egypt

Greece

Rome

Australian Aboriginals

the river, while broad transport vessels wallowed along carrying heavy commercial cargoes.

While it was always easier and cheaper to transport cargo by water, when goods had to be transported overland, the Egyptians made use of various pack animals and wheeled transport. Humble donkeys were used to carry both goods and people. Horses were ridden by government messengers and were used to pull chariots carrying nobility.

A standard method of transportation for the wealthy was a litter carried by servants. Litters could range from a simple chair attached to poles to more elaborate enclosed compartments holding multiple people and carried by a dozen attendants.

One specialized type of transportation problem in Egypt was how to move the gigantic stone blocks used in construction projects such as the pyramids. Certain other stone items, such as obelisks and colossal statues, also had to be moved. Naturally, the Nile was used to carry these burdens as far as possible by water, and specially designed barges and tugboats were constructed to manage these heavy and dangerous cargoes. When the stones had come as far as possible by water, they still often had to be dragged considerable distances overland. The Egyptians employed sledges, ropes, rollers, and abundant manpower to haul the stones to their destinations. Literally thousands of people could be harnessed to the drag ropes to move particularly heavy stones.

~*Gregory S. Aldrete*

FOR MORE INFORMATION

David, R. *Handbook to Life in Ancient Egypt.* New York: Facts on File, 1998.
Partridge, R. *Transport in Ancient Egypt.* London: Rubicon Press, 1987.

ECONOMIC LIFE
|
TRAVEL
& TRANSPORTATION
|
Mesopotamia

Egypt

Greece

Rome

Australian Aboriginals

GREECE

Travel was widespread in all periods in ancient Greece. From the eighth century B.C.E. onward, traders had regular contacts with non-Greeks such as Phoenicians and Egyptians. Already in the *Odyssey* we encounter itinerant experts, including bards, physicians, builders, and seers, known collectively as "those who serve the community," who, as Homer tells us (17.386), were "invited from the ends of the earth." To this group in later times should be added the Sophists, or teachers of rhetoric, who were much in demand in the fifth century B.C.E., and—a much larger group—the mercenaries. In addition, many Greeks made long journeys at some point in their lives, to either attend a Panhellenic festival, consult an oracle, or visit a healing sanctuary.

Horses were a luxury confined to the very rich. Because they were unshod, horses were incapable of traveling long distances or negotiating the steep mountain paths that dotted the Greek landscape. Stirrups and saddles were unknown, which made horseback riding extremely uncomfortable. Chariots and other wheeled vehicles were useful only over short distances. Most Greeks would therefore have been accustomed to walking considerable distances. In Xenophon's *Memorabilia* (3.13.5), Socrates talks nonchalantly of the journey from Athens to Olympia as a five- to six-day walk. The going was tough, not to mention dangerous. That is why a favorite theme of Greek myth is the "culture hero," who cleared the roads of brigands and marauders, as Theseus did for the stretch between Megara and Athens.

Road-building techniques were by no means unsophisticated. There is evidence of ramps, switchbacks, and pull-offs even in the Archaic period. All roads, however, were local; they did not join one community to another. In Athens, the principal paved road was the Panathenaic Way, which began at the Dipylon Gate and ended on the Acropolis. It served primarily as a processional way. More functional was the paved road to Athens from the marble quarries on Mount Pentelicon. Goods were conveyed to and from the port of Piraeus along a cart road that began on the west side of the city. During the Peloponnesian War, when it was no longer safe to travel outside the city walls, a road running the entire length of the Long Walls that joined Athens to its port served in its place.

The most impressive road-building project in Greece was the *diolkos* or slipway, built by the Corinthians about 600 B.C.E. The *diolkos* enabled ships to be towed across the isthmus of Corinth, rather than having to circumnavigate the Peloponnese. It remained in use until the ninth century C.E.

The most common means of long-distance travel was by sea, although both weather conditions and piracy made this dangerous. The sea god Poseidon's enmity to Odysseus, which delays the hero's homecoming and causes him the loss of all his ships, reflects a genuine paranoia about sea travel, notwithstanding its importance to Greek culture.

Because the many mountains made the terrain unsuitable for wheeled traffic, and because there are no navigable rivers in Greece, most goods had to be conveyed by sea. No part of Greece is more than 60 miles from the sea, and safe harbors are numerous around the entire coastline. Goods were conveyed loose, in sacks, or in earthenware jars known as amphorae.

The busiest commercial port in the Greek world was the Piraeus, situated about five miles southwest of Athens. The Piraeus functioned not only as a center for the export of Athenian merchandise and the import of goods destined for Athens but also as an entrepôt or place of redistribution and trans-shipment for traders who found it more convenient to use its unrivaled facilities than deal directly with the source of supply. Given the unpredictability of the Aegean during the winter months, the commercial port, which was known as the *emporion*, buzzed with frenetic activity for half the year and was practically idle for the rest.

The volume of traffic that passed through the Piraeus required an extremely efficient system of loading and unloading to prevent a backlog of ships from clogging up the harbor with spoiled cargoes. After unloading their wares, merchants were under considerable pressure from the harbor authorities to sell their cargoes and depart as quickly as possible. The majority of dockers were slaves, hired out to shipowners on a contractual basis. Smaller merchant vessels unloaded from the stern, whereas larger vessels remained at anchor in the harbor basin while their merchandise was transferred onto barges. From the sixth century B.C.E. onward, cranes were used to unload the heaviest commodities such as marble and timber; pulleys were not in use until the fourth century B.C.E. Loose merchandise was removed from the hold by means of a swing-beam, with a weight attached to one end and a bucket to the other. Amphorae had to be removed singly with the assistance of a wooden pole supported at either end. Most cargoes were probably mixed. A duty was levied on all cargoes entering or leaving the Piraeus, which in 399 B.C.E. amounted to more than 18,000 talents.

As early Greece knew nothing of inns, an institution known as "guest-friendship" or *xenia* developed. This meant that aristocrats offered board and lodging to other aristocrats when they were on the road. Zeus Xenios protected the rights and responsibilities of guests and hosts alike. Inns are not heard of until the early fifth century B.C.E. At the end of the century, Panhellenic shrines were offering public accommodation for visitors, with separate quarters for foreign dignitaries (Thucydides, *The Peloponnesian War* 3.68.3).

Even in a major commercial and tourist center like the Piraeus, the standard of accommodation was deplorably low. Aristophanes implies that its inns had a reputation for discomfort, prostitution, and bedbugs (*The Frogs*, lines 112–15). By the middle of the fourth century B.C.E., the lack of decent facilities led Xenophon in *Revenues* (3.12) to recommend "the construction of more hotels for shipowners . . . around the harbors . . . as well as public hostels for visitors" (my translation). Whether his advice was followed is not known. By the Roman period, the situation had deteriorated even more. Cicero, in *Letters to Friends* (4.12.3), relates that when a certain Servius Sulpicius journeyed to the Piraeus to collect the body of a friend who had died there, he found the latter stretched out under a tent. Evidently, his friend had been unable to find any other accommodation in the port (Garland, 156–58).

FOR MORE INFORMATION

Casson, L. *Ships and Seamanship in the Ancient World*. Princeton, N.J.: Princeton University Press, 1971.

Garland, R. *Daily Life of the Ancient Greeks*. Westport, Conn.: Greenwood Press, 1998.

———. *The Piraeus*. Ithaca, N.Y.: Cornell University Press, 1987.

ECONOMIC LIFE

|

TRAVEL
& TRANSPORTATION

|

Mesopotamia

Egypt

Greece

Rome

Australian Aboriginals

ROME

One of the most famous aspects of Roman civilization is its roads. The Roman road system constituted the best-built roads up until very recently. Roman roads were carefully constructed with foundations that went down four feet and were graded so as to drain water away from them. The roads were also paved, and the Romans were proud of making their roads go straight even when this meant constructing long bridges over deep valleys or tunneling through solid rock mountains.

The first major Roman road was the Via Appia, which was begun in 213 B.C.E. by the man who gave his name to this road, Appius Claudius. It connected Rome with Brundisium at the heel of Italy, which was a departure point for ships to the east. By the end of the second century B.C.E., additional roads such as the Via Flaminia and the Via Aurelia had been constructed running up and down the length of Italy and joining the cities of the peninsula by a web of well-built roads. As the Roman Empire expanded outside of Italy, the Romans doggedly extended their network of carefully built roadways into the provinces. Legions stationed around the Mediterranean spent much of their time constructing roads, and a typical Roman soldier spent far more time digging than fighting. These soldiers left records of their construction work in the form of thousands of stone mile markers, which proudly record the name of the military unit that built that section of road.

These roads served many purposes. They helped the Romans keep control of their empire by enabling troops to be rushed to trouble spots. They encouraged and facilitated long-distance trade and bolstered the economy. They sped up communication among the different regions of the empire, a function that was aided by an imperial messenger service. Finally, they served as a powerful symbolic marker that a territory was indisputably Roman. Like an animal marking its territory, the presence of Roman roads was an unmistakable signal that an area belonged to Rome.

Travel along these roads was fraught with dangers, however. Bandits were very common, and anyone venturing outside of large cities was literally risking his life. Roman literature is full of examples of people who simply disappeared, who set out on a journey and were never heard from again. Presumably, they fell victim to bandits along the road. Rich Romans would travel with bodyguards and with armed slaves, but even such protection was not proof against bandits. One senior magistrate and his entire party vanished only a few miles from Rome. Even the Bible provides good evidence of the ubiquity of bandit attacks. The parable of the good Samaritan centers around a man who is beaten and robbed. He was traveling along the road from Jerusalem to Jericho, a distance of about 15 miles, in the daylight along what was perhaps the most heavily traveled road in the province (Luke 10:25–37). A common phrase on tombstones is *interfectus a latronibus*, "killed by bandits." In a list of the duties of a Roman governor, the first thing mentioned is to suppress bandits.

The Roman word for bandits is *latrones*. The Roman definition of bandit, however, was more inclusive than our modern one. It encompassed not merely outlaws but also anyone the Romans were fighting against who was not a member of a diplomatically recognized state. Thus many barbarians were referred to as bandits. Another common usage of the term occurred during a civil war, when inevitably each side would attempt to label the other as bandits. Therefore the real definition of a bandit to the Romans was an armed person with illegitimate authority, who, by implication, was in conflict with the legitimate authority, the Roman state. The Church Father Augustine wrote: "What are states but gangs of bandits on a large scale, and what are bandit gangs but states in miniature?" (*City of God* 4.4). Bandits were viewed as a direct challenge to the authority of the emperor and, in the countryside at least, constituted an alternate power structure. It is not surprising that because of the threat they posed to legitimate authority, captured bandits received the ultimate punishment: crucifixion.

Just as bandits owned the countryside, pirates for most of Roman history ruled the seas. Piracy was simplified in the ancient world by the fact that most ships did not venture out of sight of land but instead crept along the coastline. This made it easy for greedy or desperate men to keep watch for such ships and, when they were sighted, to dash out to sea and seize them. They would often kill the crew or sell them into slavery and steal the goods to be sold later. If the pirates captured a wealthy or important person, they would hold him or her for ransom. In some coastal areas of the Mediterranean, piracy was a way of life. The most infamous area was along the coast of Asia Minor in a region called Cilicia. Piracy was most rampant in periods when central authority was weakest. The late Republic was one of the worst times, when pirate gangs attained the power and size of small kingdoms.

No one was safe from pirates, as is illustrated by the fact that when Julius Caesar was young, he was captured by pirates who held him for ransom. He was insulted that his captors only asked for 20 talents of ransom when Caesar thought that he was worth at least 50. He told his captors that as a result of this offence, he would have them all crucified. As soon as his ransom was paid and he was released, he gathered together some ships and soldiers, tracked down the pirates, and—true to his word—had them all crucified (Suetonius, *Life of Julius Caesar*, 4). Eventually, piracy became so bad that the Romans had to act. In 67 B.C.E., a special law called the Gabinian Law was passed, giving the general Pompey an extraordinary command. He was awarded absolute power over all the Mediterranean Sea, as well as the coasts to a distance of 50 miles inland, 20 legions, and 270 ships, and was ordered to solve the pirate problem. He divided the sea into 13 regions and set up blockades so that no one could pass from one region to another. He then began at one end of the Mediterranean and swept across it, capturing and destroying all the pirates' strongholds on the coasts while driving the fleets ahead of him. In only three months, Pompey succeeded in purging the Mediterranean of piracy. Piracy naturally came back, but after the establishment of Roman naval bases, it was never as much of a threat as it had been in the late Republic.

Because it was much faster to go by sea than by land, most people traveling long distances took a ship. There were no passenger vessels, so someone who wished to travel had to arrange passage on a merchant ship. Since most long-distance travel was concerned with the food supply of Rome, these were the ships that passengers would travel on.

The motivation for such travelers was varied. Often people undertook trips to famous temples in attempts to cure an illness. Large international contests such as the Olympics also attracted travelers. And finally, many people simply went on holidays. Rich Romans liked to spend the summer on the coast, and in particular, the Bay of Naples was a kind of resort area for the rich. Passengers on a merchant ship had to bring all their own equipment, including their bed, the food they would eat, the pots and pans to cook it in, and the servants to do the work.

Because of the harshness and unpredictability of winter storms at sea, ships mainly sailed in the summer. A few traveled in the spring and fall, but very few would risk sailing in the winter, when storms were most frequent.

Travelers along Roman roads were advised to conceal their valuables in a pouch under their shirt, and women were told not to wear any jewelry that might attract robbers. Travelers stayed at inns, and since they did not want to be caught on the road after dark, it was vital to know where these inns were located. Documents called *itineraria* were available, which listed the locations and characteristics of different lodgings. There were a fair number of people whom today we would call tourists. These tourists were mostly interested in the past, in seeing famous sights or monuments. The Seven Wonders of the Ancient World were tourist destinations, as were sights associated with mythological events and stories, particularly the Trojan War. Some tourists would go to see the graves of heroes, while others would visit the houses where famous men had lived, such as the house of Socrates in Athens. Like today, art attracted tourists. The ancients did not have museums, but most temples were almost like museums in that they were stuffed with sculptures, paintings, and war trophies. Certain statues became very famous, such as the cult statue of Zeus and a famous, extremely lifelike sculpture of a bronze cow by Myron in Athens.

A milestone in ancient travel occurred in the second century c.e., when a Greek named Pausanias wrote the first comprehensive guidebook to a country. He penned a book describing all the famous sites and monuments of Greece. His guidebook is organized by regions and cities, and for major places like Athens, he even offers directions for different walking tours that will take you to the notable places in the city.

~*Gregory S. Aldrete*

FOR MORE INFORMATION

Casson, L. *Travel in the Ancient World*. Baltimore, Md.: Johns Hopkins University Press, 1974.

Chevallier, R. *Roman Roads*. Rev. ed. London: Batsford, 1989.

Laurence, R. *The Roads of Roman Italy*. New York: Routledge, 1999.

Shaw, B. "Bandits in the Roman Empire." *Past and Present*, no. 105 (November 1984): 3–52.

AUSTRALIAN ABORIGINALS

Australian Aborigines possessed no domesticated animals on which they could ride or load a pack, or with which to pull a cart or sledge. The only domesticated (or semidomesticated) animal was the dingo, the small native Australian dog, but it had only been in Australia a few thousand years. The main means of movement or transport of goods was by humans on foot.

The exception to this was transport by water, and a variety of canoes and rafts were used throughout most of Australia. There were limitations to the range of water transport, however, since with the exception of the Murray, Murrumbidgee, and Darling Rivers (all of which join), no rivers in Australia were suitable for long-distance movement. There were also few sheltered areas along the coast where long-distance trips could be conducted safely. Therefore, canoes were mostly used for fishing rather than transportation, and instances of long-distance water transport were more the exception than the rule. On both sides of Cape York, in the relatively sheltered waters inside the Great Barrier Reef, and in the Gulf of Carpentaria, long trading voyages were made by people from the Torres Strait and New Guinea. Elsewhere, offshore islands were visited to exploit resources such as seal colonies and seabird rookeries.

Most of the time, people moved on foot. The distances traveled varied from a few miles on a hunting expedition to many miles for moving to a new camping site to hundreds of miles for trading goods or attending a ceremony with neighboring groups. People traveled lightly, carrying only essential tools and finding or making new ones when they arrived and building a new house from scratch. If traveling rapidly or in unknown territory, they carried some preserved food, perhaps dried fruit or bread, as a reserve. Generally, however, food could be found quickly and easily no matter how strange the territory. Aboriginal peoples would carry fire sticks for starting fires or sometimes carry fire itself in the form of smoldering tinder. Additionally, they might carry, either on the head or in a bag, goods intended for trade, such as spears, drugs, ornamental shells, ochre, or quality stones for spear or axe manufacture.

> *Landmarks were learned by children through songs or stories of the travels of ancestral heroes.*

Travel required knowledge of landmarks along the way, especially the location of water holes in dry country. These landmarks were learned by children through songs or stories of the travels of the ancestral heroes. Knowing these songs and stories was a matter of survival, particularly in drought conditions when accidents could happen and people could become trapped when waterholes dried up.

The first arrival of Aborigines in Australia must have involved water travel because there was always a gap between Australia and Indonesia too wide for land to be seen on the other side. Crossing this strip of water was perhaps the first extended trip human beings made by sea anywhere in the world. During the last 50,000 years, the sea level has risen and fallen, so that some pieces of land that were once hills on a coastal plain are now islands. Certain of these islands show evidence of human occupation from the times when the sea level receded. The canoes used in different parts of Australia ranged from simple rafts consisting of a few logs lashed together, or rudimentary one-man canoes crafted from a single piece of bark folded over and sealed at each end, to large dug-out canoes made from a single log, or even sophisticated watercraft with one or two outriggers attached for stability.

~*David Horton*

FOR MORE INFORMATION

Baker, R. M. "Yanyuwa Canoe Making." *Records of the South Australian Museum* 22 (1988): 173–88.

Berndt, R., and C. Berndt. *The World of the First Australians*. Canberra: Aboriginal Studies Press, 1988.

Horton, D., ed. *The Encyclopedia of Aboriginal Australia*. Canberra: Aboriginal Studies Press, 2001.

Mulvaney, J., and J. Kamminga. *Prehistory of Australia*. Sydney, New South Wales: Allen and Unwin, 1999.

ECONOMIC LIFE: WEB SITES

http://www.epas.utoronto.ca/amphoras/project.html
http://www.mc.maricopa.edu/~reffland/anthropology/lost_tribes/agriculture.html
http://www.indiana.edu/~kglowack/athens/sites.html
http://www.mic.ki.se/Mesop.html
http://www.digitalegypt.ucl.ac.uk/foreignrelations/trade.html
http://www.umich.edu/~kelseydb/Exhibits/Food/text/farm.html

4

INTELLECTUAL LIFE

The human mind is an amazing thing that allows people to reflect on ideas so abstract that we can imagine things we could never see or touch. We can think about things as complex as philosophical considerations of ethics, justice, and even thought itself. The study of ideas is called intellectual history and includes science, philosophy, medicine, technology, literature, and even the languages used to record the ideas.

At the basic level, the capacity for abstraction permits people to impose order on (or to see order in) the astonishingly complex universe. As Stone Age people looked at the dark night sky dotted by millions of stars, they organized the view into patterns of constellations, which allowed them to map and predict the movement of the heavens. They then echoed the heavenly order in such earthly monuments as Stonehenge in Britain or the Mayan pyramids in Mexico. Through time, this capacity to order extended from the heavens to the submicroscopic particles that dominate twenty-first-century physics and the development of mathematics as the language to express these abstractions. An important part of intellectual life throughout history has been the growing evolution of science, but this is only one aspect of the accomplishments of the mind.

Some people have applied their creative capacity for abstract thought to technology, finding ways to make their lives easier. Technological innovations have spread more rapidly throughout the world than even abstract scientific explanations. Horse collars from China, windmills from Persia, and Muslim medical advances transformed medieval western Europe, while the Internet dominates world culture in the twenty-first century.

What makes these escalating advances possible is not an increase in human intelligence. Instead, the ability to record abstract ideas in writing and preserve past accomplishments in education have allowed human knowledge to progress. As one medieval thinker (John of Salisbury) noted, if we can see farther than the ancients, it is only because we build on their knowledge. We are as dwarfs on the shoulders of giants, and through our intellectual life, we can look forward to even greater vision.

The people of the ancient world may have had the least inherited knowledge, but they were certainly not lacking in intelligence or creativity, creating nearly every-

INTELLECTUAL
LIFE
|
LANGUAGE
& WRITING

EDUCATION

LITERATURE

CALENDAR & TIME

SCIENCE

ART

thing we consider part of intellectual life for the very first time. Nothing existed; everything had to be invented. The history of intellectual life in antiquity is a long sequence of revolutionary firsts—the first writing, the first calendars, the first mathematical systems, the first maps, the first literature, the first monumental buildings, and so on.

The motivation for these inventions usually stemmed from a combination of curiosity and necessity. Ancient humans were both curious about the natural world around them and desperate to understand it to enhance their chances of survival. A farmer who did not have at least a crude understanding of the cycle of the year and the turning of the seasons would not know when to plant his crops, and the price of a wrong guess would be starvation. Such necessity led to the development of calendars geared to the solar and lunar cycles, and the calendars employed by the earliest civilizations in Mesopotamia are not so vastly different in sophistication and accuracy (within 3 percent) from the ones we still use today.

The invention of written language was another huge step, one that enables us to directly experience the thoughts, emotions, and histories of people from the ancient world as expressed in their literature and records. The challenge of finding a way to express in consistent, visual symbols the complexity of spoken language is an impressive achievement that in retrospect seems obvious; yet for the first person to conceive of, let alone accomplish, such a procedure was a great intellectual leap forward. The early crude pictographic writing systems rapidly evolved into extraordinarily sophisticated written languages such as ancient Greek, which has a more complex grammar with more subtleties and varieties of tenses, moods, conjugations, inflections, and declensions than most languages used today.

The sciences also have their origins in antiquity, and although the distinctions that ancient thinkers made among science, religion, philosophy, and mysticism were not clear-cut, all were part of the movement to interrogate the world around them and to create order and understanding out of chaos and mystery.

~*Joyce E. Salisbury and Gregory S. Aldrete*

FOR MORE INFORMATION

Tarnas, R. *The Passion of the Western Mind: Understanding the Ideas That Have Shaped Our World View.* New York: Ballentine Books, 1991.

INTELLECTUAL
LIFE

LANGUAGE
& WRITING

Mesopotamia

Egypt

Greece

Rome

India

Australian Aboriginals

Language and Writing

The invention of a written language, which seems to have first occurred in Mesopotamia about 3000 B.C.E., is one of the classic milestones in the history of civilization. Prior to this, memories and knowledge could be handed down orally from one person to another, but such a method was easily subject to corruption of the message and required an unbroken chain of carriers. The invention of writing made it possible for hard-won knowledge to be reliably preserved, so that future generations could benefit from and build on it. For the first time, people could record for posterity their deeds, ideas, beliefs, fears, and hopes.

Through writing, the actual words and thoughts of someone who lived thousands of years ago can be read and experienced directly by a modern reader. Writing not only allows a storehouse of data to be established and built upon, but in a sense, it conveys a kind of immortality upon those ancient authors whose words have not been forgotten. Could the ancient Greek poet known as Homer have imagined that millions of people living thousands of years after his death would still be reading his poetry, debating and discussing its meaning, and discovering relevance in it to their own lives? This is the power of writing.

The earliest forms of writing, such as cuneiform in Mesopotamia and hieroglyphics in Egypt, tended to employ pictographs, drawings of objects. These quickly developed into systems in which signs came to stand for phonetic sounds, and a true alphabet was created. The modern alphabet today used in Western societies still incorporates elements of these earliest writing systems. Our letter A, for example, transmuted and adapted through the Phoenicians, Greeks, and Romans and turned upside down, is basically the ancient Sumerian symbol for the head of a cow.

In most civilizations, including Mesopotamia and Greece, the earliest application of writing was not to record great philosophical ideas, religious beliefs, or even works of literature but instead to make inventories of possessions. While it is a somewhat depressing thought that writing was first put to use to create what are essentially tax records, it was swiftly employed to record the full range of human thoughts and experiences. Because it forms the permanent basis of all knowledge, writing truly is one of the most significant inventions in history.

~Gregory S. Aldrete

MESOPOTAMIA

INTELLECTUAL
LIFE
|
LANGUAGE
& WRITING
|
Mesopotamia

Egypt

Greece

Rome

India

Australian Aboriginals

The invention of writing is credited to the Mesopotamians and is dated to the end of the fourth millennium B.C.E. It was triggered by economic necessity—to keep a reliable record of grain, sheep, and cattle entering and leaving the warehouses and farms that belonged to the palaces and temples. Once developed, writing was the most efficient and comprehensive solution for recording information.

Writing was invented in Mesopotamia about 3100 B.C.E. But writing was not the first method developed by humans to keep track of information. Early lists of accounting devices note wooden sticks, a loom, and even an abacus. In the "Debate between the Sheep and the Grain," a second-millennium text, we find early recording devices alongside writing:

Every day an account of you [the sheep] is made,
The tally sticks are planted in the ground;
Your shepherd tells the owner, how many ewes and how many little lambs.
How many goats and how many little kids there are. (cited in Civil, 168)

Among the earliest forerunners to actual writing were clay tokens or counters, called "stones." The tokens were mostly made of clay and were usually the size of small marbles. They came in a variety of shapes: spheres, discs, cones, and rods. The token system can be dated to approximately 10,000 B.C.E. Initially, tokens were used for simple household and market bookkeeping. Later, with the development of cities, the token system evolved, displaying a proliferation of markings to record numbers as well as an increasing variety of goods—a kind of ancient three-dimensional writing system.

The earliest writing is found at Uruk in Mesopotamia. Slightly later examples of writing systems using similar signs have been excavated at sites from Syria to Iran. The early Uruk tablets contained both numerals and pictographs (drawings of objects). The tablets included approximately 1,200 signs. Some of these signs may have had their origin in clay tokens, but most were pictographs, from which cuneiform signs later developed. For example, the drawing of an ox's head (sometimes even the whole ox) is used as the sign for ox, and an ear of barley is used as the sign for barley. Approximately 85 percent of the tablets recorded goods, food, or animals delivered either by individuals or by the city's temples. The other 15 percent of the tablets are lexical (word) lists of officials, commodities, and animals. The same lists are still found 600 years later, showing the continuity of a tradition.

The first texts we can read are from the first half of the third millennium B.C.E.—they were written in Sumerian. At this point, the scribes used grammatical elements that clearly indicate that the language was Sumerian. They achieved this by assigning phonetic values to signs that were ideograms. This happened in two ways. First, ideograms (symbols used to represent words) were extended to include a constellation of meanings by association; for example, the sign for foot also meant "stand" or "walk." Second, the range of sounds for ideograms was extended by punning, much the way the sign for "sun" could be extended to "son." Thus, a collection of syllabic signs was created, and scribes could indicate grammatical elements so that the script corresponded to the language. Sumerian is an agglutinative language. Each idea, whether nominal or verbal, was expressed by a single unchanging syllable (or polysyllable). This fixed syllable or root could be modified by long chains of prefixes and postfixes, signifying specific grammatical elements.

By the middle of the third millennium B.C.E., the Akkadians used the writing system developed by the Sumerians. Akkadian was an inflected language, relying on the addition of prefixes, infixes, and suffixes to form a single word. Therefore, a single cuneiform sign could not convey the meaning of an Akkadian word. So for the most part, Akkadian scribes wrote words out phonetically, even though they continued to use Sumerian ideograms to express some Akkadian words.

Other writing systems were influenced by Mesopotamia's cuneiform system and developed soon after. They include Egyptian hieroglyphics, proto-Elamite from Iran (which remains undeciphered), the Indus Valley script from Pakistan and India (also undeciphered), Minoan Linear A from Crete (still undeciphered), Hittite hieroglyphics (used in central Asiatic Turkey), and Chinese writing. Each nation put its own unique stamp on the writing system that came from Mesopotamia.

With so many values for each sign, as well as the same value for several signs, how did the ancient scribe manage to choose the correct value or meaning for each sign? Scribes used determinatives, that is, signs used either before or after a word as classifiers to indicate the category of objects to which the word belongs, for example, wood, deity, human being (male or female), river, city, fish, bird, and so on. Other aids to reading were provided by context, by signs preceding and following, and sometimes by variant writings that clarified the possibilities of reading the sign. Also, a scribe did not use all the theoretical possibilities of the sign in writing texts.

In the second millennium B.C.E., as writing spread to other areas within Mesopotamia's cultural (and political) sphere of influence, certain problems arose because the scribes often spoke another language and were not as well trained as scribes from Mesopotamia. But records of transactions were still needed in the international community. As a solution, the district scribes simplified the script, either by giving it a quasi-alphabetic character or by eliminating duplication of phonetic values by reducing the number of signs. Also, cuneiform was adopted in simplified form to write other languages.

Clay tablet with cuneiform writing. This tablet is a typical example of record-keeping—its columns list daily food distributions. © Copyright The British Museum.

Numbers were written in all categories of cuneiform texts, from the earliest, circa 3100 B.C.E., to the last datable text in 75 C.E. Like the rest of the cuneiform script, the method of writing numbers also evolved. Initially, numbers were formed by pressing the ends of a reed stylus into the clay either vertically (to make larger or smaller circles) or at a slant. Later, when the script became stylized and took on the appearance of cuneiform, the numbers took on a more angular form.

A stylus was made from a cut reed, trimmed to form a round, pointed, or sloping end; the stylus was then used to draw signs and to mark horizontal lines and vertical columns on lumps of clay that fit into the palm of the hand. The materials for writing were easily found in the river valleys of the Near East and were simple to use. We do not know how the scribes actually chose, prepared, and stored the clay and kept it sufficiently moist for writing. Clay could be worked into a flat shape, which could be written on while moist and then dried in the sun to last. Many tablets in the libraries of Assyrian kings were actually baked to the same hardness as pottery that had been fired. In other words, once dried, tablets could not be altered; this made them an excellent medium for final records in legal and administrative transactions. Also, many tablets that survive today in museum collections were burnt in antiquity when a city was conquered and sacked. Unwanted tablets were reused, thrown away, or sometimes used as floor packing.

When an impression, whether writing or a seal, was made on clay, it could not be altered once the clay hardened. The practice began in the fifth millennium B.C.E. with the use of stamp seals on lumps of clay and continued with cylinder seals throughout Mesopotamian history. In the second and first millennia B.C.E., even the illiterate could authenticate a legal document by using a seal. Seals could even be rolled on lumps of clay to seal doors, pottery jars, and goods. Some seals belonged to a city official or, in the case of legal proceedings, a judicial authority. Seals could be carved on stone, bone, metal, or shell. Different designs and inscriptions were used to indicate their owners. Later, the practice changed, and the party (or parties) to a legal action impressed a seal or a substitute such as a fingernail or garment hem.

About the time of Sargon (2334–2279 B.C.E.), envelopes were invented; they were slips of clay formed around the tablet. Envelopes protected the contents from damage and even fraud; that is, the envelopes safeguarded against someone moistening the clay and changing the numbers. Sometimes the text was repeated on the envelope and also sealed. In the case of a dispute, the envelope could be opened and the contents examined and compared. Some envelopes opened in modern times have been found with information written on them different from that of the tablets inside.

The cuneiform script evolved through time, becoming more standardized during times of strong centralized government. Eventually, the form of the signs became unrecognizable from the pictographs of the past. The end of the reed used for writing was cut at an oblique angle, forming a triangular cross-section. As a result, the signs came out wedge-shaped, hence the term *cuneiform*, a Latin word meaning "wedge-shaped." By the second millennium B.C.E., the signs became less complex—only three or four kinds of wedges were used to form signs. Even the number of signs was reduced: similar signs merged, and rarely used signs were deleted. As a result, the number of cuneiform signs known from the Uruk writing was cut in half to about 600 signs. Nonetheless, many signs still had multiple word and phonetic values. From the beginning of the second millennium B.C.E. a scribe could have done his job by using less than 200 signs.

The stylus was also used for other markings; for example, ornamental rulings might be incised around the outer edge of tablets. Check marks might be placed next to every tenth person in account texts and against every tenth line in literary texts. From the second millennium on, numerous literary tablets have "firing holes," made by pressing the stylus (or a similar object) straight through the tablet from front to back or side to side, often in an ornamental arrangement. A tablet could be canceled by using a stylus or a similar instrument to draw a mark across it.

Tablets were stored in a variety of ways. Private individuals stored tablets by wrapping them in either a piece of cloth or a reed mat or by putting them in a jar, basket, bag, or chest. Private archives were sometimes stored in palaces for safekeeping. The systems for storage described indicate that tablets were meticulously filed to be readily available for reference. Tablets could be placed on shelves or benches, or in jars, baskets, or other receptacles, according to contents, date, place, and so on. The tablets were placed on shelves or in clay banks tied with strings, with tags attached noting the contents. Some large tablets from the Ur III period and the Old Babylonian period contained memos on the edge of the tablet, similar to the spine of a book today. In the first millennium B.C.E., notations were added in Aramaic, Greek, and Egyptian to business documents with a stylus or pen using ink or paint (Nemet-Nejat, 48–54, 62–64).

FOR MORE INFORMATION

Civil, M. "The Sumerian Flood Story." In *Atra-hasis: The Babylonian Story of the Flood*, ed. W. G. Lambert and A. R. Millard. Oxford: Clarendon Press, 1969.

Nemet-Nejat, K. R. *Daily Life in Ancient Mesopotamia*. Westport, Conn.: Greenwood Press, 1998.

Walker, C. B. F. *Cuneiform*. London: British Museum Publications, 1987.

EGYPT

INTELLECTUAL
LIFE
|
LANGUAGE
& WRITING
|
Mesopotamia

Egypt

Greece

Rome

India

Australian Aboriginals

A common misconception about Egyptian writing is that hieroglyphs picture the subjects written about—that the appearance of a bird or a rabbit in a text, for example, indicates a discussion of those animals. Hieroglyphs are actually phonetic, like our own letters, in which signs represent word sounds. When an ancient Egyptian sculptor carved a hand followed by a rectangular reed mat and a loaf of bread on a temple wall, he was indicating the sounds *d*, *p* and *t*, spelling the word *dpt*, ancient Egyptian for "boat." If he wanted to make the meaning doubly clear, he could add the boat hieroglyph at the end of the word. Hieroglyphs used this way are called determinatives because they help the reader determine the meaning.

Although Egyptians did not write vowels, some signs could be used in their place when writing modern names. Thus the Egyptian vulture sign is not an exact equivalent of our letter *a* but may be used in its place. The arm hieroglyph may be used in place of our *e*, and so on.

In addition to an alphabet of single sounds, other hieroglyphs, called biliterals, represented two consecutive sounds. The hieroglyph of a house plan represented the combined *p* and *r* sounds, pronounced something like *per*. Our word *pharaoh* comes from an Egyptian word made up of two biliterals. The bottom biliteral was pronounced "aha" and meant "great." Thus the *per-aha* was the one who lived in the great house. Another group of hieroglyphs represented three sounds—triliterals, such as the hieroglyph pronounced *ah-n-kh*, the ancient Egyptian word for life. A scribe used about 500 common hieroglyphs in all, but several thousand others were written only occasionally or rarely.

Papyrus—the material on which all official writing was done—constituted a necessary commodity in Egypt. Papyrus was a natural marsh grass that grew abundantly in the delta, and it could reach as tall as 10 feet high. Its harvest provided not only a living for marshmen but the material for their boats and homes as well. Thanks to the pockets of air inside its cellular

Hieroglyph	Sound	Object
	a	vulture
	b	foot
	ch	placenta
	d	hand
	e	arm
	f	horned viper
	g	jar stand
	h	twisted flax
	i	reed
	j (dj)	snake
	k	basket
	m	owl
	n	water
	p	reed mat
	q	hill
	r	mouth
	s	folded cloth
	sh	pool of water
	t	loaf of bread
	tch	tethering ring
	u (or w)	quail chick
	y	two reeds
	z	door bolt

The Egyptian alphabet.

Example of hieroglyphic writing. This relief is from the tomb of the pharaoh Unas. Photo courtesy of Pat Remler.

stem, cut papyrus served as a fine material for boats, which were made by lashing together enough lengths to create a kind of punt that could be poled through the still, shallow water. When the same papyrus was stood upright, laced together, and plastered with mud, it provided a simple shelter for the marshman and his family.

Each day, a marshman punted through natural stands of papyrus, cutting stems below the waterline, and then stacking them onto his boat. These bundles would be delivered to papermakers who sliced the stems lengthwise into thin strips and cut them into foot-long lengths before placing them in layers, first side to side horizontally and then side to side vertically. When beaten with a wooden mallet, the two thicknesses compressed to paper-thin dimensions while exuding a sap that acted as a natural glue when dried. The end result was sheets of paperlike writing material called papyrus—the origin of our word *paper*—that were trimmed and smoothed with a polishing stone before use. Sheets could be glued together to make continuous scrolls of any length desired, which in some cases measured more than a hundred feet long (Brier and Hobbs, 87–89, 193–95).

FOR MORE INFORMATION

Betro, M. *Hieroglyphics: The Writings of Ancient Egypt*. New York: Abbeville Press, 1995.

Brier, B., and H. Hobbs. *Daily Life of the Ancient Egyptians*. Westport, Conn.: Greenwood Press, 1999.

INTELLECTUAL
LIFE
|
LANGUAGE
& WRITING
|
Mesopotamia

Egypt

Greece

Rome

India

Australian Aboriginals

GREECE

By the thirteenth century B.C.E. at the latest, the inhabitants of the Greek mainland and the island of Crete were speaking Greek. Although its origins are unclear, Greek belongs to the Indo-European family of languages, which extends from Iceland to Bangladesh. Until the Hellenistic period, it existed in a number of different dialects, the most important of which were Aeolic, Doric, Ionic, and Attic. These dialects do not, however, invariably correspond to ethnic divisions within the Greek "race." For instance, the inhabitants of Halicarnassos, modern Bodrum on the Turkish coast, who were Dorians, spoke in an Ionic dialect. Following the conquests of Alexander the Great, a dialect called *koinê,* or "common," became the educated tongue of the entire Hellenistic world. *Koinê* is the dialect in which the New Testament was written.

The evidence for the existence of the Greek language during the Bronze Age derives from a prealphabetical Greek script called Linear B, so named to distinguish it from an earlier, still-undeciphered script called Linear A, which may or may not have been Greek. Linear B was based on the principle that each sign represented one syllable.

Clay tablets engraved in Linear B by means of a sharp instrument have been found at Mycenae, Tiryns, Thebes, Pylos, and Knossos (Crete). With the collapse of the Mycenaean world circa 1200 B.C.E., the script died out, and the art of literacy was lost.

Greece subsequently remained illiterate for more than 400 years. Then, in the early eighth century B.C.E., the Greeks came into contact with a seafaring people called the Phoenicians, who inhabited the coast of Syria. They adapted the Phoenician alphabet to their own language by adding seven vowel sounds (i.e., *a*, short and long *e*, *i*, short and long *o*, and *u*) to the original 16 consonants, making it a much more flexible script. Many of the Phoenician names for the letters entered the Greek alphabet virtually unchanged, including *aleph* (alpha) meaning "ox-head" and *beth* (beta) meaning "house." The same letters also functioned as a numerical system and were used for musical notation.

The earliest surviving examples of the Greek alphabet are dated circa 740 B.C.E. Although some states had their own local variants, the alphabet had become standardized by the early fourth century B.C.E. The Greek alphabet was destined to become the basis for many European scripts, including Latin, modern Greek, and Cyrillic.

Because Greek is an inflected language, the significance of each word is determined not by its order in the sentence but by its ending. Each noun, pronoun, and adjective consists of a stem, which never changes, and an ending, which does. Endings take the form of cases. For example, the genitive case is the case of possession, as in the phrase "the bone *of the dog*" or "the *dog's* bone." Because Greek is an inflected language, it tends to be more economical than English in the number of words it employs. In addition, the definite and indefinite articles (the, a, and an) are frequently omitted, particularly in verse.

A	α	alpha	a
B	β	beta	b
Γ	γ	gamma	g (always hard as in "get," not as in "gent")
Δ	δ	delta	d
E	ε	epsilon	short e (as in "get")
Z	ζ	zeta	z
H	η	eta	long a (as in "ate")
Θ	θ	theta	th
I	ι	iota	i
K	κ	kappa	k
Λ	λ	lambda	l
M	μ	mu	m
N	ν	nu	n
Ξ	ξ	xi	x
O	o	omicron	short o (as in "top")
Π	π	pi	p
P	ρ	rho	r
Σ	σ, ς	sigma	s
T	τ	tau	t
Y	υ	upsilon	u
Φ	φ	phi	ph
X	χ	chi	ch
Ψ	ψ	psi	ps
Ω	ω	omega	long o (as in "porter")

The Greek alphabet.

It is not known what percentage of the Greek population could read and write. What is abundantly clear, however, is that mass literacy never existed on the scale that it exists today. William Harris (1989) has estimated that no more than 30 percent of the Greek population was literate at any one time. Levels of literacy inevitably varied from place to place and from one social group to another. One of the highest levels was achieved by Classical Athens, whose democratic constitution was based on the principle that a majority of the (male) citizenry could read the often lengthy and extremely detailed documents that were recorded on stone. In Sparta, by contrast, where few written records were kept, most of the population was probably completely illiterate. Literacy is likely to have been practically nonexistent among women, those who belonged to the lower social classes, and slaves, apart from those whose job it was to keep accounts of financial transactions or to read aloud to their masters and mistresses.

The most common Greek writing material was *Cyperus papyrus*, a plant that grows in the swamps of Lower Egypt, which was used for writing in Egypt from 3000 B.C.E. onward. The Greeks called this plant *biblos*, from which the word *Bible* derives. Stalks of papyrus were laid out in horizontal and vertical strips and were then entwined and pressed flat to form a scroll. The earliest surviving Greek papyrus, a commentary on the Orphic poems, dates from the fourth century B.C.E. It was found at Derveni, near Thessalonici, in Macedonia. The overwhelming majority of papyri have come to light in Egypt, whose dry soil provides ideal conditions for their preservation. The largest cache has been retrieved from the rubbish dumps of a town called Oxyrhynchus (the name means "the city of the sharp-nosed fish"), situated about 100 miles south of modern Cairo. Oxyrhynchus has so far yielded over 50,000 papyri. They include tax returns, death certificates, and private letters. Many are written on scraps that contain fragments of Greek literature on the reverse. It is thanks to papyrology (i.e., the study of papyri) that many lost works of Greek literature have come to light. Among the most important finds are Sophocles' satyr play *Detectives*, Menander's comedy *The Ill-Tempered Man*, and Aristotle's *Constitution of Athens*.

Papyrology provides us with a slice of Greek life that would otherwise be completely unknown to us. It is the life of the Greek population that settled in Egypt following its conquest by Alexander the Great. It sometimes comes across to us in heart-rending detail. We hear, for instance, of a slave called Epaphroditos, eight years old, who fell to his death out of a bedroom window when he was leaning out to watch the castanet players down below in the street. On a more light-hearted note, we also hear of a schoolmaster called Lollianos, who complained that he never received his salary "except sometimes in sour wine and worm-ridden corn."

Because papyri were relatively expensive to purchase, broken pieces of pottery, known as *ostraka*, frequently served for writing as well. From *ostrakon* comes *ostrakismos*, which give us our word *ostracism*. An *ostrakismos* was a vote cast by the Athenian assembly to banish a person who was judged to be harmful to the state. If more than 6,000 votes were cast, the leading candidate would be exiled from Athens for 10 years. The ballot papers took the form of *ostraka* on which the citizens wrote the name of the candidate of their choice—or rather nonchoice. Thousands of *ostraka* have been preserved in the soil of Greece because, unlike papyri, they are practically indestructible (Garland, 35–40).

FOR MORE INFORMATION

Chadwick, J. *Linear B and Related Scripts*. London: British Museum Publications; Berkeley: University of California Press, 1987.

Garland, R. *Daily Life of the Ancient Greeks*. Westport, Conn.: Greenwood Press, 1998.

Harris, W. V. *Ancient Literacy*. Cambridge, Mass.: Harvard University Press, 1989.

ROME

INTELLECTUAL
LIFE
|
LANGUAGE
& WRITING
|
Mesopotamia

Egypt

Greece

Rome

India

Australian Aboriginals

The Latin language seems to have been widely spoken in ancient central Italy by a number of groups, including the Romans. As the Roman Empire expanded, Latin was the official language of law and government and spread along with Roman conquest. The Romans did not force subject peoples to speak Latin, but ambitious local aristocrats were encouraged to learn the language, and many were eager to do so to further their own goals. The process of Romanization in the provinces further spread Latin, particularly due to the establishment of Latin-speaking Roman colonies, which were often populated by veterans from the army. Once Rome became exposed to Greek culture, upper-class Romans began to learn Greek as well, and a well-educated Roman was expected to be conversant in both languages.

Because nouns in Latin have case endings indicating their grammatical purpose in a sentence, word order in Latin is much more flexible than in English. Graffiti written by ordinary Romans suggest that the daily spoken language was more informal, and less grammatically complex, than the sophisticated Latin found in literary texts. The Latin alphabet is derived from a mixture of Greek letters and some Etruscan ones and has 23 letters (*j*, *u*, and *w* are missing as compared with English). Latin was written from left to right and usually lacks either punctuation or spaces between words. Although Latin is today regarded as a "dead" language, it has been enormously influential, contributing a substantial percentage of root words to English and surviving in evolved form in the Romance languages, including Spanish, French, and Italian.

~*Gregory S. Aldrete*

FOR MORE INFORMATION

Adkins, L., and R. Adkins. *Handbook to Life in Ancient Rome*. New York: Facts on File, 1994.

INDIA

INTELLECTUAL
LIFE
|
LANGUAGE
& WRITING
|
Mesopotamia

Egypt

Greece

Rome

India

Australian Aboriginals

Despite a large number of documents discovered in the ruins of the cities of the Indus Valley, the language and script of this civilization remain as yet undeciphered.

From the time of the *Rig Veda*, Sanskrit has been the primary religious and liturgical language of India. Sanskrit is a language of the Indo-European family of languages, often compared to Latin or Greek. The name *Sanskrit* roughly means "perfected" or "refined," owing largely to the efforts of the ancient Indian grammarian Panini to formalize the language in his fourth century B.C.E. work *Astadhyayi*.

Seal from Mohenjo-Daro. The bull with the prominent hump is a common Indian motif. The meaning of the inscription is uncertain because the writing of the Indus Valley civilization remains undeciphered. Borromeo/Art Resource, NY.

The original revelations of ancient India, the Vedas, were orally transmitted for centuries. To preserve and apply this oral wisdom, ancient India developed six branches of learning. These were the Vedangas, the "limbs of the Veda." Given the necessity for accurate oral transmission of Vedic revelation, and India's emphasis on the sacrality of the Sanskrit language, it is natural that four of the Vedangas dealt with the use and preservation of the language of the Vedas. These disciplines were *siksa*, phonetics and correct pronunciation of Sanskrit; *chandas*, methods for correct metrical and prosodic recitation of the Vedas; *nirukta*, the etymology of Vedic words; and *vyakarana*, grammar. These together were the impetus in ancient India for the emphasis on linguistics. The next Vedanga, *kalpa*, detailed the proper performance of the Vedic sacrifice.

Other languages of ancient India that were derived from Sanskrit are known as *Prakrit* ("natural," "unrefined") languages. The best-known Prakrit language was Pali, in which the original teachings of Buddhism were preserved. After the beginning of the Common Era, however, with the rise of Mahayana texts, many Buddhist writers resorted to using Sanskrit. Other Prakrit languages survive through dramatic literature.

In southern India, the Dravidian language Tamil had a role similar to that of Sanskrit in northern India. In the first centuries of the common era, a corpus of poetic literature developed in Tamil, with its own styles, tropes, and commentary.

~*Matthew Bingley*

FOR MORE INFORMATION

Burrow, T. *The Sanskrit Language*. London: Prometheus, 1955.

INTELLECTUAL
LIFE
|
LANGUAGE
& WRITING
|
Mesopotamia

Egypt

Greece

Rome

India

Australian Aboriginals

NUBIA

Because encounters between Egypt and Nubia were frequent, the Nubians adopted much that was Egyptian, including hieroglyphic writings. See the Egypt entry in the section "Language and Writing" in this chapter for a discussion of the hieroglyphic script that ancient Nubia shared with Egypt.

AUSTRALIAN ABORIGINALS

Verbal communication was enhanced by pervasive multilingualism. All Aborigines needed to have a good working knowledge of the different languages used by neighboring groups. Also, particularly at ceremonial events, communication was carried out through songs and storytelling. Aborigines did not have written language, but they did use a number of nonverbal forms of communication.

About 50,000 years ago, when the first people traveled to Australia, they had to sail across an ocean passage so wide that when they departed, there was no visible land on the horizon, and when they arrived, the land they had left behind had disappeared. The original trips may have been accidental, but it is possible that people set off toward the smoke from fires burning in Australia that were visible although the land was below the horizon. The first travelers perhaps assumed that this smoke indicated that people were living in an unknown land over the horizon. In fact, there had been natural fires as a result of lightning strikes in Australia for millions of years. Fires did, however, signal the existence of land, and people arrived safely on the new shore. From that time, some of the fires that they lit might have been seen by later voyagers and would have served as an incentive for others to try to join them.

In later times, smoke was employed for signaling over long distances. Sometimes this signaling was passive—people might see a cluster of smoke columns from campfires, or the more extensive smoke from a hunting expedition, and work out from the size and number of fires, their direction and distance, and the time of year, who was likely to be present at the site where the fires were lit. Smoke could also be used deliberately to send signals summoning people to attend a ceremony or join a hunt for abundant resources. Nuances of meaning could be conveyed by changing the color of the smoke or the character of a smoke column according to some mutually agreed upon manner.

Most communication over long distances, however, had to be accomplished by personal contact. If a neighboring or related group needed to be informed about a ceremony or funeral, the elders would construct a "message stick" to be carried by a messenger. The stick was notched or marked in a specific fashion, not as a form of written language but as an aid to its carrier, who had memorized the message. The stick functioned almost as a passport or a guarantee of the man's bona fides. If the messenger needed to travel through the territory of neighboring groups to reach his goal, the message stick explained his reason for being on their land. When he arrived, the stick served to remind him of categories of information and of important facts or figures, such as the number of days until a ceremony.

Communication could also occur between members of a group without direct contact. One band of people on a hunting expedition would be able to follow the signs left by another group and in addition might be able to ascertain who was in the group, how fast they were traveling, and what they were doing. Some signs might be left behind deliberately while others were simply the accidental footprints, bent grass, broken twigs, and so on left by any party of travelers.

Communication also took place through painted and engraved trees, rocks, and caves. Such visual symbols might indicate ownership of a particular area or warn travelers that they were approaching sensitive or dangerous (in the religious sense) sites. Tattooed or painted symbols on human bodies and on weapons such as shields could indicate to a knowledgeable observer qualities such as that person's status or affiliation.

~David Horton

FOR MORE INFORMATION

Berndt, R., and C. Berndt. *The World of the First Australians.* Canberra: Aboriginal Studies Press, 1988.

Dortch, C., and B. Muir. "Long Range Sightings of Bush Fires as a Possible Incentive for Pleistocene Voyages to Greater Australia." *Western Australian Naturalist* 14 (1980): 194–98.

Hamlyn-Harris, R. "On Messages and 'Message Sticks' Employed among the Queensland Aborigines." *Memoirs of the Queensland Museum* 6 (1918): 13–36.

Kendon, A. *Sign Languages of Aboriginal Australia.* Cambridge, England: Cambridge University Press, 1988.

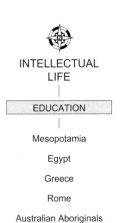

INTELLECTUAL
LIFE

EDUCATION

Mesopotamia

Egypt

Greece

Rome

Australian Aboriginals

Education

In the ancient world, formal education to acquire even a basic literacy in general was only available to a small number of people. Those who did learn such skills were overwhelmingly male, which accounts in part for the predominance of male authors in surviving texts.

Literacy rates were probably lowest in Mesopotamia and Egypt, where even kings and priests were often illiterate. These civilizations solved the need for those with the ability to read and write by developing a special class of people called scribes who made a living by taking dictation, inscribing texts, and reading them. Prospective scribes would attend classes starting from around the age of seven to learn how to read and write. Writing was often done on clay tablets, and a fair amount is known about this educational system because many of these tablets written by students and teachers survive. Repetitive exercises and drills formed a large part of the educational process, and students who did not master their lessons or who were inattentive in class suffered corporal punishment. More advanced lessons focused on mathematics and the study of literature. Those pupils who graduated from this system became valued members of the government or temple bureaucracy, and frequently, their sons would follow in their footsteps.

In Greece and Rome, literacy seems to have been somewhat more widespread, although just how much is a matter hotly contested among scholars. Fifth-century Athens, with its democratic form of government requiring participation from its citizens, perhaps placed a greater premium on literacy than other states. The Greek and Roman systems of education were usually not state run but were left to the initiative and resources of individual families who contracted with freelance teachers to educate their children. Students would progress through a series of instructors who would impart knowledge ranging from learning the alphabet, through reading and writing and the study of literature, and eventually perhaps even instruction in verbal debate skills and logical argumentation. The most famous of these pedagogues were the Greek Sophists, who were sometimes suspected of teaching argument for its own sake and techniques of verbal trickery, such as how to make a good thing appear bad and vice versa. The condemnation of the great philosopher Socrates at his trial, where, among other things, he was found guilty of corruption of the youth, was at least partially based on the questionable assumption that he was such a Sophist.

As soon as writing was invented, education became an important activity, and although literacy is far more widespread today, the basic types of activities practiced by students and the roles of their teachers have changed surprisingly little over the centuries.

~Gregory S. Aldrete

MESOPOTAMIA

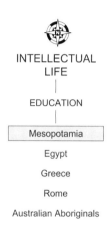

Sumer's great achievement was the invention of writing, and an organized system of education was its natural outgrowth. Most people were not literate. With approximately 600 signs with multiple values, education was confined to the few. Even priests, kings, governors, and judges were illiterate, with few exceptions. Letters were dictated to a professional scribe and would be read to the addressee by another professional scribe. Literacy was highly prized, and only a few rulers, among them, Shulgi, Naram-Sin, Lipit-Ishtar, Assurbanipal, and Darius, boasted of their scribal accomplishments.

The oldest documents, the Uruk tablets, consist primarily of economic and administrative records. But we also find lexical lists used by scribes to learn signs to study elementary vocabulary for use in administrative texts and to categorize the world in which they lived so that an archaic society could better understand itself. The same lists are found about 500 years later at Shuruppak, thereby showing the continuity of a tradition.

The archaic texts offer little information about the education or professional activity of scribes. However, the unity in both the appearance of tablets and the writing conventions from different regions of Babylonia suggests the existence of some kind of regulated system of education circa 3000 B.C.E. The first detailed information concerning the scribal profession and its social status comes from the Ur III period (2112–2004 B.C.E.). Most probably, the purpose of the official Ur III schools was to provide necessary specialized personnel at a time when the demand for scribes was great. From this period come tens of thousands of clay tablets that are administrative in nature, encompassing all aspects of economic life in Sumer. From these texts, we learn that there were thousands of scribes, specializing in all branches of the temple and royal administrations. From this, we can infer that scribal schools must have thrived.

The organization and operation of schools in Mesopotamia are known from the numerous student-teacher exercises, lexical lists, essays on school life, examination texts, and royal hymns in which kings refer to their education. This information comes from the first half of the second millennium B.C.E. After this, small groups of tablets appear at different periods, often retaining the intent of the old tradition but revamping the format.

The student attended school, called a "tablet-house," whose headmaster was called "expert" or "father of the tablet-house." A dean enforced the rules and regulations of the tablet-house, called "supervisor of the tablet-house," and there was even a "man in charge of the whip." Teaching assistants were referred to as "older brothers"; their jobs included writing new tablets for the students to copy, checking the students' work, and listening to memorized lessons. Other faculty members included "the man in charge of Sumerian" and "the man in charge of drawing," as well as proctors in charge of attendance and discipline. Mathematics was a separate part of the curriculum, taught by the "scribe of accounting," "the scribe of measurement," and the "scribe of the field." We know neither the hierarchy of the school nor how salaries were paid. When finished, the student became a scribe, literally, a "tablet-writer."

Education was undertaken only by wealthier families; the poor could not afford the time and cost for learning. Administrative documents from about 2000 B.C.E. list about 500 scribes who are further identified by the names and occupations of their fathers. Their fathers were governors, "city fathers," ambassadors, temple administrators, military officers, sea captains, important tax officials, priests, managers, accountants, foremen, and scribes, in other words, the wealthier citizens of the city. There are references to poor orphan boys adopted and sent to school by generous patrons. There is only one reference to a female scribe at this time. However, cloistered women, celibate devotees of the sun god Shamash and his consort Aya, served as scribes for their own cloister administration. Celibate priestesses may also have devoted themselves to scholarly pursuits.

The Sumerian school may have begun as a temple annex during the third millennium B.C.E.; it was attached to some palaces in the second millennium and later privatized. The first Mesopotamian schools we know of were founded or subsidized by King Shulgi at Nippur and Ur at the end of the third millennium. The actual learning process involved memorization, dictation, writing new lessons and reviewing old ones, reading aloud from a written document, and spelling. The students learned signs, language, and vocabulary through syllabaries (syllabic lists) and lexical lists. The lexical lists provided compilations of botanical, zoological, geographical, and mineralogical information; they also provided important linguistic tools for the study of grammar, bilingual and trilingual dictionaries, and legal and administrative vocabulary. The methods of teaching have given us thousands of "school tablets," often round in shape, with the teacher's copy on one side and the pupil's work on the other. We have the tablets students wrote themselves, from the beginner's first copies to those of the advanced student, whose work could hardly be differentiated from the teacher's. Not every scribe completed the "full course." In fact, the student was probably not required to complete the entire series before attempting the next text of the curriculum. The student copied tablets not only as exercises but at times to build a private library for himself or his teacher.

Despite its professional orientation, the Sumerian school was also a center for literature and creative writing; the Mesopotamian literary "classics" were studied and copied, and new compositions were written. Later, the Akkadians not only used the Sumerian script but also studied the literature of the Sumerians, even imitating their works. The "dictionaries" became useful tools for learning the Sumerian language, which was no longer spoken by the beginning of the second millennium B.C.E. but enjoyed enormous prestige, much like Latin in Western culture.

The student attended classes daily from sunrise to sunset. The student began school between the ages of five and seven years and continued until he became a young man.

We do not know if scribes were expected to have a varied background or to what degree they were expected to specialize as preparation for assuming their posts.

We have several essays on school life, which have been named in modern times (1) "Schooldays," (2) "School Rowdies" (or "The Disputation Between Enkimansi and Girnishag"), (3) "A Scribe and His Perverse Son," and (4) "Colloquy between an Estate Superintendent and a Scribe." "Schooldays" deals with the daily life of the schoolboy as recounted by an alumnus. It was composed by an anonymous schoolteacher about 2000 B.C.E. and tells a story of school life, not unlike today. It begins with the question, "Old Grad, where did you go (when you were young)?" The alumnus answers, "I went to school." The schoolteacher-author asks, "What did you do in school?" The old grad replies:

I recited my tablet, ate my lunch, prepared my (new) tablet, wrote it, finished it; then my model tablets were brought to me; and in the afternoon my exercise tablets were brought to me. When school was dismissed, I went home, entered the house, and found my father sitting there. I explained my exercise-tablets to my father, recited my tablet to him, and he was delighted . . . . When I arose early in the morning, I faced my mother and said to her: "Give me my lunch, I want to go to school!" My mother gave me two rolls, and I set out; my mother gave me two rolls, and I went to school. In school the fellow in charge of punctuality said: "Why are you late?" Afraid and with pounding heart, I entered before my teacher and made a respectful curtsy.

> ### 📷 *Snapshot*
>
> **An Exam Given to a Mesopotamian Student Wanting to Become a Scribe**
>
> A: Come, my son, sit at my feet. I will talk to you, and you will give me information! From your childhood to your adult age you have been staying in the tablet-house. Do you know the scribal art that you have learned?
>
> B: What would I not know? Ask me, and I will give you the answer.
>
> A series of questions follows:
>
> 1. "The element of the scribal craft is the simple wedge; it has six teeth (directions in which it could be written). . . . Do you know its name?"
> 2. Secret meanings of Sumerian words (cryptography).
> 3. Translation from Sumerian to Akkadian and the reverse.
> 4. Three Sumerian synonyms for each Akkadian word. . . .
> 6. Sumerian conjugation of verbs.
> 7. Various types of calligraphy and technical writing. . . .
> 9. To understand the technical language of all classes of priests and other professions, such as silversmiths, jewelers, herdsmen, and scribes.
> 10. How to write, make an envelope, and seal a document.
> 11. All kinds of songs and how to conduct a choir.
> 12. Mathematics, division of fields, and allotting of rations. . . .
>
> On this occasion, the ill-prepared candidate failed the exam. (as cited in Nemat-Nejat, 57–58; originally in Landsberger)

In school, the student misbehaves and is caned by different staff members for a variety of offenses, such as poor class work, sloppy dress, speaking without permission, rising without permission, going to the school gate, not speaking Sumerian with his Sumerian instructor, and poor penmanship (Kramer, 237–40).

Despite a less-than-innovative curriculum, the discipline, and rivalries between classmates (the essay "School Rowdies" depicts a bitter verbal debate between two classmates), the students who persevered graduated from the school. They found jobs, often in the service of the palace or temple, since the goal of the school was to train scribes for various administrative positions in these institutions, as well as other positions, such as royal scribe, district scribe, military scribe, land registrar, scribe for laborer groups, administrator, public secretary to a high administrative official, accountant, copyist ("deaf writer"), inscriber of stone and seals, ordinary clerk, astrologer, mathematician, or professor of Sumerian (Nemet-Nejat, 54–64).

FOR MORE INFORMATION

Kramer, S. N. *The Sumerians: Their History, Culture, and Character.* Chicago, Ill.: University of Chicago Press, 1963.

Landsberger, B. "Scribal Concepts of Education." In *City Invincible: Urbanization and Cultural Development in the Near East,* ed. C. H. Kraeling and R. McAdams, 94–123. Chicago, Ill.: University of Chicago Press, 1960.

Nemet-Nejat, K. R. *Daily Life in Ancient Mesopotamia.* Westport, Conn.: Greenwood Press, 1998.

INTELLECTUAL
LIFE

EDUCATION

Mesopotamia

Egypt

Greece

Rome

Australian Aboriginals

EGYPT

The largest group of workers in Egypt after farmers, scribes included cadres of thousands of bureaucrats, private individuals who handled accounts and correspondence for large estates, and freelancers. Because no public school system existed, the average Egyptian could neither read nor write. The sons of scribes, higher officials, and occasional precocious farm children attended local temples for instruction in letters. Except for separate classes convened for royal or otherwise socially prominent girls, all scholars were male. Each set out in the morning carrying a small basket of bread and beer from home and returned again in the late afternoon.

Beginning instruction consisted of copying hieroglyphic signs over and over until they were committed to memory. Because papyrus was too expensive for this repetitive task, thin slabs of erasable limestone or wood boards with replaceable gesso surfaces were used instead. After learning his ABCs (or, in this case, his vulture, foot, and baskets), a worthy child graduated to papyrus and longer classic texts—generally consisting of moral platitudes. These skills were not easily mastered. In addition to 20 single-syllable picture signs, more than 100 two-syllable signs (*pr, wr,* etc.) and an equal number of three-syllable signs (*nfr,* etc.) had to be committed to memory, along with almost the same number of "determinatives"—endings indicating whether a word's meaning had to do with an activity, an animal, an abstract thought, and so on. With the language, which included a grammar and three tenses, mastered, a student had learned only one of the three forms of Egyptian writing. In addition to hieroglyphs—the picture symbols we most often associate with Egyptian writing—a more cursive form called hieratic was employed for handwriting, and a more abbreviated version called demotic was used for quicker notes.

When all three symbol systems had been committed to memory, a pupil who showed aptitude could move to advanced courses in mathematics and basic building practices, both of which were taught by practical examples rather than abstractions. Problems such as computing the number of bricks needed for a wall of a certain dimension, the amount of provisions a specified number of troops needed for an expedition of given duration or the number of men required for moving an obelisk of a given size prepared graduates for high civil positions in the army or on government construction projects, although most students progressed no farther than mastering the reading and writing appropriate for more mundane occupations.

Such repetitive instruction surely bored most children. Letters abound from fathers who, looking toward the rewards awaiting their son's graduation, urge them to persist, criticizing those who play hooky in local bars and brothels. Since a number of dated and corrected student exercises survive, it seems that assignments were a principal teaching tool. Instead of grades providing motivation for good work, one father reminded his son that "a youngster's ear is in his back; he only listens to the man who beats him" (Montet, 256).

Despite the difficult course of instruction, some students graduated to don the dress of the scribe's trade—a long skirt, rather than the normal short kilt. They carried foot-long scribal palettes—rectangles of wood with two depressions in one end and a slot in the other. The slot held writing brushes; the depressions served as pots for mixing black and red ink. Black was used for the body of a text, and red indicated chapter headings or an especially important phrase. As a scribe, a young man enjoyed opportunities for advancement. Certain orders of priests required scribal skills, as did the quartermaster corps of the army and a host of government jobs above the lowest level. The vast majority of scribes, however, filled the ranks of clerks or simple accountants for the duration of their professional lives (Brier and Hobbs, 82–84).

FOR MORE INFORMATION

Brier, B., and H. Hobbs. *Daily Life of the Ancient Egyptians*. Westport, Conn.: Greenwood Press, 1999.

Lechtheim, M. *Ancient Egyptian Literature*. Vol. 2. Berkeley: University of California Press, 1976.

Montet, P. *Everyday Life in Egypt in the Days of Ramesses the Great*. Translated by A. R. Maxwell-Hyslop and M. Drower. Reprint, Philadelphia: University of Pennsylvania Press, 1981.

GREECE

Prior to the fifth century B.C.E., education was in the hands of private tutors; therefore, only the very wealthy could afford it. Most schools were extremely small, accommodating perhaps no more than about 10 or 15 pupils. We do hear, however, of a few exceptions. Herodotus (*The Histories* 6.27) tells us of a school on the island of Chios that had 120 pupils. In 494 B.C.E., the roof caved in while the boys were learning their letters; tragically, only one survived.

Most Athenian boys began their schooling around the age of seven. They continued as long as their parents could afford to pay their fees—or as long as the parents did not require their sons to be economically productive. There is no record of the fees that were charged. Because democratic Athens required its citizens to be functionally literate, few boys were completely unlettered. Aristophanes makes it clear in *The Knights* (line 188f.) that even an ignorant lout such as a sausage seller knew how to read and write. As Protagoras points out in Plato's dialogue of that name, it was a general rule that "the sons of the most wealthy went to school earliest and left latest" (326c). Not until the Hellenistic period was a system of universal public education

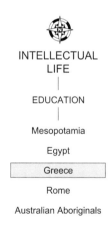

INTELLECTUAL
LIFE

EDUCATION

Mesopotamia

Egypt

Greece

Rome

Australian Aboriginals

established in some cities for all boys, thanks to foundations that funded teachers' salaries.

Basic Athenian education consisted of reading and writing, physical training, and music. Reading and writing were taught by the *grammatistês*. Pupils practiced their letters on waxed tablets, using a pen called a *stylos*. Broken shards of pottery, called *ostraka*, served as scrap paper. The *grammatistês* also provided their pupils with a grounding in literature, by requiring them to learn passages from epic, lyric, and dramatic poetry. Memorization was a key element in the educational process. Niceratus, who figures in Xenophon's *Symposium*, claims that his father made him learn by heart the whole of the *Iliad* and *Odyssey*—some 27,000 lines in all (3.5). Learning by rote sometimes paid off in later life. The Athenians who were taken prisoner by the Syracusans after the disaster of the Sicilian expedition were removed from the stone quarries and given domestic work if they were able to recite passages of Euripides. The most popular musical instrument was the lyre or *kithara*, which was taught by a musician known as a *kitharistês*. It was regarded as such an important part of education that in Aristophanes' *Wasps*, the hero Bdelykleon seeks to excuse a dog's thievery on the grounds that "he never learnt the lyre" (line 959). Only a few children learned how to draw. Little attention was given to mathematics.

Although the Athenian state did not require children to be educated or involve itself in the school curriculum, it legislated to ensure that proper standards of conduct were upheld. The orator Aischines (1.9–12) cites an Athenian law that forbade parents to send their children out of the home before daybreak and insisted that they be collected before sunset. With the exception of slaves called *paidagôgoi* who accompanied their young masters to school and sat behind them during instruction, no adult was allowed to enter the school. If any did, it was a capital offense. Class size was prescribed by law. Publicly sponsored competitions sought to encourage high standards of accomplishment. At the festival known as the Apatouria, for instance, prizes were given to boys for recitation.

The education of Athenian girls was almost completely neglected. The majority received merely a basic training in running the household, generally from their mothers. Girls may even have been actively discouraged from becoming literate to keep them "unspoiled." A fragment from a lost play by Menander states axiomatically, "He who teaches his wife how to read and write does no good. He's giving additional poison to a horrible snake." Although some women could play a musical instrument, as we see from depictions in Greek art, few would have been sufficiently well informed to express an opinion about the political issues of the day. Xenophon's fictional Ischomachos therefore probably speaks for a number of middle-class Athenians when he declares,

When I married my wife, she was not yet fifteen and had been so carefully supervised that she had no experience of life whatsoever. A man should be content, don't you think, if his wife comes to him knowing only how to take wool and make clothes and supervise the distribution of spinning among slaves. (*Household Management* 7.5–6, my translation)

Herodotus (6.60) informs us that in Sparta, some trades and professions were exclusive to certain designated families, including those of herald, flute player, and cook. In Athens, too, many skills and professions were handed down from father to son, due partly to the fact that the lawgiver Solon prescribed that an Athenian father should teach his son a skill if he expected to be supported by him in old age. For instance, the Athenian sculptor Praxiteles was the son of a sculptor, and both his sons and grandson were sculptors as well (Garland, 102–4).

FOR MORE INFORMATION

Beck, F. A. *Greek Education 450–350 BC*. London: Methuen, 1962.
Garland, R. *Daily Life of the Ancient Greeks*. Westport, Conn.: Greenwood Press, 1998.

ROME

In traditional Roman society, and particularly before Rome's overseas conquests, education was conducted by the father, who taught the child whatever he thought was necessary. The stern patrician Cato is the example of this. He personally taught his son to read, to write, to use weapons, and to swim. In this period, a basic level of literacy and military training was the totality of education thought necessary. Education was primarily restricted to male children.

The great change in Roman education happened, as did so many other major changes, when Rome conquered Greece. Exposure to Greek literature and culture raised expectations of what an aristocrat should know. Now they would be expected to know both Greek and Latin, to be familiar with the literature of both cultures, and to be able to give formal orations in public.

The hundreds of thousands of Greek citizens who were enslaved by Rome provided a ready source of teachers. From this time on, the structure of Roman education was that the student passed through a series of teachers, and the highest goal toward which all their education aimed was to produce an eloquent speaker.

The first of these teachers was known as the *paedagogus*. This was a household slave to whom the young boy was entrusted. Ideally, the *paedagogus* was an educated Greek slave and could give the boy his preliminary instruction in Latin and Greek. Technically, the main duty of the *paedagogus* was to look after and protect the child. Thus whenever the boy went out in public, he was always accompanied by his *paedagogus*. Another of the *paedagogus*'s duties was to restrain and discipline a mischievous child, usually either by twisting his ear or beating him with a cane. Depending on their relationship, Romans tended to look back on their *paedagogus* with either fondness or hatred. There are many examples of men who once they became adults, freed their old tutor out of gratitude. The emperor Augustus is one example.

Around the age of six or seven, the student began to go to a more formal type of school. The new teacher was not a family member but was a man who made individual contracts with parents to instruct their children in reading, writing, and arithmetic. He was known as the *litterator*. Often a boy would go through a series of these teachers, learning basic reading, writing, and counting from one, gaining more sophisticated knowledge of the same from a second, and then focusing on literature from a third. A teacher of the more advanced levels was called a *grammaticus*.

INTELLECTUAL
LIFE

|

EDUCATION

|

Mesopotamia

Egypt

Greece

Rome

Australian Aboriginals

On a typical school day, classes began at dawn, so the boy had to get up long before this, get dressed, eat a simple breakfast, and then, accompanied by his *paedagogus*, walk to wherever the school was being held. A very young boy might be carried on the shoulders of the slave.

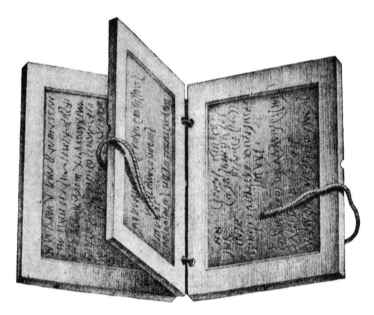

Drawing of wooden tablets with wax panels, which were used by the Romans to write on. Letters were scratched in the wax, and the tablet could be reused by smoothing over the wax. Reproduced from the collections of the Library of Congress.

There were no actual school buildings, so classes might be held anywhere. Sometimes a teacher would rent a shop or an apartment, sometimes he would set up school in a corner of the forum or in a colonnade. This would certainly have made for a distracting academic environment since the teacher and students might find themselves trying to hold classes surrounded by the bustle of people buying and selling and of officials conducting state business and trials. The teacher sat on a thronelike chair, while his pupils sat on simple benches gathered around him. There were no chalkboards or paper, and students would have small wooden tablets with a shallow indentation filled with wax to write upon. Into this wax they would scratch out their lessons. The instrument they used was called a *stilus*, a metal cylinder pointed at one end and flattened at the other. For doing math, students might use an abacus.

Since texts were extremely expensive and fragile, only the teacher would likely have any, and much of Roman education consisted of the teacher reading aloud from these, with the students memorizing long passages by heart. The lack of visual aids could sometimes be overcome by imaginative teachers. One *grammaticus* who specialized in teaching the alphabet had a large troop of slaves, each of whom had strapped to his back a giant wooden copy of one of the letters of the alphabet.

Classes lasted from dawn until noon, but there were some holidays on which the students did not have to go to class. The main break was summer vacation, which usually started around early June and lasted until the middle of October. This was not a fixed schedule, however, but depended on the individual teacher; one particularly zealous *grammaticus* kept his students in class almost all the way through July.

The two main characteristics of this phase of schooling were endless amounts of memorization reinforced by brutal beatings whenever a student failed to perform properly. The teacher had a wide range of punishments available. The most common and simplest was to have the student hold out his hands or lay them flat on a piece of wood; the teacher would then beat them with a cane made of reeds. For more egregious offenses, the teacher would beat the student with a whip consisting of multiple strips of leather. The ultimate punishment was the *catomus*, in which the student was stripped naked and stretched out across the backs of two other students, one of whom would grasp his legs and the other his arms. The unfortunate victim was then savagely flogged by the teacher with a wooden stick. It is not surprising in view of this, that many Romans' memories of school were not pleasant and that they referred to their old teachers not by their names, but by suggestive nicknames, including "The Whacker."

The last couple years of this instruction focused on literature, particularly on Homer and on Roman historical literature such as Virgil. This phase of education usually ended around the age of 13 or so.

There were no colleges or universities, but the wealthiest, most ambitious, or most promising of students then went on to a third class of instructor known as the *rhetor*. The *rhetor* was a specialist who trained students to be effective public speakers. Oratory, or the art of public speaking, was a central component of the life of anyone who wanted to be in the Roman government or army. Since everything about Roman life was public, the ability to get up in public and persuade others of your opinion was a highly prized talent.

The students began by composing and delivering short speeches about mythological topics. These were simply descriptive essays. In the next phase, students prepared comparisons. Some topics that were assigned included comparing Homeric heroes such as Achilles and Odysseus or comparing seafaring and agriculture or town and country life. The next step up in complexity was for the students to put themselves in the place of a famous mythological character and compose the speech he might have given in a certain situation. This exercise emphasized psychological insight and imagination. One popular topic was Achilles talking over the body of his dead friend Patroclus. The ultimate level of their training was to do the same thing with actual historical events, as this was felt to be the best preparation for the speeches they would actually have to give.

~*Gregory S. Aldrete*

FOR MORE INFORMATION

Bonner, S. F. *Education in Ancient Rome*. Berkeley: University of California Press, 1977.

AUSTRALIAN ABORIGINALS

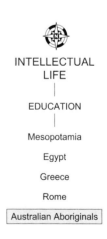

INTELLECTUAL
LIFE
|
EDUCATION
|
Mesopotamia

Egypt

Greece

Rome

Australian Aboriginals

For Aboriginal people, education was an ongoing process that lasted from cradle to grave. Although there were separate categories of knowledge to be gained, such as technological, economic, religious, and artistic, all of them were interwoven into the regular social and cultural life of their society. There was not a universal body of knowledge to which all members of a group were granted equal access. Knowledge was made available in successive units throughout life as individuals passed through various initiation processes to gain access to the next stage. Men and women had parallel bodies of knowledge that overlapped to some degree in technology and economy, but to a minimal extent in matters of art and religion.

One's place of birth and the locations of other significant life events also determined one's rights and access to particular stories or ceremonies, to the use of hunting grounds, to hunting certain animals, and to sacred places. Additionally, the relationships acquired through birth or marriage, and one's consequent place in the complex web of kinship comprising every Aboriginal group, also helped to determine one's access to certain types of knowledge.

Although every Aboriginal person had the ability to carry out the basic functions of tool making, hunting and gathering, food preparation, shelter building, and so on, there were specialists recognized for their particular expertise. Some typical areas in which people possessed special skill included flaking stone tools, making baskets, painting, singing, dancing, canoe making, and kangaroo hunting. With age came the knowledge and wisdom that made elders responsible for deciding such matters as the selection of campsites, hunting grounds, and ceremonies, and the finding of raw materials. They were also in charge of supervising religious observances such as burials and initiation ceremonies.

The young learned in two main ways. No formal schools existed, but there was the equivalent of on-the-job training. From birth, babies accompanied their mothers on food gathering expeditions and were expected to observe what food was collected and how. From a few years of age, children were also expected to help with food gathering. Young boys played games with toy boomerangs and spears to learn the skills that would be necessary later in life. When they were old enough, they began to accompany men on the hunt.

The second educational approach was for children to learn essential texts by heart. It was an oral rather than a literate society, so the transmission of knowledge relied totally on each generation passing on information to the next. Young children watched while artists painted or mapped out water holes and other important sites, and they learned the songs or stories that enabled people to remember the sequence and location of such sites. The stories were often told in the form of legends of the Dreamtime, in which ancestral figures moved from one part of the landscape to the next, creating natural features as they went. Learning such stories or songs meant that when traveling, or during difficult times, people had knowledge of where the next permanent waterhole or food source was located. Similarly, they learned stories about other aspects of life, including the enormous complexity of kinship relationships, behavior that was not permitted, the habits of animals, and the origins of natural features or types of weather.

Learning was not theoretical in style or content but practically based in a kind of apprenticeship system and firmly rooted in example. By the time adulthood was reached, the education that a young Aboriginal person had received fully equipped him or her to earn a living, survive difficult times, function in society, take part in the cultural and religious life of the group, and eventually make a suitable marriage and raise his or her own children.

~David Horton

FOR MORE INFORMATION

Berndt, R., and C. Berndt. *The World of the First Australians*. Canberra: Aboriginal Studies Press, 1988.

Harris, S. *Two Way Aboriginal Schooling*. Canberra: Aboriginal Studies Press, 1990.

Horton, D., ed. *The Encyclopedia of Aboriginal Australia.* Canberra: Aboriginal Studies Press, 2001.

Thomson, D. *Children of the Dreamtime: Traditional Family Life in Aboriginal Australia.* Ringwood, Victoria: Viking O'Neill/Penguin Books, 1983.

Literature

Although writing was first used for tax records and accounting, people eventually began to exploit its potential for expressiveness and for recording emotions and reactions to the world around them. Language could be used to praise the gods in the form of hymns and prayers such as the Vedas of India, to shape a love song, or to describe the beauty of nature. The origins of literature are probably found in the stories that people made up and told to one another. In ancient Greece, oral poetry was memorized and recited at public performances by traveling bards, but over time these epics were written down and became more finalized in form. Instead of just being performed, poems, epics, and plays could also be read by those who were literate and preserved for future generations.

While ancient literature was often preoccupied with the exploits of gods and heroes, as in the Mesopotamian epic of *Gilgamesh,* the Indian masterpiece the *Mahabharata,* Homer's *Iliad,* and Virgil's *Aeneid,* literature also addressed the lives and concerns of everyday people and even at times provided escapist entertainment. The poet Hesiod wrote the *Theogony,* about the creation of the universe and the origins of the gods, but he also wrote *The Works and Days,* about a farmer's life and its trials. Literature could be used to describe the world but also to analyze and criticize it. The Greek tragedies of Sophocles, Aeschylus, and Euripides and satires by such Roman writers as Juvenal and Martial offered sharp critiques of contemporary society.

Then as now, language could be used to describe both exalted emotions and everyday events. We still read letters written by Cicero to his friends as well as his philosophical tracts. Literature has always been employed, in a wide variety of genres, to examine the entire spectrum of human concerns.

~Gregory S. Aldrete

INTELLECTUAL
LIFE
|
LITERATURE
|
Mesopotamia

Egypt

Greece

Rome

India

MESOPOTAMIA

We do not know the real origins of Sumerian literature. Our only knowledge comes from Berossus, a third-century B.C.E. priest of Marduk who lived in Babylon. At the request of the Seleucid king Antiochus I, Berossus wrote *Babyloniaca,* a book about ancient Mesopotamian cultural traditions and history.

The earliest literary texts found so far date to approximately 2400 B.C.E. and are from Ebla, Abu Salabikh, and Fara. We do not know the role of oral tradition in the formation of these compositions. It is possible that generations of storytellers and scribes were involved in creating the final product.

INTELLECTUAL
LIFE
|
LITERATURE
|
Mesopotamia

Egypt

Greece

Rome

India

Some scribes signed their names to tablets as early as 2600 B.C.E. Generally, the authors of literary texts remained anonymous; however, a catalog from Nineveh lists authors and editors of some well-known compositions, such as the *Epic of Gilgamesh*. Later scribes listed their lineage, giving the names of their fathers and even earlier ancestors. Scribes usually described themselves by the simple term "scribe," but sometimes they qualified this with further titles, such as "junior scribe," "exorcist," "astrologer," and so on. A few compositions appear to have been composed by a single author; these works show uniqueness in language, subject matter, and artistic development. In some cases, the texts actually identify the author in the narrative or in an acrostic.

Sumerian literature is about equivalent to biblical literature in size, but much of Sumerian literature still remains to be discovered. Most is written in the main Sumerian dialect. However, the speeches of women and goddesses in myths and erotic poetry, as well as lamentations recited by male singers, were written in "the language of women." Most Sumerian literature we have today comes from later copies. The Babylonians and Assyrians imitated, revised, and translated Sumerian literature. There are also numerous Sumerian texts with interlinear translations into Akkadian. Sumerian literature influenced Akkadian literature in style, viewpoint, and choice of subject.

> *"He gave me dagger and sword—'it becomes you,' he said to me."*

During the second half of the second millennium B.C.E., Kassite scribes, the last great authors and editors of Babylonia, standardized many literary works. New texts entered the canonical corpus at a later date; some were very popular and became widely distributed. As texts were copied and recopied, the scribes sometimes edited the compositions by adding or deleting.

Poetry was generally favored over prose. The language of the texts tended to be simplified over time. Texts that could be either shortened or expanded usually survived.

In Mesopotamian tradition, literary compositions are generally named according to the first few words of the text, so that *When Above* is the native title for *The Epic of Creation*, and *He Who Saw Everything* is the native title for *The Epic of Gilgamesh*. The ancient Mesopotamians did not divide literature into specific categories, although modern scholars prefer to classify texts as myths and epics, prayers and hymns, essays, wisdom literature, and historiography.

Incantations, the first category of literature to be discovered at Fara and Ebla (ca. 2400 B.C.E.), were written throughout the third millennium B.C.E. By the beginning of the second millennium, incantations were compiled, organized by subject (such as those against evil spirits), and later provided with interlinear translations into Akkadian. Here is an incantation against an attack by rabid dogs:

It is fleet of foot, powerful on the run,
Strong-legged, broad-chested.
The shadow of a wall is where it stands,
The threshold is its lurking place.
It carries its semen [that is, foam] in its mouth,
Where it bit, it left its offspring.

(Incantation to survive a dog's bite, incantation of Ea [the god of wisdom and benefactor of mankind].) (as cited in Foster, 127)

Hymns to the gods and their temples are also found at about the same time. Some of the best were composed by the first known author, Enkheduanna, high priestess of the moon god Nanna and daughter of King Sargon of Akkad. She wrote a cycle of 42 short hymns. In a hymn titled "The Indictment of Nanna," Enkheduanna used her considerable literary skill as a poet to describe being forced from office and escaping to Ur.

As for me, my Nanna takes no heed of me.
He has verily given me over to destruction in murderous straits.
Ashimbabbar has not pronounced my judgment.
Had he pronounced it: what is it to me? Had he not pronounced it: what is it to me?
(Me) who once sat triumphant he has driven out of the sanctuary.
Like a swallow he made me fly from the window, my life is consumed.
He made me walk in the bramble of the mountain.
He stripped me of the crown appropriate for the high priesthood.
He gave me dagger and sword—"it becomes you," he said to me. (as cited in Hallo and van Dijk, 29)

Myths and epics narrate events about major and even minor deities, as well as semilegendary rulers such as Gilgamesh. Wisdom literature has been given this name because of its affinity to Proverbs, Job, and Ecclesiastes in the Bible. The focus of this literature is humankind and a concern with moral and ethical problems. Instructions, proverbs, and riddles are the earliest known subcategories of wisdom literature.

Riddles are as old as proverbs, and sometimes their puns and allusions elude the modern reader; for example:

(What is it?)
A house with a foundation like heaven,
A house which like a copper kettle has been covered with linen,
A house which like a goose stands on a (firm) base,
He whose eyes are not open has entered it,
He whose eyes are (wide) open comes out of it?
Its solution is: It's the school. (as cited in Sjöberg, 159, and Kramer, 236)

While the last three lines are clear—the purpose of school is to educate—the beginning of the riddle is completely obscure to us. Perhaps, unlike other wisdom categories, riddles do not always bear the test of time.

Next we find royal hymns, celebrating the events and accomplishments of the king. Many hymns to the gods also ended with a prayer for the ruling king, much like the invocation "God save the Queen!" The king was regarded as being of both human and divine parentage, with the human partners representing Ishtar, the goddess of love, and her lover, Tammuz, the shepherd god. From poetry celebrating this sacred marriage grew secular love poetry, sometimes addressed to the king or to be read by him and his bride.

Hymn writing became such an important creative effort in Sumer that the scribes themselves actually categorized the hymns, adding a special note to the end of each composition, such as "harmony hymn," "musical hymn," "hymn of heroism." Some hymns were classified according to the accompanying musical instruments, such as lyre, drum, and unidentified string instruments. There are also choral refrains and instructions to bow.

Later philosophical works should be included in the category of wisdom literature. The concept of justice and just rewards evolved slowly in Mesopotamia. Mesopotamians assumed that the gods ruled the universe and that humans were punished for neglecting the gods and rewarded for serving them.

After the fall of Ur (ca. 2000 B.C.E.), Sumerian became a dead language, learned only by the educated scribes, who cataloged, copied, and translated Sumerian texts into Akkadian; the scribes even continued to compose texts in Sumerian. The prestige of Babylonian learning went beyond Mesopotamia's borders. Some compositions continued in bilingual and even trilingual versions, while others disappeared. An Akkadian literature developed, sometimes revising Sumerian works. New works appeared, such as "The Poor Man of Nippur" in Assyria, a humorous piece about a poor man cheated by the mayor, whom he later outwits to exact revenge.

We do not know if the general public was familiar with written literature, since only scribes could read and write. Perhaps literature was written by the scribes as part of their curriculum and even for their own amusement. We know that there was court poetry. Some hymns and epics were recited at religious celebrations. In general, literature was passed down by the scribes to subsequent generations of scribes.

Sumerian myths and epics lack an intensification of feeling and excitement as the story progresses, so the story does not build to a climax. The characters appear to be flat. In the case of epic tales about heroes, the Sumerians did not always integrate individual episodes into a larger whole. However, Akkadian myths and epics have an awareness of storytelling techniques. For example, the hero hesitates before the big battle, thereby intensifying our experience once he ventures forth to fight his opponent. Also, unlike the Sumerians, the Akkadians integrate various stories about Gilgamesh (some with Sumerian antecedents), as well as the beloved Flood story, into an epic tale of 12 tablets. *The Epic of Gilgamesh* contains adventures and encounters with strange creatures, both men and gods. But also central to the story are human relationships and feelings, such as loneliness, friendship, love, loss, revenge, regret, and fear of death. Some myths from first millennium B.C.E. Assyria also have a political slant to combat the pro-Babylonian factions at the royal court.

The Mesopotamians loved to write letters, many of which have survived. Most were related to business matters, but occasionally we find a personal letter. Royal correspondence is some of the most interesting, giving information on many facets of court life and the daily business of running the government, such as repair of flood damage, transportation, and neglect of duties. There were references to war, reports on enemies by the king's spies, and reports on missing persons.

Economic and administrative documents are known from the beginning of writing in Mesopotamia. Economic documents concern a variety of topics, such as sales contracts, warranty deeds, marriage settlements, adoption contracts, inheritance documents, loan agreements, receipts, court decisions, wage memos, and so on. Administrative documents were a bureaucratic tool for recording the movement of goods and the responsibility of personnel; taxes, tribute, yields of temple lands, accounts of animals and animal products, and distribution of goods and rations were among the records kept by officials.

Writing was created by economic necessity. Developed for administrative purposes, it was soon used in the creation of myths and other categories of literature (Nemet-Nejat, 64–76).

FOR MORE INFORMATION

Dalley, S. *Myths from Mesopotamia*. New York: Oxford University Press, 1992.

Foster, B. R. *Before the Muses: An Anthology of Akkadian Literature*. 2nd ed. 2 vols. Bethesda, Md.: CDL Press, 1996.

Hallo, W. W., and J. J. A. van Dijk. *The Exaltation of Inanna*. Yale Near Eastern Researches 3. New Haven, Conn.: Yale University Press, 1968.

Kramer, S. N. *The Sumerians: Their History, Culture, and Character*. Chicago, Ill.: University of Chicago Press, 1963.

Nemet-Nejat, K. R. *Daily Life in Ancient Mesopotamia*. Westport, Conn.: Greenwood Press, 1998.

Sjöberg, A. "The Old Babylonian Eduba" In *Jacobsen Festschrift*. Assyriological Studies 20. Chicago, Ill.: University of Chicago Press, 1975.

EGYPT

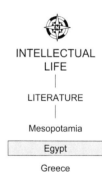

INTELLECTUAL
LIFE

LITERATURE

Mesopotamia

Egypt

Greece

Rome

India

Although probably less than 5 percent of its population was literate, Egypt, like any other great civilization, employed a large bureaucracy to collect taxes, record business transactions and preserve the country's history—all tasks that required writing. Besides being crucial for the business of the country, written work provided the literate minority with both instruction and pleasure.

In addition to record keeping and religious writing, literature, where the craft was as important as the content, existed as well. Wisdom literature, simply called "Instructions" by their authors, were texts that first appeared during the Old Kingdom to guide younger generations. Their aristocratic authors, princes and viziers, thus instructed their sons how to attain and prosper in high offices. The "Instructions to Kagemni" advise modesty:

The respectful man prospers.
Praised is the modest one.
The tent is open to the silent. (as cited in Lichtheim, vol. 1, 59–61)

In a set of 37 maxims, the vizier Ptahotep gives his son, and us, a view of the moral system of the ancient Egyptians. One should know one's place:

If you are among guests
at the table of one greater than you,
Take what he gives as it is set before you. (as cited in Lichtheim, vol. 1, 61–80)

And one should follow reason rather than emotion:

The trusted man does not vent his belly's speech,
He will himself become a leader . . .
The great hearted is god-given,
He who obeys his belly belongs to the enemy. (as cited in Lichtheim, vol. 1, 61–80)

Ptahotep also counsels against women and greed. "In whatever place you enter, beware of approaching the women!" "Guard against the vice of greed. . . . The greedy has no tomb." Mixed with the advice of restraint—in lovers, eating and speech—runs the belief that justice will prevail. In an equivalent of our "Crime does not pay," Ptahotep proclaims, "Crime never lands its wares, In the end it is justice that lasts."

Marsh workers along the Nile River gather papyrus plants, which will be used to form papyrus sheets to write on. Drawing by Rivka Rago.

The Egyptian sense of order, with everything and everyone in its proper place, led to the highly structured society reflected in wisdom literature. Know your place and be restrained; the rich are supposed to be rich, so do not rock the boat. The pharaoh Khety counseled:

Don't reduce the nobles in their possessions.
Beware of punishing wrongfully,
Do not kill, it does not serve you.
Punish with beatings and detentions,
Thus will the land be well ordered. (as cited in Lichtheim, vol. 2, 97–109)

By the time of the New Kingdom, a growing class of well-to-do nonaristocrats required their own wisdom literature that encouraged the same virtues as in the Old Kingdom texts but preached those values from the mouths of scribes, rather than kings and princes. Any, a scribe of Queen Ahmose-Nefertari, instructs his son:

Don't indulge in drinking beer,
lest you utter evil speech,
and don't know what you are saying.
If you fall and hurt your body,
none holds out a hand to you;
Your companions in drinking
Stand up saying: "Out with the drunk!" (Lichtheim, vol. 2, 135–46)

This was the way a working-class man told his son to stay out of bars.

Although wisdom literature had the practical purpose of instruction, a large body of fictional literature was written purely for entertainment. Because most Egyptians were unable to read, and those who could, in most cases, were unable to afford a papyrus for mere entertainment, these short stories were probably read at gatherings, much as Middle Eastern storytellers entertained the illiterate until modern times. Egyptian short stories deal with magic and mystery, heroes and bravery, and almost always have happy endings. Probably the most famous is the "Tale of Sinhue"(see Simpson, 57–74).

Sinhue, an aristocrat and a loyal courtier of the Middle Kingdom pharaoh Senusert I, flees Egypt for the northern lands of Syria-Palestine when his pharaoh dies. He endures hardships, almost dying of thirst and hunger, but is finally rescued by a local prince who recognizes Sinhue, having met him on an earlier trip to Egypt. Sinhue's skills and virtues enable him to prosper in his new land, and the tale chronicles his rise to respectability. He marries a princess and becomes an owner of cattle and large tracts of land, but as in any good tale, he is waylaid by a villain. A local warrior, jealous of Sinhue's wealth and status, challenges him to mortal combat. After preparing his bow, arrows, shield, and dagger, Sinhue marches toward his enemy with a crowd cheering him on. The villain fires first from a distance that allows Sinhue to sidestep the arrow and continue forward until he draws close enough to fire back. Sinhue pierces his enemy's neck. Moving in for the kill, Sinhue dispatches him with his battle ax. As is traditional, Sinhue appropriates his rival's cattle and goods to become even more wealthy. He fathers numerous children and enters his twilight years as one of the most respected men of his adopted tribe.

Despite Sinhue's successes, he remains an Egyptian at heart, realizing that if he dies abroad and is not mummified, he will lose his chance for immortality. When the son of the pharaoh Sinhue originally served hears of Sinhue's desire to return to Egypt, he sends an entourage to escort Sinhue home. The story proclaims Sinhue's joyful and triumphant return, as he is welcomed by the new pharaoh and his children and is given land and a grand house so he can spend his final days in comfort. Although the "Tale of Sinhue" is intended as entertainment, it contains the clear message that there is no place like home, especially if home is Egypt.

> ### 📷 Snapshot
>
> **An Egyptian Love Song**
>
> My love is over on one side,
> the river between us.
> The river is high now,
> and there's a crocodile on the sandbank.
> I dive into the river and brave the current.
> My heart is strong.
> The crocodile seems small to me,
> the torrents are like ground under my feet.
> Her love makes me strong;
> It makes a water spell for me. (as cited in Brier and Hobbs, 198–99; originally in Foster, 193)

Love poetry also existed in Egypt, becoming particularly popular during the New Kingdom. As in all love poems, separated lovers pine for their loved ones, extolling the pleasures of ecstasy (sometimes in graphic detail). Women are compared to the beauties of nature, and couples scheme how to meet (Brier and Hobbs, 195–99).

FOR MORE INFORMATION

Brier, B., and H. Hobbs. *Daily Life of the Ancient Egyptians*. Westport, Conn.: Greenwood Press, 1999.

Foster, J. *Love Songs of the New Kingdom*. Austin: University of Texas Press, 1992.

Lichtheim, M. *Ancient Egyptian Literature*. 3 vols. Berkeley: University of California Press, 1973, 1976, 1980.

Simpson, W. K. *The Literature of Ancient Egypt*. New Haven, Conn.: Yale University Press, 1972.

GREECE

Probably the works that the Greeks would have identified as their most important literature were the great epic poems of Homer: *The Iliad* and *The Odyssey*. These were originally oral poetry recited by wandering bards during the Dark Ages of Greece and were eventually written down about 750 B.C.E. *The Iliad* tells the story of a great war involving all the Greek city-states against the Trojans on the coast of what is present-day Turkey. The Greeks lay siege to Troy for 10 years, at the end of which the city is captured and burnt. *The Odyssey* describes the fantastic adventures and tribulations experienced by one of the Greeks, Odysseus, during his 10-year journey home from the Trojan War. Homer's poems are set in the time prior to the Dark Ages, and these half-remembered figures and events have become mythical and larger than life in his poems. Homer became the great benchmark work of literature for subsequent civilizations. Greeks, and later, Romans, would memorize long passages from his writings, and his poems and their mythology became a common frame of reference in art, literature, and even everyday interactions.

Today, the types of Greek literature that are perhaps still the most vibrant are the tragedic and comedic plays produced in Athens in the fifth century B.C.E. These plays remain a staple of theater today, and the way in which modern audiences and actors can still reinterpret them and find relevance in them speaks to their greatness as timeless works of literature. We have complete plays from only three Attic tragedians. Of the works of Aeschylus (525–456 B.C.E.), the earliest of the three, we possess only seven. Aeschylus introduced a second actor into Greek plays, which enabled a dialogue between two actors to take place on stage. He described his work as "slices from the great banquet of Homer," although his earliest surviving play is the *Persians*, a historical drama that deals with the Persian naval defeat at Salamis in 480 B.C.E. Aeschylus's masterpiece is the *Oresteia*, which was produced in 458 B.C.E. when he was 67 years old. The *Oresteia*, his only complete trilogy that we possess, traces the fortunes of the house of Atreus from the murder of Agamemnon by his wife Clytemnestra through to the acquittal of his son Orestes for avenging his father's death. Aeschylus, who fought at the battle of Marathon, allegedly met his death when an eagle dropped a tortoise on his bald head in the belief that it was a stone.

Aeschylus's successor, Sophocles (495–406 B.C.E.), is also represented by only seven tragedies. His introduction of a third actor enabled more complicated dramatic interchanges between actors to take place. This also had the incidental consequence of reducing the chorus to the role of spectator. His most celebrated drama, *Oedipus the King*, traces Oedipus's discovery of the fact that he has inadvertently killed his father and married his mother. At the end of his life, Sophocles was said to have been taken to court by one of his sons, who tried to have him declared insane. The poet successfully refuted the charge by reading out one of the choruses from the play that he was currently working on. He then turned to the jury and inquired, "Do you consider that to be the work of a madman?" Despite the fact that his plays illustrate the inscrutable will of the gods, Sophocles was a humanist. The following lines, which are delivered by the Chorus in *Antigone*, seem to echo the poet's own judgment on human achievement:

Wonders are many, but none is more wonderful than man, who traverses the grey deep in wintery storms, making his way through waves that crash around him, wearing away the oldest of the gods, Earth, the indestructible, ploughing the soil year in and year out with his horses . . . . Only Death he has found no way to escape, though from irresistible sickness he has devised a way out. His ingeniousness and contriving are beyond everything. Now he makes his way to destruction, now to greatness. When he establishes laws and divine oaths and justice, his city rides high. (lines 332ff., my translation)

Nineteen extant dramas written by Euripides (480–406 B.C.E.) survive. Euripides, Sophocles' younger contemporary, consistently depicted the gods as violent and inhumane. There is a tradition that he caused so much offense in Athens that he was prosecuted for atheism, though we do not know for certain whether this is true. In *Bacchai*, one of his last plays, the god Dionysos takes terrible revenge on the royal house of Thebes, which has denied his divinity, by causing a mother to tear her son limb from limb. The poet became so alienated and embittered at the end of his life that he abandoned Athens for Macedon, where *Bacchai* was performed. It is said that he met his death by being torn apart by hunting dogs—another tradition of dubious authenticity.

The majority of tragedies are set in Greece's heroic past and depict the fortunes of her royal houses. Only a minority are set in Athens, and none at all in contemporary Athens. This does not mean that they were devoted to the exploration of outworn themes. Rather, the heroic past served as a backdrop for the lively investigation of contemporary political, moral, and social issues. Aeschylus's *Eumenides*, for instance, which was produced in 458 B.C.E. as the third play in the *Oresteia*, contains a clear and ringing endorsement of the democratic revolution that took place in Athens four years earlier.

All tragedy, like comedy, is written in a variety of meters. The choral passages are punctuated by "episodes" that resemble the scenes of a modern play. A central feature of many plays is the *agôn*, which takes the form of a contest or dispute between two characters, each of whom seeks to defeat his opponent in argument. In Sophocles' *Antigone*, for instance, the *agôn* between Creon and his son Haemon turns upon the justice of Creon's decision to wall up Antigone alive in punishment for having given burial rites to her brother, who has been condemned as a traitor.

Although the majority of tragedies are concerned with violent and destructive actions, the audience never sees any violence perpetrated on stage. Instead, it was common practice for a messenger to provide an extremely detailed description of a murder, suicide, self-mutilation, or other grisly occurrence that he has just witnessed offstage.

Evidence for fifth-century comedy is even more meager than for tragedy. We possess only 11 plays by a single dramatist, Aristophanes (ca. 450–ca. 385 B.C.E.). Highly topical in subject matter, they contain plentiful references to events and personalities in contemporary Athens, many of which are lost on the modern reader. They are also extremely ribald and scatological. Frequently, the plot turns upon a solution to a contemporary problem, such as how to end the Peloponnesian War. In *Acharnians*, for instance, the hero, who is a very average Athenian citizen called Dikaiopolis, achieves his goal by making a private peace with the Spartans. Similarly in *Lysistrata*, the women of Athens decide to jump-start the peace process by refusing to have sex with their husbands. Other plays are even more fantastic. *Birds*, for instance, is a fantasy about two Athenians who, fed up with all the pressures of modern life, attempt to set up a new city among the birds, called Cloudcuckooland. In *Frogs*, Dionysos descends to Hades to bring back Euripides from the dead, although in the end he decides instead to resurrect Aeschylus, since Euripides' poetry is partly responsible for Athens' current troubles.

In the fourth century B.C.E., a new style of comedy evolved that was almost entirely shorn of chorus and contained no contemporary allusions. Its greatest exponent was Menander (342–ca. 293 B.C.E.). Only one of his plays, *The Ill-Tempered Man*, has survived in complete form. Most of his plots explore the theme of romantic love through a complex intermingling of improbable devices including identical twins, broken families, and abandoned children. The genre, which is known as New Comedy, was taken over and adapted by the Romans. New Comedy was destined to provide the basis for comic inventiveness for centuries to come, an obvious example being Shakespeare's *Comedy of Errors*.

Tragedy and comedy may be said to be two sides of the same coin. The principal difference was that whereas tragedy explored the tragic consequences of conflict, comedy envisioned the possibility of some kind of reconciliation or resolution, however far-fetched it might be. Between these extremes, there was little place for melodrama or sentimentality (Garland, 186–89).

FOR MORE INFORMATION

Baldock, M. *Greek Tragedy: An Introduction*. Bristol, England: Bristol Classical Press and Focus Publishing, 1989.

Baldry, H. C. *The Greek Tragic Theatre*. London: Chatto and Windus, 1978.

Garland, R. *Daily Life of the Ancient Greeks*. Westport, Conn.: Greenwood Press, 1998.

INTELLECTUAL
LIFE
|
LITERATURE
|
Mesopotamia

Egypt

Greece

Rome

India

ROME

In the Roman Republic, there was relatively little literature. For much of Republican history, the Romans were farmers and soldiers and had little time or inclination for poetry. After Rome had conquered Greece and was in turn conquered by Greek culture, Rome began to take a greater interest in literature. Until the very late Republic, however, most Roman literature consisted of imitations of Greek authors. The area in which Roman authors were most successful at imitating the Greeks was theater, and in particular in writing comedic plays. The Romans produced several great comedic playwrights. The most prolific was Plautus. He wrote more than 130 plays, many of which directly imitated Hellenistic new comedy, specifically the plays of Menander. Plautus's plays were filled with jokes, slapstick, and buffoonery and usually addressed themes of frustrated love affairs and mistaken identity. The characters in his plays were stereotypes, such as the disloyal scheming slave, good-natured prostitutes, unfaithful wives, and dirty old men. His plays were frequently named after these characters, such as one that was called "The Braggart Soldier."

The late Republic witnessed several talented writers. Among these was the poet Catullus, who wrote memorable poems about the joys and pains of love. The most prolific author was the politician and orator Cicero, who in addition to manuals on oratory and the texts of his speeches, wrote many works of philosophy. He even published seven books of the letters he wrote to other people. More writing survives from Cicero than any other author in the ancient world, and at least partly because of him, the late Republic is one of the best documented periods in Roman history.

The next phase of Roman literature is known as the Golden Age, and it corresponded with the reign of the first emperor, Augustus (31 B.C.E.–14 C.E.). This short period produced no less than three poets of great talent. Augustus strongly desired to have his achievements memorialized in poetry and thus took a very active role in promoting poets and attempting to direct their efforts. In one way or another, the works of all three of the Golden Age poets are reactions to Augustus's patronage.

The most obvious example of this patronage can be seen in the works of the poet Horace. The son of a freed slave, Horace became a favorite poet of the emperor. He wrote patriotic poems praising the reign of Augustus and composed poems to celebrate various events in the emperor's life and achievements. He also wrote satires that contrasted with his court poetry, being written in conversational tone and using everyday language. These satires poke fun at various human behaviors but were usually meant in a good-natured rather than a cruel way.

The next of the three poets, Ovid, wrote a work called the *Art of Love*, which is basically a practical manual of advice on how to seduce women. Another major work of Ovid's was the *Metamorphosis*. This compilation and retelling of Greek and Roman myths became important in later times as one of the main sources for ancient mythology. Augustus was very concerned with public morality and in consequence was quite upset by Ovid's *Art of Love*. He was so offended that he banished Ovid and sent him to live in exile north of the Black Sea.

The last of the three great poets of this time was Virgil. Augustus wanted Virgil to write a great epic poem celebrating the emperor's reign. His hope was that Virgil would be the Roman version of Homer and produce a great national epic that would become the cornerstone of Roman literature. Augustus got what he wanted, and Virgil did write the great Roman epic, but not on the subject that the emperor wanted. Instead of writing his epic poem about Augustus, he wrote about Rome's earliest history. This epic poem, called the *Aeneid*, was about the foundation of Rome. Virgil deliberately imitated Homer's works, and his hero experiences most of the same adventures that Homer's did. Despite the superficial similarities with Homer, however, the poem has a distinctly Roman flavor and praises Roman virtues. The two main messages of the work are that Rome's rise to power was the will of the gods and that the hero of the poem, whose name is Aeneas, displays the Roman virtues of determination, piety, and self-sacrifice for the good of the state. Virgil died before he had finished the poem, and because he did not want it to be published in less-than-perfect form, in his will he ordered that it be burnt. Augustus personally intervened to save the manuscript and had it published in its incomplete form.

The next era of literature was called the Silver Age, which lasted for about 100 years after the death of Augustus. One significant writer of this time was Seneca—the same Seneca who lived through the reigns of Caligula and Claudius and was the personal tutor of the emperor Nero. Seneca was an interesting person in that during an age of excesses he advocated a return to simpler values and lifestyles. He was a philosopher of the Stoic school and wrote a number of philosophical *Moral Essays*, such as one called "On Anger," which, as one might expect, advocates that people should control their baser emotions. In addition to his philosophical works, Seneca wrote a number of tragedic plays that are particularly gruesome variants of traditional Greek mythological themes. In the end, he could not control his pupil, Nero, and determined to commit suicide before the emperor could kill him. Despite the many works on suicide he had written, he did not seem to manage his own very well. First he cut his wrists, but after a while he wasn't bleeding profusely enough, so he then cut the veins in his ankles. This still didn't kill him, so he next cut the arteries behind his knees. Since he was still not dead, he took the opportunity to dictate another essay to his secretaries while he waited to bleed to death. Becoming exasperated, he ordered some poison to be brought and drank it, but this didn't work either. Finally, he was suffocated in the bath.

Some of the earliest surviving examples of another type of literature, the novel, date from the first two centuries of the Roman Empire. Extended prose works of fiction were not thought of as a high or even reputable form of literature at the time. One novel that survives in its entirety is called the *Metamorphosis*. This is its formal title, but it is more popularly known as *The Golden Ass*. The author, a man named Apuleius, lived in the second century C.E., when Rome was at its height. The protagonist of this comic novel is Lucius, a lustful and opportunistic man. He is staying at the house of a sorceress, and after witnessing the sorceress's powers, he attempts to copy them but of course gets the spell wrong with the result that he is transformed into an ass (donkey). All it will take to change him back is to eat some rose petals, but before he can do this, robbers plunder the house, and not knowing that the ass is really Lucius, they steal him. This sets Lucius off on a series of misadventures in ass form in which he changes owners many times and suffers many indignities. Over the course of the novel, various characters tell many other stories, ranging from accounts of Greek myths to the description of a soldier who encounters a werewolf. The ass's adventures become ever more outrageous, until at the end, the goddess Isis appears to him in a vision. The book concludes with him restored to human form and being inducted as an initiate of Isis in a mysterious ritual.

Despite the many works on suicide he had written, Seneca did not seem to manage his own very well.

Another novel surviving from this time is the *Satyricon*, written by the author Petronius. The *Satyricon* is the comic account of the adventures of two bumbling men and the beautiful young slave boy with whom both are infatuated. The centerpiece of the novel, and its most famous scene, is when they manage to get an invitation to the extravagant dinner party of a former slave, Trimalchio, who has gained both his freedom and an enormous fortune. The dinner of Trimalchio, which takes up nearly half the book, is an incredible orgy of food and excess. Unfortunately, the end of the manuscript is lost, so we do not know the outcome of the novel.

A notable poet of the empire was Juvenal, who lived in the second century C.E. and wrote *The Satires*, a series of bitterly scathing poems about aspects of Roman culture. The most important of these is probably his third satire, "Against the City of Rome," because it gives us one of the most vivid portraits of what everyday life was like for the poor inhabitants of the city. In the course of walking down a street, the narrator of the satire is elbowed by some passing slaves, has his toes stomped on by the boots of a soldier, is nearly crushed beneath the toppling cargo of an overloaded wagon, and is menaced by pots, garbage, and excrement being thrown out the windows of high-rise apartments.

Rome also produced some memorable writers of history. Livy, who was a rough contemporary of Augustus, wrote a monumental *History of Rome*, which outlines all of Roman history from the foundation of the city until his own time. He wrote 142 books of this history, of which only 35 and some fragments survive. His history is perhaps the best record of the legendary heroes of early Rome, who defined Roman virtues and values. Tacitus (ca. 56–ca. 117) was a senator as well as a historian. A member of a provincial aristocratic family probably from southern Gaul or northern Italy, he was consul in 97 C.E. and proconsul of the province of Asia in 112. His literary works are the *Dialogus*, a work on orators and oratory, the *Agricola*, a biography of his father-in-law, Agricola, who conquered much of Britain, the *Germania*, an account of Germany and its inhabitants, the *Annals*, a history of Rome from the death of Augustus in 14 C.E. to 68 C.E., and the *Histories*, a history of Rome from 68 C.E. to 96 C.E. Only portions of these last two works are extant. Tacitus is famous for his abrupt, gnomic, and cynical style.

Another interesting Roman senatorial author is Pliny the Younger, who was an eyewitness to the eruption of Mount Vesuvius in 79 C.E., which buried the city of Pompeii. He made a name for himself in the law courts, then had a successful senatorial career, and finally was appointed governor of Bithynia and Pontus. His important writings include his lengthy *Panegyric* to the emperor Trajan, which he delivered during his consulship, and 10 books of *Letters*, of which the final book preserves his correspondence while governor with Trajan and offers important insight into the roles of Roman administrators and their relationships with emperors.

~*Gregory S. Aldrete*

FOR MORE INFORMATION

Kenney, E.J., ed. *The Cambridge History of Classical Literature*. Vol. 2. *Latin Literature*. Cambridge, England: Cambridge University Press, 1982.

Ogilvie, R. M. *Roman Literature and Society*. Totowa, N.J.: Barnes and Noble, 1980.

INDIA

Despite a large number of documents discovered in the ruins of the cities of the Indus Valley, the language and script of this civilization remain as yet undeciphered, and so little is known of their literature.

From the time of the *Rig Veda*, Sanskrit has been the primary religious and liturgical language of India. Ancient India is famous for its contributions to philosophy and spiritualism. The scriptural literature of India comes in two categories: *sruti*, what is "heard" or "revealed," and thus eternal and divine; and *smriti*, what is "remembered" and is the work of great sages. Thus the earliest literary works in Sanskrit are the four Vedic *Samhitas* (hymns), the original *sruti*. The four are the *Rig*, *Sama*, *Yajur*, and *Atharva Vedas*, compiled 1500–800 B.C.E. They contain collections of hymns, spells, mythology, and cosmology of the earliest Indian orthodoxy. Following the Vedas historically were commentaries dealing with their interpretation and sacrificial use. These were the *Brahmanas* and *Aranyakas*. A fourth class of ancient *sruti* were written in the mid- to late first millennium B.C.E.: the *Upanishads*, which frequently dealt with more esoteric topics and reveal a trend away from sacrifice and toward inward contemplation for salvation.

It is worth noting that the primary definition of *sruti* is that of revelation and that not all groups accepted the Vedas as possessing the sole claim to revelation. Saiva Siddhantins, for example, regarded a class of texts known as the *Agamas* as *sruti*, as direct revelation from Siva.

The *smriti* literature, on the other hand, frequently addressed more mundane topics, such as politics, social order, proper conduct, and so on. Some examples include the *Manu Smriti*, dealing largely with conduct of members of the various classes of society, and the *Arthasastra* of Kautilya (third century B.C.E.), a key text on political life in ancient India.

The philosophical texts of the six schools of orthodox thought, each claiming their roots in the Vedas, are also classified as *smriti*. These emerged in the late centuries of the first millennium B.C.E. Two dealt with largely analytical aspects of philosophy. The *Nyaya Sutra* of Gotama was concerned with aspects of logic to arrive at a conclusion. This text established the four valid means of knowledge: intuition and perception (*pratyaksa*), inference (*anumana*), analogy (*upamana*), and verbal authority (*sabda*). The *Vaisesika Sutra* of Kasyapa took an atomic view of reality, positing that nine elements comprised all things: earth, air, fire, water, space, time, mind, light, and self (*atma*).

Two closely related schools of orthodoxy were Yoga and Sankhya. The *Yoga Sutras* of Patanjali describes the methods and purposes of yoga, which was to still the mind and reveal the self as it truly is. The *Sankhya Karikas* of Isvarakrsna, a late text (third century B.C.E.), draws a distinction between *prakrti*, which is nature or matter, and *purusa*, immortal and unchanging spirit.

The final two orthodox schools are the Purva and Uttara Mimamsa. The former dealt primarily with ritual and ethical duty (*dharma*), and its textual origins begin with the *Mimamsa Sutras* of Jaimini. The Uttara Mimamsa, through Badarayana's *Brahma Sutra,* is the foundation of later Vedantic speculation on the nature of the self and its essential identity in Brahman.

But the ancient Indians also developed a materialistic view of the world. In the six systems of philosophy created by the Indians, elements of materialistic philosophy appear in the Sankhya system of Kapila, who was born about 580 B.C.E., and in the Lokayatha system of Charvaka, who lived in the sixth century B.C.E. The ancient Indians thus developed both idealist and materialist systems of philosophy at a time when no philosophers in any other country were delving so deeply into this problem.

Of great importance for the literary culture of India are the two epics the *Ramayana* and the *Mahabharata.* The former tells of the life of Rama, an *avatar* of Vishnu, and his efforts to rescue his wife Sita from the demon Ravana. It has often served as a model for devotion, virtue, and proper governance. The *Mahabharata,* on the other hand, is a veritable compendium of ancient Indian mythology and lore, loosely set in the plot of a cataclysmic war between two wings of a royal family. A key character in the epic is Krishna, another *avatar* of Vishnu, whose divine identity as source and salvation of all beings is highlighted in a short but famous section, the *Bhagavad-Gita,* which taught devotion to Lord Krishna and stressed the proper performance of ritual functions.

The original teachings of Buddhism were preserved in the Pali language, one of the Prakrit languages derived from Sanskrit. The Buddhist canon is called, in Pali, the *Tipitaka,* the "Three Baskets," containing *Vinaya,* the monastic code; *Sutta,* the discourses of the Buddha; and the *Abhidhamma,* philosophical commentaries. After the beginning of the common era, however, with the rise of Mahayana texts, many Buddhist writers resorted to using Sanskrit. Other Prakrit languages survive through dramatic literature.

In south India, the Dravidian language Tamil had a role similar to that of Sanskrit in northern India. In the first centuries of the common era, a corpus of poetic literature developed in Tamil, with its own styles, tropes, and commentary. This corpus is known as the *Sangam* literature. The chief themes of the poetry can be divided into "internal" (*agam*), dealing with motifs of love, and "external" (*puram*), focusing on the deeds and glory of kings. The tropes that were developed used natural settings, flowers, animals, and so on in a metaphorical code for situations, events, and moods. Thirukural of Thiruvalluvar is a Tamil book of philosophy consisting of 1,330 couplets. Considered the bible of the Tamils, the work is a real moral code that has been translated into many languages throughout the world. The later mystic poet-saints, the Alvars and the Nayannars, took up the naturalistic themes of Tamil literature to describe their experiences of God's manifestation in and through the world.

~Matthew Bingley

FOR MORE INFORMATION

Narasimhan, C. *The Mahabharata.* New York: Columbia University Press, 1965.
Ramanujan, A. K., trans. *Poems of Love and War.* New York: Columbia University Press, 1985.

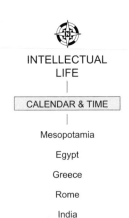

INTELLECTUAL
LIFE
|
CALENDAR & TIME
|
Mesopotamia

Egypt

Greece

Rome

India

Calendar and Time

The systems that humans have produced to keep time are simply codifications and quantifications of the rhythms provided by nature. The most obvious is the daily sequence of the sun: it rises, passes across the sky, and sets, and after a period of darkness, it appears once more. Thus is created the basic and universal timekeeping unit of the day. Longer units of measuring time are the products of agrarian societies in which the rhythms that mattered most were those that affected the growing of crops. Even without a formal calendar system, the annual cycle of the seasons—spring, summer, fall, and winter—provides a structure to life and collectively forms another natural unit of timekeeping: the year. In Egypt, where the flooding of the Nile was by far the most significant event in the agricultural year, the various water levels of the river took the place of seasons in the local calendar.

From these underlying natural rhythms, all the cultures of the ancient world settled on solar calendars of approximately 360 days in length. It was a natural further step to subdivide this period into months based on the cycle of the phases of the moon. For many cultures, this was really all the degree of precision that was needed. Such fine units as minutes, seconds, or even hours were difficult to measure and often not that relevant in the everyday lives of ordinary people.

Days were frequently divided up into 24 hours, but the standard method of doing this was to divide the amount of time that it was light on a given day into 12 equal hours and the amount of time that it was dark into another 12. Since the amount of daytime and nighttime varies over the course of the year, the length of an hour was not fixed and fluctuated considerably. This variation does not seem to have bothered ancient peoples, whose notions of temporal precision were by necessity more forgiving. Some cultures did group a set of days together to form a week, but because these were not based on natural cycles, the number of days that constituted a week varied among different civilizations.

When there was some pressing necessity to measure out short, definite intervals of time, the usual recourse was to specify the time it took for some easily repeatable physical event to take place—the amount of time it took for a length of candle to burn down, for example, or for a quantity of water to drip out of a hole in a container. Such water clocks were widely used, as in the law courts of Athens, where they measured how long speakers had to state their cases before the jury.

Ancient scientists and philosophers computed impressively precise calendars based on astronomical observation, and their work is the basis of our modern timekeeping systems, but in day-to-day life, people of the ancient world were much less subject to the tyranny of the clock than are the inhabitants of the modern world.

~*Gregory S. Aldrete*

INTELLECTUAL
LIFE
|
CALENDAR & TIME
|
Mesopotamia

Egypt

Greece

Rome

India

MESOPOTAMIA

By the seventh century B.C.E., precise astronomical observations influenced the development of a more accurate calendar. The Mesopotamian calendar was lunar, based on observation of the moon throughout its history. Each lunar month consisted of 29 or 30 days, and a year was approximately 354 days. The month names usually referred to an important ritual observance or agricultural event. An extra month (called an intercalated month) was added approximately every three years to align the lunar and the solar calendars.

The ancient Mesopotamians were aware of both the lunar and solar calendar, but the lunar calendar took precedence. In fact, in their mythology the Sumerians depicted the moon as the father of the sun. An intercalary month was added to guarantee that the religious festivals, which were connected to the lunar calendar, were observed at the proper time. By the eighth century B.C.E., a regular intercalation of 7 months every 19 years was established; its accuracy in reconciling the lunar and solar calendars is still admired. By the fourth century B.C.E., mathematical astronomy was used for this intercalation. The calendar produced was called the Metonic Cycle, which was the basis of the later Jewish and Christian religious calendars. The lunar month of the Mesopotamian calendar had 29 or 30 days, of which 6 days were designated holidays, 3 days lunar festivals, and 3 more for relaxation.

Besides the seasonal and lunar cycle, the Mesopotamians were influenced by the cycle between the equinoxes, the period during which the sun and moon competed for time in the sky. The two six-month equinox cycles were important in instituting a cultic calendar and were reinforced by the seasons—the summer, which began around March, and the winter, which began around September. The equinox refers to the two times during the year when the sun and moon cross the celestial equators and both the night and day are approximately the same in length.

The division of the hour into 60 minutes is a Babylonian legacy. However, the division of the day into hours was influenced by both the Babylonians and the Egyptians. The Babylonian day, which began at sunset, comprised 12 "double hours," each consisting of 60 "double minutes." Each day was also divided into six equal parts for calculation and observation. At the same time, the Egyptians divided the day, that is, from sunrise to sunset, into 12 unequal parts, depending on the season of the year. Hellenistic astronomers took the next step—they divided the 12 double hours into 24 units of equal length. Thus, the 24-hour day was created.

In everyday life, water clocks were used to measure units of time. Water clocks were either cylindrical or prismatic. Time was calculated by filling a vessel of specified height to a marked line with water and then letting the liquid escape through a hole in the bottom (Nemet-Nejat, 87–88).

FOR MORE INFORMATION

Bickerman, E. J. *Chronology of the Ancient World*. London: Thames and Hudson, 1980.
Nemet-Nejat, K. R. *Daily Life in Ancient Mesopotamia*. Westport, Conn.: Greenwood Press, 1998.

EGYPT

Because most work in ancient Egypt was motivated by a need for sustenance rather than a desire for acquisitions, it followed rhythms radically different from our own.

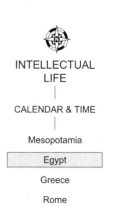

INTELLECTUAL
LIFE
|
CALENDAR & TIME
|
Mesopotamia
Egypt
Greece
Rome

India

For most Americans, each day of the week has a different character: Monday is the first day of work, Friday is the end of a work period, and Saturday begins two days of nonwork activity. Most of us sleep later, dress differently, and have more control over our time on weekends than during the previous five workdays. Life marches to these seven-step patterns, punctuated by recurring holidays that serve as bonus free days, along with special periods of two weeks or more for vacations of our choosing.

Nothing similar existed in ancient Egypt. Egyptians had no weekends. Most worked every day, with few exceptions. Special holy days of the year called for all the inhabitants of a given area to lay down their tools and gather at a local temple to watch a procession of idols, after which they feasted on bountiful free food supplied by the temple. The most festive of these holy days were *Opet*, when the idols of Mut and Khonsu traveled from Karnak Temple to Luxor Temple to celebrate their marriage; the Five Yearly Days, which celebrated the end of one year and hopes for a successful next year; and birthdays for each god of Egypt. For practical reasons, most of these holidays occurred when the Nile was in flood, making farming impossible in any case. During the rest of the year, one day followed another in much the same way. No regular day of rest existed until it was introduced much later by the Jews in Palestine and borrowed by the Christians. Indeed, names for individual days of the week did not exist in the language, nor did the seven-day grouping we call a week. The character of work periods was instead determined by what nature demanded—weeding, repairing canals, plowing, or harvesting. No calendar told a farmer how to schedule his time when he woke each morning.

The year was divided into three seasons, marking nature's rhythms, each consisting of four 30-day months. "Inundation" began the year around our September, when the Nile overflowed and flooded the farmland. "Emergence," which referred to the reappearance of the land from the receding water, was planting time and was followed by "harvest." Each season called for work appropriate to environmental circumstances. During inundation, when the waterlogged land could not be worked, the farmer repaired his tools and house. Emergence began with reconstructing the canals that brought essential Nile water to the fields, after which came plowing, planting, then tending the crops as they grew. During harvest, farmers reaped and processed the crops before storage. Of course, three seasons of four 30-day months added up to only 360 days, which left five days unaccounted for. This yearly five days provided Egyptians with the closest they ever got to a sustained holiday: no one worked during the long new year's celebration.

Despite being nameless, each day was marked in calendars as representing specific theological events that occurred on that particular day. Thus, the first day of the second month of emergence was considered the day Ra had lifted up the sky, whereas day 26 of the first month of inundation marked the time Sekhmet's ferocious eyes first caught sight of her human prey. These mythical events lent every day a quality, marking it as auspicious, if some fortunate event had occurred, menacing, if the contrary, or neutral. Egyptians took these matters seriously, planning important events to coincide with auspicious days and taking extra care on menacing ones.

The average farmer needed no more indication of time than the position of the sun or the moon, and none of his countrymen understood divisions finer than an hour. The word for minute—let alone the ultraprecision of a second—did not even exist in the language.

Living under a sky unobscured by industrial smoke or bright city lights, ancient Egyptians became keen stargazers, using the movements of the stars for their nighttime clock. They learned that the hour of the night could be determined by observing where each of their 36 major constellations appeared in the sky at that time. If an ancient Egyptian priest wanted to determine the end of the last hour of the night and a particular star appeared on the horizon just before dawn, he might try to use this star to fix the end of the 12th hour of the night. But because of the annual eastward motion of the sun, this star would rise earlier each day until it no longer served as a usable indicator of the end of night. Priests learned to select a larger object, the constellation next to this star, instead and use that as the indicator of the end of the last hour of the night. Despite Egyptians' keen observations of the night sky, their records contain no predictions of lunar or solar eclipses. They used their astronomy for practical purposes and saw no reason to involve themselves in abstract theories (Brier and Hobbs, 76–77).

FOR MORE INFORMATION

Brier, B., and H. Hobbs. *Daily Life of the Ancient Egyptians*. Westport, Conn.: Greenwood Press, 1999.

Montet, P. *Everyday Life in Egypt in the Days of Ramesses the Great*. Reprint, Philadelphia: University of Pennsylvania Press, 1981.

GREECE

The Greek day was divided into 12 hours of daylight and 12 hours of darkness, meaning that the daylight hours were longer in the summer than in the winter. Hours were not subdivided into halves and quarters. In fact, the only way to tell the time accurately was by means of the sundial, which was introduced into Greece in the sixth century B.C.E. The natural divisions of the day—dawn, midday, and dusk—served for most purposes.

Only in the Athenian law courts was accurate timekeeping necessary; from the fifth century B.C.E. onward, speeches were timed down to the last second. This was done with the aid of a water clock known as a *klepsydra*, a clay vessel that could be filled up to the level of an overflow hole just below the rim. When the speaker began his delivery, a plug was removed from a small hole at the base of one of the jugs. As soon as the water ceased to flow, the speaker would be required to sit down. This simple device guaranteed that both parties spoke for exactly the same amount of time.

Hesiod's *Works and Days*, which was composed in the seventh century B.C.E., is a kind of farmer's almanac. It uses signs from the natural world, such as heliacal risings and settings, to mark the passage of the seasons, which in turn serve as a guide to the farming year. The time for plowing and harvesting, for instance, is indicated by the rise of a constellation known as the Pleiades:

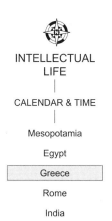

When the daughters of Atlas [the giant who supports the earth on his shoulders] are rising [i.e., early in May], begin the harvest, and when they are setting begin your plowing. These stars are hidden for forty nights and forty days, but they appear again as the year revolves again, which is when iron [i.e., for the blade of the plow] must first be sharpened. (lines 383–87, my translation)

Similarly, the moment to harvest grapes coincided with the appearance of particular stars:

When Orion and Sirius are in the middle of the sky, and rosy-fingered dawn sees Arcturus [i.e., in September], then cut off all the grapes . . . and bring them home. (lines 609–11, my translation)

Hesiod also uses animal behavior as an indicator of the changing seasons:

When the house-carrier [i.e., snail] leaves the ground and climbs up plants [i.e., in the middle of May], fleeing the Pleiades, then is not the time to dig vineyards, but to sharpen your sickles and rouse your slaves. (lines 571–73, my translation)

The blossoming of plants served as a further guide:

When the artichoke comes into flower [i.e., in June], and the chattering cicada sits in a tree and pours down his sweet song in full measure from under his wings and wearisome heat is at its height, then goats are fattest and wine is sweetest. Women are in heat, but men are at their weakest, because Sirius saps the head and the knees, and the flesh is dry because of the heat. (lines 582–88, my translation)

There was no universal method of reckoning the passage of years in the Greek world. Rather, each community adhered to its own system. So when the historian Thucydides is trying to indicate the year in which the Peloponnesian War broke out, he tells his readers that hostilities began "fourteen years after the capture of Euboea, forty-seven years after Chryses became priestess of Hera at Argos, in the year when Ainesias was ephor at Sparta, and in the year when Pythodoros was archon in Athens" (2.2.1, my translation).

The earliest preserved date in Greek history is 776 B.C.E., the year when the Olympic Games were first celebrated. However, Olympiads, which marked the four-year intervals between successive celebrations of the games, were not adopted as a basis for chronology until the third century B.C.E. Nor did city-states seek to establish the year of their foundation. All that they were interested in proving was that their city had been founded earlier than its rivals, since this could lend legitimacy to territorial claims.

Athens's written records begin in 683 B.C.E., the year it instituted a system by which a magistrate known as the eponymous archon gave his name to the year. There was, however, nothing inherently significant about this date. It merely marked the adoption of a procedural convenience. Moreover, although the Athenians annually celebrated the birthday of their principal state deity, Athena Polias, on the 28th of the month of *Hekatombaion* (i.e., shortly after the summer solstice), they did not know the year in which the goddess had been born. They also held a festival called the *Synoikia* earlier in the month in commemoration of the *synoikismos* or unification of Attica, which they ascribed to their legendary King Theseus. However, since Theseus's reign could not be dated, this event did not provide a fixed date either. It was not until the Hellenistic period that a determined attempt was made to establish a foundation date for Athens. The author of an inscribed marble column, known as the Marmor Parium, who claimed to have "written up the dates [of Athenian history] from the beginning," maintained that Cekrops, the first king of Athens, came to the throne 1,218 years prior to the setting up of the inscription in 264/3 B.C.E. In the same century the geographer Eratosthenes devised a dating system that took as its departure the fall of Troy, which he assigned to 1183 B.C.E.

The Athenians did not celebrate the new year, mainly because their calendar, which was based on the phases of the moon, was in a state of almost-constant turmoil. A lunar calendar is extremely convenient in a subliterate society for arranging the dates of monthly festivals, payment of debts, and so forth. As a basis for marking the passage of the seasons, however, it is virtually useless, because the lunar year is 11 days shorter than the solar year. Since, however, the success of the harvest was thought to depend on ritual activity performed at precise moments of the year, the Athenians, like other Greeks, had to intercalate (or add) an extra month from time to time to keep their calendar in line with the annual circuit of the sun. In fact, over a 19-year cycle, they had to intercalate seven extra months (Garland, 30–34).

FOR MORE INFORMATION

Bickerman, E. J. *Chronology of the Ancient World.* London: Thames and Hudson, 1980.
Garland, R. *Daily Life of the Ancient Greeks.* Westport, Conn.: Greenwood Press, 1998.

ROME

Each day was divided for the Romans into two periods: the time when it was light outside and the time when it was dark. Each of these periods was then subdivided into hours. Superficially, this sounds much like our modern system of 24 hours in a day. However, there was one rather significant difference: Roman hours were not of a fixed length; they were simply the amount of light or darkness on a given day divided by 12. Because the amount of daylight varies greatly from day to day over the course of the year—with perhaps as many as 15 hours of daylight in the summer and only 8 or 9 in the winter—a Roman hour in the summer might be equivalent to a modern hour and a half. Similarly, in the winter, a Roman hour might only be 40 of our minutes long. When telling time, the Romans referred to the hour after sunrise as the "first hour of the day," the next as the "second hour of the day" and so on up to the 12th. The 12 nighttime hours worked in the same way except that the starting point was sunset. Thus they would have the first or second hour after sunset and so on. The length of an hour would change from day to day, and meetings could only be set very approximately. If, for example, someone said "Meet me at the fifth hour," you simply had to make your best guess when that might be.

To indicate the year, the usual method was to refer to the names of the two consuls elected for a given year. Thus, for example, to indicate the year 59 B.C.E., the Romans would have said "in the consulship of Caesar and Bibulus" since those two men were the consuls for that year. In practice, this meant that one had to carry around a mental list of all the pairs of consuls in Roman history to tell dates—an impressive feat of memorization and clearly a somewhat awkward system. To get around this, the Romans also sometimes used an alternate numbering system for the year. In this system, they dated things from the foundation of the city of Rome, which in our numbering system was 753 B.C.E. Thus, a Roman might say so and so happened in the 480th year since the city was founded. The Latin phrase for "From the foundation of the city" is *ab urbe condita*. When the historian Livy wrote his account of the entire history of Rome, he titled this work *Ab Urbe Condita*, indicating that he was going to tell everything that had happened since the city was founded.

Like us, the Romans divided the year into 12 months. In the Republic, they only had 355 days in a year. Since, as we know, there are really 365.25 days in an astronomical year, after a few years, the calendar would begin to get severely out of line with the natural seasons. If left uncorrected for long enough, this could have disastrous consequences for farmers since it would lead to their planting crops at the wrong time of year, if they went by the calendar. The solution that the Romans devised was to have the priests every so often declare an intercalary month. This was a month without a name inserted between two existing months to bring the months back into line with the natural seasons. Because there was no set time table for inserting intercalary months, in times of crisis when the priestly colleges were not regularly meeting, the calendar could get greatly out of line. The most obvious example of this occurred in the Late Republic during the civil wars between Julius Caesar and his rivals. By the time Caesar emerged as sole ruler of the Roman world, the calendar was off by a full six months and Caesar had to insert six intercalary months all at once. Thus in the late 40s B.C.E., there was one extra-long year that was, in reality, one-and-a-half years long.

To make sure that this did not happen again, Caesar undertook a major reform of the Roman calendar. He added 10 days to the calendar, thus making a year 365 days long. Like our own months, each of the Roman months had between 28 and 31 days. To take care of the extra quarter of a day, Caesar instituted the leap year, where every four years there would be one extra day added. This reformed calendar was known as the Julian Calendar and is essentially the same one we use today.

The modern names of the months are all derived from the Roman ones. The Roman names were Januarius, Februarius, Martius, Aprilis, Maius, Junius, Julius, Augustus, September, October, November, and December. The names of January through June refer to Roman gods: for example, January is named after the Roman god, Janus. The months of July and August were named by the Romans to honor Julius Caesar and the emperor Augustus. (Originally, July was Quinctilus, literally, "the fifth," and August was Sextilus, "the sixth.") The names for September through December are derived from numbers, with September meaning "the seventh," up to December, "the tenth." The reason December was called the 10th month rather than the 12th is that the Romans began each year on March 1 rather than January 1.

To indicate a day within a month, the Romans would not say, as we would, "on the 17th." Instead, they picked three days of each month and gave them special names and indicated all other days by their relationship to these three. The first day of each month was known as the *kalends* (or *calends*) of the month. The day of the month on which the moon was full was called the *ides*; the ides usually fell on what we would call the 13th or the 15th of the month. Finally, the *nones* was the day nine days before the ides. Because the Romans used an inclusive numbering system, the nones fell on what we would call the fifth or the seventh. One of the more famous dates in Roman history, for example, is the ides of March, the day on which Julius Caesar was assassinated. This would mean, in our calendar, March 15. For all days that were not one of these three, the Romans would indicate the day by the number of days before the next of the special days. Thus, for example, if the Romans wanted to indicate March 13, they would say three days before the ides of March.

Much is known about Roman calendars because the Romans were fond of putting calendars on the sides of their public buildings or temples, either actually carved into or painted on the stone. The letters were painted in red on a white background. These calendars not only included the dates, but almost always there were also comments included about important days. Such a calendar is known as a *fasti*. All *fasti* consisted of 12 vertical columns, one for each month. Each month column was further subdivided. First came the name of the day. Next was a column of the letters A through H, repeating. This was to keep track of when market day came. For the Romans, every eighth day was market day, called *nundinae*. This cycle of days was the equivalent of our week. Thus, while we have a seven-day week because of Christianity, the pre-Christian Romans had an eight-day week. In a third column was an abbreviation that gave further information about what type of day it was. There were many types of days, but four were particularly important. The first type was symbolized by the capital letter "F." This stood for *dies fasti*, and there were 42 of these each year. These were the

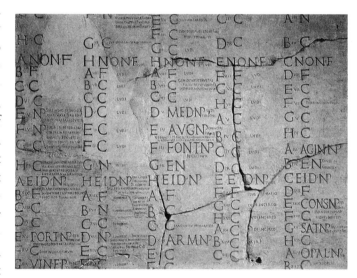

Fragment of a Roman calendar. Such calendars used abbreviations to note the days of the month, holidays, market days, and other important dates. © The Art Archive/Museo della Civilta Romana Rome/Dagli Orti.

only days on which it was legal to institute a legal action. Second were days labeled "N," which stood for *dies nefasti*, of which there were 58 per year. On these days, it was forbidden to conduct any legal business. The third type was marked with a "C" for *dies comitiales*, and there were 195 of these per year. These were the only days on which the Comitia, the voting assembly, could meet. Finally, there were days marked "NP," meaning *dies nefasti publici*. These were public holidays on which no business should be conducted and everyone should have the day off to celebrate. There was no set number of holidays.

The Romans believed that certain days were luckier than others. Odd-numbered days were thought to be luckier than even, and thus all holidays began on odd-numbered days. The days after the kalends, the ides, and the nones were called "black days" and were thought to be particularly unlucky. Superstitious people would try to do as little as possible on these days and certainly would never begin any new endeavor on such a "black day."

~*Gregory S. Aldrete*

FOR MORE INFORMATION

Bickerman, E. J. *Chronology of the Ancient World*. London: Thames and Hudson, 1980.

INTELLECTUAL
LIFE
|
CALENDAR & TIME
|
Mesopotamia

Egypt

Greece

Rome

India

INDIA

The last of the six Vedangas, or traditional branches of learning, was *jyotis*, which generally refers to astrology. The proper purpose of this branch of learning was the study of astronomy for setting the calendar and thereby performing sacrifices and festivals at the appropriate time. It also developed into astrology as it is commonly understood: studying the movements of stars, planets, the sun, and moon for horoscopes and divination. Astrology relied on the movements of the *navagraha*, "nine graspers," so called because it was thought their actions influenced events by "seizing" individuals. These nine were the five visible planets (Mercury, Venus, Mars, Jupiter, and Saturn) plus the sun and moon, as well as Rahu and Ketu, two halves of a demon responsible for eclipses.

Astronomy, a subcategory of *jyotis*, developed into a high science. By the fourth century B.C.E. Aryabhatta argued that the Earth revolved around the sun and was a sphere, tilted on its axis. In the fifth century B.C.E. the prominent astrologer Varaha Mihira compiled the knowledge of both Indian and Western civilizations and argued that solar and lunar eclipses were caused not by demons, but by the shadow of the moon and Earth, respectively.

Mathematics supported this astronomical knowledge. From the necessity of properly constructing the altar of the Vedic sacrifice grew knowledge of geometry. India as well developed abstract mathematics, and invented the concept of zero as a number. The zero notation was later imported into Islamic and Western mathematics.

The Indian calendar was based on the phases of the moon. The year was divided into 12 lunar months of 30 days each. Each month was further subdivided into "bright" and "dark" halves, depending on whether the moon was waxing or waning. Since this calendar yielded a year of 354 days, every 30 months an extra month was added to correct the discrepancy. Although a number of methods of dating years developed, the most common was the Vikrama era, dated from 58 B.C.E. For example, the year 2000 C.E. in the Western calendar would be year 2058 of the Vikrama era.

Time, on a grand scale, was measured by the *yuga* (age) and the *kalpa* (aeon). Time moves in great cycles of creation, evolution, and destruction, followed by a new cycle, and in each cycle the world moves from a golden, perfect time to one of degeneration and corruption. There are four *yugas*, or "ages," that comprise the basic cycle: the

Krta, the *Treta*, the *Dvapara*, and the *Kali*. According to this mythology, the world is currently in the *Kali Yuga*, the most corrupt age.

~*Matthew Bingley*

FOR MORE INFORMATION

Auboyer, J. *Daily Life in Ancient India*. London: Phoenix Press, 1965.
Basham, A. L. *The Wonder That Was India*. London: Sidgwick and Jackson, 1967.

Science

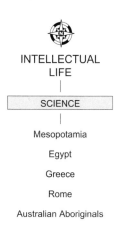

INTELLECTUAL
LIFE
|
SCIENCE
|
Mesopotamia

Egypt

Greece

Rome

Australian Aboriginals

In the ancient world, there was considerable overlap between the fields that we would today label science, philosophy, and religion. Ancient science had its start when people began to be curious about the natural world around them and began to attempt to understand how things worked and why they happened.

Before it is possible to analyze or understand the natural world, it is necessary to have a consistent way to describe natural phenomena. To record even the most basic data, however, such as the size or weight of an object, first requires that there be widely accepted and consistent standards of measurement. But even before one can have standard weights and measures, it is necessary to have a workable system of mathematical notation. The first scientists therefore were literally starting from scratch, and their initial great inventions were simply coming up with the language and mathematics necessary to begin describing the world around them. Mesopotamian mathematicians developed fairly sophisticated mathematical systems up to workable algebraic computations. They also laid the foundations for geometry, working out fundamental principles and formulas.

One of the earliest practical applications of these newly developed theoretical systems was to use them to analyze the movements of the planets and stars in the night sky. Mesopotamian astronomers' understanding of the heavens grew so sophisticated that they eventually were even able to predict astronomical events such as eclipses.

Living in a world so filled with unexplained and often dangerous phenomena, a natural goal of early scientists was to find some way to be able to predict future occurrences. This is where ancient astronomy blurred seamlessly into what today we would label as astrology, as these scientists tried to find a link between phenomena in the skies and events on earth.

The ancient Greeks built on the knowledge of the Mesopotamians, and the group known as the Ionian Rationalists began to work out the forerunner of the scientific method based on the application of logic and reason to close observation of the natural world. Above all, these men (the ones we know of were all men) asked questions and were not content with traditional answers. This process could be controversial because it led them to question contemporary religious beliefs about the nature of the gods and their interactions with the world.

Ancient Egypt and Rome did not perhaps push the theoretical boundaries of science as much, but both civilizations shone in its practical application, especially in the field of engineering. Monuments such as the pyramids of Egypt, the Pantheon, and the aqueducts of Rome still stand today as testimony to the engineering skills of their builders.

If measured against modern notions of scientific methods and procedure, the scientists of the ancient world would often come up short, but the revolutionary way in which they set about questioning the world around them formed the basis of all subsequent science.

~*Gregory S. Aldrete*

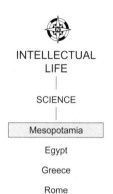

INTELLECTUAL
LIFE
|
SCIENCE
|

Mesopotamia

Egypt

Greece

Rome

Australian Aboriginals

MESOPOTAMIA

Numbers were written on cuneiform texts from the earliest, circa 3100 B.C.E., to the last text found in 75 C.E. The method in Mesopotamia for writing numbers developed as did the rest of the cuneiform script—becoming more stylized and angular through time.

The number system was always a combination of the decimal system (counting by 10s) and the sexagesimal system (counting by 60s). Babylonian mathematics used the sexagesimal system; the decimal number system was rarely used in mathematical calculations. Base 60 is preserved in the way we tell time, that is, 60 seconds to a minute and 60 minutes to an hour, and in measuring a circle as 360 degrees. From 2000 B.C.E. to 75 C.E., Babylonian numbers used place-value notation or a positional number system, which was developed in the fourth millennium B.C.E. Place-value notation uses a very limited number of symbols whose magnitude is determined by position (the higher values on the left and the lower values on the right). That is, for every place a number moved to the left, its value was multiplied by 60, and for every place it moved to the right, it was divided by 60.

The Babylonian system had two inherent disadvantages: (1) it was confusing and, therefore, not used in many daily economic activities, and (2) there was no special sign for zero, to separate the different units. To understand the difficulties that arise from not having zero, a number like 353 could be read as 3,053 or 3,503 or even 3,530. Some Old Babylonian mathematicians sometimes compensated by leaving blank spaces for zero or by using a special sign that indicated a space between words. A sign for zero was eventually invented sometime in the first millennium B.C.E., although it was never used at the end of a number. The lack of the zero sign was probably tolerated because of the amplitude of base 60, which included a large number of factors (1, 2, 3, 4, 5, 6, 10, 12, 15, 20, 30).

Babylonian mathematicians developed a mastery of algebraic skills, even though there was no graphic symbol for the unknown. Instead, the Babylonians used a method called false value. Here the unknown is provisionally designated by 1 to find the coefficients and thus solve first-degree (linear) and second-degree (quadratic) equations. Examples of first- and second-degree equations in Babylonian mathematics show that the scribes had all the necessary algebraic tools, such as reduction of similar terms, elimination of the unknown by substitution, completing the square, and, in second-degree equations, containing two unknowns, using ± in a single algebraic statement.

The Babylonians never took additional steps to prove statements and formulate theorems. Rather, the scribes merely performed the operations leading to the solution without explaining them. Algebraic problems in school exercises were constructed with an eye to their solution, so that ancient mathematicians rarely encountered an irregular number, that is, a prime number that is not a factor of base 60.

The Babylonians displayed a considerable knowledge of geometric shapes and geometric formulas. They even used the Pythagorean theorem more than a thousand years before Pythagoras and applied principles of similarity.

The Babylonians surpassed their neighbors in the ancient Near East in their knowledge of astronomy and mathematics. The Babylonians and Assyrians kept detailed records of their observations of the position and movement of heavenly bodies. They combined these observations with their mathematical proficiency to give birth to mathematical astronomy.

Basic knowledge of astronomy was collected and organized into a three-tablet series. This series was found in Assurbanipal's library; it includes a list of stars arranged in three parallel "roads," with the middle one following the equator, along with references to the planets, to complexities of the calendar, and to observations of Venus's disappearance and reappearance behind the sun. From the seventh to the second century B.C.E., astronomical "diaries" were kept; they were primarily based on monthly or yearly observations but contained a number of predictions, in particular relating to the moon, the planets, solstices, equinoxes, Sirius phenomena, meteors, comets, and so on. In addition, the diaries noted the weather (rain, thunder, lightning, fog, haze, cold, cloudburst, hail, overcast, etc.), prices of various goods, the river level, and historical events. The astronomical diaries of previous years were collected in goal-year texts to predict astronomical phenomena in the coming year, that is, the goal year. Included in the diaries for 164 and 87 B.C.E. are references to Halley's Comet. The Assyrians kept records of lunar eclipses, which they were able to predict.

Astronomical computations were also essential to the invention of the zodiac and horoscopic astrology. The Mesopotamians believed that what happened in the heavens was mirrored on earth. Thus, Mesopotamians believed that the movements of heavenly bodies could be connected with gods, kings, and countries to make predictions. At first, astrological omens were used to explain only the future of the country and its ruler. However, the shift to horoscopic astrology required a method for relating celestial phenomena to individuals. The zodiac came into play here, and along with it, a year of 12 30-day months was created. By the fifth century B.C.E., the zodiacal belt was partitioned into 12 zodiacal signs of 30 degrees each. The first known Babylonian horoscope was cast for a child born April 29, 410 B.C.E. Astrology and mathematical astronomy were associated with separate social and intellectual circles. Astrology was the basis for the reputation of "Chaldean" science, which extended through the whole of Europe.

We know about Babylonian science and technology from cuneiform tablets. The technical vocabulary is extensive, but unfortunately, many of the words cannot be translated. We also have archaeological evidence confirming both advanced knowledge and technology in many fields. However, technological equipment is often not recognized by archaeologists because they do not know exactly what they are looking for.

The ancient Mesopotamians tried to understand and organize the world around them. To this end, they made inventory lists of animals, plants, minerals, and so on. They even made lists of the gods. Lists of objects were recorded as early as the third millennium B.C.E., but a definite sequence within categories was not established until much later.

During the second millennium B.C.E., some lists became canonized. A series of about 40 tablets was organized and named after the first line, "interest obligations." The work is an exhaustive survey of the world the Mesopotamians knew, including real and mythical animals, foods, manufactured objects, and so on. The organization is not always clear. For example, trees are listed in Tablet 3, but the rest of the plants are in Tablet 17. Later, during the first millennium B.C.E., explanations or commentaries were added to bridge the gap between Sumerian and Akkadian.

Early attempts to deal with the natural sciences produced the Sumerian lists, which were expanded by the Babylonians. The Babylonians were aware of a variety of species, although their categories differ from ours. For example, a comprehensive list of land animals was extended to include insects and worms. Body parts of both humans and animals were grouped together. During the first millennium B.C.E. there were lists of drugs made from animals, flowers, and minerals, along with the illnesses they were meant to cure. The lexical lists did not clearly define the boundaries between animal, vegetable, and mineral. Less information was given about birds and fish in these lists. Nevertheless, animals, birds, and fish were accurately depicted in the reliefs.

The lexical lists are not our only source of information about the natural sciences in Mesopotamia. Lists of terrestrial omens describe animals and their behavior. Real and fantastic omens are included, such as a lamb with 10 feet. Other texts tell us of animals living in the wild at the time (for example, the small horse of the steppes, with a head resembling that of a camel and a short, thick, stiff mane) or animals that have now become extinct (for example, a long-bearded ram with widely separated curving horns). Certain literary texts give useful information about identifying birds and even spell out bird calls. Also, we have a list of 18 varieties of edible fish sold at a market in Larsa (near the Persian Gulf) circa 2000 B.C.E.

The Babylonians drew maps of local areas, such as field plans, estate plans, and ground plans of temples and houses, as well as maps of more distant regions, such as larger areas, districts, and towns. They also gave us the famous *mappa mundi* or world map, which portrays the Babylonians' vision of the world with Babylon as its center. The maps were of practical value in daily life. They could be used for surveying, building, conducting business transactions, taxation, traveling, and waging campaigns. Sometimes maps were cited in litigation.

Surviving Babylonian maps are limited in number. Nevertheless, they exhibit common characteristics through the millennia. Most important, they were drawn as if seen from above, that is, what we today call a bird's-eye view. The maps were drawn with little attention to angles, scale, and orientation. They used mostly straight lines, since curved lines were difficult to draw on clay. Even rivers and canals were depicted as angular forms rather than winding curves. But sometimes canals were portrayed by parallel lines filled by wavy ones (a convention still used by cartographers and called "water lining"). The name of the canal was inserted with the designation "canal" to remove any ambiguity. Cities, camps, fields, and so on were designated by rectangles or circles. Streets or highways were indicated by double or single lines with the name of the street written inside or along the lines. Only one map, from Nuzi, has a rather pictorial drawing of mountains as a series of semicircles drawn closely together and in two rows.

Maps of immediate localities included building plans and field plans. Ground plans were usually of private houses, but there were also plans of public buildings and temples. Field plans were the most common type of survey and occurred throughout Mesopotamian history. The field plans ranged from simple areas of land to complex ones, which, in turn, were subdivided for calculation. The drawings were usually rough sketches, and the fields were depicted as rectangles, triangles, or trapezoids. The amount of information given on the field plans varied considerably and could include compass directions, notations in the field plan or along the border (to show adjacent fields, canals, or buildings), the name of the field, the year in which the survey was made, the commissioner of the survey, a summary of calculations, and the name of the surveyor. However, frequently the only information given included measurements of the sides and the area.

Clay tablet used for mathematical calculations. The keen Mesopotamian interest in geometric principles is plainly illustrated in this tablet. © Copyright The British Museum.

Maps of large areas of the country consisted of both district and city maps. For example, a map found at Nippur and dated to the second millennium B.C.E. shows nine towns, three canals, and a road. City maps presented either cities or sections of cities as, for example, in maps of Babylon, Nippur, and Assur. Temples, palaces, rivers, canals, walls, and fortifications were indicated. Sometimes distances and areas were given. No private houses were noted. A city map of Nippur, dated to the second millennium B.C.E., is particularly interesting because it was drawn to scale with such remarkable accuracy that it proved similar to plans drawn by an American expedition during their excavation of the city. The careful portrayal of this well-fortified city may indicate a military use for this map.

The *mappa mundi* reveals the Mesopotamian, indeed the ancient Near Eastern, view of ancient cosmography. The earth was seen as a round disk encircled by the ocean (depicted by a double ring), with Babylon at its center and the Euphrates flowing through the middle of the Earth. Other cities and districts were marked on the map, but they were not placed in geographical order. The text on the tablet explains the map as a chart of the "Seven Islands," regions lying between the "Earthly Ocean" (also called the "Bitter River") and the "Heavenly Ocean." The signs of the zodiac, belonging to the "Heavenly Ocean," are also described in the text. These seven islands beyond the "Bitter River" were drawn as triangles around the edge of the circle. The cartographer noted the exact distance between them and added a descriptive note about the fifth region, "country where the sun is not seen." We may conclude that the Babylonians knew of the polar night, at least by hearsay. The concept of the cosmos as portrayed by this map was accepted for a long time, but each nation saw its own capital as the center of the universe (Nemet-Nejat, 82–97).

FOR MORE INFORMATION

Nemet-Nejat, K. R. *Daily Life in Ancient Mesopotamia*. Westport, Conn.: Greenwood Press, 1998.

Neugebauer, O., and A. Sachs. *Mathematical Cuneiform Texts*. American Oriental Society 29. New Haven, Conn.: American Oriental Society, 1945.

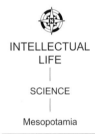

INTELLECTUAL
LIFE
|
SCIENCE
|
Mesopotamia

Egypt

Greece

Rome

Australian Aboriginals

EGYPT

Physics, chemistry, and biology were never studied by ancient Egyptians; true science with its controlled experiments, careful observations, and testable results did not exist until long after. Still, Egyptians approached injuries and diseases more objectively than did their contemporaries, and mathematics, essential for the complex and precise buildings that the Egyptians erected, was taught in every school (Brier and Hobbs, 223).

Egyptians built massive temples, palaces, and pyramids without the sophisticated mathematics engineers would use today; simple arithmetic was all the Egyptians knew. Their expertise extended only to addition and subtraction, not even multiplication or division. Lacking a theoretical understanding of numbers, they substituted clever tricks and found practical ways to arrive at the solutions they needed.

Multiplication was achieved by clever addition, called the method of doubling. If a scribe wanted to multiply 18 by 7, he started by writing 18 once, then below it doubled the number and continued doing so, while to the left of each doubling he wrote the number of times it had occurred. When the numbers in the left column added up to 7, he knew the total of the right column would be the correct answer, 126:

Doublings	Sum
1	18
2	36
4	72
7	126

Division was accomplished by a similar procedure, just a bit more complicated. If a scribe had to divide 184 bronze chisels among 8 workers, he treated the problem as a doubling (multiplication) problem and, after asking himself what he had to multiply 8 by to get 184, he began his doubling.

Doublings	Sum
1	8/
2	16/
4	32/
8	64
16	128/

He stopped at 128 because he knew the next doubling (256) would be larger than the 184 he had to work with. He next asked, what in the right-hand column adds up to 184 without going over it? The answer is 128 + 32 + 16 + 8 = 184. He then put a slash mark next to those numbers and added the left column entries beside them; that is, he added 16 + 4 + 2 + 1 to get 23. Thus, 8 goes into 184 23 times: each worker gets 23 chisels.

The Egyptians worked with a base of 10, using hieroglyphs only for the number 1 and for numbers that are powers of 10. As to fractions, the Egyptians worked only with numerators of 1. They had no 3/4 or 6/7. Rather, 3/4 was written as 1/2 + 1/4, and 6/7 was 1/2 + 1/4 + 1/14 + 1/28. Here too the scribe resorted to his doubling techniques to draw up long tables he could consult rather than redoing the tabulation each time.

Fractions were written by placing the hieroglyph that meant "part," represented by a mouth, above the denominator. The only hieroglyph with a numerator other than 1 was 2/3. The fractions 1/2, 1/4, 1/8, 1/16, 1/32, and 1/64 used special hieroglyphs based on the myth of Osiris. After Osiris was killed by Seth, Osiris's son Horus (the falcon) avenged his father's death but lost his eye in the battle. Fortunately, the fragments were collected and restored by the god of magic, Toth. The distinctive markings of the feathers around Horus's falcon eye became the hieroglyphs for well-being and, when broken into components, represented the fractions: 1/2, 1/4, 1/8, 1/16, 1/32, and 1/64. The Egyptians realized that these fractions added up to only 63/64, instead of 64/64 or unity, so they claimed that the missing 1/64 was supplied by Toth's magic.

Egyptians used mathematics not for abstract intellectual exercises but only for practical problems: fields had to be measured, quantities of grain recorded, and supplies divided among workers. Such problems required standards for size, weight, and volume that could be used with their arithmetic.

Since construction workers constantly had to measure, cut, and mark off distances, they used parts of their bodies—hands, palms, fingers—for measurement. We call their basic unit the cubit: the distance between the elbow and the tip of the middle finger (*cubitum* is Latin for "elbow"). Although the length of a cubit or width of a palm varied from worker to worker, such standards proved adequate for many small projects. Major projects, such as temples or pyramids whose thousands of blocks had to be uniform in size, required greater precision. The royal cubit was set for this purpose at 52.3 centimeters (20 5/8 inches), slightly longer than the average Egyptian's elbow to middle fingertip. This royal cubit was divided into seven palms, approximately the width of four fingers without the thumb. Palms were further divided into fourths, called "fingers," making 28 fingers to the cubit. The smallest unit Egyptian craftsmen used was 1/16 finger. Architects for major construction projects supplied cubit rulers for their overseers to maintain uniformity.

Land was measured by ropes cut in 100-cubit lengths, called a *khet*. An area one *khet* (100 cubits) on all four sides was a *setat*, the basic unit of surface area, about two-thirds of a modern acre. Volume was measured in *hekats*, which contained slightly less than a modern liter. The standard unit for liquids was the *hin*, a small jar about one-tenth of a *hekat*.

In a society that had no coin or paper money, commodities were the means of exchange and were measured for each transaction. For bread and beer, the staples of the Egyptian diet and of exchanges, there was even a measure of quality, the *pesu*. A *hin* of diluted beer was not worth as much as one that was full strength, nor was a heavily aerated loaf of bread equal to a dense loaf. The *pesu* indicated the number of jars of beer or loaves of bread obtained from one *hekat* of grain.

One equivalent of a mathematics textbook survives, *The Rhind Mathematical Papyrus*, a 15-foot-long scroll. Copied in the 33rd year of the pharaoh Apophis by a scribe named Ahmose, it presents dozens of math questions and their answers, which lend some insight into the kinds of problems that had to be solved. Included were such simple matters as dividing 6 loaves of bread among 10 men. Because the Egyptians did not use fractions with numerators other than 1, they could not give the easy answer of 6/10 of a loaf. Each man got 1/2 of a loaf plus 1/10 of a loaf. If there were 7 men for the 10 loaves, then the scribe got to use his one fraction with a numerator other than 1 (2/3), so each man got 2/3 plus 1/30 of a loaf.

In other problems, the student was asked to calculate the relative values of gold, silver, and lead, or how much bread was needed to force-feed a certain number of geese for a certain period. There are even problems about the volume of a truncated pyramid. Overall, the impression conveyed by the *Rhind Papyrus* is of the utter practicality of Egyptian mathematics. It served the purpose well, even though, lacking a foundation in number theory, it contributed little to modern mathematics (Brier and Hobbs, 236–39).

FOR MORE INFORMATION

Brier, B., and H. Hobbs. *Daily Life of the Ancient Egyptians*. Westport, Conn.: Greenwood Press, 1999.
David, R. *Handbook to Life in Ancient Egypt*. New York: Facts on File, 1998.

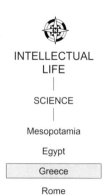

INTELLECTUAL
LIFE
|
SCIENCE
|
Mesopotamia

Egypt

Greece

Rome

Australian Aboriginals

GREECE

Between the years 600 and 500 B.C.E., in a variety of places around the world, a number of people began to question the traditional ways of doing things and of thinking about humans and their place in the world. In India this was the era of Buddha, in China it was the time of Confucius, in Persia of Zarathustra, and in Greece it was the time of a group of men whom we now call the Ionian Rationalists. Ionian Rationalism has a number of characteristics, including an interest in measurement, precision, standards, math and geometry, experimentation, logic, reason, critical thinking, skepticism, and attempting to find explanations for natural phenomena. Above all, rationalism was about asking questions. The movement embodying these characteristics began and thrived in Ionia, the region on the coast of Asia Minor including the islands just offshore. The Ionians were located in an interesting place geographically: on the border between the Greek and the Mediterranean worlds and the older inland civilizations of the Near East and Asia. They were at the crossroads of trade routes and ideas between East and West. Ionia was the one place where very disparate philosophies, religions, and cultures came together. Not only was Ionia a place characterized by a volatile intellectual climate, but its political life was similarly unsettled. The region was constantly being claimed by both Greece and Persia, claims that were often backed up by military force. In addition to the threat of external invasion, Ionia was troubled by civil war and class strife. All of these factors perhaps contributed to the Ionians of the sixth century being prone to asking questions and reconsidering tradition.

The first of the Ionian Rationalists is usually considered to be a man named Thales of Miletus. He was a merchant who, in pursuing his business, had traveled to Egypt, where he probably was exposed to Egyptian and Chaldean ideas and knowledge about mathematics and astronomy. His biggest contribution was simply to question the traditional explanations regarding the natural world. He posed questions that would obsess all subsequent Ionian rationalists and philosophers: What is the world made of? What is the basic unit that composes all other things? Thales called this "the antecedent of all things" or "the first element" and reasoned that since all things appeared to be nourished by water and to need it to survive and grow, water must be the first element. He also speculated about the universe. He believed that the earth was a flat body that floated on top of water like a raft. He supposedly used his knowledge of mathematics to predict a total eclipse of the sun in 585 B.C.E. Even after he became a philosopher, he did not lose his instincts as a merchant, and according to legend, he used his knowledge of astronomy to predict the ripening of the olive crop, which enabled him to corner the market and make a financial killing.

One of Thales' students, Anaximander, expanded on his teacher's theories. He is known to have made a map, which in itself reveals his interest in geometry and measuring the world. He was also the leader of a colony and enjoyed wearing fancy and impressive clothing. His variant of the structure of the universe was that the earth was originally covered in water, which dried up under the heat of the sun, exposing the land. He speculated that humankind therefore was descended from fish. The earth floated in a void of "undefined" matter and was surrounded by several circles of fire. A sort of barrier pierced by holes separated the earth from the rings of fire. In his cosmology, stars were the glimpses of these rings of fire seen through the holes, and the differences in brightness among stars are determined by how far away the fires are.

Another important Ionian Rationalist was Xenophanes. By profession, he was a poet, and the main direction of his theories was to challenge conventional notions of the gods. He ridiculed the idea that the gods looked just like people and argued that this concept of the gods was an egotistical manmade creation. When it came to the prime element, Xenophanes leaned toward earth as the most likely.

One of the most colorful and important figures of the next wave of Ionian Rationalists was Pythagoras. He liked to call himself a lover of wisdom or a "philo-sophos," from which come our terms philosopher and philosophy. Pythagoras's ideas fall into the two categories of mathematics and mysticism, although he himself did not see these as being different. He came up with many of the cornerstones of geometry, including the Pythagorean theorem. He thought the first element was number. He called the number one the Monad and said that it was male, and two was Dyad and was female. Ten was the most perfect number. He made important advances in astronomy as well regarding the movement of the planets. To Pythagoras, the universe was put together along mathematically precise lines. In addition, he believed that mathematics and music were interrelated, which led to his famous idea that the movement of astronomical bodies along perfect harmonious paths created beautiful sounds—"the music of the spheres."

Pythagoras was highly superstitious. He remarked that you should never poke a fire with a knife because you might injure it, and you should always spit on your nail clippings to prevent them from being magically used against you. He was a believer in transmigration of souls, even into animals, and in reincarnation. He claimed that he could remember his four past lives, including one in which he had lived at the time of the Trojan War. One story about him is that he once saw a neighbor beating a dog and asked him to stop, saying that he recognized the dog as the reincarnation of a friend. He advocated vegetarianism so that you could avoid unintentionally eating deceased friends and relatives. Some sources say that he is said to have counseled people not to eat beans on the grounds that if you cut open a bean, it looked like a human embryo, suggesting that eating beans was tantamount to cannibalism. Pythagoras was a colorful figure who habitually dressed in an outfit much like the modern stereotype of a wizard—a tall gold hat and long white robes.

Another time of intense interest in science came during the Hellenistic era. The earliest and perhaps most famous of the scientifically inclined thinkers of this period was Aristotle, who had been Alexander the Great's tutor. Aristotle's father was a doctor, and Aristotle eventually became a student of the philosopher Plato at Plato's Academy at Athens. In addition to many works on philosophy, Aristotle wrote about biology, politics, literature, ethics, physics, and the natural world. Aristotle emphasized the collection and organization of data. He marks the real start of systematic science with its reliance on cataloging and classifying. His method was to collect data and then draw conclusions from it.

The Hellenistic era was a time of experimentation into the natural world and the attempt to measure and define it. The geometer Euclid wrote *Elements*, probably the most successful school textbook ever written, in which he laid out many of the basic geometric principles. Up until the twentieth century, his book was still used to teach geometry to students.

One of the most brilliant applied scientists was Archimedes. He invented numerous clever devices including pumps, pulleys, and military machines. He established the value of pi. Perhaps his most famous saying was, "Give me a lever and a place to stand and I can move the world." His single-minded concentration on scientific problems unfortunately led to his death. The town in which he lived was attacked by Romans, and the Roman general gave specific orders that Archimedes should not be hurt. When soldiers broke into his room, however, he was so deeply involved in solving a problem that he ignored their requests for identification, so they killed him, not knowing who he was.

The Hellenistic era also was a time of great scientific invention. Some of the many devices produced at this time include cogged gears, pulleys, the screw, glass blowing, hollow bronze casting, surveying instruments, an odometer, water clocks, and the water organ. Despite the great creativity of these inventors, often their ingenuity was not applied to practical concerns but for trickery. Hero of Alexandria, nicknamed "the Mechanic," constructed an automatic puppet theater, doors that appeared to open on their own, statues that seemed to come to life and move their arms, and apparently never emptying bowls, which poured out wine from invisible reservoirs. Many of these would today be considered the kinds of things used by magicians or illusionists. The Greek word *mechane*, from which "mechanic" is derived, originally meant "a trick."

Finally there was Eratosthenes, the geographer, who described the ancient world and laid the foundation for cartography. He was also the first person we know of who attempted to put together a chronology, a timeline of important events.

~*Gregory S. Aldrete*

FOR MORE INFORMATION

Barnes, J. *Early Greek Philosophy*. London: Penguin, 1987.

———. "Hellenistic Philosophy and Science." In *Oxford History of the Classical World*, ed. J. Boardman et al. Oxford: Oxford University Press, 1988.

ROME

The area of science in which perhaps the Romans were most proficient was engineering. The Romans were master builders who, although they only developed a few new techniques, used these to their fullest potential.

When one thinks of Roman buildings, one envisions structures of shining marble, but this was only the exterior of buildings, a surface layer. The truly brilliant innovation of the Romans was that they developed usable concrete. This was a huge step forward, since concrete could be poured in any form. It opened up new possibilities of architecture because now structures could be made in many shapes with curves and irregularities. The Romans even invented a special form of concrete using volcanic stones that would harden underwater. They used it to build gigantic harbors and breakwaters to protect the ships. The concrete revolution was very important. Build-

INTELLECTUAL LIFE
|
SCIENCE
|
Mesopotamia

Egypt

Greece

Rome

Australian Aboriginals

ings would have a core of concrete that was then covered up by a layer of marble or brick, depending on how lavish or expensive a building it was.

A second Roman innovation was the widespread use of the vault. A series of stones were cut so that when put together, they form a curved arch. This form is self-supporting because the stones' own weight holds them together. Architects soon realized that if they put two vaults together meeting at right angles, they would create a roof form that could span huge rooms without needing columns.

The best-preserved Roman building is also one of the most dramatic. This is the Pantheon, whose name means "a temple to all the gods." It was built in the second century c.e. by the emperor Hadrian. It had a truly original design. From the front, it looked like a standard rectangular temple with columns, doorways, and a triangular pediment on top. Walking inside the doors, however, visitors were in for a shock. Instead of finding themselves in a rectangular hallway lined by columns, they found themselves inside a vast round room with an enormous dome overhead. At the top of the dome, a round opening lets in light. The proportions are such that if you extended the half-sphere of the dome overhead downward, the complete sphere would exactly fit inside the building. Around the edges were statues to all the gods, and the floor was covered in rich colored marbles. Ancient Romans were astounded by the fact that the dome, which was 150 feet in diameter, did not fall in. The secret was that the architects distributed the weight downward, and they built the dome in layers using lighter and lighter concrete for each layer. The highest layer was made mostly from concrete mixed using pumice, a volcanic stone that is very light. At the bottom of the dome, the walls are 18 feet thick, but by the time they reach the opening at the top, they are only 4 feet thick. Not only was the building visually impressive, but it was built well, having stood for 2,000 years. The Pantheon is one of the more influential buildings as well; its temple-facade-with-dome-behind design has been copied over and over again, particularly for important government buildings, including the Capitol Building in Washington, D.C., as well as many state capitol buildings.

~Gregory S. Aldrete

FOR MORE INFORMATION

Adams, J.-P. *Roman Building Materials and Techniques*. Bloomington: Indiana University Press, 1994.

AUSTRALIAN ABORIGINALS

For Aboriginal people, science was part of their everyday life, and scientific knowledge was a common inheritance of all members of a group. As in the West, science had the twin roles of explaining the world in which people lived and of enabling them to make effective use of that world. An understanding of the properties of rocks and soils, the ecology of plants, the behavior of animals, pharmacology, and weather patterns was all part of the knowledge needed not only to survive but to thrive in an often-difficult environment.

The theoretical background to this knowledge was the Dreamtime, a period in the distant past when the earth and sky were formed and when the ancestors, who possessed intimate links with all life on earth, established the characteristics of the natural and physical worlds. Within that background, Aboriginal science was the result of some 50,000 years of observation and experimentation, and this knowledge was passed on from generation to generation.

Although everyone knew the fundamental attributes of plants, animals, and rocks, there were recognized experts among the elders who had particular knowledge of, for example, the location, preparation, and use of medicinal plants or in finding and working stone. Children learned by a combination of observation, instruction, and experimentation. These processes repeated the way that Aboriginal people in general had learned. They observed which fruits were palatable to birds or kangaroos, tested related plants to see if they shared the same qualities, gained information from neighboring groups, and used trial and error.

These methods enabled Aboriginal peoples to even make use of plants with unpalatable or poisonous fruits and nuts. Over a long period, these potential foods (with valuable stores of carbohydrates) were incorporated into the diet after the development of sometimes complex processing sequences that removed the toxins. In some regions, they learned how to treat certain kinds of stone with heat to make them more workable. Complex traps relied on careful observation of fish and bird behavior. Navigation in desert or semidesert areas where the landscape seemed very uniform for hundreds of miles required observation of the stars and of subtle differences in landforms. In dry seasons, people had to be able to recognize surface indicators of underground water and to know how to find plants that stored water. Tracking animals involved noting changes in the way that grass lay, detecting the traces of faint footprints, interpreting scratches, and being able to see surface traces of a covered burrow.

Aboriginal medicine involved no surgery; instead, healing depended on confidence in the elders and their knowledge of a range of plants and animals containing chemicals with useful properties. Illnesses, broken bones, burns, and wounds were healed with dressings and treatments. Many medicines were applied externally as creams or in smoke. Healers were thought to possess the ability to sense the cause of an illness and to treat it by removing objects or substances through the skin after manipulating the limbs or torso. Although most healers were men, knowledge of medicines tended to be the province of women, especially when a woman needed to be treated for problems during pregnancy. Aboriginal people believed that all illnesses and death had a cause, and unless the cause was obvious, such as the death of a very old person, the elders of the society would seek who was to blame for the illness or death.

To read about science in the early British colony in Australia, see the Australia entry in the section titled "Science and Technology" in the "Intellectual Life" chapter of volume 4 of this series, *Seventeenth and Eighteenth Centuries*.

~*David Horton*

FOR MORE INFORMATION

Berndt, R., and C. Berndt. *The World of the First Australians*. Canberra: Aboriginal Studies Press, 1988.

Flenniken, J., and P. White. "Heat Treatment of Siliceous Rocks and Its Implication for Australian Prehistory." *Australian Aboriginal Studies* 1 (1983):43–48.

Isaacs, J. *Bush Food: Aboriginal Food and Herbal Medicine*. Sydney, New South Wales: Weldons, 1987.

Latz, P. *Bushfires and Bushtucker: Aboriginal Plant Use in Central Australia*. Alice Springs, Northern Territory: IAD Press, 1995.

INTELLECTUAL
LIFE

| ART |

Mesopotamia

Egypt

Greece

Rome

Australian Aboriginals

Art

Anyone who goes to museums to look at the art of ancient civilizations will find that the term *art* encompasses a wide range of objects. Museum exhibits are likely to include, in addition to sculptures and paintings, objects produced for everyday use: pieces of pottery, dishes, glassware, jewelry, coins, and even sarcophagi, burial stones, and mummy cases. Such objects were often elaborately decorated and intended to be aesthetically pleasing as well as to serve a practical purpose. The split between mass-produced household items and pieces of art was not as pronounced then as it is now since each object had to be individually made by hand, which offered the opportunity for embellishment and individual expression.

In the ancient world, the people who produced these objects, however, were usually not seen as artists but instead as craftsmen on the same level as blacksmiths or makers of barrels. The ancient craftsman/artist often worked in concert with fellow artisans, either in a workshop or gathering together in a guild. The objects they produced were frequently collaborative creations as well rather than reflecting the vision of one individual.

As such, ancient art is often useful for gaining insight into the civilization which produced it. Although, for example, much of the art of Australian Aboriginals depicts episodes explaining their spiritual beliefs, scenes of everyday life on pots and in tomb paintings help us envision the society of the time—how people looked, dressed, and interacted. Artistic styles can be used to assess a society's attitudes and values. For instance, the fact that Classical Greek sculptors strove to create the perfect anonymous, idealized male form shows that their priorities differed from those of Roman sculptors of the Republican era, who specialized in hyper-realistic portrait busts depicting real people, complete with all their imperfections and wrinkles.

Finally, some of the most impressive works of ancient art were the result of state patronage, intended to glorify or commemorate the rulers who funded them.

~*Gregory S. Aldrete*

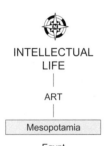

INTELLECTUAL
LIFE

ART

| Mesopotamia |

Egypt

Greece

Rome

Australian Aboriginals

MESOPOTAMIA

Some of the best-known objects of Assyrian art are the bas-reliefs from the walls of the palaces in Nimrud, Nineveh, and Dur-Sharrukin. The early reliefs actually converted wall painting into stone. There were ritual, ceremonial, and mythological scenes centered on the king in addition to scenes of hunting and war. At first, each slab was treated as an individual entity. Later, a series of slabs was used to tell a running story.

In bas-reliefs, little attention was given to perspective. Every item was carved as though the artist were standing in front of it, so that buildings never receded into a three-quarters view and soldiers scaling ladders in the assault and capture of a town were never represented in profile. Human figures were portrayed according to their rank or importance, with kings larger than courtiers, who were larger than ordinary people. The head was usually portrayed in profile, and the upper part of the body was shown full frontal or at a slight angle. But the Assyrian beard, which was square, was shown head-on even though its wearer was in profile. Like the head, the pelvis and legs were shown in profile, with the feet one behind the other in the same plane. The arms were always shown. At the beginning of the Neo-Assyrian Dynasty, the people were larger than life and the details clear and well proportioned, but the landscape was often disregarded. The north was indicated by the vine, with twisting branches forming a decorative pattern. The south was indicated by a few common trees, such as date palms, dwarf palms, and conifers. By the end of the Neo-Assyrian period, the human figures were carved on a smaller scale. Battle scenes were portrayed, with chariots, horses, and fighters tangled among the dead and the wounded.

Certain conventions were followed. For example, galloping horses were drawn with legs extended. The artist suggested the required number of persons or horses, up to four, by carving one or more lines exactly following the outline of the principal figure. As for the sculptural treatment of the bull colossi that guarded the palace gates, the spectator was assumed to look at the bull colossi either facing him or sideways. To achieve a two-dimensional aspect for the four feet, but to correspond with the three-dimensional view of the forequarters, an extra front foot was added for a total of five feet. The reliefs, like the frescoes, were never colored completely. Only certain features were highlighted, such as beards, ornaments, and garments with red or blue. Assyrian sculpture in the round consisted mainly of life-size stone statues of gods and kings. The figures stood stiffly at attention, the body shown by regular curves.

The quarrying of hard stones made large-scale building projects possible. Stone was quarried as near as possible to the construction site. After quarrying, the blocks were cut roughly to size or shape to facilitate handling and transportation. The stone was transported to the construction site using boats, wooden rollers, sledges, and ropes, and various draft animals such as oxen and donkeys. At the construction site, ramps made of wood, earth, and bricks were used to build walls or to erect colossal statues or obelisks. Blocks or sculptures were also moved by human labor. Massive building projects required both unskilled and skilled laborers, such as stonemasons or wood-workers, whose marks have sometimes been preserved on worked blocks or on the background of carved reliefs.

Artisans involved with stone included the stoneworker and picture carver. Finished sculptures, including relief carvings and statues in the round, were very often painted to make them appear more lifelike. For the same reason, eyes were frequently inlaid with other materials, such as shell and lapis lazuli, set in bitumen. There were a great many lists of magical stones from Babylonia and Assyria.

The earliest painting on built walls is dated to the Neolithic era. Throughout historical times, the interior walls of houses, temples, and palaces were often decorated with painted patterns or scenes with figures applied over layers of fine white mud plaster. Paint was made from finely ground minerals, mixed with water and an adhesive, often gelatin or glue, gum, or albumen (egg white). Carbon, azurite, ochre (iron oxide), and malachite were used to create pigments of black, blue, brown or red, and green. Artificial pigments have been found. Variations and muted shades, although rarely used, could be made by mixing the primary materials. Paints were applied to surfaces with brushes made of pieces of fibrous wood bruised at one end to separate the fibers and form bristles. Beeswax was also used as a binding medium and as a protective coating on the surfaces of paintings.

Statues and bronze surface panels made by metalworkers have survived. Bronze was used for artistic works, particularly for larger sculptures, because gold and silver were too expensive. Between 650 and 600 B.C.E., the kingdom of Urartu was a center of metal artwork, where new techniques were continuously developed.

The statue of Napir-Asu, queen of Elam, in its present mutilated condition, weighs nearly two tons. When the statue was made in the second millennium B.C.E., numerous crucibles, all heated simultaneously to the same temperature, would have been needed when the molten metal was poured. The statue was cast in two sections—front and back—and then soldered together and filed for smoothness. Although the statue was very thick, more metal was poured inside to make it sufficiently solid. Spreading the metal evenly inside was not completely successful. When Susa was plundered, the shoulder and the left arm were knocked off by a blow from a club. The technical skill shown in this statue, reliefs, and jewelry achieved a degree of excellence that was unsurpassed until the end of the nineteenth century in western Europe (Nemet-Nejat, 289–91).

FOR MORE INFORMATION

Collon, D. *Ancient Near Eastern Art.* Berkeley and Los Angeles: University of California Press, 1995.

Nemet-Nejat, K. R. *Daily Life in Ancient Mesopotamia.* Westport, Conn.: Greenwood Press, 1998.

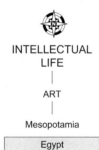

INTELLECTUAL
LIFE
|
ART
|
Mesopotamia

Egypt

Greece

Rome

Australian Aboriginals

EGYPT

Egyptian artists would be intrigued that we consider their work art. They toiled in anonymity, signed none of their works, and attained no fame during their lifetimes. Their society recognized no difference between fine art forms, such as painting and sculpting, and "lesser arts," such as pottery or cabinetry. Practitioners of any of these skills were regarded as simple workers on a level with, say, builders. Art was produced cooperatively in workshops, in a kind of assembly line. One worker chiseled a statue's arm, another smoothed the curve of its cheek, while still another etched the line of a toenail—all worked at the same time on one statue. In the case of a painted wall, one crew filled in a single color, followed by the next crew with a second color, and so forth, until a last crew added the fine details. With rare exceptions, no artist could point to anything and boast, "I made that myself." Art was a team project supervised by an overseer responsible—much as a modern-day general contractor schedules workers and monitors production—for the quality of the work, not the level of creativity.

Because recognition of an individual artist's work was unheard of and regard for creative endeavors was low, artists felt no pressure to innovate. Although a few were recognized for superior work, it was their craftsmanship rather than their imagination that earned them praise and rewards. When Egyptians found a style of portraiture they liked, all their artists repeated it over and over, creating an art of canons—set proportions, gestures and subjects—that they refined for thousands of years.

Egyptian artists developed their methods with different goals in mind from those of artists who work today. Statues, carvings, or paintings first and foremost were created for utilitarian purposes, rather than to generate enjoyment for the viewers or to excite their admiration. Some of the finest art, in fact, lay in tombs intended to be sealed for eternity from the eyes of any living person. Because most Egyptian creations were commissioned by individual citizens to serve their needs in the afterlife, artists had to maintain a certain realism in their work. A statue for a tomb owner might be more handsome, lean, and muscular than the subject was in life, but it had recognizably to resemble that person. Scenes in his tomb that depicted feasting, hunting, and so on had to portray those activities clearly to the gods on judgment day. (Egyptians fashioned animals with particular care, as well, because of their reverence for the god represented by each creature.) The need for accuracy and realism, however, did not destroy the beauty of Egyptian art: the more pleasing the portrayals, the better its utilitarian purpose was served.

In ancient Egypt, only a pharaoh commissioned art for a purpose we would find familiar—to enhance a building or monument and thereby gain admiration for the donor. Commoners commissioned artwork to ensure the afterlife they desired. Their religion instructed that a portrait statue of the deceased, their "double," be placed inside the tomb to receive the food offerings required for the next life. Commoners also had scenes painted on the walls of their tombs for a different, although still religious, purpose—to show the gods what they enjoyed so that similar pleasures would be available to them throughout eternity.

Sculpture, the preeminent Egyptian art form along with architecture, evolved from humble origins. Before 3000 B.C.E., crude animal figures, of which only a few survive, were carved clumsily in soft stone or barely molded from clay. Then, just before the dawn of the First Dynasty, a remarkable series of royal palettes and mace heads, vigorously carved in low relief, appeared. For the first time, figures of people and various animals, especially a large bull, were represented with sinews and muscles in the act of moving. The skills required to achieve such realistic depictions were not discovered suddenly but evolved from the related art of stone carving. Egyptians had mastered the hardest granite and dolerite by the fourth millennium, molding it to a desired shape as if it were pliable clay.

Sculpture in the round, however, did not achieve real competence until the Third Dynasty. The first known masterpiece, a seated, life-size limestone statue of the pharaoh Zoser, posed magisterially on his throne in a ceremonial robe, his head covered with the *nemes* kerchief and his chin adorned with a fine beard, was carved for his Step Pyramid enclosure. Offerings were made to this statue from outside—behind a wall pierced with two holes at the level of the statue's eyes, symbolically allowing it to observe the gifts being presented. The statue retains great dignity even today, despite the fact that its eyes, doubtless carved of valuable rock crystal, were gouged out in ancient times.

In the Fourth Dynasty, literally hundreds of almost-perfect statues in the round demonstrate that tomb portrait statues had become commonplace within the higher levels of society. Notable among many others, a pair of life-size, seated limestone statues of Prince Rahotep and his wife Nofert, although heavy in the legs and trunk, present sensitive facial portraits. Rahotep sports a narrow mustache above a determined mouth; Nofert wears a serene expression despite a fat wig that allows a bit of her own hair to show below. Both look out through translucent rock crystal eyes that seem eerily real.

Excellent bas-reliefs also became common during this exceptional era. Competent artists were sufficiently abundant by this time that mere courtiers and government officials could embellish their tombs with high-quality carving. Monumental statuary, embodied by the colossal Sphinx, appeared for the first time as freestanding work—as in the case of the two-foot-tall head of the Fifth Dynasty pharaoh Userkaf, which is all that remains of an over-life-size seated statue. The first metal sculpture was produced in the Sixth Dynasty. Finer work lay ahead, when the more easily cast bronze arrived in Egypt during the Middle Kingdom.

The collapse of central authority during the First Intermediate period disrupted the training of artists and resulted in crude work throughout most of that era. But with the return of a stable central government in the Middle Kingdom came a resurgence of interest in art. Strikingly, pharaohs' statues began to portray faces with lines of age and expressions of concern, as opposed to the idealized portrayals of the Old Kingdom: for the first time, real people look back at the viewer. A previous delicacy of expression was replaced by a better sense of proportion and composition, as exemplified by statues of seated scribes, knees held to their chests, in a posture that appropriately earned them the name "block statues," while the nuances of older bas-reliefs gave way to more elegant, simpler forms. In a continued democratizing trend, more citizens began to commission artists to produce work for their tombs, including charming wood and clay models—produced by the hundreds in heights ranging from less than a foot to over two feet tall—of servants bearing offerings, soldiers arrayed for battle, houses, and workers engaged in various occupations, such as cattle feeding, or bread and beer making. These models were placed in tombs to enable the gods to recognize what pleasures the deceased looked forward to in the next world.

As fine artwork continued to proliferate during the New Kingdom, pictures replaced these tomb models at the same time that monumental statuary attained superhuman scale. The mighty conquests of its divine pharaohs were underscored by wall carvings depicting the pharaoh as 10 or 20 times the size of ordinary people. Egypt's augmented position in the world demanded new artistic symbols.

Exemplifying this trend, obelisks, imposing gifts from pharaohs to adorn temples, emerged as the new art form. Consisting of one massive piece of solid rock—unlike the stone bricks of the United States' national obelisk, the Washington Monument—the granite spires of the Egyptians passed 100 feet in height and approached 400 tons in weight. Lines of hieroglyphs covered all four faces, and the point, sheathed in electrum, an alloy of gold and silver, shone like the sun. The hieroglyphs, of course, all describe how wonderful the pharaoh was to donate such a mighty monument.

Outdoing all his predecessors, Ramses the Great erected a 65-foot-tall, 1,000-ton statue at his funerary temple and followed it with a rock-cut temple at Abu Simbel, whose four gigantic images of the pharaoh were designed to erase all thought of conquest by any enemy approaching Egypt from the south. Increased contact with art styles of other countries during this period influenced Egyptians to portray clothing and coiffures more sensuously. Lines in painting, bas-relief, and sculpture became more fluid.

When Ramses became pharaoh, his love of the colossal resulted in an unequaled spate of building, which severely strained the resources of the country. Religious wall carvings began to show an obvious haste in execution, as the loving care previously lavished on them gave way to a debased style that sacrificed elegance for dramatic effect. But out of this arose a new technique—sunk relief—which was faster to carve, eliminating the need to chisel away the entire background surface, and, in the stark Egyptian sunlight, emphasizing outlines by causing them to fall into deep shadow.

Sometime after Ramses' death, when the court moved north to the delta, pharaohs' tombs ceased being built in the Theban Valley of the Kings. Although royal burials continued in the delta, its high water table destroyed much art of the Late period. What survives, mostly in the form of statuary, demonstrates the Egyptians' continued facility for carving all types of stone but without their earlier fine aesthetic.

As fine art became democratized, its quality declined—a trend exemplified particularly by Egyptian bronze statues. Bronze was brought to Egypt in the Middle Kingdom primarily for weapons, but gradually it became a favored medium for statues as well. The material, particularly well suited to casting, flowed into a mold's every crevice to produce replicas exact to the thinnest line, and the cheapness of the material allowed everyone to purchase bronze statues of their favorite god(s). Egyptians learned to cast bronze statues using the lost-wax method. First they carved a figure in wax, then coated the wax with moist clay. After firing, the wax melted and ran out a hole left for the purpose, while the clay skin hardened into pottery. When molten bronze was poured through the same hole that had allowed the wax to escape, it solidified into an exact replica of the original wax image. Early single-piece ceramic molds, shattered to release their bronze statues, had evolved by the New Kingdom into reusable molds, formed of separate halves, which could be used to produce countless replicas. During the remaining thousand years of Egypt's existence, hundreds of thousands of bronze statues of various gods were produced. Generally, they stand less than a foot high but decrease in size to as small as an inch or so, with the same themes repeated. Finer are specially

Ramses the Great erected a 65-foot-tall, 1,000-ton statue at his funerary temple.

commissioned bronzes, sometimes inlaid with gold or with components in semiprecious stone, created for wealthy patrons.

The appearance of Egyptian statuary differs markedly today from its initial state. Originally, wood or soft-stone statues were covered with a thin coat of gesso—a plasterlike material composed of chalk and glue that dried to a smooth, white coating and provided a perfect surface for painting. The figures we see now, most of which retain only faint traces of their previous colors, would have been so brightly painted, given the primary hues favored in the Egyptian palette, that we would find them garish by modern standards. Even hard stones that took a smooth polish were fair game for highlights of paint or gilt. While eyes and lips might be colored appropriately, jewels, belts, and head wear provided opportunities for serious embellishment.

Egyptian painting began as a medium separate from sculpture, but the two came together in temple and tomb reliefs that required both subtle three-dimensional modeling and a brightly painted finish.

Early drawings, elementary stick figures scratched on rocks in about 7000 B.C.E., depicted people, animals, and birds. By 4000 B.C.E., drawings with the same stick figures, but now with boats, began to appear on pottery vessels. Sometime before 3000 B.C.E., the oldest Egyptian mural had been installed in a house in southern Hieraconpolis; enigmatically, it portrayed several groups of men engaged in land-and-sea battles.

Given paint's fragile nature, it is remarkable that a masterpiece of color as old as the early Fourth Dynasty has survived. Nevertheless, beside the pyramid of Meidum, deep inside the tomb of a courtier named Itet, stands a damaged wall painting of his sons netting birds in a marsh. Miraculously, a row of two ganders and a female goose have survived intact, their sure lines and strong color preserved, with every feather still in place and as fresh as the day they were painted.

Despite an entirely different intention and a traditional lack of imagination, Egyptian artists often conveyed a feeling that still touches us today, an especially surprising fact given the limited materials available to them. Egyptians employed a palette of only a few, mainly pure, colors. Black, white, blue, red, yellow and brown came directly from a bowl; green, pink, orange and gray were mixed from two of those basic colors. Almost no other colors appear, except gilding with gold. That these colors were produced primarily from natural minerals accounts for the vividness that wall paintings retain thousands of years later. Brown, red, and yellow came from different oxides of iron, white from powdered chalk or gypsum, and blue from frit: finely ground blue glass. Black, however, derived from soot, sometimes turned brown or reddish over the centuries.

As with every society, fashions—even artistic fashions—changed. Early in the 18th Dynasty, for example, light gray backgrounds were generally chosen to set off painted subjects; later, a bright white background gained favor, with yellow as an infrequent alternative. Yellow had become the primary background choice by the 19th Dynasty. As time passed, the time-consuming carving necessary to produce bas-reliefs became less common, and it was replaced, as in the tomb of Tutankhamen, by paint alone (Brier and Hobbs, 171–89).

FOR MORE INFORMATION

Aldred, C. *Egyptian Art in the Days of the Pharaohs 3100–320 B.C.* New York: Oxford University Press, 1980.

Brier, B., and H. Hobbs. *Daily Life of the Ancient Egyptians.* Westport, Conn.: Greenwood Press, 1999.

GREECE

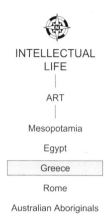

Most major works of art in ancient Greece were commissioned by the state and served a religious function, whether as temples, dedications to the gods, or monuments erected in commemoration of victorious athletes or the dead. The Greek artist often found himself in the pay of the state and had to work to a strict set of specifications and guidelines. We know the names of very few artists and virtually nothing about their private lives.

Greek sculpture originated about the middle of the seventh century B.C.E. Its initial inspiration owes much to Egypt. Marble, limestone, bronze, terra-cotta, wood, and a combination of gold and ivory known as chryselephantine were the chief materials. The 36-foot-high statue of Athena Parthenos, housed inside the Parthenon and designed by the sculptor Phidias, was covered in ivory and gold to represent flesh and clothing. Stone statues were painted, which lent them a very vivid appearance. Accessories, including jewelry and eyes, were often reproduced in a different material. Statues were not cheap to purchase. It is reckoned that a bronze statue would have cost 3,000 drachmas.

The Greek sculptor of the Classical era in Greece did not see it as his goal to produce works of art that reflected the accidental and true-to-life deficiencies of authentic human anatomy. The chief artistic inspiration for these Greeks was the physically perfect, naked male body, as exemplified by the god Apollo, who is invariably depicted as a youth in peak physical condition. A superb example of this is the Apollo who presides over a battle between the civilized Lapiths and the half-human, half-animal Centaurs on the west pediment of the temple of Zeus at Olympia. Unperturbed and impassive, Apollo extends his right arm horizontally in a gesture that indicates his support for the Lapiths. Greek sculptors attempted to identify the ideal proportions of the male body, and a preponderance of statues of this era are of naked, young, athletic males.

Portraiture inspired relatively few works of Greek art. Many sculptures that purport to be portraits were produced long after the subject's death. Their resemblance to the sitter is therefore questionable at best. A notable exception, the portraits of Socrates probably do convey an authentic likeness. The Hellenistic era saw the birth of a much more realistic style of art, and one that depicted a wide range of human body types, not just idealized young males. Famous Hellenistic sculptures include depictions of careworn philosophers, aging athletes, and old women. Hellenistic kings seem to have

The *Doryphoros* (spear-bearer) sculpted by Polyclitos. The Classical Greeks were obsessed with finding the proportions of the perfect human figure, and this statue was thought to embody this ideal. © Scala/Art Resource, NY.

been accorded a truly individualistic identity, especially in the profiles on coins. One of the most memorable coin portraits is that of Euthydemos I of Bactria, dated circa 200 B.C.E., which gazes at us across the millennia with disillusionment and disarming candor.

From the very beginning of full-size Greek sculpture about 660 B.C.E., males were depicted naked. Statues, known as kouroi (i.e., boys or youths), stand frontally with one foot advanced, hands at side, fists clenched. The earliest examples are based on a sculptural formula that had been used by the Egyptians for 2,000 years. Statues of women, called korai (i.e., girls), which have no antecedent in Egyptian art, are by contrast invariably clothed.

Not until the second half of the fourth century B.C.E. did female nudity become common in statuary. Even then, nudes are usually shown covering the genital area with a hand or piece of drapery. A celebrated example is Praxiteles' sculpture of Aphrodite taking a bath, which was described by the Roman writer Pliny (the Elder) as "the finest statue in the whole world."

In the later Hellenistic era, Greek sculptors began to carve a much wider range of human types than idealized young men. Some of the most famous statues of this time are of old women or men who are portrayed in a much less idealized way.

Until recently, our knowledge of the great paintings that decorated the interior walls of Greek temples and public buildings relied wholly on literary descriptions, which failed to convey any real sense of the technical quality of the originals. Recently, however, thanks partly to the discovery of the Macedonian tombs at Vergina, we have direct evidence of these murals.

Even so, when we talk about Greek painting, we tend to think of the humble medium of vase painting. Vase painting is a major source of information about Greek life. Especially popular subjects are drinking parties and visits to the tomb because most painted pottery was intended either to be used at a symposium or to be deposited in the grave. Other popular subjects include athletic activities and scenes taking place in the women's quarters. Earlier vases are decorated in the black-figure technique against a red background. About 525 B.C.E., however, the process was reversed, and the background was painted in black, leaving the figure in red. Most scenes of daily life are rendered in red-figure.

Although art was predominantly religious in function and although its subject matter was largely confined to the mythological, it was often used to make a political statement. When, for instance, in 447 B.C.E., the Athenians made the historic decision to rebuild the temples on the Acropolis destroyed by the Persians, they incorporated into the sculptures a number of barely disguised references to Athens's heroic struggle for freedom. The Parthenon metopes, for instance, which depict the battle between the Lapiths and the Centaurs, can be read as representing the conflict between Greeks and non-Greeks. It is possible, too, that the great frieze that ran around the outer wall of the *naos* (the innermost shrine containing the statue of the god), whose principal feature is a cavalcade of Athenian cavalry, is intended to depict the 192 Athenians who died at the battle of Marathon, here shown as the heroized dead.

Greek artists were constantly learning new techniques and addressing new problems. As a consequence, even in the absence of an archaeological context that would enable us to date a given artifact with chronological exactitude, we are often able to situate it to within a single decade. Coupled with this inherent innovativeness, however, was an inherent conservatism. For instance, although the different orders of architecture underwent refinement over the centuries, the temple remained the preferred medium of architectural expression (Garland, 192–99).

FOR MORE INFORMATION

Boardman, J. *Greek Art*. Revised ed. London: Thames and Hudson, 1973.
Garland, R. *Daily Life of the Ancient Greeks*. Westport, Conn.: Greenwood Press, 1998.

ROME

The earliest Roman sculpture reflected Rome's Etruscan origins. One of the most famous early sculptures is a depiction in bronze of the she-wolf feeding Romulus and Remus, the legendary founders of Rome. During the Republic, one notable type of sculpture that developed was the portrait bust, the head of a man. In the Republic, these busts were noted for their realism. The Classical Greeks had wanted to show idealized humans, the perfect man and woman, but the Romans took the opposite approach—they concentrated on showing real, recognizable people. Busts often seem unflattering because they depict people with wrinkles, warts, or big noses, but Republican sculpture reflected old-fashioned, simple, republican values. The clearest expression of this idea is a portrait of a Roman nobleman clad in a toga holding the busts of his ancestors.

Under Augustus, Roman sculpture began to change somewhat. It became more classical in the sense that it imitated Greek models. People were shown in more idealized ways, although they are still recognizable as individuals. A famous example of this is a statue of Augustus found in his wife's house, called the Primaporta Augustus. Augustus is clearly recognizable, but his features are somewhat idealized. The statue shows him in general's clothing, with his hand raised in an oratorical gesture. His armor is entirely covered with intricate carvings of mythological figures and historical scenes, all of which in some way glorify or commemorate his reign. This statue is an example of the way that under Augustus, art became used for propagandistic purposes.

Another Roman art form was the mosaic. These are pictures formed by gluing tiny colored pieces of stone onto a floor to form geometric patterns or even pictures. Romans liked these as floor decoration and often had them in the main public rooms of their houses. Mosaics could depict nearly any subject; popular ones included animals or mythological scenes. Roman houses had mosaics on the floor, with the walls covered with paintings. Many of these paintings were preserved by the volcanic ash that engulfed the houses of Pompeii. Common subjects for these paintings also included mythological scenes, fantastic architectural scenes, and illusionistic paintings. The idea of these was to create the impression that you were looking out a window at an amazing landscape when, in reality, you were staring at a solid wall. Roman wall paintings featured many colors, but dark red, black, and white tend to dominate.

~Gregory S. Aldrete

FOR MORE INFORMATION

Kleiner, D. E. E. *Roman Sculpture*. New Haven, Conn.: Yale University Press, 1992.
Strong, D. E. *Roman Art*. 2nd ed. New York: Penguin, 1988.

NUBIA

Sons of Nubian rulers often went north to Egypt, where they received an Egyptian education at the court of the pharaoh. In the process, they also acquired a taste for Egyptian art forms. Nubians adopted many of the artistic conventions featured in the north, which showed in their temples and in their exquisite gold jewelry. See the Egypt entry in the section "Art" in the present chapter for a description of Egypt's influential artwork.

INTELLECTUAL
LIFE
|
ART
|
Mesopotamia

Egypt

Greece

Rome

Australian Aboriginals

AUSTRALIAN ABORIGINALS

Australian Aboriginal art was inspired by the land, and the materials from which art was made were also derived from the land. Art was a part of everyday life and was functional, decorative, religious, and educational. It was owned both by individuals and groups, it involved duties and responsibilities, and it could be secret or public. Almost every type of surface, including rocks, trees, sand, bark, animal skins, and the human body, was used for artistic expression. The materials used to make art came from the ground in the form of red, brown, and yellow ochres and white clays, and from fire in the form of charcoal. Few objects, whether worn on the body or used as tools or weapons, were not decorated in some artistic way, and every ceremony, whether large or small, restricted or open, incorporated art. All members of society were involved in some way in the production of art, although some were recognized as great artists while others were merely helpers. Paintings depicted figures from the Dreamtime, animals, hunting scenes, ceremonies, symbolic figures, weapons, or even just stencils of hands. Designs made on the ground included maps showing the travels of ancestors, the location of water holes, or other important features of the landscape. While painting, the artist might tell the story he was illustrating or sing a related song. Engravings were carved into the walls of rock shelters or onto flat expanses of rocky outcrops.

Artistic styles varied over time and across the continent and often depended on the materials that were available. In northern Tasmania, there were ancient engravings of symbols and faces, whereas in the south, people decorated the insides of houses with bird feathers. In Victoria, people painted human and animal figures in rock shelters and had possum-skin cloaks decorated with incised and colored designs. In New South Wales, rock engravings on sandstone outcrops showed whales and giant emus, whereas trees were carved with complex clan designs. In Queensland, there was wonderful rock art consisting of whole galleries of stencils and paintings of animals and ancestors, and people also painted their war shields with intricate clan designs. In South Australia and the Northern Territory, intricate patterns were made from colored sands. There were many designs, including some found on rock shelters, bark, coffins and burial poles which showed, in "X-ray" style, the internal organs of animals. In Western Australia, galleries of engraved and painted human figures depicted hunting and ceremonial scenes from the past.

Bark paintings, which were used for secret ceremonial purposes, in burial rituals, or to decorate the interiors of houses, were found over most of Australia, including Tasmania. Everywhere, people decorated their bodies with ornate designs for particular ceremonies and performances, and they wore elaborate headdresses of plant and animal materials.

Rock art is probably at least 30,000 years old and may well date back to the first entry of Aborigines into Australia. It is generally thought that some of the engravings are the oldest rock art in Australia, whereas styles such as X-ray art are among the youngest. There were, however, probably paintings from earliest times, but pigments do not survive well in many localities. Some art is so old that Aboriginal people in certain areas speak of its having been made in the Dreamtime and do not know its meaning. Other art is so recent as to have been done by still-living artists. The latter might also involve retouching paintings because rock art is seen as living and needs to be constantly refreshed to fulfill its religious functions. Some forms of art, such as burial poles, were seen as temporary, meeting an immediate purpose and then being left to rot away. Aboriginal art represents the longest continuous artistic tradition in the world and provides a unique, varied, and rich body of work.

~David Horton

FOR MORE INFORMATION

Berndt, R., and C. Berndt. *The World of the First Australians*. Canberra: Aboriginal Studies Press, 1988.

Brandl, E. *Australian Aboriginal Paintings in Western and Central Arnhem Land*. Canberra: Aboriginal Studies Press, 1988.

Flood, J. *Rock Art of the Dreaming: Images of Ancient Australia*. Sydney, New South Wales: Angus and Robertson, 1997.

Layton, R. *Australian Rock Art: A New Synthesis*. Cambridge, England: Cambridge University Press, 1992.

INTELLECTUAL LIFE: WEB SITES

http://www.fordham.edu/halsall/ancient/asbookfull.html
http://classics.mit.edu
http://physics.nist.gov/GenInt/Time/ancient.html
http://metmuseum.org/explore/First_Cities/firstcities_splash.htm
http://www.clubs.psu.edu/aegsa/rome/romecbib.html
http://www-etcsl.orient.ox.ac.uk/
http://www.unc.edu/courses/rometech/public/frames/art_set.html

5

MATERIAL LIFE

Material life describes all the things we use, from the houses that give us shelter to the food that sustains us, the clothes that protect us, and the items that amuse us. It also includes the luxury items that set us apart from others less fortunate than we. Studying material life is fascinating in the details it provides. We learn that hand-kerchiefs were a luxury item in sixteenth-century Europe designed to set the wealthy apart from the peasant who used a hat or sleeve, or that underwear was only widely adopted in Europe in the eighteenth century.

Aside from the delicious details that bring the past to life, the study of material life reveals much about society as a whole. For example, cultures that rely on rice as a major staple have to invest a great deal of labor into its cultivation, whereas societies that thrive on corn (maize), which is not labor intensive, have ample spare time. People who had access to raw materials, such as iron ore, developed in ways different from those who did not, and groups that had domesticated animals or large plows had different organizing principles from others. If we know what a culture uses, we know a great deal about those people's lives.

As we study material life, it is important to remember that humans want much more than the bare necessities of life. Indeed, we are creatures of desire rather than need, and this longing has fueled much of the progress in the world. We want spices to flavor our food, not just nourishment; we want gold to adorn us as much as we want clothing to cover us. Cultures (such as in the West) that have acquired a taste for change in fashion transform themselves (not necessarily for the better) in all areas much more rapidly than those (such as in Asia) that preferred a more conser-vative approach to clothing. All in all, the details of our daily life matter. From the Stone Age, when humans adorned themselves with cowrie shells as they wielded stone tools, to the modern world shaped by high technology, humans have been defined by the things we use. Our material life reveals and shapes who we are.

The material life of the ancient world was profoundly shaped by the environment, probably to a greater degree than in subsequent eras. The necessities of life had to be fashioned or grown from resources that were locally available and cheap. This was particularly true of groups that inhabited areas with minimal natural resources, such as the Australian Aborigines. Climate determined what crops could be grown,

MATERIAL LIFE
|
FOOD

DRINK

HOUSING

HEALTH & MEDICINE

CLOTHING

APPEARANCE

and this meant that all the cultures around the Mediterranean basin depended heavily on varieties of cereal crops, chiefly wheat and barley, for basic subsistence. Within the range of crops that could be cultivated, there was some latitude for choice, so that Mesopotamians and Egyptians preferred to drink beer made from grain, whereas for Greeks and Romans, wine made from grapes was the beverage of choice. Climate and available resources similarly dictated that the universal building material in all these cultures was mud, which was fashioned into bricks to construct houses for shelter. Because cotton did not grow naturally in these countries, wool and linen were the predominant materials for clothing. Today, technology has allowed rapid, cheap international trade, which has resulted in many of the same items and foodstuffs being available throughout the world. In contrast, the ancient world required that the vast majority of people made do with what was available in their immediate surroundings.

What people owned and consumed—their houses, clothing, ornaments, and the quality and variety of their food and drink—also revealed their social status and place in society. How people dressed could indicate their profession, their degree of wealth, and whether they were free or enslaved. In Egypt, priests shaved their heads; in Greece, free men wore beards and slaves were clean shaven; and in Rome, stripes of varying thickness on their clothes proclaimed people's net worth. Just like today, people used material goods to compete with one another and boost their social standing. Among the wealthy, the limitations of local environment did not apply, and rich individuals proclaimed their status by importing exotic foods, spices, and fabrics from far-off lands.

Medical care and sanitation only existed in rudimentary forms, and in medical theory and practice, the scientific and the supernatural mingled freely. To cure a disease, doctors were as likely to prescribe an herbal concoction as they were to recite a magical incantation, and in most instances both approaches were probably employed.

For the average person, possessions and diet were extremely basic; poverty, over-crowding, and starvation were constant companions, and the quality of life was often distressingly poor.

~*Joyce E. Salisbury and Gregory S. Aldrete*

FOR MORE INFORMATION

Braudel, F. *The Structures of Everyday Life.* New York: Harper and Row, 1979.

Diamond, J. *Guns, Germs, and Steel.* New York: Norton, 1997.

Horden, P., and N. Purcell. *The Corrupting Sea: A Study of Mediterranean History.* Oxford: Blackwell, 2000.

MATERIAL LIFE

|
FOOD
|

Mesopotamia

Egypt

Greece

Rome

India

Nubia

Australian Aboriginals

Food

Food, of course, is one of the absolute necessities of life. Its primacy is demonstrated by the fact that the full-time efforts of most of the inhabitants of the ancient world were devoted exclusively to food production. Even with probably about 90 percent of the populace dedicated to growing food, there was barely enough. Food was life, and the struggle literally to put bread on the table consumed most people's full attention.

The diet of the inhabitants of the ancient world presents an interesting contrast. On the one hand, ancient sources list an astonishing variety of meats, fruits, vegetables, spices, and other foodstuffs that were consumed, and surviving recipes testify to the creativity and elaborateness of the dishes that ancient chefs concocted. The range of food that, at least in theory, was available for consumption in the ancient world was quite impressive. On the other hand, the actual day-to-day diet of the vast majority of people consisted of an extremely limited set of options. In fact, in all of the Mediterranean cultures, probably more than two-thirds of a person's caloric intake was derived from a single food—grain. The average person's diet was composed of a frighteningly (and unhealthily) monotonous round of bread, bread, and more bread, broken up by bowls of porridge, which was also made from grain. Barley was the dominant grain grown in Mesopotamia, and wheat in Greece and Rome, but the cereal family was the staple of life for the ancient world as a whole. In contrast to the agricultural societies of Europe and Asia, the Australian Aborigines subsisted entirely by practicing a hunter-gatherer lifestyle, roaming over huge expanses to gather enough food to survive.

Meat, which is often the centerpiece of meals in the modern industrialized West, was a rarity for most people in the ancient world. When eaten, it was usually in the form of fish, pork, or goat meat. When available, beef from cattle was a true luxury item. The only time that average people of the ancient Mediterranean probably tasted beef was at religious festivals when a cow was sacrificed to the gods and the carcass was roasted and eaten by the worshipers. Because of the scarcity and cost of meat, vegetarianism was a lifestyle of necessity for many, but it was also chosen by some for religious or moral reasons, especially in ancient India.

Fruits and vegetables would have been welcome variations to the diet and would have been at least occasionally widely available when in season. Cane sugar was not available, and so the universal sweetener in the ancient world for those desiring sweets was honey. Particularly in Greece and Rome, olive oil was an important part of the average person's diet and, because of its high calorie count per ounce, may even have contributed a significant percentage of one's total caloric intake. Overall, the average person of the ancient world did not starve but would have suffered from various diseases such as rickets caused by the lack of variety in his or her diet.

The rather grim and monotonous image of the typical diet stands in sharp contrast to the sumptuous feasts enjoyed by the wealthy elite. Nearly everything that walked, flew, swam, or could be grown was incorporated into ancient meals at some point. There really were instances when Roman banquets featured exotic dishes such as ostrich stew or flamingo brain pie, but these colorful feasts were the exception, not the rule.

Finally, while food is a basic necessity of life, and studying eating habits is a necessary part of understanding the practical aspects of people's material lives, food can tell us about culture as well. The way that a society goes about the preparation, presentation, and ingestion of food can serve as a form of cultural expression. The etiquette of an Egyptian banquet or a Roman dinner party can reveal much not just about what they ate but also about the people who performed these social rituals and their economic and social status.

~*Gregory S. Aldrete*

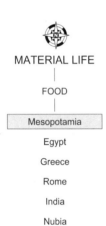

MATERIAL LIFE
|
FOOD
|
Mesopotamia

Egypt

Greece

Rome

India

Nubia

Australian Aboriginals

MESOPOTAMIA

The diet of the people of Mesopotamia was based on barley, which was used to make unleavened bread and beer. Barley and other cereals were ground with portable millstones to produce various grades of flours. The flour was then mixed with water (usually without any leavening agent) to produce assorted breads. Other grains, such as millet, emmer wheat, rye, and in the first millennium B.C.E., rice, were also used to make bread or cereal. The breads were described as first quality, ordinary, black, or white. In the Royal Cemetery at Ur in the tomb of Queen Puabi, there were pieces of unleavened bread made from finely ground flour.

Specialty breads were made by beating in various fats, such as sesame oil, lard, mutton "butter," and fish oil. The oil was sometimes seasoned or flavored to disguise the rancid taste that the fat would have quickly acquired in the heat of ancient Mesopotamia. Honey, ghee, sesame, milk, fruit juices, cheese, and fruits could be added to the dough. High-quality breads and cakes were meant for the royal table.

Soups were prepared with a starch or flour base of chickpeas, lentils, barley flour, or emmer flour. Other ingredients were onions, lentils, beans, mutton fat or oil, honey, or meat juice. The soups were thick and nourishing—a meal in a bowl.

Onions were basic to the ancient diet; the onion family included leeks, shallots, and garlic ("white onion"). The onions were described as sharp, sweet, or those "which have a strong odor." Lentils and chickpeas were staples in the ancient diet. Other vegetables included a variety of lettuces, cabbage, summer and winter cucumbers (described as either sweet or bitter), radishes, beets, and a kind of turnip. Fresh vegetables were eaten raw or boiled in water.

Dates were a source of sugar, and the date palm was used to make date wine. Other fruits commonly grown were apples, pears, grapes, figs, quince, plums, apricots, cherries, mulberries, melons, and pomegranates.

Meat was also a part of the ancient Mesopotamian diet. At Drehem in southern Mesopotamia, massive barns housed numerous flocks and herds, which were then redistributed for sustenance and cultic needs. The animals were delivered alive and then slaughtered by a butcher. But some animals were dead on arrival. Both types of meat were considered fit for human consumption. The meat from already-dead animals was fed to soldiers, messengers, and cult personnel. Among the many deliveries recorded, workers at the textile workshop at Lagash received six sheep with bread and salt.

Meat was expensive. Mutton, beef, and goat meat were part of the ancient Mesopotamian diet. The gods and the king received large rations of meat. Cattle allocated for food or sacrifice were fattened. There was no prohibition against the consumption of pigs, still found in great numbers in southern Iraq's marshes. In

Sumerian times, pigs were tended in large herds, their scavenging supplemented by barley feed. Fatty meat was prized because it was in short supply; for this reason, pork was valued. Because of the shortage of pasture land, there were few cattle. Horse flesh was eaten. A lawsuit in Nuzi (ca. fourteenth century B.C.E.) records a case in which the defendants were accused of stealing and eating a horse. Dead asses were fed to the dogs. Poultry, geese, and ducks were raised for meat and eggs; the hen was introduced in the first millennium B.C.E.

The rivers were filled with fish, turtles, and eggs. A Sumerian text (ca. 2000 B.C.E.) describes the habits and appearance of many species of fish. Fish was an important source of protein in the diet, and many kinds were listed from the third and second millennia. Fish was served to the king. But ordinary citizens also ate salt and fresh-water fish, although they preferred fish bred in "fish ponds" or reservoirs. After the Kassite period (1595–1158 B.C.E.), fish became less popular.

Many herbs and spices were available, such as salt, coriander, black and white cumin, mustard, fennel, marjoram, thyme, mint, rosemary, fenugreek, watercress, and rue (an acrid, green leafy plant).

The Sumerians did not use sugar; instead, they used fruit juices, particularly grape and date juice as sweeteners. Only the very rich could afford honey, which may have been imported. "Mountain honey," as well as "dark," "red," and "white" honey, is mentioned in texts. "Date honey" actually refers to a syrup made from the dates, not a real honey.

Many foods were preserved for times of need. Cereals were easy to keep. Legumes could be dried in the sun. A variety of fruits were pressed into cakes. Fish and meat were preserved by salting, drying, and smoking. Ice was brought from the highlands and stored in icehouses for cooling beverages.

Some fruits and vegetables could be eaten raw, but breads, cakes, and meats all required cooking. Meat could be cured, dried, roasted, boiled, and "touched with fire." Fish was described as "touched by fire" and "placed upon the fire," possibly referring to glowing coals. Even some breads were cooked in the coals. A grill could be used for cooking over the flames. The vocabulary for cooking pots, whether clay or metal, was extensive. The Sumerians used several types of ovens such as a clay oven and a kind of barbecue. Some pottery molds unearthed from the kitchen area of the Mari palace (ca. eighteenth century B.C.E.) were circular, with designs of animals; others were shaped like fish. These molds were probably used to prepare dishes for the king.

The Sumerians ate two meals a day. They bragged about their highly developed cuisine and compared it to that of desert nomads, whom they believed had no idea of the ways of civilized life. They described the nomads as eating raw food and having no idea how to make a cake with flour, eggs, and honey. Despite their boasts, we have no way to evaluate the Sumerians' culinary ability—to date, not a single recipe from them has been found.

We are fortunate to have a series of recipes on three tablets from Babylon dating circa 1700 B.C.E. Dubbed the Yale Culinary Tablets because they are part of the Yale Babylonian Collection at Yale University, these tablets contain 35 recipes. Many dishes were cooked in water to which fat was added, but the consistency of the liquid after cooking—broth, soup, vegetable porridge, or sauce—was never described. Meat broths were often named after the kind of meat used—that is, "venison broth," "gazelle broth," "goat kid broth," "lamb broth," "ram broth," and even "spleen broth." The list also includes both pigeons and francolins (wild hens). There were even vegetable broths. All broths were seasoned with a variety of mineral, plant, and animal products. Some recipes indicate their geographical or cultural origin, such as Elamite or Assyrian.

A recipe for preparing francolins in broth provides us with the following information:

Split the birds open, clean well with cold water and assemble in a cauldron to "sear" them. Remove from the fire and clean well again with cold water. Sprinkle with vinegar and rub all over with crushed mint and salt. Put beer in a clean cauldron and add fat. Clean the birds well with cold water and assemble all the ingredients in the cauldron. When the cauldron is hot, remove from the fire, sprinkle with vinegar and pat with mint and salt. Variant: clean a cauldron, put in clear water as well as the birds, and put it on the stove. Remove from the fire, clean well in clear water, and rub all over with garlic from which you have squeezed out the juice. . . .

Assemble the ingredients in a pot with water; a piece of fat from which the gristle has been removed, a carefully measured amount of vinegar, and, as desired, pieces of "aromatic wood" soaked in beer, and stripped rue leaves. When it comes to a boil, add samidu (a spicy plant), leek and garlic mashed with onion. Put the birds in this broth and cook. (as cited in Bottero, 13–14)

In this recipe, as in others, hygiene was a matter of great concern. After each step in preparing the dish, the cooked piece was washed well and wiped. The recipe included side dishes and garnishes. Because presentation was important, prepared meat was accompanied by fresh greens, garlic, and vinegar or salt and garnished with a porridge of grains and legumes. Another recipe includes five or six garnishes and a pastry crust.

The Yale Culinary Tablets comprise the first cookbooks. Because only scribes could read and write, these recipes may have been read to the cook. Texts refer to professional cooks, "the great cook," and "the chief cook." One chef even left the mark of his seal, which he claimed King Ibbi-Sin gave to him personally. Women played almost no role in royal kitchens. Female servants were employed only to mold barley.

The Yale Culinary Tablets do not include the amounts of ingredients and the necessary cooking times, information that may have been learned by observation and oral instruction. Also, instructions for preparation of many foodstuffs we know to have been eaten in large quantities, such as fish, eggs, crustaceans, turtles, locusts, and so on, are not included in these tablets. Traditional methods of cooking are rarely mentioned, for example, radiant heat in a closed chamber (the "domed oven"), indirect heat in hot ashes or roasting, direct exposure to flame (broiling or grilling), and spit-roasting. Possibly these tablets belonged to a library of similar texts dealing with the "science" of cooking, which a teacher used to instruct a student (Nemet-Nejat, 157–62).

FOR MORE INFORMATION

Bottero, J. *Textes Culinaires de Mari.* Winona Lake, Ind.: Eisenbrauns, 1995.

Limet, H. "The Cuisine of Ancient Sumer." *Biblical Archaeologist* (1987).

Nemet-Nejat, K. R. *Daily Life in Ancient Mesopotamia.* Westport, Conn.: Greenwood Press, 1998.

EGYPT

Rich and poor did not set exactly the same tables. Most farmers dined infrequently on meat and never tasted expensive imports. A cow in ancient Egypt cost the equivalent of an entire year's income for a craftsman or the annual harvest of a small farmer. The average citizen would not waste such a precious commodity on dinner. On the other hand, a goat—valued at only a 16th of a cow—might be an appropriate menu choice for a special occasion, such as a wedding or a birth, even for a poor person. Everyday protein was obtained from fish or other nonanimal sources.

Just as we use the phrase "meat and potatoes" to describe a basic meal, ancient Egyptians referred to the staples of their diet as "bread and beer." One list of troop provisions specifies 20 bread rolls per soldier per day; the jugs of beer are not mentioned (Darby, 2:502). Because bread and beer were manufactured from grain, the greatest source of energy and nutrients for the Egyptian lower classes came from cereal products.

Bread came in a multitude of forms, from crescent, round, oval, pyramidal, disk, and hexagonal shapes to exotic shapes of women, animals, and birds for special ceremonies or magical use. These could be baked in a variety of ways. Sometimes tall ovens were used; other times a flat stone heated by a fire beneath it acted as a sort of griddle for flat bread. There were also conical stoves, similar to Indian tandoori ovens, on whose inner surface dough was placed for fast grilling, and heated pottery molds. Additives, such as honey, anise, or cumin, were sometimes used to flavor the basic wheat and barley breads.

So important was bread to ancient Egyptians that they gave it up during times of mourning, a custom similar to the Christian period of Lent, a meaningful sacrifice only because of the food's importance. Otherwise, bread figured in every meal—from a farmer's breakfast of bread and perhaps milk to the most elegant feast set by a mighty pharaoh. Both commoner and king ate toasted bread, enjoyed it as a stuffing with roasted animals and fowl, and partook of sweet cakes made by adding honey to the bread. In their use of grains, the main difference between farmers and the upper class was that the latter washed his meal down with wine, the former with beer.

Bread and beer did not exhaust the Egyptians' uses of grain; it was also stewed to produce gruel, baked as groats to accompany the main course of a meal, and even used as a religious symbol. Mummies sometimes wore necklaces braided from wheat leaves, and tombs often contained full-sized beds spread with mud in which barley had been planted in an outline of the god Osiris. When it sprouted, even in the dark tomb, it symbolized both the regeneration of the god and the hopes of the deceased for their own rebirth.

Other than grain, the poorer classes depended mainly on fish supplemented by wild fowl for their protein, both of which cost only the time required to catch them.

Egyptian bakery. The man on the right pours dough into the mushroom-shaped molds, while the worker on the left pries the cooked bread from the molds. Drawing by Rivka Rago.

Fish abounded in both the Nile and in Egypt's one true lake, located in an area called the Fayum today. Only a small percentage of saltwater fish was consumed; the majority came from fresh water.

Because Egypt's warm climate caused rapid spoilage, fish generally were salted, pickled, or split open and sun dried until used. Recipes included simple roasting and boiling or stuffing with bread and spices. Fish roe counted as a delicacy, as did newly hatched fry, cultivated for that purpose in artificial ponds. Fish cakes made from shredded flesh also constituted a treat. One recipe from Ptolemaic times called for a marinade of oil, onion, pepper, coriander, and other herbs spread over a large fish as it baked (Darby, 2:399), a recipe that could please any modern-day fish lover. The Nile also yielded turtles, clams, and even crocodiles. Crocodiles could be caught on hooks, trapped in nets, or speared. Some tomb paintings record men wrestling crocodiles.

Thanks to a large population of birds native to Egypt's marshes, fowl provided variation in the diet of both rich and poor. Because Egypt lay on the main migratory route between Europe and lower Africa, hundreds of thousands of fowl, tired and easy to catch, alighted each season in Egypt both before and after their long flight across the Mediterranean. Egyptians showed their passion for birds by creating 24 separate hieroglyphic signs for various species, with many more represented by signs in combination. Ducks, geese, pigeons, and doves were regularly consumed, along with countless smaller species. Chickens found their way to Egypt from western Asia around the time of the New Kingdom and were far from common during much of ancient times.

Vegetables form a large part of the diet of most farming countries, and Egypt was no exception. Its farmers grew onions and garlic, which they used extensively, along with radishes, lettuce, celery, leeks, parsley, several kinds of squash, cucumbers, and various beans, including fava beans, chickpeas, lentils, peas, and possibly, lima beans. Aquatic plants also found their way to the table. Egyptians were fond of the lotus plant for its perfume and attractive large flower, but they also ate its root and the beans of a related species, which taste like nuts. Papyrus, a water weed in the swampy Egyptian environment that provided material for writing, was also chewed for the sweet sap in its stem.

A special place in the Egyptian diet was reserved for sweet fruit. Figs were enjoyed for both their fruit and juice, which could also be fermented into a fig wine. Abundant grapevines yielded grapes, wine, and, when sun dried, raisins. Melons, including the special summer treat of watermelon, were harvested. Of course, plentiful date palms provided their sweet fruit, fresh or dried. Another species of palm, the dom palm, supplied a tasty nut that could be eaten raw or ground into flour. More exotic fruits included jujubes, pomegranates, and *Perseas*, with juniper beans and almonds imported as exotic foods for the wealthy. A few unclear references suggest that apples may have existed, although they formed no great part of the diet. The olive, although not sweet, was a common cultivated fruit enjoyed both for itself and for its oil. A kind of chocolate pudding was made by grinding carob beans into milk, which then jelled.

There was nothing bland about the Egyptian diet. The availability and variety of spices used in Egyptian cuisine of the period would impress any modern cook. The licorice taste of anise found constant use, along with the "sweet" flavor of mint. Cumin was much used, especially as a coating for fish, but dill, marjoram, rosemary, thyme, and sage each added its distinct taste and perfume. Mustard plants yielded their seeds, although they were not ground with vinegar into the mustard mixture we use today, and safflower existed as well. Celery seeds were commonly used for seasoning. Of course, salt brought out the flavors of whatever it was sprinkled on, but pepper was not yet cultivated in Egypt. For the wealthy, two imports—cinnamon and coriander—added exotic flavors.

Unlike poorer classes, the well-to-do dined regularly on meat; however, even the richest did not eat meat every day. Vast herds of cattle of several species roamed the grassy delta to satisfy the carnivorous appetites of those who could afford them. Temple and tomb scenes show one species of long-legged cow with wide-spreading, lyre-shaped horns, perhaps akin to the early longhorned cattle of Texas. Other scenes depict a squatter, shorter-horned species. Both types ranged in color from brown to red to dappled. Perhaps the tall type was raised primarily for its meat, and the shorter for milk. Demonstrating their fondness for beef, tomb owners commissioned butchering scenes for their tomb walls, all showing a steer on its back with its four legs trussed together. First the legs were hacked off, then the head was removed with long knives, and finally, the body was cut into various chops and hung to bleed out and cure.

Both goats and sheep, called "small cattle," were eaten by the Egyptians, despite the fact that rams were associated with the god Amun and worshiped in various temples. Sheep of two varieties existed. The most common species grew a pair of horns that curled around almost in a circle. A different species had straight horns that spread several feet wide and was portrayed as the head of the ancient ram-god Khnum. However, this second species is seldom depicted as an animal, so it may have become extinct early in historic times. Sheep were certainly domesticated in the earliest days of Egypt, and they roamed in large herds throughout the country; one record refers to a flock of 5,800 (Darby, 1:221). These utilitarian animals supplied wool, in addition to their milk and meat. Goats also existed in great numbers. Since pictured goats all have short hair, Egyptians must have used these animals for milk and meat but not for wool.

In addition to these meats, which were available in regular supply, wild animals provided food on a more irregular basis. Ancient paintings show that many species of animal roamed what is now a desert adjoining the cultivated land, supported by a climate moister than today's arid one. Gazelle, antelope, ibex, hartebeest, oryx, addax, wild donkeys, and deer were avidly pursued by hunters. In early days, before horses were imported into Egypt, hunts consisted of groups of men either driving their prey into a netted area or of a smaller number of men hunting with dogs. Egyptians were possibly the first people to domesticate the dog from a wild species that resembles the modern saluki hound. They followed a pack of these rangy dogs and finished off with bows and arrows whatever prey the dogs hamstrung. Lone hunters sought smaller game, such as rabbits or hedgehogs.

When the horse and chariot came to Egypt after the Second Intermediate period, dangerous game, including lions and leopards, became part of the quarry. In addition, speedy ostriches, fierce wild cattle, and even elephants fell to Egyptian sportsmen. Hyenas, too, are shown both being hunted and trussed by ropes and being hand-fed in a pen. Their flesh is bitter, and they have never been raised for hunting or domesticated as pets, nor were they ever sacrificed by the Egyptians, so it is difficult to imagine the use made of them.

The end of a meal called for something sweet. Pure sugar, which we obtain from sugar beets or sugar cane, did not exist in ancient Egypt, but honey did. Egyptians learned to cultivate bees and even how to use smoke to drug the bees so they could collect the honey without paying the price of stings. Based on the fact that an ancient royal title for the pharaoh was *bity*, "He of the Bee," some writers contend that honey was a royal prerogative (Darby, 2:430). This theory is contradicted by the ease and negligible cost of producing large supplies of the sweet nectar that would naturally be desired by many, as well as by the difficulty of enforcing such a restriction in the case of wild bees.

Additional sweetness came from fruits and their juices. Sweet pastries and cakes existed as well. One recipe comes from the tomb of Rekhmire, a vizier during the New Kingdom, who must have relished a particular cake—by inscribing the recipe on the wall of his tomb, he assured himself pieces of it for eternity. First, "tiger nuts" (tubers of *Cyperus* grass, which grew wild in the marshes) were ground into flour. The flour was then mixed with honey and baked. Where one recipe survives, there must have been others.

When Egyptians prepared for death, they covered their tomb walls with scenes of whatever they enjoyed most during life, believing that the gods, seeing these pictures, would provide more of the same in the next life. The most common of all scenes are meals. Most show only a husband and wife eating while they gaze at each other, but many show festive banquets, replete with guests. Egyptians loved to eat and adored feasting with their friends.

A typical, lavish banquet consisted of a group sitting on the floor or at individual round tables. Often, they reposed on low chairs or stools under which lay a basin for washing their hands, sometimes with a pet cat or monkey beside it. Men and women ate together, both dressed in flowing linen gowns that reached the floor. The women held lotus flowers in one hand for the perfume and wore a perfume cone on their head made of a fatty substance that released a pleasing aroma as heat from the head slowly melted it during the course of the evening. Heaps of food completely covered the small tables. There were breads of several shapes and varieties, whole roasted trussed fowl and joints of meat, several kinds of vegetables, and assorted fruit. The mountains of food seem impossibly high as depicted, and each item is shown whole and singly, none on a plate or in a bowl. Because the owner of the tomb wanted no ambiguity about the food he desired for eternity, each bit is depicted unequivocally, if not realistically.

At an actual banquet, rather than a pile of food, various courses would have been served one after another in containers. Plates were not used, but ceramic bowls or, more likely at such formal affairs, blue glazed and painted faience dishes would have held the food. Cups of similar material stood ready for wine and were continually refilled from large pitchers carried by circulating servant girls. Other servant girls whisked away each bowl from a finished course, replacing it with the next. Supplemented with a knife for cutting mouth-sized morsels, the primary eating utensil was the eater's hand, which explains the water pitcher below each chair.

As dish after dish arrived at the table and cups were replenished, an ensemble of lute, harp, and drum accompanied one or more singers. Professional dancing women, naked except for a slim waist sash, moved energetically to the music, their activity emphasized by round weights at the ends of their long hair. With so much to eat and especially to drink, accidents were expected. Paintings show servant girls holding basins beneath the mouths of celebrants who had eaten or drunk too much.

The greatest problem with this diet was its effect on the teeth, evident in severe wearing and signs of dental abscesses in mummy after mummy. Making bread from grain swept off the ground introduced quantities of sand in the final loaf, an abrasive that would wear away granite, let alone the dentine of teeth. A diet of such bread eventually ground the teeth away, exposing their roots to decay. On the other hand, normal cavities were rare because of the absence of pure sugar (Brier and Hobbs, 99–114).

FOR MORE INFORMATION

Brier, B., and H. Hobbs. *Daily Life of the Ancient Egyptians*. Westport, Conn.: Greenwood Press, 1999.

Darby, W. J., P. Ghalioungui, and L. Crevetti. *Food: The Gift of Osiris*. 3 vols. New York: Academic Press, 1977.

Ikram, S. "Food for Eternity: What the Ancient Egyptians Ate and Drank." *KMT* 5, no. 2 (1994).

GREECE

The Greeks did not just eat to live; on the contrary, from earliest times, dining had enormous social importance. Homer tells us in the *Iliad* that as long as Achilles is grieving for his dead comrade Patroclus, he refuses all offers of food and drink. The hero's eventual acceptance of nourishment signals the abatement of that grief. Each day ends with a description of the warriors dining. Dining fills a bodily need and provides a necessary interruption to war. In historical times, the conditions of soldiers were less agreeable. On short campaigns, Athenian hoplites were required to bring their own provisions with them, whereas rowers were fed on a sparse diet of barley meal, onions, and cheese. At home, the whole family probably dined together. The most lavish dining parties were the symposia (discussed further in the section "Drink").

The basic Greek diet was both frugal and monotonous. Athenians ate two meals a day—a light lunch, known as *ariston,* and dinner, known as *deipnon,* their main meal. Well-to-do Greeks ate reclining on couches, leaning on an elbow and using their free hand to take food from a small table in front of them. This had important consequences for the preparation of food, which had to be served in small pieces. Although knives and, possibly, spoons were commonplace, forks were unknown. Many Greeks probably made do with their fingers. A piece of flat bread would also have conveniently served as a kind of spoon.

> **Well-to-do Greeks ate reclining on couches.**

In summer, meals were prepared in the open over a wood fire or charcoal grill, as is the case today in many rural parts of Greece. In winter, cooking was done inside the house on a portable brazier, which also provided the only source of heating. Because chimneys were unknown, the only way that the smoke could escape was through a hole in the roof. For this reason, charcoal was preferred, because it creates far less smoke than wood. Almost all cooking utensils were made of unglazed or partly glazed clay. The most common were kettles, saucepans on stands, shallow frying pans, casseroles, and grills. Although such mundane objects are rarely put on display in museums, they often have more to tell us about daily life in ancient Greece than the most beautifully painted pottery. Boiling and roasting were the most common ways of cooking, but much food was served raw.

From the end of the fifth century B.C.E., the Greeks began to develop an interest in culinary art. The lead in this was taken by Greek colonies in Sicily, a region famed for its luxury, where a number of cookbooks were produced. *Professors at Dinner,* written by Athenaeus, a Greek from Egypt, circa 200 C.E., culls numerous extracts from these books and provides a vast storehouse of information on the subject of dining. As in much of the modern world, the most celebrated chefs tended to be men.

Homer characterizes the human race as "bread eating," and bread remained the basis of the Greek diet throughout antiquity. It has been estimated that cereals provided 70 percent of the needed daily caloric intake. As a result of a serious shortage in cereal production over extensive areas of the eastern Mediterranean in 328 B.C.E., it became necessary to make free distributions of grain. This, however, was an exceptional occurrence.

The grain was separated from the chaff in a shallow mortar by pushing a flat stone back and forth across the millstone. The mortar was either made of baked clay or improvised from a hollowed-out tree trunk. There were two kinds of bread: *maza,* made from barley flour, and *artos,* a white bread made from wheat. Because barley was more plentiful than wheat, *artos* was something of a luxury, largely confined to the wealthy or served to the populace at festivals. The Greeks ate bread with honey, cheese, and olive oil. They also cooked it up in a porridge or broth. The word *opson* described any type of food that was eaten with bread or other cereal.

Meat was a rarity, particularly for those living in the city. Although most Greeks ate a simple casserole of game or poultry on a fairly regular basis, the only occasion on which they would have tasted roasted meat was on feast days. The climax to every religious festival was the ritual slaughter of a large number of animals, including bulls, cows, sheep, goats, and oxen. This may be another reason meat was rarely served in the home, being so closely associated with ritual. Although the ostensible purpose of a sacrifice was to honor the gods, the Greeks gave only the thigh pieces to the gods. The rest they devoured themselves. All those who attended a sacrifice received a portion of meat, the choicest parts of which were reserved for the priests.

Fish, both fresh and dried and salted, is more frequently mentioned than meat in cookery. Some of the best fish, including mackerel, sturgeon, tuna, sea bream, and mullet, was imported from the Black Sea region. In Athens, a particularly common seafood was the anchovy or sardine, which was harvested close to the Attic coast. Archestratus of Gela, a mid-fourth-century B.C.E. poet who had a reputation for being a master cook, speaks of it as follows:

Value all small fry as undesirable apart from the Athenian variety. I'm referring to sprats, which the Ionians call foam. Get hold of it fresh from the sacred arms of Phaleron's beautiful bay. What you find in wave-girt Rhodes is also good, if it happens to be local. If you'd care to taste it, you should also buy leafy sea anemones. Mix this in and bake it all in a pan, grinding the fragrant flowers of the greens in olive oil. (Athenaeus, *Professors at Dinner* section 285b)

Eels from Lake Kopaïs in Boeotia were a favorite delicacy. Aristophanes facetiously suggests that one of the greatest hardships that the Athenians had to face during the Peloponnesian War was the lack of Kopaïc eels, since the Boeotians had sided with the enemy. Kopaïc eels were accorded a quasi-religious status by the Boeotians:

The Boeotians sacrifice to the gods Kopaïc eels of extraordinary size, putting garlands on them, and praying over them, and casting barley seeds upon them, just as they do with other sacrificial victims. When a foreigner expressed amazement at the custom, a Boeotian replied that he had only one explanation for it, that one should observe ancestral customs. It wasn't his business to justify such things to other people. (Athenaeus, *Professors at Dinner* section 297d)

Popular vegetables included cabbages, asparagus, carrots, radishes, cucumbers, pumpkins, chicory, celery, and artichokes. Onions, garlic, and olives were also eaten in large quantities and provided the staple diet for those serving in the army and navy. Legumes, although high in protein, do not appear to have been regarded as an important foodstuff. Fruits included grapes, figs, apples, pears, and dates. Nuts were generally harvested wild. Almonds, walnuts, hazelnuts, and chestnuts were among the most widely distributed.

Olive oil, used in the preparation of many meals, was the principal source of fat. It also served in religious rituals and was applied to the body after exercise. The importance of olives to Attica is indicated by the fact that the goddess Athena caused an olive tree to spring up miraculously on the Acropolis when she was competing with Poseidon for the guardianship of the land. The use of butter was regarded as a mark of the barbarian. Cheese, which was mainly produced from the milk of sheep and goats, did not figure prominently in the Greek diet. Salt was used both as a preservative and as a condiment. Silphium, sage, and rosemary also served as flavorings. In place of sugar, which was unknown, the Greeks used honey and dried figs. The honey that came from Mount Hymettos in Attica was particularly highly prized in antiquity, just as it is today. Notable absentees from the Greek diet included potatoes, rice, tomatoes, citrus fruits, and bananas (Garland, 91–95).

FOR MORE INFORMATION

Dalby, A. *Siren Feasts: A History of Food and Gastronomy in Greece.* New York: Routledge, 1996.
Garland, R. *Daily Life of the Ancient Greeks.* Westport, Conn.: Greenwood Press, 1998.
Wilkins, J., D. Harvey, and M. Dobson, eds. *Food in Antiquity.* Exeter: Exeter University Press, 1995.

MATERIAL LIFE

FOOD

Mesopotamia

Egypt

Greece

Rome

India

Nubia

Australian Aboriginals

ROME

The diet of the vast majority of inhabitants of the ancient Roman world would have consisted of a simple routine of grain, olive oil, and wine. The grain was usually consumed either as bread or as a kind of porridge or gruel. This diet would sometimes be supplemented by fruits or vegetables when available; meat, especially red meat, would have been a rarity. Pork and veal were the two most readily available meat products. Fish and poultry were probably more commonly eaten than animal meats.

Adding some flavor to this diet was a kind of fish sauce called *garum* that seems to have been much loved by the Romans. The recipe for making *garum* was to take many of the undesirable parts of the fish, such as the entrails, heads, and fins, and mix them together with herbs and olive oil. This concoction was placed in a barrel or pot and put in the sun, where it was allowed to ferment. The resultant smelly paste was strained and served hot over bread or added to other foods. There were even the Roman equivalent of fast food restaurants, where pedestrians could come up to a counter and purchase a bowl of *garum* with some bread.

While the culinary lives of most Romans was monotonous, it was a different story for rich, upper-class Romans. Their wealth enabled them to eat a vast array of exotic comestibles and to hold lavish banquets. Breakfast and lunch were usually light meals, whereas dinner, or *cena*, was the principal meal of the day and the occasion for sometimes very elaborate meals.

At a formal Roman dinner party, the guests arrived, removed their shoes, and were led to a dining room called the *triclinium*. Romans lay on couches when they ate, leaning on their left elbows. Around three sides of a square table were placed low benches or beds called *triclinia*. Each held three diners, so that a full dinner party consisted of nine people. If there were more guests, the host had to set up another set of triclinia. Romans used knives and spoons but not forks. The first course of appetizers consisted of little treats such as olives, snails, vegetables, eggs, or shellfish. Main courses were elaborate meat dishes. Boar and pig udders were very popular. Particular delicacies were eels and lampreys. Many Roman aristocrats owned heated fishponds in which they raised eels, and the aristocrats competed to see who could grow the biggest and tastiest eels. Dessert was fruit, such as apples, pears, nuts, and figs.

Some wealthy Romans were famous for their gluttony, and there are many well-known instances of ostentatious banquets. The best source for elaborate Roman recipes is a cookbook written by a famous glutton named Apicius. He is said to have spent 100 million sesterces on food, and when he realized that he only had a few million left, he decided that he couldn't dine properly and so committed suicide. He left behind a book of recipes that range from familiar dishes such as omelets and sweet and sour pork to recipes for ostrich brains, flamingo tongues, sheep's lungs, and pig's wombs.

Roman gourmands paid enormous sums for the perfect fish, such as the 8,000 sesterces that were spent for one mullet (Pliny the Elder, *Natural History* 9.67), and periodically the Roman state actually passed laws making it illegal to spend more than a certain amount on one meal or to make overly elaborate dishes. Julius Caesar sent soldiers and lictors into people's dining rooms to make sure that their meals were not too ostentatious and to confiscate excessively elaborate dishes (Suetonius, *Life of Julius Caesar* 43.2). The emperor Caligula once spent 10 million sesterces on a single dinner party (Seneca, *Consolatione ad Helviam* 10.4).

~*Gregory S. Aldrete*

📷 *Snapshot*

Roman Recipe for Peas Supreme Style

Cook the peas with oil and a piece of sow's belly. Put in a saucepan: broth, leek heads, green coriander, and put on the fire to be cooked. Dice tid-bits [finely chopped meats]. Similarly cook thrushes or other small game birds, or take sliced chicken or diced brain, properly cooked.

Further cook, in the available broth, Lucanian sausage and bacon; cook leeks in water. Crush a pint of toasted pignolia nuts; also crush pepper, lovage [herbs], origany [herbs], and ginger. Dilute with the broth of pork.

Take a square baking dish, suitable for turning over; oil [it] well. Sprinkle [on the bottom] a layer of crushed nuts, upon which put some peas, fully covering the bottom of the dish. On top of this, arrange slices of the bacon, leeks, and sliced Lucanian sausage. Again cover with a layer of peas, and alternate all the rest of the available edibles in the manner described, until the dish is filled, concluding at last with a layer of peas.

Bake this dish in the oven, or put it into a slow fire, so that it may be baked thoroughly. [Next, make a sauce of the following]: Put yolks of hard-boiled eggs in the mortar with white pepper, nuts, honey, white wine, and a little broth. Mix and put it into a saucepan to be cooked. When done, turn out the peas into a large [dish], and mask them with this sauce, which is called white sauce. (as cited in Matz, 32; originally from Apicius, *De Re Coquinaria*)

FOR MORE INFORMATION

Apicius. *De re coquinaria.* Translated by J. Vehling. New York: Dover, 1936.
Dupont, F. *Daily Life in Ancient Rome.* Oxford: Blackwell, 1989.
Edwards, J. *The Roman Cookery of Apicius.* Point Roberts, Wash.: Hartley and Marks, 1985.
Matz, D. *Daily Life of the Ancient Romans.* Westport, Conn.: Greenwood, 2001.

INDIA

Looking at the Indus Valley civilization (as compared to the Vedic and Brahmanic era and the Epic and Puranic era), it is difficult to sketch with certainty what their material culture might have looked like. Indus culture apparently enjoyed a robust economy, based primarily in agriculture.

MATERIAL LIFE
|
FOOD
|
Mesopotamia

Egypt

Greece

Rome

India

Nubia

Australian Aboriginals

Food was derived from grains and domesticated animals. Water was immensely important to the Indus civilization, playing a role not just in drinking and cleanliness but in religious ritual as well. Wheat, barley, and some rice were grown, and in Mohenjo-Daro, granaries were central. Agricultural fertility was apparently linked with civic authority. Grains served as the base of the economic system, although herding of cattle, sheep, and goats also was significant. Food consisted mostly of grain products and included some rice. People drank not only water, milk, and wine but also a ritual psychoactive drink called *soma*, perhaps sweetened with honey.

The city of Mohenjo-Daro. This important urban center of the Indus Valley civilization in India contained substantial granaries. © The Art Archive/The Art Archive.

Vedic and Brahmanic material culture was partially a function of the transition from urban life to scattered tribal life. Religious beliefs and concerns for purity—especially ritual purity—reframed Vedic society's views about physical needs and material life, although Vedic material culture closely resembled Indus Valley culture. The authors of the *Shatapata Brahmana*, for instance, developed homologies between life, death, time, and the gods—especially with the creator god Prajapati (the "lord of creatures"). In Vedic and Brahmanic thought, the universe was maintained by the proper performance of Vedic rituals. In the early Vedic era, this was understood to be the physical ritual itself, whereas throughout the *Brahmanas* and eventually in the *Upanishads,* the ritual was internalized within the body. Food, then, properly belonged to the gods, and this led to the view that all preparation of food was both a holy act and a way to continue the rituals prescribed in the early Vedic texts. The pastoral influence of the Aryans can be seen in a diet that included milk, ghee (clarified butter), and oxen and sheep. Some vegetarian practices developed very late in this era, especially as reverence grew for certain animals such as the cow.

By the era of the Epic and Puranas, material culture in the subcontinent had returned to an urban, though Sanskritic, setting. Texts of this era describe richly furnished royal palaces and well-fortified cities and countries. Vegetarianism was well developed, especially under the influence of Buddhism and Jainism and their teaching of nonviolence (*ahimsa*).

To read about food in nineteenth-century India, see the India entry in the section "Food" in chapter 5 ("Material Life") of volume 5 (*Nineteenth Century*) of this series; for twentieth-century India, see the India entry in the section "Food" in the "Material Life" chapter of volume 6 (*The Modern World*).

~*Eric Rothgery*

FOR MORE INFORMATION

Allchin, B., and R. Allchin. *The Rise of Civilization in Indian and Pakistan*. Cambridge, England: Cambridge University Press, 1982.

Auboyer, J. *Daily Life in Ancient India*. London: Phoenix Press, 1965.

Basham, A. L. *The Wonder That Was India*. London: Sidgwick and Jackson, 1967.

NUBIA

Discussions of the cuisine and diet of the ancient Nubians are hampered by the almost-complete absence of contemporary texts on these subjects and by the infrequent analyses of floral and faunal remains unearthed during archaeological excavations.

As hunter-gatherers, the early Nubians doubtless foraged for edible plants. It has been suggested that these included melons, the fruity meat of which was prepared as a kind of soup perhaps served within the rind itself. They caught and ate fish found in the Nile River and probably the wild fowl, principally ducks, that abounded in the river's marshes. These Nubians also hunted, felling the giraffe, wild ass, and zebra for their hides, as well as large wild oxen, horned antelope, gazelle, and ibex. On the basis of scenes in Egyptian tombs dating from the Old Kingdom, there apparently were attempts, ultimately unsuccessful, to domesticate antelope, gazelle, and ibex as alternative food sources.

The Neolithic period (after 10,000 B.C.E.) witnessed the transition of Nubian society from one of hunter-gatherers to one of settlements, occasioned by the domestication of animals and plants. Sheep and goats were among the earliest of these domesticated beasts, as were oxen and cattle, suggesting that the meat and milk of these animals became staples of the Nubian diet.

It seems that millet played a role in the diet as well, but scholars are presently unable to determine whether it was wild or domesticated millet, the two strands appearing morphologically so close as to preclude classification. In time, the Nubians cultivated barley, wheat, peas, and lentils.

The accelerated mercantile interactions between the Egyptians and the Nubians of the A-Group culture (about 3250–2800 B.C.E.) witnessed the Nubian's exchange via barter of Africa's natural resources for typically Egyptian products. These included beer, wine, cereals, and oils, which were introduced into the Nubian diet. A Nubian effort to raise grapes is recorded during the reign of the Nubian pharaoh Taharqa of Dynasty 25 (about 690–664 B.C.E.), who reportedly enlisted the advice of Syrian vintners. The prominence accorded cattle by the Nubians of this period persisted into the late Meroitic period, as evidenced by a rare genre scene on a bronze bowl now in the Egyptian Museum, Cairo, that depicts milking. The importance attached to cattle by the Nubians has been interpreted by some as an early manifestation of the East African cattle culture that still dominates the life of the Maasai.

The diet of the Nubians appears not to have changed drastically over time. Classical sources contemporary with the late Napatan and Meroitic periods record the cultivation of traditional cereals, with an emphasis on the importance of millet and barley, as well as of sesame, pressed into oil. Other Classical authors report that the Nubians had no oil and relied instead on suet and butter. Many of these same authors maintain that the Nubians had no fruit, except the date palm, the trees of which were planted in gardens within sanctuaries to the god Amun in both Napata and Meroe by the Napatan king Harsiyotef (about 400–365 B.C.E.).

Scholars studying Greek papyri from the Roman period found in Egypt remark that the continuing presence of Greeks in Egypt from the time of Alexander the Great in the late fourth century B.C.E. had a profound effect on the cuisine of the native Egyptians, who ate proportionately more classically oriented dishes as time went on at the expense of traditional Egyptian cuisine. This dietary transformation may have continued, but perhaps to a lesser degree, during the Meroitic period as well.

The rare mentions of Nubian cuisine in ancient Egyptian texts of the Late period (after 664 B.C.E.) are unflattering in the extreme, but these must be placed in the context of ancient Egyptian attitudes toward foreigners in general. The poor opinion about Nubian cuisine expressed in temple inscriptions and echoed by the Greek historian Herodotus is but one of the many cultural criteria by which the Egyptians attempted to differentiate themselves from their neighbors and promote their nationalism.

~*Robert S. Bianchi*

FOR MORE INFORMATION

Adams, W. *Nubia: Corridor to Africa.* Princeton, N.J.: Princeton University Press, 1977.

O'Connor, D. *Ancient Nubia: Egypt's Rival in Africa.* Philadelphia: University of Pennsylvania, 1993.

Trigger, B. *Nubia under the Pharaohs.* Boulder, Colo.: Westview Press, 1976.

Welsby, D. A. *The Kingdom of Kush: The Napatan and Meroitic Empires.* London: British Museum Press, 1996.

MATERIAL LIFE
|
FOOD
|
Mesopotamia

Egypt

Greece

Rome

India

Nubia

Australian Aboriginals

AUSTRALIAN ABORIGINALS

Australia was the only continent that had no edible domestic plants or animals (the only domesticated animal being the dog), so all food was obtained by harvesting environmental resources as they became available. It was also the only continent with no pottery, so that cooking was done either by grilling or baking, and there were no boiled or liquid foods. There was generally very little storage of food; food was consumed when available and while fresh.

The same types of foods were part of the diet as elsewhere, but compared with western diets, a greater range of species was eaten within each class of food. Among mammals, for example, almost every species from mice to the largest kangaroo was eaten, the only exceptions being some of the carnivores. Because native, undomesticated species were consumed, individual items such as fruits or the seeds of cereal grains were relatively small. Aboriginal diets were relatively low in fat and carbohydrates. As a result of the cooking style, a much higher proportion of nutrients was retained in the foods.

There were some food taboos, but these generally applied to specific groups within each Aboriginal society. Pregnant women, for example, were prohibited from eating certain foods, while old people might be preferentially given others. Some species had religious connotations for particular clans or individuals, so that one person might not be able to hunt or eat possums, while another had to avoid certain bird species. The only example of a general prohibition was in Tasmania, where, about 3,000 years ago, no bony fish were eaten by anyone. Other marine resources, however, such as stingrays, shellfish, lobsters, and seals, were important items in their diet. This example was so unusual in the Australian context that much has been written about the reasons for it.

In general, Australian plant foods were much more important than animal foods, meat from small animals was much more important than meat from large animals, and the food obtained by the efforts of women was much more important than the food obtained by men. Because of their ability to move whenever necessary to exploit new resources, people rarely went hungry. In some seasons in certain regions (for example, winter in Tasmania or summer in the desert), food became very scarce, and normally undesirable foods would be consumed. Conversely, when a suitable resource was available in great abundance at a particular time of the year, people took advantage of this bounty to hold ceremonies at which many thousands of people might congregate.

Because carbohydrates were relatively scarce, or only available in small seeds, the few foods with large concentrations of carbohydrates—such as yams and the large seeds of cycad palms—were exploited even though they were either unpalatable or actually poisonous. Complex and time-consuming processing was needed to remove the toxins from cycad palm seeds.

Although a similar diet was eaten all over Australia (except for Tasmania), the particular species consumed, and the proportions of different kinds of species, varied greatly. People living on the coast had a considerably different dietary composition from those in deserts, in mountainous areas, or along rivers. Diets in the tropical north were somewhat different from those in the cold south. These differences were reduced to some extent at least by the movement of people. Coastal people would move up into the mountains to exploit the local resources at certain times of the year, and vice versa. The large ceremonial gatherings also provided a chance to obtain foodstuffs not available in one's own region, so that such gatherings constituted a mechanism for sharing abundant resources.

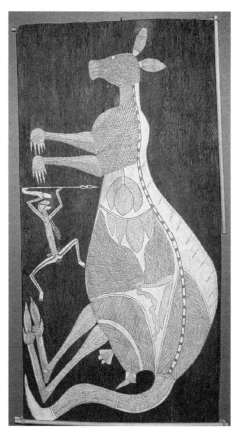

Kangaroo being hunted. This painting done on bark illustrates the large marsupials that Aboriginal hunters pursued. Werner Forman/Art Resource, NY.

Food was also shared on a small scale. When a large animal such as a kangaroo was successfully hunted, the hunter allocated portions of the meat to relatives according to a formula. Meat might also be shared with people who were not kin. All these customs had the aim of ensuring that everyone within a group received some food, even if he or she had been unlucky in a hunt or was sick. Such a system also meant that the successful hunter's family today could count on getting food another day from a different successful hunter. This sharing both strengthened bonds within Aboriginal society and ensured survival on a continent where food supplies were unreliable.

To read about food in the early British colony in Australia, see the Australia entry in the section "Food" in chapter 5 ("Material Life") of volume 4 (*Seventeenth and Eighteenth Centuries*) of this series.

~David Horton

FOR MORE INFORMATION

Berndt, R., and C. Berndt. *The World of the First Australians*. Canberra: Aboriginal Studies Press, 1988.

Brand Miller, J., K. James, and P. Maggiore. *Tables of Composition of Australian Aboriginal Foods*. Canberra: Aboriginal Studies Press, 1997.

Cherikoff, V., and J. Isaacs. *The Bush Food Handbook*. Balmain, New South Wales: Ti Tree Press, 1989.

Horton, David, ed. *The Encyclopedia of Aboriginal Australia*. Canberra: Aboriginal Studies Press, 2001.

MATERIAL LIFE

DRINK

Mesopotamia

Egypt

Greece

Rome

Drink

The cultures of the ancient Mediterranean world fall into two camps when drinking habits are considered: those who drank beer and those who drank wine. The Mesopotamians and Egyptians were avid beer drinkers, while the Greeks and Romans were just as devoted to wine. These drink preferences were not merely taste preferences, but they took on cultural significance as well. The Romans, for example, considered drinking beer to be uncivilized and to be a characteristic trait of barbarians.

Beer and wine may actually have been available in more varieties than are standard today. Mesopotamian beer makers brewed a wide assortment of light and dark beers. Wines came in a range of strengths and flavors, from powerful vintages that had to be heavily diluted with water to dessertlike wines sweetened with honey and served warm.

Beer or wine was drunk in large quantities not just by men but by women and children as well. The appeal of these alcoholic beverages was not only their mood-altering nature but the fact that the fermentation process and their alcohol content served to purify them and eliminate at least some of the sickness-causing contaminants that would have been common in untreated water. In a world where waterborne diseases and parasites were common, drinking alcoholic beverages was not just enjoyable; it was also healthy. Water was, of course, widely drunk as well. Milk was another significant drink, more commonly obtained from goats than from cows.

One final aspect of ancient dining that should be stressed is that meals were important social events. The clearest example of this is the Greek symposium, which possessed a complex set of rules governing behavior and was more than just a dinner party. A symposium could be an occasion for philosophical discussion, for political intrigue, for recitations of poetry, and most of all, for social interaction. Although other cultures may not have had as formal an institution as the symposium, meals always tended to serve as a way to bring people together to socialize, to worship, to debate, and to think, as well as simply to eat. In this way, the ritualized consumption of food and drink really did unite the mind and the body and hold societies and families together.

~*Gregory S. Aldrete*

MATERIAL LIFE
|
DRINK
|
Mesopotamia

Egypt

Greece

Rome

MESOPOTAMIA

An important part of the Mesopotamian diet was the many varieties of beer; the literal translation was "barley beer" because there were no hops. The Sumerians at Ur enjoyed dark beer, clear beer, freshly brewed beer, and well-aged beer, as well as sweet and bitter beers. Until Hammurabi's time, women brewed beer, and the craft was protected by female gods.

In taverns, beer was drunk from a common vat and had to be strained. The ends of drinking tubes were perforated by small holes that acted as filters. Ration lists for palace employees record the distribution of one quart to one gallon a day of beer, depending on the rank of the recipient.

Unlike beer, wine could be made only once a year, when the grapes ripened, but wine had a longer shelf life when stored in a sealed jar. Surviving Sumerian texts do not describe how wine was manufactured. They refer to it as an expensive and rare commodity, found in areas of natural rainfall in the highlands. Many wines were named after their places of origin. Although wine consumption increased over time, it was still a luxury item, served only to the gods and the wealthy. Women ran wine shops (ca. 1800 B.C.E.), which certain priestesses were prohibited from entering upon penalty of death.

Wine was readily available in ancient Assyria. About 2,000 liters of wine were stored in special vessels at the Nimrud palace. Many tablets from Nimrud dating between 791 and 779 B.C.E. describe the daily wine ration to the royal household as less than a half-pint per person. Other products of the vine included grape juice, wine vinegar, and raisins.

The Sumerians also drank milk: cow's milk, goat's milk, and ewe's milk. Milk soured quickly in the hot climate of southern Iraq. Ghee (clarified butter) was less perishable than milk, as was the round, chalky cheese, which could be transformed back to sour milk by grating it and adding water. The texts do not mention the processing of sheep's milk before the Persian period, at which time it was made into a kind of cottage cheese. Other dairy products included yogurt and butter. Many kinds of cheeses were produced: a white cheese (for the king's table), "fresh" cheese, and flavored, sweetened, and sharp cheeses (Nemet-Nejat, 158).

FOR MORE INFORMATION

Limet, H. "The Cuisine of Ancient Sumer." *Biblical Archaeologist* 50 (1987).

Nemet-Nejat, K. R. *Daily Life in Ancient Mesopotamia.* Westport, Conn.: Greenwood Press, 1998.

EGYPT

Beer was an important beverage from the earliest days of Egypt. Whether beer was first brewed in Sumer or Egypt is still argued—the timing was close, whichever country won the race. One difference in the beers of these two ancient countries is that the Egyptians strained theirs as we do before drinking, whereas the Sumerians instead sipped theirs through a straw. Although beer's chemistry is complex, simple, natural procedures produced acceptable versions. Grain and malt in solution produce alcohol; the carbonation caused by the fermenting action of the yeast is a by-product. When ancient Egyptians exposed moistened, unmilled grain to the air in warm conditions, it germinated and, after crushing, became malt. By baking bread of coarse flour lightly enough to prevent the heat from destroying the yeast, crumbling the loaves into water and adding some of the malt for flavor, they produced—after allowing time for the yeast in the bread to ferment the mixture and straining it through a sieve—beer of about 7 percent alcohol. Both barley and wheat beers were brewed in this manner, sometimes with such additives as date juice for a sweetener or red dye for special holidays.

Beer contained nutrients and, because of the sanitizing action of the alcohol, was safer to drink than still water, which could harbor any number of harmful microbes. It was also, of course, intoxicating if drunk to excess. Abundant tomb scenes depict the results of overindulgence (although wine was the more likely culprit in these upper-class tombs), but sober people deplored the condition. A scribe named Ani, who warns against visiting a house where liquors are served, describes drinking's effects:

Boast not that you can drink . . . a jug of beer. Thou speakest, and an unintelligible utterance issueth from thy mouth. If thou fallest down and thy limbs break there is no one to hold out a hand to thee. Thy companions in drink stand up and say "Away with that sot." If there cometh one to seek thee in order to question thee, thou art found lying on the ground and thou art like a child. (as cited in Darby, 2:583)

Although average Egyptians could not afford meat regularly, they consumed milk in great quantities. Egyptians, until they were weaned at three, drank milk as their only food and continued to consume it throughout their lives. Cows, goats, and even asses supplied substitutes after a mother's milk had ceased. No evidence of butter or cheese exists, although it seems likely that cheese, which easily could have accidentally occurred as a by-product of old milk, was available.

The wealthy considered beer the beverage of working people and preferred the smooth taste of wine for themselves. Grapes—either as low pruned bushes or as trellised vines—grew abundantly, especially in the delta region famed for its vintages.

Demonstrating the extent to which wealthy Egyptians favored this drink are the numerous tomb paintings that depict the harvesting and pressing of grapes to extract their juice. Egyptians used the age-old method of trampling grapes with bare feet in vats large enough to hold four to six people, a process that, unlike heavy presses, does not add the bitter, acidic flavor of crushed stems. To prevent falling into the grape mixture, workmen grasped ropes tied to a beam above the vat. Sometimes they were encouraged in their work by children who beat a rhythm with sticks. As the juice began to flow, it ran into a container set below a spout near the bottom of the vat, although some liquid would remain even after vigorous dancing on the grapes. The residue, called must, was shoveled into a cylindrical cloth bag up to four or five feet in length. Sticks attached to each end of the bag were vigorously twisted by several men to squeeze the last drop of juice through the cloth fibers. To prevent the torque of the twisting motion from bunching up the sack, a boy sometimes stretched horizontally from one stick to the other—hands on one, feet on the other—holding them apart. Alternatively, an end of the sack was fixed to a pole so only the other end turned.

Because grapes carry natural yeasts on their skin, fermentation was instigated by setting the juice in a warm environment—no difficulty in steamy Egypt. The juice was poured into pottery jars that stood about two feet tall, in which the conversion of grape sugar to alcohol took place. After fermentation, the opening was sealed with a conical stopper of mud and straw and left to dry hard in the sun. If any sugar remained, continued fermentation would generate a gas that would burst a sealed container. To eliminate the problem, a small hole drilled in the stopper or the neck of the jar was left uncovered until it could be safely sealed. The mud stopper was stamped with vintage information, including the vineyard that had produced it, the year of production, and the quality of the contents, which ranged from "good" to "very good" to "very, very good." Sometimes the name of the producer was also included, as is done today with fine wines.

The tomb of Tutankhamen gives further evidence of the Egyptians' appreciation of wine. Included among the great treasures found at his famous burial site were 26 amphorae of wine. Jar labels indicate their origin to be from the delta region, which boasted the finest vineyards in Egypt. The fact that only four of the two dozen had contents labeled "sweet" indicates that Tutankhamen preferred his wine dry. Twelve jars differed from the others in having long necks incorporating long handles. Because these were Syrian-style jars, it may be that the wine inside was imported; but jars were commonly reused, so we cannot know for certain whether Tutankhamen drank domestic or imported blends. Vintages were indicated by citing the year of a pharaoh's reign, without mentioning which pharaoh. One jar bore the vintage "year thirty-one," although Tutankhamen is known to have ruled only nine years. Either this wine was a rare old vintage from the time of his grandfather (Tutankhamen's father reigned only 17 years) or it was in a reused jar with its form label still affixed (Lesko, 23).

The unanswered question about Egyptian wine is whether it was red or white. Abundant scenes show the color of the grapes, which ranges from dark purple to light rose, but grapes of any skin color yield the same white juice. What determines the color of the wine is whether the juice ferments in its skins, which produces red versions. What type Egyptians made is not known, although later Greek writers remarked on the dark color of Egyptian wine.

Other kinds of wine were produced in smaller amounts from the juice of figs, perhaps of dates, and certainly of pomegranates. Grape juice was also drunk as an unfermented syrup by boiling the juice down to a very sweet drink. Because wine turns to vinegar when exposed to the air, Egyptian knowledge of this acidic liquid, by accident if not by design, was unavoidable because the clay containers in which wine was stored admitted air through their pores—in fact, wine jars found in tombs today all contain nothing but dried residue. Whether Egyptians used vinegar in cooking or in salads is not known (Brier and Hobbs, 101–7).

FOR MORE INFORMATION

Brier, B., and H. Hobbs. *Daily Life of the Ancient Egyptians*. Westport, Conn.: Greenwood Press, 1999.

Darby, W. J., P. Ghalioungui, and L. Crevetti. *Food: The Gift of Osiris*. 3 vols. New York: Academic Press, 1977.

Lesko, L. H. *King Tut's Wine Cellar*. Berkeley, Calif.: B. C. Scribe, 1977.

MATERIAL LIFE
|
DRINK
|
Mesopotamia

Egypt

Greece

Rome

GREECE

The favorite Greek drink was wine, which was almost invariably served diluted and often artificially sweetened. The Greeks preferred to drink in quantity only after they had finished eating. The islands of Chios, Lesbos, Rhodes, and Samos had the reputation for producing the best wine. Wine was transported in clay storage jars called amphorae. The handles of these amphorae were stamped with seals bearing the name of the merchant and that of the city in which the wine was produced, rather like the label on a modern bottle of wine. Beer was associated exclusively with barbarians. Milk, though used in cooking, was not a common beverage. It is thus a sign of savagery in the *Odyssey* that the cyclops Polyphemus drinks goat's milk and has never tasted wine.

When the Greeks wanted to relax at the end of the day, they did this foremost through the symposium, a word that means literally a "drinking together." A symposium was not, however, the ancient equivalent to a few guys getting together to shoot the breeze and down a few drinks. On the contrary, it was a highly ritualized institution with its own precise and time-hallowed rules.

Strictly speaking, *symposium* refers to the communal drinking of wine that took place at the conclusion of a dinner. Only after the tables containing food had been cleared away, garlands of flowers distributed, libations performed, and a hymn sung was it permitted to begin drinking. Symposiasts did not sit on chairs but reclined on couches, a custom that the Greeks probably learned from the Near East around the turn of the seventh century B.C.E. Although a symposium served a variety of purposes, for definition we can hardly do better than quote Plutarch, a Greek writer living in the Roman era, who described it as "a passing of time over wine, which, guided by gracious behaviour, ends in friendship" (*Moral Precepts* section 621c).

The most famous drinking party of all time is the one recorded by Plato that was supposedly held at the house of a young tragic poet called Agathon in 416 B.C.E. and is described in Plato's work the *Symposium*. Because some of the company were suffering from hangovers, they elected to consume only a modest amount of wine. They also decided to dispense with the services of a flute girl whom Agathon had hired for the evening. Instead, they entertained themselves by each delivering an encomium in praise of Eros, the offspring of Aphrodite, goddess of love. The last to speak was Socrates. Just when he reached the end of his delivery, a young aristocrat called Alcibiades burst into the room. Alcibiades, already somewhat the worse for drink, tried to make the other guests tipsy by forcing them to consume large quantities of wine. Eventually, he settled down and agreed to follow the procedure adopted by the company by delivering a speech in praise of Socrates. The party continued till dawn, by which time everyone had fallen asleep with the exception of Socrates and Aristophanes, who were still conversing on the subject of poetry. Socrates alone was completely unaffected by the alcohol that he had consumed, and around dawn, he rose, departed, took a bath, and went about his daily business.

As we know from references in literature, any excuse could be used for a party in ancient Greece: birth, marriage, or death, the departure or arrival of a loved one from abroad, a feast day, a birthday, or merely a change in the seasons. Probably in most cases, however, no pretext was required. While we might suppose that drinking parties were an everyday occurrence, we do not know whether they were exclusive to aristocratic society or whether poorer Athenians also held formal symposia.

Greek symposium depicted on a painted Athenian cup. Musicians often entertained the diners at such events. Réunion des Musées Nationaux/Art Resource, NY.

It was customary for the host to inscribe the names of his guests on a wax tablet, together with the day and hour appointed for the symposium, and then hand the tablet to a slave, who would make the rounds of the guests' houses. Generally, the ideal number of guests was nine, including the host. In Athens in the fourth century B.C.E., however, symposia grew so large that it became necessary to appoint a commission to ensure that the number of guests did not exceed the legal limit. Wives and daughters were not permitted to attend symposia; the only females present were prostitutes known as *hetairai*.

The growing importance of the symposium was such that from the fourth century B.C.E. onward, well-appointed houses possessed a special room for reclining and drinking known as an *andrôn*, or men's quarters. An *andrôn* can be identified in the archaeological record by its off-center doorway, so located to enable the room to accommodate the couches, which were arranged alongside one another and set against the walls. The basic *andrôn* held four couches, although some were considerably larger. The couches were made of either wood or stone. In front of each was a three-legged table on which food was laid out and the drinkers placed their cups. As private houses became more elegant, *andrônes* acquired mosaic floors, and their walls were hung with tapestries.

Every stage of the symposium was marked by a traditional religious observance. Before being mixed with water, a few drops of wine were drunk in honor of the *Agathos Daimôn*, or "good spirit." In a fragment from a lost work, Theophrastus states that the purpose of this toast was "to serve as a reminder, through a mere taste, of the strength of the god's generous gift." He continues, "Having bowed three times, they take it from the table, as though supplicating the god that they may do nothing indecent or have too strong a desire for the wine." This toast was followed by three libations, to Zeus Olympios and the other Olympian gods, to the heroes, and to Zeus Soter (savior). While these libations were being performed, a hymn was sung to the gods. Before the party broke up, a triple paean was sung to Apollo. This was followed by a hymn to Hygieia, the personification of health, which began thus: "Hygieia, most revered of the blessed gods, with thee may I dwell for the rest of my life and may thou be a gracious inmate of my house." A purificatory rite was performed both before the commencement of the symposium and at its close. So ingrained was the sense of religious occasion that Hesiod, as he sits alone under his shady rock in the heat of summer, his belly filled with good food, does not omit to perform a libation before drinking a cup of wine (*Works and Days* lines 592ff.).

There were strict rules that all symposiasts were required to follow to ensure that the drinking did not get out of hand. Several Greek writers even compiled books of symposiastic laws, although none has survived. The philosopher Theophrastus, however, provides us with a number of instances of bad form. It was, he tells us, the mark of an uneducated lout to drop his cup while the rest of the company was at prayer and burst out laughing, to tap or whistle in accompaniment to the flute girl, or to spit across the table at the wine pourer. The enforcement of these rules was in the hands of the symposiarch, or master of drinking. The ideal symposiarch, according to Plutarch, had to be "the quintessence of conviviality," neither inclined to drunkenness nor averse to drinking. He had to be aware how each of his fellow symposiasts was affected by wine to determine what was conducive to the promotion of good cheer. He should be cordial, friendly, and objectionable to no one. Election to this office was made on the throw of dice, which meant that it generally fell to one of the guests. The symposiarch had the authority to inflict a penalty on any drinker who infringed on the rules. In exceptional circumstances, he could even order a guest to depart. Because the Greeks did not drink undiluted wine, his inaugural duty was to determine the proportion of parts of wine to water—an important decision that would affect the tone of the whole evening. In addition, he decreed how many cups should be drunk, since only on rare occasions, as at Agathon's symposium, were symposiasts permitted to drink as much or as little as they wished. The purpose behind this rule was to ensure that everyone attained approximately the same degree of inebriation. Finally, the symposiarch proposed the entertainment and fixed penalties for those who failed to distinguish themselves in the games and competitions.

Despite these precautions, much no doubt happened that was not in accordance with the rules. A popular Greek saying, "I hate a drinker with a good memory," suggests that whatever was said or done by a symposiast when under the influence of alcohol was not to be held against him when he sobered up (Garland, 95–99).

FOR MORE INFORMATION

Garland, R. *Daily Life of the Ancient Greeks*. Westport, Conn.: Greenwood Press, 1998.
Slater, W. J., ed. *Dining in a Classical Context*. Ann Arbor: University of Michigan Press, 1991.

ROME

Wine was the Roman's drink of choice. The Romans, like the Greeks, usually diluted their wine with water before drinking it. Romans also enjoyed some wines that were served warm, and these often had spices added to it. A popular hot wine was *mulsum*, which was sweetened with honey.

Fine wines were allowed to age before being drunk, and the Romans recognized that some vintages were superior to others. Imported wines from Greece, such as Chian or Lesbian, were regarded highly. Among Italian wines, Falernian was particularly prized, as well as being considerably more expensive than run-of-the-mill vintages.

Water was also drunk, although even relatively poor people probably had access to some amount of wine. Consuming beer was frowned upon and indeed was considered to be the mark of a northern barbarian. Mediterranean-based peoples such as the Romans defined themselves by their beverages, so that a Roman governor of a northern province along the Danube was driven to bitterly complain that the locals led a wretched existence because they did not cultivate grapes to make wine.

~*Gregory S. Aldrete*

FOR MORE INFORMATION

Tchernia, A. *Le vin de l'Italie Romaine*. Rome: École Française de Rome, 1986.

Housing

Housing provides shelter from the extremes of the elements, privacy, and a place to keep one's possessions. Housing in the ancient world fulfilled these three basic requirements, although often in only the most rudimentary fashion.

Shelter from heat, cold, wind, and water is the most basic function of housing. In Mesopotamia, Egypt, Nubia, and around the shores of the Mediterranean, protection from the scorching rays of the sun was usually the most important environmental challenge for early builders. The universal building material that was available and affordable to ancient builders was mud. From this people fashioned mud bricks, which they piled together to make dwellings. Thatch or twigs covered with more mud was used for the roof. Not only was this a cheap method of construction, but thick mud walls functioned as a fairly effective method of providing a cool shelter from the sun. The basic mud-brick house was the standard dwelling for people in Mesopotamia and Egypt and was common in many regions of Greece and the Roman world as well.

The temporary shelters of Australian Aborigines were crafted out of whatever materials were available. In mountainous Greece and Italy, where rock was plentiful, structures created by piling up stones to form walls were frequently encountered.

MATERIAL LIFE
|
DRINK
|
Mesopotamia

Egypt

Greece

Rome

MATERIAL LIFE
|
HOUSING
|
Mesopotamia

Egypt

Greece

Rome

Australian Aboriginals

Perhaps the most elaborate construction methods were encountered in the villas of Rome's elite, which employed a variety of styles and materials, including concrete.

As usual, the dwellings of the wealthy were vastly different from those of average people. Palatial mansions such as that owned by the Roman Pliny the Younger or the Egyptian residences covering 25,000 square feet were luxurious by any standard. At the extreme end of the scale were the sumptuous palace complexes of rulers, which could cover as much territory as a small city and feature hundreds of ornately decorated rooms.

When it came to providing privacy, on the whole, inhabitants of the ancient world probably had far less of it than we are accustomed to today. In a typical farmhouse with only a few rooms, several generations of the family would live in very close proximity, likely sharing the same rooms and often the same beds. Adding to the general crowding, farm animals, especially valuable ones such as cattle or pigs, frequently were lodged in the house as well. Separate bathrooms were extreme rarities; a pot in a corner seems to have been the usual solution. Average houses appear to have been modest in size.

In cities, the density of people per dwelling would have been even higher. The ultimate example of this was the high-rise apartment buildings of ancient Rome, the *insulae*. These massive tenements could reach more than 10 stories high, packed solid with a teeming mass of humanity.

While the remains of houses survive, the furniture and objects that filled them were primarily made out of wood, which quickly rots away. Nevertheless, some idea of what furniture was like can be gleaned from mentions in literature and depictions in art. In all cultures, people seem to have had the fairly standard assortment of chairs, tables, benches, chests, and beds.

For most people in these civilizations, home was a place that provided a bare minimum of shelter and privacy, but it also always remained the center of family life.

~*Gregory S. Aldrete*

MATERIAL LIFE
|
HOUSING
|
Mesopotamia
Egypt
Greece
Rome
Australian Aboriginals

MESOPOTAMIA

Houses in ancient Mesopotamia were built of the same materials as those in Iraq today: mud brick, mud plaster for the walls, mud and poplar for the roofs, and wood for doors and door frames; all materials available around the city. The purpose of a house was to provide shelter from the 12 hours of unrelenting heat—the climate from May to September. Bricks were made from a mixture of clay and chopped straw, packed into molds, and then left to dry in the sun, often in the first summer month (May–June), also called "the month of bricks." Baked bricks lasted longer but were expensive to manufacture; consequently, they were used only to construct luxurious buildings. In the Old Babylonian period (ca. 1900–1595 B.C.E.), baked bricks, bitumen, and lime plaster were used to waterproof the lower parts of the wall, which were subject to deterioration from rising dampness.

Ancient houses, particularly those made of sun-dried brick, often collapsed. The Code of Hammurabi devotes five sections to this problem (§§229–233), noting in particular the builder's responsibility:

If a builder constructs a house for a man, but does not make his work sound, and the house that he constructs collapses and causes the death of the householder, that builder shall be killed.

If it should cause the death of a son of the householder, they shall kill a son of that builder. (as cited in Roth, 125)

The roof was usually constructed from planks of palm tree wood, then a cover of reeds and palm leaves, and finally a layer of earth. Stairs of wood or brick led to the roof, where vegetables could be dried in the sun, a cool breeze enjoyed, and sometimes rituals performed.

In the third millennium B.C.E., the average house was a thick-walled mud hut, usually without windows. When windows were present, they were made from clay or wooden grilles set in the wall. Artificial lighting was supplied by lamps, which were often shaped like small shoes filled with sesame seed oil and a wick made from wool, a reed, or some other plant. The rooms of these houses show little evidence of architectural planning. Doors between rooms were so low that people had to stoop as they went through. Frequently, two adjacent houses shared a common wall. Under such circumstances, both neighbors were responsible for the wall.

Usually, doors were made of wood; they were set in a wooden frame, which was painted red, the color that frightened evil spirits and kept them from entering. Occasionally, doors were made from ox hides—sometimes as many as 10 ox hides. Small, crude statues meant to ward off evil were buried beneath the outer door or inside, along the walls, in lavatories, and especially, in the bedroom.

Houses of the wealthy were often large, their rooms designed around a square courtyard. However, in cities, where space was limited, there might be rooms on only two or three sides of the courtyard. Poorer areas might not even have a courtyard. When present, second stories replicated the plan of the ground floor and were constructed on an extra-thick foundation wall for support. In larger homes, the rooms and their uses have been easier to identify, such as reception rooms, kitchen and courtyard, fireplaces, and water installations. Some houses had storage rooms for valuables. These rooms could be sealed by a metal hook attached to a doorknob; clay covered the hook and knob, over which a cylinder seal was rolled to secure the premises. Sometimes, a room might be set aside as a sanctuary.

Lavatories were found from the third millennium B.C.E.; they were designed as a platform above a pit or drain, sometimes with a seat of bitumen for comfort. The palace at Eshnunna (ca. 2300 B.C.E.) had six lavatories with raised seats of baked brick. There were even five rooms for bathing. Bathing rooms were a feature of houses of the rich. Inventories of bathing-room furnishings have supplied us with a list of their contents, namely, tubs, stools, jars, and mirrors. All lavatories and bathing rooms were connected with drains leading to a main sewer approximately one meter high and covered with baked bricks. Each lavatory had a large water pitcher, some found with a pottery dipper to help flush the waste. Assyrian palaces dated to the first millennium B.C.E. had an elaborate drainage system, which emptied its waste into the river.

Based on available data, city houses changed in size over time. No single house should be regarded as typical. For example, in the third millennium B.C.E., the houses at Uruk and Fara covered approximately 400 square meters in surface area. However, during the second millennium, the size of the average Old Babylonian house at Ur was less than 100 square meters. We also have house models from various cities in ancient Mesopotamia.

The residences of ancient Mesopotamia housed creeping things such as scorpions; a group of omens referred to scorpions that fell from the ceiling onto a man or his bed. There were even magical and herbal treatments to treat scorpion stings. Snakes also crawled through the house in search of rodents in the branches and mud that formed the roof and ceiling. Here again omen texts referred to snakes falling out of the roof onto a man or his bed—sometimes this was considered a lucky omen. Even the walls of houses were decorated with different colored species of ants and cockroaches. A number of omen texts indicated the significance to be attached to animals that might be met both inside the house and on its walls—reptiles, lizards, scorpions, cockroaches, beetles, and others.

> *The residences of ancient Mesopotamia housed creeping things such as scorpions.*

Household furnishings varied according to the time period, the location, and the wealth of the owners. The furniture of a typical private house was different from that found in palaces. Ancient furniture, like modern furniture, was most often made from wood and other organic materials that decayed over time. Consequently, archaeological finds of ancient furniture are rare, except for places such as Egypt, where the hot, dry climate inhibited decay. The furniture designs from the third millennium B.C.E. continued to be used in the second millennium B.C.E.

The greatest variety of sources for furniture comes from the first millennium B.C.E., namely, texts, illustrations, and numerous archaeological finds from Assyria. The furniture was either made in Assyria, imported, or brought back as booty or tribute from neighboring countries. In fact, records of booty and tribute often list furniture among the most valuable objects.

Stools were used for menial work at the beginning of the third millennium. They were usually made of reeds on a wooden frame. There were even folding stools with crossed legs as well as stools with carved legs and sides.

Chairs had legs, backs, and even arms. Their frames were made from various hardwoods; 17 kinds of wood were listed. Sometimes chair frames were inlaid with copper, bronze, silver, gold, or carved ivory. Chairs were often painted. Their seats were covered with leather, palm fiber, or rushes or padded with felt. Loose linen slipcovers were even designed for the chairs.

Chairs came in many shapes and sizes: thrones, sedan chairs for transportation, and armchairs (from which Sennacherib is shown watching the siege of Lachish). Reliefs from Khorsabad show Sargon II presented with two kinds of tables, a chair or throne, and a footstool with lion's paw feet set on conical bases. Assyrian furniture has been found with bronze panels of griffins and winged deities, in addition to calf-

or bull-head finials decorating the arms. Ivory fittings, the work of Phoenician and Syrian craftsmen to decorate furniture, were found at Nimrud (Calhu) and Fort Shalmaneser. The series included plaques depicting animals, sphinxes, griffins in floral settings, seated or standing figures holding branches beneath winged discs, and women at windows (perhaps prostitutes making themselves visible to potential clients).

Tables, tray tables, and offering stands were used throughout the third millennium, as confirmed by texts and art. Assyria has provided us with actual tables, models of tables, and illustrations of tables on reliefs. Like stools and chairs, tables were made of wood and sometimes decorated with metal. In first-millennium B.C.E. Assyria, the table was usually a small square on four ornamented legs, terminating at the bottom in either an ox hoof or a lion's foot.

Beds were usually made of a frame and supporting base of wood, although rope, interwoven reeds, or crisscrosses of metal strips were sometimes used. The bed provided support for mattresses stuffed with wool, goat's hair, or palm fiber. Bedding included linen sheets, mattresses, cushions, and blankets. Medical texts often mention patients who "took to their bed." Of course, not everyone owned a bed; the poor slept on straw or reed mats.

We have few illustrations of beds from the third millennium; in fact, beds were often omitted from furniture inventory lists of this period. An Old Akkadian source alludes to a wooden bed with fruit decoration and slender feet. However, by the end of the third millennium, a number of beds were described in texts as constructed from reed and wood and overlaid with gold, silver, or copper. Beds had legs that often terminated with an ox hoof or claw. But some beds looked like shallow wooden boxes.

Tablets refer to bedside mats, thereby raising the issue of floor coverings. The palace may have used carpets. Some floors at doorways were decorated by limestone slabs carved to imitate carpeting. Carpets were luxury goods that served two functions: they affirmed the wealth of their owners and decorated the wall or floor.

Household goods included containers for storing utensils and provisions. Baskets, skins, clay bins, and large wooden chests were used for storage. Crates were used for storing vegetables. Containers were waterproofed to hold liquids. Wine was stored in special jars of several gallons' capacity, which were sometimes marked with the volume (Nemet-Nejat, 121–26).

FOR MORE INFORMATION

Contenau, G. *Everyday Life in Babylon and Assyria*. Translated by K. R. Maxwell-Hyslop and A. R. Maxwell-Hyslop. New York: St. Martins Press, 1954.

Nemet-Nejat, K. R. *Daily Life in Ancient Mesopotamia*. Westport, Conn.: Greenwood Press, 1998.

Roth, M. *Law Collections from Mesopotamia and Asia Minor*. Atlanta, Ga.: Scholars Press, 1995.

Simpson, E. "Furniture in Ancient Western Asia." In *Civilizations of the Ancient Near East*, ed. J. Sasson. Vol. 3. New York: Scribner's, 1995.

EGYPT

Ancient Egyptians had to contend with enormous temperature swings. At noon on a summer day, in this country surrounded by desert, the temperature could reach 120 degrees Fahrenheit; nevertheless, because the Sahara does not hold its heat, temperatures could fall into the upper 30s on winter nights. In addition to sheltering people from both heat and cold, residential architects had to provide some sort of sanitary devices, as well as storage facilities for preserving food. Because rainfall was infrequent and slight enough, plentiful sun-baked mud (adobe) served adequately for the main construction material, as it has in the American southwest.

Thousands of years before air-conditioning or central heating was invented, Egypt developed a solution to its temperature extremes by evolving a housing plan that remained viable from the time of the Old Kingdom to the end of its history. The basic Egyptian house for all but the very poor consisted of a high rectangular enclosure wall with an entry door at the narrow end that faced north, if possible, to take advantage of the prevailing breeze. Inside, the compound was divided into three facilities. Just past the entry door lay a garden with a central pool of cool water that also irrigated the trees and shrubs planted around it. Next came a roofed area raised on columns open at the front to catch breezes and provide shade for family and guests, after which came apartments for the owner and immediate family, walled and roofed for privacy and to seal out nighttime cold. These three elements—an open courtyard, a columned portico, and private apartments—made up the architectural plan of all Egyptian houses, however large or small they might be and however many times these elements might be multiplied to incorporate additional three-part shelters for servants and, in a palace, for a harem.

Refinements to this basic structure could include stairs leading to a roof terrace where poles supported an awning—shade for family or guests to catch breezes not felt at ground level. Some of these terraces incorporated ingenious scoops that trapped daytime breezes and circulated them through vents to the apartments below. To minimize the heat, windows in inner rooms were placed high to let the hottest air exit as it rose. Windows were small in area—light was not desired when the sun shone so hot and bright—and unpaned, merely slatted with wood to keep birds out. Bedrooms incorporated raised alcoves for sleeping and adobe benches along one or more walls for sitting and supporting objects; niches in the walls held small oil lamps. Closets had not yet been invented. Bathrooms, which adjoined the bedrooms of more expensive houses, consisted of a latrine wall enclosed on three sides for privacy, with a channel running to the outside of the enclosure. A screened area beside this section held wooden stools with holes in their seats above a bowl. Poor farmers simply used outside areas near their houses for sanitary purposes.

Most houses included an area behind the private apartments that held stables for animals and silos to protect grain from predators, thus adding a fourth division to the three-part Egyptian house. The silos were domed structures of adobe brick that stood six feet high with a door halfway up for access to the grain inside and a trapdoor in the roof for filling the silo. A modest house would have four or more such granaries. Larger dwellings might also include a separate slaughterhouse where cows and other animals were butchered and their meat was hung to cure. By the time of the New Kingdom, cellars were added, providing additional spaces for storage and for work such as weaving and baking that could be performed in cool, subterranean conditions.

As in modern urban areas, housing in crowded cities grew upward rather than spreading outward: thriving Thebes and Memphis consisted of homes that typically rose three or even four stories above a narrow base and employed common walls to form row houses with granaries erected on rooftops. Houses formed orderly grids along roads or alleys that fed into main thoroughfares that crossed in the center of the city (the hieroglyph for a city is two roads crossing in the center of a circle).

In size, Egyptian homes were comparable to those of our time. While a mansion could be as large as 25,000 square feet and contain 30 rooms or more, more modest homes used about 2,000 square feet for their 6 to 12 rooms. The poorest class, however, lived in shelters of less than 1,000 square feet and 4 rooms. Complex mansions began with a huge open court and grand portico, after which came servants' quarters. Apartments for the owner were positioned in the center of the compound, with harem quarters adjoining. Each quarter had its own open court, pool, and a separate portico, in addition to living apartments, so each section of the compound reproduced the standard three-part plan. Private passages led to each separate quarter so that an owner would never have to walk through the servants' rooms at the front to reach his living compound. A kitchen, granaries, and offices—all separate structures—lay to the rear.

The main construction material for all housing, for both the rich and the poor, was adobe, a word that derives from the original Egyptian name, which was similarly pronounced. Made from inexhaustible Nile mud, mixed with sand or straw for bonding and to prevent shrinking as it dried, the moist mixture was placed in rectangular wood frames, about nine-by-four and one-half–by–three inches (larger for government buildings), to form bricks. The frame was lifted away to allow the mud to bake hard in the sun. The enclosing walls of the compound and supporting and dividing walls of the residence were all constructed of adobe bricks, including the stairs to the roof terrace. Roofs, however, were made from logs—generally, the wood of date palms—laid in a row and covered with smaller slats running in the opposite direction, all of which would be plastered with Nile mud to prevent water seepage. The plastered logs became the terrace, although they remained visible below as the rooms' ceilings. Columns for the portico were also wood—either a single substantial palm trunk or a bundle of slimmer sycamore trunks bound together. In both cases, the top would be carved into a stylized capital that depicted either palm fronds or lotus buds. Doors were wooden planks, attached not at the side wall by hinges but at the bottom with a metal spike that turned in a hole in a block of stone; a metal post anchored the top to a wood door beam. Doors were sealed with bolts, made of metal or wood, that slid into clasps.

Because of the infrequent rain, the life span of adobe was adequate for residential housing. To counter the occasional rain, roofs sloped slightly to produce a natural runoff of water into drain spouts attached to the lowest corners. Likewise, windows and doors often carried wooden hoods to force dripping water away from those openings, and the walls forming the compound enclosure were rounded on top, since flat tops would have held water and decomposed. In poor homes, floors were made of packed earth; in more elegant ones, floors consisted of adobe bricks plastered over, like all the walls of the house proper. Interior walls were painted with a white background on which bright painted designs or scenes from religion or nature provided the home's main decoration.

Furniture was scanty, even for the rich, and consisted of chairs, often set on a dais, low stools, beds, boxes for clothing and jewelry, and small, portable oil lamps. Tables, generally round, were sized for individuals rather than families. Beds, also small, were simple wooden frames on legs with twine lashing for a mattress and a separate curved headrest that supported the head at the neck. Ovens—consisting of baked clay drums, one-and-a-half feet wide at the base and equally tall, but narrowing to half that diameter to force the heat to the top—were located away from the residence area. They were plastered over with Nile mud for insulation except for a hole near the bottom that provided draft and permitted the fire to be stoked. More costly homes included a built-in fireplace, located in the outer court, shielded on three sides by walls to keep its heat away from the family. Most homes incorporated a small shrine in the portico for prayers and offerings to the family's favorite god (Brier and Hobbs, 143–47).

FOR MORE INFORMATION

Badawy, A. *A History of Egyptian Architecture: The First Intermediate Period, the Middle Kingdom, and the Second Intermediate Period.* Berkeley: University of California Press, 1968.

Brier, B., and H. Hobbs. *Daily Life of the Ancient Egyptians.* Westport, Conn.: Greenwood Press, 1999.

Clarke, S., and R. Englebach. *Ancient Egyptian Construction and Architecture.* Oxford University Press, 1930; reprint, Mineola, N.Y.: Dover Books, 1990.

MATERIAL LIFE
|
HOUSING
|
Mesopotamia

Egypt

Greece

Rome

Australian Aboriginals

GREECE

The residential area of Athens consisted of narrow, winding streets and small, poorly constructed houses. Most of it lay to the northeast of the Acropolis. Somewhat paradoxically, it was not until the fourth century B.C.E., when Athens's economy was declining, that houses began to be constructed in a more luxurious style. One ancient commentator called Heracleides was so contemptuous of Athens that in a fragmentary work he wrote, "Most of the houses are mean, the pleasant ones few. A stranger would doubt, on first acquaintance, that this was really the renowned city of the Athenians."

The cost of purchasing a house varied enormously. In Xenophon's treatise *Household Management*, Socrates says to his wealthy friend Kritoboulos, "I expect that if I found a good buyer, everything including the house itself would fetch 5 minai [i.e.,

500 drachmas], whereas your house would sell for more than a hundred times that amount" (2.2–4).

The best-preserved Athenian house was found in the Attic countryside near the modern town of Vari, a few miles to the southeast of Athens. Although it is a farmhouse, its plan is probably similar to that of many prosperous houses in Athens: a central courtyard with rooms leading off on all four sides. There was only one entrance to the house from the road. A south-facing veranda provided a place to work and relax, shaded from the summer heat or winter rain. Judging from the thinness of its walls, it is unlikely that the Vari house had a second story. In the southwest corner, however, the foundations are considerably thicker, suggesting that a tower of two or more stories once existed here. This probably served as either a workroom or storeroom.

Building materials were extremely crude. Even the more sturdily constructed houses had lower courses of irregularly shaped stones simply piled on top of one another. Exterior walls were made of baked or unbaked mud brick, sometimes coated with lime. For the most part, walls were so thin and poorly constructed that instead of breaking in by the front door, thieves merely knocked a hole through them. The word most commonly used for a burglar means literally a "wall digger." As the orator and politician Demosthenes once remarked, "Are you surprised, men of Athens, that burglary is so common when thieves are bold and walls are merely made of mud?"

Interior walls were generally covered with a coat of plaster, whitewashed on top. Some wealthy Athenians decorated their rooms with frescoes. Floors consisted of beaten earth or clay, occasionally covered in animal skins or reed matting. From the fourth century B.C.E. onward, they were commonly decorated with mosaics made out of small pebbles. Roofs were made of wood with terra-cotta tiling. Windows were very small and set close to the ceiling to afford maximum protection against the weather. In the winter, they were covered with boards or sacking to keep out the wind and rain, supplemented by shutters if the householder could afford them, since wood was both scarce and expensive. When the Athenians residing in the countryside evacuated to the city at the outbreak of the Peloponnesian War, they took their wooden doors and shutters with them.

The houses of the poor consisted of only one room, divided into different living spaces by makeshift partitions. However, since Greek husbands regarded it as a matter of honor that their wives not be exposed to the public gaze even when at home, those who could afford it provided them with a separate living area known as the *gynaikeion*, or women's quarters. A *gynaikeion* can usually only be identified in the archaeological record from the discovery of associated finds such as loom weights. It would generally have been situated at the back of the house or, if the house possessed two stories, in the upper story. There were, however, some exceptions. The speaker in an oration by Lysias describes his domestic arrangements as follows:

My small house has two stories. The layout was the same upstairs as downstairs, with the women's quarters upstairs and the men's quarters downstairs. Then our child was born, whom my wife decided to nurse herself. However, every time she wanted to bathe it, she had to come downstairs at the risk of falling down the staircase. So I decided to move upstairs and put the women downstairs. I soon adjusted to the new arrangement and my wife was frequently able to sleep with the baby, so that she could breast-feed it and stop it from crying. (Lysias, 1.9–10)

In time, well-appointed houses also came to acquire an *andrôn*, or men's quarters. The most favored location for the *andrôn* was on the north side of the courtyard, which was warmed by the winter sun. The *andrôn* was the setting for the symposium, or drinking party.

Lamps provided the main source of artificial lighting. From the sixth century B.C.E. onward, small terra-cotta lamps become extremely common in the archaeological record. They were provided with a wick that floated in olive oil. Several were required to illuminate a single room, and often they were set on tall stands.

Because wood does not survive in the Greek soil, we know most about furniture from illustrations on vases and sculpted gravestones. One of the most popular items was a chair with a curved back and curved legs, known as a *klismos*. Three-legged tables also appear regularly, as do a variety of small stools. A basic necessity was the *klinê*, which did double duty as a couch by day and a bed by night. Cupboards were unknown, but wooden chests, used for the storage of clothing and bed linen, were popular. Musical instruments and other objects are sometimes shown hanging from walls. Small terra-cotta statuettes served as popular adornments.

All water had to be fetched from outside. Many houses possessed a well in the courtyard that was cut into the bedrock sometimes to a depth of more than 30 feet. In later times, wells were lined with cylindrical drums made of terra-cotta to prevent their sides from crumbling into the water. From the middle of the fourth century B.C.E., however, following a sizable drop in the water table in Athens, bell-shaped cisterns became popular. These were designed to catch the rainwater that drained off the roof. The quality of the water obtained in this way must have varied greatly at different times in the year.

Many Athenians, and Greeks in general, relied on the nearest public fountain for their drinking water. Collecting the daily supply of water was an arduous and time-consuming task. For the most part, it was performed by slaves, although in the case of the poor, this chore fell to the mistress of the house. The public fountain was a popular place to gather and gossip, as scenes on vases indicate.

The earliest bathtub to come to light, which is of Mycenaean date, was found in the so-called Palace of Nestor at Pylos. Nearby it stood two large jars about four feet high, which probably contained water for the bath. In later times, small terra-cotta bathtubs became common. Given the scarcity of water, however, only wealthy Greeks were able to immerse themselves in a full bath. Personal standards of hygiene thus varied considerably from one social class to another. Few houses possessed drains for the disposal of waste water. Men seem to have had few qualms about relieving themselves in public. In the opening scene of Aristophanes' *Women in Assembly*, Blepyros relieves himself in the street as soon as he rises. More sophisticated Greeks used a chamber pot called an *amis*. Women used a boat-shaped vessel called a *skaphion*. Although babies could be dangled out of the window in an emergency (see Aristophanes' *Clouds*, line 1384), well-regulated houses possessed toilets. One toilet, which was found in the Agora, is provided with two holes for the baby's legs and a hole in the seat. Its detachable stand enabled its contents to be removed without disturbing the baby (Garland, 84–86).

FOR MORE INFORMATION

Garland, R. *Daily Life of the Ancient Greeks*. Westport, Conn.: Greenwood Press, 1998.

Jones, J. E. "Town and Country Houses of Attica in Classical Times." In *Thorikus and the Laurion in Archaic and Classical Times*, ed. H. Mussche et al., 63–140. Ghent: Belgian Archaeological Mission in Greece, 1975.

Richter, G. *The Furniture of the Greeks, Etruscans, and Romans*. Oxford: Oxford University Press, 1996.

Rider, B. C. *The Greek House: Its History and Development from the Neolithic to the Hellenistic Age*. Cambridge, England: Cambridge University Press, 1965.

ROME

MATERIAL LIFE
|
HOUSING
|
Mesopotamia

Egypt

Greece

Rome

Australian Aboriginals

The inhabitants of the countryside lived in houses made of stone or mud brick, often with several generations of the family sharing rooms along with farm animals. Rich people in the city lived in houses, the word for which was *domus,* from which comes our word *domestic.* The wealthy also often owned sumptuous country villas. The majority of people living in Rome, however, rented apartments. A surviving document known as the Regionary Catalogue is a list of all the different buildings in ancient Rome and includes the number of houses and apartment buildings in the city of Rome. At the time the list was made in the fourth century C.E., there were 1,797 buildings that were identified as a *domus,* but there were 46,602 apartment buildings. This discrepancy is even more shocking if one considers that each *domus* only contained one family, but an apartment building could shelter hundreds.

Roman houses in the city had few or no windows, and from the outside, a house would simply seem like a blank wall. By modern standards, Roman houses had relatively little furniture. Today, people tend to decorate a house by putting objects in the room, but the Romans had the opposite mentality. Rather than placing decorative objects in a room, they put more effort into decorating the walls and floor of the room itself. Most floors would have a mosaic, formed by pressing small bits of colored stone into wet concrete to create pictures. The walls tended to be completely covered in paintings, often of mythological scenes or landscapes.

The center of the house, and its focal point, was the *atrium.* This was usually an open courtyard with a large hole in the ceiling to admit light. The entryway to the house itself always opened onto the atrium and was called the *vestibulum.* In the center of the atrium, there was often a pool of water termed the *impluvium.* Opening onto the atrium was a raised platform called the *tablinum,* which was where the *paterfamilias* would sit when receiving visitors of lower status. For example, when a man's clients came every morning to pay their respects at the *salutatio,* the patron would greet them seated in the *tablinum.* The dining room, or triclinium, also usually opened onto the atrium. In the back of the house were a series of tiny rooms that served as the bedrooms. Each of these was called a *cubiculum*. The quarters for slaves and women were also at the back of the house. Roman houses were more or less the same range of sizes as modern houses, with the average house being about 2,000 square feet.

In Rome and other large cities, only a tiny percentage of urban Romans could afford their own homes. The rest lived in high-rise apartment buildings. The Romans called them "islands," or *insulae*, because of the way they often occupied entire city blocks. *Insulae* were located all over the city of Rome; some of the larger ones may have had 10 or more stories. Because of the destruction caused by poorly built *insulae* collapsing, emperors several times set limits on the height of *insulae*. Usually, these limits were about 60 or 70 feet. That the emperors felt the need to repeatedly pass such legislation suggests that these limits were repeatedly ignored. Ancient sources record numerous instances when *insulae* collapsed and Roman law did not offer tenants much protection.

Reconstruction of a Roman apartment building (*insulae*). The majority of the inhabitants lived crowded into such structures, which were often poorly made and prone to fires and collapse. Alinari/ Art Resource, NY.

Insulae housed a wide variety of tenants of differing socioeconomic classes. The ground-floor apartments would have been rented to the wealthiest tenants, who did not want to have to trudge up many flights of stairs to reach their dwellings. Often the row of rooms opening onto the street were rented out as shops and small businesses. As one climbed up the levels of the *insulae*, the wealth of the tenants declined and the number of people per room increased. The least-desirable rooms were located under the eaves of the roof and frequently leaked and were inhabited by vermin. A chamber pot served as a toilet, and despite more legislation prohibiting such actions, full pots were routinely dumped out the window. The owners of *insulae* included many famous Romans. The well-known orator Marcus Tullius Cicero was such a slumlord who owned several *insulae*, including one that collapsed because it was so poorly made. Cicero expressed no concern for the lives lost in the disaster but cheerfully noted that he would rebuild it and be able to charge higher rents for the new building.

~*Gregory S. Aldrete*

FOR MORE INFORMATION

Clarke, J. *The Houses of Roman Italy*. Berkeley: University of California Press, 1991.

Stambaugh, J. E. *The Ancient Roman City*. Baltimore, Md.: Johns Hopkins University Press, 1988.

Wallace-Hadrill, A. *Houses and Society in Pompeii and Herculaneum*. Princeton, N.J.: Princeton University Press, 1994.

AUSTRALIAN ABORIGINALS

The kind of housing used by Aboriginal people depended on the region in which they lived and the time of year. Of major importance in all areas was the need to travel lightly and make shelter quickly from readily available materials. The simplest shelter of all was a lean-to arrangement of two forked sticks with a cross beam between them and leafy branches or grass tussocks leaning against one side. These were usually set with the branches on the western side to protect against the heat of the afternoon sun. With a fireplace in front, such simple shelters were widely used by traveling and hunting parties.

More elaborate variations might be built if a camp was to be established for some time and if local food and water were plentiful. In the dry areas of central Australia, where people needed to be mobile much of the year, the simple lean-to was the basic house. In coastal, riverine, and tropical areas, where more abundant resources allowed permanent settlements, or in areas of southern or mountain Australia where winter temperatures were low and there were harsh cold winds, larger and more substantial houses were built. Some houses used a kind of thatching of leafy branches or grasses or, where available, sheets of paperbark or stringybark, the latter allowing much more extensive roofing and walls. Such housing designs had a more "western" look, and some were built around a central pole like a teepee.

In areas of Victoria, houses were even constructed of stone and wood, with low stone walls and wooden materials forming the upper walls and roof. In tropical areas, houses were built on stilts to escape mosquitoes and possible floodwaters. Mosquitoes were also discouraged by locating fireplaces inside the structure and keeping smoky fires permanently burning, or by building sleeping platforms directly above fires. Many of the more substantial structures might be lined with sheets of bark. These linings could be decorated, which was the origin of bark painting. At times, the inside was decorated with bird feathers or lined with animal skins.

Where natural rock shelters were available, they were invariably used for ready-made housing. They might be added to by constructing walls of branches or rocks to extend the shelter. The rock walls were always decorated—sometimes with hand stencils as an indication of ownership, sometimes with paintings of animals, but always with designs and motifs that were identifiable. In places such as rock shelters where people returned year after year, sometimes for thousands of years, large deposits of ash, bones, dirt, and shell refuse built up. Because plant food was brought back to settlements, and because the middens were rich in humus, some important food plants might grow within settlements and be harvested later for their fruit or nuts. In some marshy areas, these human-made mounds became attractive camping areas because they were elevated dry land. Such deposits are an important record of past Aboriginal lifestyles and are useful for dating their history.

In all settlements, the housing was arranged in such a way as to reflect social structures. Different clans would always occupy particular parts of a settlement. The single men might have their own large house, and kin who had to avoid each other socially would position their houses accordingly. At times of major ceremonies, when many different groups came together, each would establish a temporary settlement in a position approved by the hosts but that also related to the position and direction of their own homelands.

When a member of a group died, the house or place in which he or she had died had to be avoided for a period of time and then later be cleansed (for example, with a smoking ceremony). This ritual was believed to offer protection from harmful effects caused by "spirits."

~David Horton

FOR MORE INFORMATION

Berndt, R., and C. Berndt. *The World of the First Australians.* Canberra: Aboriginal Studies Press, 1988.

Horton, D., ed. *The Encyclopedia of Aboriginal Australia.* Canberra: Aboriginal Studies Press, 2001.

Ross, H. *Just for Living: Aboriginal Perceptions of Housing in North-West Australia.* Canberra: Aboriginal Studies Press, 1987.

MATERIAL LIFE
|
HEALTH & MEDICINE
|
Mesopotamia

Egypt

Greece

Rome

India

Health and Medicine

When we consider the attitudes of ancient civilizations toward medicine, the strongest theme that emerges is the lack of distinction that they drew between magic and science. Ancient theories of disease mingled the physical and the supernatural, and the cures prescribed to fight illness were likewise a combination of practical measures and incantations. The Mesopotamians seemed more aware of this distinction than other cultures and actually had two different types of medical specialists: the *asipu*, who primarily used magic to fight disease, and the *asû*, who concentrated on practical medicine. Even there, however, the line was blurred, and both types of physician made at least occasional use of the other's techniques. In Egypt, physicians (who were usually priests) made free use of both approaches in the quest to cure their patients, and later, Greek and Roman healers followed their example.

Because none of these cultures had developed an accurate understanding of the roles of bacteria, germs, and infections in causing illness, they struggled to find a way to explain the causes of disease. Lacking the technology to find the true causation, when confronted by such a mysterious and invisible process, their ascription of illness to supernatural forces is understandable. The explanations that they came up with were varied and show a great deal of inventiveness if nothing else. The Mesopotamians and early Romans believed that immoral behavior could sometimes result in sickness. The Vedic healers of ancient India believed demonic forces or beings caused disease. The Egyptians hypothesized that excesses of *wechdu*, a kind of toxic substance in the body, could instigate illnesses. Gods or demons could both cause diseases and cure them. The Greek god of healing, Aesculapius, was thought to cure worshipers in dreams while they slept in his temple. The most famous theory of disease might be that of the Greek philosopher Aristotle, who developed a complex and influential explanation of illness based on the imbalance of certain forces or substances, known as "humors," in the body. A physician's job was to help the patient restore the correct balance, and if this was achieved, the sickness would be cured.

When ancient doctors were confronted with more understandable types of health problems, such as cuts, broken bones, and other forms of trauma, their medical practices were, on the whole, as sound and competent as could be expected given the tools available. Ancient healers were adept at making splints, setting bones, stitching up cuts, and even some surgical procedures such as cataract removal. The specific situations faced by different cultures produced various medical specialties to deal with these problems. The Egyptians, for example, who lived in a desert infested by poisonous serpents, had a branch of medicine devoted to snakebites, while the militaristic Romans sent their legions into the field accompanied by a *medicus*, a doctor specializing in violent trauma injuries.

Disease was rampant in the ancient world, and poor sanitation and problems with unbalanced nutrition were primary contributing factors. Frequently quoted mortality statistics about the average life span of ancient peoples are deceptive because very high death rates during early childhood pull down the numbers. Roughly a third of children who survived birth probably died before puberty, with most of these deaths occurring in the first few years. People who managed to survive into their teens, however, probably had a decent chance of making it into their 30s or early 40s. People who lived into their 60s would have been quite rare, however.

Ancient medical texts demonstrate a keen interest in health and medicine, and although it took a while for science to provide physicians with the tools to fight disease effectively, ancient doctors did take important steps toward building a practical and moral foundation for the practice of medicine. Greek doctors kept carefully written descriptions of the course and symptoms of different diseases, which was the first step toward identifying and classifying them. The Greek Hippocratic Oath established the basic ethical principles that health care providers were to observe; and its precepts are still influential today.

~Gregory S. Aldrete

MESOPOTAMIA

Medical practitioners were known as early as the third millennium B.C.E. Babylonians who were sick could use two types of medical practitioners: the *asipu*, whose cures were magical, and the *asû*, whose cures were basically medical. The line between the two practitioners was not hard and fast. Thus, the *asipu* or exorcist sometimes used drugs, and the *asû* or doctor sometimes used incantations and other magical practices. In fact, the two professionals might even work together on a case.

We have little information on how the *asû* were trained. All we know about their hierarchy comes from their use of titles: physician, chief physician's deputy, and chief physician. There is little information about surgeons. Midwives were women. An

MATERIAL LIFE
|
HEALTH & MEDICINE
|
Mesopotamia

Egypt

Greece

Rome

India

early second-millennium tablet mentions a woman doctor. Also, the "physician of an ox or donkey," a veterinarian, is noted. A first-millennium tablet refers to an eye doctor.

Doctors conducted a clinical examination, taking the temperature and pulse of the patient. Also, any discolorations of the skin, inflammations, and even the color of the urine were noted. Tablets also mention contagious diseases, as in this letter written by Zimri-Lim, king of Mari, to his wife, Shibtu (ca. 1780 B.C.E.):

I have heard that the lady Nanname has been taken ill. She has many contacts with the people of the palace. She meets many ladies in her house. Now then, give severe orders that no one should drink in the cup where she drinks, no one should sit on the seat where she sits, no one should sleep in the bed where she sleeps. She should no longer meet many ladies in her house. This disease is contagious. (as cited in Roux, 370)

The Code of Hammurabi describes fees that were paid according to the social status of the patient. Private physicians were rarely mentioned at the turn of the second millennium B.C.E. Most physicians were attached to the palace. Letters from Mari and Amarna mention court physicians being sent abroad to impress foreign rulers. A military officer, writing from battle, asked that an *asû* be sent in case one of his men were hit by a slingshot. A humorous story called the "The Poor Man of Nippur" notes the physician as having a special hairstyle and carrying a fire-scorched pot (perhaps to mix his herbs). Other texts described the physician bringing a wooden box or leather bag of herbs.

People in ancient Mesopotamia were able to identify the natural origin of some illnesses that resulted from overexposure to heat or cold, overeating, eating spoiled food, or drinking too much of an alcoholic beverage. In the initial stages of the development of medical practices, the *asipu* would read over the list of sins the patient might have committed. The ancient Mesopotamians believed that sin lay at the cause of the patient's illness. Once the sin was identified, the *asipu* could exorcise the demon causing the illness. For the ancient Mesopotamians, "sin" included crimes, moral offenses, errors and omissions in ritual performance, and unintentional breaking of taboos. The offended gods or demons could strike directly; that is, "the hand" of various gods or demons was thought to cause illness. Therefore, illness indicated a kind of black mark against the patient. Incantations were recited to exorcise the demon, and foul substances were used to purify the body through enemas, induced vomiting, fumigation, and inhalation. Sometimes sympathetic magic was used. The *asipu* might substitute an animal to offer the disease another place to inhabit. Or the demon might be bribed with gifts that he or she might find useful on the journey away from the patient. At the same time, certain symptoms were also identified. Thus, disease was believed to be caused by both a demon and recognizable symptoms. Remedies were prescribed to expel that particular demon; for example, in the case of epilepsy, the doctor ordered the patient to place "the little finger of a dead man, rancid oil, and copper into the skin of a virgin goat; you shall string it on a tendon of a gerbil and put it round his neck, and he will recover" (as cited in Saggs, 260–61).

As a number of symptoms and prognoses of diseases were identified, omen series were developed. In time, medicine began to use materials of therapeutic significance. Some of the remedies were related in shape or color to the disease. For example, jaundice was treated with yellow medicine. Also, the exact time for collecting herbs was noted—indispensable knowledge even for today's herbalists.

There was a god called Ninazu, meaning "lord doctor," whose son used a rod intertwined with serpents as the insignia of the medical professional. Mesopotamian medicine was transmitted to the Greeks along with Egyptian medicine, laying the ground for Hippocratic reform of the fifth century B.C.E. However, in its 2,000 or so years of existence, Mesopotamian medicine made little progress. The doctors still resorted to superstition and magical explanations. Although they could offer rational explanations for many symptoms and diseases, they never tried to collect data and theorize.

> *"If (the exorcist) sees either a black dog or a black pig, that sick man will die."*

Medical texts are found from the third millennium B.C.E. on, but most come from Assurbanipal's library at Nineveh. Texts come from Sumer, Babylon, Assyria, and even the Hittite area. Medical texts are basically of two kinds: descriptions of symptoms and lists of remedies.

The greatest number of medical texts are part of an omen series that deals with the activities of the *asipu* and begins with the words, "If the exorcist is going to the house of the patient," followed by what the *asipu* might see on his way to the patient's house or at the door. This introductory series includes such chance encounters as, for example, the following:

If (the exorcist) sees either a black dog or a black pig, that sick man will die.
If (the exorcist) sees a white pig, that sick man will live. . . .
If (the exorcist) sees pigs which keep lifting up their tails, (as to) that sick man, anxiety will
   not come near him. (as cited in Saggs, 435)

This section is followed by a description of the disease and frequently the prognosis "he will get well" or "he will die." Treatment is rarely mentioned. In one section, the symptoms are organized according to the parts of the body, starting with the skull and ending with the toes. Usually, the diseases are attributed to the god or demon who caused them. In one section, the prognoses are arranged according to the daily progress of the illness. The last part of this omen series is assigned to medical problems of women and children, including pregnancy, childbirth, and malnutrition. Some omens try to predict the sex of the child from the pregnant woman's complexion, body shape, and so on. This section even includes favorable and unfavorable days for a pregnant woman to have intercourse.

The medical texts concerning the *asû* or doctor are organized in a manner similar to the omen texts; however, here specific symptoms are listed with directions on administering medication. The texts reveal an extensive list of herbal remedies, some of medicinal value; the texts also describe the identification and treatment of many kinds of illnesses, among them intestinal obstructions, headaches, tonsillitis, tuberculosis, typhus, lice, bubonic plague, smallpox, rheumatism, eye and ear infections, diarrhea, colic, gout, and venereal diseases such as gonorrhea. The Babylonians also recorded abnormal and monstrous births in their omen literature. They even recorded the hallucinations of a patient and their meaning. For example:

If, when he was suffering from a long illness, he saw a dog, his illness will return to him; he will die.

If, when he was suffering from a long illness, he saw a gazelle, that patient will recover.

If, when he was suffering from a long illness, he saw a wild pig, when you have recited an incantation for him, he will recover. (as cited in Saggs, 260–61)

Mental illness was certainly known. The royal family of Elam seemed to suffer particularly from what the texts describe as "his mind changed," meaning that he went insane, not a change of policy. Sexual impotence was also recognized as having a psychological basis.

The oldest medical text known to us, a list of prescriptions, was written at the end of the third millennium B.C.E. Saltpeter (potassium nitrate) and salt (sodium chloride) are the minerals most often mentioned. However, the prescriptions also make use of milk, snake skin, turtle shell, cassia, thyme, fir, figs, and dates. The samples were stored as either solids or powders to be used in preparing remedies—salves and filtrates (extracts) to be applied externally or powders, often dissolved in beer, to be taken internally. Unfortunately, these Sumerian prescriptions failed to indicate the quantities to be used, the amount to be administered, and how often this medicine should be taken. Perhaps whoever wrote this tablet wanted his professional secrets protected. Or perhaps these details were not considered important.

A tablet written in the first millennium B.C.E. is divided into three columns of more than 150 items; the tablet lists (1) what part of the plant to use, (2) the disease it is meant to cure, and (3) how to administer the medicine, that is, frequency, time of day, necessity of fasting, and so on. Methods of administering the drugs include baths with hot infusions, enemas, vapor inhalations, and blowing liquids through a reed or tube into the mouth, nose, ear, penis, or vagina.

An Assyrian handbook found in the libraries of Assur and Nineveh lists more than 400 Sumerian words for plants, fruits, and other substances, with about 800 Semitic synonyms. Approximately half of these plants have medicinal value.

We have little information about surgery. Probably medical expertise was acquired by training and observation—experiences not described in handbooks. As early as 5000 B.C.E., skeletal remains attest to trepanation, an operation involving removal of part of the scalp and a piece of the skull bone. Trepanations were performed when the skull was fractured or to relieve headaches and epilepsy. We also know that court physicians were called to affirm that any officials having access to the harem were castrated; although we assume that castration was performed by physicians, we do not know this for a fact. One surgical instrument, the lancet, was called a "barber's knife."

Dog made out of clay. Such statues from Mesopotamia were a form of apotropaic icon intended to safeguard the owner against disease. © Copyright The British Museum.

In general, the Mesopotamians knew little about anatomy and physiology; they were restricted by the religious taboo against dissecting a corpse. Animal anatomy may have helped, but the Mesopotamians dissected only the liver and lungs of perfectly healthy animals for divinatory purposes.

The liver was regarded as the seat of various emotions and the heart of intelligence. The ancient Mesopotamians recognized variations in pulse rate but never went a step further in understanding how blood circulated.

The Code of Hammurabi indicates that surgery was performed and that surgeons were able to set broken bones. The laws also tell us that the punishment for surgical mistakes was mutilation and even death.

The rate of death resulting from childbirth remains unknown. Infants were buried in jars beneath the living room floor. At Nuzi, a jar containing the remains of an infant burial was found under a private home; the jar was in the shape of a breast— a poignant memorial. Abnormal pregnancies, maldevelopment of the infant, and gross physical abnormalities of the fetus resulted in the death of mother and child. The live birth rate must have exceeded the death rate because enough children survived to maintain the population, and in fact, from the fourth millennium B.C.E. onward, the populations grew. In the third millennium B.C.E., Mesopotamia and Egypt each had a population of approximately one million; the life expectancy (with rare exceptions) was approximately 40 years. Because death usually occurred at an early age in antiquity, diseases associated with old age were rare.

Those who survived the physical dangers of early childhood could expect to enjoy a relatively long life. One late text reflects that the age of 40 is "prime," that 50 is "a short time" (in case he dies that young), that 60 is "manhood," that 70 is "a long time," that 80 is "old age," and that 90 is "extreme old age." In a wisdom text from the Syrian city of Emar, the gods allot man a maximum lifetime of 120 years. To see one's family in the fourth generation was considered the ultimate blessing of extreme old age. Surprisingly, a number of people actually reached extreme old age. Several kings had long reigns, such as Shulgi of Ur (48 years), Hammurabi of Babylon (43 years), and Assurbanipal of Assyria (42 years). We know that the mother of King Nabonidus lived for 104 years—she tells us so in her autobiography. Archives have shown that some individuals lived at least 70 years.

Battle casualties were the major cause of death among adult males. Those captured on military campaigns most probably died of exhaustion and maltreatment. Those who managed to escape from their victors died of exposure, hunger, and thirst. The people besieged within their cities suffered from disease and starvation, sometimes resorting to cannibalism.

Acts of nature such as flood, drought, famine, or plagues of locusts affected entire communities. Floods were generally local but extremely destructive, causing a high death rate. Locusts involved wider areas of land, starving both humans and animals.

Several infectious diseases were so severe that clinical patterns were observed by the ancients. Diseases that caused a high mortality rate were: (1) tuberculosis (ca. second millennium B.C.E.); (2) pneumonic and bubonic plague, the most lethal diseases to infect humans; (3) typhus, particularly the human louse-borne type of disease, often associated with famine, filth, and other disabling conditions in war;

(4) smallpox, probably a mutant of the cowpox virus affecting domestic cattle; and (5) leprosy, which was rarer and less infective but more chronic.

Southern Mesopotamia was the most heavily populated area of Mesopotamia and therefore more conducive to the outbreak of epidemics, such as bubonic plague. The word for epidemic disease in Akkadian literally meant "certain death" and could be applied equally to animal and to human epidemics. An omen reports plague gods marching with the troops, most likely a reference to typhus, which often afflicted armies. Tablets report cities and even whole countries that were struck by some fatal epidemic, sometimes lasting years. An Akkadian myth, Erra, was written as a result of a plague at Babylon; the myth was believed to ward off further attacks when hung on the wall of the house. Old Babylonian letters describe performing rituals, avoiding crowds, and purifying cities once the god had "calmed down."

The diseases caused by viruses were first reported in the second millennium B.C.E. These viruses may have infected their animal hosts earlier; however, in the second millennium, the increasing density of urban populations and the close contact between domestic animals and humans gave rise to two strains of diseases, one in humans and one in animals (Nemet-Nejat, 78–82, 145–47).

FOR MORE INFORMATION

Nemet-Nejat, K. R. *Daily Life in Ancient Mesopotamia*. Westport, Conn.: Greenwood Press, 1998.

Ritter, E. K. "Magical-Expert (= *Asipu*) and Physician (= *Asu*)." *Assyriological Studies* 16 (1965).

Roux, G. *Ancient Iraq*. 3rd ed. Harmondsworth, England: Penguin Books, 1992.

Saggs, H. W. F. *Civilization before Greece and Rome*. New Haven, Conn.: Yale University Press, 1989.

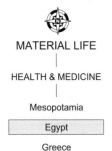

MATERIAL LIFE

HEALTH & MEDICINE

Mesopotamia

Egypt

Greece

Rome

India

EGYPT

Although ancient Egyptians were shorter than we are—the average male stood 5 feet, 6 inches tall compared with almost 5 feet, 10 inches in the United States today—in every other way they resembled modern people and consequently were subject to most of the same diseases. One scourge of countries with damp, hot climates, schistosomiasis, which still afflicts 10 percent of Egypt's population today, seems to have been rampant in ancient times. The cause is a parasite, carried by snails living in the still waters of canals and in the Nile's riverbanks, that burrows through the feet of waders, enters their veins, and then swims to the body's bladder and rectum to deposit eggs. The worms finally migrate to the urinary tract, causing blood in the urine (hematuria). After the eggs hatch, they cause severe anemia, urinary infection, and liver ailments. The ancient Egyptians never suspected that a virtually invisible worm caused these problems; all they could do was try to relieve the discomfort. Medical papyri specify a potion consisting of the tail of a mouse mixed with onion, meal, honey, and water, all strained before using and then drunk for four days.

Egyptians also suffered from a high incidence of lung disorders. Tuberculosis, in particular, was more common than in modern times. This disease, which affects the lungs, sometimes destroys bone as well and shows up in mummies as osteomyelitis of the spine (Pott's disease) because tuberculosis affects the disks between vertebrae. Even more common was sand in the lungs, which hindered breathing (sand pneumoconiosis), to be expected in a desert country in which every breeze carried sand into the respiratory system. As a result, persistent coughs plagued the Egyptians—their version of the modern black-lung disease of coal miners.

Dental problems were a major concern. Tooth decay was prevalent not because of a diet rich in sugars—Egyptians had no pure sugar, nor could the average person afford honey—but because teeth were worn away until their pulp was exposed, making them vulnerable to infection. A double dose of sand plus grit in the ancient diet, which came from bread that was made by grinding a stone against another stone to produce flour, caused the wear. Examinations of mummies, both young and old, found severely worn teeth, even abscesses that can prove fatal. Although Egyptians had specialists for many medical problems, dentistry was not one of these; Egyptians with these problems simply suffered. With dental infection so common, foul breath was a major social problem, and Egyptians invented the first breath mints: a combination of frankincense, myrrh, and cinnamon boiled with honey and shaped into pellets.

Infections of various kinds were incurable before the discovery of the penicillin family of medicines during the twentieth century. Malaria plagued ancient Egyptians who lived near marshes and lakes—a large percentage of the population—and neither its cause nor any effective treatment was known before modern times.

Egyptians took two approaches to their medical problems—clinical and magical—with the type of illness determining which was used. As long as the cause of a medical problem was known to Egyptians, as in the case of broken bones and crocodile bites, they treated it in a clinical manner. For example, the prescription for a crocodile bite was to sew the wound closed before placing raw meat over it. If, however, the affliction was something such as a fever whose cause was unknown, it was attributed to demons or malicious magic and treated with magical cures. Some afflictions, to be sure, fell entirely outside the understanding of the Egyptians and were left to a specialist in "unknown diseases."

Whether clinician or magician, most physicians came from the ranks of priests. Because Sekhmet, the lioness-headed goddess, was associated with medical arts, her priests were considered superior doctors, although some were skilled in clinical and others in magical medicine. It is ironic that Sekhmet became the patron deity of medicine because, in mythology, she had been feared for her temper that almost destroyed humankind. The gods Isis, Horus, and Toth were also associated with healing. Isis was claimed as the patron both of clinical and magical specialists because she had reassembled her deceased husband, Osiris, after he had been hacked to pieces by his evil brother Seth, and, as the goddess of magic, her supernatural powers were eagerly sought. Because an important myth told how Horus's eye was magically restored to health after it was almost destroyed in battle, he, in turn, became the patron of eye doctors. Toth, the god of wisdom, usually depicted as an ibis-headed god (but sometimes as a baboon), was the fabled inventor of writing and so was also called upon for clinical matters. Ancient Greek authors tell us that Toth inspired a series of 42 encyclopedic books, of which 36, according to Clement of Alexandria, dealt with philosophy and general knowledge; the remaining 6 concerned medicine. One volume covered anatomy, another diseases, and others surgery, remedies, diseases of the eye, and diseases of women. Because the Greeks identified Toth with their own god Hermes, these works became known as the Hermetic books.

These famous books have disappeared, but quite a few ancient Egyptian medical works survive. They fall into the same two categories—clinical and magical—as did their medical practitioners. The most famous clinical writings, the Edwin Smith Surgical Papyrus, which dates from approximately 1700 B.C.E., was a copy of a much older papyrus from the Old Kingdom. The papyrus, which deals intelligently with physical injuries, such as fractures and broken bones, indicates that whoever wrote it possessed extensive, direct knowledge of these problems. It discusses 48 specific injuries, each preceded by a title such as "Instructions concerning a Wound on the Top of His Eyebrow." This is followed by "The Examination," in which the surgeon is told how to probe the wound and what to look for. Each case ends with a "Diagnosis." The physician is told to state what the injury is, and then whether he can treat it, by saying one of three things: "an ailment which I will treat," "an ailment with which I will contend," or "an ailment not to be treated." These diagnoses divided his cases into those he could cure, those he hoped to cure, and those he could not. Fourteen cases described in the papyrus, including bulging tumors in the breast and such severe fractures of the temple that blood flowed from the nose and ears of a patient unable to speak, were so severe the physician was instructed to say they could not be treated. The intention of such a hopeless diagnosis was not for the patient's good but to protect the doctor's reputation—business would suffer if he treated too many patients who died.

The papyrus covers ailments from the top of the head to the spinal column, although blank space at the end of the papyrus suggests that if the scribe had completed his copy, he would have included injuries to the legs and feet. Three examples involving exposed brains present enough detail to show that the author had carefully observed this crucial organ. He also made a start in understanding the functions of the brain, for he mentions the possibility that a severe head injury might affect the limbs, one symptom of which could be a limp. Despite this good beginning—Egyptians developed specialists in eye ailments, gynecological ailments, and a few other medical problems—they did not develop specialists of the brain.

For the "cases to be treated," recommended remedies are surprisingly similar to modern treatments: bandages, splints, plaster, tape, and sutures to help the patient mend. Still, one curious discussion deviates from the clinical approach. In a case concerning a crushed forehead, magic is advised. A poultice of grease and ostrich egg was to be applied to the wound, probably because the shell of the ostrich egg resembled the frontal bone and the hope was that the bone would knit to form a solid sphere like the eggshell. Before the poultice was applied, a spell was to be recited:

Repelled is the enemy that is in the wound!
Cast out the [evil] that is in the blood,
The adversary of Horus [on every] side of
the mouth of Isis.
This temple does not fall down;
There is no enemy of the vessel therein.
I am under the protection of Isis;
My rescue is the son of Osiris. (as cited in Breasted, 220)

Although called the Edwin Smith Surgical Papyrus, the work contains no discussion of surgery. The practitioner is told only how to remove bone fragments, dress the wound, and so on, not what to cut or saw. Examinations of hundreds of mummies indicate that Egyptian physicians seldom practiced surgery, which would have been a difficult undertaking using only bronze knives and lacking anesthesia. Yet Egyptians did perform circumcisions. Such a scene is shown on the walls of the tomb of Ankh-ma-Hor, overseer of the works of King Teti from the Sixth Dynasty. Two adult men stand as they undergo circumcision by two others. One of the patients is held by a fifth man, to whom the circumciser says, "Hold him fast, don't let him fall." The only other evidence for surgery is what appear to be surgical instruments carved on the back wall of Kom Ombo Temple in Upper Egypt, although some doubt exists about their purpose—the hieroglyphs around the scene make no mention of surgery and do not refer to the tools in any way.

Papyrus was expensive enough that both sides were typically used. The reverse side of the Edwin Smith Surgical Papyrus consists of a second medical work based on principles of magic, consisting of a hodgepodge of spells on such diverse topics as what to do for a woman whose menstrual flow has stopped and treatments for hemorrhoids. The most intriguing is titled "How to Transform an Old Man into a Youth," the forerunner of medieval alchemists' elixirs of life. The Egyptian version consists of a wrinkle cream for smoothing the skin and made from a fruit called *hemayet* (a word still untranslated). Whatever the fruit was, it was crushed, husked, and winnowed like grain, then placed with water in a new container to boil. When the mixture reached the consistency of clay, it was removed from the fire and spooned into a jar until it cooled, then placed on linen to strain over a jar opening, after which it was stored in a vase of costly stone. The spell promises that if the cream is spread on the face, it will remove wrinkles, blemishes, and in fact every sign of age; it ends with the assurance that "it has been shown to be effective millions of times."

> *Surgery would have been a difficult undertaking using only bronze knives and lacking anesthesia.*

While this side of this papyrus contains exorcisms of demons and incantations to gods, it also hints at something very much like modern germ theory. The first eight spells concern "The Pest of the Year," an epidemic that afflicted the Egyptians annually. Spells indicate that the disease came on "the plague-bearing wind," could be carried by flies, was lodged in food and beds or bed linens, and entered the body through the mouth and throat. Of course, the text does not mention germs—malicious gods and demons, even Sekhmet, are cited as causes of the plague. Still, Egyptian doctors had made an interesting observation about how diseases spread.

Physicians of ancient Egypt grappled to understand the cause of disease as well as they could. Although they never quite grasped the ideas of bacteria or germs, they created a theory centering around a noxious substance they called *wechdu*, which resided in the lower intestine. They believed *wechdu* caused most diseases. This substance could travel from the bowel through the vascular system, they thought, coagulating the blood and changing it to pus. Such "rising" of *wechdu* produced heat (fever) that could affect the pulse rate (Steuer, 4). *Wechdu* also caused aging because its slow absorption led to body decay. Because this foul substance caused disease, the Egyptian cure was to get rid of it. When a fever or infection grew serious, doctors prescribed an enema. As a preventative, purges were recommended to rid the body of *wechdu*. Today, we can see the errors in this view of disease, but the theory shows a rational, clinical approach to trying to understand and treat ailments.

> *When a fever or infection grew serious, doctors prescribed an enema.*

Egyptian physicians had some knowledge of anatomy as well. The Edwin Smith Surgical Papyrus illustrates that some of their knowledge came from treating accident injuries: when a skull was severely fractured in a construction mishap, the attending physician could sometimes view the living brain. Additional opportunities for study were provided by war and mummification. Because physicians traveled with the troops, they could inspect internal organs and bones while they repaired battle wounds. Constrained by the need to move quickly from one battle victim to the next, however, they were unable to perform the careful examination that could lead to a precise anatomical description. Anatomy lessons learned during mummification had even greater limitations. Because the brain, for example, was intentionally pulverized inside the cranium before extraction, any possibility of discovering its structure was eliminated. On the other hand, although various internal organs were removed whole from the body and could be thoroughly inspected, embalmers, who occupied the lower end of the social scale, were not physicians.

Egyptians did not perform human autopsies because of their religious belief in resurrection; thus much of their anatomical knowledge came from animals. Most Egyptians would have witnessed animal slaughter. Hieroglyphs for various internal parts of the human body clearly show that animal anatomy was the source for information about human anatomy. Even the hieroglyph for heart is a bovine, not a human, heart. Because mummification left the heart inside the body, a cow's heart was more familiar than a human one. The hieroglyphs for many other human bodily parts—backbone, ribs, intestines—depicted animal anatomy as well. While the physicians of ancient Egypt were recognized as the most skilled of their time in the world, their knowledge of human anatomy fell far short of modern standards. They did not even have a word for the human pancreas.

The Egyptians had no hospitals, only home care, but because most of their physicians were priests, people often sought healing at temples, where they were treated with a combination of medicine, theology, and magic and then sent home to recover. In addition, several temples with reputations for effecting miraculous cures became sites of pilgrimage for the ill. Dendera in southern Egypt specialized in several types of miracle treatments. Water that dripped from statues inscribed with healing spells was channeled to basins so the diseased could bathe in holy water or drink it. Alternatively, patients could recline in small, dark crypts with special lamps, hoping to converse with appropriate gods in a dream to learn their cure. The temple at Deir el Bahri, also in southern Egypt, was another famous pilgrimage site. Priest physicians who healed were called *wabu*; lay physicians were called *sunu*. Careful regulation of the medical profession by the government with stiff penalties for improper practice ensured that whether associated with a temple or not, all doctors were thoroughly trained. The difference between priest and lay doctors was that the lay doctors could draw from all available sources for their cures, not just those connected with a single god. Those skilled at gathering the plants physicians needed were the ancient equivalent of our pharmacists.

One entire medical papyrus that survives is devoted to snake bites. Lethal cobras and vipers were plentiful in Egypt; the serpent was such a common danger in the ancient Middle East that the Bible makes it the archetype of evil. Ancient Egyptians believed that when they traveled across the sky to the netherworld, snakes would try to stop them, and magical spells would be needed to counter their venom. It is not surprising then that magical papyri are full of spells to protect the living from snake bites and that one is devoted to their treatment. "Treatment with the knife" is occasionally indicated, but merely to reduce swelling and release fluids. Sometimes the physician is instructed to bandage the wound with a poultice of salt or natron, which would indeed reduce the swelling by osmosis just like the Glauber's salt (magnesium sulfate) used today, but it would not remove the poison. Instead, the main treatment, listed 27 times in the papyrus, suggests giving the victim an emetic concoction of onions, salt, *sam* plant and beer, which would induce vomiting but not affect the venom circulating in the bloodstream. While physicians did not understand the mechanisms by which venom killed, they were certainly familiar with its effects. Several treatments were designed to "cause the throat to breathe" or "open the throat," which was a priority since cobra venom blocks impulses from the nerves to muscles, paralyzing the muscles involved in respiration.

We do not know whether obstetrics was a medical specialty, although a pregnancy test crops up in several papyri, usually under the heading "Another test to see if a woman will bear a child or if she will not bear a child." The woman urinated on two test patches of emmer and barley seeds for several days. If either grew, she was pregnant; if only the barley sprouted, she would have a boy; if only the emmer, it would be a girl. Egyptian women gave birth sitting down, so gravity assisted the baby's exit, permitting less-forceful contractions. Doctors probably did not assist at childbirth. The woman sat on a special birthing stool, generally made of bricks (giving rise to the Egyptian slang phrase "sitting on the bricks" for giving birth). The hieroglyphs for birthing, pronounced *meswet*, show a woman sitting in such a birthing position, as the head and arms of the baby emerge. A few carvings of births exist on temple walls, usually to establish the divine birth of kings and queens, but a physician is never shown. The mother is attended by females, either because of her modesty or because the process was considered so natural that it required no physician (Brier and Hobbs, 223–36).

FOR MORE INFORMATION

Breasted, J. H. *The Edwin Smith Surgical Papyrus*. Chicago: University of Chicago Press, 1930.

Brier, B., and H. Hobbs. *Daily Life of the Ancient Egyptians*. Westport, Conn.: Greenwood Press, 1999.

Estes, J. W. *The Medical Skills of Ancient Egypt*. Canton, Mass.: Science History Publications, 1993.

Steuer, R. O., and J. B. de C. M. Saunders. *Ancient Egyptian and Cnidian Medicine*. Berkeley: University of California Press, 1959.

MATERIAL LIFE
|
HEALTH & MEDICINE
|
Mesopotamia

Egypt

Greece

Rome

India

GREECE

Like other aspects of Greek life, medicine never wholly divorced itself from its religious roots. It is not therefore accidental that the growth of the cult of the healing god Aesculapius at the beginning of the fifth century B.C.E. exactly parallels the birth of the tradition of scientific medical inquiry. Sickness and its cure were now for the first time identified as areas of both professional and divine concern.

The rise of scientific medicine was largely a result of the influence of Hippocrates of Cos, a somewhat shadowy figure about whom little is known for certain yet to whom many early medical writings have been ascribed. From the fifth century B.C.E. onward, sanctuaries of the healing god Aesculapius, such as that of Epidaurus in the northeast Peloponnese, functioned as both religious and medical centers. This is demonstrated by the fact that surgical instruments and votive offerings in the form of parts of the body are commonly found together. Votive offerings were dedicated in the hope of securing the god's intervention on behalf of the part of the body so represented. Even if physicians were exclusively scientific in their approach to healing, many of their patients would have regarded their expertise as an "art," which was, at root, a gift of the god. The fact that Hippocratic physicians took their oath in the name of Aesculapius and other healing deities affords further proof of the complementarity of the two approaches.

The healing that was practiced at the sanctuaries of Aesculapius is likely to have been a potent mixture of medicine, auto-suggestion, faith healing, and divine intervention. While at night the sick slept within the temple precincts waiting for a vision from the god to reveal the source of their cure, by day they entrusted their aches and pains to human physicians. Grateful patients who were cured by Aesculapius were encouraged to erect monuments commemorating the god's intervention. A characteristic feature of these inscriptions is their emphasis on the incredulity that preceded the miraculous cure.

Although relations between the advocates of faith healing and scientific medicine seem to have been essentially benign, some rivalry did nonetheless exist. The Hippocratic author of the celebrated treatise titled *On the Sacred Disease* (2–5), for instance, vehemently opposed the prevailing orthodoxy that epilepsy was an affliction caused by the gods. Castigating "witch doctors, faith-healers, quacks, and charlatans" for seeking to alleviate the symptoms "by prescribing purifications and incantations along with abstinence from baths," he boldly asserts that epilepsy "is not more divine than any other disease." The author concludes with the claim that any skilled practitioner could cure the disease "provided that he could distinguish the right moment for the application of the remedies."

Basic first aid was practiced on the Greek battlefield from earliest times. Homer tells us that the Greek army at Troy relied on the services of two physician brothers named Machaon and Podalerius, sons of Aesculapius, who came from Thessaly, the original home of the healing god.

Not until the late sixth or early fifth century B.C.E. do we hear of professional physicians in the Greek world. One of the most famous was Democedes of Crotona, whose impressive career is reported at length by Herodotus (*Histories*, 3.129–37). Democedes, having cured Darius, king of Persia, was subsequently employed first by the Aeginetans, then by the Athenians, and finally by Polycrates, tyrant of Samos. Democedes' career indicates that there were several physicians with international reputations who were prepared to move from place to place in response to local demand. The Hippocratic treatise titled *Airs, Waters, and Places*, whose topic is the effect of climate, water supply, and location on the general health of a population, was probably written to assist itinerant physicians. It is extremely unlikely, however, that any Greek state provided free public health service to its citizens. Public physicians probably received a retainer requiring them to reside within the state's territory for a fixed period of time but were free to charge for their services.

The principal centers of medical learning and research were Crotona in southern Italy, Cyrene in present-day Libya, the island of Cos, and Cnidus on the west coast of present-day Turkey. These were not medical institutions in the modern sense of the word. Physicians did not have to undergo any formal training. Nor did they possess anything resembling a medical license. Medical students attached themselves to established practitioners on a purely informal basis. Once they had acquired sufficient knowledge, they discharged themselves and were free to practice independently. The success of their careers henceforth depended on their reputations. Given the absence of any objective criteria for determining standards of medical competence, it is hardly surprising that allegations of charlatanism and quackery are commonplace in medical texts.

Although anyone could claim to possess healing skills, some physicians organized themselves into guilds and agreed to abide by prescribed rules of medical conduct. The most important evidence for this is the well-known Hippocratic Oath, which is attributed to Hippocrates himself and which remained the cornerstone of medical ethics in the West until recently. Although we do not know what proportion of the medical profession observed it, those who took it constituted a "closed shop" because they swore to divulge their professional knowledge only to a select few.

Thanks chiefly to the Hippocratic writers and to a medical writer called Galen, we know a great deal about diseases in antiquity. Among the most common were malaria and tuberculosis. Given the extremely high incidence of infant mortality, childhood diseases, including rickets and anemia, must have been widespread. We also hear of diphtheria, chickenpox, mumps, and whooping cough, but there is no evidence for either cholera or measles. Venereal diseases such as syphilis and gonorrhea do not seem to have existed. Leprosy did not reach Greece until the Hellenistic period.

Paleopathology, the study of disease in earlier populations, provides evidence for arteriosclerosis, which in some regions affected as much as 80 percent of the population. Poor sanitation, the lack of a hygienic water supply, and malnutrition were probably the major killers. Although diagnosis was of a high quality, there was very little understanding about how diseases were transmitted because there was no notion of germs. Drugs, surgery, purges, and bleeding were the most common forms of treatment.

The best-known epidemic in Greek history was the plague that afflicted Athens from 430 to 426 B.C.E. Brought about by Pericles' decision to crowd the entire population of Athens within the city walls, the plague took perhaps as much as one-third of the entire population. Although its identity continues to be disputed by scholars, typhus and smallpox are the most likely candidates.

The majority of patients who received medical attention were those who suffered from curable illnesses and injuries. Probably the chronically sick, those suffering from degenerative diseases, and the aged would have had little reason to avail themselves of the services of the medical profession. Despite the keen interest in medicine, knowledge of the internal workings of the human body was extremely rudimentary because dissection was not employed in the study of anatomy before the Hellenistic period. Even then it was practiced perhaps only in Alexandria, Egypt, where it became common. In all the works ascribed to Hippocrates, not one is devoted to the study of anatomy or physiology. Aristotle, writing at the close of the fourth century B.C.E., frankly states: "The internal parts of the body, especially those belonging to humans, are unknown. We must therefore refer to the parts of other creatures that resemble humans" (*History of Animals* section 494b). This refusal, or at least reluctance, to perform dissection was largely a result of religious scruples—the Greeks believed that the procedure could prevent the deceased from entering Hades.

Ignorance of dissection did not prevent physicians and scientists from inventing elaborate theories about the internal workings of the human body, particularly the female body. From Aristotle's perspective, women were failed males. It was their lack of heat that made them more "formless." Aristotle goes so far as to propound the notion of a zoological hierarchy with men at the pinnacle and women one evolutionary step below. This one step nonetheless represented, in his telling phrase, "the first step along the road to deformity" (*Generation of Animals* 4.767b 7f.). Similarly, Galen states that if it were not for the fact that the menses were needed to contain the hot male seed, we might suppose that "the creator had purposely made one half of the whole race imperfect, and, as it were, mutilated" (*On the Use of Parts* section 14.6).

The fact that women needed to menstruate was proof in Aristotle's eyes that they could not burn up the residue that coagulated inside them. They were judged to be particularly susceptible to what we would call today hysteria, a word that is derived from the Greek word for "womb" (*hystera*), meaning literally "the lower parts," although the symptoms were rather different from the illness we identify by the name today. The Hippocratic school believed that the womb wandered around the body if the menses were suppressed or if women did not engage in intercourse.

Although the Greeks lacked the modern scientific terminology to systematize and explain pathological states of consciousness, they were nonetheless capable of subjecting the individual to close psychological scrutiny. Greek tragedy manifests a keen fascination with mental abnormality.

It is not just in the realm of myth that we find incontrovertible evidence for major psychological disturbances. The madness of the Spartan king Cleomenes, as reported by Herodotus, has been cited as a classic instance of paranoid schizophrenia. The king's illness, which provoked him to strike anyone whom he met in the face with his staff, was variously explained either as a punishment brought on by the gods for having burned down a sacred grove or as a consequence of his fondness for unmixed wine, the consumption of which was believed to result in madness. Cleomenes ultimately became so violent that his relatives had him placed in the stocks. While in prison, he managed to intimidate his jailer into giving him a knife, whereupon, as Herodotus relates, "He began to mutilate himself, beginning with his shins. Cutting the flesh up into strips, he proceeded from his ankles to his thighs, and from his thighs to his hips and sides, until he reached his stomach, and while cutting that up he died" (*Histories*, 6.75.3).

Although estimates about life expectancy in the Greek world vary considerably, it is possible that it was little more than half the level common in Western society today. The major source of evidence for age at death is skeletal, which is at best only approximate. Greek funerary monuments, unlike Roman ones, rarely record age at death except in the case of those who survived to extreme old age and for whom the recording of their years was thus a matter of personal pride. Despite the brevity of human life, 70 years nonetheless constituted the ideal quota of years, as is indicated in a fragmentary poem by the Athenian lawgiver Solon: "If a man finally reaches the full measure of his years [i.e., 70], let him receive the apportionment of death, without dying prematurely." Maximum life expectancy also seems to have been the same as it is today. The oldest Athenian known to us was a certain Euphranor, whose gravestone records that he lived to the age of 105. Women's life expectancy was about 10 years lower than that of men. There were many reasons for the disparity. First, other than in Sparta, girls were not as well fed as boys. This had the effect of rendering them more susceptible to disease and in certain cases, of permanently impairing their health. Second, the early age at which many girls became pregnant—shortly after puberty—imposed severe strains upon their bodies, as did the frequency with which they became pregnant. In addition, many women were required to do manual work, often of a highly demanding nature. Men, by contrast, tended to lead less strenuous lives than women, except when they went to war, which was mainly a seasonal activity.

Facilities for the disposal of refuse were almost nonexistent. As a result, rubbish piled up in the streets in vast quantities, creating a terrible stench and constituting a serious health hazard, particularly in the summer months. Where houses were built closely together, as in Athens and the Piraeus, the streets were ankle-deep in filth. Mosquitoes, rats, and flies were plentiful, carrying all manner of diseases and causing epidemics. One of the worst epidemics occurred in 430 B.C.E. when the entire population of Athens was cooped up inside the city walls. The Athenians claimed that the outbreak was caused by the Spartans poisoning their reservoirs. Although there appears to have been no substance to the charge, they were correct in their belief that the contamination of their water supply was the chief cause of the spread of the disease. We also hear of cramped and poorly constructed apartment blocks called *synoikiai*. These were surely death traps owing to the prevalence of earthquakes and the frequency of fires. *Synoikiai* were especially common in the port of Piraeus, where many poor people and foreigners resided (Garland, 64–65, 87, 104–12).

FOR MORE INFORMATION

Dean-Jones, L. *Women's Bodies in Classical Greek Science*. Oxford: Oxford University Press, 1994.

Edelstein, L. *Ancient Medicine*. Rev. ed. Baltimore, Md.: Johns Hopkins University Press, 1967.

Garland, R. *Daily Life of the Ancient Greeks*. Westport, Conn.: Greenwood Press, 1998.

Grmek, M. D. *Diseases in the Ancient World*. Translated by. M. Muellner and L. Muellner. Baltimore, Md.: Johns Hopkins University Press, 1989.

MATERIAL LIFE
|
HEALTH & MEDICINE
|
Mesopotamia

Egypt

Greece

Rome

India

ROME

As with many other aspects of their culture and arts, the Romans got their ideas about medicine from the Greeks. Most influential of these was the philosopher Aristotle, who recorded the classic interpretation of how the body functioned that would be accepted and used for hundreds of years. He believed that all things were composed of four elements: earth, air, fire, and water. These produced in the body four corresponding forces or fluids called humors, which were dry, moist, hot, and cold.

The equilibrium among these humors determined the health of the body. The ideal combination was one that favored hot and dry, and the worst, moist and cold. The Greeks believed that men were superior and hence their bodies were hot and dry, whereas women, who were inferior, were dominated by moist and cold humors.

When a person's humors got out of balance, it caused disease. Thus much of a doctor's practice was devoted to restoring the balance among the humors.

Early in Roman society, the Romans seemed to have had a disdain for physicians and relied on folk remedies for cures. For example, a cure for jaundice directed sufferers to concoct a mixture of ashes of a deer's antler and the blood of an ass diluted in wine (Pliny the Elder, *Natural History* 28.64). Not just disease but all things associated with the body received similar treatment. Sleepiness could be cured by taking calluses from a donkey, soaking them in vinegar, and thrusting them up one's nostrils, a procedure that might well jar a person awake (Pliny the Elder, *Natural History* 28.67).

The stereotypical traditional Roman was a man named Cato the Elder, who despised doctors and whose recommended cure for everything was cabbage. He wrote several books on how to run a farm, so his advice became well known. To Cato, cabbage was a miracle substance. Eating it could cure ulcers, headaches, tumors, arthritis, and heart disease. If you fried it, it cured insomnia, and if you dried it, crushed it into a powder, and inhaled it, it would cure respiratory ailments. If boiled, it cured ear problems (Cato, *On Agriculture* section 157).

Romans commonly thought that many diseases of the body were caused by diseases of the soul. Problems with the mind literally caused problems with the body. They posited a link between virtue and good health, and immorality and disease. One reason Cato thought there was no need for doctors is that they were unnecessary if you lived a virtuous life.

The only real need for doctors, therefore, were for problems clearly not caused by behavior. This included injuries such as trauma, broken bones, cuts, and wounds received in war. Because Rome was at war so often, treatment of wounds caused by weapons was a particular concern.

In 219 B.C.E., the Roman state brought a Greek doctor from Greece and set him up at Rome for the specific purpose of treating military injuries. This was the first known doctor at Rome. The Romans even granted him citizenship. At first he was popular, but he soon got a bad reputation because he was very quick to resort to the knife to cure any ailment. Because of his fondness for amputation, he was given the nickname "the executioner" (Pliny the Elder, *Natural History* 39.12).

Despite this bad experience, Greek doctors were soon coming to Rome in great numbers and setting up practices. Patients were mostly the wealthy, who were the only ones who could afford fees, which they paid either per visit or per disease. The best doctors were thought to come from the east, in particular, from Greece and Egypt. There was no official certification process and no standardized training or schooling to become a physician. Anyone who wanted to could proclaim themselves a doctor, and many quacks set up practices.

One of the most famous doctors was a man named Celsus. He wrote down a number of principles for treating patients, many of which sound quite modern. The core of his beliefs was that good health came from living a healthy lifestyle, including exercise, proper sleep, and a well-balanced diet.

Celsus was interested in the psychological aspects of medicine as well. He instructed doctors not to tell patients with a fatal prognosis the truth because it would depress them and cause them to give up. If a doctor had to tell bad news, he should break it to the patient gently. He thought that the outcome of a case depended equally on three factors: the patient, the doctor, and the disease itself. He also noted that the rich were the most trouble as patients because they constantly made demands and expected an instant cure.

The most famous and influential of all Roman doctors was Galen. Galen was born in 128 c.e. in the east. He studied philosophy and then medicine under other doctors at several cities and for five years was the doctor for a gladiator school, which would have given him firsthand experience with trauma wounds. Finally, he came to Rome, where he became the doctor to the imperial family and other aristocratic people.

Galen was very idealistic. He thought that the best physician was half doctor and half philosopher. He also wrote that a good doctor should despise money and that profit was incompatible with art. He criticized doctors who practiced medicine to get rich and thought of it instead as a philosophical art. In keeping with his philosophical bent, he was a follower of Aristotle's theory of the four humors, and he elaborated on this system. He believed the three most important organs were the liver, heart, and brain.

Galen thought that to understand how the body worked, one had to practice dissection, but because there were moral proscriptions against dissecting humans, he experimented on animals. He dissected many pigs and goats, and once even dissected an elephant. His animal of choice for dissection, however, was the ape because he thought they were most like humans. He did experiments such as feeding apes colored water and then cutting them open to see where it went. He also criticized as ignorant doctors who did not study anatomy.

Galen wrote several important texts recording the results of his experiments, including ones called "On the Uses of the Parts of the Body" and "Bones for Beginners." Physicians such as Galen still mostly prescribed treatments based on plants and potions. Actual surgery was not much used, except in the army.

Every Roman legion had one or more doctors attached to it, each of whom was called a *medicus* (the root of our words medicine and medic). For stab wounds that penetrated the abdomen and pierced the intestines, the result was almost always fatal because of the infection that would set in, and the *medicus* could do little. Thus most of his practice consisted of stitching up shallow cuts, setting broken bones, and amputating severely injured limbs. There was no good anesthesia, although sometimes Romans tried to use root of mandrake as a drug.

One specialized job of military doctors was the removal of arrows. The problem with arrows was that often the head was barbed and thus could not be pulled out without ripping the flesh. There were two solutions to this dilemma. The medicus could push the arrow more so it came out the other side. For injuries in areas of the body where this method was not practical, they developed a special instrument called the scoop of Diocles. It consisted of a set of spoon-shaped cups on long handles. These were worked into the body until the cups were positioned around the barbs of the arrowhead, and then arrow and scoops could be pulled out without tearing additional flesh.

Overall, Roman medicine was fairly primitive. The Romans had no concept of bacterial or viral causes of diseases, there was not much surgery that could be performed, and they relied heavily on magical potions. Despite all this, they did fairly well in treating trauma, and the enlightened attitudes of men such as Celsus and Galen helped to establish medicine as a real educated profession with ethical standards rather than merely a group of con artists.

~Gregory S. Aldrete

FOR MORE INFORMATION

Grmek, M. D. *Diseases in the Ancient World*. Translated by M. Muellner and L. Muellner. Baltimore, Md.: Johns Hopkins University Press, 1989.

Jackson, R. *Doctors and Diseases in the Roman Empire*. London: British Museum Publications, 1988.

INDIA

MATERIAL LIFE
|
HEALTH & MEDICINE
|
Mesopotamia

Egypt

Greece

Rome

India

Health and medicine were highly developed in the Indus Valley civilization, although the details are difficult to discern because of the mystery surrounding untranslated proto-Dravidian texts. House architecture reflected concern for purity and cleanliness, with some even having bathrooms. There was a "Great Bath" at Mohenjo-Daro that epitomized the concern for purification through bathing. This (and other evidence) indicates that water played an important role in the pre-Vedic system of medicine and that there was some concern for public health. There was apparently a strong effort on the part of Indus society to live in harmony with nature, and there is evidence that they may have had some knowledge of pharmacopoeia. There are also suggestions of the development of surgical techniques, including trepanation and the possible treatment of hydrocephaly by drilling holes in the skull (found in the remains of one boy).

Vedic medicine developed in what has been called a "magico-religious" system. Early in the Vedic era, disease was thought to derive more from external beings or forces of demonic nature. Elaborate rituals were devised to cure illnesses. Healers, however, also were trained in more mundane cures, such as setting broken bones, and administering herbs, plants, and other substances to relieve common ailments. The pharmacopoeias of the Indus Valley civilization were elaborated and perfected. Talismans were often worn with fragrant plants to ward off malevolent spirits. Surgery, catheterization, lancing, and cauterization were practiced. Ointments, salves, dyes, hydrotherapy, and salts were used. The *Atharvaveda* was a rich storehouse for all aspects of this knowledge, although many aspects of Vedic medicine derived from other Vedic and Brahmanic sources.

By the era of the Epic and Puranas, material culture in the subcontinent had returned to an urban, though Sanskritic, setting. Greek culture also apparently had some influence, as can be seen in the systems of medicine. The body was said to have channels of fluids within it called humors, and imbalances in environment, diet, digestion, and breathing were all considered to affect health. The Indian system of Ayurveda, an amalgamation of Vedic and Greek medicine, treated disease mostly through physical substances such as plants and herbs to bring the humors into balance, although it maintains some sense of its early "magico-religious" origins to this day.

To read about health and medicine in nineteenth-century India, see the India entry in the section "Health and Medicine" in chapter 4 ("Intellectual Life") of volume 5 (*Nineteenth Century*) in this series.

~*Eric Rothgery*

FOR MORE INFORMATION

Auboyer, J. *Daily Life in Ancient India*. London: Phoenix Press, 1965.

Basham, A. L. *The Wonder That Was India*. London: Sidgwick and Jackson, 1967.

Zysk, K. "Religious Healing in the Veda: With Translations and Annotations of Medical Hymns from the *Rig Veda* and the *Atharvaveda* and Renderings from the Corresponding Ritual Texts." *Journal of the American Philosophical Society* 75, no. 7 (1985).

MATERIAL LIFE

CLOTHING

Mesopotamia

Egypt

Greece

Rome

Nubia

Australian Aboriginals

Clothing

In the ancient world, clothing may have begun as a means of protection, but it gained nonpractical cultural connotations as well. From the clothes one wore, it was often possible to determine social status and role; for example, in ancient Rome, the wearing of the toga revealed Roman citizenship, and the width of its stripe indicated rank, and in Assyria, a cloak was worn to denote higher status. Even the lack of clothing could suggest one's status; for instance, prisoners of war were stripped naked by their Assyrian captors to emphasize their abject state, and Egyptian workers often wore only loincloths when toiling in the extreme heat.

Practical considerations governed the manufacture of clothes, however. Wool and linen—natural fabrics—were commonly used in ancient civilizations, but cotton was either unknown or rare. Dyes and woven designs might adorn clothes, but there were not myriads of clothes shapes and patterns, as there are today. Rather than creating items with many seams, both men and women tended to rely on large pieces of cloth that could be wrapped around the body and tied or held with pins or brooches. Cloth could be draped to create decorative folds and pleats—even pockets to carry accessories. The fact that the clothing of men and women was sometimes quite similar also suggests that practicality and ease of manufacture were concerns.

Aesthetics were also an issue in all these civilizations, as shown by the ubiquity of dyed and patterned cloth and the attention to pleats and folds, but the proper purpose of clothing varied, especially by gender. Whereas the clothes of Egyptian women were sometimes form-fitting and sheer, respectable Greek and Roman women were required to show modesty by wearing clothes that concealed the body's contours and covered them thoroughly. Inhabitants of hot climates such as Nubia or Australia often wore only minimal clothing.

Although many went barefoot in the ancient world, the most common footwear were sandals or leather boots.

One currently omnipresent item of clothing in the Western world that was noticeably absent from the ancient Mediterranean societies is pants. Ancient Egyptians, Nubians, Greeks, and Romans did not wear them, and indeed pants were seen as a mark of the uncivilized barbarian. Therefore, more modern notions of gendered clothing did not apply; men wore kilts or robes rather than trousers.

Whereas today the mass production of clothes allows for a huge variety of fabric types, weaves, and patterns, the limitations upon clothing in the ancient world remind us that people had to make their own clothes. The ability to weave and sew was seen as an indispensable skill for Greek and Roman women, and even the emperor Augustus required that his wife and daughter should apply themselves to making the household's clothing.

~Gregory S. Aldrete

MESOPOTAMIA

Clothing was worn throughout western Asia for modesty and for protection against the elements. The main sources of information have been sculptures, bas-reliefs, and cylinder seals. Unfortunately, their colors are no longer visible. The first information about clothing and grooming appeared at the end of the fourth millennium B.C.E. with the advent of sculpture and writing, where rich and powerful men were usually depicted more often than women and children.

We do not know much about clothing before the development of sculpture and writing, circa 3300 B.C.E. Before the invention of textiles, sheepskins, goatskins, and fleeces were worn, as depicted in Sumerian cultic art. Sheep were sheared or plucked for their wool. Goat's hair was also used. Men wore a belted sheepskin, which hung down above the ankles. Women wore a toga-like garment, sometimes secured by a pin from which hung a string of beads or a seal.

The materials used to make clothing were the same throughout the ancient world. Although leather was used in early times, the most common material for clothing was wool. Linen was used for better garments or for clothing for priests and statues of the gods. Felt made of low-quality wool or goat hair was used for shoes, linings, and cushions. Cotton for clothing did not become available until Sennacherib introduced it into Assyria about 700 B.C.E. Silk was introduced later. There is evidence that the warp-weighted vertical loom, which could produce a tapestry weave, was in use by the third millennium B.C.E.

The manufacture of textiles became a major industry. Letters from numerous sites of the eighteenth century B.C.E., particularly from Mari, have provided information about the use of dyes, reversible fabrics, and clothes stitched with appliqués, tiny beads, or embroidery. The famous dye produced from Maoris shells, called Tyrian purple, was produced before 1200 B.C.E. at Ugarit, where piles of shells were found.

MATERIAL LIFE

CLOTHING

Mesopotamia

Egypt

Greece

Rome

Nubia

Australian Aboriginals

At the royal tombs at Nimrud (eighth century B.C.E.), gold appliqués have been discovered. Textiles were traded and given as royal gifts.

In the Old Akkadian period (ca. 2330–2193 B.C.E.), male fashions changed; instead of being bare from the waist up, men began to wear robes draped over one shoulder. Pleated and draped material was used for robes and men's kilts. Waterproof sheepskins were replaced by wool textiles in soft folds, with intricately knotted fringes at the hems and edges. In mountainous regions, men wore shoes with upturned toes. Women's fashions also began to change. Although they continued to wear a toga-like garment wrapped around the body, the material was sometimes draped over both shoulders to form a V-shaped neckline. Short-sleeved dresses, some with rounded necklines, were introduced. During the Neo-Sumerian and Old Babylonian periods (1900–1595 B.C.E.), styles for men and women remained the same, with minor variations. Men continued to wear robes, but the ends and hems of their garments became more elaborate. The fringes of robes were sometimes impressed on contracts in place of a seal. From about 1400 B.C.E. on, both Assyrian men and women wore fringed bolts of cloth wrapped around the body and held in place by a belt, with the long, tasseled ends hanging down between the wearer's legs. Kilts were also worn, sometimes under robes.

By the first millennium B.C.E., fashions had changed again. Assyria has provided two sources of information about clothing. The main source comes from art objects, such as sculptures, bas-reliefs, plaques, carved ivories, and cylinder seals. Lexical texts also cataloged many words relating to clothing. The texts list many different qualities of textiles, from cheap materials for servants to those worn by royalty.

Men wore a tunic or several fitted tunics; these garments were short-sleeved and belted at the waist and covered men from their necks to their knees. Sometimes the upper part of the tunic had straps running diagonally from each shoulder and crossing the chest. People of higher status, such as officials and military officers, added a cloak to this outfit. The cloak was usually made of wool, or sometimes linen, in blue, red, purple, and white. There was an overgarment apart from the cloak, which had no armholes and was put on over the neck.

The Assyrians were usually barefoot, even when they went to war. When they wore footwear, they usually wore sandals with a wedge heel and straps over the top of the foot and around the big toe. Sometimes more elaborate footwear was depicted, such as calf-length boots (worn by hunters or warriors) or shoes covering the whole foot. We know less about women's footwear, although Assurbanipal's queen was shown wearing a kind of slipper, covering the front half of the foot.

Prisoners of war were often naked. The Assyrians stripped whole groups of the population during campaigns. One text describes a conquered population as so impoverished that they wore garments made of papyrus, the ancient equivalent of paper.

With the fall of Babylon to the Persian king Cyrus (539 B.C.E.), the people of western Asia wore the fashion of the conquerors—a clothing tradition based on pants (Nemet-Nejat, 153–55).

FOR MORE INFORMATION

Contenau, G. *Everyday Life in Babylon and Assyria.* Translated by K. R. Maxwell-Hyslop and
A. R. Maxwell-Hyslop. New York: St. Martin's Press, 1954.

Nemet-Nejat, K. R. *Daily Life in Ancient Mesopotamia.* Westport, Conn.: Greenwood Press,
1998.

Saggs, H. W. F. *Civilization before Greece and Rome.* New Haven, Conn.: Yale University Press,
1989.

EGYPT

What did an Egyptian man wear under his kilt or an Egyptian woman under her dress? Probably nothing. Garments designed for modesty would have to wait for people more obsessed with sex than the ancient Egyptians, who were practical to the point of working naked in hot, swampy terrain. Yet they loved clothes. A New Kingdom architect's tomb contained 17 sleeveless tunics, 26 shirts, and 50 triangular loincloths to assure his fashionable appearance in the Next World (Watson, 20). The loincloths, simple linen triangles with strings at two corners, were worn by draping the point down the back and tying the strings around the waist before pulling the point through the legs to tuck in the string at the front. Most likely, no additional layers covered them since similar loincloths are pictured as the sole attire of other workers.

Of course, loincloths represented the low end of the Egyptian wardrobe. When attired for formal occasions, Egyptians could outdress anyone with lovely, elegant gowns worn by both genders—the original unisex clothing. White—the whiter the better—was the color of choice in most eras; color was supplied by numerous accessories. In art, dresses fit close to the body. Heads were adorned, and cosmetics generously painted the faces of both women and men. As in every other culture, differences in style proclaimed differences in social status.

Fine linen remained the most-used fabric throughout all the eras of ancient Egypt. Because it "breathes," linen worked well in the warm Egyptian climate where insulation was seldom needed, and it could be loosely woven into a gauze that allowed air to circulate around the skin. In addition to being cool, it was strong and glowed with an attractive sheen. Cotton did not arrive in Egypt until Roman times. Wool clothing existed, but because it was forbidden in temples and tombs and because most surviving clothing comes from burials, actual articles of wool material are rare. (One requirement for priests was that all their hair had to be shaved. Perhaps wool was forbidden in temples because it was regarded as a kind of hair.)

Clothing manufacture constituted a cottage industry in which, after women had spun, woven, and sewn enough clothing for their families, they bartered any surplus for supplies. Tomb paintings and miniature models also depict men sewing and weaving in workshops with two or more looms, as would have been the case on a large estate with many people to dress, at a temple with its groups of priests, or especially, at the royal court.

The simplest, most common clothing for males was the Egyptian kilt, a rectangular piece of fabric that was wrapped tightly around the waist and then tied in the front with cords or belted. It extended from the waist to just above the knee. One end was wrapped over the other, but the front of the fabric, where the ends crossed, was still loose enough to permit the legs to move in a normal stride. Sometimes the bottom end of the overlapping part of the fabric was cut away in a pleasing curve, or the fabric could be cut into an arc to produce a curved slit in front rather than overlapping all the way down. A special addition for this revealing front was first added by a pharaoh but worked its way down the governmental hierarchy over time: a tapering ribbed flap fell from the waist to show beneath the parted front curve of the kilt. Alternatively, one end of a wide sash could descend down the front of the kilt. Kilt fabric was also pleated to form regular vertical lines, another reason for favoring linen, but leather examples, both solid and cut into net, are known. Beginning in the New Kingdom, kilts grew long enough to reach mid-calf, becoming male skirts. The fabric was usually cut very full to form numerous gathered folds, although it was still cut close enough to the body to reveal its outlines.

Males, from pharaohs to farmers, wore simple kilts—as often as not with bare chests—when working, resting, or fighting. To dress up a little, or to fend off a late afternoon chill, a shirt—either a short-sleeved jersey or a shoulder-strapped band around the chest—was added. A stole of fabric might be also thrown over the shoulders to cross the chest. One peculiar kilt variation featured a stiffly starched front that stood out a foot or more in an inverted "v." Of course this projection would have interfered with physical labor, which was the whole point: to demonstrate that the wearer was an overseer or a scribe who never needed to work up a sweat. A similar principle led overseers and government officials to don the long skirt style—demonstrably less practical for vigorous work than its shorter relative. Kilts did, however, even show up at formal evening occasions, but these were covered by an ankle-length overskirt of diaphanous linen and topped by a shirt.

The most common woman's attire was a sheath held up by shoulder straps, a long, narrow dress that began at the ankles and rose to just under the breasts. Often a band of contrasting material bordered the top, or the top was sashed. This almost bare-breasted version sometimes substituted wider straps that covered the breasts more completely. A longer version enveloped the whole body, like a tunic, leaving sleeveless armholes and a slightly scooped neck. Still another version added short sleeves to a tied keyhole neck. In every case, however, the apparel followed the shape of the body and reached down the leg to the ankles. These democratic dresses were worn both by the lady of the house and by her female servants.

At banquets, however, the lady of the house would never be mistaken for a servant, although she might be confused with the man of the house, for both males and females wore the same sort of fine dress, something very like the saris still worn in parts of India. The fabric consisted of nothing but a rectangle, four times as long as its width, with the manner of draping creating the garment. One corner of the rectangle was tucked into a waist cord at the

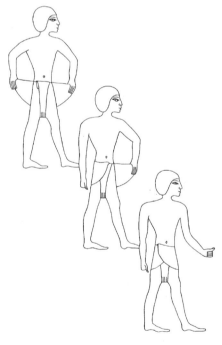

Diagram of the procedure by which Egyptian men wrapped a kilt around themselves. Such simple attire was widely worn by all classes of society because of the hot climate. Drawing by Rivka Rago.

side, and the whole fabric was wrapped completely around the waist once. Next, pleats were formed by tucking the fabric judiciously into the waist cord. The fabric was wrapped around the back again before returning to the front where it was tossed first under the far shoulder then over the other shoulder from behind. With the free end now falling down the front, it was tossed over the shoulder it had previously gone under, brought back under the other arm and finally tied in the front to the fabric's other end, the one previously tucked into the waist cord. Overall, it appeared that a shawl had been tied around the hips over an underskirt, while another shawl with a peak training down the back had been thrown over the shoulders, covering one arm to the elbow but leaving the other arm half bare. Attention would be drawn to the waist, where all the wrapping came together at the tied ends of the fabric, from which lovely folds fell to the ankles.

Variations of draping produced different looks. Instead of going under the far arm from the front, the fabric could be thrown under that arm from the back, then over the other shoulder from the front, around the back to return over the first shoulder and tie at the waist. This produced a garment that covered both arms equally to the elbow, with less emphasis on the waist. Another variation sent the fabric under the near arm from the front and over the opposite shoulder from the rear, leaving half the chest bare.

In addition to sheath and sarilike apparel, a third kind of dress, mainly but not solely for women, used two separate rectangles of fabric. One piece was about seven feet long, the other two-thirds that length; both were twice as long as their widths. Together they formed a skirt-and-shawl ensemble. The larger piece was gathered at the waist to form the skirt, and the shorter piece was thrown around the back of the shoulders while the ends were gathered together and tied at mid-chest. Less closely following the outline of the figure, this outfit often consisted of material so finely woven that the body's outline could be seen through it. A common variation en-larged the shawl into a cape. In the case of this larger second piece, the skirt too would be longer and fuller, and, rather than gathering such a large skirt at the waist, its top would be grasped at each side to form ends that could be knotted beneath the breasts. This created folds outlining the hips and waist. The cape was pulled over the shoulders and tied together with the skirt, which thereby covered both arms to the elbows and formed what looked like a single garment.

A fourth style of dress consisted of a full-length envelope of fabric, more suited to men than women. A five-foot-high by seven- or eight-foot-wide rectangle was sewn together along the short ends, forming a doubled piece of cloth. The top was sewn straight across. A scoop was then cut in the top center for the head, and slits were made at the top of both sides for the arms. This left the only large opening at the bottom, so the dress would be pulled down over the head until the head and arms stuck through their appropriate holes. It formed a very full robe, similar to a choir gown of today, but it was seldom worn in this simple manner. It was usually pulled to the body by slitting the sides so the front half could be pulled to the back and pinned at the waist, while the back half was drawn around to the front and secured with a sash. The sash was wide enough to drape the back from the waist to the bottom of the buttocks and long enough to wrap twice around the body, tie in the front, and still leave an end long enough to fall to the top of the feet. When a woman wore this type of dress, the back unsewn half was hand gathered into ends that could be tied at the waist; the front half simply fell in multiple folds. As a variation, instead of tying the back together, a sash narrower than the male version could circle the body just below the breasts and secure the back flap across the hips.

Despite their abundant folds and turns of fabric, Egyptians often dressed up what was already elaborate by adding colorful waist sashes, which dangled in the front to mid-thigh. The sash could be a simple ornamental cord, strands of colorful beads, or a solid piece of patterned fabric. Its end might be further embellished with religious symbols, such as the cow face of the goddess Hathor, or by secular motifs, such as lotus flowers. Sometimes the simple strapped tunic worn by most women was dressed up by a web of bead netting worn as an overdress. At other times, beads or buttons (never used to close openings) were sewn to the dress in patterns.

Of course, pharaohs as well as certain government officials wore special attire to indicate their rank. In addition to distinctive crowns, a bull's tail descending from the waist in the back of a kilt could be worn only by the king. Originally, the pharaoh alone was permitted to sling a leopard skin—complete with its head—over his shoulder, but that emblem was later adopted by his highest official and finally by high priests. All priests wore distinctive garb: a simple robe of white linen that fell full to the ground, clearly distinguished from the form-fitting clothing of the laity. This outfit was also adopted by high officials, who often held priestly status in addition to their government positions. Children wore nothing at all until they were old enough to walk under their own guidance; then both sexes wore a simple kilt until eight years old or so, when they donned the same apparel as the adult of their sex.

No outfit would be complete without shoes or, in the Egyptian case, sandals. Their design was so practical that they are still worn today throughout most of the world. To a foot-shaped sole, a thong was attached where the big toe and its neighbor come together. Another strip was anchored to the sole's sides about two-thirds of the way back. The wearer slipped his foot into the sandal, inching along until the front thong worked its way between his toes and the rear strip gripped the foot in front of the ankles. Such sandals, made of either rushes or leather, were produced in quantity for both genders. Those made of rushes were frequently padded for comfort. Sometimes a third strip joined the toe strap to the ankle strap which fixed their positions and made stepping into the sandal easier. The ankle strap could also be widened so it would not cut the flesh. Occasionally, another crossing strap was added between the front of the sandal and the ankle strap to form an almost-shoe; a heel strap might be sewn on as well (Brier and Hobbs, 117–30).

FOR MORE INFORMATION

Brier, B., and H. Hobbs. *Daily Life of the Ancient Egyptians*. Westport, Conn.: Greenwood Press, 1999.

Houston, M., and F. Hornblower. *Ancient Egyptian, Assyrian, and Persian Costumes*. London: A. and C. Black, 1920.

Watson, P. J. *Costume of Ancient Egypt*. New York: Chelsea House, 1987.

GREECE

Judged by modern standards, Greek clothes were uniform and utilitarian in the extreme. It was virtually impossible to make a fashion statement by adopting an exotic or provocative style of dress, although the wealthy aristocrat Alcibiades was distinguished by special shoes that were named for him and a purple robe (Athenaeus, *Professors at Dinner* 12.534c). Most clothing was made on the loom in the home, under the supervision of the mistress of the house. Almost every garment was rectangular in shape and required little stitching. Because very few items of Greek clothing have survived, our knowledge derives mostly from vase paintings and sculpture.

In earlier times, Athenian women wore a peplos, a long, heavy woolen garment that revealed little of the figure beneath. The peplos hung from the body, folded over at the top by about a quarter of its length. The turned-down material was attached to the shoulders by means of two long dress pins, and the garment was supported at the waist by a belt. Parts might be dyed purple or enlivened with woven geometric motifs. Embroidered decoration was, however, rare.

In the middle of the sixth century B.C.E., the peplos was replaced by a lighter and finer garment made of linen called the chiton. Because the chiton hugged the figure more tightly than the peplos, it was more revealing of the figure. Worn without any overfold, the chiton was held in place by a series of pins along the length of the arms. Whereas the peplos was sleeveless, the chiton had loose, elbow-length sleeves. It, too, was fastened around the waist by a belt.

The Athenians were of the opinion that the peplos was a Doric invention, whereas the chiton was Ionic. More likely, the change was a reflection of the increased wealth of the Athenians in the middle of the sixth century B.C.E., since linen, being more costly to produce than wool, had to be imported. As Herodotus reports, however, the Athenians gave a more sensational explanation for it. They claimed that after a disastrous defeat at the hands of the Aeginetans, only one Athenian managed to escape. When he returned with news of the disaster, the wives of the men who had died in the battle were so outraged by the fact that he alone had escaped, they stabbed him to death with the pins of their dresses, demanding as they did so what had befallen their husbands. Herodotus concludes:

So this man died but the Athenians thought that what the women had done was more terrible than the disaster itself. As they could find no way of punishing them, however, they made them change their dress to the Ionic style . . . which did not require any brooches. (*Histories*, 5.87)

Diagram of how a Greek woman wore typical garments, the peplos (left) and chiton (right). Originally in I. Jenkins and S. Bird, *Greek Dress.* London: British Museum Education Service. Courtesy of British Museum.

Bronze dress pins 18 inches in length have come to light in excavations. They would have been more than adequate for the task of stabbing. The peplos remained popular in other parts of Greece, however, especially in the wintertime for which it was ideally suited.

The simplest male attire was a short tunic rather less than knee-length. This *exômis*, which means "off the shoulder," was held in place by means of a brooch or knot tied at the shoulder. The *exômis* was worn by manual workers, including slaves. On formal occasions, however, men wore a chiton. Another popular garment was the himation, which was worn either over the chiton or without any undergarment. This was a rectangular piece of cloth that was generally wound over the left shoulder and under the right, with the surplus material hanging over the left forearm. There was, however, practically no limit to the different ways of attaching it to the body. Himations were often dyed and embroidered with a patterned border around the edge. In vase paintings and sculpture, those wearing himations are often depicted leaning on a stick, which suggests that it was favored by older men. Women also wore himations, usually draping them over the right shoulder and under the left arm in the same way as men. Over the course of time, the dress worn by Athenian men became simpler and less ornate. According to Thucydides, "The Spartans were the first to adopt a moderate costume, . . . and in other respects, too, the propertied class [of Athens] changed their way of life to correspond as closely as possible to that of ordinary men" (*The Peloponnesian War*, 1.6).

As an undergarment, men wore a loincloth known as a *perizôma*. A simple cloth band called a *strophion* served as a brassiere for women. Other accessories used by women include the fan or *rhipis*, a flat object with a wooden handle. Another was an umbrella, or *skiadon*, used as a shield against the sun rather than as a protection against the rain. Both men and women pulled up the fold of their himations to serve as a kind of hood. On their travels, men wore a flat, broad-brimmed hat made out of felt or straw, called a *petasos*, which they tied under the chin. When not in use, this often hung loose at the back of the neck. Workmen and slaves wore a conical cap called a *pilidion*. Women were less inclined to cover their heads than men, although in the Hellenistic period they are often depicted wearing a sunhat with a broad brim and a pointed crown.

The simplest form of footwear was the sandal. On long journeys, men wore short lace-up boots, turned over at the top. Fashionable women sometimes wore platform heels. In the home, both men and women usually went barefoot. All shoes and sandals were manufactured from leather (Garland, 64–65, 87–89).

FOR MORE INFORMATION

Garland, R. *Daily Life of the Ancient Greeks*. Westport, Conn.: Greenwood Press, 1998.
Symons, D. J. *Costume of Ancient Greece*. London: Batsford, 1987.

ROME

The Romans referred to themselves as the "people of the toga," and even today, the toga is closely identified with the Romans. It was not an everyday garment,

MATERIAL LIFE

CLOTHING

Mesopotamia

Egypt

Greece

Rome

Nubia

Australian Aboriginals

however, but was worn by citizens primarily on formal occasions. The toga was the mark of the citizen, and it was illegal for noncitizens to dress in it. A toga was made of heavy bleached wool and when unrolled was a large D-shaped piece of fabric approximately 18 feet long and 8 feet wide. This was wrapped around the wearer and over his arms in a complex fashion, with much of the excess fabric draped over the left shoulder. The toga developed over time from the republic to the empire, gradually becoming a bit larger, and with the method of folding becoming more ornate. By the early empire, the prescribed way of folding a toga included the creation of features known as the *sinus* and *umbo,* which could sometimes serve as pockets, or be pulled over the head like a hood. Beneath the toga, a belted tunic was worn.

Togas reflected the general Roman preoccupation with rank and status. The basic white toga of the citizen was called the *toga virilis.* Magistrates were entitled to wear a special toga with a purple stripe on it known as the *toga praetexta.* The width of the stripe further indicated a person's wealth and status; senators sported broad purple stripes called the *latus clavus,* whereas members of the equestrian class had to make do with thinner stripes known as the *clavus angustus.* Interestingly, male children of citizens wore miniature *toga praetextas* complete with the purple stripe.

Another type of specialized toga was the *toga candida,* a special extra-white toga that was only worn by candidates running for political office. It is from this term that our modern term *candidate* is derived. Finally, it is thought that victorious generals celebrating a triumph may have been allowed to wear an all-purple toga.

Although it was a distinctly Roman garment, the toga was by no means the only item of clothing available to the Romans. In casual everyday life, a tunic with short sleeves and extending to the knees was the standard item of clothing for Roman men, and it was widely worn by children and slaves as well. The tunics of equestrians and senators would also have carried the purple stripes. If it was raining or cold, the Romans made use of large cloaks called *lacerna* that could be thrown over the tunic or toga. Another variety of cloak was the *paenula,* which may have been a more close-fitting and waterproof variant.

Roman women were expected to dress modestly and to be largely covered up by their clothes. They wore a longer version of the tunic that reached down to their ankles and had longer sleeves as a first layer, but the stereotypical garb of the adult Roman woman was the *stola,* a full-length dress with multiple folds. Women's clothes were often dyed bright colors and were made of a variety of materials. A related garment derived from the Greeks was the peplos, which was similar to a tunic but with an extra fold of cloth over the top half of the body. When

Statue of the emperor Titus, providing a good example of a properly folded and arranged Roman toga of the imperial period. © Alinari/Art Resource, NY.

going out in public, aristocratic women donned an additional cloth covering called the *palla,* which was a large rectangular piece of cloth that could be wrapped around the body in a variety of ways.

What sort of undergarments the Romans wore is uncertain. They may well have worn nothing. Gladiators and athletes are sometimes shown in art wearing a kind of loincloth, and this may have been a variant of a standard undergarment.

Romans did not wear trousers or pants and in fact regarded the wearing of such with great disdain, as being the mark of a barbarian. This attitude caused considerable discomfort to Roman troops posted to the frigid northern provinces, and eventually these soldiers gave in to reality and began wearing leather pants.

For footwear, there was a wide range of leather boots and sandals from which to choose. The most famous Roman footwear was the *caligae*, the hobnailed boots issued to Roman soldiers.

~*Gregory S. Aldrete*

FOR MORE INFORMATION

Sebesta, J. L., and L. Bonfante, eds. *The World of Roman Costume*. Madison: University of Wisconsin Press, 1994.

MATERIAL LIFE
|
CLOTHING
|
Mesopotamia

Egypt

Greece

Rome

Nubia

Australian Aboriginals

NUBIA

Information about ancient Nubian fashions and personal adornment is derived from actual remains excavated in their tombs and from their representation in art, either in statues in the round or in reliefs or paintings from temples and tombs.

The first large corpus of Nubian clothing and jewelry comes from burials belonging to the A-Group culture (about 3700–2800 B.C.E.). They used leather obtained from their herds of domesticated animals, primarily cattle, which was then dyed and crafted into loincloths and phallus sheaths for the male members of society. We are ill informed about female fashion of the period. In addition, the Nubians painted their bodies. Jewelry for both sexes might include bracelets, anklets, and necklaces. The component elements of such jewelry were fashioned out of locally obtained stone, animal bones, and shells, as well as less commonly from ostrich egg shell and ivory from elephant tusks and hippopotamus teeth. More rare was the incorporation into this jewelry of faience, a glazed composition, in the form of beads, which were Egyptian imports.

These fashions continued to characterize the material culture of the Nubians of the C-Group (about 2300–1500 B.C.E.), whose leather garments for both sexes were more complex. They were still created primarily from leather but now were adorned with secondary materials such as bone and faience, arranged in geometric patterns.

In keeping with their acculturation to Egyptian norms, Nubians living in Egypt during the Old and Middle Kingdoms adopted local fashion. This meant kilts for men and sheaths for women that were woven from linen, in addition to multiple strands of beads in necklaces, bracelets, and Egyptian-style headbands. On occasion, economically advantaged Nubians were interred with deluxe jewelry, often of gold or semiprecious stones, the design of which incorporated common Egyptian elements. Throughout the subsequent epochs of their history, Nubians residing in Egypt or closely interacting with the administration of the land aped Egyptian fashion to such a degree that their own ethnic costumes and personal adornment were almost never depicted.

The costumes and jewelry of the Nubians of the Kerma culture (about 2500–1500 B.C.E.) reflect the opulence of other aspects of their material culture. Because this evidence is obtained primarily from their tombs, one must ask whether the fashion statements reflect daily life or are strictly religious in nature. The bodies were attired in either loincloths or long skirts, knotted at the level of the navel, with the upper body clothed in either a leather or linen garment. The upper garments of leather were adorned with either faience or shell beads finely sewn together. In exceptional cases, the deceased wore leather sandals, decorated with incised linear patterns. In some of the elite graves, ornaments carved out of mica as openwork, almost lacelike designs—often in the form of actual animals or mythological, composite beasts, primarily derived from the Egyptian pantheon—have been discovered near the head of the deceased. It has been suggested that these were sewn to caps or other articles of clothing that have not survived because of their fragile nature. These appliqués are probably funerary in nature because the beasts are apotropaic, affording the deceased metaphorical protection against all evils, real or imagined.

With the conquest of Egypt during Dynasty 25 (about 720–664 B.C.E.), specifically Nubian, as opposed to Egyptian, royal regalia begins to appear. It was primarily restricted to the costume of the Nubian pharaohs, but scholars are divided in their opinions about the physical appearance of some and the significance of most. At the top of the list is a distinctively Nubian headdress that emphasizes the round shape of the head. Identified by some as a closely cropped hair style and by others as a tightly fitting cap crown, resembling a swimming cap, this type of regalia is often depicted in both statues and two-dimensional representations of Nubian pharaohs. No actual examples are known, but the more persuasive arguments tend to suggest that one is dealing with a cap crown. This cap crown is often fronted by a double uraeus, or two cobras. A single cobra was the traditional emblem of protection on the brow of Egyptian pharaohs, but the duplication of such an emblem in the Nubian sphere is exceptional. As a result, some scholars regard this typically Nubian regalia as symbolic of Nubian suzerainty over both Egypt and Nubia, whereas others regard it as emblematic of the Kushite pharaoh's role as king of Upper and Lower Egypt. The final article of royal regalia is an open-ended lanyard worn around the neck, with each of the free ends resting on each side of the chest. The free ends and central loop around the neck feature pendants in the form of a ram's head. Depicted on statues in both stone and metal, this article of royal regalia is one of the few known from the ancient world that has survived in both gold and stone examples. The importance of the ram as a symbol of Amun both of Karnak in Egypt and of Gebel Barkal in Nubia is well attested in the Nubian record, so that the appearance of this royal lanyard can only be interpreted as placing the Nubian monarch under the protection of that god in his various manifestations.

As is to be expected, Nubian royals from the time of Dynasty 25 until the fall of the kingdom of Meroe in the fourth century C.E. wore typically Egyptian regalia in the form of crowns, scepters, necklaces, sandals, and the like. They are often depicted in typically Egyptian garments, such as the kilt for men or tightly fitting sheath for women. However, the relief decoration on the temples in Nubia also provides evidence for typically Nubian fashions, which were in vogue during the Napatan and particularly the Meroitic periods. The Nubian kings may be represented in the royal, Nubian three-piece costume, the most characteristic element of which is a shawl-like garment, often fringed, wrapped asymmetrically around the body with one free end hanging over the right leg and the other held in the right hand. Occasionally, both Nubian kings and queens are depicted with a tasseled cord tied to a belt, which was apparently first introduced during Dynasty 25. This article may allude to a primeval hunter-god worshiped by the earliest Nubians.

~Robert S. Bianchi

FOR MORE INFORMATION

Adams, W. *Nubia: Corridor to Africa*. Princeton, N.J.: Princeton University Press, 1977.

O'Connor, D. *Ancient Nubia: Egypt's Rival in Africa*. Philadelphia: University of Pennsylvania, 1993.

Trigger, B. *Nubia under the Pharaohs*. Boulder, Colo.: Westview Press, 1976.

Welsby, D. A. *The Kingdom of Kush: The Napatan and Meroitic Empires*. London: British Museum Press, 1996.

AUSTRALIAN ABORIGINALS

Australian Aborigines used a variety of natural materials for clothing and decoration. The form that these took varied considerably in different parts of Australia, according to the seasons, and between everyday and ceremonial attire. Neither native animals with fleeces nor native cottons were available, so clothing had to be fashioned from animal skins, string made from animal fur, and plant materials.

In northern and central Australia, tropical and desert conditions generally meant that little clothing was worn. In the cooler south, particularly in winter, kangaroo and possum skin coats, capes, and blankets were extensively used. These varied in complexity from simply wrapping a kangaroo skin around the waist or tossing it over the shoulders to wearing huge possum skin cloaks crafted from dozens of skins sewn together, decorated with incised designs, and colored with ochres. In the north and center, capes and aprons were usually woven from plant fibers of various kinds. String made from either bark fiber, animal fur, or human hair was used for waist-, arm-, and headbands and for sewing skins together using bone needles.

Skins (often used in conjunction with animal fat rubbed on the body to help preserve warmth) were a major factor in allowing Aboriginal people to occupy the mountains of the southeast and to survive in cold Tasmania. Animal skins must have been even more important during the colder conditions of the late Pleistocene period (25,000 years ago). People in tropical and desert regions may have simply worn a waistband, which was handy for keeping weapons and tools. A small "apron" might be suspended from the waistband for modesty or protection. In Cape York, the clothing was influenced by contact with Melanesian people and included full-size grass skirts.

Whereas clothing was mainly utilitarian (although the designs on the possum skin cloaks were significant), body decoration was symbolically important. In many areas, men in particular had cicatrices cut into the chest, arms, back, and face, which were incised with sharp implements and treated with materials to prevent fast healing. The result was rather like large tattoos, the pattern of which might indicate clan membership or status (for example, by showing that the person had completed an initiation ritual). Bodies were also painted with ochres, charcoal, and clay, creating complex designs for ceremonial performances. During such performances, costumes and headdresses, sometimes of a huge size, might also be worn. These were made from plant materials, feathers, and shells. There are rock-art pictures of people wearing enormous headdresses, skirts, and armbands, which demonstrate that some of these ceremonial clothing designs are at least many thousands of years old. Designs used in body decoration were similar to designs that have been found in rock art, carved on trees, in sand paintings, and on coffins. Different designs and the right to paint or wear them were owned by specific individuals or groups as a result of birth or kinship.

Shells, teeth, feathers, berries, bones, plant stems, and other objects were used in necklaces, and head-, wrist-, and armbands. Such ornamentation was worn for everyday as well as ceremonial use. Hundreds of tiny shells, each with a small hole drilled with a fine bone needle, could be strung on a fine string as a necklace. Kangaroo, possum, or carnivore teeth were also bored and strung on necklaces. Larger shells were used as pendants. Particularly sought after and valuable shells such as pearl shells were traded over great distances, especially to inland people. Necklaces and headbands that are thousands of years old have been found among the bones of their owners. There were various hairstyles, with the hair being colored or even plastered with clay and ochre. Bones were worn either pushed into piercings in the nasal septa or threaded into the hair.

To read about clothing in the early British colony in Australia, see the Australia entry in the sections "Male Clothing" and "Female Clothing" in chapter 5 ("Material Life") of volume 4 of this series.

~David Horton

FOR MORE INFORMATION

Berndt, R., and C. Berndt. *The World of the First Australians*. Canberra: Aboriginal Studies Press, 1988.

Bosworth, M. *Australian Lives: A History of Clothing, Food, and Domestic Technology*. Melbourne: Thomas Nelson, 1988.

Horton, D., ed. *The Encyclopedia of Aboriginal Australia*. Canberra: Aboriginal Studies Press, 2001.

Mulvaney, J., and J. Kamminga. *Prehistory of Australia*. Sydney: Allen and Unwin, 1999.

MATERIAL LIFE
|
APPEARANCE
|
Mesopotamia

Egypt

Greece

Rome

Appearance (Hair, Jewelry, and Makeup)

The limited clothing options in the ancient world were balanced by a corresponding creativity in personal adornment. In all these ancient civilizations, women paid much attention to hairstyle, cosmetics, and jewelry, and men also interested themselves in these to a greater or lesser degree. Mesopotamian and Egyptian men wore jewelry freely, and even stern Roman patriarchs wore rings and cloak clasps made from precious metals. More recent notions of effeminate appearance differ in some ways from masculine standards in antiquity; Egyptian men as well as women wore heavy makeup, much jewelry, and elaborate wigs, and long hair was common among Greek men of various periods. Perfume for both sexes was widely used, which is not surprising for a time before deodorants and personal hygiene products existed to eliminate bodily odors.

In ancient times, hair was styled using hot curling irons, stiffening agents such as wax, and even support frameworks on occasion; dyes and wigs were also prevalent. Hairstyles often function as a good indicator for dating sculptures and other artistic depictions of people. For example, the elaborate hairstyles of Roman women during the empire can be used to determine the date of a woman's portrait. The styling of men's facial hair can also be used, to a lesser extent, for dating. In addition, fashions varied among these cultures. Whereas Assyrian men wore full waved and curled beards and mustaches, Egyptian men were clean shaven; Greek men tended to wear beards and mustaches, but the Romans alternated between shaving and wearing beards, depending on the era.

Personal adornment was frequently used to indicate social status and role. Obviously, the amount and expense of the jewelry one wore revealed one's level of wealth, but the elaborateness of a woman's hairdo also told others that she had several slaves to style her hair and leisure time to devote to her appearance. On the other hand, female slaves in ancient Greece wore their hair short and up in nets because they devoted all their time to their mistress's appearance rather than their own. Profession and rank might also be reflected in one's attire. In Mesopotamia, priests, doctors, and slaves each had their own tell-tale hairstyles; Egyptian priests shaved their heads, and only the pharaoh wore a beard, albeit an artificial one; and slaves in ancient Greece were often clean shaven, as opposed to bearded freeborn men. In Egypt, hair even indicated one's level of maturity; children sported a side lock of hair up until puberty.

In addition to functioning as ornaments, jewelry often served a practical purpose. In Mesopotamia, men wore cylinder seals, which they used to sign documents, as necklaces, and Greek and Roman men wore signet rings for the same purpose. In all these societies, amulets and charms invested the wearer with magical protection from danger and diseases. Amulets depicting different gods or symbols could be used to protect against corresponding dangers—thus a fish-shaped amulet would be worn to prevent an Egyptian child from drowning, whereas a hippopotamus (symbolizing the hippo-headed goddess of childbirth) was the appropriate charm for a pregnant woman.

Personal adornments in the ancient world were never just a matter of personal taste, style, and fashion. They also served the practical functions of revealing social status, role, and identity and of protecting and preserving oneself from the vicissitudes of an uncertain world.

~*Gregory S. Aldrete*

MESOPOTAMIA

MATERIAL LIFE
|
APPEARANCE
|
Mesopotamia

Egypt

Greece

Rome

Men in Mesopotamia were usually shaved bald, but some wore their hair longer. During the Early Dynastic period (2900–2350 B.C.E.), women's hairstyles and headdresses showed great variety. The hair was worn long, but it was elaborately plaited and piled on top of the head, held in place either by a net or a scarf, or covered with a pleated headdress. Women also wore jewelry in their hair.

Excavations at the Royal Cemetery at Ur, circa 2600 B.C.E., have shown women wearing strands of gold willow leaves with beads of lapis lazuli, carnelian, and gold in their hair. Their hair nets were of gold ribbon and their hairpins silver, with large blue (lapis lazuli) and red (limestone) flowers. Also, the women wore gold and silver hair ribbons. These elaborate hairstyles may have affected the men's hairdos. A gold helmet from the Royal Cemetery was decorated with a thick metal braid wrapped around the head and coiled in a chignon at the nape of the neck. This was the hairstyle of royalty and was later worn by King Sargon.

In the Old Akkadian period, men were either shaved bald or wore their hair and beards meticulously waved. Women's hair was styled into a large chignon from the top of the head to the beginning of the neck. Women also used hairbands, hair nets, and hairpins made of bone, copper, silver, or gold. During the Neo-Sumerian and Old Babylonian periods, both men and women continued to style their hair as before.

In Assyrian reliefs, men are depicted with a full beard and mustache, waved and curled at the ends. Priests, doctors, and slaves wore distinctive hairstyles. Graying hair was treated by a lotion and an incantation. Gods, royalty, soldiers, and religious personnel wore headdresses associated with their status or ceremonial functions.

Objects made of gems and precious metals were used as decoration in life and at death. Jewelry was worn by men, women, and children and even decorated the garments of divine images and statues. Artistic representations show us how jewelry was worn at different times, as well as the styles and who wore them. Also, Sumerian and Akkadian texts have provided abundant information on jewelry and jewelers' workshops. Jewelry was exchanged as gifts between rulers, provided as wedding gifts and inheritances, and included in dowries. Tablets have also recorded precious metals (but rarely jewelry) taken as booty during military campaigns.

Perhaps the most important source of information on Mesopotamian jewelry is the Royal Cemetery of Ur. Here, hundreds of burials, mostly dating to the Early Dynastic period (2900–2350 B.C.E.), were unearthed by Sir Leonard Woolley in the

1920s and 1930s. A group of 16 tombs contained a lavish display of jewelry, weapons, and vessels made of precious metals, musical instruments, and other decorative art objects. Some of the most impressive objects were the contents of the undisturbed tomb of "Queen" Puabi. Next to Puabi's body was a lapis lazuli beaded crown with gold figures of animals, fruits, and flowers. Necklaces made from beads of gold, silver, lapis lazuli, carnelian, and agate were strung in close-fitting collar necklaces. Gold, silver, and copper pins with heads of lapis or carnelian were used to fasten clothing. All of the women at the Royal Cemetery of Ur wore crescent-shaped earrings.

Gold choker, necklace, and earrings from the Royal Cemetery at Ur. © Copyright The British Museum.

The representational arts show an increase in the amount of jewelry worn by both men and women from the Akkadian period on, particularly strings of beads and bangles worn at the wrists. By the end of the third millennium B.C.E., women wore multistrand heavy necklaces with long counterweights hanging down their backs to counterbalance the necklace.

The archaeological record for the second millennium B.C.E. has provided few examples of jewelry. Three royal tombs were found in the Northwest Palace, built by Assurnasirpal II (883–859 B.C.E.) at his new capital of Nimrud. One tomb held hundreds of pieces of gold jewelry, including a gold crown with medallions inlaid with agate "eye beads" (against the "evil eye") and cloisonné scenes executed with precious and semiprecious stones.

In Assyria, both men and women wore jewelry, such as earrings, amulets, cylinder seals, and bracelets. The ancients, like people today, passed jewelry down through the generations. Women wore ankle bracelets, a practice still surviving among peasant women in Iraq.

We know little about Neo-Babylonian jewelry, although texts refer to jewelers and goldsmiths associated with the Eanna temple in Uruk, and the house of a bead maker was discovered in Babylon.

Jewelry, including earrings, beads, pendants, bracelets, and anklets, was found in private homes together with toiletries, such as pots of unguents for the body and hair, mussel shells containing kohl (blue eye shadow), combs made from wood or ivory, and tweezers and mirrors of copper, silver, and even gold. The mirrors were usually made of highly polished bronze, which provided a reflecting surface.

The evidence for cosmetics is meager. Women used cosmetics, both for their eyes and their complexion. White, red, yellow, blue, green, and black pigments were found in cockle shells in tombs in the Royal Cemetery at Ur. Some texts refer to cosmetics, but these texts are very difficult to interpret. The base of eye cosmetics was antimony paste, which was applied with a carved ivory pin. Rouge was mentioned in a synonym list; in Sumerian it translates as "gold paste," and in Akkadian as "red pigment of the face."

Aromatic substances became a major industry in Mesopotamia; they were used for medicine, magic, ritual, and cosmetics. Women played a major role in the manufacture of perfumes. In fact, a woman is listed as the author of a series of recipes for making perfumes. Aromatic plants were steeped and simmered in water for several days, put in oil, and then skimmed (Nemet-Nejat, 155–57).

FOR MORE INFORMATION

Contenau, G. *Everyday Life in Babylon and Assyria.* Translated by K. R. Maxwell-Hyslop and A. R. Maxwell-Hyslop. New York: St. Martin's Press, 1954.

Nemet-Nejat, K. R. *Daily Life in Ancient Mesopotamia.* Westport, Conn.: Greenwood Press, 1998.

Saggs, H. W. F. *Civilization before Greece and Rome.* New Haven, Conn.: Yale University Press, 1989.

EGYPT

MATERIAL LIFE

APPEARANCE

Mesopotamia

Egypt

Greece

Rome

Colorful accents for the Egyptians' white attire took the form of abundant jewelry for both sexes. Necklaces, bracelets, armbands, ankle bands, earrings, and finger rings were worn generously by both men and women. So enamored were the Egyptians of their jewelry that even colorful dresses were dressed up by heaps of baubles, which increased in amount and complexity as the centuries passed.

Although earrings were unknown to Egyptians until they saw them on the Hyksos during the Second Intermediate period, it was love at first sight, and both women and men wore them from then on. Two types were common: rings and studs—each was attached through a hole in the earlobe. Even statues sculpted without earrings generally portrayed this hole. The ring style was usually made of metal; gold was common. Ranging from thin wires to hollow tubes three-quarters of an inch in diameter, these circles left a gap for insertion. In some cases, gold foil covered a baser metal to lend a gold look. Earrings were also carved from shell, bone, carnelian, and red jasper or were molded of faience, and they might be inlaid with turquoise or lapis lazuli. Ear studs were mushroom shaped, with only the flat end showing through the front of the ear so the bulbous stem could hold them in place through the lobe. Faience examples are common, although gold, either solid or as gilt, is also known. Examples from Tutankhamen's tomb show that intricate pendants might be hung from them as well. An unusual type of earring consisted of metal coils with several twists that dangled from the ear. Ear plugs also surface from time to time, and female mummies sometimes exhibit the dangling lobe holes caused by such large insertions. When it came to jewelry for their necks, Egyptians threw subtlety to the wind. They wore anything from chokers to single-strand necklaces to multiple strands to pectorals to pendants and broad collars up to 10 inches wide. Besides their decorative function, necklaces served amuletic and status purposes. Both sheet gold in the shape of flies—military symbols for Egyptians—strung on bead strands and heavy gold circle chains were awards for special service to the country and proudly worn by the recipient. Amulets in the shape of one god or another filled the numerous rows of necklaces. A string of hippopotamus charms, symbolizing the pregnant hippopotamus goddess Tauret, might be worn by a pregnant woman to call for protection from this goddess of childbirth. Metal, faience, or stone shaped like oyster shells ensured health, as did figures of the dwarf god Bes. Cowrie shells, either the real thing or carved facsimiles, warded off the evil eye. Young children often wore a fish amulet as protection against drowning. Indeed, 50 or more different emblems protected against as many misfortunes.

The most characteristic Egyptian neckpiece was the broad collar. This consisted of multiple strands of beads, tubes, or amuletic figures that terminated in solid ends anchoring the strands. Ties emanated from the end pieces to knot around the back of the neck, forming a collar that covered much of the chest and extended over the shoulders. Because the collar could be weighty, a counterpoise generally trailed down the back to balance and hold the piece in place. Smaller chokers formed of several bead strands tied tightly around the neck enjoyed great popularity with women in the Old Kingdom, although they fell from favor thereafter, to be replaced by looser neckwear. A single strand dangling an amulet or colorful stone was popular during the earliest times. Gradually, elements were added until the strand was covered, and several strands of different lengths could be worn at once to create the necklace of one's desire. Pendants, a single amulet hanging at the end of a cord, evolved from the New Kingdom on into pectorals to decorate the mid-chest. Pendants could be rectangular plaques telling a little story, such as a scarab holding the sun in its front paws flanked by two kneeling, worshiping gods beneath a cornice suggesting a temple, or they could be massive breastplates shaped like a falcon, a vulture or a ba-bird, the symbol of the soul. Some of the finest jewelers' work in gold and inlays was invested in such pieces, which frequently hung beneath a broad collar.

The limbs were not forgotten. Beginning in the New Kingdom, broad bands circled the biceps above bracelets ringing the wrist. Such bracelets consisted of flexible strands of beads or, more common later, rigid bands. Whether they were of rows of beads, carnelian or other stones, or bands of bronze or gold, perhaps with inlays, they added flashes of color. Originally, bead strands were simply tied to the arm, but later the ends were fixed to clasps that snapped together. The other rigid type was hinged on two sides, one of which was held by a pin that could be drawn out to remove the band. Ankles as well were circled by bands of similar construction.

A wealthy man or woman fully encased in finery would bear several pounds of jewelry.

Not one but multiple finger rings—made of stone, faience, or metal—added to the decorative scheme. If of faience or stone, they would be pierced through and attached to a metal ring or first encased in a bezel. The idea behind both methods was to allow the center piece to turn over, revealing its back. The most popular ring shape was the sacred scarab beetle, which symbolized existence to the Egyptians. Thus, the wearer's name might be inscribed on the base to symbolically wish the owner long life. Alternatively, a god or the pharaoh (a living god) might be inscribed on the base, with a request that he or she preserve the wearer. Because hard stones were difficult to carve, the most commonly used material was soft steatite, a grayish white stone glazed in blue or green. Rings were also frequently made of faience, which, although easily molded into complex shapes, broke if struck. It may be that these fragile rings were party favors, such as wedding gifts from a newly married couple to their guests.

The waist was also adorned—a woman's girded by draped strings of beads or amulets, and a man's cinched by a close fitting belt. Needless to say, a wealthy man or woman fully encased in finery would bear several pounds of jewelry.

Even with every other part of the body adorned, hair was not forgotten. Egyptians devised complex cuts, wigs, ribbons, fillets, and diadems to dress their hair up to the standards of the rest of their attire. There were several hairdos for men. Workmen wore short hair left in bangs across the forehead, then shaped to the head halfway down the neck. This produced a rounded look. Early depictions also show tight curls, but straight hair is portrayed as a norm later. In an alternative cut for men, the back was clipped straight across and the hair was pushed behind the ears, framing the head and lengthening the face. This could be combined with a ladder cut to create three or four horizontal rows. This square cut grew more complicated in the New Kingdom, when the back fell to shoulder length, sometimes including tight curls, or perhaps plaits, that ran the length of the hair. About the same time, a new cut came into vogue, angling from the nape of the neck to a longer front that spilled to just below the shoulder.

Women always wore their hair longer than men—at least to their shoulders, but generally trailing a foot or more down their backs. Bangs and a center part were popular, in both cases with the hair lining the face over the ears, instead of behind the ears as a man would wear it. The ends were cut in a straight line. As with men, fancy ladder cuts creating horizontal rows were often seen, but curling in tight spirals, or perhaps thin plaits, was also common through all eras.

Children before the age of puberty wore a distinctive cut. All the hair of male children was shaved on one side and in back leaving only one long side lock reaching below the shoulder. Female children's hair was cut to a mid-neck length except for the same side lock that fell below the shoulder—the Egyptian sign of childhood. These side locks were sometimes braided into three or so large strands twisted together.

Serious hair decoration called for complex wigs, although Egyptians did not try to fool anyone into thinking the wigs were their own hair. Statues often show a line of natural hair peeking out below a wig. Because owners of statues had the last word about how they were portrayed, they must have been proud of their wigs, suggesting that they were expensive, prized articles. Wigs were composed of human hair which, in the case of a long wig, would represent as much as a decade's worth of growth on someone's head.

One unusual early female wig, shown on a Third Dynasty statue of Princess Nofret, consisted of a big head of bobbed hair cut straight all around and standing out a good three inches when it reached the bottom of the neck. In general, longer wigs extending at least to the shoulders were most common. One version consisted of 30 or more long, dangling coils of hair emanating from a central part and tied at the end. A variation separated the coils into two lappets, each tied with ribbon to form a large mass framing each side of the face. Long hair arranged into 10 or so ladder-cut rows counted as a second type. A third type combined the first two: rows of coils laddered into layers. Two wigs could also be worn together, for example, a shorter wavy wig over a longer coiled wig. Male wigs followed female styles except that they were shorter—shoulder length or a little more—and usually lacked the center part. Beeswax seems to have been the substance that kept the cuts and curls in place, both on wigs and natural hair. Patting an Egyptian head would have felt like rubbing a large, warm crayon.

Facial hair was all removed, with two exceptions. During the early Old Kingdom, numerous statues of men show thin mustaches seldom seen after that time. Pharaohs always wore beards on ceremonial occasions, but private citizens never did. Statues and paintings of pharaohs, however, invariably show lines running from the beard to the ears, clearly indicating the artificiality of the beard. Presumably, the beard recalled an early pharaoh who sported an actual growth, and the tradition persisted long after the style had gone out of general favor. The fake beards consisted of two varieties: one was woven coarsely to show horizontal rows; in the other, two tresses were braided together. Both versions consisted of five inches or more of beard that tipped forward at the end.

Hair and wigs were adorned in various ways. A simple ribbon around the head, often tied in a bow, sometimes with long ends trailing down the back, retained favor throughout all eras. This developed into a plain fillet, or circle, of leather or gold. The Middle Kingdom achieved a height of artistic excellence in hair ornamentation. One example, belonging to a princess named Khnumet, was an airy, openwork gold diadem of tiny flowers on almost invisible wires interspersed with six Maltese crosses, all accented by touches of lapis lazuli, turquoise and carnelian. The dainty flowers would have seemed to float through her hair. Simpler, but no less elegant, was a sheet-gold diadem of Princess Sithathoriunet that was ornamented with inlayed rosettes. A gold cobra rose from the front, two tall gold plumes rose in the back, and two pairs of gold "ribbons" trailed behind. Worn with this confection were hundreds of quarter-inch gold tubes that lined her long curled hair to complete an all-over golden look. The pharaoh also indulged in diadems, as indicated by a gold circlet from Tutankhamen's tomb with a rearing inlayed cobra in front flanked by a vulture head. Gold ribbons trail behind while ribbons on each side of the head end in rearing cobras. Probably the height of fantasy headgear was a Middle Kingdom example consisting of a gold plate worn on the top of the head. From it hung 25 long rows of overlapping rosettes, originally inlayed with carnelian, turquoise, and glass. Placed over the hair (or wig), it sent stream after stream of glittering rosettes cascading past the shoulders.

Egyptian males and females wore heavy makeup. Eyes of both sexes wore a surrounding thick line that trailed out to the temple, causing the eyes to stand out brightly. Originally, the favored color was green, thought to have health-giving properties, but black grew more common after the 18th Dynasty. Small sticks of wood, bone, or ivory were dipped into the jars and used as applicators for drawing the lines.

Women reddened their lips with a brush dipped in a paste of red ochre and fat. Although not certain, it seems from the bright red on the lips of some male statues that men followed this fashion as well. Rouge consisted of red ocher again, probably with fat to make it adhere, and was applied with a pad. It is likely that henna, used today in Egypt to color the palms of hands and soles of feet red, was employed by the ancient Egyptians to dye their nails.

Makeup must also be removed in some way. Because Egyptian cosmetics were composed of fat and would not wash off with water, Egyptians concocted a cleansing cream. Powdered limestone mixed with vegetable oils gently abraded away the makeup. Beautiful cases held stone or faience cosmetic jars in individual compartments. Such cases usually included space for that essential cosmetic aid, the mirror, which in Egypt always followed the same shape. The reflecting part consisted of a highly polished metal circle slightly flattened at top and bottom. A tang inserted into a holding handle, often of wood, sometimes of metal, ivory, faience, or even stone, usually modeled an object, such as a papyrus column. The Egyptian word for mirror literally translates as "see face," which states its purpose well.

> *Women reddened their lips with a brush dipped in a paste of red ochre and fat.*

Considering that Egyptian cosmetics used fat as their base, they must have quickly turned rancid, hence requiring something to mask the odor. Perfume formed an essential component of every woman's beauty collection; it was added to cosmetics and used on its own. Egyptian versions, however, differed from modern perfumes, whose alcohol bases aid the dispersion of the scent. Egyptians never learned to distill alcohol. Their method was to soak some fragrant material in fat or oil, which would absorb some of the odor, and then wring out the fragrant oil through a cloth, much as they did with the must of grapes. Analyses of ancient remains suggest that iris roots formed the fragrance of one perfume and balsam another, but other additives included cinnamon, cardamom, myrrh, honey, and even wine and the flowers of the henna bush, sometimes in complex mixtures.

In addition to smearing perfume on various body parts, women employed a special perfuming device at banquets and parties. A cone of fat impregnated with perfume was placed on their heads that, when melted slowly by body heat, released its aroma throughout the evening. In addition, incense would burn throughout a party to freshen the air. One famed incense was frankincense, a resin that seeps through the trunks of trees that grow only in southern Arabia and Somaliland. The other famous incense was myrrh, which served as a perfume as well. A resin, like frankincense, it grew only in the same areas. Both produced fragrant fumes at parties, and both sanctified idols in temples.

The problem of unwanted hair was solved, as in our day, by razors and tweezers. These appliances originally were made of copper, until harder bronze became the metal of choice when its secret arrived in Egypt after the Middle Kingdom. Razors resembled a modern surgical scalpel; tweezers were formed exactly the same way as our own. For the sake of the face, a whetstone to hone the razor's edge was a necessary accessory. Some leather and some wooden cases survive as for carrying all three hair-removal instruments. With the Egyptians' intense interest in hair, combs abounded. Rows of long teeth were carved from wood or ivory to create a comb that differs from the modern version only in that it was held vertically to achieve greater pulling power than our horizontal types (Brier and Hobbs, 130–41).

FOR MORE INFORMATION

Aldred, C. *Jewels of the Pharaohs*. New York: Praeger, 1971.

Brier, B., and H. Hobbs. *Daily Life of the Ancient Egyptians*. Westport, Conn.: Greenwood Press, 1999.

Watson, P. J. *Costume of Ancient Egypt*. New York: Chelsea House, 1987.

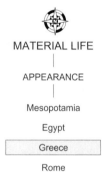

MATERIAL LIFE

APPEARANCE

Mesopotamia

Egypt

Greece

Rome

GREECE

Earrings, hairpins, necklaces (worn tight around the neck), bracelets, diadems, and rings were frequently worn by well-to-do women in ancient Greece. They were made out of a variety of materials, but the most common were gilt terra-cotta, copper, and lead. More expensive items were made of silver and gold, although it is noteworthy that few pieces of gold jewelry have survived from the Archaic period. In the Classical period, however, goldsmiths produced highly intricate work, using techniques such as filigree, granulation, and chasing. Infants were commonly provided with amulets to ward off evil. The only item of jewelry commonly worn by men was the signet ring, used to put a seal on private documents and merchandise. Expensive pieces were frequently buried with their owners.

Perfume was popular among both men and women. It was generally manufactured by boiling the petals of flowers. Guests at a symposium also liberally sprinkled themselves with perfume. A highly prized perfume container was the *alabastron*, so named because it was carved out of alabaster.

It was a sign of beauty in a woman to have a pale complexion, which is why women on vases are frequently depicted with whitened faces. Their paleness was a natural consequence of spending most of their time indoors. However, some women sought to enhance their natural appearance by applying makeup. They also applied round spots to their cheeks, and darkened their eyebrows with the soot produced by lamps. Eyes, eyelashes, and lips were also painted a variety of colors. Not everyone approved, however. In Xenophon's treatise *Household Management*, Ischomachos makes the following observation:

One day I noticed that my wife had put makeup on. She had rubbed white lead onto her face to make her complexion look paler than it really was and rouge onto her cheeks to make them look rosier than they really were, and she was wearing platform shoes to make her look taller than she really was. (9.19.2)

This drew the following stern lecture from Ischomachos:

You are to assume, my dear, that I do not prefer white paint and red dye to your real color, but just as the gods have made horses so as to give pleasure to horses, cows to cows, and sheep to sheep, so humans find the natural body most delightful. (9.19.7)

Ischomachos concludes his puritanical homily:

Mix flour, knead dough, and shake and fold the cloaks and the bedclothes. This will increase your appetite, improve your health, and add redness to your cheeks. (9.19.11)

Women arranged their hair in a variety of styles. Some plaited it in long tresses, others piled it up in the form of a bun either at the nape of the neck or on the top of the head. Athenian women only let their hair down—literally—on special occasions, notably at festivals and funerals. This gave them license to indulge in much freer behavior than was at other times permitted to them. Often, women bleached their hair or dyed it. Female slaves wore their hair short and covered it in a hairnet called a *kekryphalos*.

Freeborn men of all periods favored beards and moustaches, whereas slaves were often completely shaven. The Homeric heroes braided their hair and wore it long. This, too, is how men's hair is depicted in Archaic sculpture. In the Classical period, the Athenians cut their hair much shorter, whereas the Spartans remained conservative in their preference for long hair. Plutarch writes:

In wartime the Spartans relaxed the harshest aspects of their training and did not prevent young men from beautifying their hair and their armor and their clothing, happy to see them like horses prancing and neighing before competitions. For this reason men grew their hair long from adolescence onwards. Especially in times of danger they took care that it appeared glossy and well-combed, remembering a certain saying of Lycurgus concerning hair, that it made the handsome better-looking and the ugly more frightening (*Life of Lycurgus* 22.1)

(Garland, 89–91).

FOR MORE INFORMATION

Garland, R. *Daily Life of the Ancient Greeks*. Westport, Conn.: Greenwood Press, 1998.
Johnson, M. *Ancient Greek Dress*. Chicago: Argonaut, 1964.
Symons, D. J. *Costume of Ancient Greece*. London: Batsford, 1987.

ROME

MATERIAL LIFE
|
APPEARANCE
|
Mesopotamia

Egypt

Greece

Rome

While ordinary Roman women probably had little time or money to spend on personal ornamentation, wealthy Roman women devoted considerable effort to decorating themselves with elaborate hairstyles and thick makeup. Rich women probably had several slaves whose full-time job it was to arrange their mistress's hair. The hairstylists achieved these effects through the use of curling irons, mousselike stiffening agents, and various combs, pins, and fasteners. Roman sculpture records that various hairstyles were popular in different periods. A famous bust of a Flavian woman depicts her with an enormous fan of curls piled up on her head, probably affixed to a wood or wire underframe. In the second century C.E., a more severe hairstyle seems to have dominated, with hair piled into a tight bun or pulled back in plaits. Women also commonly dyed their hair; dying the hair red using henna seems to have been particularly popular. Experimenting with dyes was not without its risks, however. Ovid records the story of a dye job gone wrong, which resulted in a woman losing her hair (*Love Affairs* 1.14.1–46). Because few Italians naturally

Roman noblewoman of the late first century C.E. Her ornate hairstyle is typical of this period. Portrait busts of women can often be dated by the hairstyles. © The Art Archive/ Museo Capitolino Rome.

have blonde hair, blonde wigs were very fashionable. The sources for blonde wigs were German prisoners of war, and the hair of many Germans ultimately ended up on the heads of Roman women.

Roman women wore considerable makeup, starting with various foundations. Every woman had her own secret recipe that she would use; one that survives calls for a mixture of eggs, barley, ground antler, honey, lead, flowers, wheat, and crushed beans. To make the face whiter, women would apply powdered chalk or a lead-based white substance. Black would be used around the eyes, and red was applied to the lips and cheeks. Women could choose from a variety of powerful perfumes often made by some combination of flowers or herbs in an olive oil base.

Roman women also wore large amounts of jewelry in the form of rings, pins, necklaces, and earrings. Often, these earrings were very large and heavy and dangled from the ears in a succession of levels. Such jewelry was fashioned from gold and was studded with precious stones.

Roman men of the middle Republic to early empire were usually clean shaven. In the second century C.E., emperors such as Hadrian and Marcus Aurelius adopted beards, a fashion that seems to have trickled down to the average Roman man. Roman men wore rings as well, although sporting too many or too ostentatious rings was frowned upon.

Both sexes made use of a variety of metal clasps to hold their clothing together and to close their cloaks. These ranged from simple functional bronze fasteners to highly decorated and bejeweled brooches.

~Gregory S. Aldrete

FOR MORE INFORMATION

Houston, M. G. *Ancient Greek, Roman, and Byzantine Costume and Decoration.* 2nd ed. London: A. and C. Black, 1947.

Sebesta, J. L., and L. Bonfante, eds. *The World of Roman Costume.* Madison: University of Wisconsin Press, 1994.

NUBIA

The Nubians enjoyed access to gold, ivory, ebony, and gems, with which they made elegant jewelry. Because their styles were heavily influenced by the Egyptians to the north, see Egypt's entry in this section for the styles of jewelry that graced the people of this wealthy land.

MATERIAL LIFE: WEB SITES

http://www.library.yale.edu/judaica/exhibits/webarch/front/BabylonianCollection.html
http://www.ea.pvt.k12.pa.us/medant/
http://www.museum.upenn.edu/new/exhibits/online_exhibits/wine/wineintro.html
http://www.vroma.org/~bmcmanus/clothing.html
http://www.vroma.org/~bmcmanus/clothing2.html
http://www.nlm.nih.gov/hmd/greek/index.html

6

POLITICAL LIFE

The ancient Greek philosopher Aristotle (384–322 B.C.E.) claimed that humans are by definition political animals. By this he meant that an essential part of human life involves interacting in the public sphere with people who are not our intimate families. It is these relationships—along with their complex negotiations—that permit the development of cities, kingdoms, nations, and civilization itself. Throughout history, different cultures have developed different political systems to organize their lives, and all political systems are in constant states of change as they accommodate to the changing needs and interests of the populace. Political life involves two different spheres of influence: organizing the relationship among those within a political unit and negotiating the relations between different political entities (countries or tribes or kingdoms). However, at its basic level, all politics is about power—finding out who has it and who does not.

People create a political system first of all to assure themselves of internal peace and security. As the seventeenth-century political theorist Thomas Hobbes noted, without a strong authority, people's incessant struggle for power would result in a life that is "nasty, brutish, and short." This is why we want our power structures clear. Our political systems also clarify and solidify our loyalties and allegiances—nationalism has served as a sentiment that can unify people with diverse interests and backgrounds.

As people interact in ever-widening circles, our political life must negotiate the often-difficult relations with other kingdoms, countries, or empires. Diplomacy is the tool of our political life that is meant to smooth these interactions, and war is the breakdown of these negotiations. In war—which has unfortunately dominated so much of human history—we can often see the noblest and worst expressions of our human spirit. In war, we can also definitively see the struggle for power that marks our political life.

Modern maps depict neat boundaries delineating countries that are currently our primary political entities. The nation-state, however, did not always exist. Government began when people started to live in towns and villages and a leader of the group emerged and gained authority and power, ultimately becoming a source for settling disputes, making decisions, and handing down judgments. In this simple model, the seeds of monarchy can be discerned, and often monarchy was the first stage through which ancient civilizations moved. God-kings and absolute rulers in Egypt and Meso-

POLITICAL LIFE

SOCIAL STRUCTURE

GOVERNMENT

LAW

WARFARE

WEAPONS

potamia expanded their territories from cities into empires aided by warfare, intimidation, and the loyalty or fear of their subjects. For these cultures, this form of government was stable, and this political structure endured in these regions for thousands of years.

The city-state was also a common unit of government in the ancient world. Indeed, the modern word *politics* derives from the Greek term for city-state, *polis*. The city-states proved fertile ground for political experimentation, and from them arose new forms of government such as the oligarchy, democracy, and republic. The Athenian democracy and the Roman Republic have served as the models and inspiration for countless subsequent states, including the Florentine Republic of the Renaissance and the United States in the modern era.

For people to live harmoniously in groups, a set of rules to curb excesses and mediate disputes is necessary, and from this need grew the first law codes. One of the greatest legacies from the ancient world to subsequent history is the law. From basic law codes such as Hammurabi's in Babylon to the extraordinary sophistication of Justinian's Roman Code of Law, the judicial principles and legal codes that are still in use today were first developed in the ancient world.

Finally, the development of organized nations and city-states enabled warfare to be waged on a grand scale. While today peace is usually regarded as the normative state and wartime as an unusual one, this equation was often reversed in antiquity. For one 600-year stretch in Roman history, for example, there were only five brief periods during which Rome was not at war with someone. For Rome, as for many of these cultures, incessant warfare (or at least annual campaigning) was the norm. Nor were these conflicts on a small scale: armies could number in the hundreds of thousands and casualties in individual battles in the tens of thousands.

While in the realm of technology, there would be dramatic changes from the ancient world to today, in the field of politics, the basic permutations of government, law, and war were thoroughly developed and explored by the ancients, and subsequent history keeps repeating their experiences, not always wisely.

~*Joyce E. Salisbury and Gregory S. Aldrete*

FOR MORE INFORMATION

Ferrill, A. *The Origins of War: From the Stone Age to Alexander the Great*. London: Thames and Hudson, 1985.

Finley, M. I. *Democracy Ancient and Modern*. New Brunswick, N.J.: Rutgers University Press, 1973.

Maine, H. S. *Ancient Law*. 1864. Tucson: University of Arizona Press, 1986.

Van Evera, S. *Causes of War: Power and the Roots of Conflict*. Ithaca, N.Y.: Cornell University Press, 1999.

POLITICAL LIFE
|

Social Structure

People are social creatures who seem compelled to form into groups and then subgroups within those groups. The criteria for forming these groups vary from society to society, but wealth, class, age, language, rank, nationality, gender, occupation, race, status, mutual interests, and family are some of the more common factors that play into these divisions. In the ancient world, societies tended to stratify themselves into a very small number of extremely wealthy individuals who monopolized power and money, a vast majority of poor people who were primarily farmers or craftsmen, and a variable percentage of the populace who were in some form of slavery or economic bondage. With slight variations, this basic structure was found in Mesopotamia, Egypt, Nubia, Greece, and Rome. Perhaps the most rigid example of social stratification was found in India, where a formal caste system developed and one remained in the caste into which he or she was born.

All these societies either were monarchies or went through phases in which they were ruled by kings. During these periods, the top class tended to be composed of members of the royal family and their close associates. The style of monarchy that was practiced tended toward kings who were absolute rulers and who were not infrequently also believed to be divine or semidivine.

In the periods when Greece and Rome experimented with forms of democracy and republics, one of the most important distinctions that arose was between citizen and noncitizen. Citizenship was always restricted to adult men, and because women, slaves, and foreigners were by definition excluded, even the most radical democracies, such as that established in fifth-century B.C.E. Athens, only extended citizenship rights to a minority of people living within the state. Even in such instances, when power was supposedly shared among the citizens, real power and wealth still were usually concentrated in the hands of a few. This was the case, for example, with Rome's patrician families, who during the early Republic were the only people legally eligible to be elected to high political office.

Interestingly, while the inhabitants of the ancient world were keen to make economic and status distinctions among themselves, ethnic or racial divisions do not seem to have been matters of intense concern, and examples of prejudice or discrimination seem to have been more commonly based on culture than on race.

~*Gregory S. Aldrete*

MESOPOTAMIA

Hammurabi's law code furnishes much information about class and society as corroborated by contemporary documents from the ancient Near East. Mesopotamia's social structure was based on economics; that is, Mesopotamian society was divided into two groups, those who owned property, especially land, and those who depended on the wealthy—the "haves" and "have-nots." Mesopotamia did not have warrior or priestly classes. Hammurabi's law code names three basic social strata: the *awilum*, the *muskenum*, and the *wardum*; the latter means "slave," the only of the three terms that can easily be translated. Any legal distinction between *awilum* and *muskenum* disappeared after the Old Babylonian period.

Awilum, "man"—usually translated "freeman," that is, free from debt—also implied a "gentleman." Possibly the *awilum* was a landowner or head of a household. The

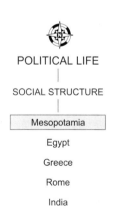

POLITICAL LIFE
|
SOCIAL STRUCTURE
|
Mesopotamia

Egypt

Greece

Rome

India

awilum had obligations to the state to pay taxes and perform military service. Upon his death, his property was divided among his sons.

Muskenum is an Amorite term, literally meaning "the one prostrating himself." Whenever *muskenum* appeared in relation to the *awilum*—the "freeman" or "citizen"—the status of the *muskenum* was inferior. The *muskenum* often served at the palace in exchange for rations or land allotments. Numerous legal provisions may have been necessary to identify the *muskenum* with the palace because he was not protected by customary law.

After 1500 B.C.E., the word *muskenum* appeared in texts with the connotation of "the poor." With this meaning, *muskenum* made its way into Hebrew, Aramaic, Arabic, and much later, into the Romance languages, namely, French (as *mesquin*) and Italian (as *meschino*).

Social distinctions were not fixed. The slave could be freed, and the freeman could be enslaved by debt. A man without land could become a landowner. There were several ways to become a landowner. Kings rewarded administrators with grants of land. A wealthy merchant could buy land. In fact, in regions where law customarily forbade the sale of ancestral land, the wealthy merchant could circumvent this prohibition by legal fiction; that is, he would be adopted by the seller and thus inherit his land. There was social mobility at the very top. For example, a man who was not of royal birth could become king. According to tradition, Sargon's father was unknown, which meant that Sargon was of humble birth. Because the king was the chief representative of the god on earth, the priests and scribes created the necessary divine link in the Legend of Sargon. The legend told that Sargon was the son of a high priestess, who bore him secretly because she was prohibited from having sexual relations with a man. A high priestess was often of royal lineage and often the consort of a god. Therefore, the son of a high priestess was certainly worthy of being king.

Ethnic divisions, with few exceptions, played no role in ancient Mesopotamia. Many ethnic groups entered Mesopotamia, and all eventually assimilated. Even former Assyrian enemies who resided in cities ruled by their conquerors were treated as "equals"; they were never called barbarians, "Asiatics," or other derogatory names, as corroborated by Neo-Assyrian royal inscriptions.

Fringe groups existed, particularly those whom the Assyrians deported as early as the thirteenth century B.C.E. Assyrian reliefs often depict women and children in wagons, while the men were on foot. Only some of the deportees became slaves; many more worked on public projects, and others, if qualified, were incorporated into the army. Craftsmen could ply their trades, particularly when their skills were in great demand. In most cases, the assimilation of resettled peoples was encouraged. Of those deported and resettled, the Aramaeans were the largest group. However, because many Aramaeans had already invaded Babylonia and Assyria through the plains, these newly arrived Aramaeans were easily assimilated (Nemet-Nejat, 116–19).

FOR MORE INFORMATION

Nemet-Nejat, K. R. *Daily Life in Ancient Mesopotamia*. Westport, Conn.: Greenwood Press, 1998.

Sasson, J., ed. *Civilizations of the Ancient Near East*. 4 vols. New York: Scribner's, 1995.

EGYPT

POLITICAL LIFE
|
SOCIAL STRUCTURE
|
Mesopotamia
Egypt
Greece
Rome
India

Modern classifications of an upper, middle, and lower class based on income have no parallel in ancient Egyptian society, where money did not exist. As in the later feudal systems of medieval Europe, Egyptian society was composed of three distinct classes: royalty, free people, and chattel, ranked according to their autonomy. At the top stood royalty, a tiny percentage of the population who wielded all official power through the pharaoh. Underneath them lay a large group of free citizens consisting of government officials, priests, soldiers, and civilians. The fact that movement was common among these four professions shows that they occupied the same tier of the social hierarchy. The sons of a free farmer sometimes entered government service, sometimes became priests, sometimes enlisted as soldiers, and sometimes followed in their fathers' footsteps. Beneath these free citizens lay two groups with little or no freedom—slaves and serfs.

Royal status depended on a blood relationship with the reigning pharaoh. His brothers and sisters, full aunts and full uncles, and mother and father automatically belonged to this class. Rarely did unrelated commoners attain membership in this group. Exceptions included Tiya, the principal wife of Amenhotep III, whose marriage raised her to royalty, and the similarly named Tey, elevated when her husband Ay took the throne, although, in general, a pharaoh's numerous wives were considered nonroyal. One could also attain royal status by marrying the eldest daughter of pharaoh's great royal wife. In the absence of a better claimant to the throne, her husband, regardless of his parentage, became the royal heir apparent but otherwise gained no royal status by the marriage.

Royal status conferred privileges, including the right to lifelong support by the state, but, except in the case of the pharaoh, it carried no automatic power. The extended royal family, who lived together in various palaces, were not required to work, although nothing prohibited them from doing so. A pharaoh's grown sons, one of whom might ascend the throne, were likely to be awarded government positions as training for such an eventuality. This held true not only for the heir apparent but for other male children as well, because circumstances, such as an heir's death or unsuitability, could always change the order of succession. In other cases, a pharaoh might award positions to family members as a way of manipulating institutions not entirely under his control. During the New Kingdom, for example, a pharaoh's chief wife or daughter generally became the god's wife of Amun, an appointment that gave the pharaoh direct control over that god's powerful and wealthy priests.

Free Egyptian citizens—both male and female—possessed two defining rights: they were free to travel and they were free to enter into contractual agreements. Although they enjoyed no other rights of modern societies, their right to make contracts permitted members of this group at least to own property and marry. Serfs and slaves were also permitted possessions, but they could not transfer them without a contract—only the free class could acquire and sell animals, property, and buildings as they wished. Although most free people merely eked out a subsistence living, some accumulated wealth and grew into citizens of substance, and a few even earned high positions in government. Little evidence indicates what percentage of the population consisted of free people. Although surely the numbers varied over time, a guess would put the percentage at something less than half of Egypt's people.

The lowest rung of society was composed of slaves and serfs, whose lives were completely controlled by other people. Slaves differed from serfs in that they could be individually bought and sold; serfs belonged to the land and hence changed masters only as the land changed hands. While neither group could enter into legal marriage, a contractual arrangement that involved inheritance rights on its disso-lution, this fact carried more technical than practical significance. Because they owned little that could be assigned to survivors in any case, serfs and slaves could enjoy most aspects of marriage, such as cooperative living and raising children. Because marriage in ancient Egypt was a social rather than religious institution, their unions closely resembled "legal" marriages. As long as they were commanded to perform legal tasks, both serfs and slaves were expected to obey their masters without question or complaint.

During every period of Egyptian history, serfs far outnumbered slaves. Serfs orig-inally comprised all the people of Egypt except for a tiny percentage of powerful elite that formed a hereditary caste. Because individuals remained serfs unless good fortune changed their situation, only slowly did their high proportion decline. A serf could be elevated through the intervention of a master who, in recognition of a special talent or ability, might assign the person to a managerial position on an estate—serf status was tied to occupation as well as birth. Marriage, too, was a way out of serfdom. Because free persons could not marry serfs, union with a serf required that he or she first be freed. In the early times of civilian armies, valor in war could also earn a serf his own land and freedom. Through one or another of these means, the percentage of serfs decreased over time, swelling the ranks of the free class until, by the height of the New Kingdom, serfs had probably declined to less than half of the population (Brier and Hobbs, 70–73).

FOR MORE INFORMATION

Brier, B., and H. Hobbs. *Daily Life of the Ancient Egyptians*. Westport, Conn.: Greenwood Press, 1999.

Trigger, B. G., B. J. Kemp, D. O'Connor, and A. B. Lloyd. *Ancient Egypt: A Social History*. New York: Cambridge University Press, 1983.

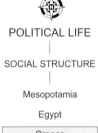

POLITICAL LIFE
|
SOCIAL STRUCTURE
|
Mesopotamia

Egypt

Greece

Rome

India

GREECE

Although the Greeks differentiated themselves from those who did not speak Greek, the idea of "Greekness" played little part in politics. They never had an agreed capital, a single ruling family, or even a clearly defined boundary. Although they did occasionally form alliances against a common enemy, these were invariably fragile and short-lived. On the cultural front, the idea of Greekness was promoted by common blood, a common language, a common set of gods, and a common set of institutions. On an everyday basis, however, being a Greek was far less significant than being an Athenian or a Corinthian or a Macedonian.

All Greeks believed themselves to be descended from one of two racial groups. Dorian communities, so named because they traced their descent to the Dorian invasion, divided themselves into three tribes, and Ionian communities, who took their name from their mythical founder Ion, son of Apollo, into four. The Athenians claimed to be Ionians, whereas the Spartans claimed to be Dorians. To what extent these tribal divisions corresponded to a genuine racial division is unknown. The distinction was emphasized at the time of the Peloponnesian War, when the Ionian Athenians fought against the Dorian Spartans. The Spartan general Brasidas even taxed the Athenians with cowardice on account of their Ionian lineage. In other periods of history the Ionian-Dorian divide carried much less weight.

In most Greek communities, citizenship was limited to freeborn adult males over the age of either 18 or 21. It is estimated, however, that no more than between 6 and 10 percent of any population were actually citizens. The most detailed information about the size of a citizen body relates to Athens. Thucydides (*The Peloponnesian War*, 2.13.6–8) tells us that at the outbreak of the Peloponnesian War, there were 13,000 hoplites on full-time duty, 16,000 of "the oldest and the youngest" who manned the garrisons, 1,200 cavalry, and 1,600 archers. This gives us a citizen body of approximately 32,000. Multiplying that figure by four to include women and children gives a total of about 120,000 Athenians. There is no evidence to indicate that men outnumbered women or vice versa except at the time of the Peloponnesian War, when there was a drastic shortage of males. The evidence for the shortage of males lies in the fact that the offspring of common-law wives were now recognized as legitimate, which was not the case at other times. The population had been seriously reduced by the plague that ravaged Athens from 430 to 426 B.C.E., but it recovered and probably remained about 120,000 until the end of the fourth century B.C.E., when it began to decline progressively.

Evidence for the size of the population of other Greek states is even more meager. Argos is thought to have had a citizen body roughly the same size as Athens, whereas Corinth's was only half that of Athens. Sparta, by contrast, had a very small citizen body. Herodotus (*Histories* 7.234.2) tells us that even in 480 B.C.E., Sparta's fighting force numbered only 8,000. By 371 B.C.E., its citizen body had dwindled to a mere 1,500. The reason for this sharp decline is not fully understood and may be complex. The most populous Greek states in the Classical period were in southern Italy and Sicily. Judging by the extent of the archaeological remains, the largest was Syracuse.

The territory of Attica, including the city of Athens, was divided into 139 local districts known as demes, many of which dated back to very early times. Some may even have predated the foundation of Athens. It was Cleisthenes who converted the demes into political units, each with its own local assembly, its own cults, its own *demarch* or local mayor, and its own treasury. Demes varied considerably in size and importance. Some were little more than hamlets, whereas others, such as Acharnai, situated on the northern borders of Attica, were substantial settlements in their own right. A few even had their own theater. Each functioned as a kind of miniature polis or city-state. Every deme was required to keep a register, in which were recorded the names of all its demesmen who had reached the age of 18. This register served as an official record of the citizen body. For all public purposes, an Athenian citizen was required to identify himself by his "demotic," or the adjective that designated the deme in which he was registered. He retained his demotic even if he went to live elsewhere in Attica. This meant that each Athenian family was identified in perpetuity by the demotic that it possessed at the time of Cleisthenes' reforms.

Cleisthenes introduced a system based on 10 tribes, which were named after 10 Attic heroes. These tribes, into which the whole Athenian body was divided, now became the basis of all civic administration. Although the Athenians continued to acknowledge the existence of the four Ionian tribes, these now ceased to play any significant part in the administrative process. The 10 Cleisthenic tribes formed the basis for election to the council, or *boulê*, which consisted of 500 citizens, 50 of whom were elected annually by lot from each of the 10 tribes. No Athenian was permitted to serve in the council more than twice during his lifetime. Its function was to prepare the agenda for the assembly and advise the magistrates. For one-tenth of the year, that is to say, for 35 or 36 days, each of the 50 members of each of the 10 tribes served on an executive committee known as a *prytany*. Each *prytany* was responsible for the welfare of the state throughout its period of office. Its members, who were on call 24 hours a day, slept and ate in a circular building known as the Tholos, situated on the west side of the Agora. Each day, a new member was elected by lot to serve as the chairman of the *prytany*. This meant that every Athenian had an equal chance of assuming the highest executive office in the land for the duration of a single day.

> *Every Athenian had a chance of assuming the highest executive office for a single day.*

Athenian citizens were divided into classes according to the economic productivity of their land. The highest property class was known as the *pentakosiomedimnoi*, so named because their land yielded 500 bushels of wheat annually. The next was the *hippeis*, or "cavalry," whose yearly yield was 300 bushels. These were followed by the *zeugitai* or "yokemen," whose yield was 200 bushels, so named because they served in close rank (i.e., yoked together) in the army. The lowest group of all was the *thêtes*, literally "hired laborers." The right of citizenship went hand in hand with the requirement to serve in the army, although military service was regarded as a privilege rather than a duty. From the time of Solon onward, all Athenian citizens had the right to attend the assembly. The belief nonetheless persisted that the attainment of full citizen rights was dependent upon wealth. The political importance of the *thêtes*, the most impoverished section of Athenian society, rose dramatically when Athens became a naval power because it was they who constituted the bulk of the sailors. Even so, members of this group were not permitted to stand for political office, either as magistrates or as members of the council, until the second half of the fourth century B.C.E.

The status of being a foreigner, as the Greeks understood the term, does not permit any easy definition. Primarily, it signified such peoples as the Persians and Egyptians, whose languages were unintelligible to the Greeks, but it could also be used of Greeks who spoke in a different dialect and with a different accent. Prejudice toward Greeks on the part of Greeks was not limited to those who lived on the fringes of the Greek world. The Boeotians, inhabitants of central Greece, were routinely mocked for their stupidity and gluttony.

Metic, which comes from the Greek word *metoikos*, meaning "one who dwells among," denoted a foreigner with the right to live permanently in the host country of his or her choice. Classical Athens, because of its empire, wealth, and commercial importance, attracted a vast number of metics. In this, it was rather unusual, as Pericles pointed out (Thucydides, *The Peloponnesian War* 2.39.1). Approximately three-fifths of the metic population lived in demes located in or around Athens, nearly one-fifth in the port of Piraeus, and the remaining fifth in demes situated in the countryside and along the coast. At least 60 different Greek and non-Greek states are represented among their ranks, as we know from sepulchral inscriptions. In the fifth century B.C.E., metics perhaps accounted for as much as 10 percent of Athens's entire population, or about from 20,000 to 30,000. It should be emphasized, however, that their numbers fluctuated in line with Athens's changing fortunes and prosperity. Very likely, many left before the outbreak of the Peloponnesian War in 431 B.C.E. Athens was not the only Greek state that encouraged the immigration of foreigners, but it was undoubtedly the one that attracted them in greatest numbers. The Spartans were notoriously xenophobic and actively discouraged foreigners from residing in their territory even on a short-term basis.

It is sometimes suggested that the Greeks more or less invented racism single-handedly by holding up their culture as a shining example of everything that was noble and praiseworthy, while at the same time denigrating everybody else, particularly the Persians. The truth, however, is rather more complex. Even if the Greeks considered their culture to be superior to others, that does not mean that they were out-and-out racists. Moreover, some Greeks saw much to admire in Persian culture. The historian Herodotus was so enamored of the Persians that he was dubbed *philobarbaros*, or "barbarian lover." Overall, the Greek attitude toward the Persians was probably a complex mixture of fascination, envy, and contempt.

The notion of the barbarian was not inherent in Greek culture. There is no trace of racial prejudice against the Trojans in Homer's *Iliad*. In fact, the regard for civilized values on the part of the Trojans is equal, if not superior, to that of the Greeks. Not until Aeschylus's *Persians*, which was produced in 472 B.C.E., are barbarians depicted as a stereotypical group with a homogeneous culture. This change came about as a result of the Persian invasion of Greece—an event that bred terror and loathing in the Greek population, similar in intensity to that felt toward the hated Hun by the Allies in World War I. The stereotype was also disseminated through art, notably in portrayals of the battle between the Lapiths and Centaurs, which we find on the metopes of the Parthenon. The lascivious and aggressive Centaurs stand for the Persians, and the innocent and abused Lapiths for the Greeks. Depictions of this mythological encounter, in which right clearly triumphed over wrong, served to bolster Greek self-esteem and self-righteousness in the aftermath of the Persian invasion.

Precisely what the category *barbarian* amounted to in practical terms is difficult to determine. The most plausible origin of the word is "the people who mutter baba-ba." Barbarians, in other words, were people who could not speak Greek. Non-Greek speakers were excluded from participation in the Olympic Games and from certain other religious ceremonies, such as the Eleusinian Mysteries. In time, however, *barbarian* also came to acquire the pejorative meaning of "ignorant, brutal, and savage."

Despite the negative view of barbarian culture that many Greeks held, there is no evidence to suggest that barbarians were unwelcome or subjected to mistreatment if they traveled to Greece. On the contrary, they figured prominently among Athens's metic population in the fourth century B.C.E. The Sidonians, who were Phoenicians, actually enjoyed a privileged status that was not extended to other metics: they were exempted from the metic tax and other financial burdens (Garland, 44–47, 73–78).

FOR MORE INFORMATION

Frost, F. J. *Greek Society*. Boston: Houghton Mifflin, 1997.
Garland, R. *Daily Life of the Ancient Greeks*. Westport, Conn.: Greenwood Press, 1998.
Whitehead, D. *The Demes of Attica*. Princeton, N.J.: Princeton University Press, 1986.

POLITICAL LIFE
|
SOCIAL STRUCTURE
|
Mesopotamia

Egypt

Greece

Rome

India

ROME

One of the most important distinctions in Roman society was that between citizens and noncitizens. The number of citizens was always a small minority of the total populace. In the early empire, when there were perhaps 50 million people living in the entire Roman Empire, it is estimated that there were only about six million citizens. To be a citizen, first one had to be an adult, free male. Thus, by definition, women, children, and slaves were excluded from citizenship. In addition, one had to have passed the census, which identified the person's age, geographical origin, family, wealth, and moral virtue. For hundreds of years, the Romans were reluctant to extend citizenship even to the thoroughly Romanized inhabitants of Italy until forced to by the Social Wars in the late Republic. Once Rome acquired overseas provinces, it often remained reluctant to grant citizenship to provincials on a large scale. A major change came in 212 C.E., when the emperor Caracalla declared that all adult male free inhabitants of the empire were now citizens.

Early in Roman history, one of the main duties of a citizen was to fight in the army. Later, once Rome's army was professionalized, the main duty of citizens was to vote. Being a citizen gave a person protection under the law, and in theory, all citizens were treated equally by the law. One of the rights of citizens was that they could not be punished without some form of trial, and this trial had to be held at Rome. For example, when Christians were being persecuted, if they were citizens, they had to be sent to Rome, but if not, the local magistrate could deal with them.

One of the most potent phrases in Roman society was "Civis Romanus sum," meaning "I am a Roman citizen," because declaring this instantly gave you certain protections and rights. This phrase entered Roman legend when a corrupt governor,

Verres, seized a Roman citizen and, ignoring the man's repeated protestations of "Civis Romanus sum," illegally ordered him to be beaten and tortured.

Roman citizens were formally divided into two groups, the patricians and the plebeians. This distinction went back to the earliest days of Rome when the society was dominated by a small number of wealthy land-owning families who collectively became known as the patricians, literally, "the fathers." This dominance became institutionalized in laws that stated that only patricians were eligible to hold high political office. The monopoly was maintained by further laws that dictated that patricians could only marry members of other patrician families. All nonpatricians, the vast majority, were labeled plebeians. These distinctions resulted in considerable social unrest, culminating in a struggle known as the Conflict of the Orders. As a result of these conflicts, the privileges of patricians were eroded and eventually eliminated, although being a member of a patrician family continued to convey a certain status throughout Roman history. From 445 B.C.E. on, patricians and plebeians were legally allowed to marry.

Another way Roman citizens were divided was by wealth. Every so often, the state appointed a special magistrate called a censor, who reviewed the wealth and moral worthiness of all citizens. If one's total wealth was more than 400,000 sesterces, that person was granted equestrian status. *Equites* wore a special gold ring and wore togas with a narrow purple stripe. Many equestrians seem to have operated successful commercial enterprises, and in the empire, a number of important government posts were allotted to equestrians.

One final significant component of Roman social structure was not delineated by a formal or legal set of rules yet played an important part in daily life. This was the patronage system, which developed as a way to link together Romans of varying status. Powerful men would serve as patrons to a group of their social or economic inferiors, who were known as the man's clients. Patrons would provide financial or legal help and protection to their clients. In return, the clients would perform actions that enhanced the prestige or reputation of their patrons. For example, clients would be expected to support their patron with their votes during an election or, if their patron was giving a public speech, to attend and to applaud enthusiastically. In a ritual known as the *salutatio*, clients would gather at the house of the patron in the morning to receive his greetings (and perhaps also some food or money).

~*Gregory S. Aldrete*

FOR MORE INFORMATION

Alföldy, G. *The Social History of Rome*. Baltimore, Md.: Johns Hopkins University Press, 1988.

Wallace-Hadrill, A., ed. *Patronage in Ancient Society*. New York: Routledge, 1990.

INDIA

The caste system has traditionally been the primary force for maintaining social order in India. One is born into one's caste and is bound to it for life. It is an essential

POLITICAL LIFE
|
SOCIAL STRUCTURE
|
Mesopotamia

Egypt

Greece

Rome

India

part of a person's identity. In this context, caste refers to two distinct but related systems. The first is that of *varna*, broad divisions of class, and the second is *jati*, particular economic and social groups that constitute caste proper. Regulation of roles within and between classes is codified in the *Manu Smriti* (Laws of Manu).

The *varna* system divides society into a hierarchy of four main classes. This hierarchy is based on notions of ritual purity and pollution; the higher levels of the hierarchy are assumed to be more "pure," whereas the lower levels are considered more "polluted." Beyond social status, other situations and events, such as birth, death, menstruation, the sight of an eclipse, and so on, may render one temporarily impure, or polluted. One may also become polluted by coming into contact with or taking food from those of lower *varna*. While there are various ritual means of removing temporary impurity, bathing is the most common, and bathing in sacred waters, such as the Ganges River, is best.

The highest *varna* is that of the Brahmans, the scholars and priests. The obligatory duties of a Brahman are to study and teach, to perform sacrifice, and to receive gifts. The status of the Brahman rests on a reciprocal relation with the next *varna*, the Kshatriya, the warriors and kings. The Kshatriya ideally protects all creatures, and his power allows him to act as patron for the priestly Brahman, who in return performs the sacrifices necessary to ensure the king's position and grant his reign legitimacy. The tension between these two *varnas*, in terms of the dichotomy between spiritual versus temporal authority, is a major theme of the epic literature of India. The third *varna* is that of the Vaisya, responsible for making up the economic life of society. Manu grants Vaisyas the role of living from the land, whether through farming or herding, as well as commerce and trades.

These first three *varnas* have the added distinction of being *dvija*, "twice-born." This implies that they are permitted access to Vedic knowledge and can take part in initiatory rites of passage. However, the learning was the exclusive domain of the Brahmans, and the roles of the other *varnas* in this sphere were not significant. The lowest *varna* is the Sudra, servants and others who perform menial or repugnant tasks, such as scavenging, butchering, or leather working. They are forbidden to study or hear the Veda.

The divisions of society are set out in *Rig Veda Samhita* X.90.11–12. There, the sacrifice of the primordial person, Purusa, is the origin of the fourfold classification. From his mouth came the Brahmans, from his arms the Kshatriyas, from his thighs the Vaisyas, and from his feet the Sudra servants.

Outside of the fourfold *varna* system are other groups of persons. One such group comprises the untouchables, who were considered to be the original inhabitants of India. These may be those who have traditionally had no place in society, or entered India from abroad, or they may be those who perform such lowly tasks that they have no place in the hierarchy of purity. As the name implies, the untouchable is one who is thought to be polluting through contact or even proximity. Another group that may be considered outside of the *varna* system consists of *sannyasins*, religious wanderers and ascetics who have renounced home, possessions, and social ties. Buddhist and Jain ascetics, too, may be considered outside of the *varna* system.

The term *jati* refers to one's birth and is the most essential feature of one's social identity. There are thousands of different *jati*, all loosely tied to the *varna* system. First, one's family belongs to a particular *jati*; hence one is born into it. Moreover, each caste tends to be endogamous, meaning that people marry within their caste. The *jati* also determines one's occupation. Each *jati* has its own specific profession, which persists through generations: one does what one's father did, and one's sons will perpetuate this tradition. By pulling together marriage, social group, and occupation into a coherent whole, *jati* defines one's social identity. This does not imply that different *jati* do not interact at all. Within any geographical territory, from a village to a town or city, different *jati* are integrated collectively, so that all benefit from the products of each occupation.

~*Matthew Bingley*

FOR MORE INFORMATION

Auboyer, J. *Daily Life in Ancient India*. London: Phoenix Press, 1965.

Basham, A. L. *The Wonder That Was India*. London: Sidgwick and Jackson, 1967.

Dumont, L. *Homo Hierarchicus: The Caste System and Its Implications*. Translated by Mark Sainsbury et al. Chicago: University of Chicago Press, 1980.

Government

While, as illustrated in many chapters of this book, the different ancient civilizations followed similar paths in many respects, in the realm of government there were sharp differences among the systems that evolved in the various cultures. The civilizations of the ancient world experimented with a wide range of types of government and with the autonomy and respect accorded to the individual and the rights bestowed upon the citizen. The inventors of these various systems were creating new institutions—they did not have models or previous examples to draw upon—and the range of solutions they came up with to bring order to their societies is a testament to their creativity.

The Australian Aborigines had a decentralized form of social organization based around kinship and with different elders serving in leadership roles in various situations.

In Mesopotamia, flat land without obstructions encouraged conquerors to carve out large empires and then to set themselves up as the rulers of their subject territories. Thus Mesopotamian civilizations were always run by kings who wielded nearly absolute power over their subjects. Absolute monarchy endured as the dominant, and indeed the only, form of government in the ancient Near East, even as a succession of different civilizations rose and fell. The Sumerians, Akkadians, Babylonians, Assyrians, Chaldeans, Persians, and Sassanians all came and went, but always these cultures were ruled by proud kings who usually were jealous of their power. In

POLITICAL LIFE
|
GOVERNMENT
|
Mesopotamia

Egypt

Greece

Rome

India

Nubia

Australian Aboriginals

India and Nubia, monarchies were also common, and strong leaders such as Chandragupta Maurya ruled over vast territories, aided by elaborate bureaucracies.

In Egypt, the institution of the all-powerful king was taken a step further, and the pharaoh became viewed not merely as an omnipotent human but literally as a god on earth. As such, his authority was unquestioned, and he was viewed as the font of blessings and punishment by his people. The enormous pyramids that they willingly built for him are testimonies to the central role the pharaoh played in Egyptians' lives.

By contrast, the mountainous terrain of Greece and the many islands in the Aegean Sea split the land into many small, separate city-states, which allowed more opportunities for local citizens to take a role in their own government and to try out different systems of rule. At various points, different Greek city-states experimented with monarchies, oligarchies, plutocracies, and ultimately—and most radically—democracies. The most extreme form of democracy came in fifth-century B.C.E. Athens, in which the members of the executive council were actually drawn by lot from the common citizens, and all citizens voted directly on important issues.

Finally, the Romans, after passing through the seemingly obligatory monarchical phase, developed a republic with a kind of mixed constitution that divided power among various elected magistrates, the advisory body of the senate, and the voting body of the people.

Although they began as experiments into different methods of structuring society, many of the political institutions that the peoples of the ancient world invented were remarkably successful and long-lived. The Egyptian state remained relatively stable for thousands of years, the Roman Republic endured for 500 years, and the subsequent Roman Empire for a comparable time. Even when states fell, the governmental institutions they invented lived on. Although the Greek form of democracy flared out after a century or so, 2,000 years later its modern heirs can be found all around the world.

~Gregory S. Aldrete

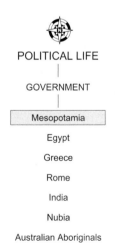

POLITICAL LIFE
|
GOVERNMENT
|
Mesopotamia

Egypt

Greece

Rome

India

Nubia

Australian Aboriginals

MESOPOTAMIA

The Mesopotamian king was considered the gods' representative on earth. An Akkadian proverb provided the metaphor, "Man is the shadow of a god, and a slave is the shadow of a man; but the king is the mirror of a god." Both political and religious events on Earth were believed to be mirrored and explained by events in heaven.

Secular government was universally in the hands of a single ruler, who was almost invariably male. The name of the ruler's position varied from city to city. For example, some rulers held the title *sanga*, "chief accountant (of the temple)," perhaps reflecting the economic basis of their authority. At other times, the king was called *en*, originating from high priestly office. In several cities, the ruler was referred to as *ensi*, "city governor." Finally, *lugal*, "king" (literally, great man), was a title accorded to the most powerful *ensi*. Hammurabi put an end to the institution of the *ensi* once and for all by using its Akkadian equivalent, meaning "farmer." The kings also held various titles, such as "the strong king" (meaning the legitimate king), "the legitimate king" (in reality, a usurper), and "the king of the four corners (of heaven and earth)" (emphasizing the king's expansionist policies).

Unlike the Egyptian pharaohs, who were regarded as gods, the kings in Babylonia and Assyria were usually considered mortals. In exceptional cases, certain kings had themselves divinized. Cultic structures similar to those of the traditional gods were built for some kings. Mesopotamian kingship had a religious dimension. Mesopotamian theology incorporated the concept that kingship was one of the basic institutions of human life, designed by the gods for humankind. The gods were described as choosing the king, that is, "taking his hand." They were even credited with some role in his creation, birth, and upbringing. Divine approval was necessary because there were no unequivocal secular criteria. Rulers often cited the fact that their father or other ancestors preceded them as ruler. Ancestry constituted some form of legitimacy, but inheritance of office by the eldest son was not strictly followed. Rulers could be succeeded by their brothers. Members of the royal family who had no claim to the throne defended the legitimacy of their usurpation through divine calling.

Safeguarding the king was of great importance. A large number of omens referred to safety or danger to the king, and divination was used to protect the monarch. The king was subject to various religious strictures to safeguard him against an evil day or an evil omen. On some occasions, the Assyrian king had to fast for several days until the new moon appeared. The king wore the clothes of a nanny, remained indoors, donned a white robe for several days, and stayed for a week in a reed hut like a sick person.

In earliest times, the ruler was chosen from among the population of the city, and his acceptance by the people was important. The king's rule could come to an end if his people revolted. The inscriptions of Uru-inimgina, a usurper (from Lagash, ca. 2350), described his reform of social injustices and his concern for the welfare of the

Hypothetical reconstruction of an Assyrian throne room. The individual motifs, such as the human-headed lions, are all attested. Originally in A. H. Layard, *The Monuments of Nineveh*. © Copyright The British Museum.

citizens, particularly the orphan and the widow, as part of his claim to legitimacy.

Installation ceremonies were held at Ur, Nippur, and Uruk and involved three symbolic acts similar to those used by today's monarchies: coronation, enthronement, and taking a mace or scepter. A Sumerian epic explained that when kingship was brought to earth after the Flood, it was represented by three symbols: the crown, the throne, and the scepter—images that recurred numerous times in hymns addressed to the king.

Reigning, or even powerful, queens were the exception. Normally, the queen was the king's consort and had no royal functions. Short inscriptions by queens were rare but indicated that a few strong women often exercised considerable influence, also documented in letters. In Assyria, King Sennacherib deeply loved his Syrian-born wife, Naqiya-Zakutu, and even ensured that her death was recorded in the

Babylonian Chronicle—an extraordinary event. When Sennacherib was murdered by one of his own sons, the crown prince, Esarhaddon, could not be installed for three weeks. So for three weeks control of Assyria fell into the hands of the queen mother, Naqiya-Zakutu. She continued to wield considerable power during the early years of the reign of Assurbanipal, her grandson. Royal officials feared her.

The secular bureaucracy in the palace was probably modeled on the traditions of the temple. The major temples created a bureaucracy to administer and keep detailed records of its employees and of the commodities under its supervision. As territories expanded, each independent state became a province. The bureaucracies of the former regime were maintained, but usually an outsider was selected to govern. By the middle of the second millennium B.C.E., the old system of provincial governors evolved into petty kingdoms in which larger states were administered as districts, each with a governor—a policy adopted by Hammurabi, among others. The king retained some form of limited sovereignty by appointing a trusted nominee.

In the Old Babylonian period, the king regulated most of the palace activities both inside and outside the palace, such as craft industries, agricultural estates, and business activities. Reports were made to King Hammurabi himself about the collection of revenues from both the temple and the palace. Tax collectors were forced to collect the full tab or make up the deficit themselves. King Hammurabi paid attention to even the smallest details in his letters, describing time and labor devoted to building and maintaining canals and defense walls. The king also kept a close eye on his officials, who in their letters defend themselves against charges of negligence.

As the palace organization grew, the complexity of palace architecture came to reflect new requirements, such as the installation of a throne room and audience hall. Within the royal court, there might be several subcourts, such as that of the queen mother or crown prince, along with their staffs. The crown prince sometimes had his own palace, called the "House of Succession." The provincial governors might even have a palace in the capital, apart from the royal palace.

The palace complex served a variety of functions. It was the residence of the king, his family, and household servants. It housed the government and administrative offices as well as workshops. Household goods and royal treasure were stored there. Ceremonies of state took place there. Provincial officials sent regular provisions for the palace personnel and livestock.

The king was chosen by the gods to provide prosperity and righteousness. As ruler, he was responsible for the welfare of all subjects, especially the poor and the weak. Temple offerings made by the king had both religious and political overtones; that is, the temple personnel accepted the king's offerings because he was the recognized ruler. Divine approval of the king's actions resulted in prosperity.

Mesopotamian rulers built and rebuilt temples. Rulers were depicted carrying a basket of earth or builders' tools thrown over their shoulder. Sometimes rulers carried the first basket or molded the first brick of a temple. The king ordered the fashioning of images of the gods. He also provided income to maintain the temple staff and took part in festivals.

The king could delegate responsibilities. He could not participate in every local ritual in person as required, so he sent representatives from his family, much like kings and queens of present-day monarchies. The king also took part in emergency rituals to avoid evil omens.

The political map reflected a lively diplomatic scene. Messengers traveled widely both within and beyond the borders. Some messages were conveyed orally, but rulers generally used extensive written documentation to regulate their officials and to communicate with their allies. Because of written correspondence, ambassadors were able to represent their rulers in making agreements. Nevertheless, high-level meetings still took place between rulers. The crossing of frontiers must have required careful advance planning. Kings probably traveled with an entourage, some of whom were armed.

Kings sent ambassadors on special occasions or as residents at other courts to establish and maintain diplomatic relations. They usually brought a gift of great rarity or of high-quality craftsmanship. The exchange of gifts was one part of the reciprocal relationship between the king and his guest. Particular gifts were requested, and sometimes the recipient complained about a gift. Dynastic marriages also were a feature of international relations, used to cement relations between ruling families everywhere.

The king fed and housed any visitors from outside the state at royal expense, even if they were not accommodated in the palace itself. The Mari archives recorded the daily royal menu on thousands of tablets. In addition, there were banquets for special events such as religious festivals and visits by foreign ambassadors. Occasionally, we find mention of more distinguished guests, such as the Hurrian ruler of Nineveh and his entourage of more than a hundred followers.

Ambassadors enjoyed certain diplomatic immunities: their property was protected, and they were sometimes exempt from customs duties. Sometimes their activities made them unwelcome, and their rulers were requested to remove them. But regardless of the ambassador's popularity, his person was inviolate.

Gifts were also brought by strangers and subjects alike when permitted an audience with the king, but the king was not easily accessible to all the people because he was subject to many taboos. Usually, only the superintendent of the palace had direct access to the king, much like the chief of staff to the president of the United States. The crown prince could have an audience with the king when the astrological omens were auspicious. Courtiers often received gifts to speak to the king on behalf of suppliants.

> *The king was not easily accessible to all the people because he was subject to many taboos.*

From the second millennium B.C.E. onward, rulers frequently corresponded by mail. The language commonly used was Akkadian, the language of diplomacy. Kings used kinship terms such as "father," "son," or "brother" in addressing each other. For example, calling a ruler "my father" implied his seniority, and "my brother," equality. Some rulers were touchy about their status and took offense at familiarity. On appropriate occasions, such as accession or illness, vassals were expected to send congratulations or inquiries about the king's health. Failure to do so was considered a serious breach of conduct. The treaties between rulers called for reciprocity—each ruler was responsible for the safety of the other king's subjects. Also, every ruler was held liable for any criminal offenses committed by his subjects abroad. The king took responsibility for foreigners living in his land (Nemet-Nejat, 217–21, 240–43).

FOR MORE INFORMATION

Edwards, I. E. S., et al., eds. *The Cambridge Ancient History*. 3rd. ed. 2 vols. Cambridge, England: Cambridge University Press, 1970–1975.

Nemet-Nejat, K. R. *Daily Life in Ancient Mesopotamia*. Westport, Conn.: Greenwood Press, 1998.

POLITICAL LIFE
|
GOVERNMENT
|
Mesopotamia

Egypt

Greece

Rome

India

Nubia

Australian Aboriginals

EGYPT

Religion was such a powerful force in ancient Egypt that it determined both the structure of government and the organization of society. Unlike our modern Western idea that government and religion should be separate, Egyptians believed that their ruler was a god with unlimited power and who spoke with divine authority. Egyptians viewed the pharaoh as their protector, the guardian of the country, and they believed that society's order and prosperity depended on their unquestioned obedience to him.

It was up to every pharaoh to ensure that proper order, or *maat*, was maintained. But the Egyptians' view of order was calculated strictly along class lines. If good fortune came to a poor person, it was not considered a blessing or a credit to him but a sign that something was wrong with the world. As long as the rich and powerful prospered while slaves and the poor remained in their places, *maat* was maintained.

Besides ensuring order, pharaohs performed a unifying function. Egyptians believed that their land had once consisted of a northern and a southern kingdom until Narmer (Menes), a mighty hero from the south, conquered the north, married its queen, and by assuming the crowns of both kingdoms, unified Egypt into a single nation. Even after 2,000 years as a unified country, the title "Lord of the Two Lands," along with his Horus name, was a pharaoh's most important designation. To the Egyptian mind, their union existed solely in the person of the pharaoh—Narmer and his successors—and it was to him, rather than to country or flag, that all loyalty was owed.

As both a god and the embodiment of Egypt, a pharaoh wielded great power. Were he to ask his subjects to build an impossibly massive tomb, they would toil for decades to make the impossible real, receiving no pay, just enough food to sustain them. They believed praise from their pharaoh when he joined his ancestors in the netherworld would be their ample reward, just as later people devoted vast time and resources to raising cathedrals to ensure their personal salvation.

A pharaoh was regarded with awe and fear. Ordinary citizens prostrated themselves in his presence, and the upper classes knelt and bowed until their heads touched the ground, waiting for permission to stand. Those closest to the pharaoh might, as a singular honor, be allowed to bow from the waist, but this was an innovation of the more "democratic" New Kingdom. All except his most-favored courtiers feared looking directly on the pharaoh's face, and no one spoke unless he granted them that right.

The pharaoh's authority was boundless with every government position filled by his appointees, at least in theory. In fact, given the hundreds of appointments a pharaoh had to make, it was often expedient simply to replace a father with his son. In this way, more and more government positions became hereditary over time and outside a pharaoh's control. As the pharaoh's authority waned, so did Egypt's power, as exemplified by the First and Second Intermediate periods. When strong pharaohs regained control, they consolidated their power base by reverting to the practice of making their own appointments.

As the lineal descendant of the conqueror Menes, the pharaoh owned all of Egypt—the land, the livestock, and the people—and governed by a feudal system like that of medieval Europe. Private property did not exist in such a system because one person controlled everything. The king alone granted the right to manage a farm, town, or pond, and whoever received that right exercised it on the king's behalf—what was produced belonged to his lord and master. So it was in the beginning in Egypt: whoever tilled an acre, fished the Nile, or mined for gold did so with the pharaoh's permission. Yet, over centuries, the landholdings of the pharaoh gradually diminished. If a farm had been worked by a family for several generations, tradition eventually ceded them a title that could be upheld by the courts, creating a new category of land separate from a pharaoh's estates, although he could levy whatever tax he wished on these farms. Pharaohs themselves contributed to the decrease in their own estates by transferring land in perpetuity to certain temples, a practice that enriched the temples but diminished the pharaoh's landholdings. They further decreased their estates by using land as incentives to service, awarding acreage to those who pleased them. Once land came into the possession of a private citizen, he controlled its use and bequeathed it to whomever he pleased. Decreasing royal landholdings added private property to the economy, sometimes, but not always, subject to a pharaoh's national tax. What began as a pharaoh's literal ownership of the country slowly evolved into his right to tax and otherwise distribute the produce, so that, by the end of the New Kingdom, although the pharaoh remained Egypt's largest single landholder, temples collectively controlled more land than he did, and even more acreage was held by small farmers.

Although central to the Egyptian system, a pharaoh could not manage the country without a substantial, professional government. Evidence from early times, such as the Fourth Dynasty, shows son after son of a reigning monarch bearing titles of high government positions. Generally, for example, a prince was designated as the overseer of works, the chief engineer of the pharaoh's pyramid and mortuary temple. This suggests that Egypt's government originally consisted of the family of the pharaoh, although this changed as its population and power grew. By the end of the Old Kingdom and through the remainder of Egyptian history, nonroyals, nominated by the pharaoh, invariably bore the titles of government officers. From then on, royal children who did not inherit the throne generally became high priests and priestesses rather than officials in the civil government.

The evolved government consisted of four major branches. One managed the royal court and pharaoh's estates; another, the armed forces; another, the religious hierarchy; and the remaining branch, civil government. Each consisted of a pyramidal hierarchy (or, in the case of civil government, of two pyramids) that established a chain of authority and command and provided a structure by which a pharaoh could convey his wishes to all the citizens of his sprawling country. The government's overriding principle was that an Egyptian citizen should receive his distant pharaoh's orders from a local person whom he knew and respected. This neat structure could become confused when multiple titles were awarded to the same individual, effectively placing him in more than one branch of the government at once.

Viziers bragged about how the least important citizen could approach them with his problems.

Civil government was headed by a *tchety*, conventionally translated "vizier," the highest civil official after the pharaoh. Two viziers, one for the north and another for the south, split the job and presided over separate central bureaucracies and the governors of their respective sections of the country. The godly pharaoh stood far above practical details of management, so viziers bragged about how the least important citizen could approach them with his problems, and how they oversaw the construction of magnificent temples and pyramids. Such boasts were exaggerations. The vizier did not serve as a sole judge to adjudicate complaints—a complex legal system took care of such matters. Nor did most viziers possess the necessary architectural and construction skills to supervise personally the construction of large buildings. The truth behind the boasts is that the *tchety* held ultimate responsibility for the justice system and for securing the talents required to build whatever a pharaoh commanded. The vizier was responsible for all civil business, which he conducted through ministers—most important, treasury, tax collection, judicial appeal, and regional governors—who, in turn, managed numerous functionaries.

Headed by an official whose title translates as "overseer of the house of gold," the treasury collected crops and animals as payment-in-kind for taxes and handled their accounting and management. Beneath this minister, an overseer of granaries and an overseer of cattle supervised numerous bureaucrats who managed facilities for provisioning the army, feeding workers on national projects, and maintaining surpluses against lean years.

Taxes were levied and collected by another department, whose many members roamed the country assigning an obligation to every citizen. Levies were not based on how much an acre had produced that year, which would have encouraged farmers to hide part of the crop to lower their tax. Instead, a careful record was kept of how high the Nile rose during its annual inundation using "nilometers," stone markers set along the river's course. The height of that year's flood determined what, compared with the previous year, each farm *should* have produced regardless of what it *did* produce and set the tax rate. Those who did not hand over their levied amounts were beaten or imprisoned. The treasury and tax departments were considered so important that their heads reported directly to the pharaoh, like the vizier. Both departments employed thousands of scribes to compute and record every transaction.

Regional government consisted of 42 areas of the country called *nomes*, corresponding to American states, presided over by a local governor called a *nomarch*. *Nomarchs* maintained order in each territory and ensured that its assigned portion for national projects was supplied, whether in the form of taxes or labor. As the local official with ties closest to the national government, *nomarchs* exercised great authority in their territory, sometimes acting as local kings. Below each *nomarch* stood town mayors, village chiefs, constabularies, and district councils, or *kenbets*.

Such a large bureaucracy required extensive management and supervision. Leading the religious establishment was the overseer of the temples and prophets of all the gods, a minister who functioned not as a priest but as the civil overlord of an institution that controlled great national wealth. So entwined were Egypt's civil and religious affairs, however, that in addition to his civil post, a vizier often held the position of overseer of the temples. Ranked directly below the overseer stood high priests—one for each god of Egypt.

The pharaoh's staff constituted a major segment of society in a country whose ruler controlled immense amounts of land, officiated at innumerable official ceremonies, and personally communicated with heads of foreign states. Hundreds of functionaries managed royal estates, and thousands of families worked his land. Under the supervision of a governor of the palace, another special group of officials oversaw the affairs of the king's two official residences. Each palace compound housed a troop of royal guards, a kitchen staff including serving women, musicians and dancers, groundskeepers, carpenters and other artisans, horsemen, and even zookeepers for the exotic animals most pharaohs enjoyed. A separate diplomatic staff of hundreds of emissaries and scribes conducted foreign affairs from offices in a separate structure inside or near the royal compound.

One special group lived inside the palace to care for the pharaoh's personal needs. An overseer of royal clothes would supervise a chief bleacher, chief washer, and chief rober; an overseer of wigs supervised upper and lower wig makers; and a royal sandal bearer cared for the royal footwear (it seems that sandal bearer symbolized royal authority). Even the royal harem had its own administration, governed by an overseer of the secluded who managed both scribes and attendants who served the needs of the women, in addition to a group of doorkeepers who were responsible for their management. The doorkeepers arranged nightly appointments with the pharaoh, as he desired. Teams of musicians trained the women to entertain their king by singing to the musical accompaniment of their sisters in seclusion. Royal children were housed in a separate section of the palace apart from the adults and raised by tutors, called royal nurses, who generally were women relatives of the child's mother or of an important government official, such as the vizier (Brier and Hobbs, 59–70).

FOR MORE INFORMATION

Brier, B., and H. Hobbs. *Daily Life of the Ancient Egyptians.* Westport, Conn.: Greenwood Press, 1999.

Montet, P. *Everyday Life in Egypt in the Days of Ramesses the Great.* Translated by A. R. Maxwell-Hyslop and M. Drower. Reprint, Philadelphia: University of Pennsylvania Press, 1981.

Trigger, B. G, B. J. Kemp, D. O'Connor, and A. B. Lloyd. *Ancient Egypt: A Social History.* New York: Cambridge University Press, 1983.

GREECE

The most distinctive political unit in the Greek world was the polis, or city-state, from which our word *politics* is derived. Although no two poleis were identical in physical layout, all by definition possessed an urbanized center and surrounding territory. Each polis formulated its own law code, kept its own army, developed its own system of government, and recognized its own set of gods. The polis system prevailed in the heartland of the Greek world. The mountainous terrain of Greece encouraged each separate city to develop as a distinct political entity. Thus, even though the Greeks shared a common language, they were not a unified country, but dozens of separate city-states. The large number of states also perhaps encouraged experimentation with different forms of government. The polis system proved to be remarkably resilient. Even after the Greeks had lost their independence, first to Macedon and later to Rome, it continued to flourish. Its success over such a long period of time was in part a result of the inherent particularism of the Greeks—their preference, that is, for living in politically independent communities. It is for this reason that the notion of "Greekness" was largely confined to the linguistic, religious, and social spheres. As a political concept, it amounted to very little.

From the mid–seventh to the mid–sixth century B.C.E., although rather later in the case of Athens, many Greek states were ruled by tyrants. The majority of tyrants were disaffected aristocrats, who nursed a grudge against their peers. Their rise depended on the support of the common people, with whom they allied themselves against aristocratic power and privilege. This coalition of interests typically lasted for two or three generations, after which the ruling tyrant, having lost popular support, found himself isolated and beleaguered. Although the Greeks vilified their tyrants in later times because of their detestation of unconstitutional power, tyrants played an important part in the progress toward democracy by serving as a catalyst at the point of transition from aristocratic to popular rule.

The title "father of democracy" is most appropriately applied to the politician Cleisthenes, who in 507 B.C.E. devised a way of undermining the grip over the Athenian constitution that was being exercised by powerful aristocratic kin groups known as *genê* (singular, *genos*). Cleisthenes, who was himself an aristocrat, made each citizen's political identity dependent upon the Attic deme or village to which he belonged. Henceforth, each citizen was required to identify himself as "X, son of Y, of the deme Z." Cleisthenes then assigned each of the 139 demes to one of 10 new tribes. In this way, he broke the stranglehold previously held by the *genê*—regions that had earlier been dominated by a single *genos* were now divided among several tribes. Aristocrats could no longer manipulate or intimidate ordinary citizens as they had done in the past. The new Cleisthenic system was complicated and artificial, but it was wholly successful in making the Athenian political system more representative.

In the late 460s and early 450s B.C.E., Athens took the final steps along the road to becoming what is known as a radical or participatory democracy. It was a political system for which there exists no modern parallel. The Greek notion of *dêmokratia,* or "power in the hands of the people," was very different from the modern system of democracy. In the Greek world, there was no menacing equivalent of big government. Nor were policy decisions made by faceless bureaucrats accountable only to their immediate superiors. On the contrary, the Athenian citizenry or *demos,* which consisted of all adult males over the age of 21, was completely sovereign. The demos wielded its formidable power through a voting assembly known as the *ekklêsia,* which met approximately four times a month, although extraordinary meetings could be called during times of emergency. Each citizen exercised one vote and had the right to speak on whatever issue was under debate. Magistrates and junior officials were in the strictest sense its servants; they were subject to investigation both before taking up office and upon laying it down. It was also the demos, sitting in court as the *hêliaia,* who constituted the supreme judicial authority.

Sparta, which is situated in the south-central Peloponnese, was a highly distinctive city-state that developed along a different path from other Greek city-states. At the head of the Spartan state was a dual kingship. The kings, who had equal power, led the Spartan armies in time of war. Aside from their military role, however, their powers were strictly curtailed. They were subject to constant scrutiny by five magistrates known as ephors, who were elected annually. If found guilty of impropriety, the kings could be deposed or exiled. The aristocratic feature of the constitution was the *gerousia,* or council of elders. This consisted of the kings plus 28 citizens over the age of 60 chosen from the aristocracy. Finally, there was the *apella,* or assembly, which all citizens, who were known as *homoioi,* or "equals," attended (Garland, 6–13).

FOR MORE INFORMATION

Garland, R. *Daily Life of the Ancient Greeks.* Westport, Conn.: Greenwood Press, 1998.
Jones, A. H. M. *Athenian Democracy.* Baltimore, Md.: Johns Hopkins University Press, 1986.
Meier, C. *The Greek Discovery of Politics.* Translated by D. McLintock. Cambridge, Mass.: Harvard University Press, 1990.
Sealy, R. *A History of the Greek City States.* Berkeley: University of California Press, 1976.

ROME

Roman history has traditionally been divided into three periods according to the type of government in place at the time. The Monarchy, which lasted from 753 B.C.E. to 509 B.C.E., was succeeded by the Republic, which lasted until 31 B.C.E., the beginning of the empire. The end point of the Roman Empire is a much-disputed topic, with plausible arguments being made for many different dates ranging from the death of the emperor Marcus Aurelius in 180 C.E. to the fall of Constantinople in 1453 C.E.

POLITICAL LIFE

GOVERNMENT

Mesopotamia

Egypt

Greece

Rome

India

Nubia

Australian Aboriginals

The traditional founding date of the city of Rome is April 21, 753 B.C.E. This is the starting point both of the Roman calendar and of Roman history. Despite the importance that the Romans attached to the foundation of their city, it is difficult to determine what the truth of the story is; no contemporary account survives, and the later ones are heavily weighted with propagandistic purposes. Archaeological evidence tells us that the site of Rome was inhabited from at least 1000 B.C.E. and that starting around 700 B.C.E., the population increased very rapidly and the first signs of major urban structures in stone began to appear.

According to legend, the founder of Rome was Romulus, who became the first king and gave his name to his new city. He was succeeded by a series of kings, the latter of whom had Etruscan names, suggesting that at some point, the Etruscans imposed their own rulership on the Romans. Thus Rome went through a period when it was in essence ruled by foreign kings. The resentment caused by this left deep scars on the Roman psyche and would have long-reaching consequences. A rebellion was staged against the seventh king, supposedly in reaction to the arrogant behavior of the king and members of his family and resulting in their expulsion from Rome and the establishment of the Roman Republic.

The governmental institutions of the Roman Republic evolved over several hundred years and persisted into the period of the empire, when the emperors had effectively reestablished one-man rule. The core of the government centered around a series of magistracies. All of these magistracies shared a number of characteristics: officeholders obtained their positions by election, served one-year terms, and had to meet minimum age requirements for each office. In addition, each office was collegial, meaning that more than one person held the same title at the same time. Ambitious aristocrats aspired to be elected to each of these offices in turn, and the entire sequence became known as the *cursus honorem*, "the course of honor."

The lowest magistracy was the quaestorship. Under the fully developed system, quaestors were supposed to be 30 years old and were in charge of various financial affairs. Originally, only two quaestors were elected each year, but over time, as there was need for more and more officials, the number grew to 20. Different quaestors had varying specific duties, with some, for example, in charge of monitoring taxation, others overseeing financial matters in a province, and others controlling government finances.

The next magistracy was the aedileship. Aediles had to be 36 years old, and four were elected each year. The aediles were responsible for a variety of urban affairs, including the maintenance and repair of urban infrastructure, monitoring markets to ensure fair trade and enforce uniform standards of weights and measures, and staging public festivals.

Above the aediles were the praetors, who had to be 39 years old. Like the quaestors, the number of praetors gradually increased over time from one to as many as eight. Praetors mainly served judicial functions, overseeing law courts and the running of the judiciary system.

The most prestigious post of all was the consulship. Consuls had to be 42 years old, and only two were elected each year. They acted as the chief executives of the state and, at least during most of the Republic, served as the generals of Rome's armies.

In extreme emergencies, when the state itself was threatened, the Romans might appoint a dictator, who held almost absolute power. Because the Romans were very uncomfortable with the idea of one man monopolizing power, this office was only to be invoked in dire circumstances, and a dictator could hold office for no longer than six months.

A dictator could hold office for no longer than six months.

One other important elected office was the tribuneship. The number of tribunes varied, but they were charged with protecting the interests of the plebeians. To fulfill this duty, they had a number of unusual powers. Tribunes could propose legislation, and they enjoyed a special status of immunity intended to protect them. The tribunes' most potent prerogative, however, was the tribunician veto. This gave them the right to declare laws invalid, to revoke actions of other officials, and to overturn legal decisions. This powerful privilege was rarely invoked but was intended, by its very existence, to serve as a curb upon the worst excesses of patrician power.

Each of the main magistrates was appointed a number of assistants, or *lictors*, whose job was to enforce their orders. The number of lictors granted to each magistrate varied, with the highest office, consul, having the most and the junior magistrates having fewer. As a symbol of the magistrates' power, each lictor carried a fasces, an ax surrounded by a bundle of rods tied together with a purple ribbon. In theory, the magistrate could order lictors to dispense punishment by beating offenders with the rods or cutting off their heads with the ax.

The Roman senate, composed roughly of 300 members, was not an elected body, and it possessed no legislative powers; rather, its function was advisory. Membership in the senate was obtained by having held one of the higher magistracies, so that the senate was a body composed of ex-magistrates. Membership was for life. Because it consisted of Rome's political and financial elite, its advice on matters both domestic and foreign was usually taken seriously.

The body of Roman citizens was divided into three separate voting assemblies, which elected different officials. Patricians were simultaneously members of two of these assemblies, and plebeians were members of all three.

The first was called the *comitia centuriata*. This assembly gathered together to elect consuls, praetors, and censors. It also presided over trials for treason and, before the Punic Wars, voted on most legislation; after the wars, another assembly became responsible for legislation. Citizens were divided into 193 groups called centuries; which century a citizen was placed in was according to his net worth as determined in his census. In the actual election, each century had one vote. Thus there were 193 total votes. To determine how the century would cast its vote, the members of each century voted among themselves, and whatever the majority of the members decided was how the century's vote was cast. Thus the system was similar to the United States' electoral college, in which all the electoral votes of a certain state are given to just one candidate.

The process at first glance seems democratic, but it really was not because citizens were not divided evenly among centuries. The small number of wealthy Romans controlled the majority of the centuries. In essence, the vote of a rich man was weighted much more than the vote of a poor man. Not everyone voted at the same time; instead, they would start with the richest centuries, who would cast their vote, and then move downward. As soon as a majority (97) was reached, the election was over. Therefore, poor voters were often deprived of the opportunity to cast their ballot.

The next assembly was called the *comitia tributa*. In this assembly, instead of being divided by wealth, all citizens were divided by geography into 35 tribes. There were 4 urban tribes and 31 rural ones. The *comitia tributa* elected aediles and quaestors and voted on most legislation.

The system was similar to the *comitia centuriata* in which each tribe voted among itself and then the entire tribe cast a single vote. Thus in this election, there were 35 total votes, and whoever got 18, a majority, won. Once again, even though it looks democratic, the system favored the rich, though in a more subtle way. Elections were held at Rome, and a citizen had to be physically present to cast a vote. There were no absentee ballots, and everyone voted in one place. Thus if a citizen wanted to vote, he had to travel to Rome, which required time and money, things only the rich had. The poor people who lived in Rome could certainly vote, and did, but because they were all grouped into the four urban tribes, they only had 4 out of 35 votes.

The final important assembly was the *concilia plebis*. It was organized in the same way as the *comitia tributa*, with 35 tribes, and voted in the same way. The only difference was that all patricians were excluded, and its main function was to elect tribunes.

~Gregory S. Aldrete

FOR MORE INFORMATION

Abbott, F. F. *A History and Description of Roman Political Institutions*. 3rd ed. New York: Ginn and Co., 1963.

Nicolet, C. *The World of the Citizen in Republican Rome*. Berkeley: University of California Press, 1980.

Talbert, R. *The Senate of Imperial Rome*. Princeton, N.J.: Princeton University Press, 1984.

POLITICAL LIFE
|
GOVERNMENT
|
Mesopotamia

Egypt

Greece

Rome

India

Nubia

Australian Aboriginals

INDIA

In the late third century B.C.E., a minister of Emperor Chandragupta Maurya compiled a treatise containing the political wisdom of ancient India. This legendary minister was named Kautilya, and the treatise was the *Arthasastra*, which became— in principle, if not always in practice—the template for governance for centuries to follow.

At the center of the state is the king. Key to the rule of the king is that he rule judiciously, in accordance with the dictates of the *dharma* (righteousness). The king is as the god Indra on Earth, and his chief duty is to provide protection to the people.

The *Arthasastra* enumerates a number of bureaucratic and executive offices in government, but of paramount importance to the king was legitimation of his rule in accord with the *dharma*. To this end, an important minister of the king was the *purohita*, who was always of the Brahman community. This minister had no temporal authority, according to Kautilya, but functioned as a teacher and advisor, as well as ritual priest. Primary among legitimating rites for the king that the *purohita* officiated were the Rajasuya, the rite of royal consecration, and the Asvamedha, the horse sacrifice.

The religious legitimation of the rule of a king cemented his authority over the people as well as ensuring the welfare of the people by affirming the kingdom's harmony with cosmic order. Moreover, with the emphasis in many Indian traditions on the doctrine of *ahimsa* (nonviolence), religious legitimation frequently sanctioned such kingly necessities as warfare, capital punishment, and meat eating. There are several instances, however, where the king relied on nonorthodox traditions to legitimate rule. For example, Chandragupta's grandson, the Emperor Asoka, after expanding his rule through conquest to govern the greatest ancient empire in India's history, reputedly converted to Buddhism and erected tablets proclaiming the Buddhist *dharma* as law of the land.

In northern India, and especially in tribal areas, a different form of government frequently prevailed. In these cases, rule was by a council of elders, often called a republic, although the term *oligarchy* might better describe this arrangement.

The converse of religious duty for the king was the protection of the kingdom, accompanied by expansion of the state and its resources through conquest. The typical Indian army rested on four components: elephants, cavalry, chariots, and infantry. The elephant, mounted by several spearmen or archers, was an awesome sight on the battlefield, useful for breaking up enemy formations. However, elephants frequently proved unpredictable, and once one took fright, a stampede or flight from the battle was likely. Cavalry was often underutilized in Indian armies, to their detriment. Kautilya saw cavalry's role as primarily means of scouting, raiding, and flanking the enemy, leaving the fore of the army to the elephants. The chariot was the main fighting force from the Vedic period through the Epic period but declined in the early centuries of the common era. The light chariot of the Vedic period evolved from two wheels, carrying a warrior and a driver, to a more elaborate vehicle with four wheels and carrying up to four warriors. Infantry was the mainstay of the army, and soldiers were typically armed with spear or sword, although some employed maces or axes.

Column capital with lions. This sculpture is from the palace of the Indian king Asoka at Sarnath. The wheels represent the Buddhist concept of existence as a repeating cycle of life and death. Christine Osborne/ Painet Inc.

Outside the authority of the state, and on the fringes of a weak state, ancient India was frequently seen as a dangerous place. Bands of thieves were abundant, and local chieftains occasionally raided villages and towns. Moreover, according to the *Arthasastra*, a king's adjacent neighbor was to be viewed as a natural enemy, while nonadjacent kingdoms bordering an enemy were natural allies. This reflected the norm of aggressive warfare for conquest and expansion of territory as a means to increase the state's power, despite the condemnation of such practices by many religious texts.

~*Matthew Bingley*

FOR MORE INFORMATION

Allchin, B., and R. Allchin. *The Rise of Civilization in India and Pakistan*. Cambridge, England: Cambridge University Press, 1982.

Altekar, A. S. *State and Government in Ancient India*. 3d ed. Dheli, India: Motilal Banarsidass, 1958.

Kautilya. *The Arthashastra*. Edited and translated by L. N. Rangaranjan. New York: Penguin Books India, 1992.

Kenoyer, J. M. *Ancient Cities of the Indus Valley Civilization*. New York: Oxford University Press, 1998.

NUBIA

To understand the governing structure of the Nubians in the more distant epochs of their history, it is important to consider the data gleaned from their excavated graves and the goods found within them over a period of time. These graves, first encountered in numbers during the Neolithic period (after 10,000 B.C.E.), reveal differences in their design and dimensions, the number and quality of their accompanying grave goods, and their position within the cemetery itself. So, for example, at Kadera one can distinguish elite graves, which are both cut deeper into the earth than others and contain deluxe grave goods in the form of ivory artifacts and Red Sea shells, together with weapons including stone mace heads. The latter, termed *powerfacts*, were symbols of decorum used by Nubian society as an index of social status. Such graves belonging to the Nubian elite are estimated to account for no more than 10 percent of the population as a whole. They suggest a society based on tribes or interrelated families, with the elders serving as an oligarchy, one of whom exercised primacy over all. With the passage of time, these elite groups consolidated their control over their immediate geographic area and soon came into conflict with competing elite groups from other regions.

By the time of the A-Group culture (about 3700–2800 B.C.E.), these elite groups were warring not only against one another, as a scene carved into the rock at Gebel Sheikh Sulimen suggests, but also with Egyptians. These military engagements decided suzerainty over territories as well as control of trade routes. The A-Group culture came to a close with the ascendancy of Egyptian military power in Nubia.

The pattern of competing elites characterized the subsequent history of Nubia, culminating in the kingdom of Kerma (about 2500–1500 B.C.E.). Excavations of the settlement of Kerma itself, as well as of the tombs of its elite members, reveal a highly organized state with international connections. After the pharaohs of Egypt, the rulers of Kerma can be considered Africa's first true kings. Their power is reflected in their burials, which included sacrifices of human victims and the burial of their horses.

With the extensive Nubian acculturation to pharaonic Egyptian norms during the New Kingdom and early Third Intermediate period (about 1550–720 B.C.E.), the Nubians seemed to lose their ethnic identity in the archaeological record. But that presence is emphatically reaffirmed with the founding of the Nubian dynasty of pharaohs in Egypt (about 750–664 B.C.E.).

The records from this period, however, are difficult to interpret. As a result, the process by which any particular Nubian became king during Dynasty 25 are contentious issues. Some have argued that succession was predicated on primogeniture, passing on leadership to the next eligible male issue of the current ruler, while others argue for the successor's relationship to the primary, dominant female member of the oligarchy. When the succession was in doubt and the oligarchy could not reach consensus on any given candidate, as was the case with Aspelta of the following Napatan period (about 575 B.C.E.), divine intervention in the form of an oracle delivered by the god Amun decided the issue.

Once established as pharaoh, the Nubian kings presented themselves in accordance with ancient Egyptian norms, ruling their kingdom by the divine grace of the god Amun and intent on maintaining cosmic order and harmony. Contemporary inscriptions of pharaohs Piankhy and Taharqa of Dynasty 25 describe their reigns in terms of piety toward the gods and depict the suppression of military opposition to their authority as battles against the inimical foes of the divine. They allowed themselves to be depicted on the walls of their temples and official stelae in traditional roles relative to the gods of the land, granting to them offerings of tangible commodities, various products, and land in return for intangibles such as a long reign, peace, and triumph over one's foes. They ruled as absolute monarchs, occasionally allowing a coregent to oversee affairs in Nubia while they resided in Egypt at Memphis. They habitually staffed their administration with members of their immediate families and other elite members of society. They were reverential toward the deities of both Nubia and Egypt and gained additional religious and political leverage by elevating their female relations via adoption to the prestigious office of divine wife of the god Amun at Thebes. In keeping with Egyptian norms, they were themselves the chief celebrants of every temple in both Nubia and Egypt and enlisted the assistance of a bureaucracy whose members simultaneously served in important clerical and secular offices. In battle, they fought at the head of their armies and risked death, as the wounds sustained by Taharqa demonstrate. In death, they were buried with all the pomp and circumstance attendant upon the position of ancient Egyptian pharaohs.

At some point during the course of the third century B.C.E., a schism developed among the Nubians regarding the overweening influence the priesthood exercised in matters of royal succession. One ruler managed to break the power of the priesthood and assert his own claim to the throne. He then moved the capital from Napata to Meroe and elected to be called *qore*, "commander," a title already current for Nubian leaders during the Egyptian New Kingdom. The Nubian monarch behind this political change that ushered in the Meroitic period has not been identified but may have been the Ergamenes mentioned by the Classical authors or Arkamani I, the first royal Nubian to have been buried at Meroe. The Meroitic *qore* appears in depictions on temple scenes to be the equal of two other individuals, one a man called a *pqr*, the exact meaning of which remains elusive, and a woman, whose title is *kdke*, equated by the Classical authors with that of queen.

The *kdke* seems to have been highly regarded in Nubian society, as were women generally. Some *kdke* appear to have exercised supreme positions of power in the Meroitic period, as the remarkable case of one of these rulers reveals. Classical authors refer to her only as Candake, assuming her title—in this, its Classical form—was her actual name. The historical person behind the title in this episode of Nubian history has not been unequivocally established. Her story is as follows.

Shortly after the death by suicide of Cleopatra VII (30 B.C.E.) and the subsequent conquest of Egypt by Augustus, the first emperor of Rome, the situation in Upper Egypt in the region around Aswan deteriorated, perhaps over issues of Roman taxation. At the same time, dissent within Roman possessions in Arabia across the Red Sea forced the Romans to dispatch their legions, stationed in Egypt, to this hot spot. The removal of the Roman garrison encouraged the Nubians to revolt, but the arrival of Roman legions could not decide the issue. The two armies were stalled as they faced one another in Nubia. The hostilities were amicably resolved when an embassy of Candake, the Nubian queen, was granted safe passage to the Greek island of Samos, where Augustus had been temporarily headquartered. The Nubians extracted concessions from the Romans, which included the remission of taxes and the establishment of a buffer zone between the southern border of Roman Egypt and the kingdom of Meroe. This episode reveals the power and prestige of Nubian rulers and the status attained by their queens.

~*Robert S. Bianchi*

FOR MORE INFORMATION

Adams, W. *Nubia: Corridor to Africa*. Princeton, N.J.: Princeton University Press, 1977.

O'Connor, D. *Ancient Nubia: Egypt's Rival in Africa*. Philadelphia: University of Pennsylvania, 1993.

Trigger, B. *Nubia under the Pharaohs*. Boulder, Colo.: Westview Press, 1976.

Welsby, D. A. *The Kingdom of Kush: The Napatan and Meroitic Empires*. London: British Museum Press, 1996.

POLITICAL LIFE

GOVERNMENT

Mesopotamia

Egypt

Greece

Rome

India

Nubia

Australian Aboriginals

AUSTRALIAN ABORIGINALS

Aboriginal society was at the same time extremely democratic and strongly hierarchical, with both local and regional structures. Power was based not on amassing wealth but instead on accumulation of knowledge. Men were accorded power because of their gender, but women too had their own power structure. There were no titles of rank such as king or chief, but everyone possessed a set of titles that identified their place in society. Goods were not inherited, and the names of the dead were not even spoken after death, but individuals inherited their position in society.

Decisions and actions were based on detailed observation of the environment as it changed each day.

Laws were handed down unchanged from the beginning of time and were as unchanging as the land. The role of elders was not to make laws but rather to remember the laws passed down from the ancestors. Law was not remote from everyday life and indeed was derived from and affected every aspect of the land and human behavior. The purpose of government was to maintain the law, and law was concerned with religion. Unlike in Western societies, there was no separation between secular law and religious law. All law had to do with observing the rules for correct behavior in society and in relation to the spirit world. As with most aspects of Aboriginal life, everything was intertwined with everything else.

As children grew up, they were instructed in what they needed to know to function in society and to obey the laws. An understanding of the law was gradually obtained throughout life, marked along the way by stages of initiation into new levels of knowledge.

Elders were distinguished by their attainment of the whole body of knowledge of law and religion. They therefore possessed the expertise to make judgments about the actions of individuals or the group as a whole. In addition, they had accumulated experience about survival and the environment. Although old men and women could no longer hunt, they were supported by the younger members of society in return for providing governance of the political, economic, and religious life of the community. Their rule, however, also depended on the input of ideas and opinions from all the adults in the group. Authority varied according to context, and those who had power in one ceremony might be subservient in another, so that power was shared across society. Some ceremonies were undoubtedly viewed as larger or more important than others, and the elders who played key roles in important ceremonies would be seen as being more powerful. Similarly, while all clan groups were in theory equal, some would inevitably be bigger than others, and their leaders consequently of more importance.

Government and the laws by which society was regulated served to determine ceremonial affairs as well as matters such as marriage or the settling of disputes. Sometimes mediation failed, and the group (or two related groups) might become embroiled in a cycle of revenge. Eventually, however, a settlement would be reached, perhaps through holding a special peacemaking ceremony. Aboriginal society is a striking example of a form of government and social organization that is totally different from that of current Western society, but which thrived for 50,000 years.

~David Horton

FOR MORE INFORMATION

Berndt, R., and C. Berndt. *The World of the First Australians*. Canberra: Aboriginal Studies Press, 1988.

Elkin, A. *Aboriginal Men of High Degree*. St. Lucia, Queensland: University of Queensland Press, 1977.

Stanner, W. *White Man Got No Dreaming*. Canberra: Australian National University Press, 1979.

POLITICAL LIFE
|
LAW
|
Mesopotamia

Egypt

Greece

Rome

Law

Anytime people begin to live communally in densely packed groups, as in cities or towns, conflicts among them will be inevitable. To prevent a situation whereby the strong simply prey on the weak, rules to govern behavior and to mediate conflict are quickly developed. This is the origin of law codes—they are what make living together possible.

While some sort of formal or informal codes establishing rules of conduct and laying out penalties for deviations from the standard no doubt existed even in the first human settlements, the earliest such systems to have been written down and survived come from Mesopotamia. By far, the most famous is the Code of Hammurabi, dating to about 1700 B.C.E. Hammurabi's code and other early law codes, such as the Twelve Tables of Rome, tend to share a number of characteristics. They usually reflect their origins in agrarian communities through numerous laws dealing with establishing property boundaries, provisions for accidents involving farm animals, and so on. They typically were retaliatory codes, prescribing a system of punishments based on the eye-for-an-eye principle, whereby whatever crime you inflict on another person is done to you in turn. These law codes also reveal the inequalities found in the societies that produced them, so that the law was not the same for all persons but varied by one's gender, age, and status. Finally, the punishments prescribed are frequently quite harsh, with beatings, mutilation, death, and torture being meted out to wrongdoers. Incarceration as a punishment was almost never practiced, and most ancient societies had nothing like modern prisons, in which criminals are kept locked up for long periods of time.

In the ancient monarchies, all justice usually derived in theory from the king, but because of the obvious impracticality of the monarch personally presiding over all trials, various local courts, such as the Egyptian *kenbet* system, were established to deal with everyday cases. Greece and Rome both developed trial by a randomly selected jury of peers in at least some circumstances, and these juries could sometimes make up a not insignificant percentage of the total citizen body, as with the 600-person juries used in some Athenian trials. Trial procedures involved the giving of evidence and the presentation of witnesses. The ultimate goal of most trials is to determine the truth of what happened and then to address any injustices. All ancient juridical systems placed an emphasis on testimony by witnesses and used oaths to try to compel truthful testimony. In Greek and Roman trials, the testimony of slaves could only be legally admissible if it was obtained by torture, the assumption being that slaves would otherwise habitually lie.

However harsh or at times unjust the early law codes might seem to us now, their creation was an important step forward for civilization as a whole. Without laws to regulate social interaction, it would be impossible for people to live together and to create civilizations and cultures. The law is one of the clearest and most important legacies of the ancient world to the modern one. The majority of the world's legal systems today can either be directly traced back to the Roman code of law or were influenced by it.

~Gregory S. Aldrete

MESOPOTAMIA

POLITICAL LIFE
|
LAW
|
Mesopotamia

Egypt

Greece

Rome

The king was directly responsible for administering justice on behalf of the gods, who had established law and order in the universe. The king was considered the final judicial authority for all appeals within his realm. Although appeals were made to him, he often referred them back to the lower authorities. Mesopotamian judicial institutions had clear procedural guidelines for settling disputes. The facts had to be clearly established before a verdict was rendered. Oral testimony was taken from two contestants; witnesses were called from either side; and documents, if available, were presented. If the facts of the case were not clear, judges might write to local authorities to have witnesses sent or request further investigation locally. At the end, the penalty had to suit the crime. Judicial tasks were carried out by local councils, judges and courts, and the king.

The court of first resort in early Mesopotamia was the local council, which included the elders and mayor of the village or city quarter. Their decisions, both judicial and administrative, were announced by a public herald. Correspondence shows that although the local council passed judgment, the council (and even the litigant) could refer the case to a higher court.

Judges presided by the Early Dynastic period, sometimes in conjunction with the ruler of the city-state. Attorneys were never mentioned. In the Old Babylonian period, the town mayor and elders usually settled minor local disputes, while other cases were brought before the whole town to render a decision. At times, one party and his witness(es) were required to testify under oath, usually in the presence of the god's symbol, which was rented from the temple. Lying under oath was hindered by the fear of divine vengeance in cases of perjury. When there was contradictory evidence, the divine judges of the river were summoned to decide the case by the "river ordeal." Immersion in the "Divine River" brought a verdict of guilt (drowning) or innocence (survival). The river ordeal was reserved for cases in which grave accusations could not be decided by any other means, for example, perjury, sorcery, adultery, and homicide. Evidence for execution of the death penalty is almost wholly lacking. Both the death sentence and mutilation were perhaps oral pronouncements, and only civil cases involving compensatory damages were transcribed.

There was no Akkadian word for "court," and the term used implied that the case was brought before a judge or benches of judges who sat at the gate or in the temple courtyard. We do not know the credentials of these judges or how they were chosen. Some judges seem to have been appointed when necessary, possibly from among the "elders" and prominent secular and temple officials. There is some evidence for the appointment of more permanent judges, known as "judges of the king," who were also responsible for administrative duties. By the beginning of the Old Babylonian period, some men were given the professional title of "judge." Judges were expected to display high standards of professional conduct, as noted in the Code of Hammurabi (§5): "If a judge tried a case and made a decision and had a sealed document executed, but later changed his judgment, they will convict that judge of changing his judgment: he will pay twelve times the claim involved in that case, and they will remove him in the Assembly from his judgment seat, and he will not sit in judgment with the judges again."

A good deal is known about the administration of justice. There were court officials who ensured that the court's decision was executed. The Old Babylonian courts had a sheriff (literally, "soldier") whose duties included recovering property and bringing a baby to court to record its birth. Another official attached to the court was a barber, who gave slaves the hairdo

---

📷 Snapshot

A Mesopotamian Trial

In this lawsuit, Ilusha-khegal, a priestess, claimed that she had not received full payment for land sold to the current owner, Belessunu, a priestess and wife of Addi-liblut:

> The judges requested from Ilusha-khegal (to provide) witnesses that Belessunu, the *naditum* (priestess), had not paid her the silver, or (documentation for) the debt-document which they had made out to her for the remainder of the silver, but they (that is, the documents) did not exist and she did not produce them; whereas Addi-liblut did produce the sealed deed for 1 sar of house, and the judges read it, and questioned the witnesses who were written in the deed and they gave evidence before the judges in front of Ilusha-khegal that she had received 15 shekels of silver as the price of 1 sar of developed property (literally, "a built house"), and Ilusha-khegal conceded it.

> The judges examined their case, and because Ilusha-khegal had disowned her seal they imposed a penalty on her and made out this tablet renouncing her claim. (Nemet-Nejat, 222)

---

characteristic of their status. Later, the barber performed unrelated tasks such as destroying tablets nullified by a royal edict. A herald also was an official at the court; his duties involved announcing official information. It was the herald who publicized the loss of a seal and its dates, so any documents sealed after that date would be deemed invalid. He also advertised a runaway slave, announced government conscriptions, and presided over house sales. The king himself could hear cases, and any citizen could appeal directly to the king. The lower courts might refer a case to the king. Murder trials traditionally were the king's domain.

The king might require that the two opposing parties take oaths. Letters describe Hammurabi judging and supervising cases. Sometimes penalties affected the entire community; for example, §23 stipulates that if a man was robbed but the robber was not caught, the local authorities had to compensate the victim for his loss. The code included both civil and criminal matters. Preserved also are the texts of some "decrees" considered to be royal decisions. After about 1500 B.C.E., the kings of both Babylonia and Assyria issued decrees of exemption from various kinds of conscripted service such as military obligations and corvée labor as well as a moratorium on debts to certain cities.

At the beginning of a king's reign, edicts were announced, rather than recorded, to provide short-term relief from social and economic injustices. The first known edict was from Uru-inimgina. Royal edicts have been found through the reign of Hammurabi and after, when they became a regular institution.

The next step taken by the king was recording collections of laws. The law codes began with a prologue written in the style of a royal inscription, followed by a collection of laws, which formed the main body of the text. An epilogue contained curses against those who should try to deface or alter a stele. Each collection was a new, independent legal work, but some laws were quoted verbatim from previous collections. Most of the laws were formulated like omens, including a conditional clause and a statement: for example, "If a man has committed robbery, he will be killed." None of the legal collections was organized systematically; cases of penal, civil, trade, and work laws alternated with each other.

The most complete law code by far was the Code of Hammurabi (ca. 1750 B.C.E.). A relief of King Hammurabi of Babylon (1792–1750 B.C.E.) receiving the insignia of royal power from Shamash (the god of justice) was portrayed at the top on the front of the stele. The last seven of these columns were erased by Shutruk-Nakkhunte, the Elamite king, who took the monument as part of his booty (ca. 1595 B.C.E.). There were 282 cases, taking into account the missing portion in the middle. The penal law was much harsher than older laws. The death penalty was a common punishment. Mutilations (such as cutting off a hand) and beatings were frequently prescribed. Hammurabi termed his laws "cases of justice." Many copies of the Code of Hammurabi were made on stelae and clay tablets and have been found from the time of Hammurabi through the Seleucid period. Late texts included commentaries to facilitate understanding of the code.

The Code of Hammurabi may have represented a collection of decisions, customary law, legal innovations, and designations of areas in need of amendment. The code may have standardized traditional practices. We do not know for certain to what extent it was actually implemented in judicial practice.

In both the prologue and epilogue, the word used for laws is "decision," perhaps referring to royal decisions. The key to understanding the purpose of the legal code may be found in the epilogue: "Let the wronged man who has a case go before my statue (called) the 'King of Justice' and have my inscribed stele read and hear my valuable words. Let my stele reveal his case; let him see the law which applies to him, and let his heart be at rest." The stele was placed in Babylon before a statue of Hammurabi, erected in the 22nd year of his reign.

Alternatively, the code may have been a model for just royal decisions, as also described in the epilogue: "To the end of days, forever, may the king who happens to be in the land observe the words of justice which I have inscribed on my stele . . . let that stele reveal to him the accustomed way, the way to follow, the land's judgements which I have judged and the land's decisions which I have decided." Hammurabi's laws were not statutes in the modern sense; to date, only one reference has been found to his laws among thousands of court records, in a contract

Stone stele inscribed with the Law Code of Hammurabi. The stele is approximately 7 feet tall, and the carving at the top depicts Hammurabi and the god of judgment, Shamash. Louvre © Photo RMN–H. Lowandowski.

dealing with the cultivation of land (dated in the fifth year of Hammurabi's successor). Some cases in public documents were settled in a completely different way from the code. In comparing the Code of Hammurabi with contemporaneous administrative and legal documents, we find numerous omissions and contradictions in the law code.

As for Assyrian laws, Old Assyrian documents and letters cited laws that were part of a merchant statute, based on either Assyrian or local laws. Middle Assyrian laws have been found in a fragmentary state. The first tablet, almost completely preserved, concerned women. The second dealt with property rights, and the third dealt with slaves, livestock, and goods. According to the Middle Assyrian laws, the status of women was low. Punishments in all cases were exceedingly harsh, including the death penalty, beatings up to one hundred blows, forced labor, and various mutilations. River ordeals were frequently used by judges to decide guilt or innocence. There was no further codification of law in Assyria after the second millennium B.C.E. (Nemet-Nejat, 221–27).

FOR MORE INFORMATION

Nemet-Nejat, K. R. *Daily Life in Ancient Mesopotamia.* Westport, Conn.: Greenwood Press, 1998.

Roth, M. *Law Collections from Mesopotamia and Ancient Aisa Minor.* Atlanta, Ga.: Scholars Press, 1995.

POLITICAL LIFE

LAW

Mesopotamia

Egypt

Greece

Rome

EGYPT

Although the pharaoh was the ultimate authority, on a practical day-to-day basis, *kenbets,* or district councils, appointed by the area *nomarch* from the most-respected citizens in each community, functioned as Egypt's legal system, deciding most disputes, which generally concerned property. Most criminal cases and inheritance controversies also fell within their scope. Because the government did not operate through laws (no legislative body existed), *kenbets* functioned less as judges of a codified legal system than as investigative committees to uncover the truthfulness of allegations. They took depositions from those who knew the character of a person bringing suit, searched voluminous archives for old records that might bear on the case, and then rendered a decision.

If the decision did not satisfy both parties, the suit could be resubmitted, but an unusual device was employed to end perennial litigation. The *kenbet* could relay the evidence to the statue of a god, who would render a verdict either by communicating to a priest or, more often, while carried on priests' shoulders by stopping in front of one of the litigants to indicate the god's favor. Usually, the "divine" authority of such a verdict ended the dispute.

Kenbets used several remedies to rectify wrongs. They could order property to be seized and transferred to the injured party. They could inflict physical punishment such as beatings (usually a hundred blows with a stick) or mutilation (cutting off an ear or nose). Although no prisons existed in Egypt, the *kenbet* could sentence offenders to fixed periods of heavy labor in mines or quarries and could also exile serious criminals.

Because Egypt functioned with two capital cities, Memphis and Thebes, each maintained a Great *Kenbet*, which served as a higher court for the lesser *kenbets* of the respective northern and southern territories. Each vizier held a seat on the Great *Kenbet* of his area, along with the top officials of the state, temple, and army. Capital offenses were assigned to the Great *Kenbets* alone, but because these councils consisted of busy men of great responsibility, capital cases could not have been as frequent as in our day (Brier and Hobbs, 67).

FOR MORE INFORMATION

Brier, B., and H. Hobbs. *Daily Life of the Ancient Egyptians*. Westport, Conn.: Greenwood Press, 1999.
David, R. *Handbook to Life in Ancient Egypt*. New York: Facts on File, 1998.

GREECE

POLITICAL LIFE
|
LAW
|
Mesopotamia

Egypt

Greece

Rome

Our knowledge of crime in ancient Greece is meager. We know much more about legal procedure than about criminals. Although we hear about burglary, theft, mugging, rape, and murder, we know only of isolated cases. Comparing the prevalence of such crimes in antiquity with their occurrence today is not possible. Most of our evidence comes from law-court speeches written on behalf of well-to-do clients embroiled in cases of disputed adoption, inheritance, and the like. What follows, therefore, inevitably reflects the limitations of our sources.

No Greek community had a police force in the modern sense of the term. The Scythian archers that Athens possessed had the primary task of keeping the peace. In the absence of any state-run means of law enforcement, it was up to the injured party to arrest any criminal caught in the act and to bring him (or her) before the magistrates. This must have been extremely difficult in the case of victims of violent crime, especially if they happened to be elderly or female. An injured party who was incapable of arresting the criminal could summon the magistrate, who would then make an arrest on his or her behalf. In the case of a wrongful arrest, a fine of 1,000 drachmas was imposed. Other than in cases involving theft, murder, rape, and adultery, the accused received a written summons naming the day that he or she was required to appear before a magistrate.

Athenian law was divided into public and private actions. Public actions involved the community as a whole, whereas private actions concerned individuals. There was no public prosecutor. Although in practice many cases would have been brought to the courts by magistrates or other officials, Solon legislated that "anyone who wishes" was free to initiate prosecution in a public action or *graphê*. In the case of a private suit or *dikê*, it was the responsibility of the injured party to bring the action. In cases of homicide, the relatives of the victim were required to prosecute the killer.

A preliminary hearing called an *anakrisis* took place before a magistrate. Oaths were exchanged by the plaintiff and the defendant, the former swearing that his accusation was genuine, and the latter either admitting guilt or swearing that he was innocent. The defendant was free at this time to enter a counterplea. The case was then assigned to a particular court on a particular date. All trials, irrespective of the severity of the charges, were confined in scope to the space of a single day. Only a limited amount of cross-examination took place. The testimony of slaves could be obtained only under torture.

Although magistrates presided over trials, they did not serve as judges in the modern sense of the term. They gave neither advice nor directions to the jury nor did they sentence those who were found guilty. They merely supervised the proceedings in a general way. Juries, composed of citizens over 30 years of age, were often extremely large because it was believed that this reduced the likelihood of bribery. In exceptional cases, the jury could even include 600 members. After the speeches had been delivered by the prosecution and defense, the jurors voted without deliberation. In the fifth century B.C.E., jurors cast their votes in secret. Each juror was provided with two tokens, one for conviction and the other for acquittal. The juror deposited one of these in a wooden urn, whose tokens were disregarded, and the other in a "valid" bronze urn, whose votes were counted. Judgment was passed on a majority verdict. In the fifth century B.C.E., a tie meant an acquittal. In the following century, odd-numbered juries were the norm.

Imprisonment was applied only on a short-term basis to those awaiting trial or execution. Prisoners were supervised by a group of junior magistrates known as the Eleven, who also had the task of supervising the execution of condemned criminals. Athens's state prison has tentatively been identified with a building located in the southwest corner of the Agora. It consisted of 12 small rooms that possibly served as cells. The identification is strengthened by the discovery of 13 miniature bottles. These may have contained the hemlock that condemned prisoners such as Socrates were required to drink.

Execution was mainly reserved for crimes such as murder, larceny, theft, picking pockets, housebreaking, kidnapping, and temple robbing. As Socrates' trial indicates, however, any serious offense was punishable by death if the prosecution saw fit to demand it. In extreme cases such as treason and tomb robbery, the condemned was denied the rite of burial. After being hurled off a rock, he was left to rot in the *barathron* or pit, a rocky gully that probably lay a short distance west of the Acropolis. In Sparta, a similar practice took place at a site called the Kaiades. This practice ensured that the dead would never be granted access to Hades but would wander disconsolately up and down the banks of the river Styx for all eternity. In Macedon, hanging was the preferred form of execution. There is little evidence to suggest that decapitation was ever practiced.

There were several weaknesses in the Athenian legal system, excellent though it was by the standards of the day. First, a trial resembled a public spectacle, with skillful oratory playing a disproportionate part in the outcome. In addition, the large size of many juries increased the possibility of a verdict being subject to crowd hysteria. We know of at least one instance in which the citizen body, sitting in assembly, made a decision in the heat of the moment and reversed it the next day; it is likely that comparable changes of heart among jurors occurred from time to time. As there was no procedure for lodging an appeal, however, only exceptionally was a verdict overturned.

Although the legal system was intended to uphold the rule of law, in practice it continued to countenance, if not actively encourage, the pursuit of a family vendetta. This was particularly true in cases of homicide, where it was the duty of the relatives of the murdered victim to prosecute the killer. Many actions of lesser import are also likely to have been motivated by revenge. In one, a prosecutor admitted as much, confident that his honesty would not count against him in the eyes of the jury (Garland, 149–53).

FOR MORE INFORMATION

Gagarin, M. *Early Greek Law*. Berkeley: University of California Press, 1986.
Garland, R. *Daily Life of the Ancient Greeks*. Westport, Conn.: Greenwood Press, 1998.
Garner, R. *Law and Society in Classical Athens*. London: Croom Helm, 1987.
Todd, S. C. *The Shape of Athenian Law*. Oxford: Clarendon Press, 1995.

ROME

POLITICAL LIFE
|
LAW
|
Mesopotamia

Egypt

Greece

Rome

The Romans liked to keep records, and one of the things they kept very good records of was the law and law cases. From these, we know a great deal about Roman law. In the 500s c.e., the emperor Justinian collected vast numbers of these cases and had them compiled into something that became known as the Digest of Roman Law. It took several years to collect all of these, and they were finally published in 533 c.e. This collection of cases and commentaries by jurists became the basis for many of the world's legal systems. Nearly every country in Europe and many others around the world can trace their law codes directly back to Justinian's Digest. England, however, developed its own code called English Common Law, and the United States copied this, although most of the terminology and concepts were still derived from Roman law. The Digest represents the end point of Roman law, and by this time, Roman law was fully as complex as our modern legal system, with laws and precedents to cover nearly every possible situation. This complex legal system did not spring up overnight but was the result of hundreds of years of accumulated legal practice. The origins of Roman law date back almost a thousand years prior to the Digest, to 450 b.c.e., when the first law code was formally written down.

Soon after Rome had expelled the kings and become a Republic, it became obvious that in a democratic type of government, all citizens would demand protection under the law. A commission of 10 was appointed to come up with a law code, which became known as the Twelve Tables.

Each table addresses a part of the law, such as crimes, inheritance, property, and so on. The tables were literally bronze tablets inscribed with the law and were set up in the Forum. The Twelve Tables were quite simple and were plainly the product of an agrarian society. Many were concerned with settling disputes between farmers over boundaries, use of animals, and so on. Punishments were retaliatory, meaning that whatever a person did to someone else was usually done to the perpetrator as punishment, and the code is harsh, with many things resulting in the death penalty.

From these basic beginnings, Roman law developed and grew more complex. The Roman term for law is *ius* (the root of our word *justice*). The law was divided into two parts: *ius publicum*, which concerned the relationship of the individual to the state, and *ius privatum*, which concerned the relationship of individuals to one another. As with most other things in Roman society, a person's status meant everything. Thus all people were classified under different categories. The first was whether they were free or slaves. The second was whether they were *sui iuris* or *alieni iuris*. Only people who were *sui iuris*, literally, "under their own law," had power and could bring a lawsuit.

One drawback of the Roman legal system was that there was no real police force. Hence, to bring someone before the praetor on a charge, you had to capture him yourself and take him to the praetor. One of the praetors had the job of sitting in the Forum and dealing with legal cases that were brought to him. A few crimes, such as treason, required trials before one of the assemblies, but for most day-to-day crimes, the praetor had power to settle the case. Praetors were supposed to follow legal precedents in making judgments, but the system was not formal, and there was room for arbitrariness.

Rome had no professional lawyers, and legal trials often took on the nature of public spectacles, particularly in the late Republic when a number of high-profile Roman citizens were involved in a series of sensational public trials. Law cases were judged out in the open, often in the Forum itself, so that anyone could gather and watch. In this time, law cases became almost a form of entertainment. People came and watched the speakers perform. Men such as Cicero who were gifted public speakers could make their political careers by presenting celebrity cases. Because of the public nature of trials, such speakers played as much to the audience as to the jury. Audiences were quite vocal and would shout out comments, abuse, and praise.

Rome did not have a prison system. The only jail in Rome was a single cell, which was used to hold people until they could be executed. The standard punishments were fines, flogging, decapitation, crucifixion (for slaves who had revolted, incest, and treason), or burning (for treachery and arson). Citizens could also be stripped of their status as citizens and become slaves or gladiators. Another punishment was to be sent to the mines, which entailed incredibly hard and dangerous labor; this really amounted to a delayed death sentence. A final option was exile. The Romans termed this to be interdicted from fire and water. It was a capital offense to help or harbor an exile, and an exile who returned could be killed with impunity.

The Romans had a few special punishments for crimes they found especially offensive. Given the reverence, status, and power accorded to fathers, it is not surprising that the Romans were particularly horrified by children who killed their fathers. The punishment for this crime was to be sewn up in a sack together with a live rooster, dog, snake, and monkey; the sack was then thrown into the ocean.

If a defendant was found to owe money as punishment for a crime and was unable to pay the debt, his body became the property of the wronged person—in other words, he became the slave of that person. A person who killed someone else's slave or animal had to pay the highest value that the property had possessed in the past year. A person who burned, broke, or smashed anything had to pay its highest value in the last month. For theft, the wronged party received double the value of the object stolen. If the theft was accompanied by violence, the victim received four times the value.

For personal injuries, such as one person hitting another, an estimate was made of the damage and a money award was given to the injured person. This type of crime had a one-year statute of limitations, meaning that if the wronged person did not bring suit within one year, he could no longer do so. There were four cases in which the injured party would receive extra money because of the outrageousness of the crime: (1) if the injured person was of high rank, such as a senator; (2) if the act was unusually brutal, such as clubbing with a heavy stick; (3) if the crime took place in a very public place, such as the theater; and (4) if the injured body part was particularly sensitive, such as the eye.

Romans were very concerned with leaving their property to the desired person. About 20 percent of surviving legal writings concern wills and what makes them valid. The main purpose of a will was to designate somebody as the heir. This is different from modern wills, in which the main purpose is to distribute property. The heir not only inherited all or most of someone's property, but they almost literally assumed the testator's identity and status. Thus, normally, the oldest son was made the heir. The first duty of the heir was to see to the funeral of the deceased. An heir not only assumed the property and the rights of the testator, but he also inherited any debts. This did not mean that debts were paid out of the estate and that he got what was left over if anything. Instead, he was now legally responsible for the deceased person's debts, even if these exceeded the value of the inheritance.

The only jail in Rome was a single cell, used to hold people until execution.

The shortest will consisted of just four words: Be X my heir ("X mihi heres esto"). This did all that was necessary. The first line of a will was always the designation of the heir. If a man had multiple children or did not want any of his children to be his heir, he had to next specifically list their names with the formula "Let X be disinherited." To be valid, a will had to name an heir, disinherit anyone who might be eligible, and then be written at a special ceremony with seven witnesses observing. The witnesses had to be adult males and could not be blind or insane. One of the witnesses was designated the *libiprens*, who held up a set of scales while the will was being written and signed; all witnesses had to sign for the will to be valid. The one exception to this ceremony was for soldiers on the eve of a battle, who were allowed to orally declare their will before three comrades; this would be a legally binding will. If the heir was someone who could legally refuse to accept the inheritance, the testator had to list a time limit and a secondary heir if the first did not accept. If a will was defaced, it was invalid.

As time went on, the Romans became concerned that too many people were leaving their property to persons other than their children and that as a result, families were falling into ruin. Therefore laws were added that declared that if children were disinherited in favor of "base persons," they could challenge to have the will declared invalid.

If a person wished to include in his will specific gifts of money or property to people other than the heir, he had to add a line, called the legacy, to the will, describing the property or the amount of money and the person to whom it should go. There were two types of legacies. The simple legacy immediately transferred the property or money to the designated person. The second type ordered the heir to pay out the legacy from his inheritance. This was called a damnation legacy, and the formula was "Let my heir be damned to give X to Y." Again, so many people were giving away large portions of their estates through legacies that the laws were changed so that a testator could give away no more than three-quarters of his inheritance via legacies. Another very common part of a will was the posthumous manumission, or freeing of the testator's favorite slave or slaves.

A will could include a variety of other statements. One common item was directions for the type funeral, and in particular the size and expense of the funeral monument that the heir was required to provide. A person could also leave people whom he hated a legacy of a rope and a nail; the message was for them to tie the rope to the nail and then hang themselves from it. It was illegal, however, to slander the emperor in any way.

Finally, someone making a will could make requests. The most famous of these requests was in the poet Virgil's will; in it, he demanded that his epic poem *The Aeneid* be burnt and all copies destroyed because he had not quite finished it. The emperor Augustus ordered that this request be ignored, which is the reason we still have *The Aeneid* today.

~*Gregory S. Aldrete*

FOR MORE INFORMATION

Champlin, E. *Final Judgments: Duty and Emotion in Roman Wills*. Berkeley: University of California Press, 1991.

Crook, J. A. *Law and Life of Rome*. Ithaca, N.Y.: Cornell University Press, 1967.

Nicholas, B. *An Introduction to Roman Law*. Oxford: Oxford University Press, 1962.

POLITICAL LIFE
|
WARFARE
|
Mesopotamia

Egypt

Greece

Rome

Nubia

Australian Aboriginals

Warfare

Most of the civilizations discussed in this book were very proficient at warfare. It is not much of an exaggeration to say that it is actually because they were better than their neighbors at waging war that they are in this book at all, since they were the ones who, by military force, carved out large and long-lasting empires. In ancient Italy alone, there were dozens of vibrant, creative, ambitious cultures, such as the

Samnites, the Volsci, the Tarentines, and the Sabines, who might have risen to dominate the peninsula. In the end, however, they all were defeated in warfare by the Romans, and so rather than being household names today and having books devoted to their daily lives, they have been relegated to the status of being footnotes to Roman history. There is truth in the saying that the victors write the histories, but perhaps even more significant, it is often only the victors that history remembers at all.

Warfare seems to be an inevitable part of human nature, and in the ancient world the goals of warfare were fairly straightforward: to expand territory, to gain resources, to acquire booty, and to win glory. The earliest empires in Mesopotamia were formed when ambitious leaders conquered their neighbors and expanded their empires to the natural limits of local geography. Egyptian history really began when a warrior first united Upper and Lower Egypt. To gain wealth was always a strong motivation for war, and it was standard practice after a city had been captured for the soldiers to plunder it and carry off whatever they could, including human captives who were sold into slavery. Gaining fame was a motivation for some warriors, none more so than the Greek warrior Achilles memorialized in Homer's *Iliad*. Men such as Achilles valued the glory to be won by arms literally more than life itself.

The methods of ancient warfare show a great deal of sophistication. Not only was a vast array of weaponry employed, but the armies of the ancient world could rival modern ones in both size and professionalism. At the height of their empire, the Romans kept half a million highly trained professional soldiers in the field, and the organizational structure of the Roman war machine was as impressive and complex an achievement as their famous aqueducts and amphitheaters.

Although missile weapons such as bows and arrows were commonly used, sometimes with great skill and efficiency such as by the Nubians, the core of most ancient warfare was face-to-face combat. Men chopped and slashed at one another directly, and the resulting butchery was every bit as horrifying as anything experienced on modern battlefields. The number of Americans killed at the battles of Gettysburg, Pearl Harbor, Iwo Jima, and D-Day combined is less than half the number of Romans who were hacked to death in one afternoon by the Carthaginians at the battle of Cannae in 216 B.C.E. Ancient generals made use of psychological warfare as well. The Assyrians deliberately practiced extreme brutality and advertised the results to intimidate prospective future enemies.

The often-gruesome story of ancient warfare may not be the most noble aspect of these civilizations, but warfare has been a constant companion throughout human history. To leave it out or to downplay its significance would be a misrepresentation.

~*Gregory S. Aldrete*

POLITICAL LIFE

WARFARE

Mesopotamia

Egypt

Greece

Rome

Nubia

Australian Aboriginals

MESOPOTAMIA

Warfare in Mesopotamia often arose as the result of wealth, control of the Tigris and Euphrates for transportation and irrigation, boundary disputes, and the need to acquire luxury goods such as timber, stone, and metals. City walls originally may have been built to protect livestock from wild animals and poachers. Some early walls did not encircle the city fully and were perhaps used as barriers against flooding. Once erected, the walls displayed the wealth and power of the ruler; sometimes they were even richly decorated.

The people of the ancient Near East explained warfare as the will of the gods. In 714 B.C.E., Sargon II attacked his northern neighbor, Urartu; he issued a report to the national god, which was probably read publicly at the New Year's festival, justifying his invasion and claiming divine approval. Each step of the campaign was checked in advance by extispicy, which was accompanied by very specific questions, such as, "Will Kashtaritu (ruler of Karkashi in Media) and his troops, or the troops of the Cimmerians, or the troops of the Mannaeans, or the troops of the Medes, or of any other enemy capture that city Kishassu?" (Dalley, 422). Diviners probably accompanied the army on all its campaigns.

All nations developed practices to curb the savagery of war; unfortunately, the conventions were not uniform, thus giving one army an advantage. For example, the Egyptians had a ban against surprise attacks, even postponing a battle until the enemy was ready to fight. However, the Hittites accepted the element of surprise as a legitimate military tactic, as is known from their attack against the headquarters of the Egyptian king. The Assyrians publicized their atrocities in reports and illustrations for propaganda purposes. In the tenth and ninth centuries B.C.E., official inscriptions told of cruelty to those captured. Most were killed or blinded; others were impaled on stakes around city walls as a warning. The bodies were mutilated; heads, hands, and even lower lips were cut off so that counting the dead would be easier. These horrifying illustrations, texts, and reliefs were designed as a warning to frighten the population into submission.

Assyrian strategies for conquering foreign territories included siege warfare, pitched battles, and psychological warfare. The Assyrians did not have a navy and turned to the Phoenicians when they had to go to sea. Because sieges and pitched battles took much energy, time, and manpower, the Assyrians preferred psychological warfare whenever possible. When the Assyrians decided to conquer an area, they first tried rhetoric to persuade or threaten people into submission without a fight. When surrounding the capital city and

Relief of Assyrians besieging a town. On the left, assault troops attempt to scale the walls using ladders; in the center, a covered battering ram pounds at the walls; and on the right, archers keep up a covering fire. © Copyright The British Museum.

shouting to the people inside failed, the Assyrians' next tactic was to select one or more small cities to attack, usually ones that could be easily conquered. Then the Assyrians committed extreme acts of cruelty to show how the entire region would be treated if the inhabitants refused to surrender peacefully. Houses were looted and burned to the ground, and the people were murdered, raped, mutilated, or enslaved—acts all vividly portrayed in the Assyrian stone reliefs and royal inscriptions in the palaces. The Assyrian troops regarded looting and rape of a conquered city as partial compensation. The largest and choicest share, of course, went to the king.

Controlling conquered areas was often a problem, with vassal states either withholding annual tribute or in open rebellion. If repeated attacks failed to quell the population, the Assyrians transported large numbers of people to another area. Assyrian kings began deportation in the thirteenth century B.C.E., but the practice became state policy during the ninth century B.C.E., with numbers reaching half a million deportees. The Assyrians found mass deportation beneficial; it provided labor colonies to work on the monumental building programs, to cultivate new farmland, and to produce more food for the growing urban population. People were also deported to curb nationalistic longings. Persistent rebellion was treated with harsh retribution.

Early dynastic monuments clearly illustrate battles fought and armies conscripted. The texts from the Early Dynastic period describe frequent armed confrontations both within "The Land" (Sumer) and against external invaders; other documents record lists of those in the military, chariots, and weapons. The first clear reference to a standing army comes from the Akkadian Dynasty. King Sargon (2334–2279 B.C.E.) spoke of 5,400 soldiers eating before him. For all periods, documents describing the administration of the army are few. Such texts usually involve the conscription of soldiers and efforts to avoid the draft. The most successful method of conscription, the *ilkum*, was devised during the Old Babylonian period. This practice involved exchanging land ownership in return for military service. However, in times of peace, state service was substituted. If a citizen was conscripted for the royal campaign and failed to appear, he would be executed. The Code of Hammurabi forbade hiring substitutes to perform military duties.

Throughout Mesopotamian history, soldiers were allocated plots of land in return for military service by the military administration. Such land could be inherited. The Code of Hammurabi allowed certain classes of society, namely, priestesses and merchants, to sell their *ilkum* plots, but other citizens could not.

Military units consisted of 10, 50, and 100 men. Larger units were formed according to the needs of warfare. As the Assyrians conquered foreign territory, part of the male population was incorporated in the Assyrian army. Near the end of the Neo-Assyrian Empire, the majority of the troops were not Assyrian. Eventually, these population groups received all the economic and social rights of native Assyrians. The size of military forces increased through the Iron Age as the Neo-Assyrian Empire expanded. Shalmaneser III (858–824 B.C.E.) mentions a force of 44,400 men; a century later, an inscription of Tiglath-pileser III mentions a force of 72,950 men. The militia of Sargon II (721–705 B.C.E.) numbered 90,580 and grew to 208,000 under his son Sennacherib (Dalley, 418). The reliability of these figures remains open to question.

Sennacherib divided the royal corps into two or three contingents, perhaps headed by the queen and by the crown prince. Usually, we expect the queens' roles to have been nominal in military affairs. An unpublished inscription referred to Sammuramat (Greek, Semiramis), wife of Shamshi-Adad V, mother of Adad-nirari III, and daughter-in-law of Shalmaneser III, as being instrumental in a victorious campaign that established the boundaries among three territories.

Once the Assyrians conquered a region, systematic administration took place as an extension of the military. The king himself took on a dual role; he was head of state and commander-in-chief of the army. Three officers served immediately under the king: (1) the field marshal, who executed the king's military orders and led the troops in the king's absence; (2) the vice-chancellor, who advised the king on affairs of state; and (3) the majordomo, who alone had direct access to the king.

The king's bodyguard was drawn from the chariot corps. The army included cavalry, chariotry, engineers, infantry, and supply personnel. When the king did not lead the army into battle, his commanding officers spearheaded the campaign. The major cause of death among adult males was death during war in the line of duty. Terms distinguishing the different types of soldiers have been difficult to understand. Various types of foot soldiers depicted on reliefs also appear in royal inscriptions. Foot soldiers served in various capacities, for example, as swift messengers on horseback, as laborers cutting new roads before the advancing Assyrian army, and at the front breaking through city walls.

Assyrian troops considered loot and rape from a conquered city as part of their pay.

With the growth of the Assyrian army, a new building known as the "review palace" was developed. An inscription of Esarhaddon clearly states its purpose: "For the ordinance of the camp, the maintenance of the stallions, chariots, weapons, equipment of war, and the spoil of the foe of every kind" (as cited in Dalley 418). The review palace had huge internal courtyards, ideal for mustering the troops, as well as numerous storage rooms and living quarters.

Historical records describe armies in pitched battle, long-term sieges around fortified cities, long-distance campaigns to foreign countries, bedouin razzias, and invasions by barbarian hordes. Because war was a seasonal activity, sedentary communities drew on greater manpower during nonagricultural periods.

Siege warfare developed as a special category of military strategy. Outer and inner walls were often built in front of a fortification wall, which had towers and a complicated design of gates to thwart the enemy. Sometimes these fortifications were built next to a river. There were more elaborate fortifications in mountainous regions. The attacking army might redirect the courses of rivers to make both walls and buildings collapse. The battering ram was used to pierce enemy fortifications. Mari correspondence is full of references to siege towers that were preassembled and floated downstream. Wooden scaffolds and ramps were also used to scale the battlements.

At the end of the battle, cities, houses, and individuals were looted. In the local wars in Sumer and Akkad, the city temples were treated with respect because their gods were members of the same pantheon. However, booty was taken from temples of enemies. The Lamentation over the Destruction of Ur describes the Elamite desecration of the innermost temple sanctuaries and destruction of decorations. The Hittites boldly carried Marduk's statue into exile upon their capture of Babylon.

There were conventions governing the distribution of the spoils of war. The king took the largest and most valuable share of the booty for himself; these items were enumerated in royal inscriptions and depicted on reliefs. The king's portion consisted of luxury goods such as gold, silver, and ivory, used to decorate the Assyrian palaces and temples. Military leaders often shared in the division of spoils with the king; in addition, they received large estates of agricultural land as a reward for prowess, valor, and victory. Assyrian troops considered loot and rape from a conquered city as part of their pay. The kings of Akkad presented at least token gifts to the gods from their booty. Stone bowls, inscribed "booty of Elam" or "booty of Magan," have been found at various sites. The tradition of making a dedication to the appropriate temple survived into Assyrian times, in fact, even into the Classical world.

One of the most valuable spoils of battle was the people. From the Ur III period, some tablets record long lists of women and children. Males are not included in these lists, perhaps because they were often killed, tortured, or mutilated. Occasionally, captured soldiers were sacrificed to the gods. Sometimes women and children were included as part of the general massacre, but usually they became slaves.

Prisoners of war were often taken on long marches. Often naked, they were put in neck stocks, their hands bound behind their backs; or they were enmeshed in a net. Because heavy chains were expensive, the prisoners were often blinded en masse. When brought to their captors' land, they could still perform certain tasks, such as carrying water from a well or canal with a bucket and a rope.

In peace treaties, both parties swore by the gods to obey the terms of the treaty. If one side attacked the other, the gods would punish the offending party. Prospective agreements included these clauses, thereby promoting future cooperation rather than settling past differences. International treaties also secured succession. Parties to the treaty agreed to support their allies militarily. The treaties also included extradition clauses.

A minor kingdom usually became a vassal of a major one because vassalage was its only hope of survival or because it offered economic advantages. The king would formally initiate his vassal by anointing his head with oil, and then he would announce the terms of the treaty. Both parties accepted the treaty under oath. Such terms limited the vassal's right to an independent foreign policy and sometimes even economic activities. Vassals had to pay annual tribute and serve in the army. In return, the overlord defined and defended the boundaries of his vassal states. Babylonia was a special case. It could not be treated by the Assyrian imperialists as a territory to oppress and exploit. Historical, ethnic, religious, and cultural ties would have neither allowed the Assyrians to treat their southern neighbor in this way nor permitted the Babylonians to accept such a subordinate status. The Assyrian Empire needed secure borders in Babylonia for their armies to march through on the way to conquer western Asia. The Assyrians tried to use puppet kings, whom they married to their daughters, to manipulate the Babylonians.

During the Neo-Assyrian period, the annual campaign usually began in spring, once the army met at a given point. A show of force was usually sufficient to ensure voluntary payment of tribute. Tribute and taxes levied on conquered areas included costly goods, as well as more practical items such as horses for the military and grain stored locally as rations for the troops. Vassal territories paid tribute as part of their treaty obligations. Major provinces paid large sums, but peripheral areas, such as the Anatolian states, usually sent token gifts (Nemet-Nejat, 227–40).

FOR MORE INFORMATION

Dalley, S. "Ancient Mesopotamian Military Organization." In *Civilizations of the Ancient Near East*, ed. J. Sasson. Vol. 1. New York: Scribner's, 1995.

Nemet-Nejat, K. R. *Daily Life in Ancient Mesopotamia*. Westport, Conn.: Greenwood Press, 1998.

POLITICAL LIFE

|

WARFARE

|

Mesopotamia

Egypt

Greece

Rome

Nubia

Australian Aboriginals

EGYPT

Pharaohs in Egypt demonstrated their greatness by raising imposing buildings or by waging successful wars—and then boasting over and over again about their accomplishments. None ever bragged that his reign was peaceful. Successful military campaigns increased a pharaoh's prestige because they reinforced all Egyptians' view of their country as superior to others and served the economy by ensuring a flow of foreign goods to Egypt.

Wars recurred in ancient Egypt because of the nature of their military operations. The Egyptian army invaded to seize whatever booty was available, not to annex land. The army marched south into Nubia for gold and north to Syria for cattle and slaves, but as soon as victory was achieved and the booty collected, everyone returned home to Egypt. Seldom were garrisons of troops stationed in conquered territories, and the government usually remained, as before, in local hands. Before leaving, Egyptian leaders exacted a promise from the invaded country to send an annual tribute, but without a continued army presence there was little incentive to comply. So each year, the troops sallied out again to force payments. This system of raid and retreat meant that Egypt never built a true empire—it dominated its neighbors but did not expand its territory.

Amazingly detailed accounts of battles, with numbers of casualties, enemy killed, prisoners taken, and even the names of the king's horses have come down to us, thanks to the pharaohs' custom of carving boasts on temple walls to tell their people how brave and mighty they had been. As a result, battles are better recorded than any other Egyptian events.

No records from the early period of Egyptian history describe the original armies, but undoubtedly they were composed of conscripted or volunteer farmers who went to war when the Nile's inundation made farming impossible, although Egypt's ability to grow surplus food did eventually support a standing army. While not a profession of great status because of the long marches, difficult conditions, and dangers, soldiering attracted men for the captured booty, which, with the pharaoh's share subtracted, was disbursed among the troops.

Ancient cities, fortified by massive walls, typically could withstand sustained attacks for years. Kamose's brother Ahmose, for example, spent three years laying siege to a fortified city in Palestine before it fell (Joshua 19:6). Because cities generally crowned hills and water supplies lay in valleys outside the walls, a city's greatest survival problem during a siege was the need for water. One solution was to dig a deep pit inside the city leading to a tunnel running uphill to a well so the water could flow to the pit by gravity. Because food could be gotten from animals stabled within the walls and some crops could be grown, the addition of a secure water supply meant a long wait for a besieging army. To allow defenders to rain missiles safely on besiegers from the tops of walls—arrows, stones, or boiling oil—battlements were designed with what looked like rows of giant teeth, whose gaps, called "embrasures," provided spots through which archers could fire at the enemy and then quickly retreat behind the "teeth," called "caps" or "merlons."

Egyptian armies employed two strategies for attacking a foreign city: penetration and siege. Penetration could be achieved from above, from below, or through the wall, but none of these methods was easy. To penetrate from above, ladders were brought so the walls could be scaled. Naturally, the defenders attempted to throw down the ladders and hurled stones on the men as they climbed; at the same time, the attacker's archers tried to maintain a steady volley of arrows to chase the defenders from the parapet. Tunneling through a massive wall, on the other hand, was time consuming and inevitably led to a considerable loss of men. All manner of tools were used—including axes, picks, and spears—but battering rams were the primary weapons. A metal tip at the end of a long wooden beam was shoved into the wall and maneuvered up and down, left and right, to dislodge stones and bricks, thereby creating a breach through which the army could charge. The major problem with the battering ram was that it exposed the men who worked it to attacks from the wall. Before long, a portable shelter was devised under which the men could work, protected from the rocks and arrows hurled from above. Some of these shelters fixed the battering ram to ropes hanging from their ceilings so it could be swung into the wall repeatedly with minimum effort. Because penetration could also be attempted through the gates to the city, the doors were usually covered with metal so they could not be set on fire; however, troops could attack the hinges in an effort to remove the doors completely. Penetration from beneath the wall was probably the least dangerous of the three possible routes, but it could prove disastrous. Miners would tunnel underground, often at night, to surprise the enemy within their walls. Of course, if the defenders discovered the tunnel, they organized an appropriate reception committee. The alternative to taking a fortified city by penetration was to besiege it: surround the city and starve the defenders into submission. Although it was time consuming, it was generally the least dangerous method.

After expelling the Hyksos, the Egyptian army grew large and hierarchical, with commanders, generals, divisions, corps, and so on beneath its commander-in-chief, the pharaoh. The 18th Dynasty managed an unprecedented period of military successes as its second pharaoh, Amenhotep I, began his reign with a military expedition as far south as any expedition had ever gone—to the third cataract of the Nile. Egypt's southern frontier had been established. A later pharaoh, Tuthmosis III, easily earned his reputation as Egypt's greatest military leader. Within a period of 16 years, he led 14 separate campaigns into Syria-Palestine, crossed the Euphrates River, and conquered the land of the powerful Mitanni.

Not surprisingly, with one notable exception, Egyptian battle records all describe land engagements because Egypt had no navy. Hemmed in by deserts on the east and west and the Sudan in the south, Egypt's only water border was the Mediterranean to the north, but the Egyptians, skilled in plying the placid Nile, developed no open-water navigational or sailing skills and seldom sailed the Mediterranean. Their ideal river conditions had spoiled them. In fact, their extensive trade with both Greece and Cyprus depended on sailors from those seafaring lands.

The only Egyptian record that describes a real naval battle is an account of a battle fought by Ramses III against a mysterious group called the Sea Peoples. This enemy comprised populations of different nationalities who came from the islands of the Mediterranean and from Asia Minor. One segment of the Sea Peoples was called the Peleset, who gave their name to Palestine. They wore distinctive feather-topped helmets, their primary weapon was the long, straight sword, and they carried round shields. A smaller, but important group of the Sea Peoples, called the Sherdens, gave their name to Sardinia. They too carried round shields but wore horn-topped helmets. Ramses depicted two battles with the Sea Peoples on the walls of his temple at Medinet Habu: one on land, another on water. According to the text accompanying the battle scenes, "[T]he foreign countries made a conspiracy in their islands . . . they were coming forward toward Egypt." A powerful confederation had set their sights on Egypt which would have to fight for its existence. The land battle, shown in traditional style, was a complete victory for the Egyptians and total defeat for the enemy. Two details are of interest, however. Behind the enemy infantry and chariots, carts are pictured carrying noncombatants—women and children. This suggests that the Sea Peoples intended to settle in Egypt if they won. That they were migrating is the reason different groups of Sea Peoples settled in different Mediterranean countries after their defeat. The other interesting detail is that the Sea Peoples are depicted without an archery corps; they could engage in nothing but close combat.

Although Ramses boasts that he destroyed the Sea Peoples on land, the records show that a sea battle was also necessary, even if it was not the sort of naval encounter we normally think of because there was no maneuvering on open water. The conflict probably took place in the delta where the Nile branches out into the Mediterranean. Because narrow streams provided no space to sail, ships on both sides served merely as platforms for infantry. The temple wall account of the battle shows several important differences between the Egyptians and the opposing troops, any one of which could explain Ramses' victory. First, the Egyptian ships were fitted with both sails and oars; those of the Sea Peoples had only sails, giving the Egyptians the advantage of greater control and maneuverability in close river fighting. Egyptian archers were able to inflict damage at a distance, but the Sea Peoples, lacking archers, could only try to board Egyptian ships, which maneuvered out of their way while raining arrows on them. Finally, while more Egyptian archers shot arrows from the shore, men with slings hurled stones at the Sea People from the crow's nests of their ships. The temple walls show the outcome in graphic detail: no hand-to-hand combat, only enemies pierced by arrows falling into the Nile.

The Egyptian armament and style of campaign served the country well for a thousand years, allowing Egypt to dominate surrounding countries during that time with superior manpower. Egypt's power was finally reduced by new superpowers with more modern methods who raised warfare to a science. Egypt endured through the rise and fall of one militant superpower after another, rebelling when it could, joining forces with other countries in opposition, or simply biding time when conquered (Brier and Hobbs, 201–2, 210–20).

FOR MORE INFORMATION

Benson, D. S. *Ancient Egypt's Warfare*. Ashland, Ohio: Bookmasters, 1995.

Brier, B., and H. Hobbs. *Daily Life of the Ancient Egyptians*. Westport, Conn.: Greenwood Press, 1999.

Sandars, N. K. *The Sea Peoples: Warriors of the Ancient Mediterranean*. London: Thames and Hudson, 1978.

Yadin, Y. *The Art of Warfare in Biblical Lands*. 2 vols. New York: McGraw Hill, 1963.

GREECE

Homeric warfare, which probably resembled the style of fighting that was actually current in Homer's day, was highly ritualistic. Although mass engagements are occasionally described, it is the individual encounters between heroes such as Achilles and Hector that account for most of the action and ultimately determine the course of the war. The plot of the *Iliad* rests on the pretension that the prowess of a single warrior is such that his withdrawal from the battlefield causes a complete reversal in the fortunes of the two sides. Likewise, the death of Hector at the end of the poem portends the destruction of Troy, since Hector was Troy's most valiant defender.

Heroes only did battle with warriors of comparable rank and fighting ability. They were seemingly oblivious to the possibility of being struck by a stray arrow or a rock hurled by one of the mob. Although usually conveyed to the battlefield in chariots, they fought almost exclusively on foot. Their chariots remained parked while the encounter took place, ready to provide a means of escape if their owners were forced to retreat or when they went in search of a new opponent. Having found a suitable opponent, heroes revealed their identity and issued a challenge. Ritual insults often preceded the exchange of blows. On rare occasions, combatants might have declined to fight with one another if they discovered that there existed a long-standing tie of friendship between their families. This happened in the case of the Greek Diomedes and the Trojan Glaucos in the *Iliad,* book 6. After learning of each other's pedigree, the two men actually exchange armor with each other, "so that everyone will realize that our families have provided hospitality for one another in days of yore" (line 230f.).

The vanquished warrior, if not killed outright, typically offered the victor a ransom to spare his life. If the victor rejected his appeal, he might follow up the killing with an attempt to strip his victim's corpse of its armor. Where particular animosity existed, the victor might even have despoiled the corpse. Achilles engaged in this barbaric practice when he attached Hector's corpse to his chariot and then dragged it around the walls of Troy under full view of his victim's parents. The death of a major hero on either side caused such disruption that it interrupted the whole war. Even on the battlefield, the aristocratic hero required a full-scale aristocratic funeral. Seventeen days were devoted to the obsequies of Achilles, nine for Hector, and two for Patroclus. The extent of funeral rites conducted on behalf of any individual reflected his social standing and value to the army. Ordinary soldiers received only minimal rites of burial. The only method of disposing of the dead was cremation.

The primary objective of the Homeric hero was to win "imperishable glory" so that his deeds of prowess would be celebrated forever in epic verse of the kind written by Homer himself. His goal was "always to excel in battle and to outstrip others," as Peleus explains to his son Achilles (Iliad 11.784). The value of the prize or *geras* that he received when the spoils of war were distributed to the army reflected his individual worth and thus symbolized the honor in which he was held. Only marginally was the hero concerned with the collective good of the whole army. Warfare, in other words, primarily presented an opportunity for status enhancement and personal enrichment. At the beginning of the *Iliad*, Achilles, after being insulted by his commander-in-chief Agamemnon, withdraws to his tent, secure in the knowledge that this decision will cause the deaths of many of his comrades. What matters to him foremost is the public recognition of his own worth. Although he is criticized by his peers for his lack of judgment, none of them ever suggests that his behavior is selfish or immoral.

Even though Homeric warfare was highly ritualistic, the poet's description of what Achilles calls "blood and slaughter and the choking groans of men" (Iliad 19.214) is virtually unsurpassed for its realistic evocation of the brutality of the battlefield. It provides an unforgettable picture of the type of warfare that depended primarily on a thrust of the spear. Homer describes the deaths of 240 warriors in the *Iliad*, of whom 188 were Trojan and 52 Greek. An almost-infinite variety of wounds are described. We are told, for instance, that "the brain ran along the socket of the spear-head in blood-spurts" (17.297f.) and in another that "the point of the spear shattered the collarbone, tore through it, and stuck out by the base of the shoulder" (17.309–10). Despite the poet's evident fascination with war, the *Iliad* is by no means a glorification of war. Brutality is constantly exposed for what it is, while the achievements of the heroes are evocatively contrasted with the plight of the innocent, including women, children, and the elderly.

About 700 B.C.E., a new style of warfare called hoplite was introduced, named for the *hoplon* or round bronze shield with which soldiers were equipped. These soldiers were heavily armored with shield, greaves, breastplates, and helmets, and their primary weapon was a spear, although they also carried swords. Hoplites fought in a formation called a phalanx in which they lined up with their shields overlapping. In this type of warfare, close coordination and keeping formation was essential.

Service in a hoplite army was regarded as a privilege rather than an obligation, since only citizens were eligible. It is not accidental, therefore, that the introduction of hoplite warfare coincided with the rise of the city-state. Success in battle now depended not on individual deeds of prowess but on the collective discipline of the whole army, whose members were rewarded for their services by being given a role in the politics of the community they defended. However, because armor was expensive to purchase, service remained confined to the well-to-do.

Before a general gave orders for his army to engage in battle, a seer took the omens to determine whether they were favorable. Sacrificial victims were then slaughtered to the gods in the hope of securing their goodwill. The Spartans drove whole herds of goats onto the battlefield for sacrifice. Armies advanced singing a paean or hymn in honor of Apollo. As they often closed in on each other at a trot and as each hoplite was

> *Because armor was expensive to purchase, service remained confined to the well-to-do.*

carrying approximately 70 pounds of bronze, the initial engagement must have resembled a head-on collision between two heavy vehicles. When the Athenians advanced against the Persians at the battle of Marathon, they did so, Herodotus tells us, at a run. This tactic so unnerved the Persians that although they heavily outnumbered the Athenians, they were instantly thrown into a panic. After the battle the Athenians established a cult in honor of Pan, the god of panic.

After the battle, the victorious side often erected a monument called a *tropaion* at the spot where the keenest fighting had taken place. A *tropaion* was the trunk of an oak tree decorated with the spoils of victory. These consisted mainly of the weapons and armor that had been taken from the losing side.

It was a universally upheld law throughout the Greek world to allow the defeated side to return to the battlefield to retrieve its dead. Only very rarely was this law violated since sensibilities touching burial ran extremely high. During their retreat from Syracuse, the demoralization of the Athenians was greatly increased by the fact that they were unable to care for their dead and wounded (Thucydides, *The Peloponnesian War* 7.75.3). The dead were usually cremated on the field of battle. Their ashes were then placed in individual cinerary urns identified by name tags and brought home. The Athenians arranged their dead in 10 piles according to their 10 tribes and publicly interred their remains at the end of each campaigning season. Only rarely, as in the case of the 192 Athenians who died fighting the Persians at Marathon, did they accord the war dead the honor of burial on the battlefield. Likewise the Spartans buried the 300 who died with their king Leonidas, while guarding the pass of Thermopylae, where they fell.

Legend reports that the Greeks besieged Troy for 10 years and succeeded in taking it only by using the device of a wooden horse, which they left outside the city, ostensibly as a peace offering. Although this story may well be pure fantasy, the supposition that Troy was able to resist for a whole decade the entire military capability of the Greek world is by no means inconsistent with what we know about the ineffectual nature of Greek siegecraft, which even in the fifth century B.C.E. remained rudimentary. Virtually the only way to achieve success was by starving a city into submission, which was why Pericles was so confident that the Peloponnesians would never be able to defeat Athens if its population withdrew within the walls, because its navy could guarantee its supply routes. In the fourth century B.C.E., siegecraft became more sophisticated with the development of catapults and mobile towers. In response to these improved techniques, walls and towers became thicker and higher. Curtain walls, ditches, and postern gates were also introduced. At the conclusion of a successful siege, the defeated population tended to be treated much more harshly than when hostilities were confined to the battlefield. This was no doubt partly because of the protracted nature of siege warfare and partly because of the fact that besieging armies often suffered great hardship, notably from plague and other diseases.

When Athenian youths reached the age of 18, they were required to serve for two years in the army as ephebes in the company of other members of their tribes (*ephêbos* means "poised at the moment of youth"). Their first year was devoted to training in hoplite and light-armed warfare. Light-armed warfare included the use of the bow, the javelin, and the catapult. At the end of the year, a review was held, at which each ephebe was presented with a shield and spear. During their second year, ephebes served as patrolmen at forts situated along the borders of Attica. Then, probably at the end of their second year, they were required to take an oath of loyalty to the Athenian state.

📷 *Snapshot*

Oath Sworn by Athenian Soldiers

I shall not disgrace my sacred weapons nor shall I desert my comrade at my side whenever I stand in the rank. I shall fight in defense of both sacred and secular things and I shall not hand down a fatherland that is reduced in size but one that is larger and stronger. . . . I shall be obedient to the laws that are established and to any that in the future may be wisely established. . . . I shall honor the sacred rites that are ancestral. (as cited in Garland, 165)

Having completed their two years of military service, ephebes became full citizens. They remained eligible for service until the age of 59, although it was between the ages of 20 and 30 that they were most liable to be called up. Although proficiency in warfare was an essential attribute of any state, Athens did not let it dominate its entire existence. As we see from the speech delivered by Pericles in honor of the dead who fell during the first year of the Peloponnesian War, Athenians took considerable pride in the fact that, whereas their enemies submitted themselves to a rigorous system of military training, they by contrast "pass the time without such restrictions but are still just as ready to face the same dangers as the Spartans" (Thucydides, *The Peloponnesian War* 2.39.4).

From the end of the fifth century B.C.E. onward, Greek states increasingly relied on the services of mercenaries, particularly in specialist capacities as light-armed troops or as archers. This development first came about during the Peloponnesian War, whose duration caused a shortage of manpower on both sides. Many of those who enlisted as mercenaries came from such poverty-stricken regions as Arcadia. Others came from outside the Greek world proper, such as the Thracians who were hired by the Athenians to assist their expedition to Sicily. Although it was economic hardship that primarily drove increasing numbers of men to seek mercenary service, new modes of fighting were now rendering hoplite warfare increasingly obsolete; many engagements took place in rough terrain where hoplites were virtually useless.

As a result, the previously indissoluble bond between service in the army and citizenship was undermined for all time.

In the fourth century B.C.E., Greek mercenaries came to enlist in the armies of both Greeks and non-Greeks. Theoretically, therefore, Athenians could find themselves fighting in the same battle against other Athenians, although whether this actually ever happened is not known. Because they had an excellent reputation for discipline, Greek mercenaries were in considerable demand. In 397 B.C.E., a Persian prince called Cyrus hired 10,000 mercenaries from the Greek mainland in his bid to seize the throne from his brother. When Cyrus was killed in battle, the mercenaries succeeded in making their way from the Persian heartland back to friendly territory without suffering serious losses. The march, which is stirringly described by Xenophon in a work called *Anabasis*, or *The March Up-Country*, demonstrated the military superiority of Greeks over Persians. This was to be proven even more dramatically when Alexander the Great invaded Persia in the 330s B.C.E. at the head of an army that consisted largely of mercenaries attracted by the promise of rich rewards.

With the exception of siegecraft, which had its own rules, warfare tended to adhere to fairly civilized standards of behavior. Unlike their Homeric counterparts, hoplites did not make a habit of stripping their opponents' bodies or mutilating them in the way that Achilles mutilated Hector's body. Nor was it their practice to despoil temples, sanctuaries, or tombs, which were regarded as sacrosanct. The destruction of property, whether public or private, was extremely rare, in part because warfare was confined largely to the battlefield. A notable exception was the Persians' destruction of the temples and statues that stood on the Athenian Acropolis in 480 B.C.E. The Athenians were so outraged by this act of vandalism that they left their temples in their ruined condition for 30 years as a living testimony to Persian savagery.

Hostilities between Greek states were suspended for the duration of the Olympic Games in accordance with a sacred truce known as the *ekecheiria*, which means literally "a restraining of hands." Ambassadors were placed under the protection of the gods, and their persons were regarded as inviolate. Although local squabbles leading to bloodshed were endemic, wars tended to be short in duration. The campaign season began in the spring and ended in the fall. In Athens, its conclusion was marked by the mass burial of all those who had died in the preceding season.

Not until the Peloponnesian War did the Greek world experience anything akin to the modern notion of total war. Thucydides constantly emphasizes the decline in moral standards that this brought about. In 413 B.C.E., a contingent of Thracian mercenaries, who had been hired by the Athenians, ran amok and killed all the inhabitants of the town of Mycalessos in Boiotia, slaughtering "even the livestock and whatever other living creatures they saw," including all the pupils at a boys' school (*The Peloponnesian War* 7.29.4). When the town of Mytilene on the island of Lesbos revolted from the Athenian Confederacy and was forced to surrender in 427 B.C.E., the Athenians decided to execute all the men and enslave the women and children. The next day, however, they revoked their decision and opted instead to execute only the ring leaders, 1,000 in number (3.50). Just over 10 years later, the island of Melos, which was neutral, declined to join Athens's alliance. After a short siege, the Athenians did not think twice about carrying out the punishment that they had originally reserved for the Mytileneans. They slaughtered the men, enslaved the women, and repopulated the island with 500 of their own citizens (5.116).

Greek warfare was conducted on a miniscule scale in comparison with its modern counterpart. It has been estimated that at no time in history were the Greeks able to put more than 50,000 soldiers onto the field. Another major difference is that it was not conducted under the glare of publicity as it is today. Once an expedition had departed, only general reports of its fortunes reached home. Aeschylus in *Agamemnon* (lines 437ff.) memorably describes Ares, the god of war, as the "gold-broker of corpses," who accepted soldiers in exchange for the ashes that were brought back from the battlefield in cinerary urns. Just as relatives waved goodbye on the quayside as the fleet set sail at the beginning of a campaign, so, too, they awaited the arrival of "urns in place of men" announcing the death of a husband, brother, or son (Garland, 158–70).

FOR MORE INFORMATION

Garland, R. *Daily Life of the Ancient Greeks.* Westport, Conn.: Greenwood Press, 1998.
Hanson, V. D. *The Western Way of War: Infantry Battle in Classical Greece.* Oxford: Oxford University Press, 1989.
Hanson, V. D., ed. *Hoplites: The Classical Greek Battle Experience.* New York: Routledge, 1991.
Rich, J., and G. Shipley, eds. *War and Society in the Greek World.* New York: Routledge, 1993.

POLITICAL LIFE
|
WARFARE
|
Mesopotamia

Egypt

Greece

Rome

Nubia

Australian Aboriginals

ROME

Because the Romans managed to conquer most of the known world, it is clear that they were doing something right with regard to their army. Throughout Roman history, the main characteristics attributed to Rome's military forces, both by the Romans and by their opponents, were determination, organization, and discipline.

Particularly during Rome's conquest of Italy and the western Mediterranean, Rome often did not have superior technology or tactics, but they did have a fanatical dedication to continue fighting until victorious. One famous example of this was when Rome attacked a wealthy Greek city in southern Italy. The city was defended by an excellent mercenary general named Pyrrhus and his troops. The Romans and Pyrrhus fought a bitter battle, but in the end, Pyrrhus's professionalism won the day, although his army suffered heavy casualties. The Romans raised another army, and again Pyrrhus was victorious, although again with heavy casualties. At this point, Pyrrhus is said to have exclaimed, "If I win another victory like this, I'm lost." He simply could not match Rome's deep manpower reserves and determination to keep fighting until they achieved a final victory. Similarly, in the First Punic War, Rome lost several entire fleets of ships but kept building new ones, and in the Second

Punic War, the Carthaginian military genius Hannibal wiped out three Roman armies in quick succession, but Rome never gave up and ultimately won the war.

From the time of the Punic wars on, Rome's army was what we would today call a professional army, meaning one in which the members are full-time soldiers who have no other job. A full-time army could devote all of its effort to training and produce much more professional soldiers. Also, for most of Rome's history, soldiers were recruited from the ranks of citizens and thus had a stake in what they were fighting for. The Roman army was perhaps the first in which organization was raised almost to an art form. All aspects of the soldier's daily schedule were regulated, his equipment was standardized, and he knew exactly his place and role within the army.

The easiest way to illustrate this is to consider the way that Roman military units were organized. The basic army group was the legion. During the civil wars of the late Republic, there were some 60 legions that had been gathered by the end of the wars. Once Augustus emerged in sole control, he pared this number down to 28, and this became, with minor variations, the standard size of the Roman army for the next several centuries. Each legion was elaborately subdivided into smaller and smaller groups. The smallest unit of men was the *contubernia*, which consisted of eight men. The word *contubernia* can be translated as "those who share a tent," and this was exactly what it was since Roman army tents held eight men. *Contubernia* were collected together into groups of 10, and each group of 10 was called a century, which despite the title, contained 80 men. Six centuries were grouped together to form a cohort (480 men), and 10 cohorts formed a legion (4,800 men).

Trajan's Column in Rome, ca. 1900. © Library of Congress.

The first cohort contained five double centuries, adding another 400 men to the total, and there were 120 cavalrymen attached to each legion, plus a number of clerks, supply officers, surveyors, orderlies, and of course, the officers for the legion. Added all together, a legion at full strength was about 6,000 men. Thus Augustus's 28 legions meant that there were about 168,000 citizens serving in the Roman army. Six thousand is an ideal number, however; in practice it is thought that the average legion probably had about 4,500 men.

This elaborate organization was one of the keys to Rome's success because, in battle, a legion could maneuver either as a whole or be broken apart into units ranging from 8 to 480 men; also, each of these units was trained to act independently or together with others as the need arose. This gave the Romans great flexibility since the legion could react quickly to new situations, such as during a famous battle that Rome fought against Macedon. At a crucial point in the battle, one of the Roman commanders recognized that the Macedonian flank was exposed to attack, and he was able to instantly detach a couple of cohorts to assault the weak point and take advantage of the momentary opportunity.

Each legion was commanded by a man called the legate, who had to be of senatorial rank. Under him were six officers called military tribunes. Both legates and tribunes were in essence political appointments. They were held not by soldiers for whom the army was a lifetime career but rather by politicians as one stage in their political career on their way toward the consulship. Serving for a year or two as military tribune was informally regarded as the step just before being elected to the lowest magistracy, the quaestorship. This was perhaps one of the greatest weaknesses in the Roman military system because it meant that the high-ranking officers in the legion were not professional soldiers. Sometimes their inexperience bordered on incompetence, with disastrous results. Most surprising about this system is the number of politicians who actually turned out to be competent generals.

Legates and tribunes came and went fairly rapidly, and thus continuity and professionalism in the Roman army were provided not by the senior officers but by the junior officers, called *centurions*. As the name implies, each legion had one centurion per century, and thus there were 60 per legion. Centurions were promoted from the ranks and were therefore the best and most experienced of the soldiers. Among the centurions, there was a strict hierarchy of seniority from the most junior centurion all the way up to the most senior, who was called the *primus pilus*, literally, "the first spear." In the modern U.S. army, the centurions would be the equivalent of sergeants, and they were the ones who really supervised and trained the men and got most things done. As a symbol of their authority, each centurion carried a vine stick; this was more than just a symbol since he would use this to beat the soldiers whenever he was displeased with them. One centurion was nicknamed "Bring me another" because he had the habit of beating his soldiers so hard with this stick that he was constantly breaking it, causing him to always be shouting, "Bring me another!"

> *Most surprising is the number of politicians who turned out to be competent generals.*

Other important posts that were not technically officers but were regarded as positions of honor to be held by the bravest soldiers were the men who carried the standards of the legion. Standards, called *signa*, were the Roman equivalent of flags and consisted of long poles with some sort of carved symbol at the top. A man who carried one of these was called a *signifer*. Common symbols found on a signa included mythological creatures, bulls, boars, and an open human hand. One *signa* was far more important than all the rest, however. This was the *aquila*, "eagle." This special standard had at the top an eagle with its wings spread and clutching a thunderbolt in its claws. Each legion had one eagle, which was given to it by the emperor himself, and because of the importance of eagles and thunderbolts as symbols of Jupiter, this was a very potent icon. The man who carried the eagle was known as the *aquilifer*. These eagles over time became symbols for the legions themselves, and one of the greatest disgraces that could befall a legion was to allow its eagle to be captured by an enemy. The standards were also the center of religious ritual for the legion. Whenever the legion camped, the standards were placed on a special raised platform in front of the legate's tent at the center of the camp, and any prayers or sacrifices performed by the legion took place beneath these standards.

The third characteristic of the Roman army was discipline. Above all else, soldiers were expected to perform their duty, and if they failed, the punishments were predictably harsh. Offences such as insubordination or falling asleep while on watch were punished by death. A particularly Roman institution that illustrates this attitude was the procedure known as decimation. If an entire unit, whether a century or a legion, was judged to have failed to perform its duty, then a special lottery was held and 1 out of every 10 men was selected to receive the punishment. The chosen 10 percent were clubbed to death by their remaining comrades. Astonishing as this seems, there were multiple occasions when decimation was actually used, most commonly when a unit was thought to have shown some form of cowardice in the face of the enemy.

For most of its history, Rome had a volunteer army. Because there were more people attempting to join than there were spaces, it was a selective process. Preference was traditionally given to the sons of soldiers, and hopeful recruits would also try to get letters of recommendation from current soldiers or people with political influence. They would then go to an interview at which they would present their letters along with proof that they were full Roman citizens. Usually at this stage, there was also a medical exam. Ideally, the Romans tried to recruit soldiers who were at least five feet eight inches in height, although in practice there seem to have been large numbers of shorter men serving. If they passed all these tests, they were assigned to a legion and had to travel to wherever the legion was located.

Upon reaching the legion, the recruits had to swear the military oath and then began training. The first phase of their training emphasized physical fitness, and the recruits spent most of their time marching. They were expected to be able easily to cover 24 Roman miles in full equipment in five hours. The next phase of their training was weapons training, and as in gladiator schools, they initially practiced with wooden weapons. These swords, shields, and spears, however, were all twice as heavy as the real weapons to build up strength. Drills and training never stopped in the Roman army, and units spent much of their spare time perfecting formations and maneuvers.

Throughout most of the empire, the standard pay for a common legionary was 900 sesterces per year. However, out of this was deducted money for their food and equipment, and so the amount they actually received as cash was probably less than 100 sesterces per year. Soldiers were obligated to serve 20 years, and this was later raised to 25. The real reward for serving as a legionary did not come until a solider was discharged from service. If a soldier managed to survive his 20 years and chose to leave the army, upon discharge he received a metal diploma stating that he was a veteran and granting him certain privileges. In addition, he received either a large lump sum of cash amounting to several thousand sesterces or title to a plot of land. The Roman military system was odd in that a soldier never received much money the whole time he was serving, but upon getting out he got a huge reward.

One source of resentment among soldiers was the fact that by law they could not get married while in active service. In practice, most soldiers had wives and families, but technically, these were concubines and illegitimate children until after the soldiers' discharge, when they could then marry and adopt their own children. Eventually, this law was changed.

In addition to the legions composed of citizens, the Romans also maintained a large group of noncitizen soldiers. These were called the *auxila*, meaning auxiliaries or allies. They were supplementary military units composed of noncitizens. The Romans specialized in heavy infantry, but armies need other types of troops such as archers, horsemen, and lightly armed skirmishers. The Romans chose to train their citizens only as heavily armed infantrymen and filled these other positions with non-Roman units. Certain ethnic or geographic groups were thought to be particularly skilled at specialized forms of warfare. For example, North Africans were excellent horsemen, and thus Romans raised cavalry *auxila* from North Africa. The inhabitants of the island of Crete were considered to be unusually skillful archers, and so Rome raised cohorts of Cretan archers. The inhabitants of the Balearic Islands were experts at the use of slings, and so contingents of Balearic slingers were highly valued.

Auxila units were organized in groups of either 500 or 1,000, and the total number of *auxila* employed by the Romans was roughly equal to the number of legionaries, about 170,000. Roman armies usually also had a roughly equal mixture of legionaries and *auxila*. *Auxila* received slightly less pay than legionaries and were required to serve 25 to 30 years. The big incentive to serve as an *auxila* was that if an *auxila* survived his 30 years, upon discharge he received full Roman citizenship. The *auxila* became one of the principal forces of Romanization in the empire.

One other group of soldiers was the *praetorian* guard. This was the only unit stationed at Rome, and it was supposed to serve as the emperor's personal bodyguard. *Praetorians* received double pay but in practice were more often responsible for assassinating the emperor than protecting him.

One famous characteristic of the Roman legions was the marching camp. When a legion was in the field traveling through unsettled territory, every night they would build an elaborate camp. They would clear a series of roads, with the two main roads forming a cross and dividing the camp into four quadrants. The other roads were laid out on a grid pattern. The design of these temporary one-night marching camps was copied by Roman surveyors when building new cities. Eventually, the grid pattern became the model for nearly all cities and was used by urban planners as the model for laying out a city until very recently. Thus most of our modern street systems are the direct descendants of the Roman army's marching camp. These camps were also surrounded by a ditch five feet wide and three feet deep behind which was piled up an earth wall six feet high. In addition, Roman soldiers on the march each carried two sharpened stakes, which were set in the ground outside the wall. Thus each night the Romans built for themselves a secure fortress within which to sleep. Even though these camps were abandoned after only one night's occupancy, they were built so well that even today it is possible to fly over the fields of England and spot the outlines of the marching camps. Archaeologists have found that they can actually trace Roman campaigns by following the trail of camps. As these camps show, another characteristic of the Roman soldier was that he was an excellent digger. Every soldier carried a pick-ax called the *dolabra*, which was as essential a piece of equipment as his *gladius* (sword) and was certainly used far more often.

In open ground, where the Romans could use the flexibility of their organization and could form their troops into battle lines, the army was nearly invincible. The weakness of the Roman system was that it did not work well in terrain that was not open or where the troops could not maneuver easily. In particular, they ran into trouble in northern Europe, which at that time was covered in thick forests and deep swamps. This was terrain better suited for the guerilla warfare that was practiced by the local Germanic barbarians.

Rome's greatest military defeat occurred late in the reign of Augustus in 9 C.E. The causes were a combination of difficult terrain and the other flaw already mentioned: incompetent, nonprofessional officers. A politician named Varus was put in charge of three legions in Germany. The leader of the barbarians, called Arminius, pretended to be an ally of Varus and lured him deep into one of the most impenetrable German forests, the Teutoberg Forest. There, with the Romans stretched out along miles of swampy forests, Arminius and his army ambushed the Romans and wiped out all three legions. This was such a disgrace that the numbers of these three legions were never used again.

~Gregory S. Aldrete

FOR MORE INFORMATION

Rich, J., and G. Shipley, eds. *War and Society in the Roman World*. New York: Routledge, 1993.

Watson, G. R. *The Roman Soldier*. Ithaca, N.Y.: Cornell University Press, 1969.

Webster, G. *The Roman Imperial Army of the First and Second Centuries*. 3rd. ed. Totowa, N.J.: Barnes and Noble, 1985.

NUBIA

There is evidence of warfare among the Nubians as early as the Neolithic period (after about 10,000 B.C.E.), as is revealed by the numerous weapons crafted of stone that are dated to this epoch. These weapons include arrow heads and axes, which admittedly may have served other functions, as well as mace heads. These were used in the internecine battles between competing elite oligarchies to establish suzerainty over their emerging domains. Although the organization and chain of command of these fighting forces cannot be adduced, mace heads and hand axes appear to have been ways to indicate power and authority. This suggests that the leading member of each elite was simultaneously the political and military head of the community. Among the earliest direct evidence for warfare in Nubia is a relief contemporary in date with the Nubian A-Group culture (about 3700–280 B.C.E.), which depicts an Egyptian triumph over the Nubians. The motifs used there were to become stereotypes for such representations of victory and included the image of the triumphant pharaoh and defeated enemy, with the result that its value as a record of actual events is limited.

By the time of the C-Group culture (about 2300–1600 B.C.E.), the Nubians had become proficient archers, as is indicated both by the archery equipment, found together with daggers and axes in their graves, and by a remarkable model of a troop of 40 Nubian archers discovered in an Egyptian tomb of the same period. From this period on, the value of the Nubians as warriors was recognized by the Egyptians, who engaged Nubians as mercenary forces.

It was doubtless because of their skills with bow and arrow that the Nubians of the Kerma culture (about 2500–1500 B.C.E.) were able to storm and take the Middle Egyptian fortresses erected along the Nile River to protect their mercantile interests. Elite cemeteries excavated at the settlement of Kerma have revealed warriors buried with quivers full of arrows and daggers still in place in their belts, where they were worn in life. That the rulers of Kerma could successfully challenge the military might of Egypt testifies to their ability to conduct war. Their autocratic position within Nubian society is emphasized by the human sacrifices that accompanied their burial rites.

Model of Nubian archers. These 40 archers were found in the tomb of Mesehti in Egypt and may depict Nubian mercenaries in Egyptian service. © The Art Archive/Egyptian Museum Cairo/Dagli Orti.

The warrior pharaohs of the New Kingdom (after 1550 B.C.E.) successfully subdued Nubia to ensure the uninterrupted flow of African luxury goods. The sustained Egyptian presence so masked Nubian ethnicity beneath a seemingly impenetrable Egyptian veneer that it is difficult to identify the material culture of the Nubians in their homeland. Occasional Egyptian punitive campaigns were deemed necessary for maintaining the status quo. Although scenes from the period recording these episodes are stereotypical in the extreme, certain depictions of Nubians in the Memphite tomb of Horemheb depict the Nubians as somewhat taller in stature than their Egyptian captors. Whether this discrepancy in scale is a reflection of the natural order of things or whether it is an Egyptian convention aimed at enhancing Horemheb's victory by emphasizing the physical superiority of the Nubians remains uncertain.

It is only with the official documentation of the Nubian pharaohs of Dynasty 25 (about 747–656 B.C.E.) that one gains a firsthand understanding of the Nubian military, at whose head stood the Nubian pharaoh. The earliest of these records is the Victory Stela of Piankhy (about 747–716 B.C.E.), which records his suppression of the revolt of Egyptian Delta princes and his taking by storm of Memphis, their principal stronghold. All the weapons of ancient warfare were at his disposal, including war horses, the indispensable Nubian bow and arrow, chariots, earthen embankments, siege towers, slingers, and men-of-war capable of attacking city walls from the river. Details of the actual strategy and tactics are passed over in silence, but the account is redolent with metaphors likening the Nubian king to a raging panther and his forces to a flood unleashed.

The importance of the Nubian military establishment during the reign of his successor, Taharqa (about 690–664 B.C.E.), is well known. A contemporary inscription describes how Taharqa trained his forces by making them run a desert course. He personally led his armies twice against the Assyrian attacks on his kingdom, during which he sustained wounds. He is twice mentioned in the Hebrew Bible as a defender of the kingdom of Judah against the Assyrians, but scholars disagree about whether these references are historical.

The Assyrian defeat of the Nubians and the suggested sack of Egyptian Thebes forced the Nubians to retreat to their ancestral homelands, where they continued to rule as members of the Napatan Dynasty (about 656–310 B.C.E.). With the exception of a punitive military campaign against the Nubian Napatans under the

Egyptian pharaoh Psametich II of Dynasty 27, ostensibly to maintain the status quo of the region, the subsequent records seem to pass over the Nubian military in silence.

Classical texts making reference to the Meroitic period are replete with accounts of repeated clashes between the Nubians and their enemies, but the lack of specificity and the generic nature of the hostilities render it virtually impossible to identify either these peoples or the theaters of conflict. It may well be that these references are harbingers of the escalating conflicts between the Meroites and the marauding nomadic tribes identified as Blemmyes and Megabaroi, some of whom had been fighting against the Nubians since about 600 B.C.E.

During the reign of the Roman emperor Augustus between 30 and 21 B.C.E., the Meroities revolted and stormed the area around Aswan. They toppled statues of the Romans and carried off to Meroe a head from a bronze statue of Augustus himself, which they intentionally buried beneath the threshold of one of their palaces so that the ruler, upon entering and exiting, would habitually be treading upon the fallen Roman ruler. The hostilities ended in a stalemate when the opposing forces opted for a diplomatic settlement rather than a military strike. An embassy of the Meroitic ruler, called Candake in the Classical texts, was escorted to the Greek island of Samos, where Augustus was temporarily headquartered. There the Meroities extracted from Augustus a pledge to remit taxes and establish Aswan as the frontier between the two realms. This Candake, which is the Classical rendering of the Meroitic title *kdke*, was, in fact, the queen of the Meroites, although her identity has not been established.

Dislocations throughout the Roman Empire and repeated assaults upon both Roman interests and Meroitic territory by marauding bands of nomadic peoples, including the Blemmyes, compelled the Roman emperor Diocletian to remove garrisons from Upper Egypt. Their withdrawal created a power vacuum. The kingdom of Meroe ultimately fell, but the causes of its collapse around 300 C.E. and the role played by the kingdom of Axum remain obscure.

~*Robert S. Bianchi*

FOR MORE INFORMATION

Adams, W. *Nubia: Corridor to Africa*. Princeton, N.J.: Princeton University Press, 1977.
O'Connor, D. *Ancient Nubia: Egypt's Rival in Africa*. Philadelphia: University of Pennsylvania, 1993.
Trigger, B. *Nubia under the Pharaohs*. Boulder, Colo.: Westview Press, 1976.
Welsby, D. A. *The Kingdom of Kush: The Napatan and Meroitic Empires*. London: British Museum Press, 1996.

AUSTRALIAN ABORIGINALS

Although there were conflicts between groups in Aboriginal Australia that were settled by what could be described as warfare, there were no wars in the sense that

POLITICAL LIFE
|
WARFARE
|
Mesopotamia

Egypt

Greece

Rome

Nubia

Australian Aboriginals

the term is commonly applied in the rest of the world. Perhaps because society and culture were linked so closely and inextricably with the land, war over territory, economy, or religion did not make sense to Aboriginal people. Individuals and the group of which they were a part claimed rights to the land they occupied by virtue of their place of birth and kinship ties. The economy was based on a safety net of reciprocal obligations determined by relationships and prior exchanges of food and other goods. During hard times, people could call upon those obligations and know that they would never go hungry. In turn, each person would feed others when he or she had a surplus.

All of Australia shared essentially the same system of beliefs, although the details of these beliefs, particular ancestral figures, and the rules of social behavior varied across the country. No one would have considered it sane behavior to kill another person for having slightly different beliefs or to force him or her to conform to one's own beliefs. There were regular gatherings in ceremonies involving large numbers of the people living in a region, which helped to diffuse tensions by creating marriages between individuals from different groups and developing future reciprocal obligations. These interactions meant that people were constantly forced to view their neighbors as fellow human beings.

Disputes were the result of such matters as trespassing, accusations of sorcery, or the perception that a marriage was improper. Revenge might be sought through an expedition of warriors, who would attempt to wound or kill the offending individuals or group. Often, however, a dispute would merely result in two groups meeting and shouting much abuse at one another. There might be a shower of spears or a fight between representative individuals. Generally, such "wars" were more symbolic than real, although injuries and deaths did result, and the rules of engagement were well understood.

Formal peacemaking ceremonies existed, including a ruling about who was in the wrong and what recompense should be paid. Sometimes an offending individual might allow himself to be wounded by the aggrieved individual as payback for some wrongdoing. When fights broke out, the weapons employed, such as spears, knives, throwing sticks, boomerangs, and clubs, were the same weapons used for hunting game. Such weapons could and did inflict great damage, and the use of shields, the only tool specifically crafted for war and fighting, is testament to this. There may have been disputes and fights, but there were also mechanisms in place to ensure that they did not usually affect the survival of the group.

~*David Horton*

FOR MORE INFORMATION

Berndt, R., and C. Berndt. *The World of the First Australians*. Canberra: Aboriginal Studies Press, 1988.

Horton, D., ed. *The Encyclopedia of Aboriginal Australia*. Canberra: Aboriginal Studies Press, 2001.

Tacon, P. *Australia's Ancient Warriors: Changing Depictions of Fighting in the Rock Art of Arnhem Land*. Cambridge, England: Cambridge University Press, 1994.

Wild, S. *Rom: An Aboriginal Ritual of Diplomacy*. Canberra: Aboriginal Studies Press, 1986.

Weapons

POLITICAL LIFE

WEAPONS

Mesopotamia

Egypt

Greece

Rome

Australian Aboriginals

The simplest weapons in the ancient world were farm implements such as scythes and pitchforks, which could be turned against people as well as crops. Weapons used in hunting, such as spears and bows, were also readily adaptable to warfare. More specialized weapons and methods of using them were eventually developed, and when a culture came up with such an innovation, it frequently gave them an edge over their opponents. The history of warfare is closely linked to the history of weapons and of technology. The ancient world witnessed a sequence of military revolutions, usually based around a new type of weapon or style of fighting that temporarily gave military superiority to the group that developed it.

One example is the chariot, which became a kind of ultimate battlefield weapon for the Egyptians and gave their armies an edge when pitted against non-chariot-equipped foes. Chariots were also used with great success by some Near Eastern armies such as the Hittites and Assyrians, who valued them for their speed and power. The Egyptians also refined the use of the bow in warfare, and Egyptian archers enjoyed great success against lightly armored foes.

The Greeks took infantry tactics to a new level when they developed the hoplite style of warfare based around a heavily armed and armored infantryman who acted in concert with similarly armed men to form an irresistible battlefield force. All Greek states quickly adopted the new hoplite style of warfare, and even when the Greeks were tested against the military superpower of the time, the Persians, hoplite warfare proved superior, granting the Greeks a stunning series of upset victories. Later, the Macedonians further refined hoplite warfare, introducing a longer spear and ultimately beating the Greeks at their own game, and incidentally conquering Greece in the process.

Roman military success did not rest so much on vastly superior weapons as it did on improved training and tactics. By the mid-Republic, the Roman army was a full-time professional standing army that trained year-round. Their high degree of discipline and training, standardized equipment, and meticulous organization gave them the advantage when confronting less-orderly enemies.

Styles of naval warfare were also determined by technology. The standard warship in the ancient world was a slender vessel propelled by banks of oars. The preferred method of sinking enemy ships was by ramming them with a bronze ram placed on the front of the ship.

Ancient civilizations showed considerable creativity in inventing new and more effective tools and methods with which to kill one another. Some of the most sophisticated technology and the cleverest inventions developed by the ancients were devoted to military applications. This tendency for the cutting edge of technology to be used not for the betterment of people but to kill them more effectively seems to be a general human characteristic that continues to be amply illustrated in more recent times, when jet aircraft, computers, and countless other innovations saw their first practical applications as weapons.

~*Gregory S. Aldrete*

POLITICAL LIFE
|
WEAPONS
|
Mesopotamia

Egypt

Greece

Rome

Australian Aboriginals

MESOPOTAMIA

In Mesopotamia, the soldiers' weapons were often used as tools in their daily life. Hunters used slings and nets. Nomads were probably well armed and kept supplies of metal. Sedentary communities brought elaborate military equipment such as chariots, carts, and protective armor. Different contingents were distinguished by their clothing and weapons.

Each troop had its own patron deity and standards of other gods accompanying the king in battle. For example, Old Babylonian texts mention the gods Nergal or Erra on the right and Adad on the left, that is, a right and left wing. Weapons used by kings and gods were deified and given names. Starting with the Early Dynastic period, foot soldiers or infantrymen used a variety of weapons such as axes, adzes, large shields, spears, maces, and bows and arrows. Daggers, sickle swords, and homemade-looking blades wrapped around the end of a wooden shaft were followed by swords, invented in the second millennium B.C.E. Defensive weapons included small round shields, round helmets, and protective armor, even used for the horses, particularly at the neck.

Later texts list lance bearers, shield bearers, and archers. Palaces and administrative centers sometimes supplied military equipment. In the first millennium B.C.E., iron became the metal of choice for weapons. Engineers were important for building bridges and roads for the army, primarily during the first millennium in Assyria.

Chariotry became important during the second half of the second millennium, when the Hurrians and Hittites first introduced masses of light, spoke-wheeled chariots drawn by teams of horses—usually racehorses, which were well trained. Originally, the chariots carried only a bowman and a driver; later, a shield bearer was added to the group. There were two main types of chariots: the four-wheeled "battle-car," a heavy vehicle with wheels of solid timber, and the two-wheeled chariot, which may have been made for the hunt. In the first millennium, horses from Nubia were used to pull the heavier chariots.

Charioteers wore body armor made from copper or bronze platelets that overlapped and were attached to leather garments, the whole gear weighing as much as 57 pounds and issued by the palace treasury. Scale armor protected the charioteers from arrows. Helmets were sometimes plumed and covered in metal scales or made from hammered sheet-iron; one set of body armor required 400 large copper scales for the corselet, 280 small scales for the sleeves, and 190 scales for the helmet. Such precise information has come to us mostly from texts and reliefs (Nemet-Nejat, 233–34).

FOR MORE INFORMATION

Dalley, S. "Ancient Mesopotamian Military Organization." In *Civilizations of the Ancient Near East,* ed. J. Sasson. Vol. 1. New York: Scribner's, 1995.

Nemet-Nejat, K. R. *Daily Life in Ancient Mesopotamia.* Westport, Conn.: Greenwood Press, 1998.

POLITICAL LIFE

WEAPONS

Mesopotamia

Egypt

Greece

Rome

Australian Aboriginals

EGYPT

By the time of the Middle Kingdom, Egypt's army was professionally disciplined and divided into units. Tomb models display units marching in orderly columns of 10. Archery divisions were considered elite troops, and entire units of these were composed of Nubians who were famed for their skill with the bow. (Egyptians referred to Nubia as the "Land of the Bows.") Most archers were right-handed, so they held their bow with the left—the arm generally protected from the snap of the string by a leather arm guard—and drew the string with the right hand. The bow, consisting of two basic parts, the body and the string, is the first tool in history designed to concentrate energy. When an arrow is notched on the string and drawn toward the archer, the bow's body stores the tension that propels the arrow forward upon release. The bow's advantage over a mace or sword was its ability to kill at a considerable distance—how far depended on the amount of tension. If your bow had greater range than your opponent's, you could injure him while standing safely out of his range, an advantage that led to the world's first arms race.

The earliest Egyptian versions of bows were made from the acacia tree, one of the few native sources of wood available, and were simply convex in shape. By putting a curve in the bow—shaping it like an upper lip—the string lay closer to the body of the bow, increasing the amount of tension and hence the distance it traveled when drawn back. This invention armed Egypt's oldest troops. But an ideal bow would combine strength with flexibility, which no single wood can do. Woods that bend easily store little energy; those that store more energy break rather than bend. The solution was to combine different materials in one bow, thus extending its range. These "composite bows," made of animal horn, animal tendons, wood, and glue, were constructed by first gluing together woods from several types of tree to produce a core. The part facing the string (called the belly) was strengthened with two sections of strong animal horn, one on either side of the hand grip. The back of the bow (the part away from the string) was covered with animal sinews for flexibility and to prevent the wood from splitting. After the composite bow was shaped into a double convex form to add power, its effective range became nearly a quarter of a mile.

Of course, a bow is useless without well-made arrows. Because the shaft had to be straight, light, and strong, it was generally made of wood, occasionally of reed. The arrowhead, which

An Egyptian archer draws his bow. The Egyptians were particularly proficient archers and used the bow both in hunting and warfare.

needed to be hard, was made of flint or metal and was either leaf shaped or triangular. The arrow shaft fit into the head (socket), or else an extension of the head (tang) was inserted into the shaft. To ensure that the arrow flew straight, feathers of various birds—eagle, vulture, or kite—fletched the end. Because the archer fired many arrows during a single battle, Egyptian leather quivers, holding from 20 to 30 arrows, were worn over the shoulder to free both hands to load and shoot what the Persians called "messengers of death."

Slings were similar to bows in purpose. Originally designed by shepherds to keep foxes from their herds, these simple weapons composed of a rectangular piece of leather with two strings attached could inflict damage at a distance. A stone was placed on the leather, which became a pouch when the ends of the strings were held together in one hand. The sling was swung round and round to build momentum, and then one of the strings was released, which opened the pouch and sent the missile on its way. Corps of slingmen served in conjunction with archers to rain missiles on massed enemies.

For closer combat, the arsenal expanded. Javelins were medium-range weapons, similar in principle to an arrow but propelled by hand. They consisted of a wooden shaft (approximately five feet long) with a metal tip fixed to it with either a socket or a tang. When hurled by a skilled thrower, javelins could be deadly at more than 100 feet. Spears, larger and heavier than javelins, were intended for thrusting, rather than throwing.

The oldest hand-to-hand weapon was the mace featured on Narmer's Palette, a stone tablet depicting the first king of Egypt. This simple but lethal weapon consisted of a stone fixed to the end of a stick whose short handle, about 18 inches long, allowed quick swings. The lethal end consisted of a carved pear-, disk-, or apple-shaped rock about the size of a fist with a hole in one end for the handle, like a modern ax head. Unlike an ax, however, the mace was designed to smash rather than cut. Although it was an impressive weapon, it was replaced by the battle ax when enemies began to protect their heads with metal helmets. The close combat arsenal also featured lethal-looking but overrated swords. Two basic kinds were employed. A straight version was intended for stabbing, so its metal blade was pointed at the tip and honed sharp along both edges. A striking sword, on the other hand, was sharpened only along one edge and curved, like a sickle, to slice as it was pulled back. The problem with both versions was that they consisted of long pieces of bronze, which ancient metalsmiths could not forge strongly enough to do damage without bending, chipping, or breaking. Battle axes, which evolved over the centuries in response to changes in warfare, were preferred for hand-to-hand combat because they carried a smaller, more durable metal blade. The first axes were cutting weapons, so their blades were broad and often curved for a larger cutting surface. The blade was attached to a short wooden handle either by the tang or the socket method and reinforced with cord so it would not fly off during battle. Armor caused the axe's undoing: cutting blades made no dent in mail or metal helmets. A more pointed blade, better suited for piercing, was developed later.

To counteract all these weapons, soldiers carried shields as barriers between themselves and the enemy's weapon. Always something of a compromise, they were either large and heavy, providing excellent protection but slowing the soldier's attack, or small and light, affording little protection. A shield light enough to carry in one hand but strong enough to ward off an enemy's blows eventually was developed by combining materials. Egyptian shields were round-topped rectangles that extended from the chin to the knee. Wood formed their core, hardened by a tough animal-hide cover, a combination that made the shield difficult to penetrate while keeping it light and maneuverable. Soldiers held shields in their left hands to ward off arrows, axes, and swords, while attacking with a weapon in their right. Because each country's shield shape was distinctive, ancient representations of battles distinguish the good guys from the bad not by the color of their hats but by the style of their shields.

For more than 700 years, the Egyptian arsenal hardly changed, until the unthinkable happened.

For more than 700 years, the Egyptian arsenal hardly changed, until the unthinkable happened: a foreign army invaded Egypt and won. There are no records of the invasion—the Egyptians never recorded defeats—so Egyptologists have reconstructed a probable scenario. The invaders, called Hyksos by the Egyptians, or "foreign rulers," arrived from the north and ruled Egypt for more than a century (1663–1555 B.C.E.). This enemy brought a new superweapon with them: the chariot. Until the Hyksos, the Egyptians had never seen a horse; no word for this animal existed at the time in their language.

Three factors determined the outcome of any battle: firepower (arrows, axes, spears, and so on), defense (shields and armor), and mobility. The chariot was never intended as a troop transport since an army's rate of march is constrained by its slow infantry. Rather, the chariot was a mobile platform from which javelins could be hurled and arrows shot. Pulled by two horses, these light, two-wheeled vehicles provided a tremendous advantage against foot soldiers. A weakness in the lines could be reinforced by chariot troops before the enemy could take advantage; a weakness in the enemy lines could be overcome by horse-driven reinforcements before more foes arrived. Even if endangered, a chariot could quickly retreat to safety and fire from a distance. Chariots held a pair of soldiers—a driver and an archer, or sometimes a javelin thrower. A skilled driver controlled his horses with one hand while his other held a shield to fend off enemy arrows, allowing his partner to fire away in safety. In addition to the chariot, the Hyksos may have introduced the composite bow into Egypt. Such a twofold advantage—in firepower and mobility—would give them an unbeatable edge.

The experience of the Hyksos wars so clearly proved the power of the chariot that, ever after, chariot divisions formed the heart of Egypt's army. These forerunners of light tanks required skilled woodworkers for their manufacture, a craft to which Egyptians brought centuries of experience in working with imported woods. Their skill at wood bending enabled them to make a spoked rather than solid wheel, reducing the weight of the chariot to aid its maneuverability. While elm, which bent easily, was used for the wheels, ash formed the carriage because of its strength. The floor on which the archer and his driver stood was woven from leather, which acted as a shock absorber in stabilizing the platform. Chariots involved considerable investment. In addition to the expense of imported woods and skilled craftsmen, stables of horses and horse trainers had to be maintained. Egyptians bred their horses only for war, so all the raising, feeding, and training expenses counted as military expenses. Because chariots also required continual maintenance—they broke easily despite the care that went into their production—military campaigns included hundreds of wheelwrights, chariot builders, spare horses, and trainers. When an army marched out with its chariot corps, it displayed the kind of significant military investment only a superpower of the time could afford.

Whereas Narmer, the first king of Egypt, portrayed himself smiting enemies with his mace, kings of the 18th Dynasty are shown terrorizing their foes in chariots. As evidence of their prowess, they are often depicted controlling the chariot alone, without a driver, and pharaohs are even shown managing their horses with the reins tied around their waists so they could use both hands to shoot arrows. Chariots had become a status symbol, the ultimate weapon in Egyptian warfare (Brier and Hobbs, 202–10).

FOR MORE INFORMATION

Brier, B., and H. Hobbs. *Daily Life of the Ancient Egyptians*. Westport, Conn.: Greenwood Press, 1999.

Davies, W. V. *Catalogue of Egyptian Antiquities in the British Museum: VII Tools and Weapons*. London: British Museum Press, 1987.

Littauer M. A., and J. H. Crouwel. *Chariots and Related Equipment from the Tomb of Tutankhamen*. Oxford: Griffith Institute, 1985.

McLeod, W. M. *Self Bows and Other Archery Tackle from the Tomb of Tutankhamen*. Oxford: Griffith Institute, 1982.

POLITICAL LIFE

WEAPONS

Mesopotamia

Egypt

Greece

Rome

Australian Aboriginals

GREECE

The armor described in the Homeric poems was made of bronze, as is consistent with the Bronze Age context of the Trojan War. It consisted of greaves (i.e., leg guards), a corselet, and a helmet with a crest of horsehair. There was also a special kind of helmet worn by a few warriors that was made out of ox hide, to which were attached plates made out of boar's tusk. Shields were made of ox hide stretched over a wooden frame. The most common type of shield was small and round. Ajax, however, who was the tallest of the Greek warriors, had a rectangular shield with a rising curve on its top edge. Heroes fought mainly with a pair of throwing spears or a single thrusting spear, although at close quarters they also used the sword, frequently described as "silver-studded." The bow and arrow were chiefly limited to the common soldiery and a very few heroes, including Paris and Odysseus.

In the seventh century B.C.E., there was a military revolution in Greece that brought a new way of fighting and specialized equipment. This new style of fighting was known as hoplite warfare, after the large circular shields, the *hoplon*, carried by the soldiers who were called hoplites. The *hoplon*, which was made of wood or stiffened leather with a bronze covering, was about three feet in diameter and designed to cover half the entire body. It had a double grip and could be rested against the right shoulder, since it was concave on the inside. It was intended to protect not only its bearer but also in part the man standing to his left. For this reason, hoplite armies showed a tendency to drift to the right while they were advancing, as each hoplite sought protection on his exposed side from the shield of his companion on the right. Like Homeric heroes, hoplites wore helmets, corselets, and greaves made of bronze to a thickness of about half an inch. The principal weapon of attack was the thrusting spear, which was eight feet in length and tipped with iron. As the unit advanced, the spears held by the hoplites standing in the first five ranks all projected beyond the front line. If a spear broke, it could be turned around, since the reverse end possessed an iron spike. Hoplites also carried a short sword, which they could use if they lost their spears. Hoplite gear, although essentially uniform, was likely highly individual in appearance. Because there was no government issue of arms or armor, individuals were at liberty to request from the armorer whatever modifications to the basic design they desired.

A Greek hoplite. He is equipped with bronze helmet, spear, and *hoplon* (shield). Designs painted on shields were intended for identification or for intimidating the enemy. © The Art Archive/Acropolis Museum Athens/Dagli Orti.

The unit in which hoplites fought was known as a phalanx. This was a rectangular formation with a long battlefront usually eight ranks deep. Most hoplite battles took place on level terrain because only thus could a phalanx maintain its cohesion. The objective was to break through the enemy ranks en masse. Most battles resembled a kind of tug-of-war, with both sides evenly balanced for some time, while much pushing and shoving took place. Complicated maneuvers were rarely attempted, as these made it difficult for a phalanx to retain its formation. Because hoplite helmets had only small eye slots and no piercings for the ears, it was practically impossible for generals to give precise orders. Once battle had commenced, they could do little more than bark out words of encouragement.

When one army finally began to yield, a swift outcome generally ensued, since it would have been practically impossible for a broken phalanx to regroup. However, because the victorious side also put itself at risk if it broke rank and began pursuing a fleeing army, it was usually content merely to occupy the field. Thus most hoplite battles ended in a tactical victory. The victors rarely sought to annihilate the enemy or render them incapable of waging further war.

Ships and naval warfare also played an important role in Greek warfare. In 483 B.C.E., Athens made the historic decision to build a fleet and become a naval power. Prior to that date, it possessed only a skeletal navy of about 50 ships. It was with a navy that Athens helped the Greek alliance defeat the Persian invasion two years later and that it subsequently acquired a maritime empire. Athens achieved naval supremacy with the aid of a warship known as a *trireme*. The word *trireme* is derived from the Greek *trierês*, meaning "three-fitted," a reference to its three banks of oars.

Two banks of rowers sat in the hold of the ship and one on the crossbeams. The trireme was designed to achieve maximum speed and maneuverability with minimum weight. Its hull was about 170 feet in length, and its width a mere 15 feet, giving it a ratio of 9 to 1. It provided accommodation for 170 rowers, with 10 hoplites, 4 archers, and 16 crew members, making a complement of 200. Its objective was to ram the enemy by means of an iron ram mounted on its prow. It is estimated that a trireme could maintain an average speed of about 8 knots and ram at 12 knots. In the Hellenistic period, much larger warships, such as *quadriremes* (four bankers) and *quinqueremes* (five bankers), became common throughout the Greek world.

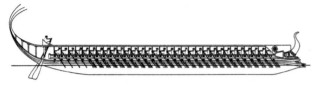

Drawing of a Greek trireme. Similar ships powered by rowers and equipped with rams were the standard warships of the ancient world. Originally in J. S. Morrison, *Greek Oared Ships* (Cambridge: Cambridge University Press, 1968), 184. Courtesy of Cambridge University Press.

The headquarters of the Athenian navy was in the Piraeus, whose three harbors were equipped with more than 370 ship sheds. The discovery of a circuit wall marking off the naval zone from the rest of the port suggests that entry was reserved for naval personnel. Aristophanes evocatively tells us that when an expedition was about to set sail, the Piraeus reverberated with the sound of "oars being planed, pegs hammered, and rowlocks banged into place, and all to the accompaniment of shouting, flutes and whistles of boatswains' orders" (*Acharnians*, lines 552–54). At the outbreak of the Peloponnesian War, Athens possessed 300 seaworthy triremes. By the terms of the treaty in 404 B.C.E., Athens was required to surrender all but 12. The size of the fleet increased during the fourth century, reaching an all-time peak of more than 400 in 322 B.C.E.—ironically, just before Athens's sea power suffered a fatal reverse at the hands of the Macedonians (Garland, 160, 162–63, 167–68).

FOR MORE INFORMATION

Garland, R. *Daily Life of the Ancient Greeks*. Westport, Conn.: Greenwood Press, 1998.

Hanson, V. D. *The Western Way of War: Infantry Battle in Classical Greece*. Oxford: Oxford University Press, 1989.

Hanson, V. D., ed. *Hoplites: The Classical Greek Battle Experience*. New York: Routledge, 1991.

Snodgrass, A. M. *Arms and Armor of the Greeks*. Baltimore, Md.: Johns Hopkins University Press, 1967.

POLITICAL LIFE

WEAPONS

Mesopotamia

Egypt

Greece

Rome

Australian Aboriginals

ROME

In the early Roman Republic, weapons were not standardized, and soldiers probably only had leather vests and shields for protection. Later, protective shirts made of chain mail were added. By the Punic Wars, equipment began to be more standardized, and the Roman legions specialized in heavy infantry. In the late Republic and the first few centuries of the empire, when resources were at their greatest, the Romans were able to outfit their soldiers with good standardized armor.

A typical soldier would have been equipped with a *lorica segmentata* protecting the chest and belly, which consisted of bands of steel tied together with leather strips. The overall effect was somewhat like the plates of armor protecting a lobster.

To protect the head, Roman soldiers had helmets in all periods. The high point of helmet development had cheek guards to protect the face, an extension at the back to protect the neck, and a reinforcing bar across the front to help save the skull from chopping blows from above.

To improve mobility, Roman soldiers did not have armor on their arms or legs. This left the entire lower half of their bodies exposed, although they did wear a specialized type of belt called the *cingulum* from which were hung strips of leather studded with metal disks to offer at least some protection.

On their feet, Roman soldiers wore boots made of leather straps and a thick hobnailed sole. The Roman term for these boots was *caligae*. The emperor Caligula was really named Gaius, but when he was a young boy, his father commanded an army unit and the soldiers made a miniature pair of military boots for him. The term for these miniature boots was *caligula*, which we might translate as "bootikins," and the nickname stuck with him throughout his life.

For offence, the Roman legionary had two main weapons. First was the famous Roman short sword, called the *gladius*. It is edged on both sides and can be used either to cut or thrust. It is made for combat at close quarters and is designed to kill in a most efficient manner. It is not a flashy or romantic type of sword for fencing, but like the Romans themselves, it was highly practical for the style of fighting they practiced.

Each legionary also carried two spears. The spear was about seven feet long and was called a *pilum*. The spears were specially designed so that they would bend on impact, making it impossible for an enemy to throw them back at the Romans.

In battle, the legion would advance to close range, perhaps 10 or 20 feet, throw their spears in unison, and then draw their swords and charge forward.

A final part of the soldier's standard equipment for battle was the shield, known as the *scutum*. The *scutum* was three or four feet high, two or three feet wide, rectangular in shape, and curved slightly outward so that the legionary could hide his body within the curvature. These shields were painted; the most common design was to paint them red with a golden lightning bolt symbol.

Other items found on veteran soldiers were decorations for bravery. Usually, these took the form of round disks called *phalerae*. Soldiers who had won many of these would have a special harness on top of their armor displaying all of their disks. There were rewards for specific acts, such as the first man over the wall of an enemy city or for one who had distinguished himself in a naval action. There was also an award given to those who saved the life of a fellow citizen on the battlefield.

The Romans much preferred to fight on land rather than at sea. The Romans were never good sailors, and in normal circumstances, they only maintained a small

Bronze statue of a typical legionary of the Roman Republic with standard equipment of helmet, chain mail, body armor, boots, sword, spear, and shield. © The Art Archive/Museo della Civilta Romana Rome/ Dagli Orti.

navy whose primary duty was to attempt to deter pirates. The basic Roman warship was more or less the same as that used by the Greeks, a long narrow vessel propelled by hundreds of rowers. These ships would carry around 300 oarsmen, 30 sailors, and 100 soldiers. The larger ships were equipped with turrets from which archers could shoot down arrows and small catapults that would throw rocks or fire bombs at enemy ships. At the front of the ship was a large iron ram called a *rostra*, and the main goal in a naval battle was to ram an enemy ship. Ramming was most effective if the ship could hit the enemy ship's side. Because the enemy would try to keep the front of their ship facing the ram, this was a difficult maneuver to achieve. Contrary to most movies and books about Rome, the rowers were not slaves. Instead they are thought to have been poor Romans who were hired to serve as rowers.

In the early days of Rome's history, when they were building their first fleets to fight Carthage, the Romans were completely incompetent as sailors. Aware of this, they came up with a clever way to turn naval battles into land battles, at which they excelled. They equipped all their ships with a long wooden bridge with an iron spike at the end, and when a Carthaginian ship came in to ram them, they dropped the bridge, literally nailing the two ships together. Then the Roman soldiers ran across the bridge and fought the Carthaginians hand to hand. The name of this device was the *corvus*, "raven," so named because the iron spike reminded them of a raven's beak.

~Gregory S. Aldrete

FOR MORE INFORMATION

Starr, C. G. *The Roman Imperial Navy*. Ithaca, N.Y.: Cornell University Press, 1941.
Watson, G. R. *The Roman Soldier*. Ithaca, N.Y.: Cornell University Press, 1969.
Webster, G. *The Roman Imperial Army of the First and Second Centuries*. 3rd ed. Totowa, N.J.: Barnes and Noble, 1985.

POLITICAL LIFE

WEAPONS

Mesopotamia

Egypt

Greece

Rome

Australian Aboriginals

AUSTRALIAN ABORIGINALS

Australian Aborigines had a range of tools that were used for making a living. The weapons that were used for punishment or warfare were also usually employed for hunting, although some were modified versions of hunting spears, boomerangs, or clubs. One tool specifically associated with warfare was the shield. Australia was the only continent on which no tools and weapons were made from metals; instead, all were crafted from stone, wood, bone, shell, or various combinations of these materials.

Whereas stone tools survive indefinitely, wooden tools or components seldom last for long in Australian conditions. As a result, it is difficult to form a history of tools and weapons in Australia. A rare set of ancient wooden tools some 10,000 years old, including spears, sticks, and the earliest known boomerang, was found in a swamp in South Australia and is the only such find of wooden implements of any great age. Very old rock-art paintings depict boomerangs and spears. People would use any sharp piece of stone or suitably shaped natural piece of wood that served their purpose; it can be difficult to determine whether such objects had been used when they are found in ancient archaeological deposits.

Tools used for making other tools included heavy rocks for flaking stone, sharp-edged flakes for planing or shaving wood, pointed stones for drilling holes, bone and shell needles for sewing and weaving, and abrasive stone for sanding. Tools and weapons employed for obtaining food included digging sticks, boomerangs, throwing sticks, spears of many kinds, axes, nets, traps, fishhooks and lines, bags, and waterbags. Food preparation involved the use of equipment for lighting fires and tools for cutting, chopping, winnowing, and for grinding seeds.

One criterion of weapon and tool design in Australia was that the implements had to conform to an economic and social system that required moving great distances over the course of the year. A man needed to carry either in his hand or stuck in his belt all the weapons needed for hunting, butchering, and lighting fires. Weapons had to be light and portable and preferably multipurpose as well. A woomera (spear-thrower) for example, might have a sharp flake fitted on the opposite end for chiseling wood, while the body of the woomera could be used for holding food during preparation. Women also needed to carry their implements (and often a baby as well). They might place some tools in a bag, but grindstones, essential for grinding seed, were too heavy to be carried far. Often grindstones would be left at all of the different campsites used by a group so as to be available wherever the group moved. Other cumbersome tools, such as spearshafts or the stone blanks used for making knives and axes, might be hidden away in rock shelters so that they could be used the next time a group arrived.

Tools were used, reused, or modified for new purposes in an almost-endless recycling process. The types of tools have changed over the last 50,000 years, but the reasons for these changes are not clear. There were variations in weapons used in different parts of Australia probably as a result of diverse environments and kinds of food, shelter, and transport, but the complete reason for these variations is not always evident.

~David Horton

FOR MORE INFORMATION

Berndt, R., and C. Berndt. *The World of the First Australians*. Canberra: Aboriginal Studies Press, 1988.

Davidson, D. "Australian Throwing Sticks, Throwing Clubs, and Boomerangs." *American Anthropologist*, n.s., 38 (1936): 76–100.

Hayden, B. *Paleolithic Reflections: Lithic Technology and Ethnographic Excavations among Australian Aborigines*. Atlantic Highlands, N.J.: Humanities Press, 1979.

POLITICAL LIFE: WEB SITES

http://www.fordham.edu/halsall/ancient/hamcode.html
http://www.dalton.org/groups/Rome/RPol.html
http://samuseum.sa.gov.au/aacg/speakingland.htm
http://www.roman-emperors.org/lindexxx.htm

7

RECREATIONAL LIFE

Play is serious business. All mammals play, but humans have cultivated recreation to a high art. After family and work, most of our energies and time are devoted to recreational activities, and as any modern sports enthusiast knows, we can play with as much passion as we work. What are recreational activities? There are several characteristics that all play shares. First, it is voluntary—one cannot be forced to play. As such, it is in fact the very essence of freedom, and even slaves and prisoners treat themselves to games or music or dance for the sheer voluntary quality of the activities. Second, recreation is outside of "real" life, limited in time, duration, and space. Thus playtime by contrast almost defines "work" time; recess at school not only offers a break from study—it marks the serious times when one is to learn. Third, recreation has its own rules, which are more rigorous and predictable than anything we can find in our more complex "real lives." At the end of the game—and there is a definitive end—there is a winner and loser, and the rules are clear. Of course, cheating is always a possibility (archaeologists have even found loaded dice in Anglo-Saxon settlements), but even unsportsmanlike conduct is recognizable. It may be that we love games precisely for the clarity of the rules. Finally, recreational life builds a group identity among the "players," and this is true even of individual sports such as archery or bicycling, for "archers" see themselves as linked with others who share the pastime.

While recreational activities throughout history share these general characteristics, the particular forms of play we choose shed light on who we are and what we value. In play, we prepare ourselves for the rest of our lives. For example, games from the Olympics to chess hone our skills for war, while music and art stimulate our creativity. Violent sports from dog fights to boxing steel us to face violence in life, and team sports like American football prepare us to work together in an economy of separation of skills. In studying the games people play, we can more fully understand the society they are creating.

In the ancient world, the line between real life and recreation was sometimes ambiguous. The play that children engaged in was often meant to prepare them for their adult roles. Then, as now, dolls were popular toys for young girls, and boys honed their hunting skills as training for warfare. In the realm of entertainment,

RECREATIONAL
LIFE
|
HUNTING, SPORTS,
& GAMES

DANCE, MUSIC,
& THEATER

HOLIDAYS, FESTIVALS,
& SPECTACLES

such events as gladiator games, featuring a spectacle of death that was real, further blurred the boundary between reality and play. Entertainment often closely reflected the serious concerns of a society. The Roman obsession with violence can be seen as mirroring their almost-constant warfare, and the Greek preoccupation with politics can be detected in their plays, which frequently commented upon or critiqued current events and those in power.

Games of a less grandiose nature were always played by individuals for the sheer fun and excitement they brought. Throwing dice and wagering on the outcome were popular in all societies and among all social classes, and playing surfaces and pieces of complex board games have been recovered everywhere people lived, from the sands of Egypt to the bogs of northern Europe.

Human beings love to compete—to test and to measure themselves physically and mentally against an opponent. The foe might be another person, an animal, or even one's own endurance and will, but the urge to take part in the struggle is an addictive one. A central appeal of such contests is that they elicit strong emotions, and the competitive drive is fueled both by the ardent desire to experience the exaltation of victory and by the equally powerful desperation to avoid the agony of defeat. In light of this strong motivation within the human psyche to engage in forms of play, it is interesting to note that the modern English word *agony* is, appropriately enough, derived from the ancient Greek word *agon*, meaning "a contest" or "a competition."

~*Joyce E. Salisbury and Gregory S. Aldrete*

FOR MORE INFORMATION

Huizinga, J. *Homo Ludens: A Study of the Play Element in Culture*. Boston, Mass.: Beacon Press, 1964.

RECREATIONAL
LIFE
|
HUNTING, SPORTS,
& GAMES
|
Mesopotamia

Egypt

Greece

Rome

Nubia

Australian Aboriginals

Hunting, Sports, and Games

Contests of athletic ability, intellectual skill, and chance have great appeal to humans who wish to test themselves, their abilities, and their luck against one another, and the ancient world was no exception to this desire. Such activities were common in all these cultures and were played by all levels of society.

Perhaps one of the most basic and universal games of all was throwing dice and guessing and wagering on the outcome. The poorest peasant to the most godlike emperor or pharaoh all found fascination and amusement in games of chance using dice. Archaeologists have found numerous dice made of everything from bone, wood, and clay to precious metals. The simplest (and probably the first) six-sided dice were the knucklebones of animals marked with crudely inscribed or painted spots.

More complex types of games involved boards and game pieces that were maneuvered according to sets of rules and using various strategies. Such boards and pieces survive from Mesopotamia, Egypt, Greece, and Rome, although the rules that governed their use can sometimes only be guessed at. These board games were clearly popular and engaging ways to pass time for many people, as evidenced by the game grids that bored idlers hacked into the fine marble steps of public buildings in ancient Rome.

The competitive nature of humans found an outlet in a variety of familiar and not-so-familiar athletic sports. One of the most basic forms of athletic contest that is attested in all these cultures is wrestling. Contests involving running, throwing, and jumping were also common. The most glorious and longest-lasting institutionalization of athletics is the Greek Olympic Games, which were held every four years for a thousand-year span. Along with other great international athletic contests, such as the Pythian or Nemean Games, the ancient Olympics were every bit as popular as major sporting events such as the World Cup today, and the victorious athletes were just as idolized. One significant difference, however, is that these ancient athletic contests had a religious component. Olympia was a religious sanctuary, the games were held during a religious festival, and they were viewed as a way of honoring the gods. The Greeks raised athletics to a particularly high level, and every self-respecting Greek town had a gymnasium in which its citizens could exercise and train.

Another popular pastime was the pursuit of wild game. Hunting and fishing were popular among average people not just as a way of supplementing the diet but also for the challenge and the thrill of the chase. Hunting for the Aboriginal peoples of Australia was more than a game; it was a necessity for survival because they did not cultivate crops. Hunting, especially of large or dangerous animals, had a special status, seen as a way of honing and displaying skills that were useful in war. In Assyria, the kings engaged in ritual lion hunts specifically as a way of asserting their fitness to be military leaders. Such hunts probably also occurred in Nubia, where the range of large dangerous animals included such formidable beasts as elephants and hippopotamuses.

Uniting all these forms of entertainment is their general accessibility to the average person. Almost everyone could race his peers, play board games, or try to catch a fish, and while particularly talented individuals could gain fame and fortune through their skills, the real appeal of these activities was that the average person could play them and experience for themselves "the thrill of victory and the agony of defeat."

~Gregory S. Aldrete

MESOPOTAMIA

Both boxing and wrestling were depicted in Mesopotamian art. Terra-cotta plaques showing boxers imply that boxing was a popular sport. In one plaque, the boxers are beside two men who are beating an enormous drum, perhaps in time with the boxers' motions. In *The Epic of Gilgamesh*, there is a reference to a wrestling match between Gilgamesh and Enkidu.

Game board and counters found at Ur. The intricately crafted board and pieces are made of a variety of fine materials, including lapis lazuli, shell, and stone. © Copyright The British Museum.

A form of polo may also have been played, but with men astride the shoulders of other men rather than on horses, as in Mesoamerica. Again, in *The Epic of Gilgamesh*, there is a reference to Gilgamesh oppressing his subjects by tiring the young men with endless contests of this type of polo and then taking sexual advantage of the young women.

Board games have been recovered through archaeological excavation. The boards were usually made of stone or clay (in Egypt and ancient Israel, they were made of wood or ivory). Some are from Esarhaddon's palace and display the royal legend. Board games were played with various kinds of pieces and even dice. Two of these games were similar to those of ancient Egypt. The first, the game of 20-squares, involved a race using pieces that moved according to rolls of the dice. That the game of 20-squares was played not only by the rich is indicated by the discovery of large clay bricks with the board crudely drawn. Palace guards even passed their time playing the game of 20-squares; in fact, a game board was scratched into the pedestal of one of the pair of bull-colossi guarding King Sargon's palace gates at Khorsabad.

The second type of board game, the game of 58 holes, is an early model for cribbage. Two lot boards, one connected with the 12 signs of the zodiac, contain instructions on the back about how the game was played. They explain how to draw the 84 sections on the ground and the names of the pieces (eagle, raven, rooster, swallow, and an unidentified bird). In fact, the lot boards used a word for game piece, "doll, figurine," similar to "man" in chessman. The pieces were moved when dice made from astragals (the joint bones of oxen or sheep) were thrown. This game, called *asha,* is still played today by women in the Jewish community of Cochin in southern India.

In general, games were accompanied by objects that were thrown and objects that were moved. Thrown objects included dice, probably of Indian origin, which have been dated to all periods and found at sites throughout Mesopotamia. The dice are cubes of bone, clay, stone, and even glass. They have the numbers 1 through 6 incised on them. However, unlike modern dice, on which the sum of the opposite sides is always 7, ancient dice have opposite sides that are usually numbered consecutively. Other objects thrown included joint bones, throw sticks, and stones. Stones, described as desirable or undesirable, were put as lots into a container, drawn, and played once certain prayers were made to the gods to oversee the game. Moved objects included the game piece referred to as "doll, figurine," as well as birds, dogs, circular pieces, and other shapes such as small clay cones and pyramids.

The Assyrian kings were famous hunters of lions, elephants, ostriches, wild bulls, and other beasts. Although the king preferred to hunt the larger, more aggressive animals, other beasts would do. The sport had both religious and political implications: as a successful hunter, the king proved that the gods favored him and that his power was therefore legitimate. Good triumphed over evil.

The Syrian plain was often the scene of the Assyrian royal hunt, but lions were also caught in Africa and brought to Assyria, where they were kept in game reserves until the hunt. The hunts were carefully orchestrated. From a booth above the wooden cage, a servant raised the door and released the lions, who were attacked by dogs and beaters. The beaters' job was to beat the lions with sticks and drive them toward the king. The king killed the lions from his chariot with a bow or spear. Sometimes the king was shown on foot, killing the lion by holding its mane and

Relief of Assyrian king hunting lions. Displaying prowess as a hunter was a way to demonstrate military skills. Erich Lessing/Art Resource, NY.

thrusting a sword into his prey. The hunt became a public event. After the hunt, as part of a religious ceremony, the king poured a libation over the dead lions to atone for the harm he had done them and to appease their angry spirits. He also recited a devotional speech attributing the success of the hunt to his patron goddess. At the end of the hunt, the servants picked up the dead animals. The formal hunt was continued by the Persian kings. The popularity of this sport is attested by both information in the tablets and lifelike hunting scenes carved ad nauseam on Assyrian palace walls (Nemet-Nejat, 163–66).

FOR MORE INFORMATION

Anderson, J. K. *Hunting in the Ancient World.* Oxford: Oxford University Press, 1985.

Contenau, G. *Everyday Life in Babylon and Assyria.* Translated by K. R. Maxwell-Hyslop and A. R. Maxwell-Hyslop. New York: St. Martin's Press, 1954.

Nemet-Nejat, K. R. *Daily Life in Ancient Mesopotamia*. Westport, Conn.: Greenwood Press, 1998.

EGYPT

Games existed in great variety in ancient Egypt, from sedate board types to more physical ones, with most of the latter being played by children. They loved their version of tug of war, in which one team's captain grasped the wrists of the other captain while, behind, each team formed a human chain to try to pull them apart. "Your arm is much stronger than his! Don't give in to him!" one team urges its captain on a tomb wall from 4,000 years ago. Another favorite game resembled the buck-buck game played by modern-day Boy Scouts. A standing group of from six to eight boys formed a tower by linking their arms over their shoulders. The object of the game was for the other members of their team to leap on top—not an easy feat—and settle on all fours. Then the other team had its turn. One scene illustrating this game includes the score: two children succeeded. Another game consisted of seating two children back to back with their arms grasping the ankles of their outstretched legs. The object was for a third child to jump over this human obstacle, a challenge complicated by the obstacle's attempts to trip the jumpers. Although the seated children kept their eyes closed, the jumper was required to yell a warning as he ran toward them. Also popular was the universal odds and evens, in which two players shot out as many fingers as they wished after yelling either odd or even; a count of the combined fingers determined the winner.

Wrestling, beloved of both men and boys in ancient Egypt, achieved a great degree of complexity and required long training. Tombs of Middle Kingdom nobility in modern Beni Hassan show hundreds of vignettes of paired wrestlers—with only a ribbon around their waists—illustrating as many different holds and throws, from half nelsons to hip rolls. A match began, as in our own day, with two opponents coming at one another in a semicrouch, reaching for a first hold.

Marshmen and other boating people substituted a kind of joust for wrestling in which, as spectators rooted for their favorite, the crew of one small punt tried to knock the other crew in the water with long poles. Other games taught military skills, as in one in which contestants wielded short sticks simulating swords or battle axes and used small boards fixed to one lower arm to ward off an opponent's blows. Others involved aiming arrows and spears at targets. Given the Nile's proximity, swimming, of course, was a favorite pastime for all children. Egyptians enjoyed sailing for its own sake, with no objective other than to enjoy the cool breeze of the Nile.

Girls and young women enjoyed their own varieties of games. Many involved balls carved from wood or made by sewing leather around a packed wad of straw. Juggling two or three balls was popular, as was a simple game of catch. To make tossing a ball more interesting, one girl rode piggyback on another and threw the ball to a similarly mounted rider, attempting to keep three balls moving at once. Perhaps the first girl to drop the ball became the "horse" in the next round. In another, more gymnastic, exercise, two participants stood back to back with outstretched arms while two others grasped their arms and leaned back almost horizontally with their feet resting on those of their standing partners. The entire ensemble then spun around as often as they could until overcome by dizziness.

More sedate activities included four board games known from examples found in tombs—an indication of how much they must have been enjoyed. The oldest, called *mehen*, consisted of a serpent etched on a board and whose body, divided into segments, coiled to the center. Pieces representing three lions and three lionesses were found in a drawer in the board, along with a red and a white ball. Because no instructions were included, its rules are unknown, but most likely it was an antecedent of such modern games as Chutes and Ladders, in which a piece moves from square to square, some with rewards, others with penalties, and the objective is to reach the end before one's opponent. Other board games came with either ivory or wood wands, each about eight inches long, some with round ends, others with foxlike heads. One side of the wand was curved; the other was flat and inscribed with three bands of lines. The way in which the wands fell when they were thrown probably decided the move.

Equally old was a game of many squares and multiple pieces that looks remarkably like our checkers. The top and bottom of a game box from the early New Kingdom gives us information about two other board games. One board layout, called *senet*, consisted of three rows of 10 squares each. The other, called *tjau* (robbers), consisted of three rows of four squares at one end of the board, from which eight more squares formed a line toward the other end. This "tail" row was bordered by a hound facing a lion above and a lion facing two gazelles below. Six dome-shaped ivory game pieces were found inside the box, along with six spool-shaped pieces, three pairs of game wands, and a pair of knucklebones. How these games were played remains unknown, but they appear to be games of position much like Go or Parcheesi.

Drawing of an Egyptian fisherman seated in a boat made out of bundles of papyrus. Drawing by Rivka Rago.

Much like today, fishing and hunting were pursued for the pleasure of the catch as well as for food. Marshes provided a favorite arena for the activity. Often, couples are portrayed enjoying the outing together, both simply and practically dressed—probably a relief from the formal attire usually worn by this class. Some scenes show a husband drawing a bead on a duck with his bow while his faithful wife holds the next missile ready. Others reproduce a couple posed in the same attitudes but substitute a curved throwing stick as the weapon, and yet others show the husband poised to hurl his harpoon at underwater prey, also under the admiring gaze of his wife.

Desert hunting provided the thrill of the chase. Egyptians, mounted in chariots, usually in groups of three or four to corral their prey, pursued speedy game such as rabbits, antelope, and gazelles with bows or spears. Even the most dangerous animals—fierce lions and leopards—were hunted in a desert more verdant than it is today. Sometimes a tied cow was used as bait, and hunting dogs, swifter over short distances than chariots, were employed as well. Indeed, Egyptians are the first people on record, though not necessarily the first in fact, to have domesticated the dog, a greyhound-like species known today as the saluki. More certain and surprising is the fact that they first domesticated cats and used them as hunting animals in the marshes.

Children practiced with bows, spears, and throwing sticks by the hour to gain enough proficiency to hit live targets, and adults honed their skills regularly as well. Bullfighting was the one known Egyptian spectator sport. The Egyptian version pitted bull against bull rather than man against beast, but referees with short sticks watched, ready to step in to prevent fatal injury to either animal (Brier and Hobbs, 89–90, 93–95).

FOR MORE INFORMATION

Brier, B., and H. Hobbs. *Daily Life of the Ancient Egyptians*. Westport, Conn.: Greenwood Press, 1999.

Montet, P. *Everyday Life in Egypt in the Days of Ramesses the Great*. Translated by A. R. Maxwell-Hyslop and M. Drower. Reprint, Philadelphia: University of Pennsylvania Press, 1981.

RECREATIONAL
LIFE

HUNTING, SPORTS,
& GAMES

Mesopotamia

Egypt

Greece

Rome

Nubia

Australian Aboriginals

GREECE

Few peoples have attached so much significance to the cult of physical fitness as the Greeks. The notion of physical perfection was so central to their sense of self-hood that they seem to have been almost incapable of conceiving of themselves in any other terms. Greek art is saturated with images of perfectly formed men and women. Theirs was a culture that made no differentiation between what was *kalos* (beautiful) on the one hand and *agathos* (good) on the other.

The adoration of the human body found many outlets. Greek art, especially sculpture, gave it uninhibited expression. It was the Greeks who first identified the naked human body as the primary object of artistic attention. No less important, physical perfection was exemplified through competitive athletics, which occupied a central place in a number of major festivals. The apparent assumption was that the gods, who themselves exemplified physical perfection on the divine plane, took delight in observing their human counterparts.

Athletic training was a vital part of education for boys from wealthy families. As soon as they began school at about the age of seven, Athenian boys were entrusted to a professional trainer known as a *paidotribês*, who worked in a *palaistra* or "wrestling school." Athens contained many *palaistrai*, but none has been fully excavated. Their general layout was similar to that of a Greek house. The training ground was probably enclosed by a wall with a veranda to provide shelter from the rain and sun. Most *palaistrai* possessed a changing room, a bathroom, and a place to store equipment.

More mature athletes exercised naked in the gymnasium, a Greek word whose root is the adjective *gymnos* (naked, or lightly clad). Although many gymnasiums were equipped with changing rooms and other facilities, the basic requisite was a piece of level, open terrain, where athletes could practice javelin and discus throwing, as well as running. Gymnasiums tended to be located near a river, enabling athletes to refresh themselves and bathe after exercising. Although only their foundations have survived, they were probably verdant oases with well-shaded walks. By the end of the sixth century B.C.E., Athens had acquired three principal gymnasiums—the Academy, the Lyceum, and the Cynosarges—all situated outside the city. These were used by Athens's ephebes, as well as by its hoplites.

Socializing also went on in the gymnasium. Not only aspiring athletes but also older men would gather there to converse, gossip, and argue, while sitting in the shade beside running water. Here, too, itinerant professors, known as Sophists, would talk and give lectures. In the fourth century B.C.E., the gymnasiums of Athens came to acquire a new identity as centers for philosophical discussion. Plato established his school in the vicinity of the Academy. The name, which derives from a local hero called Academos, is the origin of our word *academic*. Half a century later, Plato's pupil Aristotle established a rival philosophical school in the Lyceum. Aristotle's followers were dubbed peripatetics (from the verb *peripateô*, "to walk up and down") because of their habit of pacing up and down as they pursued their philosophical inquiries. The geographical coincidence between intellectual and athletic excellence testifies to the Greek conviction that the two aspirations are complementary.

Competitive athletics was one of the principal means by which the Greeks promoted a sense of cultural unity. Although there were probably hundreds of local athletic festivals, four Panhellenic, or "all-Greek," games attracted athletes from all over the Greek world. These were the Olympic and Nemean Games, both held in honor of Zeus; the Pythian Games, held in honor of Apollo; and the Isthmian Games, held in honor of Poseidon. The most prestigious of these were the Olympic Games, held every four years from 776 B.C.E. to 261 C.E. It is a remarkable testimony to the Greek ability to rise above politics at least on a temporary basis that in the course of this thousand-year period never once, so far as we know, were they canceled. By contrast, our modern series, which was first held in 1896, has already been canceled three times, quite aside from being regularly exploited for propagandist or commercial advantage.

There were a number of reasons why the ancient Olympic Games were successful in promoting the spirit of Panhellenism. First, Olympia, because of its location in a politically unimportant region of Greece, never fell prey to the ambitions of any neighboring power. For most of its history, the sanctuary was controlled by the neighboring city of Elis. Consequently, the games were never used for self-promotion by the host country, in the way that the Nazis used the Munich games in 1936 to promote an image of racial superiority. The ancient Olympics did, however, occasionally serve the propagandist aims of individuals, notably in 69 C.E. when they were postponed for two years to enable the Roman emperor Nero to compete. To the credit of the Olympic authorities, his victories in the chariot race and musical contest were later expunged from the record books.

Another reason the Olympic Games genuinely embodied the Olympic ideal is that they formed part of a religious festival held in honor of Zeus Olympios. Olympia was the chief sanctuary of Zeus on the mainland. The religious component, which accounted for two-and-a-half out of the five days devoted to the festival, was never overshadowed by the kind of hoopla that characterizes the modern series. A sacred truce, known as the *ekecheiria*, which remained in effect for one month, was observed to allow spectators and competitors to travel to and from Olympia in safety. In later times, this was extended to two months and finally to three months. Only once was the truce broken, by Sparta in 420 B.C.E. As a punishment, Spartan athletes were prohibited from participation in the games that year.

> *All Olympic contestants participated naked and barefoot.*

All Greek speakers were eligible to participate, and there was virtually no distinction between professionals and amateurs. Most cities subsidized the training of their athletes. Participants had to spend the entire month preceding the games training at Olympia under the supervision of the *Hellênodikai* or "Judges of the Greeks."

The first day of the Olympic Games was devoted to oath taking, checking the qualifications of the competitors, sacrifices, and prayers. So important was winning that competitors prayed "either for the wreath or for death." All contestants participated naked and barefoot. The origin of this practice is attributed to a certain Orsippos, who was in the lead in a footrace when his loincloth fell off. Orsippos tripped and lost the race.

On the second day of the festival, the chariot race took place in the hippodrome. This was the most spectacular, as well as the most dangerous, event. It consisted of 12 laps up and down a straight track. The chariots had two wheels and were drawn by a team of four horses. Because there was no dividing barrier between the up and down track, and because charioteers were required to perform 180-degree turns when they reached the end of each lap, head-on collisions were frequent. Increasing the likelihood of serious injury was the fact that charioteers tied their horses' reins around their bodies, so that if they fell they were dragged along the ground. Pindar, who wrote many odes commemorating victors in the games, claims that in one race at Delphi, "forty drivers were laid low" (*Pythian Ode* 5.49). The chariot race was followed by a horseback race without stirrups or saddles over the same course. The victor in both events was not the charioteer or the jockey but the owner. Because horses were extremely expensive, this was almost invariably a wealthy aristocrat or tyrant.

The remaining events took place in the Olympic stadium. This was named for the stade, a unit of measurement approximately 210 yards in length. The stadium consisted of a level piece of ground covered with sand. Spectators watched from a raised bank of earth on either side. Only the judges were provided with seating. The first event was the pentathlon, which took place on the afternoon of the second day. The pentathlon consisted of five events: discus, long jump, javelin, footrace, and wrestling. The javelin was thrown with the aid of a thong to give it more momentum. For the long jump, athletes carried weights, enabling them to lengthen their jump. On the morning of the third day, more religious celebrations took place, culminating in the sacrifice of a hundred oxen on the great altar of Zeus. In the afternoon, competitions between boys aged between 12 and 18 took place. These consisted of a footrace, wrestling, and boxing. On the morning of the fourth day, adult footraces were held over various distances, the longest being 12 laps. (There was no equivalent of a modern marathon.) The afternoon was given over to body-contact sports, including wrestling, boxing, and *pankration*. The *pankration*, which can be best translated as "all-out combat," was a combination of wrestling and boxing. There were no rules, and serious injuries, even deaths, were not uncommon. On one occasion, the prize was awarded to an athlete called Arrachion, who was strangled to death. His opponent gave in just as Arrachion was expiring because the latter had broken his toe. The final event was a race over two laps run by competitors dressed in full hoplite armor, helmets, and greaves and carrying large, round shields. Proficiency in this event may have contributed to the Athenian victory at the Battle of Marathon, in which the heavily armed hoplites unnerved the Persians by charging from a distance. The only competition for unmarried girls was a footrace in honor of Hera.

On the fifth and final day, prizes of olive wreaths were awarded to the victors. There were no prizes for those who finished second or third. Victors were permitted to erect statues in the sanctuary and were feted lavishly by their own cities when they returned home. Some were granted free meals at public expense for the rest of their lives. States whose athletes won prizes gained enormous prestige. Alcibiades boasted that "the Greeks believed that Athens had even greater power than was the case because of my success in the Olympic Games, although earlier they had thought they had entirely worn us out in the war" (Thucydides, *The Peloponnesian War* 6.16). The most successful state was Elis, where Olympia was situated. Elis produced the first recorded Olympic victor, Coribos, in 776 B.C.E. Sparta was also prominent, whereas Athens, even at the height of her power in the mid–fifth century B.C.E., won far fewer victories. The most successful athlete was Milo of Croton, who won the wrestling prize in five successive Olympiads between 536 and 520 B.C.E. Milo, a notorious show-off, used to challenge people to bend back his little finger—apparently, no one could. He was also in the habit of tying a band around his head, taking a deep breath, and snapping the band with the aid of the veins of his head (Pausanias, *Guide to Greece* 6.14.7).

Women were not permitted to enter the sanctuary of Zeus while the games were in progress. Pausanias (*Guide to Greece* 5.6.7) tells us that the ban was introduced after a woman called Callipateira managed to disguise herself as an Olympic trainer to watch her son compete. She was exposed (literally) when she jumped over the trainers' enclosure. The judges decided not to punish her out of deference to her brothers, father, and son, all of whom had been Olympic victors. Although women could not watch the games in progress, handsome athletes had their fans, who hung about the entrance to the site, eager to catch a glimpse of their favorites. Although only a minute proportion of the Greek population actually participated in the games, young men were inspired to train in the *palaistra* in the hope that they might one day have the distinction of representing their city. The games thus functioned as a general incentive to achieve physical excellence (Garland, 171–77).

FOR MORE INFORMATION

Finley, M. I. *The Olympic Games: The First Thousand Years*. London: Chatto and Windus, 1976.

Gardiner, E. N. *Greek Athletic Sports and Festivals*. London: Macmillan, 1970.

Garland, R. *Daily Life of the Ancient Greeks*. Westport, Conn.: Greenwood Press, 1998.

RECREATIONAL LIFE
|
HUNTING, SPORTS, & GAMES
|
Mesopotamia

Egypt

Greece

Rome

Nubia

Australian Aboriginals

ROME

The Romans entertained themselves with a wide range of leisure activities ranging from board games to athletic training to hunting. Many of these activities took place at the public baths, which, contrary to their name, included much more than just bathing facilities. Full-fledged Roman bath complexes such as those at Rome included within their walls not only bathing pools with different temperature waters but also exercise fields for ball games and wrestling, tracks for running, rooms for lifting weights, massage parlors, libraries, food vendors, displays of art, poetry readings, and gardens. In the city, the entrance fees for major public baths were modest, enabling even poor Romans to make regular use of the buildings and their amenities. Men and women usually did not bathe together but instead had separate facilities or else used the same bath at different hours.

Bathers had a selection of rooms to choose from, including the *caldarium*, which would have been much like a hot tub inside a sauna, the *tepidarium*, with a pool of heated, but not hot water, and the *frigidarium*, whose waters were cold. Bathers usually proceeded from one room to the other in one of several designated sequences. A popular accompaniment to a bath was rubbing olive oil over the body and then scraping it off with a curved metal instrument called a *strigil*. Wealthier bathers might bring slaves with them to do the oiling, scraping, toweling, and massaging, or they could hire attendants at the bath. Bathers of more modest means had to tend to themselves. Baths were important social centers where people gathered to gossip, debate, exchange news, broker deals, and mingle with their peers.

A vivid image of the lively nature of Roman baths is provided by a letter written by the philosopher Seneca, who lived for a while in an apartment situated over a bath complex. He complains about having to endure a variety of unwelcome noises, including the grunting and gasping of weight lifters, the slapping sounds of people getting massages, the babbling of noisy drunks, and the caterwauling of people who, despite a lack of talent, liked to sing in the bath. Adding to the cacophony were the strident and repetitive shouts of vendors selling drinks and snacks, and the shrieks of people having the hair plucked from their armpits (Seneca, *Letters* 56.2.2).

Unlike the Greeks, the Romans did not establish purely athletic contests, but they were concerned with physical fitness. Much of their interest in strength, agility, and endurance probably stems from concern to be ready for warfare. Adolescent Roman boys took part in a number of staged displays of athletic fitness with military overtones. Adjoining the city and encompassed within a bend of the Tiber River was a wide field known as the Campus Martius, literally the "Field of Mars." Eventually, this area became built up, but in Republican Rome, it was the site at which Rome's armies would muster for war, and the name no doubt refers to Mars' role as the god of war. This field was also used as a kind of all-purpose exercise ground where people raced horses and chariots, played ball games, ran foot races, and wrestled (Strabo, *Geography* 5.3.8). Hunting was also a popular pastime among Roman aristocrats and was similarly viewed as a useful activity because the skills it honed were directly applicable to war.

One common form that exercise took was playing various types of games involving balls. There were games using balls, small and large, played in teams or in pairs. One of the most popular was a contest called *trigon* in which three players stationed themselves at the points of a triangle and threw balls at one another. Points were scored when a player failed to field a ball thrown at him. Apparently, multiple balls might be in play at the same time, and players could throw and catch with both hands. This game obviously favored those with quick reflexes and good hand-eye coordination, and players who could use both hands skillfully were admired. At least one type of ball game seems to have been played in a specially constructed court, but most seem to have needed only an open expanse.

Women also exercised with weights and played ball games, although whether as much as men is unlikely since many women's baths did not include open fields like men's. A famous mosaic from Sicily, however, depicts young women clad in garments resembling bikinis throwing balls, running, and using dumbbells.

In addition to physical contests, Romans enjoyed games of skill and chance. One often finds in Roman colonnades crude board games hacked into the fine marble stairs or flooring. Many visitors apparently felt comfortable modifying their surroundings to suit their personal taste. These permanent boards presumably replaced more temporary versions drawn on the ground where people gathered to pass the time. The creators of many such carved game boards were probably the merchants who habitually set up their wares nearby and who played games with each other to pass the idle time between customers.

The Romans—young and old, rich and poor—were avid gamers and enjoyed a variety of board games, of which many examples survive. Most of these appear to be variations on backgammon, involving the movement of counters around a board. Two of the most popular of these board games were *Duodecim Scripta* (Twelve Lines) and *Latrunculi* (Robbers). *Duodecim Scripta* seems to have been a game involving 15 pieces per side, which were moved on the board according to the throw of three dice. *Latrunculi* was a simulated war game in which the players maneuvered different types of pieces around a board divided into squares, with the goal of attacking their opponent's pieces and breaking into his territory while defending his or her own. Another game featured six words with six letters each arranged in a pattern, and the players presumably moved game pieces around the words. The exact rules of all of these games are a matter of contention, but in these and other board games, play was dictated by a variety of types of dice, of which the most common was the familiar six-sided die marked with one to six spots.

In fact, such dice are one of the most common archaeological finds at the sites of Roman legionary encampments, where soldiers then as now often gambled away their earnings to stave off the boredom of garrison life. Gambling at dice was a popular pastime at all levels of society, and although technically illegal, it seems that this injunction was seldom enforced. Many emperors are known to have been particularly avid gamblers. Augustus provided generous amounts of cash to his dinner guests so that they could gamble with abandon, while on the other hand, Caligula was notorious for cheating at dice (Suetonius, *Life of Augustus* 70.2; *Life of Caligula* 41.2). The emperor Claudius was so addicted to dicing that not only did he write a book on the subject but he even had a board specially built into his imperial chariot so that he could pursue his passion while traveling (Suetonius, *Life of Claudius* 33).

In general, the Romans loved games and contests of all kinds and this attitude is summed up well by a mosaic that bore the inscription, "Hunting, bathing, gaming, and laughing constitute living" (*C.I.L.* [Corpus Inscriptionum Latinarum] 8.17938).

~*Gregory S. Aldrete*

FOR MORE INFORMATION

Balsdon, J. P. V. D. *Life and Leisure in Ancient Rome*. New York: McGraw Hill, 1969.

Fagan, G. *Bathing in Public in the Roman World*. Reprint, Ann Arbor: University of Michigan Press, 2002.

Harris, H. A. *Sport in Greece and Rome*. London: Thames and Hudson, 1972.

NUBIA

The picture of Nubia during the prehistoric epochs is still far from clear. It is assumed that the earliest artifacts, in the form of hand axes, were created about 300,000 B.C.E. and that in the interval between 70,000–40,000 B.C.E., hunting and fishing were practiced by the Nubians. Stone implements of various types were manufactured, but implements from the later epochs of about 40,000–10,000 B.C.E. do not differ significantly in design and manufacture from contemporary tools created in the Maghreb of northwestern Africa, the Levant, and central Africa.

Climatic changes in the period between 10,000–5000 B.C.E. compelled the Nubians to become more dependent upon hunting and gathering, and these pursuits were practiced as animal husbandry and agriculture were being developed.

The Neolithic revolution of the sixth millennium B.C.E. transformed Nubian society as more and more of their attention was turned toward the exploitation of domesticated animals. Knowledge of this period is derived from continuing archaeological excavations of both town sites and cemeteries.

These excavations have unearthed spear tips and harpoon points crafted of either bone or ivory, as well as fish hooks, suggesting a continuing interest in fishing. Such implements would continue to be employed by the Nubians for fishing, and in time they may even had recourse to nets.

The presence of hippopotamus tusks and elephant ivory among their cultural remains indicates that the Nubians hunted these beasts, but the archaeological record is silent about the specific methods by which the Nubians felled their prey. It might be possible that the hippopotamus was hunted with harpoons in boats on analogy with depictions of the hippopotamus hunt in later two-dimensional representations in Egyptian tombs.

The Nubians were famed as archers for most of their history. The painted wooden model of a troop of 40 archers from an Egyptian tomb of about 2000 B.C.E. and the ubiquitous presence of thumb guards in graves of the Meroitic period attest to their skills as archers over a long period of time. It is possible that the bow and arrow were the primary weapons of the hunt and may have been employed against the big cats of Africa, the hides of which formed a staple of Nubian-bartered luxury goods. The bow and arrow were doubtless the weapons of choice for the Pan Grave Nubians, who first appeared about 2200 B.C.E. and who were so named because of the resemblance to a cooking pan of the shallow, circular graves in which they were buried. Their material culture includes the horns and frontal bones of gazelles, which were painted and presumably employed as talismans over the entrances to their huts or tents to protect them from harm.

It is not known how the Nubians hunted elephants, although in the pharaonic periods, elephant tusks were habitually designated an African product in the Egyptian record. During the early Meroitic period, which was contemporary in part with the Ptolemaic Dynasty of Egypt, (305–30 B.C.E.), there is evidence that the Nubians were engaged in capturing African elephants for use by the Ptolemaic armies in war. The attempt was, however, short-lived, and the assertion by certain Classical authors, chief among them Arrian, that the Kushites employed elephants in war is clearly in error. The suggestion that the great enclosure within the site of Musawwarat es-Sufra was a staging area for rituals involving elephants has been dismissed in favor of regarding it within the pilgrimage program of the site's seven temples.

The capture of live elephants by the Meroitic Nubians contemporary with the Egyptian Ptolemaic Dynasty must be correlated with the New Kingdom evidence, particularly from the tombs of the elite Egyptians of Dynasty 18 (about

Nubian pot with giraffes. This example of Meroitic pottery illustrates the kind of large animals available to the Nubians to hunt. University of Pennsylvania Museum (neg. #E8183).

1550–1300 B.C.E.), in which Nubians are habitually depicted bearing live African animals as tribute. These beasts included simians of all types, giraffes, and big cats as depicted in the tombs of both Rekhmire and Huy. These examples adequately reveal the ability of the Nubians not only to capture beasts alive but also to care for and transport them over long distances.

The importance of the hunt in Nubian civilization has been asserted by at least one scholar, who interprets the tasseled cord—an article of royal and divine regalia—as emblematic of some primeval hunter-warrior god, later identified with Onnuris, whose attributes might also include a lasso. In later periods, Onnuris is closely identified with the god Arensnuphis, and both shared the characteristics of this putative hunter-warrior deity of old. Nubian kings and queens are often depicted in art wearing this accessory, by means of which they are symbolically linked with this fundamental Nubian deity.

~*Robert S. Bianchi*

FOR MORE INFORMATION

Adams, W. *Nubia: Corridor to Africa.* Princeton, N.J.: Princeton University Press, 1977.

O'Connor, D. *Ancient Nubia: Egypt's Rival in Africa.* Philadelphia: University of Pennsylvania, 1993.

Trigger, B. *Nubia under the Pharaohs.* Boulder, Colo.: Westview Press, 1976.

Welsby, D. A. *The Kingdom of Kush: The Napatan and Meroitic Empires.* London: British Museum Press, 1996.

RECREATIONAL
LIFE
|
HUNTING, SPORTS,
& GAMES
|
Mesopotamia

Egypt

Greece

Rome

Nubia

Australian Aboriginals

AUSTRALIAN ABORIGINALS

Australia was the only continent on which all protein was obtained by hunting and fishing and none from farming. It was also the only continent with no herd animals, although kangaroos can occur in big groups. It possessed a relatively small area of dense forest, so that most hunting had to be done in circumstances in which the hunter could be seen a long way off. No Aboriginal groups had boats capable of venturing far out to sea, so deep-sea fishing played no role in the diet. It is also the only continent that lacked very large land mammals, the biggest kangaroos weighing no more than 100 kilograms (220 pounds). In addition, it is the only continent on which there were neither wheeled vehicles nor domesticated animals that could carry packs. These facts affected hunting styles and the way meat could be used. In many parts of Australia, there is a wide continental shelf, thousands of offshore islands, and coral reefs of enormous extent. All these factors encourage the use of marine resources (including shellfish, seabirds, and mammals, as well as fish). Conversely, Australia has few large rivers and lakes, and much of it is very dry, greatly reducing the access to freshwater resources in most areas.

Australia was the only continent where bows and arrows were not used (except in the far northern Torres Strait, where they were derived from New Guinea); instead, a combination spear and spear-thrower (woomera) was employed. In most, but not all, parts of Australia, boomerangs were used either as a missile to kill or wound prey or to frighten them into nets or traps.

Because of the difficulties of hunting and fishing, Aborigines used a wide range of trapping devices. These varied from rock walls many hectares in extent covering reef areas and trapping fish at low tide to small basket traps shaped like horizontal lobster pots deployed in small streams. Birds and mammals were caught in nets suspended over water or in rocky valleys. Sharpened stakes were a simple means of catching wallabies in Tasmania, and fire was also used to drive kangaroos and wallabies into traps or toward ambushing men with spears. In Victoria, swamps in which eels bred were joined to other swamps by ditches in which traps were placed to catch the migrating eels.

Sea mammals and turtles were hunted with harpoons from canoes in northern Australia and by women with clubs in breeding colonies in Tasmania. Fish were caught in traps, and various nets, hooks and lines, and spears were used. Because of the relatively small size of even the largest prey, men usually carried the carcasses from successful hunts back to camp, sometimes after preliminary butchery to divide up the load. Although whales were not hunted, a beached whale could feed people for many days, and groups would camp on the beach while the meat was consumed, until it became too rotten.

Generally, women collected plants and small animals (for example, insects, lizards, and bird eggs) and men hunted larger prey, but there was some overlap, with men collecting food opportunistically while hunting and women sometimes helping pursue larger prey (for example, seals in Tasmania). There were prohibitions on certain people collecting or hunting particular species, and some areas were set aside as what amounted to nature preserves to protect notable species. Conservation over long periods of time resulted from hunter-gatherers moving on to a new area when a resource became scarce, unlike the commercial overexploitation of animal species by Western societies. Some have suggested that over-hunting in the late Pleistocene period caused the extinction of giant marsupials in Australia, but there is no direct evidence for this, and the theory is hotly disputed by scientists.

~David Horton

FOR MORE INFORMATION

Berndt, R., and C. Berndt. *The World of the First Australians*. Canberra: Aboriginal Studies Press, 1988.

Godwin, L. "Around the Traps: A Reappraisal of Stone Fishing Weirs in Northern NSW." *Archaeology in Oceania* 23 (1988): 49–59.

Gould, R. *Yiwara: Foragers of the Australian Desert*. New York: Scribner's, 1969.

Horton, D., ed. *The Encyclopedia of Aboriginal Australia*. Canberra: Aboriginal Studies Press, 2001.

Dance, Music, and Theater

The performing arts have their origins in the ancient world. Not only were music, dance, and theater all invented during this time, but they frequently developed to a high degree of sophistication. The tragedic plays written and performed by the

RECREATIONAL
LIFE

DANCE, MUSIC,
& THEATER

Mesopotamia

Egypt

Greece

Rome

India

Australian Aboriginals

Greeks, for example, are still being performed today and can speak as vividly and with as much relevance to modern audiences as they did to their original spectators.

Human beings are drawn to rhythm and even as babies seem to have an innate ability and desire to create repeated rhythmic noises and sounds. The origins of music can be found in this deeply rooted human characteristic. Ancient Mesopotamians developed not merely a wide variety of devices for producing music, including wind, percussion, and string instruments, but even the beginnings of music theory and scales. The Egyptians, Indians, Greeks, and Romans followed in their footsteps and likewise enjoyed producing music and creating new instruments. Some of the most commonly encountered instruments of the ancient world were flutes, drums, trumpets, and the lyre, a stringed instrument. There were even instruments that were particularly associated with certain religious cults and rituals, such as the sistrum, which was employed by worshipers of the goddess Isis and in fact was so strongly associated with her that statues of Isis often depict her holding a sistrum. Some of the lyrics written by ancient musicians have survived and run the expected range from love songs to drinking songs to hymns of worship.

Just as people enjoy rhythmic sounds, they also take pleasure from rhythmic movements, and dance was a significant part of ancient people's lives. Dances were performed for pleasure but also constituted a central part of many religious rituals. Mesopotamian devotees of Ishtar danced in her honor, while Roman worshipers of Mars performed a special dance as part of their rituals. Indian dancers conveyed meaning through elaborate stylized body movements and gestures. Bodily movements were appreciated in secular contexts as well. Dancers were a typical entertainment at Greek banquets, and mimes and pantomimes that acted out comedic sketches were wildly popular forms of entertainment in Rome, especially among the common people.

One of the most highly developed of the performing arts in the ancient world was theater. The Greeks created the most notable form of theater. The earliest Greek plays only had a single actor delivering monologues, which a chorus would comment upon. Eventually, they added up to two additional actors, making possible dialogue and more complexity. The fifth century B.C.E. witnessed the golden age of Greek theater, when the tragic playwrights Sophocles, Aeschylus, and Euripides and the comic playwright Aristophanes produced their great works. Greek plays were much more than simple entertainments, however. These authors used mythological subjects to explore contemporary (and timeless) concerns, such as the relationship of the individual to the state, the allure and price of vengeance, and the interactions of men and women and of citizens and foreigners. As with music and dance, plays were linked to religion, and the famous plays by Athenian authors were staged as part of an annual religious festival, the Dionysia.

~*Gregory S. Aldrete*

RECREATIONAL
LIFE
|
DANCE, MUSIC,
& THEATER
|
Mesopotamia

Egypt

Greece

Rome

India

Australian Aboriginals

MESOPOTAMIA

Modern music theory has roots in ancient Mesopotamia. Seven-tone and eight-tone musical scales, including our standard modern major scale, were used as early as the Old Babylonian period (ca. 1800 B.C.E.). Music theory and practice spread to the Levant and ancient Greece by the first millennium B.C.E. Pythagoras claimed that he learned his mathematics and music in the Near East, and he probably did. The style in which music was performed remains unknown. Wind, percussion, and stringed instruments were known.

The selling of songs (sacred and secular), a minor trade, was always popular but poorly paid. Among the catalogs of titles is a collection of song titles, such as "He appears, the god of fire, the Lord of battles," "Your love is like the scent of cedar wood, oh my Lord," "Come to the king's garden: it is full of cedar trees," "Oh, gardener of the garden of desires," and "In the streets, I saw two harlots" (Contenau, 100).

From the Early Dynastic period, if not before, music was a part of royal and religious festivals. Singers and musicians were featured at festivals, as were snake charmers, bear trainers, and jesters. Singers were both male and female; they sang in the royal courts and in the temple, where they sometimes functioned as priests. Their repertoire consisted of celebratory music, laments, and literary works. Singers were often accompanied by musical instruments.

Musical instruments belonged to the string, wind, and percussion families. Stringed instruments, pipes, and a clay whistle were even recovered from excavations. Eight lyres and two harps, including an elaborate example of a lyre inlaid with shell and trimmed in gold, were found at the Royal Cemetery of Ur. There are also many examples of both the harp and the lyre throughout the Near East, but there are fewer examples of the lute. The pipe, a wind instrument, existed as either a single or double pipe. Trumpets were used for communication (as in battle) rather than for music. Three kinds of drums are known: a hand drum or tambourine, a drum in the shape of a sandglass, which was used by the temple priest to appease the god, and a kettledrum, which was beaten in the temple courtyard during eclipses of the moon. Also, cymbals and bells were used. Second-millennium tablets from Babylonia, Assyria, and Ugarit in Syria describe music theory, naming nine strings of the harp and using a heptatonic scale. A whole psalm praising the moon goddess Nikkal was found complete with libretto and score at thirteenth-century B.C.E. Ugarit. Complete scores were also kept on file.

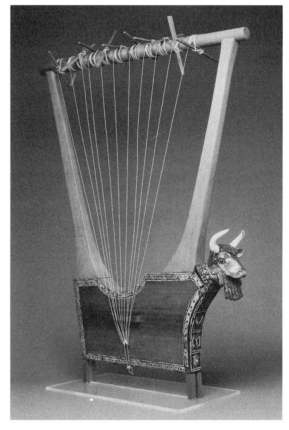

Restoration of a lyre with gold and lapis lazuli decoration from the Royal Cemetery of Ur. © Copyright The British Museum.

In art, musicians were sometimes shown playing solo, but often several musicians were pictured together, carrying harps, lyres, and various other instruments, suggesting an ensemble. The musicians might also accompany dancers or singers in royal and religious festivals. Sometimes musicians were even shown dancing. Musicians were also depicted in military scenes, accompanying the army as they marched.

Reliefs show dancing done in time to music, singing, and clapping. Dancing was mentioned in the tablets but usually in reference to the cult and not as an independent activity. At the annual feast for the goddess Ishtar and other goddesses, whirling dances were done in her honor by both men and women. Circle dances were usually performed by women. Acrobatic dancers took part in cultic activities (Nemet-Nejat, 167–70, 299–300).

FOR MORE INFORMATION

Contenau, G. *Everyday Life in Babylon and Assyria.* Translated by K. R. Maxwell-Hyslop and A. R. Maxwell-Hyslop. New York: St. Martin's Press, 1954.

Nemet-Nejat, K. R. *Daily Life in Ancient Mesopotamia.* Westport, Conn.: Greenwood Press, 1998.

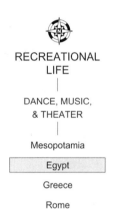

RECREATIONAL
LIFE
|
DANCE, MUSIC,
& THEATER
|
Mesopotamia

Egypt

Greece

Rome

India

Australian Aboriginals

EGYPT

Music provided a favored entertainment in ancient Egypt. Festive scenes almost always depict an orchestra, generally with dancers swaying to its rhythms. Old Kingdom bands consisted of harp, drums, oboe, and flute, with a variety of mandolins and lyres; a double flute was added by the New Kingdom. While a type of straight bugle existed, its shrill tones only issued commands for troops and never figured in musical ensembles.

Harps, ranging from half the size of a man and played kneeling to taller than man-sized and played standing, had 4 to 7 cat-gut strings in the smaller versions and as many as 10 to 22 in the larger. All were tied to an oversize sounding board that used stretched leather to amplify the sound. Blind harpists, probably because their handicap gave them better memories for the lyrics they sang, are often depicted. Flutes, or more correctly, reed pipes, were blown from their ends rather than their sides as with the modern flute. Surviving examples include instruments with between 3 and 14 holes; another common type joined two pipes together, probably producing a semblance of harmony. Mandolins, thin oblong sounding boxes with from six to eight strings attached to a long arm, were held vertically like guitars; a pick was used to strum the instrument.

Percussion instruments were many and varied. Drums consisted of a sort of tom-tom several feet long, slung over the shoulder with a cord and played with drumsticks. Not only used to set a beat for a band, this style of drum was employed in the military to give Egyptian troops their marching cadences. Other drums were shallow in depth and struck with the hand. Both the tambourine and the forerunner of castanets, a pair of five-inch sticks clicked rhythmically in one hand, were also popular. A special percussion instrument called a sistrum was made of metal

Drawing of an all-female Egyptian band playing a variety of instruments. The woman on the far left is keeping time by clapping while the others play (from left to right) a small harp, double flute, lute, lyre, and standing harp.

in the shape of the head of the cow goddess Hathor, patron of music. Her horns were elongated so that several wires on which metal disks were loosely strung could be attached crosswise, producing a metallic rattle sound when shaken.

Dancers' rhythmic clapping added more percussive sounds to a performance. Only women, most often naked or with only a sash around their waist, danced at banquets. They are often portrayed bending backward in gymnastic-like contortions as their long hair, tied at the ends with weights that swayed to the music, touched the ground. One scene shows part of a troop of dancers, their hair pulled high to simulate the tall, white pharaonic crown, posing in the familiar attitude of a pharaoh smiting his enemies while others in the group acted the role of victims. In a solemn dance performed for funerary processions, dancers with caps hiding their hair slid their right feet forward, with arms, palms up, forming a circle over their heads, then slid their left feet ahead while their right arms moved to a 45 degree angle and the left descended behind the body. Step by slow step, the dancers made their way to the tomb, followed by singers, mourners, friends, relatives, and servants.

No notation to record Egyptian music existed, but lyrics were written out, and some have been found. Their bittersweet tales generally encourage enjoying the moment because of life's fleeting nature. One New Kingdom song advises:

Men's bodies have returned to the earth since the beginning of time
And their place is taken by fresh generations.
As long as Ra rises each morning
And Tum sinks to rest in Manou,
So long will men beget and women conceive
And through their nostrils they will breathe;
But one day each one that is born must go to his appointed place.
Make a happy day, Oh priest. . . .
Pass thy day in happiness. . . .
Think on the day when thou must fare to the land where all men are as one.
Never a man hath taken his possessions with him to that land,
And none can thence return. (modified from Montet, 96–97)

Another, of similar sentiment, counsels:

Follow thy heart and thy happiness as long as thou art on earth.
Consume not thy heart until there cometh for thee that day
When man begs for mercy,
Unless the god whose heart beats no longer hears them who call upon him. (as cited in
    Montet, 97–98)

Although both these songs were inscribed in tombs, their philosophy was also commonly embraced by the living. In the Late period, most festive banquets ended with a fake mummy in a small coffin being paraded around the diners and making, in a more graphic manner, a similar point about human mortality (Brier and Hobbs, 90–93).

FOR MORE INFORMATION

Brier, B., and H. Hobbs. *Daily Life of the Ancient Egyptians*. Westport, Conn.: Greenwood Press, 1999.

Montet, P. *Everyday Life in Egypt in the Days of Ramesses the Great*. Translated by A. R. Maxwell-Hyslop and M. Drower. Reprint, Philadelphia: University of Pennsylvania Press, 1981.

RECREATIONAL
LIFE
|
DANCE, MUSIC,
& THEATER
|
Mesopotamia

Egypt

Greece

Rome

India

Australian Aboriginals

GREECE

The Greek word *mousikê* identified a much broader range of cultural activity than does our word *music*. It included all of the arts that came under the patronage of Apollo and the nine Muses—that is, singing and dancing, as well as philosophical discourse. The epithet *mousikos*, which means "muse-ish," was synonymous with good taste. Conversely, *amousikos* described a person who lacked refinement or education. This section considers the word *music* in its limited, modern sense.

Music was a central part of Greek daily life. It was a feature of all social gatherings, including births, weddings, and funerals. Songs were sung by laborers to lighten the workload, especially at harvest and vintage, and by women in the home while they were grinding the grain or weaving. Soldiers and athletes trained to the sound of pipes. Every religious event was marked by the singing of hymns. Nearly every genre of poetry, including epic, lyric, and dramatic, was written to be sung. Music was also an essential accompaniment to the drinking party. The various modes of music were believed to exercise a profound impact upon the mind. The so-called Dorian mode, being solemn and martial, was thought to induce courage, whereas the Phrygian mode, which was wild and perhaps atonal, was thought to encourage impetuosity. In Classical Athens, musical proficiency was a basic part of every boy's education. Philosophers were of the opinion that it contributed to a well-balanced and disciplined personality. Plato, however, was extremely skeptical of its influence and banished it from his ideal state. Greek vases depicting scenes at the tomb suggest that delight in music was not interrupted by death.

Professional musicians were commonly employed in the Greek world. The earliest were the itinerant bards, who traveled from one aristocratic house to another, reciting tales about heroes and gods that they improvised, relying heavily on the formulaic structure of epic verse.

The most popular instrument was the lyre or kithara, which resembled a modern guitar. In its simplest version, the sound box was made out of a tortoise shell with a hide stretched over the hollow underside. The sound was produced by plucking the strings, usually seven in number, either with the fingers or with a plectrum. A variant on this instrument was the *barbiton*, which had longer strings. The *barbiton* was associated with scenes of revelry that were held in honor of Dionysos. Another stringed instrument was the harp, whose use seems to have been confined largely to professional musicians.

The most popular wind instrument was the *aulos*. This is often identified with the flute, although the sound it produced was actually closer to that of the oboe. The *aulos* consisted of a hollow pipe made out of wood, bronze, bone, or reed. It was pierced with holes for the fingers and fitted with a reed mouthpiece. *Auloi* were usually played in pairs. The chorus of Greek drama sang and danced to the accompaniment of an *aulos* player, who also piped soldiers into battle. Another wind instrument was the *syrinx*, which consisted of a number of pipes bound together. Variations in pitch were made by blocking the inside of the pipes with wax at different intervals. The *syrinx* was a somewhat crude instrument, whose invention was attributed to the goat god Pan. It was especially popular among shepherds.

The nearest approximation to a brass instrument was the *salpinx*, a long slender instrument terminating in a bell-shaped aperture. It was used primarily to herald the beginning and end of religious and other ceremonies. Several percussion instruments are known, including the *kymbala*, from which our word "cymbals" is derived, the *tympanon*, meaning a small drum, the *krotala* or castanets, and the *sistra* or rattles. These were used in ecstatic cults, notably those that were imported into Greece from the East.

Some 46 musical scores, mostly fragmentary, have survived. Despite all the work that has been done by scholars, however, it would be overbold to suggest that we actually know what Greek music sounded like.

When we talk about Greek drama, we usually mean Athenian drama, both tragedy and comedy. Only a few non-Athenian playwrights are known to us by name, and none of their plays has survived. Drama was both an invention and an integral aspect of Athenian democracy, so much so that it is quite impossible to talk about it other than as an expression of the distinctive political and civic realities of the Athenian state. The origins of Greek drama are

Drawing of Greek musicians copied from a vase painting. From left to right, they play the *aulos,* harp, and kithara. Originally in I. Jenkins and S. Bird, *Greek Music.* London: British Museum Education Service. Courtesy of British Museum.

imperfectly understood, but they probably derived from an opposition between the chorus and a single actor. From earliest times, the Greeks held choral performances in honor of the gods, in commemoration of military and athletic victories, and in mourning for the dead. *Tragoidia*, the Greek word for tragedy, which derives from *tragos*, "goat," and *oidê*, "song," probably owes its origins either to the fact that choruses were originally dressed in the loin skins of goats or to the fact that the prize for the song was a goat. The Athenians attributed the invention of tragedy to a shadowy figure called Thespis, who is credited with having won first prize in the first contest for tragedy held circa 534 B.C.E. *Kômoidia*, which gives us our word "comedy," means "*kômos* singing." A *kômos* was a band of tipsy revelers who wandered about the town, crashing drinking parties.

The promotion of drama to the level of Athenian national pastime par excellence owed much to the tyrant Pisistratus, who accorded it a central position in a new festival instituted in honor of Dionysos, the patron god of drama. It was at this festival, known as the Great or City Dionysia, that plays were staged that rank today among the foremost achievements of Athenian culture, namely, the tragedies of Aeschylus, Sophocles, and Euripides and the comedies of Aristophanes. The Dionysia was a four-day festival held in March.

Each tragedian had to submit three tragedies to a magistrate known as the archon eponymos (i.e., the Athenian magistrate who gave his name to the year). He also had to write a satyr play, so named because of its chorus of half-animal, half-human creatures, whose drunken and licentious antics provided an uproarious coda to the serious business of tragedy. Comic poets submitted only one drama. It was the archon's duty to choose which plays should be performed. Once he had made his choice of three tragic and three comic productions, he allocated to each a *chorêgos* or chorus master, who was a wealthy Athenian or metic. It was the responsibility of the *chorêgos* to pay all the expenses of the production, chief of which was the training and costuming of the chorus. It is estimated that the services of some 1,500 persons were needed to stage all the plays produced at the City Dionysia each year. Plutarch actually claimed that the Athenians spent more money on dramatic productions than they did on their defense budget (*Moral Precepts* line 349a).

If a play failed to attract state sponsorship, its chances of being performed in Athens or elsewhere were virtually nil. In the first half of the fifth century B.C.E., playwrights were required to be composers, choreographers, designers, directors, and actors as well. Increasingly, however, these roles were taken over by specialists, although the playwrights still had to write the music for the chorus. Being a playwright hardly amounted to having a profession in the modern sense of the word because they received payment only if they won first prize.

A Greek theater consisted of a *theatron* or "seeing space," which was frequently cut into a hillside in the form of steeply raked tiers of seats, and a circular *orchêstra* or "dancing space" about 20 meters in diameter, almost entirely surrounded by the *theatron*. Seats were arranged in the form of wedges and divided from one another by vertical gangways. In the fifth century B.C.E., the seats were wooden, but in the next century stone became commonplace. The raised stage was an invention of the fifth century B.C.E., as, too, was scenery. The Greek *skênê*, meaning "hut" or "tent," from which our word *scenery* derives, describes the actors' changing room, the outside of which could be painted to resemble the facade of a palace or temple and thus provide a sense of place. There was no other form of stage setting.

The Theater of Dionysos in Athens could probably accommodate about 20,000 spectators. Even if only 10,000 attended, this probably amounted to a quarter of the citizen body. The front rows were reserved for priests, magistrates, and distinguished visitors. In the center of the front row was the throne of the priest of Dionysos Eleuthereus (liberator). Special areas were reserved for ephebes, members of the council, and metics. Probably the rest of the audience sat in blocks allocated to each of the 10 tribes. The price of admission was two obols, although from the fourth century B.C.E. onward and possibly earlier, citizens were admitted free. We do not know for certain whether women or slaves were permitted to attend.

Going to the theater was hardly a relaxing experience in the modern sense of the word, since the audience was expected to sit through four plays a day at least, or five if the tragic plays performed in the morning were followed by a comedy in the afternoon. That amounts to about 10 hours of uninterrupted performance per day. There were no intervals, except between plays. Not surprisingly, audiences became extremely restless if they were bored or displeased. We hear of several instances when a hostile crowd pelted the performers with stones and fruit. In the fifth century B.C.E., plays received only a single performance. The only exception was Aristophanes' *Frogs*, whose political message was judged to be so relevant that the play was put on a second time. In the fourth century B.C.E., revivals became commonplace.

Because theatrical performances took place in broad daylight, there was no opportunity to focus on a particular spot through lighting effects. Only two items of stage equipment were in regular use. One was known as the *ekkyklêma*, or "object that is rolled out." This low platform on wheels was projected into the *orchêstra* from the central doors of the scene building to reveal the interior of a place or temple. The

> *Going to the theater was hardly a relaxing experience.*

ekkyklêma was undoubtedly used by Aeschylus in *Agamemnon* to display the bodies of Clytemnestra and her lover Aegisthus after they had been murdered by Orestes. The other device was the *mêchanê*, a word that simply means "machine." The *mêchanê* was a kind of crane that enabled a character to be transported on- or offstage by being swung through the air. The Latin phrase *deus ex machina*, literally, "a god from a machine," which has entered into our language, is a reference to the overworking of this device by dramatists who used it to extricate their characters from an otherwise-insoluble plot.

The Greek word *chorus*, which to us suggests collective singing, literally means "dance" (as in our word *choreography*). Most Greek choruses were a combination of music, dance, and song. Choral performances generally took place at religious festivals in honor of the gods, although some were secular. These include the encomium (*enkômion*), whose name derives from the fact that it was originally a song sung at a revel or *kômos*; the victory ode; and the dirge. The earliest surviving choral poetry was written by Alcman, who composed songs for choruses of Spartan girls in the seventh century B.C.E. The central importance of the chorus in Greek drama is indicated by the fact that it was the *orchêstra* that formed the focus for a theatrical production. In earlier times, choruses numbered about 50, but about the middle of the fifth century B.C.E., they were reduced in size to 12 or 15. The training of a chorus was a lengthy and expensive undertaking. Costumes were often costly and elaborate. In comedy, the costumes worn by the chorus were often extremely exotic, as suggested by the names of some of Aristophanes' comedies, such as *Birds*, *Wasps*, *Clouds*, and *Frogs*.

The chorus entered the *orchêstra* at the end of the first scene and remained there throughout the whole performance. During the choral passages, its members would sing and dance to the accompaniment of the *aulos*, a double-pipe with reeds. The chorus leader might converse with the actors from time to time. One of the primary functions of the chorus was to comment on the action and urge caution. Its reactions also helped the audience to reach its own verdict about events, though the chorus was not the mouthpiece of the poet. At a more mundane level, it enabled the actors to change costumes between scenes. Its significance declined over time, and in many of Euripides' late plays it is little more than an adjunct. The exception to this rule is *Bacchai*, where its role is central to the drama. Even Menander, however, writing in the late fourth century B.C.E., did not abolish the chorus altogether.

Greek theater at Epidaurus. Despite seating at least 12,000 spectators, the acoustics of the Greek theater design enabled all of the audience members to hear the performers clearly. © The Art Archive/Dagli Orti.

All the speaking parts in both comedy and tragedy were performed by a maximum of three male actors. Because there could be as many as eight different dramatis personae in a play, however, actors frequently had to change parts. They did this both by switching masks and costumes and by altering the pitch of their voices. Masks, which were probably made out of stiffened linen, were fairly naturalistic in the case of tragedy but grotesque caricatures in the case of comedy. Because actors could not rely on facial expressions to convey their emotions, they had to be far more expressive in both voice and gesture than their modern counterparts.

Tragic actors wore brightly colored robes decorated with elaborate patterns. They also wore a calf-length boot known as the *kothornos*, which was loose enough to fit on either foot. In later times, the *kothornos* was fitted with a high heel to make actors look more impressive. Comic actors were heavily padded so as to make them look completely ridiculous. Beneath their short tunics, they sported huge phalluses to depict the erect male organ, strapped around the waist by means of a belt. Actors were also provided with role markers, such as a scepter in the case of a king or a club in the case of Hercules.

Drama was a highly competitive activity. The prizes for first, second, and third place were decided by panels of 10 *kritai* or "judges." It is from *kritês* that our word *critic* is derived, although the English word is something of a misnomer since Athenian critics were elected by lot from the citizenry as a whole and in no sense constituted a panel of experts. Each of the judges wrote his decision on a tablet. The 10 choices were then placed in an urn, from which the archon eponymos drew out only 5. This system was intended to leave some part of the decision making to the gods. Regrettably, there is no way of telling to what extent the judges' verdict was based on dramatic content and structure and to what extent it was influenced by the quality of the production. Several of what today are regarded as the finest examples of Attic tragedy were not awarded first prize.

The victorious dramatist received a wreath and a small cash prize, and the winning *chorêgos* was permitted to erect a column in his own honor. Of the three tragedians whose works survive, the most successful was Sophocles, who wrote 123 plays, won first prize 18 times, and never dropped lower than second place. From 449 B.C.E., the judges also awarded a prize to the best protagonist.

Publicly funded, profoundly civic in orientation, and fundamentally sacred in character, Attic drama might at first sight strike us as a covert means of reinforcing social conformity. The truth was far different. Although drama took place in a religious context, the playwrights did not see it as their objective to offer pious platitudes or promote supine obedience to the will of the gods. On the contrary, they were anything but shy of depicting the Olympians as degenerate and even morally repellent, whenever it suited their purposes. What drama chiefly did was to provide a context in which issues of public and private concern could be literally aired in the open. Its purpose, in other words, was not to promote some kind of party line or function as a moral arbiter but rather to give expression to the hard moral choices that define human existence, to explore the problematic nature of humankind's relationship with the gods, and to demonstrate the human (and divine) capacity for evil. As such, it frequently served subversive rather than conformist ends (Garland, 180–92).

FOR MORE INFORMATION

Garland, R. *Daily Life of the Ancient Greeks*. Westport, CT: Greenwood Press, 1998.

Green, J. R. *Theatre in Ancient Greek Society*. New York: Routledge, 1996.

Kitto, H. D. *Greek Tragedy*. New York: Routledge, 1939.

West, M. L. *Ancient Greek Music*. Oxford: Clarendon Press, 1993.

ROME

RECREATIONAL
LIFE
|
DANCE, MUSIC,
& THEATER
|
Mesopotamia

Egypt

Greece

Rome

India

Australian Aboriginals

In ancient Rome, theater, music, and dance were often combined as one synthetic experience rather than being presented as independent art forms. From the third century B.C.E. onward, plays were performed on the model of Greek theater, with masks and without women actors. The male actors, who were usually slaves or freedmen who had been specially trained for the stage, played the female parts as well. Roman playwrights are today best known for their comedies, which relied on stock characters, coincidences, and mistaken or hidden identities.

However, from the first century B.C.E. on, mimes and pantomimes outstripped plays to become the most popular forms of theatrical entertainment. Ancient mime is different in style from what is currently practiced, since the performers had speaking roles. Mimes sang, danced, and acted without masks, whereas pantomimes wore masks, acted, and danced but didn't sing; instead, musicians or a chorus offered musical accompaniment. Also, women were permitted to act in mimes and pantomimes. In a general sense, the two forms can be distinguished by subject matter; mimes tended to be realistic, comic, and even vulgar and could deal with any topic, whereas pantomimes resembled ballet productions on themes and stories from myth and evolved into impressive spectacles full of elaborate staging, costumes, and special effects. Under the empire, pantomimes were at times literally enacted, so that a pantomime performed at the opening of the Colosseum featured a lyre-playing Orpheus being followed by trees and trained animals charmed by his music—until they ate him at the end.

Mime did not require a special setting. It was often used as entertainment between acts at the theater, where mimes would perform in front of a linen screen pulled out to hide the stage scenery. Mimes were considered more low-brow than pantomimes, as they were meant to produce laughter by any means, including physical comedy and beatings, while pantomimes were often tragic in character. Songs heard at mimes sometimes became popular among the public at large. The popularity of these forms of entertainment was probably at least partly due to the relative unimportance of language; Rome's diverse populace and its many foreigners could appreciate the stories being told through the actors' use of gestures and sign language, which were crucial to conveying the action.

Dance was not completely like dance in the modern sense, in that it often focused on stylized rhythmic and expressive movements of the head and hands. There are also mentions of athletically strenuous motions such as leaps, twists, quick turns, jerks, and suddenly freezing in place—all of which were intended to help illustrate the story being told.

Dance and dramatic performances were accompanied by music, and choral singing and solos existed in ancient times (part singing was not invented until the Middle Ages). Poetry was usually set to music (played on stringed instruments), and musicians were often also poets who did the musical arrangements for their own poems.

The most popular instruments for "artistic" musical performances were the flute and the kithara (resembling a harp without a fret board), which could be played either with the hands or a plectrum, a tool like a small wand (similar in function to a guitar pick). Other instruments were reserved for more specialized uses. Horns and trumpets, such as the cornu (similar to a large French horn) and the tuba (a trumpet more than three feet long), were employed by the army for martial music and giving commands, and noisy instruments, such as cymbals and drums, were used in cult festivals. The hydraulic or water organ, invented in Hellenistic times, was played as popular entertainment and was said to induce strong emotional reactions in audience members.

However, music, dance, and drama were not limited to theaters and odea specially built for such events. Occasions featuring professional entertainers were entwined throughout many aspects of Roman life. After-dinner entertainment at banquets usually included professional singers, dancers, or musicians or recitations of dramatic scenes or poetry. A band played at gladiator games, where satirical songs were sung along to music and the rhythmical movements of the audience. But music was also a part of most religious ceremonies as well, and there was not a sense of division between sacred and profane music. Flute and lyre players accompanied animal sacrifices to drown out any sounds of ill omen; cymbals and tambourines were used by eastern orgiastic cults such as those of Cybele and Bacchus; and a special rattle, the sistrum, was important in the cult of Isis. The leaping, or dancing, priests of Mars were well known, and dancing and music were used in the worship of Cybele. Funeral poems or songs were sung by either hired singers or the female relatives of the deceased.

Despite the ubiquitousness of music in everyday life and the admiration afforded to those musically skilled, the Romans had a mixed reaction and contradictory attitude to music and dance. Stern Roman tradition dictated that music, singing, and dancing were morally suspect, improper pursuits for freeborn Roman citizens and should be relegated to slaves and freedmen, who already suffered from lowered status. Over time, attitudes relaxed so that an amateur interest in music was acceptable; even the emperor could indulge in music. What was scandalous was to pursue music as a professional, which Nero did, to the shock of his subjects.

~*Gregory S. Aldrete*

FOR MORE INFORMATION

Beacham, R. *The Roman Theatre and Its Audience*. Cambridge, Mass.: Harvard University Press, 1992.

Csapo, E., and W. J. Slater. *The Context of Ancient Drama*. Ann Arbor: University of Michigan Press, 1995.

Slater, W. J., ed. *Roman Theater and Society*. Ann Arbor: University of Michigan Press, 1996.

INDIA

The *Natya Sastra* by Bharata is an ancient text codifying the theory of the performing arts in India. Bharata records that drama, dance, and music were gifts handed down from the gods. Performance was understood as an ordered set of structures—plots, themes, and stimuli such as speech, gestures, and costuming—intended to convey to the audience certain feelings.

The basic term necessary to understanding performance art in India is *rasa*, which means "feeling." Bharata enumerates eight basic types of *rasa*: love or passion, humor, grief, anger, heroism, fear, disgust, and surprise or delight. Another term, *bhava*, indicates the means used to evoke the various *rasas*. Acting, then, is the expression of physical gestures, words, costuming, and emotional displays to evoke in the audience particular *rasas*. For example, seeing an actor wearing armor and weapons and speaking boldly might evoke a feeling of heroic courage in the audience, and a clown telling jokes produces humor. Costuming was standardized, so that the audience could immediately identify stock characters, such as kings, clowns, courtesans, gods, and so on. The standard format for plays began with an invocation to the gods for a blessing, and the play itself frequently displayed injustices and tragedy for the heroes but almost always ended happily.

Bharata also specifies the language to be used in plays: Sanskrit for gods and kings, and Prakrit languages, or common dialects, for all other characters. The major playwrights of ancient India followed this pattern. Themes for plays and folk performances were often drawn from *puranas* (traditional stories), historical events, and epic and hagiological literature.

Kalidasa (ca. fourth century B.C.E.), who is often considered India's greatest playwright, drew on such themes in his works. His most famous drama, the *Abhijnanasakuntalam* (Recognition of Sakuntala), is considered by many as one of the hundred best literary works in the world and is drawn from a well-known *Mahabharata* story.

The basic plot involves King Dusyanta, who meets and secretly marries Sakuntala, daughter of a forest sage. The king leaves his ring with her, as proof of their union. But as a result of a curse, she loses the ring, and when she is pregnant and seeks out the king, he denies knowing her. The tension is heightened, and it is years later before the gods themselves intervene to bear witness that her son is Dusyanta's heir.

The *Natya Sastra* also treats the subject of dance (*tandava*), as a gift from the god Shiva. There are 108 basic *karanas*, or positions, that determine the movement of hands, feet, and so on. Each of these is also expressive, intended to resonate with the audience. The dancer controlled every gesture, every movement of every part of the body, to convey meaning.

Indian music is another subject treated in the *Natya Sastra*. It could be an integral part of a play or be performed on its own. Ancient Indian sources classify four types of instruments: covered, such as drums; solid, such as cymbals; hollow, such as flutes or reeds; and stringed, of which the chief example is the *vina*, the lute. Music consisted of a seven-note scale, and the notes were called *sa, ri, ga, ma, pa, dha,* and *ni,* in much the same way that Western music calls the notes of the scale *do re mi fa so la ti do*. A sequence of five or more notes in a melody was called a *raga*. Different types of ragas were specified as appropriate for different times of day and night. Ancient Indian musical theory also had rules for keeping time (*tala*). Music lacked harmony, but drumming and a basic droned note kept the tune.

To read about music in nineteenth-century India, see the India entry in the section "Music" in chapter 7 ("Recreational Life") of volume 5 (*Nineteenth Century*) of this series.

~*Matthew Bingley*

FOR MORE INFORMATION

Auboyer, J. *Daily Life in Ancient India*. London: Phoenix Press, 1965.

Basham, A. L. *The Wonder That Was India*. London: Sidgwick and Jackson, 1967.

Bharata Muni. *Natyasastra*. Edited and translated by Adya Rangacharya. New Delhi: Munshiram Manoharlal, 1996.

Coulson, M., trans. *Three Sanskrit Plays*. New York: Penguin, 1981.

RECREATIONAL
LIFE
|
DANCE, MUSIC,
& THEATER
|
Mesopotamia

Egypt

Greece

Rome

India

Australian Aboriginals

AUSTRALIAN ABORIGINALS

Aboriginal music and dance serve very different roles within Aboriginal culture than they do in modern Western society. Aboriginal music is inextricably linked to all aspects of Aboriginal society. The words in Aboriginal music are critically important, and there is no purely instrumental music; the instruments are there only to accompany the song. The words and tunes are believed to exist independently of humans, waiting to be discovered, usually in a dream. Singing the songs puts the singer and the group in touch with the power of the supernatural world to promote the health and fertility of the community.

There are particular songs and ceremonies for events such as birth and death. Some songs relate to events in the Dreamtime, recounting the travels of ancestral beings. Paintings depict similar themes visually, and painters often sing while painting. Dances accompanied by music during ceremonies also served to represent the beings and the events of the Dreaming. Other types of songs include love songs and songs used for teaching children.

Although all Aboriginal music is instantly recognizable because of its style and structure, there were nevertheless variations in style and sound across the continent. Some of this variation was probably attributable to the age of the music concerned and to ancient influences from areas such as Indonesia and the Torres Strait. In recent times, some songs and dances were copied and rapidly adopted across large parts of the country. Newer songs have also appeared that describe interactions with Europeans, suggesting that songs in the past were used to record events as they happened.

In Aboriginal groups, no one specialized in music exclusively, but some singers and musicians were recognized as being particularly talented. Men and women had different songs and ceremonies, although public ceremonies were attended by both sexes. Performances were also intimately linked with the land and ownership. Just as with paintings, certain people would own a ceremony while others would manage the performance. This pattern of owners and managers, based on ancestry, kinship, and birth, is a common feature of Aboriginal society. Managers of one ceremony might be owners of another, and vice versa.

Instruments varied across Australia, with the didgeridoo only being found in the north. Constructed from a hollowed-out branch, the didgeridoo was played in a seated posture by blowing across the mouth end. A continuous sound could be produced by breathing in through the nose and out through the mouth. Rhythm was kept by clapping, slapping hands against legs, tapping together sticks or boomerangs, or with drums fashioned from rolled skins. In Cape York, some additional instruments were found, most notably drums with stretched skin, probably derived relatively recently from Torres Strait cultures. Apart from the didgeridoo, melody was mainly provided by voices singing in a chorus and employing sounds in addition to words.

A description of Aboriginal dancing that could be applied to all of Australia was written about the Tasmanian Aborigines by George August Robinson in 1830: "Their dances are quite different, and require great exertion and agility, . . . they bound from one position to another. Legs, arms, head, and every part of the body is in motion. Their eyes are also made to act their part and at the same time they keep up a song which regulates their motions. They are certainly the best dancers of any aborigines I have yet seen." Whether it was an old man singing to himself as he painted, children singing as they learned, or hundreds of men chanting and dancing in the flickering firelight, music was an integral part of Aboriginal life.

~David Horton

FOR MORE INFORMATION

Berndt, R., and C. Berndt. *The World of the First Australians*. Canberra: Aboriginal Studies Press, 1988.

Clunies, R., M. T. Donaldson, and S. Wild. *Songs of Aboriginal Australia*. Oceania Monograph 32. Sydney: University of Sydney, 1987.

Horton, D., ed. *The Encyclopedia of Aboriginal Australia*. Canberra: Aboriginal Studies Press, 2001.

Mulvaney, J., and J. Kamminga. *Prehistory of Australia*. Sydney: Allen and Unwin, 1999.

RECREATIONAL
LIFE

HOLIDAYS, FESTIVALS,
& SPECTACLES

Mesopotamia

Egypt

Greece

Rome

India

Holidays, Festivals, and Spectacles

While work forms a central part of most people's lives, designated days when one does not have to labor usually constitute some of the most anticipated and enjoyable events. Ancient civilizations did not have the modern workweek of five days followed by a two-day weekend, but most cultures peppered their calendars with a substantial number of holidays. These days were not just meant as times of rest, however, but were almost always observed to celebrate a religious festival. Even the English word *holidays* itself preserves this intent, being a contraction of the term "holy days."

A common focal point of these religious holidays was a sumptuous procession in which the cult statues of gods were transported from one site or temple to another, often accompanied by lavish displays of wealth, sacrifices, and feasting. In Mesopotamia, such processions were thought to be enjoyed by the gods, who were able to get out from their temples, visit with fellow gods, and look around the city. The Greeks, too, featured processions as part of many of their holidays, the most important of which was the Athenian Panathenaic procession, a huge parade involving the participation of many of the inhabitants of Athens and culminating in the presentation of a new shirt to the goddess Athena to be worn by her cult statue until she got a new one at the next year's Panathenaia. In Rome, victorious generals returning to the city were sometimes granted the right to hold a triumph, a type of parade in which the general, his soldiers, and the wealth and prisoners of war that they had seized paraded through the streets of the city. To free the populace to attend the parade, the day the triumph took place was declared a public holiday. Everybody really does seem to love a parade, and the inhabitants of the ancient world found many occasions to stage them.

Another type of holiday celebrated the end of one year and the beginning of a new one. The Mesopotamians had a prominent New Year's celebration, and the five-day New Year's festival held in Egypt constituted the longest regular holiday enjoyed by the ancient Egyptians. Festivals in India were often held on the day of a new full moon and could include feasts, fasts, gift giving, and even temporary suspension of the caste system.

Food always seems to play a central part in holidays, and most religious festivals in the ancient world included an element of feasting, often at state expense. At religious festivals involving animal sacrifice, most of the meat was then roasted and eaten on the spot by the participants and observers. This tradition enhanced the popularity of these events because it was probably only on such occasions that the average person was able to eat and enjoy red meat. The feasting, drinking, singing, and general merrymaking that formed an integral part of religious sacrifices make these events seem much like a modern outdoor barbecue, an analogy that is not that far-fetched. Given the perennial popularity of food, sometimes rulers would treat their subjects to public feasts to celebrate various events. The incredible feast given by the Assyrian king Assurnasirpal II to celebrate his accession to the throne, at which thousands of cows and sheep were served up to the populace, is one example.

All these celebrations have a spectacular element to them, and some rulers also deliberately put on impressive public spectacles for the entertainment of their subjects. The most infamous of such events were the Roman public entertainments that often featured acts of extreme violence. Gladiator combats in which men fought against each other, sometimes to the death, had a long history in Roman society but really only became large-scale public spectacles in the early empire. Other forms of entertainment staged at Rome that featured bloodshed included beast hunts, public executions of criminals, theatrical performances with real violence, and chariot racing with frequently fatal crashes. Most of these violent performances were still linked with religion, however, by being held on religious holidays. These events not only were a way for rulers to please and entertain their subjects but also constituted a highly visible and impressive expression of their own wealth and power.

~*Gregory S. Aldrete*

MESOPOTAMIA

Everybody loves a good time, and the Mesopotamians were no exception. The lunar month of the Mesopotamian calendar had 29 or 30 days. Six days were designated holidays, three days lunar festivals, and three more for relaxation. Both the monthly and annual holidays were times for games and entertainment.

The cultic relationship between the city and its god was formalized at cyclical festivals, such as the New Year's festival and the festival of each temple and its god. The festivals were usually centered around a cult drama that was reenacted to institute the necessary function. The common person was only able to communicate with the deity through communal religious events such as cyclical festivals and mourning ceremonies. The role the general public played in these elaborate ceremonies remains uncertain. But at the very least, the public could observe the great processions as the divine image was carried through the spacious yards of the temple compound or through certain streets of the city.

When deities left the temple, they showed themselves to the public, took stock of their city, visited their country home, and met with the gods of other cities to determine the fate of the nation or to receive the blessings of major gods. Outdoor rituals involving the god statues of more than one city helped to maintain theological unity on a national level. With the collapse of the Ur III Dynasty, these visits

RECREATIONAL
LIFE

HOLIDAYS, FESTIVALS,
& SPECTACLES

Mesopotamia

Egypt

Greece

Rome

India

were seldom mentioned, although the gods continued to leave their temples to go on local journeys to settle legal disputes.

Myths spoke of gods and goddesses leaving their homes to visit their friends and relatives. These visits reflected actual ceremonies in which the divine statue was transported for both regular calendar festivals and special occasions. There were many regular festivals in Babylonia, including festivals of thanksgiving and sheep-shearing. Various cities had their own calendar of seasonal feasts. For example, there were special calendar days for the delivery of first fruits and the offering of the first dairy products of the year. This ritual act was recognized both as a religious celebration and as an exchange of products between the cattlemen in the south and the farmers in the north of Mesopotamia.

The most common festivals were connected with certain days of the month that corresponded to the phases of the moon. The concept of self-generation was usually associated with the moon, which waxed, waned, and finally vanished during each (lunar) month. The ancients believed that the moon actually died at the end of each month, went down to the netherworld, and then came to life again by its own efforts. Special offerings were made on the day the moon was invisible and believed to be dead, "the day of lying down." On this day, the god Nanna descended to the netherworld to render judgment and make administrative decisions there with other deities. When Nanna had completed his duties in the netherworld, he reappeared in the skies as the new moon. A partial or total eclipse of the moon was considered an ominous event. The great gods asked Sin (the moon god) how to avoid the evil omen portended by the eclipse. Purification rites were a general feature of the Mesopotamian cult to keep the moon free of defilement during eclipses.

The greatest festival of all was celebrated at the new year. In Neo-Babylonian times, the New Year's festival took place during the first 11 days of Nisan, the month of the spring equinox. For the first few days, ceremonial ablutions and prayers were performed, but on the evening of the fourth day, the whole of the *Epic of Creation* was recited in public or perhaps reenacted like a medieval mystery play. The *Epic of Creation* told how the universe was created through Marduk's victory, thereby providing assurance to the Babylonians that the world as they knew it would continue unchanged. The fifth day included more ritual purification. The god Nabu arrived from Borsippa to participate in the festival, and so did the king. The king was permitted to enter the inner sanctuary but only after the high priest had removed the royal insignia. The

---

Snapshot

King Assurnasirpal II's Public Feast to Celebrate His New Capital at Nimrud

When Assurnasirpal, king of Assyria, inaugurated the palace in Calah, a palace of joy, built with great ingenuity, he invited into it Assur (the Assyrian national god), the great lord and the gods of his entire country. He prepared a banquet of 1,000 fattened head of cattle, 1,000 calves, 10,000 stable sheep, 15,000 lambs—for my lady Ishtar (alone), 200 head of cattle (and) . . . 1,000 spring lambs, 500 stags, 500 gazelles, 1,000 ducks, 500 geese . . . 10,000 doves . . . 10,000 assorted small birds, 10,000 assorted fish, 10,000 jerboa, 10,000 assorted eggs; 10,000 loaves of bread, 10,000 jars of beer, 10,000 skins with wine . . . 1,000 wooden crates with vegetables, 300 containers with oil, 300 containers with salted seeds . . . 100 containers of parched barley . . . 100 containers of fine mixed beer, 100 pomegranates, 100 bunches of grapes . . . 100 pistachio cones . . . 100 with garlic, 100 with onions . . . 100 with honey, 100 with rendered butter, 100 with roasted . . . barley, ten homer of shelled pistachio nuts . . . ten homer of dates . . . ten homer of cumin . . . ten homer of thyme, ten homer of perfumed oil, ten homer of sweet smelling matters, . . . ten homer of zinzimmu-onions, ten homer of olives.

When I inaugurated the palace at Calah I hosted for ten days with food and drink 47,074 persons, men and women. (as cited in Nemet-Nejat, 170–71)

king was humiliated by having his cheek slapped and his ears pulled. Then he knelt before Marduk and assured the god that during the year he had not committed any sins or neglected Esagila and Babylon. After a speech by the priest, the king's insignia were returned to him, and once again he was slapped on the cheek. The more painful his slap, the better, because the tears in the king's eyes signified that Marduk was well pleased. In the evening, the king participated in a ceremony at which a white bull was sacrificed. The rest of the ritual text is lost, but from other sources we know that later ceremonies included a procession to the New Year's house outside the city. During the parade, the king "took the hand of Marduk," leading him from his shrine along the Processional Way and through the Ishtar Gate. Then the king took part in the so-called Sacred Marriage.

The Sacred Marriage was a fertility drama celebrated in select cities. The date growers in Uruk celebrated the Sacred Marriage as the power in the date palm to grow and bear fruit, and the herders, dependent on pasture and breeding, believed that consummation resulted in fertility in nature. In this rite, the ruler, the priest-king (*en*), or king (*lugal*) represented the god. His sexual union with the goddess, Inanna, played by a high priestess or perhaps even the queen, resulted in all of nature being fertilized. The Sacred Marriage was based on the myth The Courtship of Inanna and Dumuzi and was celebrated at the New Year's festival.

Kings sometimes treated their subjects to huge feasts. Such public feasts were impressive spectacles and demonstrations of kingly power and wealth (Nemet-Nejat, 163, 194–96).

FOR MORE INFORMATION

Contenau, G. *Everyday Life in Babylon and Assyria.* Translated by K. R. Maxwell-Hyslop and A. R. Maxwell-Hyslop. New York: St. Martins Press, 1954.

Nemet-Nejat, K. R. *Daily Life in Ancient Mesopotamia.* Westport, Conn.: Greenwood Press, 1998.

Saggs, H. W. F. *Civilization before Greece and Rome.* New Haven, Conn.: Yale University Press, 1989.

EGYPT

Egyptians had no weekends. Most worked every day, with few exceptions. Special holy days of the year called for all the inhabitants of a given area to lay down their tools and gather at a local temple to watch a procession of idols, after which they feasted on bountiful free food supplied by the temple.

The most festive of these holy days were Opet—when the idols of Mut and Khonsu traveled from Karnak Temple to Luxor Temple to celebrate their marriage—and birthdays for each god of Egypt. For practical reasons, most of these holidays occurred when the Nile was in flood, making farming impossible in any case. During the rest of the year, one day followed another in much the same way. No regular day of rest

RECREATIONAL
LIFE
|
HOLIDAYS, FESTIVALS,
& SPECTACLES
|
Mesopotamia

Egypt

Greece

Rome

India

existed until it was introduced much later by the Jews in Palestine and borrowed by the Christians.

The Egyptian year had 360 days, which left 5 days unaccounted for. This yearly five-day period provided Egyptians with the closest they ever got to a sustained holiday: no one worked during the long New Year's festival, the Five Yearly Days, which celebrated the end of one year and hopes for a successful next year (Brier and Hobbs, 76–77).

FOR MORE INFORMATION

Brier, B., and H. Hobbs. *Daily Life of the Ancient Egyptians*. Westport, Conn.: Greenwood Press, 1999.

Montet, P. *Everyday Life in Egypt in the Days of Ramesses the Great*. Translated by A. R. Maxwell-Hyslop and M. Drower. Reprint, Philadelphia: University of Pennsylvania Press, 1981.

RECREATIONAL
LIFE

HOLIDAYS, FESTIVALS,
& SPECTACLES

Mesopotamia

Egypt

Greece

Rome

India

GREECE

Festivals regulate the flow of life. Without them, the passage of life is in constant danger of becoming monotonous and undifferentiated. The Greeks would not have understood how society could function without a sense of shared experience. Since, moreover, they did not divide the year into periods of seven days with an appointed period of rest at the end of each week, festivals constituted the primary pretext for recreation. They also afforded the Greeks an opportunity to express their common identity as citizens, tribesmen, and demesmen and to reinforce their sense of an inherited tradition. In Athens, more than 60 days of the year were devoted to festivals annually.

Greek festivals took many forms. At the lower end of the scale were the deme festivals. At the upper end were the civic festivals, in which the entire citizen body, including in some cases resident aliens, participated. The best attended were the prestigious Panhellenic or all-Greek festivals, which attracted celebrants from all over the Greek world. In the Hellenistic period, kings founded festivals at their capitals with the object of impressing their subjects as well as their rivals. One such was the Ptolemaia, which was instituted by Ptolemy II in the early third century B.C.E. at Alexandria, Egypt, in honor of his deified father. The procession he arranged under its auspices in 270 B.C.E. was one of the grandest events ever celebrated in antiquity.

Each festival was a unique expression of worship, tailor-made to the deity in whose honor it was held. A number of features, however, were common to many: a procession to a deity's shrine with ritual stops along the way; the singing of hymns; the decorating of a wooden object that embodied the deity's power; athletic, musical, and dramatic contests; and finally, the most essential feature of all, a blood sacrifice performed on an altar in front of the deity's shrine, followed by the distribution of meat among the priests and worshipers.

Our knowledge of Greek festivals is not sufficiently detailed to permit us to fathom the precise significance that they held for the people who celebrated them. In general, the impulses that propelled the Greeks to congregate and perform these elaborate rituals incorporated anxiety and fear on the one hand and relief and gratitude on the other. Festivals connected with the agricultural year were designed to secure a good harvest, although we never gain a detailed insight into why precisely the celebrants did what they did. One of the most puzzling is the Thesmophoria, a fall festival conducted exclusively by women. This was held all over the Greek world in honor of Demeter, goddess of the wheat. The culminating ritual involved throwing the bodies of sacrificial pigs into snake-infested pits. Three days later, women were lowered into the pits to retrieve the pigs' putrefied remains, which were then placed on an altar and mixed with seed grain. This bizarre rite, which was perhaps seen as a kind of enactment of Persephone's descent to Hades, was evidently intended to facilitate the germination of the grain, but why it took this precise form is a mystery.

Other agricultural festivals included the Oschophoria, in which two youths carried branches known as *ôschoi* laden with grapes; the Haloa, held in honor of Demeter in midwinter, when cakes in the form of phalluses were eaten; the Rural Dionysia, held in honor of Dionysos, during which a giant phallus was carried aloft; the Anthesteria, a flower festival held in early spring, when wine jars containing newly fermented wine were opened and blessed by Dionysos; the Thargelia, held in honor of Apollo, during which a pot of boiled vegetables called *thargela* was offered to the god and a human scapegoat, who perhaps personified hunger, was beaten and driven out of the city; and finally, the Pyanopsia, in which branches laden with wool, fruits, cakes, wine, and oil flasks were borne by children in procession and later hung on the front doors of every Athenian home.

Because the passage from one stage of life to another was thought to be fraught with danger, the Greeks paid close attention to the junctures between these stages. The first rite of passage for an Athenian child took place on the second day of the flower festival called Anthesteria, when infants aged between three and four would be given their first taste of wine. It seems probable that this ritual signaled the formal admission of the child into the Athenian religious community, since wine, the gift of Dionysos, was a feature of almost every religious rite. Rites of passage were also conducted at later moments in a person's life, notably at adolescence and adulthood, as well as at marriage and death.

Festivals in honor of the dead formed a major feature of the calendar. The most spectacular was the annual ceremony held in honor of the war dead. Known as the *taphai* or "burials," it took place at the end of the campaigning season in early winter. Thucydides describes it as follows:

Three days before the ceremony the bones of the fallen are brought and put in a tent which has been erected, and people make whatever offerings they wish to their own dead. Then there is a funeral procession in which coffins of cypress wood are carried on wagons. There is one coffin for each tribe, which contains the bones of members of that tribe. One empty bier is decorated and carried in the procession. This is for the missing, whose bodies could not be recovered. Everyone who wishes, both citizens and foreigners, can join the procession, and the women who are related to the dead make their laments at the tomb. When the bones have been laid in the earth a man chosen for his intellectual gifts and general reputation makes an appropriate speech in praise of the dead and after the speech everyone departs. (*The Peloponnesian War* 2.34)

Other festivals in honor of the dead included the third day of the Anthesteria, or flower festival, known as the Chytroi or Pots, so named because pots of porridge were offered on that day. Chytroi, in other words, was the Athenian equivalent to All Souls Day, when the souls of the dead left their graves and wandered abroad. To counter their noxious presence, people would chew buckthorn and smear the doors of their houses with pitch. The dead were also celebrated at the Genesia and Nemeseia. The latter festival was held at night, and as its name (derived from *nemesis*, or "vengeance") suggests, it was intended to placate those who had come to a violent end.

The most prestigious Athenian festival was the Panathenaia or All-Athenian Festival, held annually on the birthday of Athena, the city's patron goddess. Once every four years, the festival was celebrated with special grandeur. This occasion is the subject of the great frieze that ran around the outer wall of the Parthenon. The procession assembled outside the city at the Dipylon Gate and proceeded through the Agora along the ceremonial Panathenaic Way in the direction of the Acropolis, its final destination.

Groups representing the entire population of Athens participated, the largest of which was a military contingent. On the Parthenon frieze, this takes the form of a cavalcade of naked horsemen. Young girls carried baskets containing barley meal to sprinkle on the heads of the sacrificial victims, as well as cushions for the gods to sit on. Youths carried water pitchers, old men brandished olive branches sacred to Athena, and metics bore offering trays. The central feature of the procession was a ship mounted on wheels with a woolen peplos rigged to its mast in place of a sail. The peplos, which was woven by Athenian maidens of noble birth who resided on the Acropolis, clothed an olive wood statue of Athena that was believed to have dropped onto the Acropolis out of the sky. The removal of the goddess's old peplos and its replacement by a new one evidently formed the climax to the entire Panathenaia, for this is the scene depicted on the portion of the frieze directly above the entrance to the Parthenon. A herd of cows was sacrificed to the goddess on the altar outside her temple, and the meat was then distributed to participants down at the Dipylon Gate, where the procession had begun.

The Panathenaia also featured competitions, including recitations of the works of Homer, contests on the flute and harp, athletic and equestrian events, dancing, and in later times, a naval competition. Victors were awarded Panathenaic amphoras containing olive oil in commemoration of the fact that the olive tree was the goddess's gift to the state. These bore the simple inscription, "One of the prizes from Athens" (Garland, 177–80).

FOR MORE INFORMATION

Garland, R. *Daily Life of the Ancient Greeks*. Westport, Conn.: Greenwood Press, 1998.
Parke, H. W. *The Festivals of the Athenians*. London: Thames and Hudson, 1977.

Robertson, N. *Festivals and Legends: The Formation of Greek Cities in the Light of Public Ritual.*
    Toronto: University of Toronto Press, 1992.
Simon, E. *Festivals of Attica.* Madison: University of Wisconsin Press, 1983.

ROME

RECREATIONAL
LIFE
|
HOLIDAYS, FESTIVALS,
& SPECTACLES
|
Mesopotamia

Egypt

Greece

Rome

India

Roman society was filled with dramatic public spectacles. The victory parade, or triumph, awarded to a victorious general, funerals of wealthy aristocrats, even speeches given by politicians to the Roman people assembled in the forum—all of these could be, and often were, the occasion for lavish and impressive rituals and performances. The Roman calendar included a large number of public holidays, called *feriae*, that increased in number as time went on. On some of these days, there would have been private rituals of worship, but more common were religious rites performed by state officials at mass ceremonies, often accompanied by public entertainments held as a part of the religious observances.

One popular Roman holiday was the Saturnalia. This was originally an agricultural festival held during the winter solstice, and in particular, it was to honor the god Saturn, who was associated with grain and the growing of wheat. The Saturnalia initially was held just after the sowing of the last wheat crop of the year. Eventually, the Romans settled on December 17 as the date to celebrate the Saturnalia, and as the festival grew in popularity, they kept adding days until by the high empire, the Saturnalia was a full weeklong holiday beginning on December 17. The official component of the Saturnalia was that on December 17, the senators performed a mass animal sacrifice at the temple of Saturn, followed by a huge banquet to which everyone was invited. The rest of the week was taken up with continuous parties and feasts. All shops, law courts, and schools were closed. Normal moral restraints were loosened, and everyone was expected to engage in all forms of revelry and fun. This was the only time in the year when people were legally allowed to gamble in public. Bands of revelers would run through the streets drinking and shouting "Io Saturnalia." Part of the custom of the festival involved inversions in status. Thus, for one day of the week, slaves were treated as equals, and often at the banquet that day, masters would wait on their slaves and serve them. During the festival, everyone wore liberty caps, either symbolizing that for the moment everyone was equal or that everyone was expected to behave with freedom and abandon. Each family would select a *princeps* of the Saturnalia, who presided over the parties. Often this was someone normally of low status. Another custom of the Saturnalia was exchanging gifts. People gave dolls made out of clay to children and wax candles to their friends. Not all Romans approved of such merrymaking. The senator Pliny the Younger supposedly had a special sound-proof room constructed at his villa, and while everyone else in his household was having a good time and partying, he would retreat to his room for the week and work.

Another popular holiday fell on February 15 and seems to have been a festival associated with the story of Romulus and Remus, the legendary founders of Rome, who were raised by a wolf. The name of this festival was the Lupercalia. That the

Latin word for wolf is *lupus* is one of the reasons it is thought to be associated with the legend of Rome's founding. On February 15, priests gathered at a cave thought to be the cave of the wolf who had raised Romulus and Remus, where they first sacrificed several goats and a dog. Two young men of aristocratic family then came forward, and their foreheads were smeared with the blood-stained knife. Other priests wiped away the blood using wool that had been soaked in milk. Next, the skins of the goats were sliced into long leather strips, and everyone had a rowdy feast. After the feast came the highlight of the celebration. Young men stripped naked, took the goatskin strips in their hands, and then proceeded to run through the streets of the city, whipping bystanders. Women in particular would line the streets to watch the naked runners and invite the runners to beat them. It was believed that a woman who was whipped by one of the Lupercalia runners would become more fertile.

One of the more serious festivals was held on May 9, 11, and 13 and was called the Lemuria. This was a ceremony to appease spirits of the dead who were walking the earth, often because they had died an untimely death. These wandering ghosts were called *lemures*. Rather than being a large public ceremony, this was a private one performed by each family. Each head of a family had to get up at midnight, his feet had to be bare, and he could not have any knots anywhere on his body. He first made an apotropaic gesture with his thumb held between his closed fingers. Then he washed his hands and walked through the entire house, spitting out black beans. As he did so, he repeated nine times the phrase, "With these beans I redeem me and mine." He then washed his hands again and clanged together bronze vessels, repeating nine times, "Ghosts be gone." Throughout this entire ceremony, he was forbidden to look behind him because presumably the ghosts were following him and picking up the beans. After the ninth repetition of "Ghosts be gone," he finally looked behind him, and this ended the ceremony.

On some public holidays, the state provided public entertainment, of which there were two broad categories. The first was *ludi*, meaning "games," and took many forms, including theatrical performances, dances, and circus races. The vast majority of entertainments were *ludi*. Much rarer were *munera*. These were spectacles that included gladiatorial combats, wild animal shows, and other unusual exhibitions. The biggest difference between the Romans' concept of entertainment and ours was that all of these events had a religious component. The Romans regarded them as a form of worship, and prayers and sacrifices to the gods were a part of all of them.

Gladiatorial combats had a very ancient history in Roman society. Probably they originated with the Etruscans, the predecessors of the Ro-

Drawing of gladiators copied from a wall painting from Pompeii. Both these men are heavily armed and armored, but the Romans usually enjoyed a battle of contrasts, pitting a lightly armed, quick man against a slower, better-armed opponent. Reproduced from the collections of the Library of Congress.

mans in central Italy. Among the Etruscans, when a king or war leader died, as part of the funeral ceremony, a pair of warriors would fight to the death as a way of honoring the warlike spirit of the leader. Over time, this practice became institutionalized, and when the Romans came along they imitated it. Throughout the next 800 years of the Roman Republic, gladiator games were very rare and on a small scale, and they were always held as part of a funeral service.

Like much else, this began to change in the late Republic, and Julius Caesar is often pointed to as the man who began to transform gladiatorial combats from primarily a religious ceremony into a form of entertainment. At an early point in his career when he was trying to gain fame, Caesar put on a gladiatorial show that included an unheard-of 320 pairs of gladiators. Supposedly this was in honor of his father, despite the fact that the elder Caesar had been dead for more than 20 years. Whatever the effects on the ghost of Caesar's father, these games made him popular with the people of Rome.

During the empire, by law the Senate could sponsor no more than two gladiator shows per year. There was no limit, however, to the number the emperor could hold. Despite this, they always remained rare and unusual events. In his 60-plus-year reign, the emperor Augustus only put on gladiator shows eight times. Thus the popular image of movies and television, in which the Romans spent all their time at gladiator shows, is erroneous.

There were three sources for gladiators. First and most commonly, they were slaves who were condemned to be gladiators either because they had committed some crime or seemed likely to be good fighters. This latter category includes prisoners of war captured in Rome's campaigns. Second, some criminals were condemned to be gladiators. The third, and by far the rarest, category consisted of free people who volunteered to become gladiators in a quest for fame and money.

When one became a gladiator, he (the vast majority of gladiators were men, although there are a few known instances of female gladiators) was sent to gladiator school, where the first thing he did was abandon his old name and take a new stage name. In the Republic, most of these schools were privately owned businesses, but in the empire, they all fell under control of the emperor and the state. The staff of the schools included weapons makers, guards, masseurs, doctors, and most important, the trainer, who was called a *lanista*. This was the man who actually taught novice gladiators how to fight.

The new gladiator first underwent general training with wooden weapons until he became familiar with basic fighting techniques. At this point, the *lanista* evaluated him and assigned him to different programs of specialized training depending on his abilities. There were at least 14 different varieties of gladiator divided up according to their type of weapons and tactics. The Romans liked to see a battle of contrasts, and thus nearly all gladiator contests matched a heavily armed and armored man against a lightly armed but more mobile opponent.

The heavily armored types of gladiators included ones called Gauls, Hoplites, Samnites, and the *secutor*. All of these were armed with a sword and helmet that completely covered their face. Some were nearly completely covered in armor, while others had lighter armor but possessed huge five-foot-tall shields. In all cases, they were well protected but slow moving. Their lighter-armed opponents came in two main categories. The first was called the Thracian. He wore little or no armor, carried in one hand a small shield made only of wood or wicker, and in the other hand had a short curved sword. The Thracian would dart back and forth, looking for a gap in his enemy's armor. In turn, his heavily armed enemy would slowly pursue him, trying to trap him against a wall where he could not use his agility to escape. The other type of lightly armed gladiator was perhaps the most skilled of all and provided the greatest battle of contrasts. The *retiarius* was completely naked except for a loincloth. In one hand, he held a net with weights at the corners, and in the other a trident. His strategy was to dance around his opponent and try to entangle him in his net, where he could be skewered by the trident. In the final stages of his training, the gladiator would switch from wooden weapons to real steel ones.

When someone wished to put on a gladiatorial show, he would rent the desired number of gladiators from one of the schools. The prices seemed to range from about 1,000 sesterces for a first-time or not very talented gladiator to about 15,000 for an experienced veteran of many combats. The most famous gladiators could command gigantic fees for every appearance, and some are attested whose fee was over 100,000 sesterces.

One rather odd part of the ritual leading up to a contest was that on the night before the fight, all the gladiators who would be attempting to kill one another on the next day ate dinner together, and curious or morbid fans could come and watch these dinners.

Some gladiators, particularly enemy soldiers captured in war, when faced with the prospect of fighting each other would commit suicide. On one well-known occasion, 29 Germans who were supposed to fight the next day strangled each other. An even more horrible method of suicide was employed by another German who found a way to kill himself when he was allowed to go to the bathroom. Romans did not have toilet paper, but instead in its place each bathroom was equipped with a sponge on a stick. The German took one of these sponges and crammed it down his throat, succeeding in suffocating himself.

On the day of the show, the festivities began with a big parade of all the participants. At the head of the parade was the person providing the funding, who was accompanied by lictors as if he were a magistrate. During this parade, and indeed all throughout the day's activities, there was a band playing. Such bands included flute players, horn players, and often an organ. In the morning, there might be exhibitions of beasts and beast hunts. This continued until noon, when there was an intermission.

During this intermission, the spectators had the choice of going to get some lunch or staying and watching executions. In this interval, particularly bad criminals were led into the arena, where they were lined up and had their throats cut. These criminals were known as *noxii*. When in the later empire there were persecutions of Christians, they were often executed during the intermission. Once at some games at which Caligula was presiding, he became bored because there were no criminals to be executed during the intermission. His solution was to order his guards to throw an entire section of the crowd into the arena to be eaten by animals.

In the afternoon came the main event, the gladiator fight. One tradition has the gladiators coming out and raising their weapons in salute to the giver of the games while they shouted the phrase, "Morituri te salutant" (We who are about to die salute you). The gladiators began by yelling abuse at one another and then, at the signal, they would begin to fight. Most fans had a favorite type of gladiator that they would root for, and they enjoyed arguing with each other over the merits and drawbacks of the different varieties. In these fights, there were no referees, no rules, and no time limit. Whenever a gladiator received a wound, the crowd would shout out "habet," meaning a hit. A gladiator could ask for mercy by dropping his shield and raising a finger of his left hand. The crowd then either called for him to be killed or if he had fought well, would ask for him to be spared. They did this using both shouts and gestures. Hollywood has decided that the thumbs-down gesture meant that he should be killed and thumbs up that he should be spared. In Latin, the relevant passage does not specify which way the thumb was turned, only that the gesture involved the turning of the thumb. Many scholars believe that the thumbs down actually was a way of calling for the victorious gladiator to drop his weapon and spare his enemy, whereas the thumbs up meant to stab him in the throat. If the crowd demanded death, then the winner would plunge his sword into his enemy's throat. The victor would receive the palm of victory, a crown, and prize money.

It is difficult to determine how many contests ended in death; the sources record some games in which nearly every contest resulted in the death of the loser, while at other games nearly everyone would be spared. Each gladiator probably fought only a couple of times a year, but nonetheless, to win more than 10 combats seems to have been exceptional. Perhaps the record was held by one gladiator who was said to have been the victor in no less than 88 combats over the course of his career. If a gladiator fought extraordinarily well, he could be freed, although it seems that many of these continued to fight even though they no longer had to. When they were freed, they received a wooden sword, called the *rudis*, which was the symbol of their freedom.

Champion gladiators were celebrities and had status similar to rock stars today. Women would throw themselves at them, and there are many stories of even rich aristocratic women having affairs with gladiators. The gladiator was a symbol of virility in Roman society. At the same time, they were also one of the most despised groups in society, and it is an interesting contradiction of the Romans that they both glorified and despised the same figure. Even though gladiator games always remained relatively rare, by the second century C.E. they could involve huge numbers of participants. In one of the greatest spectacles, the emperor Trajan gave games lasting 123 days, during which 10,000 gladiators fought.

The Romans seem to have had a real fascination with exotic animals. Oddly enough, however, there was never a zoo established at Rome; instead, they mostly

---

📷 Snapshot

An Advertisement for Some Gladiator Games

Decimus Lucretius Satrius Valens, the permanent priest of Nero Caesar, will present 20 pairs of gladiators. His son, Decimus Lucretius Valens, will also present 10 pairs of gladiators.

They will fight at Pompeii on the 6th, 5th, 4th, and 3rd, and on the day before the Ides of April. A beast hunt will also be offered. The awnings will be employed to shade the spectators.

This message was written by Aemelius Celer by himself, under the light of the moon. (*Inscriptiones Latinae Selectae*, 5145)

seem to have just enjoyed watching these animals kill or be killed. As with gladiators, this form of entertainment took off in the late Republic. Pompey started the trend with some games at which several hundred lions and leopards were killed. The Roman conquest of North Africa and Egypt made all sorts of exotic animals available. How quickly this expanded can be seen by considering a single day in the empire when the following animals were slaughtered at Rome: 32 elephants, 10 elk, 20 mules, 10 tigers, 40 horses, 60 lions, 30 leopards, 10 hyenas, 10 giraffes, 6 hippopotamuses, 1 rhinoceros, and several dozen gazelles and ostriches.

A beast hunt was called a *venatione* and usually pitted a man called a *bestiarius*, armed with a dagger or spear, against one or several animals. To make these hunts more exciting, natural settings, including forests, hills, caves, and streams, were sometimes built in the arena. When animals were pitted against each other, to make sure they would fight, the Romans would often tie them together with a chain. Favorite pairings of this sort included a bull versus a bear and an elephant versus a rhinoceros. Once again, perhaps the most amazing beast hunt was the 123-day-long games of Trajan, which in addition to featuring 10,000 gladiators saw no less than 11,000 wild animals slaughtered in the arena. In view of such statistics, it is no surprise that in about a century, the Romans caused most of the large wild animals of North Africa to become extinct.

The largest stadium in Rome was not the Colosseum but rather the Circus Maximus, which was the site of chariot races, the favorite entertainment of the average citizen of Rome. The Circus Maximus was a third of a mile long and could seat 250,000 spectators. Whereas there might only be two or three gladiator contests per year, most of the more than 100 holidays per year would have included chariot racing.

Also unlike gladiator games, chariot racing was not put on or controlled by the state. Instead, there were private enterprises called factions that trained, equipped, and entered teams in the races. In the Republic, there were just two of these, which were known as the Reds and the Whites. In the early empire, two more were added, the Blues and the Greens. Later, one of the emperors himself tried to create two new groups, the Golds and the Purples, but these did not catch on, and for most of racing history, the four big factions dominated. They were large and powerful organizations; each one owned extensive stables and breeding farms for their horses and highly organized training centers and schools for their charioteers. Naturally, they also maintained a number of grooms and veterinarians.

There were several types of chariot races. One involved two-horse chariots, which were called *bigae*. The most popular and common were races involving four-horse chariots called *quadrigae*. Nearly all races were one of these two types, although occasionally for novelty there were odd variations. One unusual variation was the *pedibus ad quadrigum*. The exact nature of this race is debated, but it clearly incorporated a footrace element into the chariot race. One theory holds that in addition to the driver, there was a passenger, and as soon as each chariot crossed the finish line, the passenger jumped out and had to run one additional lap around the Circus to win.

In a standard race, with 12 chariots in the running, each faction would have three chariots entered. The signal for the start of the race was the emperor or presiding magistrate dropping a cloth. On the straight-aways, each charioteer would urge his horses to go as fast as possible; the points of tension were the turns around the central divider. In modern racecourses, the turns are very gradual, but in the Circus, each chariot actually had to complete a 180-degree turn. The chariot that turned closest to the divider would travel the shortest distance and would have the inside track on the next straight-away. This led to the chariots bunching together, and crashes were frequent. Making races even more competitive was the fact that all the chariots from a single faction worked together as a team. To ensure the victory of one chariot from the faction, the other two might possibly sacrifice themselves by obstructing chariots from the other factions or possibly even intentionally ramming them. There were 24 races per day, meaning that one could spend an entire day at the Circus. The winning charioteer received a crown of palm leaves and the winner's prize money. These prizes seem to have ranged between 5,000 and 60,000 sesterces for first place; there were also lesser prizes for second, third, and fourth place.

The inhabitants of Rome were enthusiastic fans. Just as modern sports fans follow specific teams, Romans would choose a faction and rabidly follow the fortunes of that faction. Dressed in the appropriate color, the fans would go to the Circus Maximus in large groups and sit together. They developed elaborate cheers and songs that they would chant and sing in unison by the tens of thousands. Often these deteriorated into abuse directed at fans of other factions, and riots were not infrequent.

The most successful charioteers became phenomenally wealthy as well as famous. They were true celebrities. Typical of the more successful of these was a man named Crescens, who drove for the Blue faction. He was from Mauretania in North Africa, began racing by the age of 13, and died in a crash at the age of 22, after having competed in 686 races and winning 47 of them. His monument notes that during his career he won victory purses worth 1.5 million sesterces. (*C.I.L.* [Corpus Inscriptionum Latinarum] 6.10050)

Carved relief of a chariot race in the Circus Maximus. The triple cones were the posts around which the chariots turned (and frequently crashed). The dolphins in the upper-right corner were used to mark the laps completed. © The Art Archive/Museo della Civilta Romana Rome/Dagli Orti.

In addition to these regularly scheduled entertainments, occasionally an emperor would sponsor a special spectacle, such as a *naumachia*, a naval battle. These could be held on an existing lake, or an artificial lake might be dug. Squadrons of ships manned by slaves or criminals might be pitted against each other. The biggest *naumachia* ever was held on the Fucine Lake by the emperor Claudius. In this colossal battle, two complete fleets of ships were manned by 19,000 men.

Another category of spectacle that was always popular involved reenactments of famous mythological stories. On the simple end, this might involve dressing a few gladiators up as Greeks and Trojans to have a Trojan War, or as Spartans and Athenians to stage a Peloponnesian War. More creative reenactments told mythological stories. One popular myth was that of Icarus, a man who supposedly constructed wings made out of wax and feathers and flew. Foolishly, Icarus flew too close to the sun, and the wax melted, causing his wings to fall apart and Icarus to crash to his death. To re-create this myth, a slave was outfitted with wings and then flung off the top of the amphitheater. On one occasion, Icarus crashed so close to the couch of Nero that the emperor was splattered with blood (Suetonius, *Life of Nero* section 12). Sometimes a theatrical play would be staged, but with criminals or slaves substituted in murder scenes and actually killed. Entertainments such as these destroyed the fundamental distinction between theater and real life.

The violence and cruelty of many Roman spectacles have prompted much debate as to their purpose and morality. Even among the Romans, there were those who questioned and were disgusted by such spectacles. One traditional justification the Romans gave was that they were a warlike people and should be accustomed to violent death. Others, both ancient and modern, have suggested that the games served as a symbolic assertion of Roman dominance or as a way of keeping the masses distracted and uninterested in politics. The truth may be a complex mixture of all of these factors, but regardless, gladiator games and fantastic spectacles remain one of the best-known aspects of Roman civilization.

~*Gregory S. Aldrete*

FOR MORE INFORMATION

Beacham, R. *Spectacle Entertainments of Early Imperial Rome*. New Haven, Conn.: Yale University Press, 1999.

Cameron, A. *Circus Factions*. Oxford: Clarendon Press, 1976.

Coleman, K. M. "Fatal Charades: Roman Executions Staged as Mythological Enactments." *Journal of Roman Studies* 80 (1990): 44–73.

Köhne, E., and C. Ewigleben, eds. *Gladiators and Caesars*. Berkeley: University of California Press, 2000.

Scullard, H. H. *Festivals and Ceremonies of the Roman Republic*. Ithaca, N.Y.: Cornell University Press, 1981.

RECREATIONAL
LIFE
|
HOLIDAYS, FESTIVALS,
& SPECTACLES
|
Mesopotamia

Egypt

Greece

Rome

India

INDIA

Festivals and holidays in a traditional, agricultural society such as that of India were frequently linked to natural events, the change of seasons, and physical geography. For example, numerous places in India served as the focal points of pilgrimage. These places were called *tirtha* and were often associated with bodies of water or rivers. While the sacredness of the Ganges River is well known for redemptive powers and cleansing persons of impurity, ancient Kasi (modern Varanasi or Banares) was the most sacred town along this river. To die there meant one automatically entered heaven. Other important sites included Mathura, on the Yamuna River, and Prayaga, at the confluence of the Ganges and Yamuna Rivers. The town of Puskara was famous for a pond consecrated to the god Brahma. Typically, pilgrimage involved not just bathing in water but also *puja*, worship of the image of a god or goddess, and *dana*, giving gifts or money. At some of these more important sites, every day saw hundreds or thousands of pilgrims patronizing Brahman priests and washing in the river. In temples, Brahman priests served as intermediaries between the gods and devotees.

Bathing was also prescribed after a solar eclipse. The event of an eclipse was considered an ill omen. During the time of the eclipse, people were to refrain from ordinary activity, such as eating, working, and so on, and to avoid looking at the eclipse itself. Bathing afterward served to remove the impurity imposed by the eclipse.

Fasting could also be performed for religious merit. Various fasts are described in the *Puranas*, and typically anyone could fast for merit or to petition a deity to grant a desire. Different times of the year were better for some types of fasts than others.

In the month of *Caitra* (March–April) on the full moon day was the Festival of Spring, the *Madanotsava*. This was a festival to Kama, the god of love. This holiday was a time of ignoring distinctions such as caste, playing pranks on others, and spraying people with colored water and red dye powder. Over time, this has evolved into the modern festival Holi, and the god Kama has been dropped from association with the festival in favor of Krishna.

Another key festival was that of Divali on the new moon day of *Kartika* (October–November). It was a day for visiting temples and gift giving. At night, lamps were lighted, and the goddess Lakshmi was venerated; later, Kali was venerated with this festival. Divali followed after a holiday consecrated to the goddess Durga, variously called Navaratri (nine-night) or Dasahara (ten-day).

The festival of Shivaratri, in the month of *Phalgun* (February–March) was sacred to the deity Mahadeva, better known as Shiva. People stayed up all night and offered to the *lingam* image of Shiva various items, such as flowers, perfumes, rice, and water.

The Pitripaksa in the month of *Bhadra* (August–September) was a fortnight dedicated to remembrance of ancestors. This was seen as the best time to perform *sraddha*, funerary rites.

Large-scale Vedic sacrifices are also recorded as having been public events. Perhaps the most spectacular was the lengthy Asvamedha, the horse sacrifice, whereby a king established and increased his power. The royal consecration, the Rajasuya, was another such elaborate rite, and one that had gambling as an element. The most infamous example of a gambling contest is in the epic *Mahabharata*, whose plot turns on the hero losing his wealth, his kingdom, his family, and his wife in an ill-considered match. Gambling, whether by kings or the common people, was done with a six-sided dice, and various throws were named after the four *yugas*, namely, Krita, Treta, Dwapara, and Kali.

Sports and athletics were not emphasized as public events in ancient India as much as in other civilizations. Chariot- and bullock-racing contests did exist, as did archery contests. Some periods did have gladiatorial-style combats, as well as animal fights. In Tamil country, there were bullfighting contests in which the bullfighter was unarmed and attempted not to kill the bull but rather to subdue it. Among the upper classes, many of these contests were seen particularly in conjunction with the *svayamvara,* an event in which men competed for a particular bride.

To read about holidays and festivals in nineteenth-century India, see the India entry in the section "Holidays and Festivals," in chapter 7 ("Recreational Life") of Volume 5 (*Nineteenth Century*) of this series.

~Matthew Bingley

FOR MORE INFORMATION

Auboyer, J. *Daily Life in Ancient India.* London: Phoenix Press, 1965.
Basham, A. L. *The Wonder That Was India.* London: Sidgwick and Jackson, 1967.

RECREATIONAL LIFE: WEB SITES

http://classics.uc.edu/music/
http://didaskalia.open.ac.uk/index.shtml
http://www.mala.bc.ca/~johnstoi/euripides/euripides.htm
http://www.oeaw.ac.at/kal/agm/
http://www.scu.edu.au/schools/carts/contmusic/musicarchive/AusGeneral.html

8

RELIGIOUS LIFE

The human world is made up of more than the material and social environments that surround us. Throughout history, people have left records of their recognition of and longing for something larger than themselves, and this desire to transcend daily life forms the basis for people's religious faith. Religions have two intertwined components—belief and rituals—and the second derives from and preserves the former. Thus, through careful enactment of rituals, the faithful believe they can rise above the mundane realities of day-to-day life, and historians find that the study of religious practices offers a window into people's spiritual beliefs.

Religious beliefs have served to help people make sense of the natural world—from its beauties to its disasters. For example, an ancient Egyptian pharaoh (Akhenaton) and a medieval Christian saint (Francis of Assisi) both wrote magnificent poetry praising the blessings of this world. In addition, the Buddha and the Hebrew scriptures' Book of Job both address the deep sufferings of this life. In these ways, religion has always helped people make sense of the world that surrounds them.

At the same time, religious rituals serve the needs of society. The faithful reinforce their social ties by worshiping together, and sociologists of religion argue that religion is the symbolic worship of society itself. Sacred songs, dances, and feasts have always served to bind communities closer together, and in these ways the religious and secular lives of the people mingle. This intimate relationship between religious beliefs, rituals, and societies makes the study of religious life a fruitful one. The complex nature of societies also yields complexities in religious beliefs and practices. Throughout history, we can follow the reforms and indeed revolutions in religious ideas that have profoundly shaped our past.

Through the study of religious life, we can thus learn about how people viewed the natural and supernatural, how rituals organize people's daily lives, and how beliefs brought out the best (and the worst) in people. At the same time, we can glimpse the deep longing in human souls that has generated some of people's noblest thought.

In the ancient world, religion was tilted more heavily toward ritual than belief. Many of the dominant religions in the ancient world were polytheistic; that is, they worshiped many gods rather than one. Perhaps more significantly, because polytheism acknowledged the existence and validity of other people's gods, there was not

RELIGIOUS LIFE

RELIGIOUS BELIEFS

DEITIES

PRIESTS
& RELIGIOUS RITUAL

TEMPLES

DEATH, BURIAL,
& THE AFTERLIFE

MAGIC
& SUPERSTITION

the obsessive insistence on faith and belief that characterizes modern monotheistic religions such as Christianity and Islam.

On the other hand, the gods often did not concern themselves with the moral and ethical behavior of humanity. Also, gods tended to mirror the behavior of mortals, including the whole range of human motivations and actions, even those that were not so noble. Gods and goddesses married and had children, although, as among mortals, infidelity could be a problem. Jealousy, anger, and strife caused the gods to quarrel among themselves, go to war, and even resort to murder. Husband and wife squabbled bitterly, like Hera and Zeus in Greek mythology, and brother killed brother, like Set and Osiris in Egyptian lore.

The gods also actively interfered in human affairs, and religious rituals were often intended to attempt to make such interventions positive rather than negative. Sacrifices, the construction of temples, prayers, and offerings acted as a sort of bribery, which might compel a god to give his or her mortal supplicant something in return.

Ancient religions tended to have a public focus rather than a private one, and rituals served to promote a sense of social cohesiveness. While certain heroes might have a personal relationship with a god, the idea that the average person would do so is a more modern notion. Individuals certainly sometimes prayed to gods and in particular sought their advice through oracles or omens. In general, however, priests acted as intermediaries who worked to satisfy the gods and protect the city or state, while public religious festivals, processions, and ceremonies brought groups together and sought divine blessings on behalf of the community as a whole.

~*Joyce E. Salisbury and Gregory S. Aldrete*

FOR MORE INFORMATION

Beard, M., and J. North, eds. *Pagan Priests: Religion and Power in the Ancient World.* Ithaca, N.Y.: Cornell University Press, 1990.

Burkert, W. *Homo Necans.* Translated by Peter Bing. Berkeley: University of California Press, 1983.

Hopkins, K. *A World Full of Gods.* New York: Plume, 2001.

Religious Beliefs

The role of religious beliefs in the lives of the people of the ancient world was at the same time extremely pervasive and yet also limited in certain ways.

On the one hand, in most of these civilizations, the world was filled with gods who directly controlled both the physical environment and the events that happened in it. Often, the gods not only directed and caused the weather, but natural forces such as wind, or geographical features such as rivers, were themselves thought to be gods. The gods also frequently intervened in human affairs.

On the other hand, the relationship between mortals and gods often lacked a spiritual or moral dimension. The main focal point of most ancient religions centered not around whether a person had a strong belief in the gods, but rather on the actions a person took for the gods. Usually, the gods were not particularly concerned whether people were good or bad, or how strong their belief was, but instead on whether someone performed the right sacrifice and recited the correct prayers.

In a way, the relationship between humans and gods was a simple one of mutual favors. Because the gods controlled everything, it was in people's best interests to perform actions that benefited the gods in the hope that they in turn would bestow blessings on those who had pleased them. In light of this, it is not surprising that these religions generally lacked sacred texts such as the Bible or the Qur'an (sometimes spelled Koran), which dictate moral codes of behavior.

Common features of these religions were creation stories and myths about the gods and their interactions with each other and with humans. Many of the creation stories are similar, beginning with a time when nothing existed or there was formless chaos. These stories usually go on to explain the creation of the gods, the world, and eventually, human beings. The interactions among the gods were rarely harmonious, and myths such as those of ancient Egypt, India, and Greece tell many dramatic and colorful stories of great struggles and adventures among the gods.

The dominant religions of the ancient world were all polytheistic. One aberration to this pattern was the short-lived monotheism of the Egyptian pharaoh Akhenaton. It was during the time period of the ancient world, however, that the major monotheistic religions—Judaism, Christianity, and Islam—all had their origins, although it would not be until the medieval period that these would become widespread. Eventually, these monotheistic religions would supplant the polytheistic religions that dominated the ancient world to such a complete extent that all those once-vibrant religions are today effectively extinct.

~Gregory S. Aldrete

MESOPOTAMIA

The past 150 years of excavations have yielded remains of Mesopotamian temples, statues, and religious artifacts. Unfortunately, most excavated temples were found empty, their contents stolen or brought to a safe place. Written sources include myths, "manuals" explaining religious ideology, rituals, hymns, and prayers. Common religious beliefs were also expressed in letters and administrative documents. Even personal names could communicate religious beliefs—for example, "I-Was-Spared-on-Account-of-Ishtar," "May-I-Not-Come-to-Shame, O Marduk," and "Assur-Knew-My-Loyalty." Texts often describe the transcendence of the gods, their superiority, and rule over humanity because of their power and intelligence. Myths, in particular, answered questions for ancient peoples about origins and existence by helping ancient civilizations make sense of the world around them. These myths were often about the gods and their activities and about our world and how it was created.

Creation was an important theme in mythology and was explained by separation of the primeval matter, which was watery, solid, or a mixture of the two. According

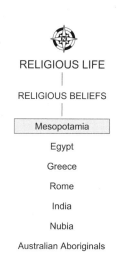

to *Enuma elish* (the Akkadian *Epic of Creation*), there was nothing in the beginning except primordial Apsu (male), the sweet waters, and Tiamat (female), the waters of ocean. The origin of the universe was traced to their union. For the Sumerians, creation began when Enlil, their chief god, separated a single body of matter into a two-level universe to prepare the world for humankind. In general, the people of ancient Mesopotamia rarely questioned how the primordial elements came into being. In all the Mesopotamian creation stories, creation always resulted in heaven and earth because the ancients clearly saw that both existed. Any creation story also included one of two basic versions of the creation of the human race. In one version, the human race sprouted from the ground like plants; in the other, people were created from clay, mixed with divine blood, and molded into figurines. In ancient Mesopotamia, divine blood, sometimes combined with divine spittle, was necessary to infuse the clay with life. Humans were created to take over the gods' work, so the gods could rest. In time, the world became overpopulated, and the gods brought a flood.

> *If an individual sinned, evils could befall the entire community.*

Trespasses against the gods were often the main topic in Sumerian sources about religion. There were numerous words for sins. The native terms distinguished their gravity. At the end of the second millennium B.C.E., the text *Surpu* (literally, burning) listed 200 acts and omissions as sins, including not speaking one's mind, causing discord in the family, neglecting a naked person, and killing animals without reason. The confessional lists of trespasses contained unintentional sins as well as ancestral sins. The gods punished the sinners they forgave, but if the gods refused to forgive the sinner, that person could not be helped. In reality, the wicked often fared better than the righteous.

Ancient Mesopotamians regarded personal well-being as being tied to correct worship of the gods. If an individual sinned or a community neglected the proper rites, disorder, plague, earthquake, fire, or other evils could befall the entire community. There was little hope for a better life after death—life in the underworld was, for the most part, miserable for all.

The religion of the priest was focused on the image of the god and on the temple. The priest was concerned with the religious service-sacrifices and hymns of praise. Royal religion differed from that of the priest and the ordinary citizen. The king alone undertook prayers, fasts, mortification, and taboos. But the religion of the common person still remains largely a mystery. For the average person, religion was ceremonial and formal rather than intense and personal. Each Babylonian had a personal god to whom he gave regular offerings and from whom he made specific requests, such as a cure from illness. The personal god also mediated with higher gods on the worshiper's behalf. The Babylonian relationship between the worshiper and the personal gods can best be described as benefits for the worshiper in return for his offerings.

Early Mesopotamians regarded the supernatural forces that controlled their world as mysterious and impersonal. Such forces are called *numina* (plural of Latin *numen*). Early humans believed that storms, rivers, lakes, marshes, mountains, sun, wind, and fire were all living beings. The religious beliefs of the Sumerians took form in Eridu, one of the oldest Sumerian settlements. For them, water was a numinous power, a supernatural life force. During the fourth millennium B.C.E., ancient Mesopotamians worshiped forces in nature, that is, the powers of fertility. Spring was brief, and its fertile powers declined as the dry, hot summer came. Myths explained the alternation of fertility and sterility. The progressive humanization of the supernatural forces emerged from the human need for a meaningful relationship with them. Eventually, this led to a growing preference for the human form over older, nonhuman forms (*numina*) and a preference for organizing the gods according to human patterns of family and profession.

The third millennium B.C.E. ushered in a period of war. Once war became chronic, the office of the king became a permanent position. Before acting, the king had to know the gods' will and how to properly carry out their orders to protect the community from divine wrath or neglect. There were "standing" orders such as cultic activities and maintenance of the temple. Sometimes the ruler received specific instructions from the gods in dreams or in omens. Occasionally, the king impiously defied divine authority as revealed through the omens. The ruler metaphor was extended to the gods. Nature gods were transformed into city gods or heads of state. In their roles as rulers, the gods were expected to protect their realms against outsiders.

In addition to their cosmic roles, the gods were assigned powers conferred on them by such high-ranking gods as An, Enlil, or the whole divine assembly. During the first half of the second millennium B.C.E., the Semites came to power and Sumerian culture came to an end. When the Sumerians disappeared from the scene, the Semites continued to develop Mesopotamia and its religion. They still maintained the ancient religious structures they had inherited from the Sumerians, but the religion took on a Semitic coloration, gods gradually becoming detached from their embodiment in nature. The majority of Semitic gods were male.

In the national cults, the great gods of the Sumerian pantheon were equated with parallel Semitic gods. The polytheistic view of the ancients allowed them to accept the gods of other nations. The rank of the gods reflected the political relationships between nations. In their political role, the gods and goddesses constituted a "Primitive Democracy," which met at Nippur in an assembly presided over by An and Enlil. Here political decisions such as war were discussed and humanity's crimes were judged. Once the gods were no longer associated with natural phenomena, they became anthropomorphized. Their cities regarded them as rulers and sought political aid and protection against external enemies and internal lawlessness.

The gods were regarded as an aristocracy of great landowners, the country's powerful upper class. The gods created humanity to serve them; this concept was expressed in numerous Sumerian and Akkadian myths, hymns, prayers, historical texts, and royal inscriptions and in art. The pantheon included various administrators and divine artisans. In this way, the humans' world was reflected in the heavenly world of the gods. In time, the gods and their world were modeled on the world of humans. The gods had wives (usually secondary figures), children, courtiers, and servants, similar to a human ruler but without human boundaries. The relations between different city gods were defined through family ties.

Descriptions of the heavens refer to seven or three heavens, each made of a different precious stone. The gods were assigned various functions, which varied in importance according to their rank in heaven. The city prince assumed a special status as the earthly representative of the city's god.

The increasing intermingling of Akkadians, immigrating Amorites, and Sumerians throughout Mesopotamia changed the theology of the time. The gods of neighboring peoples were often integrated within their own pantheon. However, the Babylonians rejected Assur, the god of the hated Assyrians. From the second millennium B.C.E. to the first millennium B.C.E. the gods were identified with the political ambitions of their nations. Marduk (Akkadian, "son of the storm"), patron god of Babylon, and Assur, patron god of Assyria, became head of their respective pantheons when their cities became the capitals of their nations and empires.

A variety of votive statues left by donors at the Square Temple at Tell Asmar. The statues are intended to represent the donors and to pray for them. The wide-eyed expression is typical. Courtesy of the Oriental Institute of the University of Chicago.

On a personal level, there was a growing closeness between humans and gods, resulting in a relationship with a personal or family god. The ancient Mesopotamians addressed their personal god (or goddess) by name, asking him or her to intervene with more powerful gods in his or her role as protector.

Various mythological themes became popular, namely, death, the demons in the netherworld, and divine wars. Death was graphically described. An was flayed and his head cut off; Enlil's eyes were plucked out. The growing cruelty paralleled the increased political roles of the gods. The gods of political enemies became the embodiment of the enemies themselves and were treated with cruelty. The gods were drawn into political conflict, with their statues and temples at the mercy of their conquerors. Politico-religious pamphlets were equally brutal.

For the most part, the Assyrians worshiped the same gods as the Babylonians, but the Assyrians' gods did not always play the same roles as their Babylonian counterparts. Assur, the patron god of the city of Assur, became the chief god of an ever-expanding empire. Oaths were taken in Assur's name, and prayers were offered to him in personal matters.

By the Neo-Assyrian period, the temple buildings and their staffs had become enormous; income from temple lands and traditional offerings were insufficient to support the temple personnel. The major cults depended on the king for extra income and upkeep of the building. The Assyrian king came to represent the god Assur. "Temple" and "palace" were no longer separate (Nemet-Nejat, 175–82).

FOR MORE INFORMATION

Dalley, S. *Myths from Mesopotamia*. New York: Oxford University Press, 1989.

Nemet-Nejat, K. R. *Daily Life in Ancient Mesopotamia*. Westport, Conn.: Greenwood Press, 1998.

EGYPT

RELIGIOUS LIFE
|
RELIGIOUS BELIEFS
|
Mesopotamia

Egypt

Greece

Rome

India

Nubia

Australian Aboriginals

Nothing affected the everyday lives of ancient Egyptians more than their religion, which differed, both in theory and practice, from any we know today. Egyptians worshiped not a single god but a vast array from which they could pick and choose. Common people took almost no part in religious rituals; that was the sacred responsibility of the priestly class. The afterlife was believed to be not an abstract spiritual realm but a concrete, real destination mirroring life in this world. Finally, attaining eternal life did not require performing good acts but simply doing no wrong.

Because no scientific principles existed to explain natural phenomena, Egyptians believed that whatever occurred in their lives or environment had a supernatural cause. Not understanding why events happened or how to control them, they considered something as familiar and central to their lives as the sun to be more than an astronomical object; it was the falcon god Ra. The Nile was not just a river obeying simple laws of nature but the god Hapi.

Egyptians depended on the good will of their gods to grant what they wanted. The disappearance of the sun each night, for example, frightened them into imagining that it made a dangerous journey past enemies who tried to prevent its reappearance in the morning. So they made offerings to the gods, prayed, and did in general whatever they believed their gods might demand to ensure its return. Lacking scientific laws to explain diverse phenomena, they regarded each natural event as the province of a separate god and assigned it personal characteristics and a physical form. Of course they did not really believe that the sun was a bird or that a river had breasts: wrestling with the impossible task of representing invisible powers in some concrete manner, they chose to symbolize a particular god as a creature or an attribute that exhibited similar abilities. At the peak of their civilization, during the 18th Dynasty, Egyptians worshiped more than a thousand gods. Some were the same deity celebrated under different names in different cities, but most were separate gods.

Ancient Egyptians were not required to choose a single god to worship, unlike later practices of monotheism. In the case of childbirth, for example, several divinities were responsible for different aspects of the process. One, a pregnant hippopotamus called Tauret, the "Great One," protected a woman through the term of her pregnancy. Another, a lion-headed male dwarf named Bes, looked after the child when it was born. When a woman became pregnant, she wore an amulet of Tauret around her neck for protection, much as Catholics wear saints' medals. After giving birth, the new mother donned a Bes amulet.

Despite an abundance of special-occasion gods, Egyptians believed that a few chief gods controlled everything in their world, including the lesser deities. In Memphis, the administrative capital of Egypt, priests credited the chief god Ptah, a human figure wearing a skullcap, with creating the world by imagining it in his mind, then uttering the word. Thebes celebrated a different major god—Amun, the "Hidden One"—with powers so great he could not be visualized; yet because he had to be represented in some way to pay him homage, he was depicted as a man with a tall ostrich plume crown.

To introduce order into their large collection of gods, Egyptians placed each within a hierarchy based on their relative powers. Relying on the familiar, they collected their pantheon into "families" of threes—a father, mother, and son—the first trinities, with the superiority of a chief god symbolized by his fatherhood. Memphis's chief god Ptah was paired with Sekhmet, a lioness; their son Nefertum appeared in human form with lotus plants on his head. Similarly, Amun's wife was Mut, a lioness-headed human; their son Khonsu took the form of a ram-headed human.

For almost all of Egypt's 3,000 years of recorded history, the same gods were an integral part of daily life. From the time an Egyptian baby was born under the protection of Bes until the time the person died and went West to Osiris, the old-time religion governed that person's life. Through thousands of years of constancy, only once were the old gods of polytheism banished and replaced with monotheism. For a brief 17-year span, all Egyptians, from high official to peasant, were forced to alter their beliefs.

Egypt had reached its greatest glory by the end of the 18th Dynasty—its temples were wealthy, its people prosperous, its army unrivaled. Amenhotep III luxuriated on his throne at this best of all times, proudly dedicating the greatest temple any pharaoh ever built to the great god of Egypt, Amun. At his death, it was assumed that his son would carry on the traditions of his forebears. Yet, after ruling only a few years, the new pharaoh changed his name from Amenhotep IV ("Amun is pleased") to Akhenaton ("It is beneficial to the Aton") and declared there was only one god, the Aton. In history's first recorded instance of monotheism, old temples and thousands of priests were no longer supported by the pharaoh, and Egyptians were told that the gods they had always worshiped had ceased to exist. The effect on society was cataclysmic.

Partly to ease social tensions, Akhenaton moved Egypt's capital from thriving Thebes, the home of Amun, to an uninhabited spot of desert in the middle of Egypt, telling his followers of a mystical vision in which the Aton himself had appeared and instructed Akhenaton to build a new city on this deserted site. Akhenaton called the city Akhetaton, the "Horizon of the Aton," and swore he would never leave. Thousands followed their pharaoh into the desert to help found the new religion and erected temples to the new god, which, unlike any others in the country, were built without roofs so the god's light could shine in. Along with the temples, houses, palaces, and office buildings, a complete city was constructed. From his new capital, Akhenaton wrote prayers to his abstract god without human or animal form: there could be no statues of a god who was light itself. As part of his new religion,

Akhenaton changed the concept of life after death. No longer was death a continuation of this world; gone was Osiris and the West. Only when the Aton rose in the east could dead souls rise along with the rest of Egypt. Most Egyptians found this shadowy sort of afterlife unsatisfying.

For a dozen years, Akhenaton kept his promise never to leave his holy city. He abandoned the rest of the country to its own devices, including their continued worship of old, familiar gods. Finally, angered, he dispatched teams of workmen throughout the land to chisel out the names of other gods wherever they appeared on statues and temple walls. Soon after Akhenaton's death, however, his holy city was abandoned, and Egypt returned to its old religion and rituals. Its brief experiment with monotheism left no lasting imprint on religion along the banks of the Nile. Not until the birth of Christ would monotheism again have a significant effect on Egypt (Brier and Hobbs, 33–36, 55–57).

FOR MORE INFORMATION

Aldred, C. *Akhenaten: King of Egypt*. London: Thames and Hudson, 1988.

Brier, B., and H. Hobbs. *Daily Life of the Ancient Egyptians*. Westport, Conn.: Greenwood Press, 1999.

Morenz, S. *Egyptian Religion*. Translated by A. Keep. London: Methuen, 1973.

GREECE

Religion was something for which the Greeks, who had a word for most things, did not have a word. What we identify as religion was not regarded by them as something distinct and separate from other departments of life. On the contrary, the secular and the profane were constantly overlapping and intersecting with one another. The gods were everywhere and in all things. They were in the home, in the crops, in the city, on the battlefield, in the body, in the birthing room, in the weather, and in the mind. There was hardly any human activity or undertaking that was not susceptible to divine influence. The Greek gods, however, were not mind readers. They were not, therefore, the least interested in whether their worshipers were, to use a Christian expression, "pure of heart."

Because most Greeks took the existence of their gods for granted, they had no use for any creed or dogma, which is why they have not bequeathed to us any sacred literature comparable to the Bible or the Qur'an. The focus of their devotion was not on belief but on action. What mattered to them principally was securing the goodwill of their gods, and what mattered in turn to the gods was what they received from mortals. Piety consisted mainly in giving the gods what they wanted. In practice, this took much the same form as giving presents to a spoiled child.

The main objective behind Greek religion was to secure advancement in this life, rather than any imagined state of blessedness in the life to come. To come to terms with it, we have to step outside the assumptions of a monotheistic worldview and conceive of a universe ruled not by a single beneficent deity but by a host of warring deities whose interests frequently conflicted and who were only marginally concerned with the good of humankind. Greek religion was an inclusive and, by and large, essentially tolerant system, which operated on the following basic principles:

1. There are many gods.
2. Any community is necessarily eclectic in its choice of which gods to worship.
3. There will always be genuine gods who are left out of the community's pantheon.

Polytheism did not have to wage war against would-be intruders, unless the would-be intruder happened to come in the form of an exclusive monotheistic religion that challenged its fundamental belief in the plurality of the divine.

Mythos, from which our word *myth* is derived, for the Greeks meant "word," "speech," or "story." Even in the sense of "story," *mythos* did not signify or imply a fiction. On the contrary, it denoted an exemplary tale that revealed a fundamental truth, whether about the nature of the world, the deeds and activities of the gods and heroes, or the composition and evolution of Greek society. The subject matter that the Greeks used for mythic treatment comprised all the events that had occurred from the beginning of the universe down to the aftermath of the Trojan War. This included the succession of divine dynasties that ultimately led to the current ruling dynasty of Olympian deities, the beginnings and evolution of human existence, the Trojan War itself, and the tales that took place in the so-called Age of Heroes.

Although myths have reached us primarily through literature, this was not how they were transmitted in antiquity. Instead, they were the product of an oral culture, a culture that passes down its lore by word of mouth from one generation to the next. Although it is impossible to reach back in time to discover a myth's origins, we need hardly doubt that many of them were rooted in Greece's preliterate past. It was a past that possessed no other means of preserving what needed to be preserved except by word of mouth. Precisely because they were transmitted orally, myths underwent considerable change in each retelling. Inevitably, some details were lost or modified, while others were invented or recast. What has survived, in other words, is the result of a long evolutionary process that took place over several centuries. It was a process that was organic in the true sense of the word.

Myths were not immutable artifacts written in stone. There was never any official version of a myth, although some versions inevitably became more popular than others. This did not prevent different versions from coexisting in different places and at different times—or even at the same time. Such a state of affairs was probably the rule rather than the exception. Although myths were the common property of all Greeks, they often bore a distinctly localized character. Each city-state disseminated its own versions and gave prominence to those myths that celebrated its own local heroes and local deities.

Our primary source for the study of Greek mythology is Greek literature. The oldest surviving myths are found in the poems of Hesiod and Homer. There is no evidence to suggest that Hesiod or Homer invented the myths they incorporated, however. Another important early source is an anonymous compilation of works called the *Homeric Hymns*, which provide us with charter myths that explain the establishment of cults in honor of the various Olympian deities. In addition, many of the best-known myths were dramatized by Athens's tragedians, who for the most part set their plays in Greece's heroic past. Most myths are preserved merely in part.

Where does the world come from? Why is there so much evil in the world? Why is the year divided into different seasons? Why in the face of all the terrible things that happen in the world do we still continue to hope that things will improve? These and other perennial questions are just a few of the issues that myths of origin seek to address.

The primary source for the mythic account of the origin of the universe is Hesiod's *Theogony*. According to Hesiod, the primordial being was Chaos, a word that roughly translates as "gaping void." Next, Earth, Tartaros (the lowest region of the underworld), and Desire came into existence. Chaos then engendered Darkness and Night, and Night by coupling with Darkness gave birth to Day. Whereas the book of Genesis ascribes the creative act to a divine being who exists outside his own creation, Hesiod proposed a model whereby the means of propagation emerged out of nothingness. In other words, it was the instinct for mating rather than a series of disconnected acts on the part of a divine will that caused the world to assume its present form.

> *The Greek hero was a morally complex individual who often failed to conduct himself honorably.*

The Trojan War represented the supreme military enterprise of all time. It was undertaken to avenge the honor of Menelaus, king of Sparta. His wife, Helen, had been abducted by the Trojan prince Paris, who was the guest of Menelaus at the time. Contingents from all over the Greek world participated in the venture, which was placed under the command of Agamemnon, Menelaus's brother and king of Mycenae. After a siege that lasted 10 years, Troy was taken and destroyed.

The Trojan War, which elicited deeds of great courage on both sides, has all the makings of an epic in the modern sense of the word. Far from being a nationalistic myth that jingoistically trumpeted the achievements of the Greeks, it served as a terrible reminder of the futility and cruelty of war. Although the Homeric poems are among the greatest legacies of Greek culture, they demonstrate a strong influence of Near Eastern epic.

Greek mythology is full of tales about heroes such as Achilles, Orestes, Oedipus, Perseus, Hercules, Jason, Odysseus, and Theseus, all of whom are of divine parentage or ancestry. Achilles was the son of the sea goddess Thetis, Hercules and Perseus were the sons of Zeus, and Theseus was the son of Poseidon. Heroes are distinguished by their physical prowess, their appetite for adventure, and their willingness to take on challenges that would overwhelm the average mortal. The greatest challenge of all was the descent to the underworld, where the hero encountered what might be described as a negation of the self.

The Greek hero was not merely an ancient version of the Lone Ranger, however. On the contrary, many of the myths connected with the hero emphasize the violent streak in human nature that is integral to humankind's lust for achievement. Unlike his popular, much-diluted modern descendant, the Greek hero was a morally complex individual who often failed to conduct himself honorably, yet whose courage and prowess, in the eyes of the Greeks, did not release him from the obligation to live as a morally responsible human being. The hero was, in other words, by no means a forerunner of the Christian saint. Nor was he primarily or predominantly a public benefactor. Although many heroic exploits did provide incidental beneficial consequences to humanity, this was by no means the only reason they were undertaken. In many cases, the principal motive for taking on the challenge seems to have been similar to that which inspires modern mountain climbers to risk their lives climbing Mount Everest: simply because it is there.

Giants with a single eye in the center of their foreheads, hideous hags with the capacity to petrify those who gazed upon them, monstrous snakes with numerous heads that doubled in number if they were lopped off—did the Greeks actually believe all this? The question does not permit a simple answer. Even the ultra-rationalistic historian Thucydides did not dismiss outright the monstrous Cyclopeans as purely imaginary. In his discussion of Sicily, where this fabulous race was thought to have once resided, he gives the following cautious pronouncement:

The most ancient inhabitants are said to be the Cyclopes. . . . I cannot say who their relatives were nor where they came from or where they went. We have to content ourselves with what the poets said and with what anyone else knows. (*The Peloponnesian War* 6.21)

Although the Greeks in general did not question the veracity of their myths, from the fifth century B.C.E. onward some effort was made to try to explain away some of their more fanciful elements. One that came in for rationalization concerned the god Dionysos, who was conceived when Zeus impregnated Semele in the form of a thunderbolt. Having at the same time incinerated Semele, Zeus rescued the embryo by sewing it into his thigh. In Euripides' *Bacchai*, however, the seer Tiresius claims that this myth is based on a verbal confusion. What Zeus really did was to make a replica of the god, which he then "showed," rather than "sewed," to Hera. This laborious pun, which can be only approximately reproduced in English, demonstrates an attempt on the part of a rationalist to explain away an extravagant mythical claim, without denying its essential veracity.

Myths express the patterns that underlie human existence; they do not, however, determine the consequences of those patterns. Rather, they admit variants in line with the Greek belief in free will. Myths allowed the Greeks to live their lives freely, while laying down certain parameters within which repetitive cycles occur. Myth played a central role as a teaching tool. In general, Greek mythology presents an exceedingly menacing and troubled landscape. Although it does not entirely banish what is generous and noble in human nature, few myths have happy endings. And such happiness as does occur is either fleeting or purchased at the cost of much misery. Through myth we encounter the dark side of human life, from which many of us would perhaps prefer to avert our gaze. Yet myth also provides us with an incomparably rich language for coming to terms with that dark side.

Within the disunited and fractured world of Greece, mythology served as a powerful cultural unifier, providing its people both with the sense of a shared past and the means of interpreting it. Nothing in the modern world performs a comparable function. Greek polytheism endured long after the rise of Christianity. As late as

395 c.e., Athens was believed to have been saved from Alaric and the Visigoths by an epiphany of Athena and Achilles, who appeared, fully armed, astride the city walls. Not until 529 c.e. were the old gods finally laid to rest, when the emperor Justinian forbade any pagan to teach philosophy in Athens (Garland, 131–32, 199–208).

FOR MORE INFORMATION

Burkert, W. *Greek Religion.* Oxford: Basil Blackwell, 1985.

Gantz, T. *Early Greek Myth: A Guide to Literary and Artistic Sources.* Baltimore, Md.: Johns Hopkins University Press, 1993.

Garland, R. *Daily Life of the Ancient Greeks.* Westport, Conn.: Greenwood Press, 1998.

Graf, F. *Greek Mythology: An Introduction.* Translated by T. Marier. Baltimore, Md.: Johns Hopkins University Press, 1993.

ROME

The religion of the Romans was different in a number of profound ways not just from modern Christianity but from the very ways that we today tend to think about the purpose, functioning, and characteristics of religion.

The most obvious difference is that Roman paganism was a polytheistic religion, meaning that there were many gods. For the Romans, the world was a place inhabited by an infinite number of gods, including many that they had not heard of. When the Romans encountered other religions, they were very open about adding these new gods to the list of those they already worshiped. Thus the Roman pantheon was constantly expanding with the addition of new gods. This attitude can be seen vividly in a ritual called the *evocatio*. This occurred when the Romans were about to attack and possibly destroy an enemy city. Before launching the assault, the Roman priests would formally invite the gods of the city to abandon it and to take up residence and be worshiped at Rome.

The pantheon of Roman gods included deities who resembled humans, such as Jupiter, personifications of abstract qualities, nature spirits, or deities usually associated with geographic places or bodies of water, and a variety of gods imported from foreign cultures, such as the Egyptian goddess Isis. Different individuals would pick different gods as their particular guardians. Because certain gods were associated with certain cities and professions, these gods would probably receive particular attention from people of that profession or who lived in that city.

There were a variety of priests and priesthoods, but with a few exceptions, this was not a full-time occupation, nor did priests receive much specialized training. They mainly performed certain public rituals and sacrifices on behalf of the state. Individuals would in essence act as their own priests and perform religious rituals for themselves or their families.

Roman religion did not have a standardized sacred text comparable to the Bible. While there were certain rituals, such as sacrifice, that were commonly prescribed for the worship of various gods, there was no central and all-encompassing theology. Roman religion was a loose collection of widely ranging gods and practices allowing a great deal of variety and personal choice.

Among the myriad belief systems were a number of cults that have been labeled mystery religions. These cults usually came from the east, had more of a focus on the individual, practiced initiation rites, and often promised worshipers some form of immortality. Among the more prominent mystery cults were Mithraism, Orphism, and the Eleusinian Mysteries. One group that was usually considered a mystery cult was the monotheistic religion Christianity, which after a very gradual spread throughout the Roman world ultimately became the religion of the Roman emperors and then the official religion of the empire. In 391 C.E., the Christian Roman emperor Theodosius I banned pagan worship.

~*Gregory S. Aldrete*

FOR MORE INFORMATION

Ferguson, J. *The Religions of the Roman Empire*. Ithaca, N.Y.: Cornell University Press, 1971.
MacMullen, R. *Paganism in the Roman Empire*. New Haven, Conn.: Yale University Press, 1981.
Ogilvie, R. M. *The Romans and Their Gods in the Age of Augustus*. London: Chatto and Windus, 1969.

RELIGIOUS LIFE

|

RELIGIOUS BELIEFS

|

Mesopotamia

Egypt

Greece

Rome

India

Nubia

Australian Aboriginals

INDIA

Because of the indecipherability of proto-Dravidian texts, little is known about the religious beliefs of the Indus Valley civilization. Only with the dawn of the Vedic and Brahmanic era, and its Sanskritic texts that provide the basis for the later Epic and Puranic period, can the religious history of the Indian subcontinent be reconstructed with greater certainty. It is known, however, that the religious life of the Indus Valley civilization was based primarily on goddess worship, although there is some evidence of reverence for male deities. Religious life was tied to the Indus agricultural setting, as is suggested by various careful depictions of flora and fauna. Goddesses were often shown with plants, such as the peepul tree, and animals, such as the water buffalo. The "Great Bath" at Mohenjo-Daro shows that religious life involved ritual bathing, but it also featured sacrifices offered to various deities. These sacrifices, usually offered on outdoor raised platforms, involved fire and occasional blood rituals, although there were some temples that housed other religious activity. There were male and female priests. Sacrifices were also offered in home hearths.

Although present, male deities in Indus society do not seem to have played a major role. One particularly intriguing case, however, comes from a seal that depicts a figure who appears to be seated in a "yogic" posture. Some scholars have called this figure "proto-Shiva" because of his resemblance to later yogic and phallic iconography of the god Shiva. There is little reason to believe that yoga was a well-developed religious practice in Indus society, and the linkages specifically with Shiva are tenuous.

With the rise of Vedic and Brahmanic culture, goddesses (*devis*) were generally marginalized in favor of male deities. The goddesses of the Indus civilization were often recast as the spouses of sky gods such as Indra and Surya, atmospheric gods such as Vayu, and terrestrial gods such as Agni and Soma. Some of the goddesses mentioned include Ushas, Vac, and Sarasvati. Vedic and Brahmanic religion has been called "magico-religious" insofar as it involved spells, incantations, and hymns offered to the gods and goddesses. Ritual sacrifice was central to Vedic religion, and fire played a key role in both public (*shrauta*) and home (*gryha*) ceremonies. Recitation of Vedic hymns or formulae (*mantras*) was thought to embody the goddess (Vac). Along with her, the lord of plants (Soma, which is also a hallucinatory ephedrine drink consumed as part of the ritual), and the god of fire (Agni) helped enable Vedic society to complete elaborate rituals that were designed to please the divinities, thereby keeping the cosmos in order. The gods and goddesses were thought to be locked in a struggle with demons, seeking order over disorder, and the battleground for this war was the Vedic altar and the fire sacrifice thereon.

Whereas early texts such as the *Rig Veda* were primarily hymns of praise to individual gods and goddesses, later texts such as the *Sama Veda*, the *Yajur Veda*, and the *Brahmanas* served to provide elaborate instructions and ideological basis for Vedic ritual. There were 30 main clans or tribes that kept these religious texts committed to memory until they were eventually written down centuries later. As the Vedic era waned, esoteric reflections were developed through texts such as the *Aranyakas* and the *Upanishads*. They recast the Vedic sacrifice as primarily an internal matter, a matter of knowledge not so much of orthopraxic ways of relating to external deities but more of a fundamental knowledge of the self (*atman*) as reflective of ultimate reality (*brahman*).

This trend toward the esoteric continued into the Epic and Puranic period, when skeptical movements sought to break away from the rigid ritualism of Vedic and Brahmanic religious practice. This orthopraxy had led to a stratification of society in which only a few rulers (*kshatriyas*) were allowed to patronize rituals that could only be carried out by ritually pure religious specialists (*brahmins*), while the merchant class (*Vaishyas*) and artisan and servant class (*shudras*) were largely excluded. This, of course, eventually came to be known as "caste," although Indian texts refer to this religio-social system as *varna* (literally, color) or *jati* (literally, class). Splinter groups such as Buddhism and Jainism, which arose after about the fifth century B.C.E., sought to break away both from the ritualism of the Vedic and Brahmanic era and from the social stratification that had developed. Instead, they followed systems that emphasized overcoming suffering (*dukkha*) in the case of Buddhism and the violent effects of actions (*karma*) in the case of Jainism. In their genesis, however, these religious systems were close offshoots from the Vedic, Brahmanic worldview.

Buddha. This carving from about the third century B.C.E. with thin limbs and protuberant ribs depicts a fasting Buddha. Scala/Art Resource, NY.

The Epic and Puranic period arose more or less simultaneously with the advent of Buddhism and Jainism. Vedic ritualism and Upanishadic speculation gave way to devotion (*bhakti*) to gods such as Brahma, Vishnu, and Shiva and goddesses such as Parvati, Durga, Shakti, and Kali (there were many more gods and goddesses than the ones mentioned here). The *Ramayana* and the *Mahabharata*, two immense epics, tell the stories of Vishnu's incarnations (*avatars*) as Rama and Krishna, and how they helped the kings of ancient India overcome evil and uphold lawful living (*dharma*). Along with *dharma*, there were three other aims of life, namely, material gain (*artha*), sexual love (*kama*), and worldly liberation (*moksha*). These trends were effectively only accessible to males of the highest castes, although later movements such as Tantrism opened up practices to women and the lower classes. Tantrism was a seventh-century C.E. yogic movement (with possible links to Indus Valley fertility religion) that taught that ultimate reality, *brahman*, had both male and female aspects, exemplified by Shiva and his consorts Shakti or Kali. In this way, Vedic practices, along with worship of gods such as Vishnu and Shiva, as well as various goddesses, have served as the foundation for most later forms of Hinduism.

To read about religion in nineteenth-century India, see the India entry in the section titled "Religion" in chapter 8 ("Religious Life") of volume 5 (*Nineteenth Century*) of this series; for twentieth-century India, see the India entry in the section titled "Religion" in the chapter "Religious Life" of volume 6 (*The Modern World*) of this series.

~*Eric Rothgery*

FOR MORE INFORMATION

Hopkins, T. J. *The Hindu Religious Tradition*. London: Wadsworth, 1971.
Keith, A. B. *The Religion and Philosophy of the Veda and Upanishads*. 2 parts. 1925. Reprint, Delhi: Motilal Banarsidass, 1970.
Potter, K. H. *Presuppositions of India's Philosophies*. Delhi: Motilal Banarsidass, 1991.
Robinson, R. H., and W. L. Johnson. *The Buddhist Religion*. 3rd ed. London: Wadsworth, 1982.

RELIGIOUS LIFE

RELIGIOUS BELIEFS

Mesopotamia

Egypt

Greece

Rome

India

Nubia

Australian Aboriginals

NUBIA

Any discussion of the religious beliefs of the Nubians prior to the Egyptian New Kingdom (after 1550 B.C.E.) is thwarted by the absence of contemporary inscriptions. Nevertheless, the persistence of certain features in their material culture and analogies with the beliefs of the ancient Egyptians enable one to suggest the following characteristics. The existence of graves furnished with goods including predominantly female figurines and pottery vessels from the Neolithic period (after 10,000 B.C.E.) suggests the belief in an afterlife. Throughout the subsequent periods of Nubian civilization, graves and their furnishings became progressively more elaborate, particularly in the Kerma period (about 2500–1500 B.C.E.), when rulers were buried in tombs on beds accompanied by sacrificed retainers, horses, and an array of vessels and furniture. Tombs of Nubians in Nubia during the Egyptian New Kingdom and of the pharaohs of Dynasty 25 (about 720–664 B.C.E.) are so close to pharaonic norms as to suggest the existence, superficially at least, of a shared funerary ethos.

During the Meroitic period, the Nubians appropriated as their own the ancient Egyptian concept of the ba-bird, namely the deceased in its manifestation as a human-headed bird. In Egyptian art, the ba-bird was traditionally depicted in two-dimensional representations and, occasionally in the Late period, as an amulet. The Nubians of the Meroitic period uniquely created statues of the ba-bird in the round as funerary monuments for both men and women. One assumes that such Nubian ba-birds, depicting the deceased transfigured, were placed outside of the tombs of the elite members of society to elicit prayers and offerings from the living for their benefit in the hereafter.

During earlier periods, the Nubians seem to have pioneered the development of rock-cut sanctuaries, the earliest of which is found at Sayala. Such sanctuaries appear to be linked to a deep-seated animism that appears to place emphasis on a numen, or divine presence, within the matrix of the living rock. A sandstone model of Gebel Barkal, which is designed in conformity with the unique hieroglyph for Gebel Barkal of the Napatan period (about 656–310 B.C.E.), clearly illustrates this concept because its hollowed-out interior originally held a statuette of Amun resting on the rectangular socket cut into its interior floor.

The *yardang*, an elongated eroded landform, at Gebel Barkal, enhanced during the reign of the Kushite pharaoh Taharqa to emphasize its serpentlike form emerging from the butte itself, is yet another manifestation of this belief system. The resulting snake was regarded as the embodiment of the god Amun of Napata resident in the Sacred Mountain, as Gebel Barkal was called in the ancient texts. Similarly, a raw piece of unworked malachite inscribed with the name of the same pharaoh was bound with knotted cords as if to control the power within its core. The ancient Egyptians themselves appropriated the form of the rock-cut shrine, or *speos*, during the course of the New Kingdom, apparently modeled on Nubian prototypes. The most famous of these are the Great and Lesser Temples at Abu Simbel erected to commemorate Ramses II and his chief queen, Nefertiti, during Dynasty 19.

Inscribing their own monuments with Egyptian hieroglyphs from Dynasty 25 on, the Nubians recorded aspects of their own religious beliefs. In so doing, they paid particular homage to the god Amun. Their reverence for this deity is, however, based on polyvalence, a system whereby different perceived divine characteristics of a godhead are divided among the manifestations of several like-named deities. In this particular case, the Nubians paid homage to Amun of Napata of the Sacred Mountain and paired him with his counterpart, Amun of Egyptian Thebes. Amun remained the supreme deity of the Nubians until the Meroitic period and was closely linked to the royal family. Amun was both the grantor and guarantor of kingship, and at least one Nubian monarch, Aspelta (about 575 B.C.E.), attributed his accession to the throne to an oracle delivered by Amun himself. Amun was variously depicted as a male figure, as a ram-headed male figure, as a ram, and as a serpent.

An interesting statue group, termed a *protome*, which was inserted over the entrance to the Lion Temple at Musawarrat es-Sufra, depicts three kneeling animals:

a ram flanked by two lions. They are distinguished by their headdresses, which suggest that the central ram is a depiction of the god Amun in oval form. The identifications of the flanking lions are moot, but their suggested equivalence with the Egyptian divine couple, Shu and Tefnut, deities of air and moisture, respectively, seems forced and denies a Nubian pedigree for the composition as a whole.

With the development of their own notational system of writing, which appeared as both a hieroglyphic and a cursive script, and gained wider currency in Nubia during the course of the second century B.C.E., the Nubians were able to communicate their religious beliefs in their own language. Despite the fact that Meroitic still presents scholars with some difficulties in decipherment, some of the main deities can be identified. Many Egyptian gods continued to be worshiped in Nubia, but the following deities appear to be more distinctly Nubian.

Apedemak is the Nubian god of war in leonine form. He may be represented in art as a striding lion wearing an elaborate crown based on Egyptian models, as well as a composite beast with lion's head, a male torso with arms and hands, and a very long, sinuous serpent's body from the waist down, which emerges from a floral bud. He is paired with a consort, but she remains nameless.

Mandulis, celebrated in the Temple of Kalabsha, had solar associations and was paired with his twin, Breith. The divine brothers were often depicted as human-headed falcons.

Sebiumeker, whose name in Meroitic appears to mean "lord of Musawwarat" and who has been identified as a creator god, is known only from images and inscriptions on the Temple of Apedemak at Musawwarat es-Shufra; he does not appear to be a principal deity in another sanctuary elsewhere in Nubia. Sebiumeker may be depicted in human form, wearing a bulging variation of the Egyptian double crown fronted by a uraeus. The attempt to identify an unfinished statue as Sebiumeker with an elephant's trunk has now been dismissed because the putative trunk is in fact the rudimentary form of what was intended to be a false beard.

~Robert S. Bianchi

FOR MORE INFORMATION

Adams, W. *Nubia: Corridor to Africa*. Princeton, N.J.: Princeton University Press, 1977.

O'Connor, D. *Ancient Nubia: Egypt's Rival in Africa*. Philadelphia: University of Pennsylvania, 1993.

Trigger, B. *Nubia under the Pharaohs*. Boulder, Colo.: Westview Press, 1976.

Welsby, D. A. *The Kingdom of Kush: The Napatan and Meroitic Empires*. London: British Museum Press, 1996.

RELIGIOUS LIFE

|

RELIGIOUS BELIEFS

|

Mesopotamia

Egypt

Greece

Rome

India

Nubia

Australian Aboriginals

AUSTRALIAN ABORIGINALS

Many common aspects of other religions were not part of the religious life of Aboriginal Australia. There were no religious buildings, religious hierarchy, or true priests. Animals were not worshiped, nor was religion aimed really at improving hunting, although there were increase ceremonies. The Aboriginal view of the universe was that humans were a part of all life, related to all other forms of life, and that all beings had a place in the universe and a right to exist.

They also viewed human life spans as just a small part of the infinite time during which the universe, the "Dreaming," had existed, and would continue to exist. At birth, human spirits emerged from the spirit world of the Dreaming, and they returned into it at death. Because of these beliefs, there was no conventional sense of history, but rather, history extended no further than the three or four generations represented by oneself, one's parents, one's grandparents, and one's children. The short lives of all these generations had emerged temporarily from the spirit world, and the spirits of all these people would return to it again, only to reemerge in other people in an endless recycling.

Aborigines believed that the ancestor spirits, which combined characteristics of humans and animals, lived in the infinite past, creating the world and all its features, and that they returned to the land at particular places of great power. Spirits were thought to come to babies from powerful places in the land, and the spirits of the dead returned to their origins in the land. Many Aboriginal religious practices are designed to ensure that the places of great power associated with life and death and the homes of the ancestors are correctly managed through ceremony and behavior. If mistakes were made, observances not carried out, or sacred places trespassed upon or damaged, then great evil could come to the community concerned. This great power, residing in the land itself, is a fundamental aspect of Aboriginal concern for sacred sites. People come from the land and return to it, so that without the land, this cycle cannot continue. The central interweaving of human destiny with land gives Aboriginal Australians extraordinarily close links to the land.

Although there were no priests, senior men in the community were recognized as having a better knowledge of the Dreaming. There was often a two-stage initiation process for young boys, first when they became adult men, and later when they began to learn religious secrets.

Correct observance of ritual was important to maintaining the health not only of a community as a whole but of individuals within the community. Sickness was believed to have an external cause, which could be identified and removed from the body. A class of elders known as the healers had particular powers to carry out such work, and they constituted the only real specialized occupation.

Responsibilities for particular species and places were spread out across the community; consequently, different people had the responsibility of organizing various ceremonies to keep everything running smoothly and to benefit all of the species in the environment, not just ones used as food sources. There were prohibitions on specific groups within a community against hunting or eating particular species, or hunting in certain places. These prohibitions were aimed at ensuring that species were protected from overexploitation.

Although there was some variation across Australia in terms of the particular form that religious beliefs took, these differences fell within a very coherent overall framework. No one conceived of imposing his or her particular set of beliefs about how the world worked—and what one needed to do to keep it working—on people from another group.

To read about religion in the early British colony in Australia, see the Australia entry in the section "Religious Practices" in chapter 8 ("Religious Life") of volume 4 (*Seventeenth and Eighteenth Centuries*) of this series.

~David Horton

FOR MORE INFORMATION

Berndt, R., and C. Berndt. *The World of the First Australians*. Canberra: Aboriginal Studies Press, 1988.

Charlesworth, M., H. Morphy, D. Bell, and K. Maddock. *Religion in Aboriginal Australia*. St. Lucia, Queensland: University of Queensland Press, 1984.

Horton, D., ed. *The Encyclopedia of Aboriginal Australia*. Canberra: Aboriginal Studies Press, 2001.

Stanner, W. *On Aboriginal Religion*. Oceania Monographs 36. Sydney: University of Sydney, 1989.

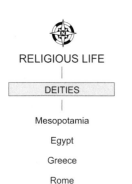

RELIGIOUS LIFE
|
DEITIES
|
Mesopotamia

Egypt

Greece

Rome

Deities

The dominant religions of the ancient world were all polytheistic, meaning that there were multiple gods, and in each culture a rich mythology developed around the numerous gods, demigods, and spirits that these cultures believed inhabited the world around them.

Despite the nearly infinite variety of gods, there were a number of similarities in the pantheon of gods created by each civilization. Most of the gods were imagined as being basically human in form, although they were often larger or more beautiful than ordinary mortals. In Egypt, many of the gods were zoomorphic and were depicted as having the bodies of humans but the heads of various animals, such as Anubis, who had the head of a jackal, or Horus, who is depicted with a falcon head.

The gods were not all the same in abilities or powers, but each typically had a geographic region or craft or concept that they were in charge of or particularly concerned with. To take some of the Greek gods as an example, Poseidon was god of the sea, Hephaestus was god of blacksmithing, and Ares was the god of warfare. Very specific geographic features were identified with a god, such as Hapi, the Egyptian god of the Nile, and in Greece even individual trees could be paired with minor gods, called tree nymphs. The abstract as well as the concrete could be deified, as with the Roman goddess of luck, Fortuna.

The gods were not united in their opinions or goals. There was frequent conflict, and even warfare, among them. In some mythologies, such as Mesopotamian, the gods could even kill one another and so were not necessarily immortal. Similarly, in Greek myth, there were several successive generations of gods who each violently supplanted the ones who had come before them. A central myth in Egyptian religion involved the struggle between the feuding siblings Osiris and Set.

The different civilizations each came up with gods for many of the same things or concepts. Every culture conceived of the sun as a deity: Utu in Mesopotamia, Ra in Egypt, Helios in Greece, and Apollo in Rome. Likewise, there was always a deity in charge of the dead or the underworld: Nergal in Mesopotamia, Osiris in Egypt, Hades in Greece, and Pluto in Rome. Gods or goddesses associated with the moon, sky, love, wisdom, arts, water, wind, agriculture, health, and war existed in all these cultures.

The gods of the ancient world usually took an active, if not always positive, role in human affairs. They brought blessings, but they could also be capricious and cruel. Human beings want to believe that things happen for a reason, and in a world filled with so much mystery and unpredictability, where there were no scientific explanations for what caused such things as illness, rain, or the rising and setting of the sun, it is not surprising that they would create a complex pantheon of actively interventionist gods in the attempt to bring some order and reason to their world.

~*Gregory S. Aldrete*

MESOPOTAMIA

The Mesopotamian gods were named in a canonical list (ca. third millennium B.C.E.), which contained almost 2,000 entries. Most of the listed gods have Sumerian names. But as a result of political events, the gods gained Semitic characteristics. The number of gods increased in the Neo-Sumerian period; the Sumerians themselves estimated that there were 3,600 (60 times 60) gods. The gods' list outlined the basic structure of the pantheon. Anu, the sky god, originally was chief god of the pantheon. Later, some of his attributes were assigned to Enlil and later to Marduk in Babylonia and Assur in Assyria.

The strongest divine personalities appealed most to worshipers, and these gods absorbed the powers of the minor gods. For example, Inanna, whom the Semites equated with Ishtar, was the goddess of love. Later, she absorbed the powers of a number of goddesses, such as the divinity of the planet Venus and the goddess of war. By the time the Mesopotamian Empire came to an end, there were about 30 major gods. Just as a human leader administered power through members of his own family and other subordinates, so the chief god in a local pantheon was envisioned as surrounded by members of his family, ministers, and servants. There was a patron deity for every profession and activity, such as a god of brick making and a god of brewing. Many local pantheons developed.

From the third millennium B.C.E. onward, An (Akkadian, Anum) was the head of the pantheon. His name meant "sky," and he was the god of the sky. All things on heaven and earth conformed to his will. As the ultimate source of all authority, An was associated with the highest authority on earth, the king, whom he designated as ruler.

According to the official pantheon, the great god list called An-Anum, An's female consort was Antum, a female derivative of An. From her breasts, the clouds brought forth her milk, the rain. Ki, "earth," was sometimes designated as An's consort as well. He impregnated her with his sperm, the rain, and she gave birth to trees, reeds, and all other vegetation.

> *Inanna was the goddess of love and sexuality, and patron of the prostitute and the tavern.*

Enlil, "lord wind," played an active role in human affairs, initially as the national god of Sumer. Enlil originally held the Tablets of Destiny, on which the fates of men and gods were decreed. Later, his role was assumed by Marduk. Enlil was the moist wind of spring and the creator of the hoe, the farmer's most versatile tool. Enlil displayed a two-sided nature, as the benign wind of spring and also as the destructive storm. His consort was the grain goddess Ninlil, "lady wind," whom, according to one myth, he raped. A tribunal of gods found him guilty, and Enlil went to the netherworld, where Ninlil followed him and bore a number of underworld deities.

Ninkhursaga was ranked number three, after An and Enlil. Her name means "lady of the stony ground" or "lady of the foothills"; originally, she was the numinous power in the alluvial stony ground, in the east at the foothills near the Iranian mountains and in the west at the stony Arabian desert. She was the goddess of birth for pregnant animals, providing shelter for them in the hut, fold, or pen. She also acted as midwife to the gods.

Enki (Akkadian, Ea) was the god of the fresh waters and a benefactor to humankind. He was the source of all secret magical knowledge. At the beginning of the second millennium B.C.E., he replaced Ninkhursaga in the ruling trio—reflecting the increasingly male-dominated society of the times. Enki was known for his cleverness—he usually prevailed in conflicts with other gods by using his brains. His name means "productive manager of the soil," and in this capacity he provided the irrigation waters for much of southern Mesopotamia. When water moistened clay, the material produced would be molded into a variety of shapes. Enki was also named "image fashioner," and in this role he was the patron god of artists and craftsmen such as potters, bronze casters, stonecutters, jewelers, seal cutters, and so on. Enki also had the power to purify and cleanse mortals. In an omen series called "The Bathhouse," Enki supervised the purification of the king from the evils of a lunar eclipse.

The older generation of gods represented the major elements of the universe: the sky, winds, foothills, and underground water.

The younger generations of gods, the grandchildren and great-grandchildren of An, represented the moon, the sun, the morning and evening star, the thunder cloud, and the rainstorm.

Nanna (Akkadian, Sin) was the full moon, the crescents, and the new moon.

Ninurta, "Lord Plow," represented the humid thunderstorm of spring, which made the soil easy to plow. He was depicted as a hybrid creature, a huge lion-headed eagle, gliding with its wings extended and thunder roaring from its mouth. A series of myths about Ninurta describes the hydraulic cycle of the waters.

Utu (Akkadian, Shamash), whose Sumerian and Akkadian names mean "sun," was entrusted with the responsibility of dispensing justice to both gods and men. Utu was placed to guard the boundaries "for heaven and earth." Thus, the universe became subject to one law and one judge—everybody and everything in existence could be brought to justice. This concept gave rise to the "just war," that is, doing battle with wrongdoers.

Inanna (Akkadian, Ishtar) was the sister of Utu. She embodied the roles of different goddesses. By the second millennium B.C.E., Ishtar became the best-known and most widely worshiped Babylonian deity, and the name Ishtar came to be the generic word for "goddess." According to various myths, Inanna was the goddess of the date storehouse, the goddess of shepherds, and the power behind the thundershowers of spring. Inanna was the Morning Star and Evening Star. As the Morning Star, she marked the awakening of man and beast. As the Evening Star, she designated the end of the day's work for men and animals. She was also the goddess of love and sexuality, as well as patron goddess of the prostitute and the tavern.

The netherworld was governed by a king, Nergal, and a queen, Ereshkigal. Their administrative staffs included, among others, minister to the queen, Namtar (literally, fate), the judges, Utu and Gilgamesh, and the gatekeeper Neti.

In Mesopotamian theology, the gods never aged or died of natural causes. They could, however, die a violent death, such as younger gods killing older gods in a struggle for succession, defeated rebel gods being punished by death, or in monster slaying.

The image of the god was central to the official religion of ancient Mesopotamia. The god was believed to be present in his or her statue. When the image of the deity was carried off in war, that god remained absent until his statue was returned. The importance of these statues has been shown by the wide distribution of cheap, clay replicas as well as statues of minor gods. In fact, a son could inherit his father's "gods." Creating a divine image was a solemn ceremonial task for the temple workshops. The statues were made and repaired in special workshops. Most temple images were fashioned from precious wood. Small decorative ornaments of gold or silver were sewn onto the clothing of the gods. Pectorals and a horned crown were added to complete the god's outfit. The clothing was changed according to ritual and ceremonial requirements. Some images were seated, evidenced by mentions of their thrones.

As early as the third millennium B.C.E., the images also underwent various rituals to sanctify them in special ways. The most elaborate ritual, the "washing of the mouth," was performed at night and accompanied by an appeal to the stars. The animation of the divine statue required several stages: mouth washing conducted in the workshop; carrying the statue in a procession to the river bank, where a second mouth washing took place; and placing the statue facing west, then facing east, and making offerings to numerous gods, planets, certain fixed stars and constellations, and finally all the stars. The role of the astral deities in the ritual was to irradiate the wooden statue, which was adorned with precious metals and stones. Also, a secret ritual of consecration was performed to endow the gods with "life" by opening their eyes and mouths to see and eat.

The divine statues were then placed on a pedestal in the inner sanctuary. Here the gods "lived" with their families and were served by a staff of minor gods who, in turn, supervised human workers such as divine musicians, handmaidens, a counselor, and a secretary who screened cases submitted to him for decision. The divine statues accumulated wealth through dedications of clothing, jewelry, and paraphernalia.

The gods of Mesopotamia were identified by their symbols or standards, horned crowns, and garments of gold. The symbols sometimes replaced or accompanied the traditional statues. If the statue was carried off or destroyed by the enemy, the symbols could substitute for the statue in all its ritual functions. Specific animals were associated with certain gods and often became their symbols, such as the dog for the goddess of healing, Gula, the lion-snake-eagle for Marduk, and the goat-fish for Ea. The symbols retained their associations for more than three millennia (Nemet-Nejat, 182–86).

FOR MORE INFORMATION

Black, J., and A. Green. *Gods, Demons, and Symbols of Ancient Mesopotamia: An Illustrated Dictionary*. Austin: University of Texas Press, 1992.

Nemet-Nejat, K. R. *Daily Life in Ancient Mesopotamia*. Westport, Conn.: Greenwood Press, 1998.

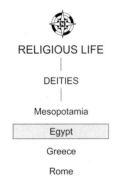

RELIGIOUS LIFE
|
DEITIES
|
Mesopotamia

Egypt

Greece

Rome

EGYPT

Ancient Egyptian religion was polytheistic, with hundreds of gods. Although some were human in form and distinguished by attributes such as their headdress, the majority were zoomorphic; they took the form of an animal, considered to be the god's soul, and were often portrayed as humans with animal heads. The Egyptians venerated these animals, showing them respect in life and frequently mummifying them after death and interring them in large necropolises (graveyards); it is probable that initially particular animals were designated as the sacred ones but that this veneration gradually extended to include entire species. In particular, many mummies of crocodiles, cats, ibises, and bulls have been discovered. The scarab beetle was identified with the sun god because of its habit of rolling its egg in a ball of dung in front of itself, reminiscent of the sun's daily progress across the sky. The divine Apis bull (believed to be the animal form of either Osiris or sometimes Ptah) was thought to be incarnated as a living animal, which was worshiped during its life and, after death, mummified and enshrined in the Serapeum, an underground burial complex.

Different localities had their own primary deity who was considered most powerful, and the god recognized as the head of the Egyptian pantheon changed on multiple occasions over time. This might have been linked to political shifts, when the capital changed location or when a new pharaoh favored a different god. For example, the god Ptah was most powerful when the capital was at Memphis (during the Old Kingdom), but when it later relocated to Thebes (during the Middle Kingdom), Amun became the head of the gods. The accession of the pharaoh Akhenaton even led to the adoption of a new type of worship and abandonment of traditional religion, which was eventually reinstated as the official one after his death. Also, gods often became associated and identified with one another, leading to hyphenated names and compound identities. For example, the two solar gods Ra and Horus combined in the form of Ra-Harakhty, Horus of the Horizon. The god Amun also became identified with Ra, forming the compound deity Amun-Ra.

Just as there was not one consistent ruler deity, there existed more than one creation myth, which arose at different locations. One popular myth originated at the city of Heliopolis. At first there was only an ocean of formless chaos, Nun; but there had always existed in this chaos a conscious element, the god Atum (meaning "the whole" or "the complete"), who managed to fertilize himself and engender the divinities Shu (god of the air) and Tefnut (goddess of atmospheric moisture or rain). In turn, this pair gave birth to Geb (the earth god) and Nut (the sky goddess), another sister-brother couple who gave birth to the gods Osiris, Isis, Set, and Nephthys (the first two and the latter two pairing off as couples). Shu intervened,

raising Nut, the sky, off of her partner, the earth, and becoming the atmosphere circulating between them. Thus Nut is represented in art as a woman with hands and feet resting on the earth and body arched to form the vault of the sky, while Geb reclines beneath her and Shu stands between them, supporting her.

The gods involved in this myth number nine and therefore comprise a divine ennead (group of nine). Another number with sacred overtones was three, derived from the notion of a family

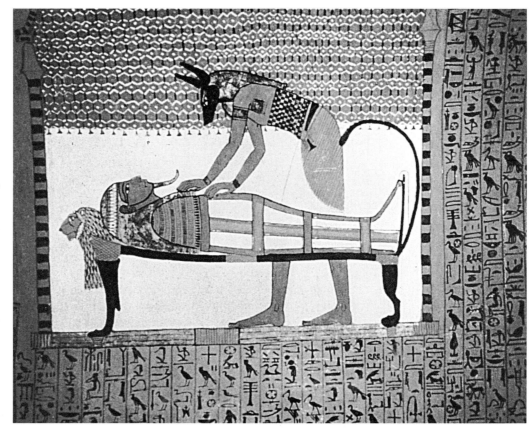

Painting of Anubis, the jackal-headed god of the underworld, embalming a mummy.

consisting of two parents and a child. Deities tended to be grouped in divine triads, like holy families. The prime example of this is the family group of Osiris, Isis, and their child Horus. Sculptures of Isis as divine mother holding her son on her lap evoke later portrayals of Mary with the baby Jesus. When Amun became the head god, not much mythology surrounded him, so he was assigned a wife (Mut, meaning "mother") and a son (Khons, a moon god) to form a divine triad.

The creation myth originating in Memphis identified the god Ptah, who existed in Nun before anything else, as creator of the universe. Through the actions of thinking and speaking, he brought into being all the other gods, humans, animals, plants, and everything else that exists. Thus a divine word was responsible for the act of creation.

> *A divine word was responsible for the act of creation.*

In another account, a cosmic egg takes the place of the primeval ocean as the starting point of life. Either a goose (known as the "Great Cackler") or an Ibis (exemplifying the god Thoth) laid the egg, or else it was made by the gods Ptah and Khnum. Another story states that the potter god Khnum first formed human beings on his potter's wheel. These are only a few of the various creation myths that arose in ancient Egypt.

The following is a list of the major Egyptian gods:

Amun—became main god during the 11th Dynasty; always shown as a man with a headdress of ostrich plumes; the ram and the goose were his sacred animals

Anubis—early jackal-headed (or jackal) god of the dead responsible for mummifying Osiris's body; developed into the embalmer of all the dead and became patron of embalmers

Bastet—cat or cat-headed goddess of fire, known as "Little Cat" in contrast to Sekhmet

Bes—god of music and pleasure; protector of children; represented as a bowlegged dwarf

Geb—earth god; husband of Nut, the sky

Hapi—androgynous god of the Nile, depicted with breasts to suggest the Nile's fertility

Hathor—goddess of love, beauty, music, and dancing, and a protector of infants; portrayed as a cow or woman with headdress of horns encircling the sun

Horus—falcon or falcon-headed man; son of Isis and Osiris, he tried to avenge his father's death by fighting his uncle Set; the gods decided their dispute, declaring Horus the King of the Living and labeling Set "the Evil One" and banishing him

Imhotep—originally a man, chief minister to the pharaoh Zoser and inventor of the step pyramid, who was deified during the Greco-Roman period; patron of science and medicine

Isis—sister and wife of Osiris; divine mother of Horus; skilled at magic; reassembled and revived her husband's dismembered body, after which he became king of the dead (and sired Horus posthumously)

Khnum—ram or ram-headed potter god, said in some myths to have created the universe

Maat—goddess of truth, justice, and both the divine order of the universe and the social and moral order governing humankind; shown as a feather or a woman wearing a feather on her head; took part in the ceremony of the weighing of the heart before Osiris, which would determine a dead person's fate in the afterlife

Min—god of virility and fertility, depicted with an erection

Nephthys—sister and wife of Set

Nut—goddess of the sky; wife of Geb, the earth god

Osiris—god of the dead, vegetation, and the flood; ruler of the kingdom of the dead; depicted as a mummified king

Ptah—creator of the universe

Ra (or **Re**)—sun god, represented as sun or falcon with sun headdress; usually shown crossing the sky in his solar barque, which represented the sun's movement across the sky

Sekhmet—lioness-headed goddess of fire, known as "Great Cat," in contrast to Bastet; wife of Ptah and mother of Nefertum and Imhotep

Set—brother of Isis and Osiris, whose jealousy drove him to kill and chop up Osiris

Sobek—crocodile god; a form of Set worshiped especially in the Fayoum region

Tauret—hippopotamus goddess of fertility, who watched over women during pregnancy and childbirth

Thoth—Ibis-headed patron of writing, learning, and the sciences, and god of the moon; also portrayed as a dog-faced baboon; invented writing and was scribe to the gods

A crucial myth in Egyptian religion, which helps to explain their funerary customs and ideas about death, involved the fate of the god Osiris and his family: his sister and wife, Isis; his brother, Set; and his son, Horus. Osiris was initially ruler of Egypt, much beloved by his subjects for his goodness and wisdom. He taught human beings about agriculture, the arts, and other life-improving knowledge. As a result, Set became jealous and decided to murder his brother. He built a chest specifically tailored to Osiris's measurements and at a party offered it to whomever best fit inside it. When Osiris tried it out, Set slammed the chest shut (obviously the prototype for a mummy case) and threw it into the Nile. Isis caused the chest to be sought and found, but then Set again interfered, dismembering Osiris's body and scattering the pieces throughout Egypt. The grieving widow Isis tirelessly searched for the pieces and then reassembled them (all except for the penis, which had been swallowed by a fish). With the help of other gods (in some versions, Thoth; in others, Anubis and Nephthys, Set's sister/wife), Isis managed to make the first mummy and through magic resurrected her husband and conceived a son, Horus. Osiris then went to the land of the dead to reign as its king. Isis in the meantime raised Horus in secret to keep him safe from Set. The son's goal was to avenge his father, and he engaged in a violent fight with his uncle in which both were grievously wounded; Set stole one of Horus's eyes, sometimes said to be the sun. The rest of the gods held court to settle this bitter feud and ultimately decided in favor of Horus and Osiris. Because Osiris had assumed the role of king of the underworld and judge of the dead, Horus took over his father's former role as king of the living. He gave his restored eye to his father and replaced it with the uraeus, a divine snake. Set, now called "the Evil One," was exiled.

This myth served an important function in offering a rationale for the nature of both the pharaoh and the afterlife. Osiris and Horus act out the transfer of power from a dying pharaoh to his son; the pharaoh was seen as the living incarnation of Horus during his life, and upon his death, he became the incarnation of Osiris. The connection of this myth to the kingship is indicated by the fact that the uraeus (the cobra substituted for Horus's eye) was symbolic of royalty, even appearing on the pharaoh's headdress. Therefore, it made sense that the pharaoh should receive the same funeral rites as Osiris; so he was also mummified in the belief that he would as a result be resurrected. Over time, the burial practices initially reserved for the pharaoh spread downward through society, with the expectation that following these rites and thus preserving one's body would allow all people to imitate Osiris's revival in the afterlife.

~*Gregory S. Aldrete*

FOR MORE INFORMATION

Morenz, S. *Egyptian Religion*. Translated by A. Keep. London: Methuen, 1973.

Watterson, B. *The Gods of Ancient Egypt*. London: B. T. Batsford, 1984.

GREECE

The Greeks worshiped a pantheon consisting of Zeus and 11 other deities who were thought to inhabit the peaks of Olympus, a mountain in central Greece perpetually shrouded in cloud. The 11 were all siblings or offspring of Zeus. The Olympian gods were not, however, identical everywhere in the Greek world, nor indeed were they held in equal honor. In addition, some major gods, such as Aesculapius, the god of healing, never joined their ranks. Arrogant, fickle, cruel, and treacherous, the Olympians have been aptly described as superhuman in power and subhuman in morality. Neither good nor evil in themselves, they were a combination of both.

The difference between the Olympian deities and, in particular, the Christian God could hardly be more extreme. The Olympians cared little for the great mass of humankind, with whom their relations were for the most part distant and somewhat strained. Although the gods were anthropomorphic—having the same physical shape as human beings—in origin they embodied aspects of the natural world and the human psyche. Apart from Hera, the first generation of Olympians—Zeus, Poseidon, Demeter, Hestia, and Hades—all personified natural forces, whereas the second generation—Hephaestus, Athena, Ares, Apollo, Artemis, Hermes, and Aphrodite—were representative of human accomplishments or attributes.

The Olympians did not create the world. They were not the first dynasty of gods to rule over it, nor was there any guarantee that they would go on ruling it forever. Cronus, who came to power by castrating his father, Uranus, sought to preserve his rule by swallowing his children alive. Likewise, his son Zeus, who acquired power by overthrowing his father in turn, took active steps to circumvent the prophecy that he would sire a son more powerful than himself. The following paragraphs describe the major deities and their spheres of influence.

Although Zeus, "the father of gods and men" as Homer describes him, was supreme among the Olympians, his authority did not go unchallenged. Hera, his current wife, constantly sought to thwart his will. (Hesiod tells us that he had been married seven times previously.) Zeus alone of the gods was sometimes thought to be concerned with justice, although he was far from consistent in his pursuit of that aim. Moreover, his own behavior fell lamentably short of setting a standard of morality for human beings. His sexual appetite was insatiable, and later tradition credits him with having adulterous relations with no fewer than 115 women, both mortal and immortal. In many cases, Zeus adopted a disguise, perhaps to try, unsuccessfully for the most part, to evade the watchful eyes of Hera and to deceive the women he pursued. He turned into a bull to pursue Europa, a shower of gold to seduce Danaë, and a swan to entice Leda.

There were more aspects to Zeus than to any other deity. He was the god of rain, hospitality, justice, and persuasion. There was even a Zeus who was the averter of flies. Although in theory above Fate, Zeus nonetheless followed its dictates. A notable demonstration takes place in the *Iliad* when, on the advice of Hera, Zeus reluctantly decides not to save his son Sarpedon from his predestined death. Zeus's weapon was the thunderbolt, which he wielded with deadly effect against perjurers.

The greatest temple built in his honor was located at Olympia, where the Olympic Games were celebrated every four years. The statue of the seated god in the temple, which was made by the Athenian sculptor Phidias, was regarded as one of the seven wonders of the world. Zeus's largest temple was erected in Athens. Begun circa 520 B.C.E., it took about 650 years to complete.

Hera, Zeus's wife and eldest sister, was the guardian of marriage and queen of Olympos. Her symbol was the peacock, the eyes of whose tail feathers were believed to be the eyes of Argos, her hundred-eyed spy. In the *Iliad*, Homer depicts Hera as a nagging wife, ever suspicious that her husband is conniving behind her back but fully capable of paying him back. Of course, she had good reason to be suspicious of his philandering. Hera's temple at Olympia was older than that of Zeus, which has suggested to some scholars that her worship on the Greek mainland predated that of Zeus. Another venerable shrine in her honor was erected at Argos. There was no significant temple in Athens dedicated to her.

Poseidon, Zeus's brother, was god of the sea. His symbol was the trident, which he used to spear fish and stir up tempests. By taking the form of a colossal bull, he became the Earthshaker, capable of making the earth rumble and quake. It was Poseidon's animosity, aroused by the blinding of his son the Cyclops Polyphemus, that caused the detention of Odysseus on the island of Kalypso for seven years. Poseidon was defeated by Athena in the contest for the guardianship of Athens. His gift to Athens was a saltwater spring that he miraculously caused to spurt up out of the Acropolis.

Aphrodite was the goddess of love and beauty. The scene of her being awarded the golden apple in the divine beauty contest by the Trojan prince Paris is one of the most popular mythological subjects in Western art. Aphrodite won the contest over her rivals Hera and Athena by promising to bestow upon the judge the most beautiful woman in the world. This promise directly caused the Trojan War since Helen, the woman in question, was married and Greek. According to Hesiod, Aphrodite was born from the semen of Uranus' castrated genitals, which his son Cronus threw into the sea. Homer, however, makes her the daughter of Zeus and Dione. According to some accounts, she was the mother of Eros, the winged boy who shoots arrows of desire into humans and gods.

Phoebus Apollo was the god of such varied things as music, healing, plague, purification, and sunlight. In wartime, he carried a bow, in peace a lyre. It was he who sent a plague upon the Greek army encamped outside the walls of Troy in response to a prayer from his insulted priest at the beginning of Homer's *Iliad*. He also afflicted Thebes with plague when its people unknowingly harbored the parricide Oedipus. Apollo's two foremost sanctuaries were located on the tiny island of Delos, where he was born, and at Delphi, where he established his oracle. In art, he is depicted as a beautiful youth eternally poised on the threshold between adolescence and manhood. Despite his good looks, Apollo was consistently unlucky in love, often choosing partners who resisted his advances. One was Daphne, who prayed to Zeus to preserve her virginity and was transformed into a laurel tree in consequence. Apollo is often regarded as the incarnation of the Hellenic spirit and embodiment of spiritual and intellectual enlightenment. This simplistic view ignores the darker side of his personality as the god of plague and unrequited love.

Artemis, Apollo's twin sister, was both virgin huntress and protectress of wild animals. She was also identified with the moon. When the hunter Actaeon inadvertently observed her bathing, the goddess turned him into a stag and set his own dogs upon him. Artemis's temple at Ephesus on the coast of Asia Minor was one of the Seven Wonders of the World.

Athena, the daughter of Zeus and Metis, was born from her father's head when he was struck by Hephaestus's hammer during a quarrel. She emerged fully adult and dressed as a warrior. She was the goddess of women's crafts and of defensive war. She became the patron deity of Athens by causing an olive tree to spring up on the Acropolis. This was symbolic of the fact that Athens's economic prosperity was based on the olive. The most sublime of all Greek temples, the Parthenon, which dominates the Acropolis, was dedicated to Athena in her capacity as a virgin or *parthenos*. It contained a statue sculpted by Phidias that was more than 36 feet high and covered in gold and ivory.

Reconstruction of the cult statue of the goddess Athena inside the Parthenon. The winged figure in her hand is a personification of victory. The original wood, gold, and ivory statue stood 40 feet tall. © The Art Archive/National Archaeological Museum Athens/Dagli Orti.

Hades, the brother of Zeus, was the god of the underworld. Together with his wife, Persephone, whom he kidnapped and raped, he ruled over the dead.

Demeter was the goddess of vegetation and the harvest. Her grief for her lost daughter Persephone, who was abducted by Hades to be his bride, was believed to cause the "death" of the vegetative cycle in winter. Conversely, her yearly reunion with Persephone was thought to usher in the spring. In the outpouring of her grief for her daughter, we see her touched by genuine emotion to a greater degree than any other Olympian deity. Demeter played a prominent part in rituals pertaining to death and the afterlife, notably the Eleusinian Mysteries, which were celebrated at Eleusis in Attica. These mysteries were open to all Greek speakers, men as well as women, slave as well as freeman.

Dionysos, the son of Zeus and Semele, was the god of wine, fertility, nature in the raw, liberation, irrationality, and drama. Semele was incinerated when Zeus manifested himself to her in his full glory as a thunderbolt. The god managed to rescue the embryo, which he sewed into his thigh. In due course, he gave birth to his infant. According to another myth, Dionysos was killed and eaten by the Titans, who were subsequently destroyed by Zeus's thunderbolt. Out of their ashes arose the human race, part human and part divine. Dionysos was a latecomer to Olympos. His origins seem to lie in Thrace, although he is also connected with Asia Minor. His entry into Greece, and the opposition that he had to overcome, is the subject of Euripides' *Bacchai*.

Hephaestus, the god of the forge, was the patron god of metalworkers. Being lame, he was the only deity who was not physically perfect. According to one version of his birth, his mother, Hera, bore him by parthenogenesis to spite Zeus. Oddly, he was married to the beautiful Aphrodite, who considered Ares a more agreeable partner. In the *Odyssey*, we learn that when the pair began an adulterous affair,

Hephaestus fashioned a miraculous net that locked them in an inextricable embrace. He then invited all the gods to come and witness the spectacle. An important temple to Hephaestus overlooked the Agora in Athens. In its vicinity, much evidence of bronze working has been found.

Hermes, the son of Zeus and Maia, was the god of trade, commerce, and thieves. He also served as messenger of the gods and guide of the dead to the underworld. For this reason, he is usually depicted wearing a traveling hat and winged sandals and carrying a herald's staff known as a *kêrykeion*. Statues of the god in the form of an upright pillar with sculpted head and erect phallus stood at street corners throughout Athens. These figures, known as herms, safeguarded gates and doorways.

Ares, the god of war, was the son of Zeus and Hera. Despite his importance, he was little venerated by the Greeks, perhaps because of his bloodthirsty nature. Even in the *Iliad* he is treated with scant respect. When he is wounded and comes sniveling to Zeus, the latter describes him as a two-faced liar and sends him packing (5.889f.). Ares received little attention in Athens despite the fact that the most venerable council, known as the Areopagus or Hill of Ares, bore his name.

Hestia, guardian of the Olympian hearth, was the most neglected of the Olympian deities. She features in no myths, and no temples were erected in her honor. Both the family hearth and the hearth that symbolized the city were sacred to her.

Other important gods who did not reside on Olympus include Pan and Aesculapius, both of whom gained entry into Athens in the fifth century B.C.E. Pan, who resembled a goat from the waist down, personified the natural world. He was worshiped in caves throughout Attica, the most prominent of which was situated on the north side of the Acropolis. The seven-reed syrinx or panpipe was his invention. He was capable of causing panic both in individuals and in armies. His cult was officially introduced to Athens after the Battle of Marathon in 490 B.C.E. The healing god Aesculapius, who began his life as a hero, was later awarded divine status. His shrine at Epidaurus in the northeast Peloponnese was the foremost healing sanctuary in the Greek world. There were also a number of minor deities who were believed to reside in streams, rivers, and lakes (naiads), on mountains (oreads), and in trees (dryads).

All the deities discussed so far dwelt in the sky, on the earth, or underwater. There was, however, another powerful group of divine beings, thought to reside underground. They are called chthonic deities, after the Greek word *chthôn*, meaning "earth." Chthonic deities were worshiped in caves and subterranean passages. We know much less about them because they have left little trace on the archaeological record. In addition, few Greek writers make reference to them. There can be no doubt, however, that chthonic deities constituted an important aspect of Greek religion, even though the state did not expend much money on their worship. Many individuals privately carried out rituals to appease their anger or invoke their assistance. They were believed to exert a profound influence on human affairs, notably in regard to fertility and food production. They were also invoked to bring evil and destruction upon one's enemy. The most persistent motif of chthonic religion is the snake because snakes were thought to be generated spontaneously inside the earth.

Whereas the Olympian deities, except for the lame metalworking god Hephaestus, were physically perfect, chthonic deities tended to be loathsome and repulsive. At the opening of the *Eumenides*, the third play in Aeschylus's *Oresteia*, chthonic deities known as the Furies, who pursue Orestes to Delphi for the crime of murdering his mother, are described as follows: "They are women—no, not women but Gorgons rather. And yet they are not quite Gorgons either. . . . They are wingless, black and they snore. Evil puss oozes from their eyes" (lines 48–54). Later, Apollo orders them from his sanctuary with the following menacing words: "Go to where heads are chopped off and eyes gouged out, to justice and slaughterings, to destruction of seed and of young men's pride, to mutilations and stonings, and to the lamentations of people being impaled" (lines 186–90).

Minor deities were believed to safeguard the security and prosperity of the home. Chief among these were Zeus Ktesios, or Zeus in his capacity as protector of property; Zeus Herkeios, or Zeus in his capacity as protector of boundaries; and Apollo Patroös, or Apollo in his capacity as divine ancestor of the Athenian race. In addition, each home possessed a hearth that was sacred to the goddess Hestia. Worship at these shrines, supervised by the head of the household, probably took place on a daily basis. Because the welfare of the entire household was placed under the protection of these gods, slaves as well as those who were free were required to participate.

Mainstream Greek religion offered a wide choice of deities from which individuals were free to choose on the basis of a variety of criteria. These included family tradition, social status, personal preference, and ease of access to the deity's shrine. The fortunes of individual deities ebbed and flowed, according to need. Cults came and went, and in extreme cases sanctuaries were leased out to new gods—or sold altogether. A new cult was accepted into the city's pantheon typically when the Greeks won a spectacular military victory, experienced a natural disaster such as drought, famine, or plague, or redefined their social and political identity. In other words, war, catastrophe, and social or political unrest were the main catalysts of change within a system of belief that was constantly in flux (Garland, 131–41).

FOR MORE INFORMATION

Adkins, L., and R. Adkins. *Handbook to Life in Ancient Greece*. Oxford: Oxford University Press, 1997.

Burkert, W. *Greek Religion*. Oxford: Basil Blackwell, 1985.

Garland, R. *Daily Life of the Ancient Greeks*. Westport, Conn.: Greenwood Press, 1998.

Graf, F. *Greek Mythology: An Introduction*. Translated by T. Marier. Baltimore, Md.: Johns Hopkins University Press, 1993.

RELIGIOUS LIFE

|

DEITIES

|

Mesopotamia

Egypt

Greece

Rome

ROME

There were hundreds, perhaps thousands, of divinities that were worshiped in Roman polytheism. Further adding to the complexity of Roman religion was the fact that there were different types of gods whose powers, inclinations, and areas of influence varied greatly. The state religion was based on worship of a subset of all these gods who were thought to be particularly concerned with the success and preservation of the Roman state, but individuals could choose any selection of gods to pay homage to.

The most prominent of the Roman gods were what might be termed the Olympian gods. These were the set of deities derived from the Greek gods said to live on Mount Olympus and included Jupiter, Juno, Mars, Venus, Neptune, Apollo, Diana, Ceres, Bacchus, Mercury, Miverva, Vesta, and Vulcan. The most important of these for the Romans were Jupiter, the king of the gods, and Mars, the god of war, who were thought to be especially interested in the success of Rome.

Often, however, these major gods were multiplied by the addition of epithets that identified some particular aspect of the god. These epithets were usually related either to a location or an activity. For example, there was Jupiter Capitolinus, the Jupiter who lived on the Capitoline Hill, and Mars Ultor, Mars the Avenger, to whom Augustus dedicated a temple in commemoration of his avenging the assassination of his adoptive father, Julius Caesar. Jupiter had at least 19 different epithets.

In addition to these gods, there were what might be called demigods, which were often men who had attained divine status, such as the hero Hercules or Romulus, the founder of Rome. There were many entities that might be called gods as well, such as spirits of streams, rivers, or trees. Such a god was a *genius loci*, literally, "the spirit of the place." Some gods were personifications of abstract qualities. The most important of these to the Romans were Fortuna, "luck," and Victoria, "victory." Finally, there were all the gods borrowed from other cultures, including Egyptian, Etruscan, and Germanic ones. The Romans were extremely open to adopting new gods that they encountered and adding them to their pantheon. Making Roman religion even more complex was the fact that when encountering new foreign gods, the Romans sometimes decided that these gods were simply local variants of gods they already knew.

Thus in Roman culture, it is almost deceptive to speak of a single notion of a god since there was such a variety of forms that divine beings or spirits could take. Nor did they fit into any clear hierarchy. Any attempt to create such a hierarchy would quickly run into problems in logic and contradictions, and even to try to do so is a modern concept and something that the Romans themselves never attempted.

~*Gregory S. Aldrete*

FOR MORE INFORMATION

Adkins, L., and R. Adkins. *Dictionary of Roman Religion*. New York: Facts on File, 1996.

Ferguson, J. *The Religions of the Roman Empire*. Ithaca, N.Y.: Cornell University Press, 1971.

Ogilvie, R. M. *The Romans and Their Gods in the Age of Augustus*. London: Chatto and Windus, 1969.

INDIA

The pantheon of deities established in early India was remarkably enduring. See the discussion in this chapter under "Religious Beliefs," then compare with the discussions about India in the nineteenth and twentieth centuries in the sections "Religion" in the chapters titled "Religious Life" in volumes 5 (*Nineteenth Century*) and 6 (*The Modern World*) of this series.

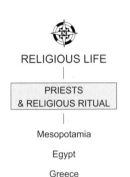

RELIGIOUS LIFE

PRIESTS
& RELIGIOUS RITUAL

Mesopotamia

Egypt

Greece

Rome

Priests and Religious Ritual

From the perspective of ancient humans, one of the trickiest aspects of religion was communication with the gods. Because of the vast power they wielded, it was essential to attempt to keep them placated so as to, at the very least, avert divinely produced disasters, and, in ideal circumstances, enlist their aid. Communicating clearly and successfully with such powerful—and often temperamental—entities was therefore of vital importance. Maximizing the chance of beneficial interactions with the gods was seen as too important to leave to chance or to amateurs, and so priests developed: professionals who specialized in knowing how best to communicate with the gods. Along with priests, ritualized practices evolved to provide a framework and a set of rules to facilitate and govern interactions between mortals and the gods.

While the basic role of priests in all these civilizations was to serve as intermediaries between the divine and the mortal, there were variations in the actual duties and activities of priests. In Mesopotamia, the priests spent much of their time and effort on rituals involving the actual cult statues of the gods. Because the statues themselves were believed to be infused with the spirit of the deity, priests lavished care on the statues. They gave the statues food and drink, clothed them, and even took them out of the temples on trips to view the city and visit the statues of other gods. In Egypt, too, cult statues received great care. The priests of Egypt were divided into two groups, one of which was devoted solely to looking after and serving the statues of the gods; because of their close contact with the gods, these priests had to observe stringent rules to avoid various forms of contamination. In Mesopotamia and Egypt, being a priest was a full-time occupation and required much specialized training. In Greece and especially at Rome, priesthoods were more likely to be part-time occupations, although there were certainly some groups and individuals, such as the Vestal Virgins, who were completely devoted to divine service. Greek and Roman priests mostly presided over and performed specific rituals.

In general, the purposes of various religious rituals were to please the gods; to receive advice, a favor, or a blessing from the gods; and to give thanks to the gods. Often rituals would combine several of these elements together. The standard formula for Greek prayers, for example, began with an invocation of a specific god and then proceeded to a reminder of the things that the supplicant has done for the god. This was followed by some sort of request made to the god, and the prayer ended with either praise for the god or a promise of further gifts to be made if the request was granted. Mesopotamian and Roman prayers followed a similar pattern of praises, petitions, and promises.

In addition to prayer, another of the religious rituals common to these cultures was sacrifice. The actual sacrifice could range from an individual's simple offering of a few drops of wine or grains of wheat to gigantic state-sponsored mass slaughterings of hundreds of cattle. Whatever the scale, the intent was the same: to give something of value to the gods to make them view the donor with favor. Human sacrifice was very rare, although some incidences of it are attested from early Mesopotamia.

One final significant type of religious ritual involved seeking advice from the gods. Sometimes this was accomplished by directly posing questions to the gods or to priests who gave divinely inspired answers. The most famous institution of this sort was the Delphic Oracle, which served as a valued source of divine advice for almost a thousand years. Another common means of determining the gods' will was through the examination of the internal organs of sacrificed animals. The Roman *haruspex*— literally, "gut gazer"—was a priest who specialized in this method of divination. Some other ways of attempting to predict the future included observing the flight or eating habits of birds, and interpreting unusual events or prodigies.

At its core, the establishment of priests and religious rituals constituted an attempt to establish communication between humans and the gods, with the ultimate goal of ensuring their favor and averting their wrath.

~Gregory S. Aldrete

MESOPOTAMIA

RELIGIOUS LIFE

|

PRIESTS
& RELIGIOUS RITUAL

|

Mesopotamia

Egypt

Greece

Rome

Ancient Mesopotamians believed that humans were created to serve the gods. This principle was interpreted literally, so the image of the god was cared for, fed, and clothed. The temple administration included the chief priest, various kinds of exorcists, singers, musicians, scribes, and the staff who supervised the temple businesses. The temple staff purified the temple. According to a detailed text from the Seleucid period, the divine statues in the temple of Uruk were served two meals daily. The first meal was served in the morning when the temple opened, and the other was served at night, immediately before the doors of the sanctuary were closed. From descriptions of divine meals, the following sequence can be reconstructed. First, a table was placed before the image. Water for washing was offered in a bowl (even the gods had to wash up before eating!). Then a variety of beverages, special cuts of meat, and fruits were brought to the table.

When the gods ate, they were hidden from both priests and human beings by linen curtains drawn around the statue and table. Music was played during the meal, and ritual fumigation was performed. At the end of the meal, the table was cleared. The curtains were opened and then drawn shut so the gods could wash their fingers. Clearly, the statues of the gods did not and could not eat. In reality, the meal of the god was scaled to feed the temple staff and their families. Also, the food from the divine meal was sent to the king for consumption, perhaps daily or only on special occasions.

Regular offerings to the gods were distinguished from those for special occasions such as the great feasts, emergencies, or celebration of joyous events. Enormous offerings were presented at annual festivals. Sacrifices included animals, incense, oil, and butter.

Human sacrifice was occasionally practiced in ancient Mesopotamia. The most striking case was found at the 16 Royal Tombs of Ur. The principal body was interred in a large pit more than 30 feet deep, lined with stone or brick. In a ritual ceremony, the king's staff was killed or drank poison—in one case, as many as 74 people, mainly women. Another form of human sacrifice was practiced in Assyria through the first millennium B.C.E. When omens foretold grave danger to the king, a substitute king was appointed to rule during this perilous time. Thus, any evil fated for the king befell his substitute. At the end of the substitute king's reign of 100 days, he and his spouse were ritually killed. An Old Babylonian chronicle reported that Erra-imitti of Isin had Enlil-bani installed as the substitute king; however, Erra-imitti was scalded with hot broth and died, so that Enlil-bani now was his successor.

To serve the god, the temple was designed like a royal palace, with well-equipped kitchens, a reception suite to receive visitors, bedrooms, additional suites for the god's family and servants, a courtyard, and stables. Many temples featured a wharf where the god's boat was moored so that he could visit other deities or his country home in spring and summer.

Enormous amounts of food were provided to temple administrators and craftsmen. The best agricultural products and the best animals (cattle, sheep, and goats) were sent to the temple, to be used in three different ways: (1) as daily food served to the divine image; (2) as income or rations for the temple staff who supervised and prepared the divine meals; and (3) to be accumulated for future use or trade. The temple also relied on funds supplied by the royals, wealthy citizens, and occasionally, booty.

Hymns and prayers have provided us with a window into the religious beliefs of the ancient Mesopotamians. Individual prayers followed a fixed pattern: (1) at the beginning there was an invocation praising the deity; (2) the middle section, which varied in length, was devoted to the complaints or petitions of the worshiper; and (3) the end included anticipatory expressions of appreciation and praised the god again. They used stock phrases, epithets, and hymnal quotations. Many examples of liturgical poems have been found; they express feelings of respect, fear, and spirituality. These liturgical poems are addressed to a particular god, before whom the worshiper bowed and appealed for mercy, sometimes through flattery. Only poems composed outside the cult show more sincere feelings and poetic style—personal requests referring to a specific and very personal experience. Prayer was used for a variety of purposes, such as imparting magical effectiveness to sacred paraphernalia and warding off the evil effects of eclipses and bad dreams. Special prayers expressed laments or complaints; others conveyed blessings. Thus, when a person enjoyed economic prosperity and spiritual peace, he or she attributed the situation to the presence of supernatural powers that either filled his or her body or guarded him or her. Conversely, a person blamed his or her misfortunes, illnesses, and failures on the absence of such protection.

Obedience to the gods was a cornerstone of religious behavior; these obligations included a large number of positive and especially negative prescriptions (taboos). The gods inevitably punished humans for their transgressions through accidents, sudden disgraces or illnesses, or unexpected catastrophes.

Prayers were mostly linked with rituals. The rituals were carefully described in a section at the end of the prayer to regulate the actions of the worshiper or priest. The ritual section included the details of sacrifice and the precise time of the offering. The links between the acts and offerings of the prayer were fixed. For example, the merchants who sailed down the Gulf to trade in Bahrain brought "thank offerings" upon their safe return home. They paid a proportion of their cargo to the Temple of Nanna at Ur, which capitalized their venture.

In times of famine, widows gave children to be temple slaves to save them from starvation.

Lists of temple personnel have given us a clearer picture of how the temple operated. The staff included cultic, administrative, and domestic staff (such as craftsmen). Cultic personnel took care of the gods' needs, placing offerings before them, keeping them clothed and sheltered, and performing rituals. According to Sumerian religious practices, priestesses served as the chief attendants to gods, and priests similarly served goddesses. However, most of the temple staff performed routine tasks such as sweeping the courtyard, guarding the doors, and managing the temple staff and property. From the Akkadian period on, the priest's head was shaved, so the barber was part of the temple staff. Another Ur III text provides a list of 180 "musicians" (both vocal and instrumental) and 62 "lamentation-priests" (who chanted) in the temples of Lagash. Music played an important part in both temple and state rituals. Musicians and lamentation-priests are often mentioned together in temple rituals.

The responsibility for arranging the songs of the rituals belonged to the lamentation-priests. The lamentation-priests had to be able to read and sing difficult rituals. They were literate and sometimes acted as scribes. A well-connected lamentation-priest could collect a variety of appointments at different temples. The duties of the musicians were to sing the songs properly and accompany them with musical instruments. Musicians, both male and female, were often mentioned in large numbers in connection with palaces, escorting the Assyrian kings on their campaigns. The Assyrian kings also captured musicians in their campaigns and brought them back as part of their booty. They included among their ranks snake charmers and bear wardens as part of a ritual circus performance.

The temple staff received regular allotments from the temple income, namely, food, drinks, textiles, wool, and silver goods. Temple personnel always included "live-in" staff. In the Old Babylonian period, the regular staff was reduced, perhaps reflecting the separation of temple and palace. Both priestly and domestic offices were treated as prebends (temple offices). Although many prebends became unnecessary, they continued to be inherited, sold, or even rented. The practice of prebends began in the Ur III period and became an elaborate institution during the Old Babylonian period, when temple offices were gradually converted into commercial shares. Certain offices changed hands every few days, but others required specialists, such as craftsmen, scribes, and permanent administrators. Temple offices were usually inherited by the eldest son upon division of the estate. But in time the prebend was subdivided so that individuals might execute their duties only one day a year. During the Seleucid period, the prebends were calculated by scribes, who divided the offices into a long and complex total of fractions to convince the purchaser that he was buying a large fraction of the day. Prebends were lucrative, so that their holders wanted the sanctuary to function according to the old rites, which gave them a guaranteed income. Female religious personnel consisted of various types of priestesses. The high priestesses (Akkadian, *entum*) were cloistered to offer prayers on behalf of their male (and female) relatives. They also took part in the Sacred Marriage as attested by cloisters containing a bedroom within the shrine at various excavated sites.

The cloister at Sippar, a large walled enclosure, served as the residence of a whole community of *naditum*-priestesses. Their cultic role was unclear. The word *naditum*, "fallow," referred to the women's unmarried or virginal status. The *naditum* was not reclusive—she was active in business and family life. The priestesses were from wealthy families, and some were even royalty. The cloister staff also included managers, officials, scribes, laborers, and personal female slaves.

Other female religious personnel, mostly in temples of Ishtar, took part in cultic prostitution as part of fertility ceremonies. Greek authors reported that every woman had to offer her body to a stranger in the temple of the goddess of love. Herodotus describes temple prostitution as follows:

The most shameful of the customs of the Babylonians is this: every woman must sit in the shrine of Aphrodite once in her life to have intercourse with a strange man. Many women who scorn to mix with the others, because they are rich and proud, drive to the temple in covered carriages drawn by teams of horses and stand there with their retinue. But most sit in the precinct of Aphrodite, wearing a wreath of string round their heads. . . . And through all the women are passages marked off running in all directions, along which the strangers walk to make their choice. Once a woman has taken her seat, she does not go home until one of the strangers has thrown money into her lap and had intercourse with her outside the shrine; and when he throws the money, he has to say, "I call you by Mylitta," because the Assyrians call Aphrodite Mylitta. The amount of the money does not matter; for the woman will never refuse, because that is against the law, as this money has thus become sacred. She follows the first man who throws money and refuses no one. After the intercourse, she has discharged her duty to the goddess and goes home, and it is then impossible to seduce her, however large the offer. So handsome, tall women can leave soon, but the ugly ones have to wait a long time because they cannot fulfill the law; and some of them stay there for three or four years. There is a similar custom in Cyprus. (Herodotus, *Histories* 1.195–200)

Another group, the "sacred women," were dedicated to the god Adad; they were expected to bear or nurse children and were probably not prostitutes.

Orphans, children of the poor, and children of insolvent debtors were dedicated as temple slaves. In times of famine, widows gave children to be temple slaves to save them from starvation, but the children stayed with their mothers until they were able to work. Marriage of temple slaves replenished the slave personnel. Privately owned slaves were sent to the temples by their devout masters. During the Neo-Babylonian period, prisoners of war were offered as slaves to the temple. Most slaves dedicated to the temple were branded, but sometimes the slave mark was a wooden or metal tag on the slave's wrist. The status of a branded slave was passed down at least to the third generation. Temple slaves were marked on the wrist or the back of the hand with symbols of the gods to whom they were dedicated; for example, a star tattoo was Ishtar's symbol; a spade, Marduk's; and a stylus, Nabu's. Temple slaves were further identified by their own name plus their father's.

When slaves or workers ran away, they were branded or marked, placed in shackles, and returned to work. Also, when slaves refused to work, they were placed in shackles. The demand for shackles was so great that the temples regularly placed orders for their manufacture. Rebellious slaves were sometimes confined to temple prisons.

Temple slaves worked under strict supervision and lived in city districts specially set aside for them, although some owned their own houses or lived in rented lodgings. Numerous texts involving judgments about temple slaves note their harsh treatment. Temple slaves often attacked their overseers and even high temple officials. Slaves who worked for the temple year-round were placed on a permanent allowance, receiving barley in the form of grain or flour, dates, and vegetable oil. Some slaves even received beer, salt, and occasionally, meat. The temples also supplied clothing and footwear to their slaves, although slaves often received wool, instead of clothing, to weave their own garments. Some slaves, who led an independent economic existence or did not work under the direct, regular supervision of temple officials, were obliged either to pay monetary remuneration or to provide the temple with finished products such as bricks and garments (Nemet-Nejat, 151–52, 186–94).

FOR MORE INFORMATION

Bottero, J. *Mesopotamia: Writing, Reasoning, and the Gods.* Translated by Z. Bahrani and M. van de Mieroop. Chicago: University of Chicago Press, 1992.

Jacobsen, T. *The Treasures of Darkness: A History of Mesopotamian Religion.* New Haven, Conn.: Yale University Press, 1976.

Nemet-Nejat, K. R. *Daily Life in Ancient Mesopotamia.* Westport, Conn.: Greenwood Press, 1998.

EGYPT

Egyptians practiced their religion differently from modern people whose attendance is expected at a church, temple, or mosque for participation in joint prayer, recitation of common beliefs, and practice of rituals. Egyptian lives were so filled with gods that they felt no need to set aside special times for praying together. Only on rare festival days might groups congregate outside a temple to witness a perfor-

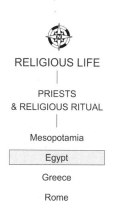

RELIGIOUS LIFE
|
PRIESTS
& RELIGIOUS RITUAL
|
Mesopotamia

Egypt

Greece

Rome

mance of holy rites. In every other respect, the business of religion was conducted entirely by proxy: only priests were permitted inside temples, and only priests were allowed to perform the rituals. In effect, being a believer required no action whatsoever.

An Egyptian temple was a dark, mysterious place considered to be the divine residence of a specific god or god's family, rather than a communal gathering place. Far inside, in the "holy of holies," the innermost room of the temple, stood a sacred statue of the temple god. These statues—usually bronze images up to two feet tall inlaid with gold and silver or, occasionally, composed of solid gold—were meticulously served and cared for by specially trained priests as if they were living gods. Each morning, the priests opened the doors to the shrine, placed food before the statue for its first meal, painted cosmetics around its eyes, perfumed it, and dressed it in white linen. These rituals complete, they closed the doors to the shrine until it was time for the next rites. The only occasion on which an average Egyptian might see a cult statue was on important festival days when people crowded into temple courtyards for rare glimpses of their god's image as it was carried outside on portable litters of gilded wood.

According to ancient texts, these cult statues could nod their heads and talk. Perhaps the reality was that priests secretly pulled strings to make the head move, spoke for the god by throwing their voices, or represented their own words as the deity's. Whatever the illusion employed, statues were consulted for their opinions on a variety of personal problems; one ancient record even credited a statue with solving a crime.

Cult statues even served as judges in courts of law. In a case involving a dispute over the ownership of a tomb, an oracle actually—somehow—wrote its decision. A workman named Amenemope had laid claim to a tomb he said belonged to his ancestor Hai, but necropolis officials who inspected the site questioned his claim when they found only a coffin with no name, funerary equipment, or offerings. To settle the matter, Amenemope appealed to his local god, who, according to his own account, "gave me the tomb of Hai in writing"—a mystery indeed. Perhaps two papyri—one supporting Amenemope's claim, the other denying it—were presented to the statue, who indicated his choice with a nod.

Although temples generally employed groups of priests to tend cult statues, say prayers, and conduct temple business, during Egypt's earliest history, pharaohs bore the sole responsibility for maintaining divine order by acting as high priest, in addition to serving as king. As Egypt grew more populous, pharaohs no longer had time to perform all the duties and rituals demanded by the burgeoning numbers of temples. The designees who were selected as stand-ins evolved into Egypt's priestly class. Because they merely represented the pharaoh, these men were not required to hold deep religious convictions. Only their duties distinguished them from other government workers. Priests, in fact, often held regular jobs as carpenters, scribes, or goldsmiths in addition to their religious responsibilities because most worked in the temple only a total of three months a year: their tours of duty lasted 30 days, followed by three months of secular life.

Because each temple needed some full-time person to manage its operations, the position of first god's servant evolved. As temples grew more complex and powerful, these men oversaw temple-owned farms, fields, cattle, and orchards and managed the temple staff. The position carried such responsibility and power that parents frequently advised their children to become scribes because it was from these ranks that first god's servants were chosen. In the case of large temples, second and third god's servants existed beneath the first god's servant; beneath them were endless other priests, each performing a specific job.

Regular priests fell into two categories: those directly responsible for the cult statue and those who performed other kinds of religious duties. *Wab* priests, held to the highest standards of cleanliness because they came in contact with the cult statue, shaved all their body hair to avoid lice and wore nothing but pure white linen clothing. Even their internal purity was monitored: they had to swear they had not recently eaten fish, considered ritually unclean, before touching the idol. Other priests, called "scroll carriers," managed the sacred scrolls in the temple library, recorded donations and estate revenues, kept inventory, and recited prayers. When the bakers, beer brewers, and cooks, who supplied each temple with offerings, and the farmers, herdsmen, and overseers of the temple estates were all counted, these thousands and thousands of religious functionaries in ancient Egypt formed the largest bureaucracy, in terms of percentage, the world had ever seen.

Priests were primarily paid—directly or indirectly—from the pharaoh's coffers. When warrior pharaohs returned from conquered foreign lands with gold and other booty, they donated a portion of their plunder to the temples, both in gratitude for the gods' favor and to ensure their continued goodwill. Foreign conquests also supplied Egypt with captives who provided an important source of manpower for temple construction and work on temple estates. Further adding to the wealth of the temples, pharaohs often donated large tracts of their own land to temples as continuing annuities until the holdings of Egypt's religious orders paralleled those of the Roman Catholic Church in medieval Europe—each grew to rival the wealth of its king.

Egyptian priests spent little time dealing with the well-being of individuals, never advising or counseling those with personal problems but concentrating instead on cosmic matters such as keeping the sun in the sky and ensuring the fertility of the land. Any individual who desired special favors from the gods could, however, pay for offerings and prayers that priests would perform on their behalf.

The only other personal service priests regularly performed for believers was to interpret their dreams—also for a fee. One might even arrange to spend the night

---

📷 *Snapshot*

Egyptian Guide to Interpreting Dreams

If You Dream About:	The Interpretation Is:
Killing an ox	Good. Enemies will be removed from your presence.
Seeing a large cat	Good. A large harvest is coming to you.
Climbing a mast	Good. You will be suspended aloft by your god.
Seeing one's face as a leopard	Good. Authority will be gained over the townsfolk.
A dwarf	Bad. Half your life is gone.
Bare buttocks	Bad. You will soon be an orphan.
Picking dates	Good. You will find food from your god.

(as cited in Brier and Hobbs, 40–41)

near a temple god, hoping to receive a divine message during sleep. All dreams were considered prophetic, so the key lay in their interpretation, a service priests performed with the help of special books. Because these books were written thousands of years before the idea of an unconscious mind, they ignore the possibility that a dream might result from the dreamer's experiences. A dream's theme, not its details, determined its meaning: Egyptians viewed their dreams as messages from the gods. Regardless of who the dreamer was, dream symbols were universal, carrying the same message for everyone (Brier and Hobbs, 36–41).

FOR MORE INFORMATION

Brier, B., and H. Hobbs. *Daily Life of the Ancient Egyptians.* Westport, Conn.: Greenwood Press, 1999.

David, A. R. *A Guide to Religious Ritual at Abydos.* Warminster, England: Aris and Phillips, 1981.

Surneron, S. *The Priests of Ancient Egypt.* New York: Grove Press, 1960.

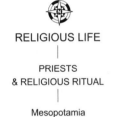

RELIGIOUS LIFE
|
PRIESTS
& RELIGIOUS RITUAL
|
Mesopotamia

Egypt

Greece

Rome

GREECE

To invoke the power of the gods, it was necessary to attract their attention, since only fitfully did they take an interest in human affairs. This being the prevailing attitude of the gods, it follows that it was something of an uphill battle to enlist their support. Their attention had to be first attracted by a prayer in which the petitioner reminded the deity of his or her pre-existing relationship with the petitioner. This was accompanied by sacrifice, libation (drink offering), votive offering, or a combination of these. A votive offering was a gift that was "vowed" or promised to the deity in recompense for his or her assistance. Sacrifices consisted of first fruits, grain, beans, cakes, wine, or milk. The most powerful sacrificial offering involved the spilling of animal blood, preferably in large quantities, since the gods were thought to derive both pleasure and sustenance from the smoke of the sacrificial victim that wafted up from the altar and entered their nostrils. The most common victims were goats, sheep, and oxen.

The largest sacrifices were performed annually in honor of the deities who were worshiped by the state as a whole. At the Great Dionysia held in Athens in honor of Dionysos in 333 B.C.E., no fewer than 240 bulls were slaughtered. Just before the axe fell, barley grains were sprinkled on the victim's head to induce the animal to nod in assent at its own killing. It was then flayed, chopped up, and roasted on top of the altar. Public sacrifices afforded one of the few occasions when the entire citizen body had an opportunity to eat meat; all of the victim, except the thigh pieces, was later distributed among the priests and the celebrants.

Votive offerings took many forms. They could be either as small as a cheap terracotta figurine or as large as a miniature temple. It was customary to offer a tenth-part of the spoils captured from the enemy after a victory in fulfillment of a vow made to the gods who were believed to have guaranteed it. The sanctuary of Apollo at Delphi was crammed full of miniature temples, called "treasuries," erected by victorious Greek states from the spoils filched from vanquished Greek states, since Apollo was invoked as a god of victory whenever states entered the fray.

The Greek word *hiereus*, which is roughly translated as "priest," denotes an official who supervised the *hiera* (i.e., sacred objects) stored within a sanctuary and who conducted sacred rites connected with the cult. The chief of these was the supervision of the sacrifices. In general, male deities were attended by priests and female deities by priestesses. Eligibility to a priesthood was based on external qualifications rather than intellectual or moral attributes, although it is no surprise to learn that prostitutes, army deserters, and debtors were forbidden to hold this office. The principal qualification seems to have been the absence of any deformity or disability, since the possession of a physical blemish was thought to constitute proof of divine disfavor. As far as we know, priests did not have to undergo any formal training. Nor were they ordained before assuming office. In the majority of cases, holding a priesthood was probably a part-time occupation. In democratic Athens, the newer priesthoods were annual appointments to which all members of the citizen body were eligible, whereas the older cults, such as that of Athena Polias (of the city), were reserved for members of a particular noble kin group or *genos* and held for life.

Priests received only a modest fee for their services, although they were entitled to a choice piece of the sacrificial meat. Their duties were primarily of a liturgical and administrative nature. They were not expected to administer to the spiritual needs of worshipers, nor did they take any part in ceremonies that had to do with birth, marriage, and death. Because there was no centralized religious authority either in Athens or anywhere else in the Greek world, priests could not exercise any influence over the political process, other than by virtue of their personalities.

One of the most terrifying inventions of the Greek mind was the belief in *miasma* or pollution. Miasma, whose workings were invisible, was analogous to a virus and capable of infecting a whole community if its course went unchecked. The belief in pollution may well owe its origins in part to the experience of contagious diseases such as plague or typhus, for which no medical explanation was available. However, miasma was not exclusively a physiological phenomenon. It had a religious dimension as well. In ascending order of magnitude, the principal causes of pollution were childbirth, death by natural causes, accidental homicide, and murder. The presence of an undiscovered murderer in a community was believed, at least in early times, to be capable of causing barrenness and blight among humans, livestock, and crops alike. To prevent miasma from seeping into the community, elaborate rites of purification were conducted by priests in consultation with religious experts. The most common purifying agents were saltwater, fire, sulfur, and blood. The most effective agent was the blood of a pig.

Not the least important reason for worshiping the gods was the fact that they had knowledge of the future, even though they did not control human destiny. Consultations mainly took place at oracles, where the gods often dispensed their knowledge through a medium who served as their mouthpiece. Ten oracular shrines are known to us. The most prestigious was at Delphi, where Pythian Apollo presided. No question was too important or too trivial to put to the oracle. Individuals might inquire,

"Should I get married?" "Should I go on a sea voyage?" or "Should I adopt an heir?" States might ask, "Should we go to war?" "Should we make peace?" or "Should we make a treaty?" Most answers came in the form of a simple affirmative or negative, but occasionally the petitioner received a more detailed and complicated response. In many cases, one suspects, he or she came to the oracle primarily to seek divine sanction for a decision that had already been reached.

An oracular response did not remove the responsibility of decision making from the petitioner, as the following anecdote told by Herodotus (*Histories* 1.53) clearly indicates. When Croesus, king of Lydia, consulted Delphi about the advisability of declaring war on the neighboring kingdom of Persia, he was informed that if he did so he would destroy a large empire. Emboldened by this response, Croesus duly declared war on Persia and fulfilled the prophecy—by destroying his own empire. What this cautionary tale reveals is that Delphi was not a place to get a "quick fix" on life's problems. On the contrary, the value of its utterances was nil if the petitioner did not interpret them with a proper sense of his own limitations. Not for nothing was the injunction "Know yourself" engraved on the sanctuary wall. The Delphic Oracle remained in operation for almost a thousand years and was still issuing pronouncements after the rise of Christianity. In 267 c.e., it was finally destroyed by a group of invading barbarians called the Heruli.

Other means of foretelling the future included examining the entrails of sacrificial victims, observing the flights of birds, and interpreting the significance of dreams. Natural phenomena such as eclipses and earthquakes were also thought to presage the future. The reading of these signs was in the hands of seers, who hired out their services to individuals as well as states. Seers played a particularly important role on the battlefield, being required to supervise the sacrifices that preceded any decision to join or delay battle (Garland, 1998, 131–34, 141–43).

FOR MORE INFORMATION

Burkert, W. *Greek Religion*. Oxford: Basil Blackwell, 1985.

Fontenrose, J. *The Delphic Oracle: Its Responses and Operations with a Catalogue of Responses*. Berkeley: University of California Press, 1978.

Garland, R. *Daily Life of the Ancient Greeks*. Westport, Conn.: Greenwood Press, 1998.

———. *Religion and the Greeks*. London: Bristol Classical Press, 1995.

RELIGIOUS LIFE

PRIESTS
& RELIGIOUS RITUAL

Mesopotamia

Egypt

Greece

Rome

ROME

In ancient Rome, there were very few professional priests. There was a great variety of types of priests, but with a few exceptions, this was not a full-time occupation, nor did priests receive any specialized training. Priests mainly performed certain public rituals and sacrifices. Priests were almost exclusively male and were members of several important priesthoods called colleges. Each college had a fixed number of places. When one member died, a new one was selected to take his place. The existing priests nominated several names to fill the vacancy. An election was then held, and the winner joined the college. Once elected to a priesthood, one held the office until death.

The most important of these colleges was the Pontifical College. It contained 16 men called pontifexes and 15 called flamens. The head of this college was known as the Pontifex Maximus. He was considered the head of religious affairs, and it is from this title that Christianity derived its title of Pope. The pontiffs' main duty was to preside over various religious festivals.

Each of the flamens was associated with one particular god. Of these, 12 were known as Minor Flamens. The remaining three were the Major Flamens and were associated with the three gods thought to have special links to the Roman people: Jupiter, Mars, and Quirinus. In keeping with the importance attached to these gods, each of their flamens had special rules and regulations governing their behavior.

The flamen of Jupiter was known as the Flamen Dialis, and because Jupiter was the king of the gods, he was the most important flamen. Jupiter was particularly associated with the city of Rome, and therefore his flamen could never spend the night outside the city, nor could he sleep away from his own bed for more than three nights. To connect the Flamen Dialis with the earth, the legs of his bed were coated in clay. To avoid contamination, he could not eat beans, touch fermented flour, raw meat, or a dog, or see a dead body, a horse, or the Roman army. He could never have any knots on his clothing. At all times, even in the privacy of his own home, he had to wear a special hat called the apex, which was like a circular disk with a rod protruding from the middle. The Flamen Dialis was the link between the city of Rome and the most potent aspect of Jupiter, known as Jupiter Optimus Maximus.

Also attached to the college of the pontiffs was a group of six women known as the Vestal Virgins. These were women who served Vesta, the goddess of the hearth and by extension the goddess of fire and of the home. In keeping with the idea that women could not be priests, when a woman became a Vestal, she in essence gave up her gender. Part of this belief was the requirement that they be virgins and that they remain virgins the entire time they served the goddess. Vestals had to serve for 30 years. In the first 10 years, they learned their duties; in the second, they performed them; in the third, they taught others. After 30 years, they had the option of resigning from the priesthood and getting married, but few did this. The ultimate crime for a Vestal was to lose her virginity. If she did this and was discovered, she was dressed in funeral clothes and carried in a funeral procession with her friends and relatives lamenting them. She was then placed in an underground room and buried alive. The most important duty of the Vestals was to tend the sacred fire. If this fire was allowed to go out, it was considered an omen foretelling the destruction of the city.

The next most important college was the college of augurs, of which there were 16. These priests had a specialized job: discerning the will of the gods through the interpretation of various signs. The three main categories of these were (1) the observation of the flight and feeding habits of birds; (2) the inspection of the internal organs of sacrificed animals; and (3) the interpretation of portents, such as lightning, disasters, and bizarre occurrences in general.

There was a special site on the Capitoline hill called the Auguraculum. The augur would sit here and designate one of the four quarters of the sky for observation. Any

Roman bronze model of a sheep's liver. It is thought that this may have been used to train novice priests how to read omens by inspecting the entrails of sacrificed animals. Scala/Art Resource, NY.

birds that flew through this zone were thought to carry a message from the gods. For ravens, crows, and owls, they studied the cries of the birds, and for eagles and vultures, they observed the direction of their flight and their number. There were specialized priests who studied specific behaviors. One of the most famous of these was the *pullarius*, who was an augur who observed how chickens ate. The more eagerly the chickens ate their food, the better, and the best omen of all was when the chickens ate so greedily that bits of food fell from their beaks. Naturally, the worst sign was if the birds refused to eat at all. This type of augury was frequently used as a test of the gods' favor before a battle. The most famous incident concerning the sacred chickens involved an admiral named Appius Claudius Pulcher, who, just before a naval battle, consulted the sacred chickens. The chickens absolutely refused to eat anything. Pulcher became enraged, saying, "If they won't eat, then let them drink," and then threw the sacred chickens overboard, drowning them. Needless to say, he lost the battle (Suetonius, *Life of Tiberius* 2.2).

Another type of augur was the *haruspex*, who specialized in examining the internal organs of sacrificed animals, especially the liver. The emperor always had a haruspex attached to his staff. The haruspex would examine the color, size, and shape of the liver. If the liver was diseased or malformed, it was a terrible omen. Archaeologists have discovered a liver made out of bronze, which was probably used as a training device to instruct novice haruspices. The bronze liver is divided into 40 sections, each of which has a certain god associated with it. The worst omen of all involving a liver was if part of it was missing. Supposedly, such a liver turned up at a sacrifice at which Nero was presiding shortly before he was assassinated. By law, all important public acts or events had to be preceded by some form of augury, and if the omens were unfavorable, the event had to be canceled.

The final form of augury was the interpretation of prodigies. Whereas the examination of birds and organs was a form of men asking questions of the gods, prodigies were unsolicited messages sent from the gods. The most common of these was lightning. Because lightning was the symbol of Jupiter, it held special significance. Any site struck by lightning became holy. If lightning was seen before a public assembly, it had to be called off. This rule was much abused in the late Republic and manipulated for political purposes. In this period, a remarkable number of magistrates seemed to see lightning that no one else noticed. On the other hand, if when a magistrate first took up his office, he saw lightning on the left, it was a good sign.

Any exceptional or bizarre event was a sign from the gods and had to be interpreted by the augurs. All Roman authors report such portents before most important events. Some of the types of portents listed include cows talking; raining stones; statues weeping tears or blood; raining blood; spears, statues, or swords bursting into flame; swarms of bees settling on standards; a bull kicking over the altar; the sky bursting into flames; animals born with multiple heads; an ox climbing up a building and committing suicide by throwing itself off; and mysterious voices speaking. Particularly dramatic omens were associated with the death and deification of emperors. Toward the end of Augustus's life, lightning struck one of his statues and melted off the first letter of the word Caesar inscribed on the base. Because C was the Roman numeral 100 and *Aesar* is the Etruscan word for god, this was interpreted to mean that in 100 days Augustus would die and become a god (Suetonius, *Life of Augustus* section 97). When Julius Caesar died, a comet appeared in the sky, which was also interpreted as a sign of his divinity (Suetonius, *Life of Julius Caesar* section 88). This interpretation was strengthened by the fact that the Romans called comets "hairy stars" and the word Caesar in Latin means "hairy." Dreams were also thought to be messages from the gods, particularly as predictions of the future.

In times of great disaster, when the state itself seemed threatened, the third of the colleges, the *Decemviri*, was called upon. They were the custodians of a group of ancient manuscripts called the Sybilline books. These were a series of manuscripts supposedly given to the Romans in the earliest days of Roman history by a prophetess known as the Sybil. The *Decemviri* would randomly pluck a page from these books and read it, and whatever it instructed, they would do. Usually this involved the introduction of a new god or ceremony.

Another type of specialized religious ceremony was called the *lustratio*. This was a purification ceremony, usually employed to cleanse a plot of land that was about to be used for some purpose of impurities, to protect it from future hazards. The way this was accomplished was by taking a pig, a sheep, and a bull and leading them in a procession all around the perimeter of a territory. The three animals were then sacrificed. This was known as a *suovetaurilia* (sus = pig, ovis = sheep, taurus = bull).

One final priestly college was the *fetials*. This priesthood had 20 members and performed religious rites involving international relations, including declarations of war and signing of treaties. When the Romans went to war, they were very concerned that it be a just war, at least in their eyes. To make it a just war, one of the *fetial* priests had to perform the following actions. He traveled to the land of the people the Romans were considering declaring war against, and to the first person he met after crossing the border, he said: "Hear me, Jupiter and Quirinus and all the gods of the sky and all the gods of the earth and of the underworld. I call you to witness that these people are unjust and do not make reparations." He then wandered around for 33 days saying the same thing to the first person he met whenever he entered a city or marketplace. If at the end of this time, the demands of the Romans had not been met, then a vote was taken and the Romans declared war. The *fetial* then took a bloody spear and in the presence of three adult men, recited another formula declaring the war to be a just war, at the end of which he threw the spear into enemy territory. This was the formal procedure by which the Romans declared war.

When the Romans signed a treaty with another nation, the *fetials* again played an important role. To formalize the treaty, they recited a long prayer to call the attention of the gods to what was happening. The prayer ended with the phrase: "If the Romans shall break this treaty, then on that day great Jupiter smite the Roman people as today I smite this pig." With these words, the priest bludgeoned a pig.

When the Romans addressed a prayer to one of the gods, they usually addressed it first to all the different names associated with a certain deity, then to the geographic locations with which he or she was thought to be associated, and finally, just to make sure they did not leave anything out, they would add the phrase, "Or whatever name you care to be called."

A major part of religious worship was sacrifice. The Romans sacrificed a number of animals to different gods, including goats, cows, bulls, sheep, pigs, birds, dogs, and horses. Male animals were sacrificed to male gods, and female animals to goddesses. White animals were sacrificed to gods of the sky, and black animals to gods of the underworld. The animal had to be perfect. Any deformities or unusual coloring or characteristics made it unsuitable. If the animal had horns, you would tie ribbons around them, or if you were rich, you would gild them with gold. When leading the animal to be sacrificed, it was a good sign if it went will-

A Roman *suovetaurilia* (sacrifice of a pig, sheep, and bull). The presiding priest is the man to the far right with his head veiled and holding his hand over the altar. © The Art Archive/Musée du Louvre Paris/Dagli Orti.

ingly. If it struggled much, you were supposed to get another animal and start over. All temples had their altars located outside, and this was where the sacrifices actually occurred. Before the sacrifice, the worshiper would go inside the temple and, if making a vow, would write it on wax tablets and attach it to the cult statue. At the actual sacrifice, everyone involved had to be sure they had washed their hands, and the priests had to cover their heads. Except for the prayers, everyone was expected to remain silent. Throughout the course of the sacrifice, one person would be playing a flute. Once the animal was led to the altar, the prayer would be recited. If it was a large animal, one of the priest's attendants would strike it on the head with a hammer or axe, and then another would cut its throat. They would cut upward if it was for a god of the skies, downward if it was for a god of the underworld. The kill needed to be done cleanly and efficiently. A sloppily performed sacrifice was a bad omen. The worst thing of all that could happen would be if the wounded animal broke free and ran off. This once happened at a sacrifice over which Julius Caesar was presiding, and because he ignored it, he received much criticism. After the animal was killed, the internal organs, in particular the heart, liver, and intestines, were removed. These were cut up and burned in a fire on the altar. This was the actual offering to the gods, and as they were burned, the priest directed the following phrase to the god being honored: "Be you increased by this offering."

If an error was made at any stage of this process, the whole ritual had to be repeated, along with an extra prayer and sacrifice to make up for the error. Sometimes the priest would make a preliminary sacrifice to atone ahead of time for any error they might make. These sacrifices could be on a gigantic scale. When Caligula became emperor, to celebrate his accession, 160,000 cows were sacrificed in a three-month period at Rome—nearly 2,000 a day (Suetonius, *Life of Caligula* section 14). This must have created quite a gory scene, since each cow would have contained more than two gallons of blood.

~*Gregory S. Aldrete*

FOR MORE INFORMATION

Beard, M., and J. North, eds. *Pagan Priests: Religion and Power in the Ancient World*. Ithaca, N.Y.: Cornell University Press, 1990.

Ferguson, J. *The Religions of the Roman Empire*. Ithaca N.Y.: Cornell University Press, 1971.

Ogilvie, R. M. *The Romans and Their Gods in the Age of Augustus*. London: Chatto and Windus, 1969.

Temples

RELIGIOUS LIFE
|
TEMPLES
|
Mesopotamia

Egypt

Greece

Rome

In an ancient city, the largest, tallest, most elaborately decorated, and most expensive structure was likely to be a temple. Only the palaces or tombs of rulers could sometimes compete with temples. In addition, temples were usually situated in prime locations in the city center. The skyline of Athens, for example, was dominated by the Parthenon, a huge temple to the patron goddess of the city, which was perched atop a high rocky outcrop in the center of the city. The most important temple of Rome, the Temple of Jupiter Optimus Maximus, was similarly situated on the crest of the highest hill, where it could be seen from all over the city. Temples were adorned with the very finest artworks and constructed out of the most valuable materials. The sculptures of the Parthenon are regarded as some of the finest ever produced by the Greeks, and the roof of the Temple of Jupiter Optimus Maximus was plated in solid gold.

In Mesopotamia and Egypt, temples were believed to function as actual dwelling places of the gods and therefore had to be appropriately luxurious and impressive. In addition to containing the cult statue of the god, temple complexes had to include space to house the god's attendants and priests, as well as the offerings that had been made to the god. Temples also usually had to provide appropriate spaces and settings for the various religious rituals that constituted so much of the day to day cult of the god. Greek and Roman temples were somewhat curious in that almost all the actual ceremonies and sacrifices were performed outside the temple. Altars were usually situated on the steps of the structure. The inside was devoted to housing the cult statue and valuable offerings frequently made of precious metals. Because of this, such temples also often doubled as the state treasury.

The prominent sites accorded to temples and the degree of expenditure lavished on them were similar in all these cultures, but the architectural forms that temples took varied considerably. In Mesopotamia, temples eventually developed into a distinctive stepped pyramid shape, the ziggurat. Egyptian temples were made up of a series of walled courtyards with attached buildings, frequently accompanied by tall engraved pylons in front of the main entrance. Standard Greek and Roman temples were rectangular structures surrounded fully or partially by columns.

While temples might look very different from one place to another, the care and resources lavished on them are testimony to the importance of the gods in the lives of ancient civilizations.

~*Gregory S. Aldrete*

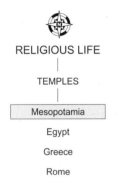

RELIGIOUS LIFE
|
TEMPLES
|
Mesopotamia

Egypt

Greece

Rome

MESOPOTAMIA

The temple represented the communal identity of each city and was usually located in the center of the city. It was both the largest and the tallest building in the city. At each temple, worshipers could meet one or more gods to make requests of them. Most gods had a dual function; they both served as the god of a particular place and as the patrons of some particular aspect of life.

The temple was built mostly of mud bricks, but the facades and walls were elaborately decorated. Mud-brick columns and half-columns graced the temple, sometimes imitating palm trunks. The most important temples had several courtyards and principal entrances, which led to the temple *cella*, the innermost chamber of the temple often containing a statue of a god. There was even an ante-*cella* in front of the *cella*. The architecture of the temple was carefully planned. Miniature bricks were found at one ancient temple—they were probably used to construct a scale model. Throughout the history of ancient Mesopotamia, there was continuity in religious architecture. In the third millennium B.C.E., temples became the symbolic focus of the city and its surrounding countryside as well as of the state and its rulers.

Stone statues were commonly placed inside temples to act as substitutes for the worshiper, standing before the gods in a state of continuous prayer. Ritual texts describe parts of the temple forbidden to outsiders and ritual actions "at a place which is not public." The immense enclosure surrounding the ziggurat at Babylon allowed the people to observe ceremonies, but only from a distance.

Architects designed stepped towers called ziggurats. The ziggurat had a rectangular base and three staircases, which met at right angles and led up to the high temple. The first proper ziggurat was built by Ur-Nammu (2112–2095 B.C.E.), the first king of the Third Dynasty of Ur. Ur-Nammu's piety and attention to building and restoring shrines led to his posthumous deification. Sanctuaries were considered public places of worship, although, in reality, only the clergy visited them. According to texts from the Old Babylonian period, individuals sometimes donated small chapels to the temple. There were also wayside shrines containing numerous votive objects.

The temple was regarded as the god's "house" or "estate" and was managed like a secular institution. The temple could own property in more than one place and take part in various productive and commercial activities. The range of the temple's economic activities included cultivation of cereals, vegetables, and fruit trees; management of sheep, goats, and cows; manufacture of textiles, leather, and wooden items; and promotion of trading links with foreign lands. These enterprises necessitated storerooms, granaries, and workshops within the temple enclosure. Some temples lacked sufficient space for expansion in the crowded quarters of the old shrine. In these cases, additional buildings were spread throughout the city and countryside.

Although the temple accumulated capital, rural estates, and craft industries, it was not only a capitalist institution. Evidence of the social conscience of the temples could be found in loans of barley made interest-free to individuals in time of famine. A few surviving sale documents record the purchase of children for an unspecified price by the high priest of the temple—transactions that implied the temple's practice of taking in poor children, illegitimate children, and orphans.

The temple also served as a forum for various judicial proceedings, particularly the taking of solemn oaths (possibly for a fee). The gods or their symbols even left the temple to go on location to settle human affairs, such as boundary disputes or the distribution of shares in a harvest (Nemet-Nejat, 187–89).

FOR MORE INFORMATION

Jacobsen, T. *The Treasures of Darkness: A History of Mesopotamian Religion.* New Haven, Conn.: Yale University Press, 1976.

Nemet-Nejat, K. R. *Daily Life in Ancient Mesopotamia.* Westport, Conn.: Greenwood Press, 1998.

EGYPT

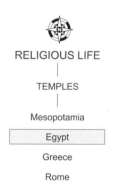

RELIGIOUS LIFE
|
TEMPLES
|
Mesopotamia
Egypt
Greece
Rome

Even though buildings for the immortal gods or for a mortal Egyptian's eternal life were constructed of permanent stone, they owed much to the design of the Egyptian house. Temples were called the "house of the god so-and-so" because they were viewed as residences for a god. Indeed, anyone familiar with the three elements of an Egyptian house will recognize the same parts in every temple. First, inside a rectangular enclosing wall, came a large courtyard, open to the sky, followed by a broad colonnaded court, roofed but open at the front. Behind stood a collection of small walled rooms with ceilings where the statue(s) of the god(s) resided. Conventionally, these parts are called the forecourt (or peristyle court), hypostyle hall, and the holy-of-holies.

The greatest difference between temples and houses, in addition to the use of stone for temples, was that the floor of each succeeding area in the temple rose as their ceilings progressively lowered. Passing through a temple brought the believer into successively more intimate and darker environments, as access became more restricted. Only priests could enter the holy-of-holies, for example. One other difference between a temple and a house (although later copied in palaces) was found at the front. Here, one of the architectural signatures of Egypt formed the temple entrance—a pair of pylons. These gently sloped, instead of perfectly vertical, walls rose from 20 feet to more than 100 feet on either side of an entrance door. Long poles, fitted into niches in the pylons, flew banners from their tops. Such flagpoles were the hieroglyphic symbol for divinity.

Other temple-related buildings, such as priests' houses, magazines for storing food, bakeries, and amulet factories, surrounded the temples, making them hives of activity rather than solemn edifices. All these parts were encompassed by a brick enclosure wall that defined the temple precinct, to which an alley formed by two rows of small sphinxes or other statues led the way.

The 20th Dynasty mortuary temple of Ramses III, named "United with Eternity," across the Nile from Luxor, serves as a clear example of a developed temple. It consisted of a walled rectangle 500 feet long by almost 100 feet wide—large enough to house a modern football field with plenty of room around it. A great pylon gateway at the eastern end served as the temple entrance. One-hundred-foot-tall flagpoles were fixed to this pylon, which stretched 210 feet wide at its base and rose 75 feet in the air and anchored a massive door in the center, 33 feet high by 12 feet wide. Inside were two successive open courtyards rather than the usual single court. The first, 125 feet deep, was bordered by columns on its north and south sides supporting a roof to create covered ambulatories on those two sides. A ramp at its west end led to a second pylon, through which stood a second open courtyard as large as the first but seeming smaller because its covered ambulatory ran around all four sides. A ramp at its western end led to the roofed temple proper. First came a large hypostyle hall, 60 feet deep by the 93-foot width of the temple. Its central nave rose on eight massive columns almost 30 feet high supporting a ceiling higher than the smaller (22 feet tall) columns to either side, thus allowing for stone windows in the gap where the roof from the lower columns met that from the taller ones. On its northern side stood four chapels, including one for Ramses III himself. A "treasury" for storing temple equipment occupied the south side of the hypostyle hall beside a small chapel for the pharaoh's namesake, Ramses the Great. Beyond this first hypostyle hall stood a second, 25 feet deep, that reached as high as the lower parts of the first hypostyle hall. Entry to a sanctuary for Ra-Harackhty ran from its northern side, and an entry to a sanctuary for Ramses III ran from its southern side. Behind this second hypostyle hall lay a third almost identical to the second except for being lined with statues of the gods Maat and Toth bearing faces of Ramses III. At the end of this final hypostyle hall stood a sanctuary (15 feet square) for Amun, the main god of the temple, flanked by sanctuaries for his consort, Mut, and their son, Khonsu. A number of small rooms behind and beside these sanctuaries served as temple storage.

Because temples endured sometimes for hundreds of years, succeeding pharaohs added embellishments, complicating their basic plans. The extreme case is Karnak Temple, which increased owing to the additions made by 20 or more pharaohs until it occupied an area of 600 acres and consisted of seven separate temple complexes, the most important of which were the complex for Amun, the one for his wife, Mut, and a third for their son, Khonsu.

The fluttering banners in front of the temples provided a festive atmosphere. Their tall masts sometimes more than 130 feet high (the first pylon at Karnak) soared above the pylons. Because no Egyptian timber grew that tall, masts of the famed cedar from Lebanon had to be imported for this purpose, then clad in a sheet of metal, most often electrum (an amalgam of silver and gold), and attached to the pylon by metal cleats near the top, while anchored at the bottom in a metal box fixed to both the pylon and the ground. Pylons were constructed of either stone or adobe bricks, and they were hollow inside to leave space for internal stairs to the top. Pairs of doors, as tall as 40 feet, fit between the pylons. Temple columns were always made of stone, formed of drums stacked on top of each other until they reached the required height. They rested on a stone base slightly wider than the column, and the column top was carved to represent palm fronds, lotus buds, or, less commonly, a papyrus cluster. Unusual types of columns included fluted examples with a simple rectangular top (forerunners of the Greek Doric style), or human shaped, in the form of a pharaoh or of the god Osiris.

Stone walls in and around the temples provided fine surfaces for carving, and they were adorned with images of gods. Temple walls were also covered with scenes of pharaohs smiting their enemies, which led early excavators to doubt that these were religious buildings, not realizing that Egyptians believed their victories in battle were ordained by the gods and evidence of their gods' might. Shrines in the holy-of-holies often included altar-shaped stone structures in the center or front. These were not for sacrifices, which Egyptians seldom performed, but for resting sacred litters until the god's statue was placed on board. Idols were generally made from metal—bronze, silver, or gold. Temples almost always bordered water—the Nile or a canal—for easy transport by boat of the massive quantities of stone used in their construction. Unlike religions such as Islam, in which temple orientation is important and prescribed, Egyptian temples pointed in a variety of directions.

> *Temple walls were covered with scenes of pharaohs smiting their enemies.*

Ramses the Great built a unique structure at Abu Simbel. This temple was carved into a stone mountain, so the outside served as the forecourt, and the hypostyle hall and holy-of-holies stood behind each other inside the cavern. Two other kinds of temple were erected during special eras, both associated with the worship of the sun. The Sun Temples of the Fifth Dynasty were mere rectangular open courtyards with a large platform at the far end on which a squat obelisk, called a *benben*, stood. According to one theory, the pyramidal top of the benben symbolized rays emanating from the sun. It seems that obelisks, whether the *benben* sort or the more familiar slender shafts, were all associated with the sun (Brier and Hobbs, 153–60).

FOR MORE INFORMATION

Brier, B., and H. Hobbs. *Daily Life of the Ancient Egyptians*. Westport, Conn.: Greenwood Press, 1999.

David, A. R. *A Guide to Religious Ritual at Abydos*. Warminster, England: Aris and Phillips, 1981.

GREECE

The Greek temple afforded the primary context for the expression of Greek artistic excellence. It was also the artistic medium on which was expended the most effort and resources. Built primarily to house a cult statue, it provided a showcase for the finest achievements of Greek art. The temple was by no means intrinsic to worship, since all cultic activity took place in the open air, around the altar. Its primary religious function was to secure the goodwill of the deity to whom it was erected.

The basic layout of the temple was established about the end of the seventh century B.C.E. A *pronaos* or porch led to a central room or *naos*. In some cases, there was a back porch or *opisthodomos* and a surrounding colonnade known as a peristyle. Temples were mostly aligned on an east-west axis, with the cult statue facing east so that it could witness the sacrifice being performed on the altar. At first, only the stepped platform on which the temple stood was made of stone, but later, stone replaced wood for both the columns and the superstructure. The first temple to be made entirely of stone was that of Artemis on the island of Corcyra (now Corfu). The best preserved is the Second Temple of Hera at Poseidonia, which was built of limestone about the middle of the fifth century B.C.E. The crowning achievement of Greek architecture is the Parthenon, located on top of the Acropolis at Athens, which uses a numerical ratio of 9:4 in all its proportions. Such are its stylistic refinements, which are intended to counteract the effects of optical illusion, that not a single line in the entire building is completely straight.

Greek temples are categorized according to the so-called orders of architecture. The principal orders are the Doric and Ionic, which both evolved in the fifth century B.C.E. A third, known as the Corinthian, came into being somewhat later. Doric columns, which are somewhat squat in appearance, rise from their platform without any base. They are decorated with 20 vertical grooves, known as flutes, in which shadows settle as the sky darkens, thereby lending a sense of drama and plasticity to the building. They are topped by capitals that resemble cushions. The Ionic column, which is considerably taller in proportion to its width, rises from a molded base and terminates in a capital that is surmounted by a pair of volutes. It has 24 flutes, separated from one another by a narrow band. The Corinthian capital also rises from a molded base, but its capital resembles bands of acanthus leaves.

The temple of Hephaestus, the blacksmith god, at Athens. This best-preserved Greek Doric temple owes its survival to the fact that it was converted into a Christian church. © The Art Archive/Dagli Orti.

The differences in style extended up into the superstructure. A Doric frieze consists of rectangular blocks called metopes, interrupted by narrower rectangles with vertical grooves called triglyphs. By contrast, an Ionic frieze is continuous. The crowning member is a triangular gable known as a pediment, which is located at either end of the temple. A few temples, notably the Parthenon, combine elements of both the Doric and Ionic orders. Metopes, pediments, and friezes are frequently decorated with relief sculpture. Because these were painted, the overall effect would have been extremely colorful. Most large temples on the Greek mainland were built in the Doric style with a surrounding colonnade, whereas in Asia Minor (Turkey), the fashion was for massive temples in the Ionic style with double colonnades.

Much of the sculpture that decorated a temple was narrative. A masterly example is to be found on the east pediment of the temple of Zeus Olympios at Olympia. Its subject is the chariot race between Pelops and Oinomaos. Pelops, who wished to wed Oinomaos's daughter, Hippodameia, had to defeat him to secure her hand. To ensure his victory, he bribed Oinomaos's charioteer to tamper with the king's chariot wheels so that they would fall off during the race. Instead of portraying the drama of the collision, however, the sculptor has chosen to depict the tense moment before the race begins. The composition, which is dominated by the commanding presence of Zeus flanked on either side by the contestants, purveys an unearthly stillness. What shatters this mood is the reclining seer who raises his clenched fist to his cheek in a gesture of alarm. We comprehend that the seer is gazing into the future and envisions the catastrophe ahead (Garland, 195–97).

FOR MORE INFORMATION

Bruno, V., ed. *The Parthenon*. New York: Norton, 1974.
Dinsmoor, W. B. *The Architecture of Ancient Greece*. New York: Norton, 1975.
Garland, R. *Daily Life of the Ancient Greeks*. Westport, Conn.: Greenwood Press, 1998.

ROME

The image that comes to mind when visualizing a Roman temple is a rectangular building surrounded by columns with a triangular pediment and a cult statue inside. Such temples were certainly a standard design and were quite similar to Greek and Etruscan patterns. Greek temples tended to be oriented toward the east and to have columns all the way around, whereas Roman temples could face any direction and often had a more frontal orientation with columns only at the end with the main entrance doors. Romans also built round temples, and altars and shrines came in a wide assortment of designs, from simple stone blocks to elaborate structures.

Unlike modern churches, important religious ceremonies usually did not take place inside the temple but rather at the altar, which was commonly located on the front steps of the temple. This is where animal sacrifices and prayers were performed. The interiors of temples were used to store votive offerings and the cult statue and, as such, often doubled as a kind of combination museum/bank where precious objects were stored for safekeeping.

The city of Rome contained dozens of temples. The emperor Augustus alone boasted that he restored no less than 82 temples in the city that were in need of

RELIGIOUS LIFE
|
TEMPLES
|
Mesopotamia

Egypt

Greece

Rome

repair. One of the oldest, most important, and most famous temples at Rome was the Temple to Jupiter Optimus Maximus (Jupiter the Best and the Greatest) located on the Capitoline hill. This temple played a central role in a number of state ceremonies. The triumphs celebrated by victorious generals ended here, and newly elected consuls performed sacrifices here when taking up their duties. As befitted the temple to such an important god, the roof and doors of this temple were adorned with a vast amount of gold, roughly equal to the entire Roman military budget for a year.

~Gregory S. Aldrete

FOR MORE INFORMATION

Richardson, L. A New Topographical Dictionary of Ancient Rome. Baltimore, Md.: Johns Hopkins University Press, 1992.

Ward-Perkins, J. B. Roman Architecture. New York: Harry Abrams, 1977.

RELIGIOUS LIFE
|
DEATH, BURIAL,
& THE AFTERLIFE
|
Mesopotamia

Egypt

Greece

Rome

Death, Burial, and the Afterlife

Most ancient civilizations believed that death was not the end of existence, although there were differing opinions on the nature of the afterlife. The customs and rituals that evolved in each culture surrounding death and the disposal of the corpse were largely geared toward either easing the spirit's transition from life to the afterlife or ensuring that the spirit would have all that it needed in the next world.

In each culture, the treatment of the body after death was a point of particular concern. One ritual common to Mesopotamia, Egypt, Greece, and Rome was a ceremonial washing of the corpse, usually performed by relatives. Often there was a public display of the body for family and friends, accompanied by expressions of grief such as crying, tearing of the hair, and lamentation. The most elaborate corpse preparation certainly occurred in Egypt, where the body underwent the complex and lengthy process of mummification, in which the internal organs were carefully saved and stored and the remainder of the body dried out and infused with preservative agents. Because the Egyptians believed that the soul would need the body again in the afterlife, it was essential that it be preserved. For the same reason, mummies were entombed accompanied by all the physical objects that people needed in everyday life; it was assumed that these would be equally necessary and useful in the afterlife. Most other cultures thought that the soul or spirit would continue to exist, although without corporeal form, so bodies were often cremated or inhumated accompanied by only minimal grave goods.

Corpses were placed in a variety of tombs. The most impressive were surely the gigantic pyramids that some Egyptian pharaohs had built to house their remains. One commonality was that tombs were almost always situated outside the city limits, usually out of fear of either physical or spiritual contamination. In Greece and Rome, the main roads leading into cities were lined with funerary monuments, and the inscriptions on them often directly address passers-by.

Overall, people seem to have been quite concerned that they receive a proper burial, and when this was in doubt, they came up with various strategies to attempt to ensure that their bodies would be disposed of with reverence. In Rome, for example, many individuals joined burial clubs, whose members paid monthly fees and promised to give any member who died a suitable funeral. Others spent vast sums on their tombs before they died so that they could be assured of an adequate final resting place.

Ancient concepts of the afterlife varied, but in general there were not really counterparts to modern ideas of heaven and hell. On the whole, cultures including Mesopotamia, Greece, and Rome did not conceive of the afterlife as a place where people would be judged on the basis of their moral behavior while alive and then either rewarded or punished accordingly. Instead, the spirits of all people, good and bad, existed in an ill-defined and not very pleasant sounding limbo status in an underworld. Sometimes people were punished by not being allowed to enter the underworld.

In Egyptian religion, however, the soul did undergo a moral evaluation after death, similar to Christian concepts of the Last Judgment. Before the throne of Osiris, the god of the dead, a person's heart (believed to be the site of the soul) was weighed against a feather representing truth. If you had been a good, truthful person, you were allowed to enter the afterlife, but if you had been false, your soul was destroyed by a monster and your existence ended.

Whatever their precise beliefs about proper treatment of the body, or what happened after death, all these cultures recognized that death marked an important moment of transformation, and they accordingly developed complex rituals to ensure that the body and the spirit successfully navigated the crucial transition from life to death.

~Gregory S. Aldrete

MESOPOTAMIA

We know a great deal about beliefs concerning death and the afterlife in ancient Mesopotamia. Numerous sources describe their funeral and mourning practices, the cult of the dead, burial practices, funerary offerings, visits from ghosts, the organization of the netherworld, and causes of death.

Many literary texts struggled with the meaning of death and dealt with the fortunes of the dead in the netherworld. Surprisingly, creation myths generally exclude the institution of death. In both *Gilgamesh* (the epic of a hero-king) and *Atra-khasis* (the Babylonian Flood Story), the gods created death. The gods solved the problem of overpopulation through sterility, miscarriage, and religious celibacy.

Death was not the end. Humans had a soul or ghost, which was inherited from the slain god whose body was used in creating humans. When one was accorded

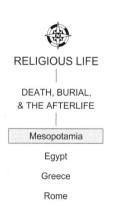

RELIGIOUS LIFE

DEATH, BURIAL,
& THE AFTERLIFE

Mesopotamia

Egypt

Greece

Rome

traditional burial rites, he or she could descend to the kingdom of the dead below the earth, the lowest realm of the universe.

The ancient Mesopotamians did not speak of death for fear of summoning it. Instead, they referred to death by using a host of euphemisms: "to cross the Khubur," "to go up to/toward heaven" (meant only for kings of the Third Dynasty of Ur), "to go to one's fate," "to be invited by one's gods," "to come to land on/reach/take refuge in one's mountain," "to go on the road of one's forefathers" (Reiner, 114). The Mesopotamians' practice was not so different from our own; we refer to death by terms such as "passed away," "no longer with us," "may they rest in peace," and so on. All things said and done, the ancient Mesopotamians accepted death as a fact of life.

> *The ancient Mesopotamians did not speak of death for fear of summoning it.*

In ancient times, people preferred to die in their own bed, surrounded by their loved ones. The dying person was moved to a special funerary bed with a chair placed at the left. A specific formula was recited to release the soul from its body, and the chair served as a seat for the soul. The soul received its first funerary offerings on the chair.

To prepare it for burial, the body was washed and the mouth tied shut. The corpse was anointed with oil or perfume, clothed in clean garments, and accompanied by as many personal items as the family could afford—weapons, toiletries, jewelry, and other objects. Most bodies were simply buried without being preserved for eternity. The body and grave goods were laid out for public viewing (the Mesopotamian version of a wake) shortly before the funeral. Of course, members of the royal family were expected to provide lavish funeral displays.

The dead were buried in a coffin, sarcophagus, or tomb. The poor were wrapped in a cloth or reed mat and provided with a few simple pottery vessels, stone beads, a copper pin, or the like. Kings and wealthy commoners buried their dead in individual or communal vaulted chambers built below the floors of the palace or house. The sarcophagi of kings were often impressive. Family members and servants who died at home were interred in the family crypt, older bodies being pushed aside to make room for new bodies. Other families buried their dead in public cemeteries. Those who carried the body to its final resting place were paid. Burial officials were also compensated with first rights to the funerary bed and chair and the clothing in which the person died (which was removed when the body was washed). The edicts of reforming kings such as Uru-inimgina (ca. 2350 B.C.E.) tried to ensure that the amounts charged for such services were not excessive.

After burial, mourning rites could last as long as seven days for a prominent person. Both relatives and close friends were supposed to display their grief openly. For the death of the king, queen, or queen mother, the subjects mourned publicly. Professional mourners, both male and female, were hired to increase the number of mourners and to lead the laments. Sometimes prostitutes were recruited for this service. Laments could be sung alone or accompanied by a musical instrument or even the rhythmic beating of the breast. A few funeral laments have been found expressing grief and eulogizing the dead, as in *The Epic of Gilgamesh*:

Hear me, O Elders of Uruk, hear me, O men!
I mourn for Enkidu, my friend,
I cry out bitterly like a mourner . . . an evil demon appeared and took him away from me!
My friend, the swift mule, fleet wild ass of the mountain, panther of the wilderness . . .
Now what is this sleep which has seized you?
You have turned dark and do not hear me. (as cited in Reiner, 63)

Mourning rites were not meant to end prematurely. Mourners also expressed their grief in the way they dressed. They were expected to remove their finery, tear their garments or clothe themselves in sackcloth, take off their turbans or cover their heads with their clothes, and move about unbathed and ungroomed. Fasting was another expression of grief. The ancient Mesopotamians accepted men openly displaying their sorrow, but only women tore out their hair or scratched their cheeks and breasts. Once the dead were interred, the official mourning period drew to a close, marked by purification ceremonies and a return to normal dress and grooming habits.

The ceremonial rites for mourning for Ishtar's spouse, Dumuzi (as for other dying and returning fertility gods), are described in detail in myths and cult songs meant to accompany rituals. During the ceremonial mourning for Dumuzi, some vessels used for offerings to the deceased were broken, torches were carried around the funeral bed three times, and incense was burned. These rites were performed to protect the living from contamination by the dead. Niches for funeral lamps were found in graves at various sites. The tombs of high-status individuals also contained a niche into which an engraved funerary inscription was placed.

The dead depended on living relatives to provide them with funerary offerings. The eldest son of the deceased was primarily responsible for providing a continuous series of funerary offerings, perhaps an explanation of why he received an additional share of the inheritance. Offerings to kings corresponded to the deluxe menus they enjoyed on earth; these offerings were made at the new and full moon and at an extended celebration during the month of Abu (July/August). War heroes received special offerings associated with the royal cult; they were portrayed as relaxing on couches while served by their family.

In the royal cult, all ancestors of the reigning king received individual offerings regularly. But ordinary people provided individual offerings to those relatives they knew personally, such as their fathers, mothers, brothers, sisters, grandfathers, and grandmothers. More distant relatives were lumped together as a common ancestor. A few legal texts, from Susa of the Old Babylonian period (1900–1595 B.C.E.) and from Nippur of the Middle Babylonian period (1595–1000 B.C.E.), specifically required a woman to perform rites of the ancestors' cult. The family ghosts of ordinary people received cold water, bread, hot broth, beer flavored with roasted grain, flour, oil, wine, honey, and occasionally, the rib section of a sacrificed animal. The food was set at the place of burial, and liquids were poured through a pipe in the earth. To ensure that the intended ghosts received the offerings, the names of the dead were called. Sometimes a statue of the deceased housed his spirit for offerings. Ghosts were usually helpful, often intervening on behalf of family members. But if the deceased were neither buried nor accorded the proper funerary rites, their ghosts were considered dangerous.

Several times a year, ghosts were permitted to leave their homes in the netherworld and return to earth for brief visits. At the end of Ishtar's descent to the netherworld, Dumuzi was said to return during his festivities in Du'zu (June/July), and there was also a general return of the dead in Abu (July/August). During these celebrations, the ghosts were wined and dined. Then they returned by a special river road to the netherworld on boats, which floated down the river.

During life in the upper world, the gods were able to control population growth, but in the realm of the dead, the population always increased. The netherworld was called "earth," "great earth," and "extensive earth." There were two traditions explaining how humans entered the netherworld. According to one tradition, the road to the netherworld passed through the demon-infested steppe land, across the Khubur River, and then through seven gates with seven gatekeepers. Another version describes a road to the netherworld crossed by boat down one of the rivers of the upper earth and across the *apsû* (the sweet waters under the earth) to the lower earth, where Ereshkigal, queen of the dead, ruled. The latter road was taken by the dead returning home from their annual visits with their families, by babies about to be born, and by the occasional demon. Situated in the bowels of the earth, the netherworld was described as a dreary place:

To the gloomy house, seat of the netherworld,
To the house which none leaves who enters,
To the road whose journey has no return,
To the house whose entrants are bereft of light,
Where dust is their sustenance and clay their food.
They see no light but dwell in darkness,
They are clothed like birds in wings for garments,
And dust has gathered on the door and bolt. (as cited in Reiner, 119)

Despite this paradigm, the dead were not always gloomy because Shamash (the sun god) visited daily on his travels through the sky. Also, the inhabitants were not reduced to eating mud; rather, they imitated life above: eating bread and drinking clear water. A complex bureaucracy similar to that of the upper world governed below. There was a royal court, presided over by King Nergal and Queen Ereshkigal, who were outfitted in royal regalia and lived in a lapis lazuli palace.

The bureaucracy of the netherworld was described in great detail, particularly in the dream of Kumma, in which he visited the netherworld, where he met many members of the bureaucracy, some described as half-man and half-animal. The Anunnaki, the court of the netherworld, welcomed each ghost, taught them the rules of the netherworld, and assigned them a place there. The female scribe of the netherworld checked the names of the newcomers against a master list so that no unexpected visitors from the upper world arrived.

Besides the court of the Anunnaki, there were two other courts of the netherworld. Gilgamesh, the legendary king of Uruk, presided over one court; however, we know little about it. The sun god Shamash presided over the other court in his daily rounds. In effect, the circuit of the sun god allowed him jurisdiction in both the upper and lower worlds. Shamash decided problems between the living and dead, such as punishing ghosts who harassed the living and ensuring that lonely and forgotten ghosts got their fair share of funerary offerings.

The netherworld courts did not render a Last Judgment as in the Christian tradition. In fact, neither the dead person's virtues nor sins on earth were considered when assigning them a place. The worst punishment dispensed to a sinner was denial of entry by the gods of the netherworld. In this way, the sinner was sentenced to sleeplessness and denied access to funerary offerings. Foreigners were permitted to enter the Mesopotamian netherworld. Lepers were allowed entrance, but they were kept safely apart from the rest of the dead (Nemet-Nejat, 141–45).

FOR MORE INFORMATION

Nemet-Nejat, K. R. *Daily Life in Ancient Mesopotamia*. Westport, Conn.: Greenwood Press, 1998.

Reiner, E. *Astral Magic in Babylonia*. Transactions of the American Philosophical Society, vol. 8, part 4. Philadelphia: American Philosophical Society, 1995.

EGYPT

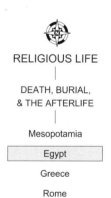

RELIGIOUS LIFE

DEATH, BURIAL, & THE AFTERLIFE

Mesopotamia

Egypt

Greece

Rome

Egyptians invested enormous faith, energy, and money in their belief in life after death. Egypt's people loved life yet made extensive and costly preparations for death because their religion promised they would live again—just as the myth of Isis and Osiris taught. No one knows whether this ancient myth gave the Egyptians their first ideas about the hereafter or whether the myth was invented later to explain existing ideas. It demonstrates the Egyptians' most important religious belief: resurrection—that a physical body would literally revive in the next world, just as Osiris was magically reanimated. To gain a perfect eternal life required an intact body. Isis went to such lengths to retrieve the corpse of her husband for a proper burial because if she had not pieced together his dismembered body—the vehicle for eternal life—he could not have been resurrected.

Certain ideas about life after death evolved over time. Originally, immortality was not thought to be parceled out equally: only the pharaoh was assured eternal life, a reasonable assumption given that he alone descended from the gods. It was believed that a nonroyal Egyptian's best chance for eternal life was to be buried near his pharaoh's pyramid in hopes that the king would take some commoners with him to the next world. Our earliest known writings about resurrection were found on the walls of the royal pyramid of Unas, the last king of the Fifth Dynasty, and include hundreds of magical inscriptions in vertical lines running from ceiling to floor. These hieroglyphic "utterances," referred to as the Pyramid Texts, detail the three stages of a pharaoh's transition to the next world: awakening in the pyramid, ascending through the sky to the netherworld, and finally, being admitted into the company of the gods. The principle behind all the spells was the same: the word is the deed. Saying something, or having it inscribed on a pyramid wall, made it so.

By the 11th Dynasty, nonroyals began inscribing similar writings on the sides of their own coffins to ensure their own immortality. Known as "Coffin Texts," they are variations of the Pyramid Texts, with the same concern—the well-being of the deceased. Eventually, these spells became so numerous that they no longer fit on the coffin, which led to their being written on rolls of papyrus that were placed inside the coffin and today are referred to collectively as the *Book of the Dead*. As customers eager for immortality increased, books of the dead became a major industry for scribes who copied thousands of editions. Many of the books were, at least for the period, mass produced. Places for the deceased's name were left blank—the first "forms" in history—until purchase, when a scribe would fill in the appropriate information.

To achieve an afterlife, Egyptians expected two final judgments, crucial tests to be passed before admittance into the next world. One was beyond the deceased's control; the other was based on the deceased's persuasive skill. The first test placed the heart of the deceased on one side of a balance scale whose other pan held a feather. Because the feather hieroglyph stood for the word *maat* or "truth," this test examined the heart to determine how truthful the person had been in life. Osiris is usually depicted presiding over the judgment to ensure fairness while the god of writing, Toth, records the result. If the dead person failed the test, their heart was thrown to a creature with the body of a hippopotamus and the head of a crocodile, who destroyed the person by eating the heart. Egyptians sent no one to Hell, only out of existence. After the balance scale test, the deceased would be ushered into the Hall of Double Truth for a second judging by a tribunal of 42 gods. The deceased would be required to "separate himself from evil doings" by making a plea, convincing each god that he or she had never done a specific wrong. By passing this second test, the deceased was declared "true of voice," earned passage to the netherworld, and became a "westerner," ready to be welcomed by Osiris.

Egyptians focused so much attention on the importance of their physical bodies that it may seem as if they lacked any concept of a soul. In fact, however, they had such an abstract concept. In chapter 125 of the *Book of the Dead*, the dead person's soul is represented as a heart, but the fully evolved theory was more sophisticated. A soul was thought to be made up of several parts, the most important of which were the *ba* and the *ka*.

The *ba* was represented as a bird with the head of the deceased. Because the *ba* of a living person was rarely spoken of, we can deduce that it came into independent existence only when someone died and so resembled modern concepts of a soul. But unlike its modern counterpart, an Egyptian *ba* had physical needs. Relatives of the deceased were supposed to leave offerings in front of the tomb to feed the *ba* until it reached the next world; paintings in the *Book of the Dead* even show the *ba* flying around the tomb or outside it. The soul's second element was called the *ka*, a kind of spiritual duplicate of the deceased that required a place to dwell—preferably the mummified body. A wealthy Egyptian would be buried with a *ka* statue, a likeness of himself that the *ka* would recognize and in which it could live, in the event that his body was later destroyed.

Preserving the physical body after death became, over the centuries, a kind of Egyptian industry. At first, the dead were simply placed in sand pits and covered with more sand. Contact with the hot, dry granules quickly dehydrated the body and created natural mummies. Later, as burials became more elaborate, bodies were placed in rock-cut tombs, but away from the drying sands, they soon decomposed. Artificial mummification was needed to dehydrate the body before burial.

When someone died, a member of the person's family ferried across the Nile to embalming shops on the west bank, where a type of mummification, which varied according to price, was chosen. Much as we hire hearses today, a special funerary boat was rented for the occasion to transport the corpse to the shop, where it was deposited for 70 days. Female mourners who accompanied the body were paid to weep, wail, and throw sand on their heads in traditional gestures of lament.

The mummification process removed the moist internal organs, which cause a body to decompose. In the most expensive method of mummification, the brain was drained out through the nasal passages after a long, needlelike instrument was inserted through the nostril to break into the brain cavity. Then a thin tool with a hook, resembling a coat hanger, was pushed into the cranium and rotated to break the brain into pieces. When the cadaver was turned upside down, the mixture ran out through the nostrils. The brain was one of the few parts of the body embalmers discarded because it was thought to serve no useful function. Egyptians believed people thought with their hearts—when thoughts excite, a person's heart beats more quickly.

Embalmers next removed the organs inside the torso through a small abdominal incision in the left side. The stomach, intestines, liver, and spleen were all pulled through this hole, but the heart was left in place so the deceased, once resurrected, would be able to think and say the magical spells necessary to become reanimated. Organs were individually stored in one of four jars specially made for the purpose, each with a lid carved in the shape of one of the four sons of Horus: Mesti, the human headed son; Duamutef, the jackal; Hapi, the baboon; and Qebesenef, the hawk. These jars were called "canopic" jars by early Egyptologists because the Greek god Canopus was worshiped in the form of a jar. A fluid, called the "liquid of the children of Horus" was poured over the internal organs to preserve them, and the jars were sealed. Finally, priests recited prayers to invoke the protection of Horus's sons.

> *The brain was one of the few parts of the body embalmers discarded.*

Now the body was ready for drying. Natron, a naturally occurring compound of sodium carbonate, sodium bicarbonate, and sodium chloride—basically, baking soda and table salt—was shoveled onto the body until it was completely covered. Given the human body's large mass and approximately 75 percent water content, more than 600 pounds of natron and 40 days were necessary to complete dehydration. The abdominal and chest cavities were then washed with palm wine and aromatic spices and packed with resin-soaked linen that would harden to maintain the body's original contours. For less-expensive mummifications, sawdust and onions placed in small linen bags were used as body-packing material, and the face was padded with linen in the cheeks and under the eyelids. (In one instance, onions were even placed in the eye sockets.)

Last of all, the body was anointed twice from head to toe with oils mixed with frankincense, myrrh, and the same lotions used in daily life—cedar oil, Syrian balsam, and oil of Libya. Next, bandages, which could come from the bedding of the deceased or other linen scraps, were torn into strips as long as 15 feet by 4 inches wide and rolled, prior to use, like modern bandages, then applied according to a fixed ritual. First, each finger and toe was wrapped individually, with wealthy clients receiving gold covers for toes and fingers as additional protection—pure gold was the metal of eternity because it does not tarnish.

Magic amulets were also usually placed within the wrappings to protect the mummy until it was resurrected in the west. When the mummification was complete, the family returned to the west bank of the Nile with an entourage of friends, mourners, and dancers. Servants carried furniture, clothing, and food to be placed in the tomb and bore the mummy to its final resting place. Next came the most important of all the resurrection rituals: the "opening of the mouth" ceremony. Involving more than a dozen participants, the ceremony was a play, perhaps the oldest in history, which took place in front of the tomb on the day of burial. Special animals were ritually killed, including two bulls (one for the north and one for the south), gazelles, and ducks. One leg from the bull of the south was cut off and, along with its heart, offered to the mummy. The play ended with a ceremonial opening of the mouth as a priest touched a special implement, shaped like a miniature adz, to the mummy's mouth and recited an incantation that the person would live again. The mummy was now ready for its resurrection in the west. The tomb was sealed while friends and relatives sat together outside to share a meal in memory of the deceased.

The first tombs, called mastabas, the Arabic word for the benches they resembled, were simple adobe rectangles whose walls angled toward the center. Inside, compartments held the owner's goods, while the body lay in a simple pit below ground, covered with logs on which sand was piled to represent either the heaped sand burials of distant ancestors or else the primeval mound of creation. Everyone who could afford the cost of such a tomb, from wealthy government officials up to pharaohs, built a mastaba for themselves.

As pharaohs increased their power, they created a special kind of tomb, beginning about 2700 B.C.E., when a pharaoh named Zoser added another, smaller, mastaba on top of a first one, then another and another until six were stacked in a 200-foot-high facsimile of a wedding cake. Called the Step Pyramid, this new kind of tomb set pharaohs in pursuit of more and more imposing burial places. The next breakthrough came with the last king of Zoser's dynasty. The pharaoh Huni stacked eight

---

📷 Snapshot

Final Incantation Spoken over Mummified Bodies

Thy mouth was closed, but I have set in order for thee thy mouth and thy teeth.
I open for thee thy mouth, I open for thee thy two eyes.
I have opened thy mouth with the instrument of Anubis, with the iron implement with which the mouths of the gods were opened. . . .
You shall walk and speak, your body shall be with the great company of the gods. . . .
You are young again, you live again.
You are young again you live again. (as cited in Brier and Hobbs, 53; originally in Budge, 185)

mastabas on top of each other 300 feet in the air and then filled the steps with dressed stone to form smooth, slanting sides. This was the first true pyramid. The sides, however, formed an angle too steep for its soft limestone cover, making the structure unstable, so the pyramid was abandoned before the burial chamber inside was completed.

Experiments continued with the first pharaoh of the Fourth Dynasty, Sneferu, whose pyramid's sides climbed at the sharp angle of 54 degrees. The angle abruptly changed to 43 degrees about half way to the top, however, marking the point at which architects learned that cracks had developed inside the burial chamber and at the pyramid base so the weight of the building had to be reduced. Despite the lower height than planned of this Bent Pyramid, it was a truly massive building that stood 310 feet tall from a base 620 feet on each side, with a volume three times Zoser's Step Pyramid. Because his first attempt proved unstable, Sneferu built a second, even larger pyramid with the new 43-degree slope that ascended 343 feet from a base 722 feet on each side. This structure counts as the earliest true pyramid that survives intact today.

Sneferu's son, Khufu, capped the Pyramid Age with the largest tomb ever built. Although today it has lost 40 feet from its top, it originally rose 481 feet in the air, on a base 756 feet square, rising at a 51-degree angle. Inside, a magnificent passageway leads a third of the way up the pyramid to a granite chamber 34 feet by 17 feet by 19 feet high, in which a polished granite sarcophagus held the mortal remains of this pharaoh. Complex devices, such as passageways that led to dead ends and massive stone plugs that sealed the true route to the burial, sadly proved to no avail. The pyramid was picked clean in ancient times.

This was only the first of three startling pyramids built at Giza. Khufu's eldest son, in a short reign of eight years, began a pyramid he did not live to finish, but his half-brother Khafra took up the pyramid challenge again at Giza with a massive effort beside his father's Great Pyramid. Because it stands on higher ground, Khafra's pyramid rises even higher than its neighbor, although it originally stood 10 feet shorter. Its gleaming casing of white limestone, transported by boats from quarries across the Nile, still covers the top. The sandstone blocks that form the interior were cut from the surrounding Giza site. Probably in the course of freeing all the stone for the Great Pyramid, quarrymen struck a seam of harder rock, which, as the more easily worked stone was quarried around it, emerged as a small hill. Khafra had this rock outcrop carved in the shape of a 200-foot-long recumbent lion bearing his own face—the famous Sphinx.

Pyramids continued to be built through the Middle Kingdom, although they were made from softer adobe with only a veneer of stone. Whether stone or adobe, all the pyramids were robbed. Something new had to be designed to prevent thieves from tampering with the body. During this time, government officials in the middle of Egypt began excavating grand tombs inside stone hills. The idea spread south, and the southern pharaohs, who began the New Kingdom, continued the practice, with their tombs excavated first in the hills and then deep under the ground of the Valley of the Kings. If a mass of stone could not protect their bodies, perhaps a secret hiding place would do the job.

An outside entrance was first plastered and then covered with dirt and rocks to hide its location after the body was safely placed inside. Inside, a short hall led to a pair of wooden doors opening to a corridor that descended for a hundred feet or so. A square pit, 20 feet deep or more, was dug in this corridor, not as a device to foil robbers but to catch the water from occasional thunderstorms so it would not flow farther. At the end of this corridor came the first room, called *stja neter* (way of the god). Doors sealed this chamber from a larger "waiting room" (*wesekhet iseq*), whose walls were covered with religious texts and pictures to ensure resurrection in the next world. Here, the opening of the mouth ceremony was performed on the dead body to enliven it magically. Through another door stood the great columned room of the tomb, the *per nebu* (house of gold), in the center of which, surrounded by veiled shrines, lay the sarcophagus for the deceased. Doors closed off a small room where *ushabtis* (worker statues) were stored, ready to answer the call of the gods to work in the next world so the tomb owner need not lift a finger. The final room, through the last pair of doors, called the *per hedj en pa neferu* (treasury of the beautiful things), held clothing, jewelry, and furniture for the departed one. The series of rooms resembled the open beginning of a house (the waiting room), followed by the columned second part (house of gold), then the smaller, sealed apartment at the rear (the treasury of beautiful things).

For decoration, the limestone walls of a tomb were smoothed and then covered with a thin coat of plaster. In the beginning of the New Kingdom, this plaster was painted white, but by the 19th Dynasty, yellow had come into favor. In any case, the corridors of a pharaoh's tomb were covered with painted scenes, usually maps of the route to the next world, indicating all the obstacles and ferocious beasts to be encountered along the way. The walls and columns of the larger "gold hall" contained scenes of the pharaoh and his wife beside various gods, but the ceiling sometimes represented the heavens with painted stars, sun, and moon.

Egyptologists still wrestle with puzzles about the astonishing constructions of the Egyptians. How, with only bronze tools, were they able to quarry and cut such hard stones as granite and quartzite? The most common building stones were soft limestone or, from the New Kingdom on, equally soft sandstone. Yet Egyptians also carved statues and obelisks of both hard granite and quartzite, which would blunt any bronze tool. In this case, the secret was simply patience: Egyptians seemed to have had a love affair with stone that began long before the first dynasty. Even during such primitive times, they carved hard slate, serpentine, rock crystal, and granite in perfectly shaped and smoothed vessels. We still admire their incorporation of a stone's natural veining in designs, an indication that craftsmen studied rocks long and hard before they began carving. Carving consisted of

The huge pyramids built to be the tombs of pharaohs during the Old Kingdom on the Giza plateau. None of these tombs escaped looting. © The Art Archive/Dagli Orti.

abrading the stone with sand, which contains sharp, hard quartz flakes—over and over—continuously studying its shape before rubbing it again.

Through the simplest methods and tools, and by their hard work and cleverness, the ancient Egyptians accomplished feats of building that continue to evoke awe (Brier and Hobbs, 41–53, 160–68).

FOR MORE INFORMATION

Arnold, D. *Building in Egypt: Pharaonic Stone Masonry*. New York: Oxford University Press, 1991.

Badawy, A. *A History of Egyptian Architecture*. Vols. 1–3. Berkeley: University of California Press, 1966–1968.

Brier, B., and H. Hobbs. *Daily Life of the Ancient Egyptians*. Westport, Conn.: Greenwood Press, 1999.

Budge, E. A. W. *The Egyptian Book of the Dead*. 1899. Reprint, New York: Dover Books, 1967.

Smith, G. E., and W. R. Dawson. *Egyptian Mummies*. London: Kegan Paul International, 1991.

GREECE

In the Greek world, death was prevalent among persons of all age groups, whether as a result of warfare, accident, or illness or, in the case of women, as a consequence of giving birth. It was incorporated into the life of the community to a degree that would strike many people today as morbid. Because there were no hospitals in Greece, most people died either at home or on the battlefield. If death occurred at home, it was the duty of the relatives to prepare the body for burial. Fondling and kissing the corpse were acceptable and customary practices. The Greeks were hardly more intimate with their deceased than their modern counterparts. At a Greek Orthodox funeral, such practices also occur. Significantly, *kêdeia*, the Greek word for funeral, which literally means "a caring for," is still in regular use.

Although we occasionally hear of undertakers, known as *klimakophoroi* or "ladder bearers," *nekrophoroi* or "corpse-bearers," and *tapheis* or "buriers," the duty of these hired hands consisted merely of transporting the corpse from the house to the grave and preparing the ground for burial. Everything suggests that the Greeks would have regarded the idea of handing over the corpse of a dead relative to strangers as offensive and incomprehensible. This attitude had much to do with the belief that in the period between death and burial, the deceased are in need of the solicitous attention of their relatives. Until inhumation or cremation had taken place, they were thought to be in what anthropologists describe as a "liminal" stage—a word that derives from the Latin for "threshold." They were between two worlds, having not yet fully disengaged from this world and awaiting incorporation into the next. Entry to Hades, the world of the dead, did not occur automatically but only as the consequence of strenuous activity on the part of the living. The primary obligation upon the living was thus to perform the burial as expeditiously and efficiently as possible. To fail in this sacred duty was to condemn the dead to wander up and down the banks of the

RELIGIOUS LIFE

DEATH, BURIAL, & THE AFTERLIFE

Mesopotamia

Egypt

Greece

Rome

river Styx, which surrounded Hades, for thousands of years. Greek culture not only tolerated but also expected highly demonstrative manifestations of grief. There are frequent references in literature to men and women tearing out their hair, rending their garments, beating and lacerating their breasts, rolling on the ground and wallowing in the dust, and going without food or drink for several days. This kind of behavior was prompted in part by a desire to honor the deceased, believed to take pleasure in witnessing the exaggerated displays of grief that their death occasioned.

Although the Olympian gods occasionally mourned the passing of their favorites, as Zeus mourned the death of his son Sarpedon, this was the exception rather than the rule. For the most part, they give the impression of being indifferent to the experience of human loss.

The Greek funeral, like our own, was a three-act drama. This comprised the laying out of the body in the home (*prothesis*), the funeral cortege from the home to the place of burial (*ekphora*), and the burial. The *prothesis* was performed by the female relatives of the dead. At the moment of death, the deceased's eyes and mouth were closed. A chin strap was commonly tied around the head and chin to prevent the unsightly sagging of the jaw. The body was washed, anointed in olive oil, clothed, and wrapped in a winding sheet. Finally, it was laid out on a couch with its head propped up on a pillow and its feet facing the door. This last-mentioned practice, which seems to be nearly universal, has given rise to the expression "to carry so-and-so out feet first." From the fourth century B.C.E. onward, there developed a tendency to dress the dead more ornately, sometimes even to place a crown made out of gold foil on the head. When the body had been laid out, relatives were permitted to view the deceased and dirges were sung.

Expenditure on the dead came very high on the list of a rich citizen's financial priorities.

On the day of the funeral, which in Athens had to take place within three days of the death, the mourners accompanied the corpse to the place of burial. Some corpses were laid in a simple wooden coffin, although because of the scarcity of wood, many had to make do with only a winding sheet, strewn with a few branches. The corpse was either borne by pallbearers or transported in a cart to the grave. The burial was performed by the relatives of the deceased. Little is known about the details. The service, such as it was, probably consisted mainly of ritualized laments. Although both inhumation and cremation were practiced with differing degrees of popularity at different times, cremation was regarded as the more prestigious since this is how the dead are disposed of in the Homeric poems. After cremation, the ashes were gathered up and placed in an urn, which was then buried. Once the grave had been filled in, a grave marker was erected. The mourners then returned to the house of the deceased for a commemorative meal.

Because a dead body constituted a strong source of pollution, relatives were required to take elaborate precautions to prevent its contagiousness from seeping out into the community. Such was the degree of public concern that many states passed detailed laws to ensure that the polluting effect of a corpse did not extend beyond the members of the immediate family. Measures to contain the polluting effect of the dead included the following: placing a bowl of water brought from outside the house so that visitors could purify themselves upon entering and leaving; hanging a cypress branch on the door (a custom that may have served to warn passersby of the presence of a corpse within); placing oil flasks containing olive oil around the couch on which the dead was laid out; and most important of all, bathing the corpse. Once the dead had been disposed of, the house was ritually cleaned.

The Greeks had no conception of a necropolis in the literal meaning of that word (though *necropolis* is, of course, a Greek word)—a city of the dead that is separate from the living. Those who dwelled in the country buried their dead on their estates, while city dwellers buried them beside the main roads. The highways leading out of Athens were lined with tombs, in much the same way as advertising billboards clutter our major highways today. The most-frequented roads provided the most-favored burial spots for wealthy families, as indicated by the number of tombs located on the west side of the city in the area known as the Kerameikos or potters' quarter.

This practice of roadside burial was partly a result of a ban on burials within the city because of the fear of the polluting effect of the dead. It may also have been occasioned by the need to conserve as much space as possible, given the fact that Athens was surrounded by a wall. Roadside burial also provided the family of the deceased with an opportunity to advertise its wealth and prestige in a permanent manner, since tombs so located were viewed constantly.

Expenditure on the dead came very high on the list of a rich citizen's financial priorities. We hear, for instance, of one family tomb erected in the final decade of the fifth century B.C.E. that cost at least 2,500 drachmas, although the defendant actually claimed that the true figure was twice that amount (Lysias, 32.1). This was at a time when a rower in Athens's navy earned merely one drachma per day. Bereaved relatives continued to maintain a close attachment to the deceased long after death had occurred, since their welfare in Hades was thought to depend on the attention that they received from the living. Women were expected to pay regular visits to the grave, particularly on the anniversary of the day of death but also at other intervals throughout the year. Because the dead were believed either to dwell in the proximity of their grave or at least to be capable of visiting it, a variety of gifts judged necessary for their physical welfare were deposited on the steps of the tomb. These included jars of olive oil, branches of myrtle, wreaths, cakes, and drink. It was also customary to anoint gravestones with olive oil and to wind colored sashes around their shafts.

The Greeks, however, were extremely reserved in their depictions of death. A frequent image is that of two persons, either seated or standing, shaking hands. In most cases, it is impossible to determine which is intended to represent the deceased and which the living.

The realm of Hades was where "the spirits of the dead dwell, the phantoms of men who are worn out," as Homer puts it. And it is here, too, so to speak, that Homer's description peters out. We learn nothing about the appearance of Hades, its size, its notable landmarks, or its divisions. All that we know is that it was dark and windy. It may strike us as something of a paradox that the Greeks had such an elaborate ritual for dealing with death and burial when their ideas about the afterlife were apparently so indistinct and colorless. Everything that Homer tells us about the dead suggests that their condition was lamentable in the extreme. They are condemned to experience for all eternity the mental anguish to which they were subjected when alive. They remain, too, in the same physical condition as in the moment of their death. Deep in the bowels of Hades was a windy region called Tartaros, to which were consigned all the most miserable sinners. This did not include serial killers and rapists—they would almost certainly have ended up among the general mass of humankind—but those who had outraged and insulted the majesty of the gods. The overwhelming majority of the dead were spared the ordeal of having to go through any postmortem judgment.

In any system, there exists a privileged minority who does not endure the same miserable lot as the rest of humanity, and Hades was no different from anywhere else. In the *Odyssey*, the old man of the sea, called Proteus, delivers the following prophecy:

In your case, Zeus-born Menelaus, it is not fated that you should die and meet your doom in horse-rearing Argos. Instead the immortals will convey you to the Elysian plain and to the bounds of the earth, where fair-haired Rhadamanthys dwells, and where life is easiest for men. There is no snow, nor heavy storm, nor rain, but Oleanus always sends the breezes of soft-blowing Zephyrus [the west wind] to refresh men. (4.561–68)

Menelaus is accorded this privileged status not because he has distinguished himself during his lifetime but because he married one of Zeus's daughters. What kind of existence awaited those who dwelt in the Elysian fields is unclear. Apart from the extremely favorable climatic conditions, which would surely pall after a while, the environment appears to have been unstimulating in the extreme.

Charon, the ferryman who transported the dead across the river Styx or Acheron, was elderly, unkempt, and disagreeable. It was certainly advisable to pay him for his services. A small coin called an obol was therefore placed in the deceased's mouth by caring relatives. Protecting the entrance to Hades was the 2-, 3-, or 50-headed dog Cerberus. (Reports differ as to the exact number of his heads.) Hades, the lord of the dead and king of the entire region, the brother of Zeus and Poseidon, has few known physical traits, apart from dark hair. He is "monstrous" and "strong," "implacable" and "relentless"—no doubt because of the absolute finality of death itself. By and large, those who ran Hades were inoffensive, if not wholly innocuous. It was the sheer boredom and dreariness of Hades that made it so awful. To be there for the duration must be hell indeed.

Although the Homeric image of Hades probably continued to exert a powerful hold over the imagination throughout antiquity, as time passed the Greeks became increasingly uncomfortable with the idea of equal misery for all. Accordingly, from the sixth century B.C.E. onward, they came to believe that those who had been exceptionally virtuous or those who belonged to certain closed sects could expect a more cheerful existence in the hereafter. Notable among these sects were the Pythagoreans and Orphics. Both advocated the belief that the soul did not perish along with the body. Exactly what Pythagoreans and Orphics had in mind by the notion of "soul" is unclear, although it was certainly a more distinctive and conscious entity than a disembodied Homeric shade. They also maintained a belief in an underworld judgment involving rewards and punishments. Abstinence from eating meat and self-discipline were important requirements. Regrettably, we have no means of knowing how widespread such beliefs were or whether they made any significant impact on popular belief.

The afterlife is a subject that is extremely resistant to clear and unambiguous conclusions. Ideas about it are inevitably a hodgepodge of contradictory and ill-thought-out hopes, fears, and fantasies. At the beginning of the *Republic*, Plato puts the following pronouncement into the mouth of the elderly Cephalus:

> When a man gets to the end of his life he becomes subject to fear and anxiety about what lies ahead. The stories told about people in Hades, that if you commit crimes on earth you must pay for them down below, although they were ridiculed for a while, now begin to disturb a man's soul with the possibility that they might be true. (1.330de)

Cephalus's observation may serve as a fitting epitaph to the instability of beliefs concerning the afterlife within the same individual at different periods of his life (Garland, 114–27).

FOR MORE INFORMATION

Garland, R. *Daily Life of the Ancient Greeks*. Westport, Conn.: Greenwood Press, 1998.
———. *The Greek Way of Death*. Ithaca, N.Y.: Cornell University Press, 1985.
Kurtz, D. C., and J. Boardman. *Greek Burial Customs*. London: Thames and Hudson, 1971.

ROME

Romans had enormous reverence for their ancestors, who were the focal point of family rituals. Naturally, the point at which someone becomes an ancestor is when he or she dies, and so it is no surprise that death and burial were subjects of great concern to the Romans.

When Romans died, however, the fate of their bodies was dependent on their economic status. The very poorest Romans sometimes received no burial at all and were simply tossed into open pits, called *puticuli*, just outside the city walls. It is thought this name derives from the verb *putescare*, meaning to rot or decompose, or from the word *putor*, meaning a terrible smell. These suggestively named pits were a mixture of human and animal corpses, garbage, and excrement. Some of these pits were quite large, and one is estimated to contain 24,000 corpses. The Roman authorities were concerned that having these pits so close did not reflect well on the city, so they attempted to pass legislation trying to force people to dump their corpses farther away from the city. All around Rome, there were stones inscribed with decrees of the Senate ordaining that corpses and garbage had to be carried farther than the marker. These do not seem to have done much good, however.

Anyone who could afford to joined a burial club. The usual entry fee was about 100 sesterces, which represented a fair amount of money for a person of modest means, and new members sometimes also had to provide a jar of good wine. In addition, members had to pay monthly dues, which appear to have been quite modest. In one club, for example, the monthly dues were only one and one-quarter sesterces. Interestingly, some of these clubs seem to have been mixes of slaves and free people. If a member of the club died, the others would pay for the funeral expenses. If someone committed suicide, however, he was considered to have forfeited his right to a funeral. Burial clubs had elaborate and formal sets of rules governing precisely what the members had to do for each other. For example, there were different requirements if someone died within the city, outside the city limits but within 20 miles of them, or at a distance of more than 20 miles from the city.

In addition to burying any members who died, the other main activity of the club was to hold a series of feasts, usually about one every other month. Some of the dues were used to fund these feasts, and at each one, several members were responsible for providing a certain minimum amount of food. Sometimes a burial club would pool its money to buy a mausoleum in which urns containing the ashes of cremated members were kept. These might be dug into the ground like caves. The term for such a structure was a *columbaria*. Some of these are quite large, with niches provided for up to 700 urns. Another way for the club to earn money was to rent out some of the extra spaces to nonmembers. Very often, attached to the *columbaria* were dining facilities, where they would hold their feasts. The purpose of these feasts is somewhat unclear. They seem to have been a combination of a way to pay honor to the dead and an excuse to have a good party.

Only the truly wealthy could afford to have an individual tomb built for themselves. These tombs were constructed along the roads leading into the city; thus, to reach the city of the living, one had to first pass through the city of the dead. Tombs were frequently very elaborate and took many forms. Perhaps the most common resembled miniature marble houses. Others took the form of columns, towers, or cones. One of the most famous, which can still be seen today, is the tomb of Gaius Cestius. He had his tomb constructed in the form of a marble pyramid 60 feet high. The inscription on the tomb notes that it took 330 days to build it. Tombs often had pipes protruding out the top of them. The idea behind these was that the family would come out and have a picnic on the tomb and would share the feast with the deceased by dropping food down the tube and pouring in wine.

It was traditional that people would not build their tomb themselves but that their heir would construct it. To ensure that heirs built a suitably impressive structure, many wills contained specific directions for the type of tomb the person wanted. Often, too, it was stipulated that the heir could not receive his inheritance until he had buried the person in the specified manner.

Because standard Roman religious beliefs did not really include a well-developed notion of an afterlife, Romans seemed particularly concerned to leave some enduring memory of themselves behind. Elaborate tombs were one way to do this. Demands placed on your descendents, that they celebrate a feast on your tomb, were another. Some men tried to make sure that they were remembered by setting up funds of money, the interest from which was to be used for certain activities. Despite all the energy that went into the attempt to leave an enduring legacy, many of these efforts were in vain. Tombs were often sold and their valuable marble reused. Poor people would break into mausoleums, throw out the corpses, and use them as dwellings.

Many Christian churches plundered Roman cemeteries for building materials; indeed, the reason many Roman funerary inscriptions survive to the present is that they were built into the walls of churches. Even the Romans sometimes seem not to have shown much reverence for their own tombs. The public toilets in the town of Ostia were constructed out of old tombstones.

A full-fledged burial ceremony for a wealthy Roman noble-man could be very complex. The deceased was dressed in fine clothing, and a wreath was placed on his head. There was then a solemn parade from his house to the Forum. The man's family, friends, and clients all marched in this. The wax masks of his illustrious ancestors were placed on current family members, who also dressed up in clothing indicating the highest rank that that person had attained. Thus, for example, if one of the ancestors had celebrated a triumph, the person wearing his mask would wear the clothes of a triumphor. When they reached the Forum, the people impersonating the ancestors would sit down on a row of ivory chairs placed on the rostra. The corpse was also placed on the rostra and propped upright. One of the sons or another close family member would deliver a eulogy in which he recounted the deeds of the deceased as well as of his ancestors. The procession then traveled outside the city boundaries, where the corpse was usually cremated. During the funeral procession, close female relatives were expected to scream, beat themselves, tear out their hair, scratch their cheeks until they bled, roll on the ground, and pound their heads against the ground. The family also hired musicians and sometimes also professional mourners. These were people who made a living by screaming and wailing as if they were family members. Males were expected to be more restrained, although particularly when a father was burying his son, the father was expected to throw himself on the corpse and talk to it, asking why the deceased had abandoned him.

Certainly the most famous of all Roman funerals was that of Julius Caesar. Marc Antony seems to have given a particularly moving speech on this occasion. The crowds at Caesar's funeral were so large that they could not see his body very well, and so a large wax copy was constructed. This figure was placed upright on a revolving platform and featured realistic depictions of the 23 stab wounds that Caesar had suffered at the hands of Brutus and the assassins. The crowd was so moved by this sight and by Antony's words that they rioted and decided to cremate Caesar's corpse on the spot. They ripped apart whatever they could find to build the bonfire, including the benches of the senators, and in the ensuing chaos they burned down the Senate house itself. Later, when Caesar had been deified as a god, the emperor Augustus built a temple dedicated to him on the spot in the Forum on which his body had been cremated.

During the funeral procession, close female relatives were expected to scream.

~Gregory S. Aldrete

FOR MORE INFORMATION

Hopkins, K. *Death and Renewal.* Sociological Studies in Roman History, vol. 2. Cambridge, England: Cambridge University Press, 1983.

Toynbee, J. M. C. *Death and Burial in the Roman World*. Ithaca, N.Y.: Cornell University Press, 1971.

RELIGIOUS LIFE
|
MAGIC
& SUPERSTITION
|
Mesopotamia

Egypt

Greece

Rome

Magic and Superstition

The terms *magic* and *superstition* did not really have the same connotations for inhabitants of the ancient world as they do for people today. These things were not thought of as dubiously valid concepts that perhaps only a foolish or uneducated person might believe in. Instead, they were simply accepted as factual aspects of the world and were often indistinguishable from religion or science. The obvious explanation for this is, of course, the rudimentary state of science, which had yet to provide rational explanations for even basic natural phenomena like weather. The cause of many illnesses was ascribed to malevolent supernatural forces, and the best way to combat such an attack was therefore with magical incantations and charms of your own.

The Mesopotamians, for example, believed that inimical demons enjoyed tormenting human beings and that sorcerers practicing black magic also might cause illness or misfortune. That such supernatural threats were accepted as a real and common hazard is illustrated by the fact that Mesopotamian law codes list specific punishments for sorcerers using magic to harm others. Early Roman law codes likewise accept the existence of sorcery as factual and prescribe appropriate punishments.

Magic was not only the provenance of the rich and powerful; it is clear that common people also employed it to try to gain an advantage over rivals, to get revenge for grievances, and to attempt to increase their luck in the game of romance. Numerous curse tablets have been found from Greece and Rome and offer fascinating insights into the hopes and fears of ordinary citizens. Given the strength of emotions, both positive and negative, provoked by love, it is not surprising that many of these tablets record the wishes of jealous lovers, unrequited lovers, and vengeful lovers. Sports, too, seem to have provoked passion, and curse tablets have even been discovered buried beneath race horses' stables by ardent fans who wished to ensure that their own favorite would come in first.

One nearly universal aspect of magic in the ancient world was the use of objects thought to be imbued with magical powers that would protect the wearer from supernatural harm. Perhaps the most beautiful of such amulets were those crafted by the Egyptians out of a variety of materials, including a ceramic called faience. Amulets in the form of the eye of Horus or a scarab beetle are common archaeological finds at Egyptian sites and were thought by their wearers to possess potent apotropaic powers.

Another area that inspired much effort was the attempt to predict the future. The ancient Mesopotamians developed sophisticated knowledge of the movements of the stars and planets, but the main motivation for these observations was that it was thought possible to use them to predict the future. Thus, in the ancient world, astronomy and astrology were inseparable and interchangeable. The continuing popularity, even today, of astrology and horoscopes demonstrates the intense appeal that such attempts to gain knowledge about the future still hold. In addition to the stars, there were numerous other methods by which it was thought one could discern clues to future events. Some of the most common include extispicy, the examination of internal organs from sacrificed animals, and divination, the interpretation of signs or omens sent from the gods.

In general for these cultures, magic was an important and often necessary part of daily life and, much like technology, could bring both great benefits and cause great harm, depending on how it was used.

~Gregory S. Aldrete

MESOPOTAMIA

Magic and sorcery were widespread; they were part of experience and faith in ancient Mesopotamia. There were no boundaries separating "magic" from "cult" and "religion." There were two major forms of magic: black magic, which brought harm to people, and white magic, which tried to turn away evil caused by demons, malevolent powers, and humans. Because black magic was dreaded, sorcerers were summoned to cancel spells that brought trouble or misfortune to an individual. Most tablets described white magical activities.

The ancient Mesopotamians lived in a world of supernatural forces that constantly threatened their lives and well-being. Both evil demons and human sorcerers could strike a person at any time. Sometimes a specific demon or sorcerer could not be held responsible for the decline of the victim's well-being. Rather, the afflicted person had committed a sin unknowingly, resulting in a "ban" or "curse," which alienated him from the favor of the god(s). Once the individual became aware of his "sin," the situation could be remedied. However, if the reason for divine anger remained unclear, magic was used.

Two compendiums, called *Surpu* and *Maqlû* (both meaning "burning"), were consulted; they contained spells addressed either to deities known for their exorcistic powers or to fire, which was used to destroy figures representing the enemies of the sufferer. The prayers varied greatly in style, content, and literary merit. They contained mythological allusions, folkloric imagery, hackneyed phrases, and abracadabra-like sequences of words.

Surpu and *Maqlû* were used for different purposes. *Surpu* contained a collection of spells and rituals that described all possible types of misbehavior, such as cultic negligence, domestic trouble, uncharitable conduct, cruelty to animals, and unintentional contact with ritually unclean people or places. *Surpu* was concerned with the purification rites for the offender-victim. Objects carrying the sufferer's misdeeds were burned or discarded. As a result, the patient was released from the evil effects of his previous actions. *Maqlû* was concerned with burning the image of the witch by fire.

The texts noted the importance of identifying the perpetrator, who, in all surviving witchcraft texts, was unknown to the victim. Several law codes referred to procedures to be followed in cases of sorcery. Because an accusation of sorcery was hard to prove, the accuser himself could face death. In cases in which evidence and testimony were not easily refutable, the standard procedure was to bring the case before the divine judges of the river. Immersion in the "Divine River" brought a verdict of guilt (drowning) or innocence (survival).

A large group of omens revealed a predetermined situation, which was avoided by magical means. Omens involved two types of divine revelation given to individuals: (1) a warning about a specific danger predicted by an observable fact; or (2) a notification of a propitious development in the future. Omens were the main way in which Mesopotamian gods communicated their intentions and decisions. These signs could be interpreted through prolonged observation and deep study. The most common forms of divination were examination of the entrails of sacrificial animals (extispicy) and observation of the stars and planets (astrology). Other forms of communication, though rarely used, were oracles, prophecy, necromancy, or incubation (that is, spending the night in a sanctuary to receive a dream message). Omens were either solicited or unsolicited. In the case of a solicited omen, a specialist examined or observed a situation he deliberately induced. The gods could then be asked for advice in a specific situation. Omens predicting disaster for an individual called for the speedy performance of a specific rite to prevent the threat from becoming reality.

Representation of the demon Khumbaba, who appears in *The Epic of Gilgamesh.* © Copyright The British Museum.

Unsolicited omens, such as a solar eclipse, the birth of a baby with two heads, or the appearance of a wild animal in the city, could be seen by anybody, and even the casual observer could be affected. If the sign foretold evil, the observer could ward off its evil effect by preventive rites. Signs observed at an individual's house related primarily to that particular person; events that happened in the community (for instance, a wolf seen in town or an untimely regional thunderstorm) affected a city or district. Events in the capital could have consequences for the state administration. Terrestrial or celestial omens, such as earthquakes or eclipses, affected the whole country and its representatives, the king, the court, and their politics or warfare. Preventive rituals were recorded in various ways. Sometimes they were written on individual tablets, each designed for a specific occurrence. At other times, the ritual instructions and incantations were part of an omen series, so the specialist had easy access to all information necessary.

The common man, upon seeing an omen, probably contacted the nearest literate person, a priest, a scribe, a diviner, an exorcist, or even the local authorities. There was no one specialist to deal with unsolicited omens. If none of these people had access to the necessary manuals, they could contact a more erudite specialist or a higher authority.

Diviners were specialists who solicited omens from the gods and interpreted the signs. A diviner (literally, examiner) communicated with divine forces through extispicy, hepatoscopy, lecanomancy, and libanomancy. Diviners also used a variety of procedures to avoid evil events, such as oral formulas, manual rituals, and prayers. The Mesopotamian diviner's most important tool was a copper kettledrum covered with the hide of a black bull. There were rituals describing the ceremonies to provide a new drumhead. The process involved the ritual preparation of a bull chosen to be slaughtered, tanning its skin, and then installing its hide on the drum. After the bull had been slaughtered and its heart burned, they prepared the animal's skin and mourned its death. The bull was given a ritual burial, but its meat supplied food for the priests—as was done with any other sacrificial animal. Unlike exorcists, diviners did not belong to the priesthood of a particular temple.

Both private individuals and state officials consulted diviners on all important matters. Diviners usually received communications from the gods through extispicy; the diviner requested the gods to "write" their messages on the entrails, especially the liver, which the diviner "read" by examining the organs. Sometimes the diviners used liver models, interpreting the signs to locate or record unusual features. The diviners had extensive handbooks that listed every conceivable deformation, mark, or discoloration, often further defined by location and significance.

Hepatoscopy, the type of divination in which the liver of a sacrificed animal was examined, continued to be the main way of consulting the will of the gods, even when astral divination gained in importance. In fact, portents from celestial omens were verified by the questions submitted to the liver diviner or haruspex.

Extispicy, the form of divination based on examination of the intestines of slaughtered animals, was used to foretell future events. Extispicy involved at least one animal for each inquiry, so private citizens probably resorted to this technique only in extraordinary circumstances. Also, prayers to the stars, particularly to Ursa Major, the Wagon of the Babylonian sky, were employed by the fortune teller to obtain a reliable omen through a dream. During first-millennium B.C.E. Assyria, there were professional "observers of birds" in the king's service. They furnished reports on omens derived from the movement of birds. The observers of birds were also interpreters of dreams. The methods of divination described here sought answers on a binary level. The client, king or citizen, through the medium of the diviner, asked for a "yes" or "no" from the gods for a specific problem or situation.

In the case of an ambiguous reading, the signs were counted, and a mathematical majority of positive or negative aspects were totaled to determine the final verdict. The handbooks used for interpreting the divine signs were organized by topic and followed a format: the omen was listed in the conditional clause (the protasis), "If such-and-such is seen (or happens)," followed by an apodosis that described the portended event in a declarative clause. The list could be expanded indefinitely by variations on the protasis. For example, multiple births were enumerated from two up to eight or nine. Some omens were traced back to historical events of the past, when the occurrences were observed for the first time. Thousands of different signs were collected, and the resulting texts were expanded into purely theoretical "science" by adding scores of conceivable or inconceivable possibilities.

Astral magic is the art of harnessing the power of the stars through prayers and rituals. Professional diviners and exorcists practiced astral magic to foretell the future, avoid evil portents (apotropaic rituals), and find the most auspicious moment to undertake a task. An extensive collection of celestial omens described the influence of astral deities on man. Eventually, the art of celestial divination became a scholarly discipline.

Prayers to stars were just a few lines or a few words that briefly stated the petitioner's appeal. The reason for turning to the particular god or celestial body was not usually stated. In dire circumstances, divine favor was requested by enumerating the names of stars, the names of gods, natural forces, various rivers such as the Tigris and Euphrates, and so on.

The descriptive names the ancient Mesopotamians ascribed to their planets confirm their astronomical knowledge. For example, Mercury was called the Leaping One; Saturn (the slowest), the Steady One; and Mars, the Red Planet or the Enemy. Observational astronomy and recognition of the periodicities of heavenly phenomena began in the Old Babylonian period, but mathematical astronomy did not emerge until the fifth century B.C.E. Babylonian constellations were named after the shapes of their configurations, specifically, human figures, animals, or common objects. These names were either similar or identical to the names of constellations in Classical Greek antiquity. Hemerologies from Mesopotamia enumerated auspicious days for undertaking a particular kind of business or activity, such as building a house, marrying, or offering prayers and sacrifices to the god or goddess. Hemerologies, even in abbreviated form, always included the "evil" days (7, 14, 19, 21, 28). Particular days were named for fasting and sexual abstinence.

There was no clear distinction between the two types of celestial observation, "astronomy" and "astrology." The specialists in these fields either worked together or were experts in both fields. In the case of celestial omens pertaining directly to the king or state, the divinatory science of astrology was generally restricted to specialized scholars associated with the palace or the main temples of the land. Mesopotamian life harnessed the powers of the stars (1) to cause harm or protect from harm, (2) for amulets and charms, (3) for confirming favorable or unfavorable times, and (4) for medicine, from acquiring the herbs or other medicinal substances through preparing and administrating the medications. Moonless nights were particularly appropriate for gathering herbs. The stars transformed ordinary substances into potent ones, effective in magic, medicine, or ritual. Stars also provided reliable answers to the queries of the diviner.

The most influential area of Mesopotamian divination was astrology. The ancient Mesopotamians combined here their belief in omens with observational astronomy, mathematical calculation, and eventually, the prediction of the movements of heavenly bodies. Western astronomy was later founded on these early records.

Mesopotamians used the native term for a "dead person" interchangeably with the word for a "ghost." A corpse was fully human in appearance (though sometimes skeletal), but a ghost was not. Old souls were recycled as new human beings; otherwise, the dead would have dangerously outnumbered the living. Unfriendly ghosts pursued, seized, bound, and even physically abused their victims; they even entered their victims through their ears. Ghosts bothered people by appearing uninvited at their homes, assaulting them in city streets, or haunting their dreams. Persons who traveled through uninhabited areas were particularly susceptible to attack by ghosts, sometimes conjured up by sorcerers. The gods sent ghosts to haunt sinners, in particular, murderers.

Even the most unhappy ghosts could be rendered harmless by performing the correct magical procedure. Methods of dealing with annoying ghosts included tying magic knots, manufacturing amulets, smearing on magical salves, drinking magic potions, pouring out libations while reciting incantations, and burying a surrogate figurine representing the ghost.

As long as offerings were made without interruption, a ghost would remain more or less peaceful. Ghosts of the dead returned to haunt the living because they had not received the proper burial rites or their share of the funerary offerings. To put a stop to their roaming the earth and perpetrating acts of vengeance, the ghosts were appeased with offerings, the same as those regularly given to the dead. Offerings usually consisted of various types of water, vinegar, watered beer, ashes, and breads or flour made from roasted grain.

The preferred method for consulting ghosts involved the preparation of an ointment. Incantations included instructions for preparing the salve, which was composed of a variety of ingredients, some unusual, such as centipede dust, frog intestines, lion fat, and goose-bone marrow. The preparation was smeared on the practitioner's face to enable him to see and speak with the ghost. Alternatively, the salve could be rubbed on a figurine or skull that housed the ghost. If the application of ointments failed, the practitioner tried another ritual, an apotropaic ritual of "undoing," called *namburbû*, for which professional ghost raisers could be hired.

Demons were shapeless forms of evil. The names of many Mesopotamian demons are known to us, but few have been individually described. A few demonic figures were described in detail, such as Lamashtu and Pazuzu. Lamashtu, Anu's daughter, brought evil on her own initiative, attacking pregnant women, young mothers, and babies. Lamashtu was depicted on many amulets, which were meant to discourage her by having the demon view her own image. The ritual texts accompanying the incantations used various magical techniques, most commonly effigies of Lamashtu being killed, destroyed, buried, dispatched downstream, or sent to the desert.

Demons had no cult, received no offerings, and exploited humans mercilessly. The demons who preyed on people were called the "Seven Evil Spirits," each one given a name such as "Evil Fate," "Evil Constable," or "Disorder." The evil spirits brought diseases on their own initiative. The counterparts to the "Evil Spirits" were the "Evil Ghosts," that is, the souls of the dead that returned to earth for food and drink. Many evil spirits were believed to be the children of two senior gods, Anu and Enlil, who were not always friendly to humankind. Not all demons and spirits were ill disposed; some were protective spirits, such as the human-headed winged lions and bulls that guarded the gates of Assyrian palaces.

Many situations in everyday life required, or at least benefited from, the use of magico-religious techniques. "Potency" rituals provide the clearest example for manipulative magic. These spells and instructions were used to seduce, to rekindle passion, and particularly to enable the male partner to sustain an erection. A little magic could go a long way by inducing sexual desire that may have not existed previously. Lovers addressed prayers to Venus, the planet of Ishtar, the goddess of love. The ritual activities prescribed in these texts employed certain objects which were magically "enriched" with the power of love, often derived from the sexual organs of certain animals. These objects were brought into physical contact with the desired partner. The spells usually referred to the strong sexual potency of animals, accompanied by vivid descriptions of sexual techniques, desires, and fantasies—all directed at stimulation and arousal before intercourse.

Magical protection was necessary for both palaces and private residences. Protective spirits were placed near windows, drainpipes, and doorways—that is, places through which demons might enter. The manufacture and use of prophylactic figurines, many of which have been found throughout Mesopotamia, were described in great detail. The statues were buried beside the threshold. A compendium called "the nature of the stone is" listed numerous stones used for appeasing divine anger, preventing migraine, and being received favorably by the king. The power of the stone was defined by its material and its nature. Besides handbooks, there were shorter lists of herbs, stones, or a combination of herbs, stones, shells, and various other magical paraphernalia. Amulets were widely used; they were found in every possible location from royal palaces to poor neighborhoods.

Male and female prophets, literally, "ecstatics" or "frenzied persons," were believed to be selected by the gods for a specific occasion or time period to convey information to an individual or group. The deity usually initiated the communication, but the recipient could also induce communication. The prophets received their information from visions, dreams, auditions, and more mechanical media such as divinatory techniques. Once the prophet received the message, he or she would repeat or rephrase it in oral or written form—often poetically—to provide inspired insight into the situation. Prophetic activity was widespread throughout the ancient Near East, although only a small number of prophetic texts has survived. After the eighth century B.C.E., prophecy became a cultic activity in Assyria—the sayings of both male and female prophets were recorded in tablet series.

Oracles were sometimes similar to prophecies and communicated by priests. At times, the professional honesty of the diviners was doubted. In diviners' reports to Assyrian kings, the diviners go to great lengths to interpret bad omens to have a favorable meaning. To obtain a true report, King Sennacherib of Assyria separated his diviners into two groups—much as today's scientists use a control group (Nemet-Nejat, 196–215).

FOR MORE INFORMATION

Farber, W. "Witchcraft, Magic, and Divination in Ancient Mesopotamia." In *Civilizations of the Ancient Near East*, ed. J. Sasson. Vol. 3. New York: Scribner's, 1995.

Nemet-Nejat, K. R. *Daily Life in Ancient Mesopotamia*. Westport, Conn.: Greenwood Press, 1998.

Reiner, E. *Astral Magic in Babylonia*. Transactions of the American Philosophical Society, vol. 8, part 4. Philadelphia: American Philosophical Society, 1995.

EGYPT

RELIGIOUS LIFE
|
MAGIC
& SUPERSTITION
|
Mesopotamia

Egypt

Greece

Rome

In the face of uncontrollable natural events, average Egyptians tried to protect themselves with magical amulets. The Egyptian word for amulet, *meket,* means "protector" and was supposed to gain a god's intervention for the wearer. These small images were usually crafted with tiny holes so they could be strung and worn around the neck.

Amulets could be made of stone (lapis lazuli, carnelian, turquoise, feldspar, serpentine, and steatite), metal (silver and gold were the most valuable, but bronze was also prized), or wood and bone (inexpensive substitutes for poorer people). Of all the materials used, the most common was a ceramic called faience, a paste of ground quartz and water molded into a desired shape, fired solid in a kiln, and then generally covered with a glassy glaze that added color. Faience amulets were produced by the thousands in factories throughout Egypt. A master amulet of some durable material, such as stone, was pressed into soft clay, which, when baked, became a hard mold into which the faience mixture could be placed. Any number of molds could be made from the master amulet, so thousands of duplicate amulets could be easily produced. Holes were made by rolling a string in quartz paste and pressing it into the mold; when fired, the paste hardened into faience and the string burned away, leaving a hole.

Amulets were designed according to strict rules. The MacGregor Papyrus lists 75 amulets with their names and functions. Another list inscribed on the walls of the temple of Dendera specifies the materials from which each should be made. Egyptians believed that an amulet made from the wrong material would be ineffective, but if a person could not afford a carnelian amulet, then a faience amulet glazed the same color would do.

Protective magic amulet in the form of a scarab beetle.

Amulets invoked the gods; for example, a cat amulet carried the protection of the cat goddess Bastet. One of the most common amulets worn in ancient Egypt was the Udjet (restored) eye, associated with the falcon god Horus. According to myth,

Horus fought his evil uncle Seth to avenge the death of his father, Osiris. During the battle, Horus's eye was torn to pieces, but Toth, the god of writing, assembled the pieces and restored his eye. Thus, amulets depicting the characteristic markings around a falcon's eye became a sign of health and well-being. The most popular amulet of all was associated with the god Khepri, who took the form of a beetle. Carved in the shape of a species of beetle called *Scarabaeus sacer*, from which the modern word *scarab* comes, these amulets enjoyed great popularity for a combination of reasons. The Egyptians were fond of puns, and the hieroglyphs for beetle also meant "to exist," so if one wore a scarab amulet, that person's continued existence was ensured. The scarab was also held in high regard because the ancient Egyptians believed this beetle produced offspring without any union of male and female. After fertilization, the female deposited her eggs in a piece of dung and rolled it into a ball, which provided their newborn with food. Because birth was the only part of this reproductive cycle Egyptians witnessed, they assumed the beetle was somewhat like the god Atum, who begot children without a female partner. Further, after the beetle fashioned its dung ball, it rolled it to a sunny place, which, to the ancient mind, resembled the journey of the sun across the sky. The top of a scarab amulet was carved to resemble the beetle's body, and the bottom was left flat for an inscription, often merely the owner's name, which symbolically requested "keep So-and-So in existence," although frequently a god's or a pharaoh's name was inscribed. Wealthy people set their scarabs in rings so they could be used as seals. The top of a wine jar sealed with moist plaster would be given a scarab imprint to keep thirsty servants at bay; a broken seal could not be repaired undetected (Brier and Hobbs, 53–55).

FOR MORE INFORMATION

Brier, B., and H. Hobbs. *Daily Life of the Ancient Egyptians*. Westport, Conn.: Greenwood Press, 1999.

Pinch, G. *Magic in Ancient Egypt*. London: British Museum Press, 1994.

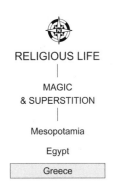

RELIGIOUS LIFE

MAGIC
& SUPERSTITION

Mesopotamia

Egypt

Greece

Rome

GREECE

Magic is a difficult concept to identify in ancient Greece because there was no category exactly equivalent to our notion. (The word *magos*, from which our word *magic* derives, referred to a Persian shaman.) It is likely that the use of magical practices was widespread in all places and at all times. Although a number of Greek philosophers, including Plato and Aristotle, as well as members of the medical profession, tended to equate magic with fraud, there was never any systematic persecution of its practitioners, as there was of witches in medieval Europe and later. This is all the more surprising in view of the negative image of witches that we receive from Greek mythology. A particularly chilling example is Medea, who in Euripides' play, *Medea*, uses her dark skills to fashion a deadly wedding dress for her ex-husband's bride and also murders her own children. As today, witchcraft seems to have been associated primarily with women, especially foreigners.

The Hellenistic writer Theophrastus provides a compelling portrait of an individual who is weighed down by a dread of both religious and magical taboos:

The superstitious man is the kind of person who . . . if a weasel crosses his path will not walk on until someone else has passed him or until he has thrown three stones across the road. . . . When he encounters smooth stones at the crossroads, he will pour oil from his oil flask upon them and go down on his knees and perform obeisance in order to be released from their power. And if a mouse gnaws a hole in a sack of barley, he goes to an expert in order to find out what to do. And if the expert tells him to go to a cobbler and have it stitched up, he won't pay any attention. Instead he'll go away and perform a sacrifice. (*Characters* 16.3–6)

There are numerous references to magic in Greek literature. The earliest is in Book 10 of Homer's *Odyssey*, where we encounter the witch Circe, who uses a variety of magical devices, including salves, potions, and a magic wand, and who is capable of transforming Odysseus's companions into swine.

From the late fifth century B.C.E. onward, individuals who wished to evoke the dark powers beneath the earth commonly used the dead as their go-betweens. Favored messengers were those who died young and those who died violently, particularly suicides and murder victims. A popular custom was to inscribe a lead tablet with the names of the persons to be cursed and then place the tablet in the grave alongside the gifts that were intended for use by the deceased in the world to come. In some cases, as many as 15 names are mentioned on a single tablet. Many tablets allude to the parts of a person's body that are to be cursed—the tongue, the eyes, the soul, the mind, the mouth, the arms, the legs, and so forth. Various underworld powers are invoked, including Persephone and Hermes. To reach the other world, the lead tablet had to be "canceled" for use by the living. For this reason, tablets are often found with a nail driven through them. A variant on this device was a kind of antique "voodoo doll"—a miniature figure made of lead whose arms were bound behind its back. The doll was sometimes transfixed through the breast with a needle. One of the most common reasons for cursing in litigious Athens was a lawsuit, as we know from the discovery of tablets that curse individuals who have allegedly given false testimony. Magic also played an important part in religious rituals, notably in regard to birth. The midwife, who in the absence of male physicians, presided unaided in the birthing room, possessed a variety of skills of a magical, religious, and quasi-medical nature.

As a protection against curses, bad luck, and the evil eye, amulets were often worn around the body, particularly in the case of young children. Many of these were made of cheap materials, although precious stones were believed to have special efficacy. Plutarch (*Life of Pericles* 38.2) tells us that when Pericles fell ill of the plague, he tied an amulet around his neck. This was taken as proof that the statesman, an avowed rationalist, really must be in a bad way "if he was prepared to put up with such nonsense." Herbs and plants were believed to possess magical healing properties. In addition, foreign and nonsense words were credited with magical powers (Garland, 127–29).

FOR MORE INFORMATION

Garland, R. *Daily Life of the Ancient Greeks*. Westport, Conn.: Greenwood Press, 1998.
Luck, G. *Arcana Mundi: Magic and the Occult in the Greek and Roman Worlds*. Baltimore, Md.: Johns Hopkins University Press, 1985.

RELIGIOUS LIFE
|
MAGIC
& SUPERSTITION
|
Mesopotamia

Egypt

Greece

Rome

ROME

Some aspects of the Romans' religion we might consider more superstitions than formal religious beliefs. Many of the present superstitions that people follow today are directly traceable to ancient ones, including black cats crossing your path and stepping under ladders as harbingers of bad luck.

The emperor Augustus was rather superstitious. If he put the wrong shoe on upon getting out of bed, he thought it was a bad omen for the day. If dew was present as he started a long journey, he considered it a good sign. At all times, he carried around a piece of sealskin, which he thought would protect him from thunderstorms (Suetonius, *Life of Augustus* 90, 92). He also liked to repeat stories about omens that foretold his rise to power. One of these was that as a very young child on the family farm, he once ordered some frogs to stop croaking, and to everyone's astonishment, they promptly stopped and never croaked again. (Suetonius, *Life of Augustus* 94). Some superstitions were associated with good luck icons. The Roman general Sulla always carried about a little statue of the god Apollo; whenever the general got in trouble, he would kiss it and pray to it.

Tiberius, Augustus's successor, was particularly superstitious. He had a favorite pet snake that he took everywhere with him. One time when he set out on a journey for Rome, he opened up its box and discovered that his snake had been eaten by ants. At this, he immediately turned around and canceled his journey (Suetonius, *Life of Tiberius* 72). Tiberius was also an enthusiastic follower of astrology and in the latter half of his reign spent all his time on an island with his personal astrologer, named Thrasyllus (Suetonius, *Life of Tiberius* 14). Many people believed that Thrasyllus really ran the empire because Tiberius would not do anything without consulting his astrologer, and if he received a negative horoscope, he would cancel that activity or decree.

Another aspect of Roman religion that seems closer to magic is the Romans' attempts to place curses on their enemies to bring them bad luck. These curses were made not just on an individual level but even on a national one. After the ritual of *evocatio* by which the Romans invited the gods of a city they were attacking to come over to the Roman side, the Romans then usually followed up with the *devotio*, which was in essence a curse pledging the enemy city to the gods of the underworld.

Individuals also attempted to place curses on their enemies. Oddly enough, the details of many of these curses are known today because of the way they were created. The curse would be written on a tablet, often by a professional sorcerer, and then it was in essence mailed to the gods of the underworld by dropping the tablet down a well, throwing it in a cave, or burying it. The usual form that the curse on the tablets took was to address one or several of the gods of the underworld, such as Pluto, promise him something for helping you, and then consign your enemy to him. To make this more explicit, it was common to list all of your enemy's body parts.

In addition to these general curses condemning an entire person, there were curses that asked for specific actions. Archaeologists have found a number of these hidden in the walls of horse stables. Chariot racing was an extremely popular sport, and fans apparently tried to curse the horses of opposing teams. Naturally, another way that people used magic was to attempt to make others love them, and a large number of magic spells and incantations survive testifying to desperate people's attempts to make the objects of their obsession return their love or lust.

> ### 📷 Snapshot
>
> **A Roman Curse Tablet**
>
> O wife of Pluto, good and beautiful Proserpina . . . pray tear away from Plotius health, body, complexion, strength, faculties. Consign him to Pluto, your husband. May he be unable to avoid this by devices of his. Consign that man to the fourth-day, the third-day, the every-day fever. May they wrestle and wrestle it out with him, overcome and overwhelm him unceasingly until they tear away his life. So I consign him as victim to thee, Proserpina, unless, O Proserpina, unless I ought to call thee Goddess of the Lower World.
>
> Send, I pray, someone to call up the three-headed dog with request that he may tear out Plotius's heart. Promise Cerberus that thou wilt give him three offerings—dates, dried figs, and a black pig—if he has fulfilled his task before the month of March. All these, Proserpina Salvia, will I give thee when thou hast made me master of my wish. (as cited in Matz, 129; *Corpus Inscriptionum Latinarum* 1.2520)

Foretelling the future was always a topic of interest. The various forms of prophecy connected to reading signs from the gods have been described in the section on priests and ritual. There was, however, even an instance of the Roman equivalent of a Ouija board. A group of people who wanted to know the future made a magic device. They fashioned a tripod of laurel twigs from the top of which they suspended a ring on a fine cotton thread. The tripod was placed over a metal dish whose outer rim was engraved with the 24 letters of the Greek alphabet. The whole thing was consecrated with spells and magic rites. They then asked it a question that they wanted answered and put the ring into motion; the ring would swing in the direction of individual letters, spelling out the answer. One of the questions they asked of it was who would be the next emperor; when word of this magic rite came to the current emperor, he had them tried for treason and executed (Ammianus Marcellinus, *Roman History* 1.25).

~*Gregory S. Aldrete*

FOR MORE INFORMATION

Betz, H. D. *The Greek Magical Papyri in Translation*. Chicago: University of Chicago Press, 1986.

Luck, G. *Arcana Mundi: Magic and the Occult in the Greek and Roman Worlds*. Baltimore, Md.: Johns Hopkins University Press, 1985.

RELIGIOUS LIFE: WEB SITES

http://religion.rutgers.edu/vri/grk_rom.html
http://www.bbc.co.uk/history/ancient/egyptians/gods_gallery.shtml
http://web.uvic.ca/grs/bowman/myth/gods.html
http://www.mnsu.edu/emuseum/prehistory/egypt/religion/religion.html
http://www.providence.edu/dwc/mesomyth.htm

PRIMARY SOURCES

This excerpt describes the declaration of innocence that souls had to make when they came for judgment before Osiris, the god of the underworld.

[The dead will say:]
Homage to you, Great God, the Lord of the double Ma'at (Justice or Truth)!
I have come to you, my Lord,
I have brought myself here to behold your beauties.
I know you, and I know your name,
And I know the names of the two and forty gods,
Who live with you in the Hall of the Two Truths,
Who imprison the sinners, and feed upon their blood,
On the day when the lives of men are judged in the presence of Osiris.
In truth, you are "The Twin Sisters with Two Eyes," and "The Daughters of the Two Truths."
In truth, I now come to you, and I have brought Ma'at to you,
And I have destroyed wickedness for you.
I have committed no evil upon men.
I have not oppressed the members of my family.
I have not wrought evil in the place of right and truth.
I have had no knowledge of useless men.
I have brought about no evil.
I did not rise in the morning and expect more than was due to me.
I have not brought my name forward to be praised.
I have not oppressed servants.
I have not scorned any god.
I have not defrauded the poor of their property.
I have not done what the gods abominate.

I have not caused harm to be done to a servant by his master.

I have not caused pain.

I have caused no man to hunger.

I have made no one weep.

I have not killed.

I have not given the order to kill.

I have not inflicted pain on anyone.

I have not stolen the drink left for the gods in the temples.

I have not stolen the cakes left for the gods in the temples.

I have not stolen the cakes left for the dead in the temples.

I have not fornicated.

I have not polluted myself.

I have not diminished the bushel when I've sold it.

I have not added to or stolen land.

I have not encroached on the land of others.

I have not added weights to the scales to cheat buyers.

I have not misread the scales to cheat buyers.

I have not stolen milk from the mouths of children.

I have not driven cattle from their pastures.

I have not captured the birds of the preserves of the gods.

I have not caught fish with bait made of like fish.

I have not held back the water when it should flow.

I have not diverted the running water in a canal.

I have not put out a fire when it should burn.

I have not violated the times when meat should be offered to the gods.

I have not driven off the cattle from the property of the gods.

I have not stopped a god in his procession through the temple.

I am pure.

I am pure.

I am pure.

I am pure.

ADDRESS TO THE GODS OF THE UNDERWORLD

Hail, gods, who dwell in the house of the Two Truths.

I know you and I know your names.

Let me not fall under your slaughter-knives,

And do not bring my wickedness to Osiris, the god you serve.

Let no evil come to me from you.

Declare me right and true in the presence of Osiris,

Because I have done what is right and true in Egypt.

I have not cursed a god.

I have not suffered evil through the king who ruled my day.

Hail, gods who dwell in the Hall of the Two Truths,

Who have no evil in your bodies, who live upon maat,
Who feed upon maat in the presence of Horus
Who lives within his divine disk.
Deliver me from the god Baba,
Who lives on the entrails of the mighty ones on the day of the great judgement.
Grant that I may come to you,
For I have committed no faults,
I have not sinned,
I have not done evil,
I have not lied,
Therefore let nothing evil happen to me.
I live on maat, and I feed on maat,
I have performed the commandments of men and the things pleasing to the gods,
I have made the god to be at peace with me,
I have acted according to his will.
I have given bread to the hungry man, and water to the thirsty man,
And clothes to the naked man, and a boat to the boatless.
I have made holy offerings to the gods,
and meals for the dead.
Deliver me, protect me, accuse me not in the presence of Osiris.

See http://www.wsu.edu/~dee/egypt/bod125.htm.

"HEKANAKHT'S INSTRUCTIONS TO HIS HOUSEHOLD," #69, P. HEKANAKHT NO. 2 (CA. 2000 B.C.E.)

This letter written by a minor official named Hekanakht giving instructions to his family in his absence is an enlightening window on the day-to-day concerns of an ancient Egyptian touching on domestic and economic concerns.

It is a son who speaks to his mother, namely, the mortuary priest Hekanakht to his mother Ipi and to Hetepe: How are you both? Are you alive, prospering, and healthy? In the favor of Montu, lord of the Theban nome!

And to the entire household: How are you? Are you alive, prospering, and healthy? Don't worry about me, for I'm healthy and alive. Now you are the case of the one who ate until he was sated having gotten so hungry that his eyes had become glassy white. Whereas the whole land has died off, [you] haven't hungered; for when I came south to where you are, I fixed your food allowance in good measure. Isn't the Nile inundation very [low]? Since [our] food allowance has been fixed for us according to the nature of the Nile inundation, bear patiently, each of you, for I have succeeded so far among you in keeping you alive.

Record of food rations for the household:

Ipi and her maidservant	8 *hekat*-measures
Hetepe and her maidservant	8 *hekat*-measures
Hety's son Nakht and his dependents	8 *hekat*-measures
Merisu and his dependents	8 *hekat*-measures
Sihathor	8 *hekat*-measures
Sinebniut	7 *hekat*-measures
Anup	4 *hekat*-measures
Snefru	4 *hekat*-measures
Siinut	4 *hekat*-measures
My's daughter Hetepe	5 *hekat*-measures
Nofre	3.5 *hekat*-measures
Sitwere	2 *hekat*-measures

Total: 6 [text: 7] *khar*-measures, 9.5 *hekat*-measures [of barley].

(Note): It is from his northern barley that rations should be meted out to Sinebniut; and until he leaves for Perhaa, they [the rations] should be at his disposal.

Lest you be angry about this, look here, the entire household is just like [my] children, and I'm responsible for everything so that it should be said, "To be half alive is better than dying outright." Now it is only real hunger that should be termed hunger since they have started eating people here, and none are given such rations anywhere else. Until I come back home to you, you should comport yourselves with stout hearts, for I shall be spending the third season here.

Communication by the mortuary priest Hekanakht to Merisu and to Hety's son Nakht, who is subordinate: Only as long as my people keep on working shall you give them these rations. Take great care! Hoe every field of mine, keep sieving [the seed grain], and hack with your noses in the work! Now if they are assiduous, you shall be thanked so that I will not have to make it miserable for you. On the first day of the month of Khentykhetyperty one shall start distributing the rations about which I have written for the new first day of the month.

Don't be unmindful then of the 10 arouras of land which are in the neighborhood and which were given to Ip Junior's son Khentykhe and hoe them. Be very assiduous since you are consuming my food.

Now as for any chattel belonging to Anup which is in your possession, give it back to him! As for what is lost, reimburse him for it. Don't make me write you about this again since I've already written you about this twice.

Now if, as you say, Snefru wants to be in charge of the bulls, you should put him in charge of them. He neither wants to be with you plowing, going up and down, nor does he want to come here to be with me. Whatever else he may want, it is with what he wants that you should make him happy.

Now as for whoever of the women or men may reject these rations, he should come to me here to be with me just to live as I live.

Now when I came to where you are, didn't I warn you not to keep a companion of Hetepe's from her, be it her hairdresser or her domestic? Take great care of her! If only you would persevere in everything accordingly. But since, as you say, you don't want her around, you should have Iutenhab [Hekanakht's new wife?] brought to me.

As this man lives for me—it's Ip I'm referring to—whoever shall make any sexual advance against my new[?] wife, he is against me and I against him. Since this is my new[?] wife and it is known how a man's new[?] wife should be helped, so as for whoever shall help her, it's the same as helping me. Would even one of you be patient if his wife has been denounced to him? So should I be patient! How can I remain with you in the same community if you won't respect my new[?] wife for my sake?

Now I have sent to you by Sihathor 24 copper *debens* for the renting of land. Have then 20 arouras of land cultivated for us on lease in Perhaa next to Hau Junior's [paying] in copper, I clothing, in northern barley, or [in] any[thing] else, but only if you shall have gotten a good value there for oil or for whatever else. Take great care! Be very assiduous and be vigilant, [since] you are on good irrigated land of the region of Khepesheyet.

Address: What the mortuary priest Hekanakht sends to his household of the village of Nebeseyet.

From E. S. Meltzer, ed., *Letters from Ancient Egypt*, trans. E. F. Wente (Atlanta, Ga.: Scholars Press, 1990).

THE EPIC OF GILGAMESH, "THE GREAT FLOOD" (CA. 2100 B.C.E.), TABLET XI

This Mesopotamian epic relates the life of King Gilgamesh of Uruk. In this passage, a man named Per-napishtim tells Gilgamesh the story of a great flood sent by the gods and how he escaped drowning by building a ship. The account has obvious parallels to the story of Noah in the Bible.

Per-napishtim then said unto Gilgamesh:
"I will reveal unto thee, O Gilgamesh, the mysterious story,
and the mystery of the gods I will tell thee.
The city of Shurippak, a city which, as thou knowest,
is situated on the bank of the river Euphrates.
That city was corrupt, so that the gods within it
decided to bring about a deluge, even the great gods,
as many as there were: their father, Anu;
their counsellor, the warrior Bel;
their leader, Ninib;
their champion, the god En-ui-gi.

But Ea, the lord of unfathomable wisdom, argued with them.
Their plan he told to a reed-hut, [saying]:
'Reed-hut, reed-hut, clay-structure, clay-structure!
Reed-hut, hear; clay-structure, pay attention!
Thou man of Shurippak, son of Ubara-Tutu,
Build a house, construct a ship;
Forsake thy possessions, take heed for thy life!
Abandon thy goods, save [thy] life,
and bring living seed of every kind into the ship.
As for the ship, which thou shalt build,
let its proportions be well measured:
Its breadth and its length shall bear proportion each to each,
and into the sea then launch it.'
I took heed, and said to Ea, my lord:
'I will do, my lord, as thou hast commanded;
I will observe and will fulfil the command.
But what shall I answer to [the inquiries of] the city, the
people, and the elders?'
Ea opened his mouth and spoke,
and he said unto me, his servant:
'Man, as an answer say thus unto them:
"I know that Bel hates me.
No longer can I live in your city;
Nor on Bel's territory can I live securely any longer;
I will go down to the 'deep,' I will live with Ea, my lord.
Upon you he will [for a time?] pour down rich blessing.
He will grant you fowl [in plenty] and fish in abundance,
Herds of cattle and an abundant harvest.
Shamash has appointed a time when the rulers of darkness
at eventide will pour down upon you a destructive rain." '
"All that was necessary I collected together.
On the fifth day I drew its design;
In its middle part its sides were ten gar high;
Ten gar also was the extent of its deck;
I added a front-roof to it and closed it in.
I built it in six stories,
thus making seven floors in all;
The interior of each I divided again into nine partitions.
Beaks for water within I cut out.
I selected a pole and added all that was necessary.
Three [variant, five] shar of pitch I smeared on its outside;
three shar of asphalt I used for the inside [so as to make it water-tight].
Three shar of oil the men carried, carrying it in vessels.
One shar of oil I kept out and used it for sacrifices,
while the other two shar the boatman stowed away.

For the temple of the gods [?] I slaughtered oxen;

I killed lambs [?] day by day.

Jugs of cider [?], of oil, and of sweet wine,

Large bowls [filled therewith?], like river water [i.e., freely] I poured out as libations.

I made a feast [to the gods] like that of the New-Year's Day.

To god Shamash my hands brought oil.

. . . the ship was completed.

. . . heavy was the work, and

I added tackling above and below, [and after all was finished,]

"The ship sank into water two thirds of its height.

With all that I possessed I filled it;

with all the silver I had filled it;

with all the gold I had filled it;

with living creatures of every kind I filled it.

Then I embarked also all my family and my relatives,

cattle of the field, beasts of the field, and the uprighteous people—all them I embarked.

A time had Shamash appointed, [namely]:

'When the rulers of darkness send at eventide a destructive rain,

then enter into the ship and shut its door.'

This very sign came to pass, and

The rulers of darkness sent a destructive rain at eventide.

I saw the approach of the storm,

and I was afraid to witness the storm;

I entered the ship and shut the door.

I intrusted the guidance of the ship to Purur-bel, the boatman,

the great house, and the contents thereof.

As soon as early dawn appeared,

there rose up from the horizon a black cloud,

within which the weather god [Adad] thundered,

and Nabu and the king of the gods [Marduk] went before.

"The destroyers passed across mountain and dale [literally, country].

Dibbara, the great, tore loose all the anchor-cable [?].

There went Ninib and he caused the banks to overflow;

the Anunnaki lifted on high [their] torches,

and with the brightness thereof they illuminated the universe.

The storm brought on by Adad swept even up to the heavens,

and all light was turned into darkness.

. . . overflooded the land like. . . .

It blew with violence and in one day [?] it rose above the mountains [?].

Like an onslaught in battle it rushed in on the people.

Not could brother look after brother.

Not were recognised the people from heaven.

The gods even were afraid of the storm;

they retreated and took refuge in the heaven of Anu.

There the gods crouched down like dogs, on the inclosure of heaven they sat cowering.

Then Ishtar cried out like a woman in travail,

and the lady of the gods lamented with a loud voice, [saying]:

'The world of old has been turned back into clay,

because I assented to this evil in the assembly of the gods.

Alas! that when I assented to this evil in the council of the gods,

I was for the destruction of my own people.

What have I created, where is it?

Like the spawn of fish it fills the sea.'

The gods wailed with her over the Anunnaki.

The gods were bowed down, and sat there weeping.

Their lips were pressed together [in fear and in terror].

Six days and nights

The wind blew, and storm and tempest overwhelmed the country.

When the seventh day drew nigh the tempest, the storm, the battle

which they had waged like a great host began to moderate.

"The sea quieted down; hurricane and storm ceased.

I looked out upon the sea and raised loud my voice,

But all mankind had turned back into clay.

Like the surrounding field had become the bed of the rivers.

I opened the air-hole and light fell upon my cheek.

Dumbfounded I sank backward, and sat weeping,

while over my cheek flowed the tears.

I looked in every direction, and behold, all was sea.

Now, after twelve [days?] there rose [out of the water] a strip of land.

To Mount Nisir the ship drifted.

On Mount Nisir the boat stuck fast and it did not slip away.

The first day, the second day, Mount Nisir held the ship fast, and did not let it slip away.

The third day, the fourth day, Mount Nisir held the ship fast, and did not let it slip away.

The fifth day, the sixth day, Mount Nisir held the ship fast, and did not let it slip away.

When the seventh day drew nigh

I sent out a dove, and let her go.

The dove flew hither and thither,

but as there was no resting-place for her, she returned.

Then I sent out a swallow, and let her go.

The swallow flew hither and thither,

but as there was no resting-place for her she also returned.

Then I sent out a raven, and let her go.

The raven flew away and saw the abatement of the waters.

She settled down to feed, went away, and returned no more.

Then I let everything go out unto the four winds, and I offered a sacrifice.

I poured out a libation upon the peak of the mountain.

I placed the censers seven and seven,

and poured into them calamus, cedar-wood, and sweet-incense.

The gods smelt the savour;

yea, the gods smelt the sweet savour;

and gods gathered like flies around the sacrificer."

From R. Johnson, ed., *Assyrian and Babylonian Literature* (New York: D. Appleton, 1901).

THE LAW CODE OF HAMMURABI, LAWS 1–4, 6, 16, 22, 25, 42, 53, 128–30, 138–43, 153, 154, 168, 175, 195–202, 215, 218, 229, 244, 282 (CA. 1700 B.C.E.)

Although its justice is unequal and can be harsh, this early law code establishes necessary rules for people to live together and to mediate disputes. Its statutes also reveal much about Babylonian society and culture.

1. If a man brings an accusation against a man, and charges him with a [capital] crime, but cannot prove it, the accuser shall be put to death.

2. If a man charges a man with sorcery, and cannot prove it, he who is charged with sorcery shall go to the river, into the river he shall throw himself and if the river overcome him, his accuser shall take to himself his house [estate]. If the river shows that man to be innocent and he come forth unharmed, he who charged him with sorcery shall be put to death. He who threw himself into the river shall take to himself the house of his accuser.

3. If a man in a case should bear false witness, or does not establish the truth of the testimony that he has given, if it be a capital trial, that man shall be put to death.

4. If a man gives false testimony for grain or money [as a bribe], he shall himself bear the penalty imposed in that case.

6. If a man steals the property of a god [from a temple] or a palace, that man shall be put to death; and he who receives from his hand the stolen property shall also be put to death.

16. If a man aids a male or female slave of the palace, or a male or female slave of a freeman to escape from the city gate, he shall be put to death.

22. If a man practices brigandage and is captured, that man shall be put to death.

25. If a fire breaks out in a man's house and a man who goes to extinguish it should covet the furniture of the owner of the house, and take the furniture of the owner of the house, that man shall be thrown into that fire.

42. If a man rents a field for cultivation and does not produce any grain in the field, they shall call him to account, because he has not performed the work required

on the field, and he shall give to the owner of the field an amount of grain equal to the average of the neighboring fields.

53. If a man neglects to strengthen his dike and do not strengthen it, and a break be made in his dike and the water carries away the farmland, the man in whose dike the break has been made shall restore the grain which he has damaged.

128. If a man takes a wife and does not arrange with her a proper marriage contract, that woman is not a legal wife.

129. If the wife of a man is captured lying with another man, they shall be bound together and thrown into the water. If the husband of the woman would save his wife, or if the king would save his male servant he may.

130. If a man rapes the fiancée of another who is a virgin and is living in her father's house, that man shall be put to death and that woman shall go free.

138. If a man would divorce his wife who has not borne him children, he shall give her money to the amount of her marriage settlement and he shall make good to her the dowry which she brought from her father's house, and then he may divorce her.

139. If there was no marriage contract, he shall give to her one mana of silver for a divorce.

140. If he is a freeman, he shall give her one-third mana of silver.

141. If a wife who is living in her husband's house shall act foolishly, neglect her house, belittle her husband, she shall be called to account; if her husband says "I divorce her" he shall let her go. On her departure nothing shall be given to her for her divorce. If her husband says: "I have not divorced her," her husband may take another woman. The first woman shall dwell in the house of her husband as a maidservant.

142. If a woman hates her husband, and says "You will not have me," there will be an inquiry into her actions and her defects; and if she has been a careful mistress and is without reproach and her husband have been going about and greatly belittling her, that woman has no blame. She shall receive her dowry and shall go to her father's house.

143. If she has not been a careful mistress, has idled about, has neglected her house, and has belittled her husband, they shall throw that woman into the water.

153. If a woman brings about the death of her husband for the sake of another man, they shall impale her.

154. If a man has committed incest with his daughter, they shall expel that man from the city.

168. If a man decides to disinherit his son and says to the judges: "I will disinherit my son," the judges shall inquire into his actions, and if the son has not committed a crime sufficiently grave to cut him off from sonship, the father may not cut off his son from sonship.

175. If either a slave of the palace or a slave of a freeman marries the daughter of a gentleman and she bears children, the owner of the slave may not lay claim to the children of the daughter of the man for service.

195. If a man strikes his father, they shall cut off his fingers.

196. If a man destroys the eye of another man, they shall destroy his eye.

197. If one breaks a man's bone, they shall break his bone.

198. If one destroys the eye of a freeman or breaks the bone of a freeman, he shall pay one mana of silver.

199. If one destroys the eye of a man's slave or break a bone of a man's slave he shall pay one-half his price.

200. If a man knocks out a tooth of a man of his own rank, they shall knock out his tooth.

201. If one knocks out the tooth of a freeman, he shall pay one-third mana of silver.

202. If a man strikes a man who is his superior, he shall receive 60 strokes with an ox-tail whip in public.

215. If a physician operates on a man for a severe wound with a bronze lancet and saves the man's life; or if he opens an abscess in the eye of a man with a bronze lancet and saves that man's eye, he shall receive 10 sheckels of silver [as his fee].

218. If a physician operates on a man for a severe wound with a bronze lancet and causes the man's death; or opens an abscess in the eye of a man with a bronze lancet and destroys the man's eye, they shall cut off his fingers.

229. If a builder builds a house for a man and does not make its construction firm, and the house which he has built collapses and causes the death of the owner of the house, that builder shall be put to death.

244. If a man hires an ox or an ass and a lion kills it in the field, it is the owner's loss.

282. If a male slave says to his master: "Thou art not my master," his master shall prove him to be his slave and shall cut off his ear.

Adapted from R. F. Harper, *The Code of Hammurabi King of Babylon*, 2nd ed. (Chicago: University of Chicago Press, 1904).

HOMER, *ILIAD*, EXCERPTS FROM BOOK 22 (CA. 750 B.C.E.)

The *Iliad* is set during the Trojan War fought between a coalition of Greek states and the city of Troy in Asia Minor. This excerpt describes the final confrontation between the greatest Greek warrior, Achilles, and his Trojan counterpart, Hector.

Then trembling seized Hector and he could no longer stand to remain there, but leaving the gates behind, he fled headlong. The son of Peleus [Achilles], confident in his swift feet, sprang toward him like a hawk of the mountains, lightest of winged things, swoops effortlessly upon a timid dove, but it darts out from beneath him and in close pursuit he utters a harsh cry and dashes upon the dove again and again with his heart within goading him to seize it. Thus Achilles flew eagerly straight at Hector, who ran away beneath the wall of the Trojans with his knees moving rapidly.

They raced by the watchtower and the wind-beaten fig tree, and they ran along the wagon road which skirted the walls. . . . A good man ran in front but a better one came behind him. Both ran quickly since they were not competing for a prize such as a sacrificial cow or an ox hide such as they award winners in the foot race, but the prize they ran for was the life of Hector the horse-tamer. Like award-winning, sure-footed horses run swiftly around the posts of a course at funeral games when a great prize such as a tripod or a woman is at stake, thus the two ran on their quick feet three times around the city of Priam.

All the gods watched, and the father of gods and men was the first to speak: "Alas! Truly I see with my eyes a man dear to me is being chased around the walls, and my heart is saddened for Hector who burned for me so many thighs of cows on Mount Ida of the many peaks and also from the towers of the city. Now godlike Achilles chases him with swift feet around the town of Priam. Now you gods must think about whether we should save him from death or despite his goodness let him be conquered by Achilles the son of Peleus."

Athena the gleaming-eyed goddess spoke to him: "Oh cloud-wrapped father of the shining thunderbolt, what are you saying? Do you want to set free a mortal man from horrid-sounding death whose doom was determined by fate long ago? Do it if you want. But all the rest of us gods will not agree with you."

Zeus the Cloud-Gatherer spoke to her in reply: "Oh Tritogeneia, dear daughter, do not lose heart. I did not speak in anger and I am well-disposed toward you. Do what you think best and do not delay." Thus speaking, he urged on Athena, who went rushing down eagerly from the summit of Olympus to carry out her plan. . . .

Father Zeus lifted up the golden scales and placed within them two fates, each weighted with death, one for Achilles and one for Hector the horse-tamer. Zeus seized it in the middle and held it up, and when the heavy fate of Hector sank down toward Hades, Phoebus Apollo abandoned him on the battlefield.

The gleaming-eyed goddess Athena came down . . . and overtook godlike Hector. She stood near Hector and took on the shape and hard voice of Deïphobos. She said: "Dear brother, truly swift Achilles presses you very hard, chasing you around the town of Priam on his swift feet. Come on, let us make a stand and defend ourselves against him. . . .

When Hector and Achilles drew near to one another, Hector of the great shining helmet spoke first: "Son of Peleus, I will not continue to run away from you as I have been doing. Three times I fled around the great town of Priam and did not dare to stand my ground to attack you. But now my heart urges me to stand against you. I will kill or be killed. Come, let us call on the gods as witnesses, since they are the guardians of treaties and are the best witnesses. If Zeus should grant me victory and let me take your life, Achilles, I will not shamefully dishonor you, but after having stripped off your excellent arms, I will give your corpse back to the Achaians. Say that you will do the same."

Then with a hateful look, swift-footed Achilles said: "Accursed Hector, do not talk to me of agreements. As there are no treaties between lions and men nor can there be harmony between the hearts of wolves and lambs, but rather they must always plot evil against one another. So between you and me, no treaty can exist, nor can there be any oaths for us two. First one of us must fall and glut with blood Ares the warrior god of battle. Summon up all your courage because now there is great need for you to be a spearman and a bold warrior. There is no escape for you because soon Pallas Athena will overpower you with my spear and you will pay at once for all the evils you have done to my friends whom you have killed with your raging spear."

So he spoke, and raising up his spear, which cast a long shadow, he hurled it. Glorious Hector saw it coming and dodged it. He ducked and the bronze spear flew overhead and stuck in the ground. Unseen by Hector, the shepherd of the people, Pallas Athena, retrieved it and gave it back to Achilles.

Hector said to the blameless son of Peleus: "You missed! And after all, Oh Achilles, you are not so like the gods. Zeus has not revealed to you my fate as you claim, but you are merely clever with words and deceitful of speech in the hope that you will frighten me and I should forget my strength and courage. You will not plunge your spear into my back as I run away, but if the god grants it to you, you may drive it through my chest as I charge you straight on. Now try to avoid my bronze spear. May it plunge clear through your body. The war would go better for the Trojans with you dead, since you are their most deadly enemy."

So he spoke, and lifting up his spear which cast a long shadow, he hurled it. He did not miss his target. He hit the shield of the son of Peleus square in the center, but the spear bounced off the shield. Hector was vexed because he had thrown his swift spear in vain. He stood there crestfallen because he did not hold an ashen spear in his hand.

He called loudly for Deïphobos of the white shield to bring him another long spear, but he was not there. Then Hector knew in his heart that he was doomed, and he said: "Ah me, the gods call for my death. I thought Deïphobos the hero was beside me, but he is within the wall, and Athena has tricked me. Now evil death is close to me. My death is not far off, and there is no way to escape it. It seems this must be the long-fated will of Zeus and the far-shooting son of Zeus who formerly protected me. Now I am overtaken by my fate. But at least let me not be killed ingloriously without a struggle. Let me first do some great thing which later men will hear about." . . . Hector sprang forward waving his sharp sword.

Achilles leapt to meet him with his heart burning with savage hatred, and holding in front of his chest the beautiful, cleverly made shield, and on his head the beautiful golden plumes of his four-horned shining helmet which Hephaestus had made so that the plumes fell thickly on both sides. Like the evening star which stands out among the other stars as the most beautiful beacon in the darkness of the night shines, so shone the sharp spear which Achilles brandished in his right hand.

His eye ran with evil intent over Hector's beautiful body searching for the most vulnerable point to strike. . . . There, in the throat, is the spot where death comes swiftest to the soul, and there, godlike Achilles drove his spear and the point sliced straight through the soft tissue of the neck, but the heavy, bronze-tipped ash spear did not sever his windpipe, so that the power of speech remained to him as he crashed down into the dust.

Godlike Achilles rejoiced, saying: " . . . I have slain you, draining the strength from your knees, and now the dogs and vultures will drag you off and mutilate you."

. . . Hector of the shining helmet spoke feebly: "I beg you, grasping you by the knees, in the name of your parents and your own soul, do not let the dogs tear me beside the ships of the Achaians. Accept the bronze and plentiful gold which my father and honored mother will give to you as gifts in order to ransom my corpse. Give them my body so the Trojans and the wives of the Trojans may burn me on the funeral pyre."

Swift-footed Achilles looked at him darkly and said: "Dog, do not beg me by parents or knees. I wish my anger and rage were great enough to drive me to chop off your flesh and eat it raw, so great are the crimes you have committed against me. There will be no one to drive the dogs away from your head, not even if the Trojans should weigh out and bring to me 10 or 20 times that amount of ransom, and promise even more, and not even if Priam the son of Dardanus should offer me your weight in gold. The honored one your mother who gave birth to you will never lay you grieving on your funeral bed but instead the dogs and vultures will tear you apart."

And with his dying breath, Hector of the plumed helmet said: "I see you and I know all too well that I am fated not to persuade you. The heart in your breast is made of iron, but you should be careful lest your treatment of me should cause the gods to be angry with you. A day will come when Paris and Phoebus Apollo will kill you before the Skaian gates no matter how brave you are." Thus speaking, death closed over him and his soul left his limbs and went down to Hades, grieving for his fate to die so young and strong.

Godlike Achilles said to his corpse: "Die! I will meet my death whenever Zeus and the other immortal gods send it to me." Thus he spoke, and he wrenched the bronze spear out of the corpse and laid it to one side . . . and devised in his mind a shameful treatment for noble Hector. He drilled through the tendons of his feet, between the ankle and the heel, and pulled ropes of ox hide through them. He tied these to his chariot and left the head dragging in the dust. He climbed into his chariot carrying the shining armor and whipped his horses to a gallop. Willingly they flew along. The dust rose around the corpse as he was dragged along with his dark hair sweeping the ground. His head, which so recently had been beautiful in men's eyes, swept deep in the dirt because on that day Zeus allowed Hector's enemies to abuse his corpse in his own land.

Translated by Gregory S. Aldrete.

THUCYDIDES (470–400 B.C.E.), *THE PELOPONNESIAN WAR,* "THE FUNERAL ORATION OF PERICLES"

This speech, delivered by the Athenian statesman Pericles at a public ceremony honoring the dead killed in battle that year, constitutes an idealized statement of the positive effects of a democratic form of government on society and culture.

"But what was the road by which we reached our position, what the form of government under which our greatness grew, what the national habits out of which it sprang; these are the questions which I may try to solve before I proceed to my panegyric upon these men; since I think this to be a subject upon which on the present occasion a speaker may properly dwell, and to which the whole assemblage, whether citizens or foreigners, may listen with advantage.

"Our constitution does not copy the laws of neighboring states; we are rather a pattern to others than imitators ourselves. Its administration favours the many instead of the few; this is why it is called a democracy. If we look to the laws, they afford equal justice to all in their private differences; if no social standing, advancement in public life falls to reputation for capacity, class considerations not being allowed to interfere with merit; nor again does poverty bar the way, if a man is able to serve the state, he is not hindered by the obscurity of his condition. The freedom which we enjoy in our government extends also to our ordinary life. There, far from exercising a jealous surveillance over each other, we do not feel called upon to be angry with our neighbor for doing what he likes, or even to indulge in those injurious looks which cannot fail to be offensive, although they inflict no positive penalty. But all this ease in our private relations does not make us lawless as citizens. Against this fear is our chief safeguard, teaching us to obey the magistrates and the laws, particularly such as regard the protection of the injured, whether they are actually on the statute book, or belong to that code which, although unwritten, yet cannot be broken without acknowledged disgrace.

"Further, we provide plenty of means for the mind to refresh itself from business. We celebrate games and sacrifices all the year round, and the elegance of our private establishments forms a daily source of pleasure and helps to banish the spleen; while the magnitude of our city draws the produce of the world into our harbour, so that to the Athenian the fruits of other countries are as familiar a luxury as those of his own.

"If we turn to our military policy, there also we differ from our antagonists. We throw open our city to the world, and never by alien acts exclude foreigners from any opportunity of learning or observing, although the eyes of an enemy may occasionally profit by our liberality; trusting less in a system and policy than to the native spirit of our citizens; while in education, where our rivals from their very cradles by a painful discipline seek after manliness, at Athens we live exactly as we please, and yet are just as ready to encounter every legitimate danger. In proof of this it may be noticed that the Lacedaemonians do not invade our country alone, but bring with them all their confederates; while we Athenians advance unsupported into the territory of a neighbour, and fighting upon a foreign soil usually vanquish with ease men who are defending their homes. Our united force was never yet encountered by any enemy, because we have at once to attend to our navy and to dispatch our citizens by land upon a hundred different services; so that, wherever they engage with some such fraction of our strength, a success against a detachment is magnified into a victory over the nation, and a defeat into a reverse suffered at the hands of our entire people. And yet if with habits not of labour but of ease, and courage not of art but of nature, we are still willing to encounter danger, we have the double advantage of escaping the experience of hardships in anticipation and of facing them in the hour of need as fearlessly as those who are never free from them.

"Nor are these the only points in which our city is worthy of admiration. We cultivate refinement without extravagance and knowledge without effeminacy; wealth we employ more for use than for show, and place the real disgrace of poverty not in owning to the fact but in declining the struggle against it. Our public men have, besides politics, their private affairs to attend to, and our ordinary citizens, though occupied with the pursuits of industry, are still fair judges of public matters; for, unlike any other nation, regarding him who takes no part in these duties not as unambitious but as useless, we Athenians are able to judge at all events if we cannot originate, and, instead of looking on discussion as a stumbling-block in the way of action, we think it an indispensable preliminary to any wise action at all. Again, in our enterprises we present the singular spectacle of daring and deliberation, each carried to its highest point, and both united in the same persons; although usually decision is the fruit of ignorance, hesitation of reflection. But the palm of courage will surely be adjudged most justly to those, who best know the difference between hardship and pleasure and yet are never tempted to shrink from danger. In generosity we are equally singular, acquiring our friends by conferring, not by receiving, favours. Yet, of course, the doer of the favour is the firmer friend of the two, in order by continued kindness to keep the recipient in his debt; while the debtor feels less keenly from the very consciousness that the return he makes will be a payment, not a free gift. And it is only the Athenians, who, fearless of consequences, confer their benefits not from calculations of expediency, but in the confidence of liberality.

"In short, I say that as a city we are the school of Hellas, while I doubt if the world can produce a man who, where he has only himself to depend upon, is equal to so many emergencies, and graced by so happy a versatility, as the Athenian. And that this is no mere boast thrown out for the occasion, but plain matter of fact, the power of the state acquired by these habits proves. For Athens alone of her contemporaries is found when tested to be greater than her reputation, and alone gives no occasion to her assailants to blush at the antagonist by whom they have been worsted, or to her subjects to question her title by merit to rule. Rather, the admiration of the present and succeeding ages will be ours, since we have not left our power without witness, but have shown it by mighty proofs; and far from needing a Homer for our panegyrist, or other of his craft whose verses might charm for the moment only for the impression which they gave to melt at the touch of fact, we have forced every sea and land to be the highway of our daring, and everywhere, whether for evil or for good, have left imperishable monuments behind us. Such is the Athens for which these men, in the assertion of their resolve not to lose her, nobly fought and died; and well may every one of their survivors be ready to suffer in her cause."

From http://www.mtholyoke.edu/acad/intrel/pericles.htm.

TITUS LIVIUS (59 B.C.E.–17 C.E.), *HISTORY OF ROME*

Livius wrote a description of Roman history from the foundation of the city until his own time. His accounts of famous heroes from Rome's early history exemplify traditional Roman values and virtues.

THE STORY OF MUCIUS SCAEVOLA

Lars Porsena, king of the Etruscans, has surrounded the city of Rome with his army and is conducting siege operations against it.

As the Etruscan blockade continued, there was a shortage of corn and the price of corn rose to extraordinary levels due to the shortage. Because of this, Porsena began to hope that by continuing the blockade, the city would fall to him. Meanwhile, Gaius Mucius, a young Roman nobleman . . . went before the Senate of Rome. "Fathers, I intend to cross the Tiber River and to sneak into the enemy camp, if possible. I do not intend to rob them or to destroy their property as they have destroyed ours, but with the gods' assistance, I hope to accomplish a greater deed." The Senate gave its approval, and with a sword hidden under his clothes, he snuck into the enemy camp.

When he arrived, the Etruscan soldiers were in the process of receiving their wages, so Mucius mingled in with the crowd. King Porsena and his secretary were busily distributing the funds, but since they were dressed in the same style, Mucius could not tell who was the king and who was the secretary. He was afraid to ask anyone in case he give himself away, and so, trusting to fortune, he drew his weapon and killed one of them.

As he fled the scene with his bloody weapon, he was seized by the guards and dragged back, where he discovered that he had killed the secretary instead of the king. Despite all the threats around him, he was fearless and declared, "I am a Roman citizen. My name is Gaius Mucius. I came here to kill my enemy and I am not afraid to die. Romans know both how to act with bravery and to show bravery in suffering. I am the first to attempt to kill you, but I will not be the last because there are many others like myself who will take up my mission. Therefore, prepare yourself to live in danger, to fear for your life every hour of the day, to find an enemy with a sword in his hand at the entrance of your tent. We, the young men of Rome, declare this war against you. Do not fear an army or a battle because the conflict will be between you alone and each one of us."

The king was both angered and frightened by these words. He ordered fire to be brought and threatened Mucius with torture if he did not immediately reveal all the Romans' plans. Mucius replied, "Watch me and learn how unimportant the body is to those who have dedicated themselves to a greater cause." Immediately after saying this, Mucius thrust his right hand into the flames and held it there. As the flesh burned from his bones, Mucius gave no sign that he felt anything. The king was dumbfounded at the astounding sight and leapt out of his throne, commanding that the fire be taken away. He said to Mucius, "You are free to go, you who have punished yourself more than I would have done. I would honor your bravery if your courage fought on my side. I let you return to Rome unharmed and with a full pardon from me."

Mucius answered him politely, saying: "Since you honor bravery, I will return your kindness by telling you what you could not have extracted from me by threats. I am one of 300 young Roman men who have sworn to assassinate you. We drew lots to see who would make the attempt first and my lot was chosen. All the rest will follow one by one as their lots are selected until fortune grants one of us success."

Mucius returned to Rome, followed by ambassadors sent by Porsena to negotiate peace with the Romans. Afterward, to commemorate the loss of his right hand, Mucius was known as Mucius Scaevola, meaning Mucius the Left-Handed.

THE STORY OF CAMILLUS

A Roman army under the command of General Camillus is besieging the city of Falerii.

A full siege of Falerii was instituted with lines of trenches dug all the way around the city. . . . It seemed that the siege might prove to be futile had not fortune given to the Roman general both victory and an opportunity to display his virtue.

As is the custom today in Greece, the Falerians entrusted their children to a teacher who not only taught them at school but also supervised them at other times as well. The teacher who seemed most knowledgeable was naturally in charge of all the children of the leaders of the city. During peacetime, he customarily took the boys outside the city walls where they could play and exercise. He continued this custom even while the Romans were besieging the city, leading them farther and farther from the walls until one day he led them into the Roman camp and to the tent of Camillus himself.

After committing this act of betrayal, he told Camillus that since these were the children of the city's leaders, by threatening them, Camillus could force Falerii to surrender to him. When Camillus heard this, he burst out: "You are an evil man but you make your shameful offering to a people and a general who are not villains like you. Although there is no formal treaty between the Falerians and the Romans, we are bound by the laws of nature, which tie together all men. There are laws that govern war as well as peace, and we Romans wage war bravely but justly. We do not fight against children but only against men who can defend themselves. You are even more despicable than those we fought at Veii, but nonetheless I will conquer Falerii by Roman skill, bravery, weapons, and hard work rather than by treachery."

Camillus had the teacher stripped naked with his hands tied behind his back. Camillus gave the boys rods to beat the teacher with and set them all free. At the sight of the teacher being beaten and driven back into the city, a crowd of Falerians gathered and a meeting of the Falerian senate was convened to discuss the extraordinary event.

The people were so moved by Camillus's actions that they demanded peace be made with the Romans. In the Senate, and in the streets, the honesty and justice of Camillus were praised and ambassadors were sent to Camillus and to Rome to surrender the city to the Romans. When brought into the Roman Senate, the Falerian ambassadors said this: "O Conscript Fathers, we are conquered by you and your general in a way that can displease neither the gods nor man. We willingly surrender ourselves to you, believing that we will live better under your laws than under our own. This war has resulted in two notable examples of behavior. You chose to wage a just war rather than to take a deceitful victory, and we in turn, in recognition of your justice, have voluntarily given you victory. We are under your rule. We will turn over to you our weapons and our hostages and we throw open the gates of our city to you. You will never regret our loyalty nor we your domination."

Camillus was thanked by both the Romans and the Falerians, and peace having been established, the army returned to Rome.

Translated by Gregory S. Aldrete.

POLYBIUS (CA. 200–118 B.C.E.), *HISTORIES,* "THE ROMAN CONSTITUTION"

Polybius was a Greek who witnessed firsthand Roman imperialism sweep across the eastern Mediterranean, and he came to believe that the secret to Rome's success lay in its form of government. His description of Rome's "constitution" and its balance of powers was inspirational for many subsequent republics, including the United States.

The three branches of government that I spoke of above all shared in the control of the Roman state. And such fairness and propriety in all respects was shown in the use of these three elements for drawing up the constitution and in its subsequent administration that it was impossible even for a native to pronounce with certainty whether the whole system was aristocratic, democratic, or monarchical. This was indeed only natural. For if one fixed one's eyes on the power of the consuls (highest elected magistrates), the constitution seemed completely monarchical and royal; if on that of the senate, it seemed again to be aristocratic; and when one looked at the power of the masses, it seemed clearly to be a democracy. The parts of the state falling under the control of each element were and with a few modifications still are as follows.

The consuls, previous to leading out their legions, exercise authority in Rome over all public affairs, since all the other magistrates except the tribunes are under them and bound to obey them, and it is they who introduce embassies to the senate. Besides this it is they who consult the senate on matters of urgency, they who carry out in detail the provisions of its decrees. Again as concerns all affairs of state administered by the people it is their duty to take these under their charge, to summon assemblies, to introduce measures, and to preside over the execution of the popular decrees. As for preparation for war and the general conduct of operations in the field, here their power is almost uncontrolled; for they are empowered to make what demands they choose on the allies, to appoint military tribunes, to levy soldiers and select those who are fittest for service. They also have the right of inflicting, when on active service, punishment on anyone under their command; and they are authorized to spend any sum they decide upon from the public funds, being accompanied by a quaestor who faithfully executes their instructions. So that if one looks at this part of the administration alone, one may reasonably pronounce the constitution to be a pure monarchy or kingship. I may remark that any changes in these matters or in others of which I am about to speak that may be made in present or future times do not in any way affect the truth of the views I here state.

To pass to the senate. In the first place it has the control of the treasury, all revenue and expenditure being regulated by it. For with the exception of payments made to the consuls, the quaestors are not allowed to disburse for any particular object without a decree of the senate. And even the item of expenditure which is far heavier and more important than any other—the outlay every five years by the censors on public works, whether constructions or repairs—is under the control of the senate, which makes a grant to the censors for the purpose. Similarly, crimes committed in Italy which require a public investigation, such as treason, conspiracy, poisoning, and assassination, are under the jurisdiction of the senate. Also if any private person or community in Italy is in need of arbitration or indeed claims damages or requires succour or protection, the senate attends to all such matters. It also occupies itself with the dispatch of all embassies sent to countries outside of Italy for the purpose either of settling differences, or of offering friendly advice, or indeed of imposing demands, or of receiving submission, or of declaring war; and in like manner with respect to embassies arriving in Rome, it decides what reception and what answer should be given to them. All these matters are in the hands of the senate, nor have the people anything whatever to do with them. So that again to one residing in Rome during the absence of the consuls the constitution appears to be entirely aristocratic; and this is the conviction of many Greek states and many of the kings, as the senate manages all business connected with them.

After this we are naturally inclined to ask what part in the constitution is left for the people, considering that the senate controls all the particular matters I mentioned, and, what is most important, manages all matters of revenue and expenditure, and considering that the consuls again have uncontrolled authority as regards armaments and operations in the field. But nevertheless there is a part and a very important part left for the people. For it is the people which alone has the right to confer honours and inflict punishment, the only bonds by which kingdoms and states and in a word human society in general are held together. For where the distinction between these is overlooked or is observed but ill applied, no affairs can be properly administered. How indeed is this possible when good and evil men are held in equal estimation? It is by the people, then, in many cases that offences punishable by a fine are tried when the accused have held the highest office; and they are the only court which may try on capital charges. As regards the latter they have a practice which is praiseworthy and should be mentioned. Their usage allows those on trial for their lives when found guilty liberty to depart openly, thus inflicting voluntary exile on themselves, if even only one of the tribes that pronounce the verdict has not yet voted. Such exiles enjoy safety in the territories of Naples, Praeneste, Tibur, and other allied cities. Again it is the people who bestow office on the deserving, the noblest reward of virtue in a state; the people have the power of approving or rejecting laws, and what is most important of all, they deliberate on the question of war and peace. Further in the case of alliances, terms of peace, and treaties, it is the people who ratify all these or the reverse. Thus here again one might plausibly say that the people's share in the government is the greatest, and that the constitution is a democratic one. . . .

Such being the power that each part has of hampering the others or co-operating with them, their union is adequate to all emergencies, so that it is impossible to find a better political system than this. For whenever the menace of some common danger from abroad compels them to act in concord and support each other, so great does the strength of the state become, that nothing which is requisite can be neglected, as all are zealously competing in devising means of meeting the need of the hour, nor can any decision arrived at fail to be executed promptly, as all are co-operating both in public and in private to the accomplishment of the task they have set themselves; and consequently this peculiar form of constitution possesses an irresistible power of attaining every object upon which it is resolved. When again they are freed from external menace, and reap the harvest of good fortune and affluence which is the result of their success, and in the enjoyment of this prosperity are corrupted by flattery and idleness and wax insolent and overbearing, as indeed happens often enough, it is then especially that we see the state providing itself a remedy for the evil from which it suffers. For when one part having grown out of proportion to the others aims at supremacy and tends to become too predominant, it is evident that, as for the reasons above given none of the three is absolute, but the purpose of the one can be counterworked and thwarted by the others, none of them will excessively outgrow the others or treat them with contempt. All in fact remains *in statu quo*, on the one hand, because any aggressive impulse is sure to be checked and from the outset each estate stands in dread of being interfered with by the others. . . .

From Polybius, *The Histories*, trans. W. R. Paton (Cambridge, Mass.: Harvard University Press, 1923).

JUVENAL (CA. 55–140 C.E.) SATIRE III, "THE CITY OF ROME"

Juvenal's bitter satire against the city of Rome reveals the dark side of living in the big city. Although somewhat exaggerated, the types of urban problems he describes would have been typical of life in any of the large cities of the Roman world.

We dwell in a city which is, for the most part, held up only by feeble props. For your apartment manager stands there in the tottering building, and while he patches up a yawning crack in the decrepit walls, he urges you to sleep securely, while the whole ruin above you threatens to collapse. It is better to live away from here, where there are not fires every night, where there are not terrified alarms every night. Other apartment dwellers shout for water, and drag out what little they own. Meanwhile, the third floor where you live is alight and smoke pours out, but you don't realize it. While the ground floor has panicked at the first alarm, upstairs, you, who live where the pigeons nest and only tiles protect you from the rain, will be the last to burn. . . . If you can live without the chariot races in the circus, you could buy a fine house at Sora, Fabrateria, or Fursino for the same price you pay to rent a single dark and squalid room in Rome.

. . . Here in Rome, sick people die from sleep deprivation. Undigested food lies in the stomach producing burning ulcers and illness. For who can get a sound night's rest in a noisy tenement? Only the rich are able to sleep well in this city. Wagons clatter through the narrow, winding streets, and their drivers shout angrily at one another when traffic backs up. Even the laziest man could not find rest under these conditions.

When a rich man has to make a social call, the crowd is forced aside as he floats above them carried in a luxurious litter by his attendants. He can read or write, or even enjoy a nap, for the enclosed litter encourages sleep. He will always arrive on time, but even though we might try to hurry, the surging crowd blocks our progress, and the dense mob crushes against us from behind. In the press, one man shoves me with his elbow, another sticks me with a pole, a third smacks a board over my head, and yet another cracks his wine jar up against my head. My legs become encrusted with stinking mud, from all sides big feet trample on me, and a passing soldier grinds my toes under the hobnails of his boots.

The mob kicks up a dust cloud as they rush forward to get a free handout. There are a hundred of them, each followed by his own beggar. Hercules himself could not endure under the weight of all the pots and kitchen paraphernalia which that poor skinny slave is carrying. He keeps his head up and runs as fast as he can hoping to keep the embers he holds burning by the speed of his passage. In the chaos, newly repaired tunics are torn to pieces. Overburdened wagons transporting construction materials loom overhead and threaten the crowd. Here comes a wagon bearing an enormous fir log, and there is another hauling an entire pine tree. If the axle of that cart carrying a load of Ligurian marble collapses, and the whole mountain of rock tumbles down on top of the crowd, nothing will be left of their bodies. Who could identify the mangled limbs and bones? The poor man's body would be crushed into nothingness just like his soul. Meanwhile at his home, unaware of the disaster, his family would be going about the daily business, washing dishes, blowing on the fire to keep it going, noisily preparing the oil, towels, and scrapers for a bath. While his sons scurry about their household tasks, their father sits newly arrived on the shores of the river of the underworld, fearful of the grim ferryman. Without a proper burial and a coin placed in his mouth, the wretched man has no way to pay for passage across the dark river and is doomed.

Consider also the many and varied hazards of the night. Look how high it is to the rooftop from which a chunk of masonry breaks off and smashes down on my head, or to the window from which someone tosses out a broken or cracked pot. See how it crashes down on the sidewalk with such force that it dents the pavement. Only a thoughtless or foolish person who is oblivious to disaster would dare to go out to dinner without having first made out their will. Each open window you walk beneath carries the potential to harbor your death. All you can do is say a prayer, and hold onto the pathetic hope that people will be satisfied with dumping down on you only contents of their chamber pots. . . . A mugger jumps in front of me and orders me to stop. What choice do I have? What can you do when confronted with a maniac who is stronger than you? . . . Whether you try to talk your way out of it, or try to run off without speaking, the outcome is the same—you are beaten and robbed. These are not the only dangers however. You can lock up your house or shop with bolts, shutters, and bars, but there will still be break-ins by robbers. Or, the prowler might simply stick his blade in you.

Translated by Gregory S. Aldrete.

RIG VEDA, HYMN I.1, "TO AGNI"; HYMN I.32, "TO INDRA"; HYMN V.85, "TO VARUNA"

The *Rig Veda* of ancient India contains more than 1,000 hymns to the gods. The three gods addressed in the following selections include some of the most important. They are Agni, the god of fire and the priest of the gods; Indra, a warrior god; and Varuna, a sky god concerned with order and justice.

TO AGNI (HYMN I.1)

I praise Agni, the chosen priest, god, minister of sacrifice,
The hotar, lavisher of wealth.
Worthy is Agni to be praised by living as by ancient seers.
He shall bring hitherward the gods.
Through Agni man obtains wealth, yea, plenty waxing day by day,
Most rich in heroes, glorious.
Agni, the perfect sacrifice which thou encompassest about
Verily goeth to the gods.
May Agni, sapient-minded priest, truthful, most gloriously great,
The god, come hither with the gods.
Whatever blessing, Agni, thou wilt grant unto thy worshiper,
That, Angiras, is indeed thy truth.
To thee, dispeller of the night, O Agni, day by day with prayer
Bringing thee reverence, we come;
Ruler of sacrifices, guard of law eternal, radiant one,

Increasing in thine own abode.

Be to us easy of approach, even as a father to his son:

Agni, be with us for our weal.

TO INDRA (HYMN I.32)

I will declare the manly deeds of Indra, the first that he achieved, the thunder-wielder.

He slew the dragon, then disclosed the waters, and cleft the channels of the mountain torrents.

He slew the dragon lying on the mountain: his heavenly bolt of thunder Tvashtar fashioned.

Like lowing kine in rapid flow descending the waters glided downward to the ocean.

Impetuous as a bull, he chose the soma, and in three sacred beakers drank the juices.

Maghavan grasped the thunder for his weapon, and smote to death this first-born of the dragons.

When, Indra, thou hadst slain the dragons' first-born, and overcome the charms of the enchanters,

Then, giving life to sun and dawn and heaven, thou foundest not one foe to stand against thee.

Indra, with his own great and deadly thunder smote into pieces Vritra, worst of Vritras.

As trunks of trees, what time the axe hath felled them, low on the earth so lies the prostrate dragon.

He, like a mad weak warrior, challenged Indra, the great impetuous many-slaying hero.

He, brooking not the clashing of the weapons, crushed—Indra's foe—the shattered forts in falling.

Footless and handless still he challenged Indra, who smote him with his bolt between the shoulders.

Emasculate yet claiming manly vigor, thus Vritra lay with scattered limbs dissevered.

There as he lies like a bank-bursting river, the waters taking courage flow above him.

The dragon lies beneath the feet of torrents which Vritra with his greatness had encompassed.

Then humbled was the strength of Vritra's mother: Indra hath cast his deadly bolt against her.

The mother was above, the son was under, and like a cow beside her calf lay Danu.

Rolled in the midst of never-ceasing currents flowing without a rest forever onward,

The waters bear off Vritra's nameless body: the foe of Indra sank to during darkness.

Guarded by Ahi stood the thralls of Dasas, the waters stayed like kine held by the robber.

But he, when he had smitten Vritra, opened the cave wherein the floods had been imprisoned.

A horse's tail wast thou when he, O Indra, smote on thy bolt; thou, God without a second,

Thou hast won back the kine, hast won the soma; thou hast let loose to flow the seven rivers.

Nothing availed him lightning, nothing thunder, hailstorm or mist which he had spread about him:

When Indra and the dragon strove in battle, Maghavan gained the victory forever.

Whom sawest thou to avenge the dragon, Indra, that fear possessed thy heart when thou hadst slain him;

That, like a hawk affrighted through the regions, thou crossed nine-and-ninety flowing rivers?

Indra is king of all that moves and moves not, of creatures tame and horned, the thunder-wielder.

Over all living men he rules as sovereign, containing all as spokes within the rim of a wheel.

TO VARUNA (HYMN V.85)

Sing forth a hymn sublime and solemn, grateful to glorious Varuna, imperial ruler,

Who hath struck out, like one who slays the victim, earth as a skin to spread in front of Surya.

In the tree-tops the air he hath extended, put milk in kine and vigorous speed in horses,

Set intellect in hearts, fire in the waters, Surya in heaven and Soma on the mountain.

Varuna lets the big cask, opening downward, flow through the heaven and earth and air's mid-region.

Therewith the universe's sovereign waters earth as the shower of rain bedews the barley.

When Varuna is fain for milk he moistens the sky, the land, and earth to her foundation.

Then straight the mountains clothe them in the rain-cloud: the heroes, putting forth their vigor, loose them.

I will declare this mighty deed of magic, of glorious Varuna the lord immortal,

Who standing in the firmament hath meted the earth out with the sun as with a measure.

None, verily, hath ever let or hindered this the most wise god's mighty deed of magic,

Whereby with all their flood, the lucid rivers fill not one sea wherein they pour their waters.

If we have sinned against the man who loves us, have ever wronged a brother, friend, or comrade,

The neighbor ever with us, or a stranger, O Varuna, remove from us the trespass.

If we, as gamesters cheat at play, have cheated, done wrong unwittingly or sinned of purpose,

Cast all these sins away like loosened fetters, and, Varuna, let us be thine own beloved.

From *Hymns of the Rig-Veda*, trans. R. T. H. Griffith (London, 1889; reprint, Varanasi, India: Chowkhamba Sanskrit Series Office, 1963).

CUMULATIVE INDEX

Boldface numbers refer to volume numbers. A key appears on all verso pages.

Ares, 1:382, 470, 481

Argentina: beef, 5:98; cattle, 5:133; "dirty wars," 6:481; Falkland Islands dispute with Britain, 6:479; government, 6:385, 387; immigrants, 5:98; wheat, 5:98. *See also* Latin America entries

Arghun Khan (Mongol ruler), 2:246

Arguedas, Alcides, 5:158

Ariès, Philippe, 2:77

Ariosto, Lodovico, 3:206, 213

Aristocracy: China (Tang Dynasty), 2:242, 306–7; England (Victorian era), 5:109, 112–13; Europe (Middle Ages), 2:54, 81, 198, 224, 236, 258, 302–4, 322, 368, 379, 460; France (17th & 18th Centuries), 4:453, 454; Middle Ages, 2:301–9, 377; 19th Century, 5:218; Polynesia, 2:299, 308–9; Vikings, 2:304–5

Aristophanes: domestic life, 1:35, 59, 67; economic life, 1:145; intellectual life, 1:187, 202; material life, 1:255, 267; political life, 1:398; recreational life, 1:426, 427

Aristotle: on economic life, 1:126, 127; on health and medicine, 1:283, 296–98; importance to Europe (Middle Ages), 2:157, 159–60, 161; importance to Islamic World (Middle Ages), 2:165; intellectual life of, 1:226; philosophies of, 1:411; on political nature of humans, 1:327; 2:287; 3:267; 4:343; 5:305; 6:369; on slavery, 1:111, 113; writing of, 1:178, 226

Arithmetic. *See* Mathematics

Arkamani I, 1:355

Armenian language, 3:166

Arminius, 1:387

Armor, military. *See* Weapons

Armstrong, Edwin, 6:244

Armstrong, Lance, 6:499

Armstrong, Neil, 6:188

Army. *See* Military service

Army Nurse Corps (U.S.), 6:62

Army of the Potomac, 5:58, 200

Arnow, Harriette, 6:222

Arpilleras, 6:77

Arranged marriages: Egypt (ancient), 1:23; England (17th & 18th Centuries), 4:36; France (17th & 18th Centuries), 4:209; Greece (ancient), 1:44; India (19th Century), 5:39; India (20th Century), 6:32, 46, 136, 590; Japan (20th Century), 6:49; Middle Ages, 2:30; Rome (ancient), 1:26. *See also* Marriage

Arrogation, 1:53

Arrowroot, 2:212

Arson: England (15th & 16th Centuries), 3:302; England (Victorian era), 5:333

Art: Africa (17th & 18th Centuries), 4:445–48; ancient world, 1:230–41; Australian Aboriginals, 1:240–41; Aztec, 3:353–56; China (Tang Dynasty), 2:11; Egypt (ancient), 1:232–37; England (15th & 16th Centuries), 3:341–44; England (17th & 18th Centuries), 4:450–53; France (17th & 18th Centuries), 4:453–55; Greece (ancient), 1:237–39, 519; Inca, 3:3, 357–58; Italy (15th & 16th Centuries), 3:346–48; Japan (17th & 18th Centuries), 4:455–57; Jesus Christ in, 3:340; life at sea (17th & 18th Centuries), 4:459–61; Maya, 3:350–53; Mesopotamia, 1:230–32; Native Americans (colonial frontier of North America), 4:448–49; New England, colonial,

4:457–59; North American colonial frontier, 4:448–50; Nubia, 1:240; Oaxacan Civilization, 3:3; Olmec Civilization, 3:3; Ottoman Empire, 3:348–50; Rome (ancient), 1:239–40; 17th & 18th Centuries, 4:443–48; Soviet Union, 6:233, 234–35; Spain (15th & 16th Centuries), 3:344–46; United States (1940–59), 6:15. *See also specific types such as Icons, Painting, and Sculpture*

Art, religious. *See* Religious art; Temple art; Temple statues

Artemis, 1:56–57, 58, 480

Arthasastra, 1:352, 353

Arthritis: Europe (Middle Ages), 2:181; United States (1940–59), 6:275; Vikings, 2:184

Articles of War (17th & 18th Centuries), 4:399

Artificial sweeteners, 6:312

Artillery: England (Victorian era), 5:371; United States (Civil War era), 5:357

Artisans. *See* Craftsmen

Art of Cookery Made Plain and Easy, The (Glasse), 4:246

Art of Courtly Love, 2:301

Art of Love (Ovid), 1:203

Art of War, The (Sun-Tzu), 2:344, 354

Arts and crafts movement in England, 5:439

Aryans, 1:11

Asante, 4:16

Ascension Day: Italy (15th & 16th Centuries), 3:134; Spain (15th & 16th Centuries), 3:134

Ascot horse race, 5:113

Ashanti religion, 4:467, 484

Ashley, William, 5:124, 230

Asian Americans, discrimination against, 6:16–17, 150, 151

Asipu, 1:283, 284

Askeri, 3:291

Asoka, 1:11, 85, 353

Aspartame, 6:329

Aspasia, 1:67

Aspelta, 1:355, 467

Assam tea, 5:248, 252

Assassinations: India (20th Century), 6:10, 47, 79; Israel, 6:483; Japan (20th Century), 6:493, 600; Latin America (20th Century), 6:592; United States (20th Century), 6:152, 380, 449, 476

As Seen on TV: The Visual Culture of Everyday Life in the 1950s (Marling), 6:340

Assemblies in England (17th & 18th Centuries), 4:451–52

Assembly lines: automobile manufacture, 6:115, 357–58, 360; 20th Century, 6:110, 111, 131

Assur, 1:159, 456, 471

Assurbanipal, 1:287

Assurnasirpal II, 1:3, 342

Assyrians. *See* Mesopotamia

Asthemia, 5:208

Astor, John Jacob, 5:125, 127

Astrolabes, 2:282, 285

Astrology: ancient world, 1:525; Europe (Middle Ages), 2:160; India (ancient), 1:216; Mesopotamia, 1:219, 526, 528–29

Astronomy: ancient world, 1:525; Aztec, 3:185, 189; Egypt (ancient), 1:211; England (17th & 18th Centuries), 4:175; Europe (Middle Ages), 2:148–49, 151, 159–60; Greece (ancient), 1:225, 226; Inca, 3:141, 142; India (ancient), 1:216; Islamic World (Middle Ages), 2:147, 166; Maya, 3:136, 189, 201, 383; Mesopotamia, 1:209, 219, 221, 528–29; North American colonial frontier, 4:173; 17th & 18th Centuries, 4:169; Vikings, 2:152, 162

Astrophil and Stella (Sidney), 3:209

Atahuallpa, 3:22

Atatürk, Mustafa Kemal, 6:423

"A" tents, 5:254, 257

Atheism: Soviet Union, 6:596; United States, 6:572–73

Athena, 1:479, 480

Athenian Empire. *See* Greece (ancient)

Athens, ancient, 1:101, 102–5; coins of, 1:135; foundation date, 1:213; grain and food importing by, 1:139; guardian god of, 1:479; housing, 1:276–77; Ionian origin of, 1:333; literacy, 1:178, 187; plays of, 1:201, 425; population of, 1:333; priesthood eligibility, 1:493; professions, 1:188; rescue from Visigoth attack on, 1:463; roads, 1:161. *See also* Greece (ancient)

Atherton Company, 4:411

Athletics. *See* Sports

Atmiya Sabha, 5:66

Atole, 3:246–47

Atomic bomb. *See* Nuclear weapons

Atomic Energy Commission, 6:364

Aton, 1:458–59

Attention deficit disorder (ADD), 6:281–82

Attention deficit hyperactive disorder (ADHD), 6:281–82

Attics, 5:263

Attorneys: England (15th & 16th Centuries), 3:271; England (17th & 18th Centuries), 4:158–59, 392; England (Victorian era), 5:111; Japan (20th Century), 6:431; Soviet Union, 6:395

Atum, 1:475

Aucassin and Nicolett, 2:485–88

Aud (Unn the Deepminded), 2:56

Auden, W.H., 6:219, 225

Augers. *See* Diviners

Auguraculum, 1:496

Augustus Caesar: arches and temples erected by, 1:106, 107, 483, 505, 523; death of, 1:497; education of, 1:189; empire of, 1:10; on gladiator shows, 1:443; on literature, 1:203; marriage laws, 1:48, 50; Meroitic opposition to, 1:389; military conquests, 1:151, 356; on military size, 1:383; on public morality, 1:71; on slavery, 1:115, 116; statues of, 1:239; superstitions of, 1:534; urban life, 1:99; on wills, 1:368; on women's role, 1:36, 37

Aum Shinrikyo, 6:600

Aun's disease, 2:90

Auschwitz, 6:406–8, 488

Australia, colonial: agriculture, 4:50, 102, 106–8; alcoholic beverages, 4:257–58; animals, 4:170; botanical study, 4:170–71; Botany Bay settlement, 4:21; bread, 4:242; cattle, 4:242; chaplains, 4:486; churches, 4:487; civil rights, 4:387; courts and judges, 4:386–87; crimes, 4:386–88; crops, 4:106–7; dance, 4:432; drink, 4:257–58; drinking water, 4:257; English settlements, 4:21; fairs, 4:432–33; fauna, 4:170–71; flogging, 4:388, 487; food, 4:49, 51, 242–43; games, 4:432–33; government, 4:50; governors, 4:386–87; grain crops, 4:106–7; hats, 4:286, 303; historical overview, 4:22; holidays and festivals, 4:432–34; insurrections, 4:388; laborers, 4:287; law, 4:386–89; maize, 4:106–7; map of (1606-1818), 4:20; marines, 4:286; marriage, 4:32–33; material life, 4:237–38; meat, 4:242; men, work of, 4:49–50; men's clothing, 4:285–87; men's roles, 4:48–52; military service, 4:387–88; music, 4:433; navigational exploration, 4:171; plows, 4:106; professions,

Chiles, 5:245

Chimalli, 3:233

Chimneys: Civil War quarters, 5:256; England (15th & 16th Centuries), 3:253; Middle Ages, 2:223. *See also* Fireplaces

Chimney sweeps, 5:75

Chimu, 3:300

China (19th Century): adultery, 5:339; ancestor worship, 5:451; antitraditionalist movement, 5:452; architecture, 5:145; boatmen, 5:94, 115; box making, 5:95; bureaucracy, 5:323; capital punishment, 5:339–40; censorship, 5:323; child labor, 5:95; Christianity, 5:13; classical literature, 5:193; clothing, 5:95, 290; colloquial literature, 5:193–94; compasses, 5:156; Confucian education, 5:157, 160, 176–77, 194; corruption, 5:339, 340; cotton, 5:94–95, 115; courts and judges, 5:338–39; crimes, 5:338–40; dockers, 5:94, 115; drink, 5:253; education, 5:176–78; factories, 5:115, 156; family life, 5:451–52; food, 5:248; gentry, 5:114; geomancy, 5:144, 157; government and politics, 5:322–24; governors, 5:323; guilds, 5:95–96, 130, 375, 376; gunpowder, 5:156; handicrafts, 5:94, 115; hierarchy, 5:451–52; historical overview, 5:11–14; holidays and festivals, 5:418; horse collars, development of, 3:155; housing, 5:144–45; jails, 5:340; labor movement, 5:96; legal systems, 5:115; literature, 5:193–95; magistrates, 5:323; maps, 5:12; marriage, 5:447; medicine, 5:157; migrant labor, 5:94–95; missionaries, 5:156; morality, 5:451–53; murder, 5:338; occupations, 5:94; opium, 5:131, 375–76; origins, 5:11; papermaking, 5:156; poppies, 5:131; population, 5:144; porters, 5:94, 115; positivism, 5:177, 452; printing, 5:156; Provincial Republican Government, 5:324; punishment, 5:339; rebellions, 5:324; religion, 5:463–65; rural life and agriculture, 5:94, 115, 144–46; science, 5:156–57; silk, 5:94–95, 115; silver, 5:375–76; social mobility, 5:115; social structure, 5:114–16; tea, 5:130–31, 253, 375–76; theft, 5:338; torture, 5:115, 339; trade, 5:130–32, 375–76; universities, 5:157, 177, 340; urban life, 5:144–46; vernacular literature, 5:193; war and the military, 5:375–77; weaving, 5:94; women, 5:94–95, 447; work, 5:94–96; work hours, 5:83

China (Tang Dynasty): acrobats, 2:395, 399–400; adultery, 2:46; age of marriage, 2:40, 45, 84; alcoholic beverages, 2:103, 217–18; animals, 2:127–28; aristocracy, 2:242, 306–7; art, 2:11; banks and banking, 2:101–3; banquets, 2:60, 83; barges, 2:139; barley, 2:204; beds, 2:272; beggars, 2:325; birds, 2:252; board games, 2:376–77; boat races, 2:455; bridges, 2:281; bureaucracy, 2:296; camels, 2:128; canals, 2:139–40; candles, 2:272–73; caravans, 2:138–39; cave dwellings, 2:229; chairs, 2:267, 271; chariots, 2:354; charity, 2:437–38, 440; children, 2:78–79, 83–84, 154; chrysanthemum, 2:456; churches, 2:444; civil service exams, 2:154–55, 296; clergy, 2:409, 437–40; clocks, 2:273, 281; clothing, 2:242–43; clothing materials, 2:243, 247, 252–54; cockfighting, 2:376; colors, 2:254,

262; combs, 2:263; compasses, 2:281; concubines, 2:46, 60; conquest by Mongols, 2:20; convict labor, 2:335–36; cooking methods, 2:206, 218; corporal punishment, 2:335; corruption, 2:59, 297; cosmetics, 2:258, 262–63; cotton, 2:252; couches, 2:271; courtesans, 2:59–60; craftsmen, 2:84, 324; crimes, 2:332–33; crossbows, 2:354; dance, 2:390–92; death and the afterlife, 2:464–67; death penalty, 2:264, 333, 336–37; demise of, 2:11; diseases, 2:185–86; divorce, 2:41, 46–47; drink, 2:213–14, 216–19; drinking water, 2:213, 216; droughts, 2:315; education, 2:84, 147, 153–55; elephants, 2:401; entertainment, 2:399–401; eunuchs, 2:11, 30, 70, 71–72; exile, 2:336; eyebrows, 2:262; fabrics, 2:252–54; famine and starvation, 2:315; feathers, 2:252–53; fermentation, 2:217–18; fertilizer, 2:128; festivals and holidays, 2:449–50, 454–57; figs and dates, 2:196, 206; fish, 2:205; fishing, 2:315; floods, 2:230, 315; floors and floor coverings, 2:272; food, 2:128, 187, 197, 204–6, 455; footwear, 2:242, 243; fortifications, 2:324; fruit juices, 2:216; fruits, 2:204, 205; furnishings, 2:271–73; games, 2:375–77; grains, 2:127, 204, 315; grapes, 2:217; guns, 2:281; hair, 2:257, 263–64; hats, 2:242, 243, 252; health and medicine, 2:11–12, 153, 178, 179, 185–88, 272; hemp, 2:253; herbs and spices, 2:138; historical overview, 2:7–12; homicide, 2:333; housing, 2:229–31; hunting, 2:315, 381–82; insects, 2:205, 206; intellectual life, 2:11; iron, 2:275, 280; irrigation, 2:127, 197; jails, 2:334; kidnapping, 2:316; lamps, 2:272; language, 2:173–74; law, 2:11, 154, 326, 332–38; law enforcement, 2:334; libraries, 2:307; life expectancy, 2:186; lighting, 2:272; linen, 2:253; literature, 2:173; lychee, 2:205; magic, 2:400; mandarins, 2:296, 454; maps, 2:8, 9; marketplaces, 2:101–3; marriage, 2:45–47; matchmakers, 2:39, 45; mathematics, 2:154; meat, 2:197, 204; merchants, 2:229, 321, 324; military draft, 2:315–16; milk and dairy products, 2:216–17; monasteries, 2:432, 437–40; money, 2:103, 281; mourning rites, 2:465–66; music, 2:60, 386, 387, 390–92; names, 2:83, 84; natural disasters, 2:315; nomads, 2:229; nuts, 2:204, 206; old age, 2:87, 90–92; omens, 2:164; oxen, 2:126–27; paddle-wheel boats, 2:281; pagodas, 2:441, 444; paper, use, 2:281; parents, care of, 2:87, 90, 91–92; parks, 2:377, 382; peasants, 2:126–28, 315–16; peddlers, 2:103; personal appearance, 2:258, 262–64; philosophy, 2:164; physicians, 2:187; pictographs, 2:173; pigs, 2:187; pillows, 2:272; plows, 2:126–27; poetry, 2:153, 173–74; polo, 2:369, 375; poor persons, 2:325; population, 2:127, 323; pork, 2:204; printing, 2:12, 101; prostitution, 2:30, 50–51; public officials, 2:154–55, 296–97, 307; punishment, 2:83, 102, 115, 140, 264, 297, 307, 316, 326, 335–37, 466; raptors, 2:382; reading and writing, 2:173–74; religious beliefs, 2:415–17; religious buildings, 2:440, 444–45; reptiles, 2:205–6; retirement, 2:90; rice, 2:127, 196–97, 204–5; roads, 2:133, 140; roofing, 2:230–31; rural life and agriculture, 2:93, 126–28, 315; salt, 2:101; school, 2:84, 147, 153–54; science, 2:158, 163–65; screens, 2:271–72; seaweed, 2:205; sexuality, 2:83; shellfish, 2:205; shipping, 2:101; ships and vessels, 2:139, 281; silk, 2:101; ships and vessels, 2:139, 281; silk,

2:138, 248, 253; slaves, 2:310, 316–17; social structure, 2:236, 254, 289, 295–97, 321, 323–25; sports, 2:375–77; sumptuary laws, 2:295, 302; tables, 2:268; tattos, 2:258, 264; taverns, 2:103; tea, 2:12, 213–14, 217; teachers, 2:154; technology, 2:274, 280–82; temples, 2:444; textiles, 2:101–3; tiles, 2:231; torture, 2:326, 334; trade, 2:101–3, 132, 138–41; travel and transportation, 2:101; trials, 2:333–34; trousers, 2:242; tunics, 2:242; turbans, 2:243; universities, 2:148, 153; urban life, 2:101–3, 321, 323–25; vegetables, 2:204; warfare and weapons, 2:71, 315, 354–55; waterwheels, 2:281; weaving, 2:272, 315; weights and measures, 2:102; wet nurses, 2:83; wheelbarrows, 2:274, 281; widows, 2:91; windows, 2:223, 231; wine, 2:217; women, 2:30, 46, 58–60, 243, 253, 315; wool, 2:253; work, 2:310; wrestling, 2:369

Chinampas, 3:92, 102–4

Chincaysuyu, 3:300

Chinese alphabet, 2:167

Chinese Exclusion Act of 1882, 6:526

Chinese Merchant Guild (19th Century), 5:375, 376

Chinese writing, 2:167, 173; 3:157

Chinggis Khan. *See* Genghis Khan

Chiriguanos, 3:24

Chitarras, 3:346

Chitracina, 5:419, 424

Chittenden, Hiram, 5:124

Chivalry in Middle Ages, 2:301

Chlorine gas, 6:266

Chlorpromazine, 6:276

Chocolate: England (Victorian era), 5:239; introduction to Europe from Americas, 3:236; Latin America (19th Century), 5:245; Spain (15th & 16th Centuries), 3:241

Cholan, 3:167

Cholera: England (Victorian era), 5:209; Latin America (19th Century), 5:213; Soviet Union, 6:288; United States (Western Frontier), 5:199, 204

Cholula, 3:104

Chonin (17th & 18th Centuries): children, 4:75; clothing, 4:295; crimes, 4:395; education, 4:194; food, 4:249; laws, 4:378; women's role, 4:60–61

Chonkin, Ivan, 6:485

Chopines, 3:227

Chopsticks, 4:250

Chosen Women of Inca, 3:55, 71–72, 125, 390

Christening (Victorian England), 5:463

Christian Commissions, 5:460

Christian Democrats, 6:385

Christianity: Africa (17th & 18th Centuries), 4:16, 184, 345, 431, 468; Africa (20th Century), 6:601, 602; captivity narratives (17th & 18th Centuries), 4:205–6; China (19th Century), 5:13; ethical behavior as part of, 2:409; India (19th Century), 5:14, 466; Inuit, 6:603; Islam, relationship with, 6:11; Japan (20th Century), 6:600; Mongols and, 2:429; monotheism (17th & 18th Centuries), 4:464–65; New England, colonial, 4:196, 440; Rome (ancient), 1:464; slaves in colonial America, 4:215, 497; Soviet Union, 6:597. *See also* Catholic Church; Protestantism; Puritans

Christianity (England, Spain, Italy): baptism, 3:31, 396; confirmation, 3:31; Eucharist, 3:206; imposing faith on Judaism, 3:10; Resurrection, 3:361–62; sacred story:

Coal: England (17th & 18th Centuries), 4:176; England (Victorian era), 5:75, 135, 141. *See also* Mining

Coalition of Labor Union Women, 6:131

Coatecoalli, 3:298

Coatlicue, 3:355

Coats: China (Tang Dynasty), 2:243; England (Victorian era), 5:281, 282; Europe (Middle Ages), 2:238; United States (Civil War era), 5:274; Vikings, 2:240

Coba, 3:120

Cobo, Bernabé, 3:249, 392

Coca: Inca, 3:105, 248–49, 390; Latin America (19th Century), 5:246

Coca-Cola, 6:329

Cochise, 5:366

Cochuah, 3:420

Cocidos, 3:240

Cockcrow, 3:128

Cockfighting: China (Tang Dynasty), 2:376; England (15th & 16th Centuries), 3:330; England (17th & 18th Centuries), 4:421; Europe (Middle Ages), 2:371; Middle Ages, 2:369; United States (19th Century), 5:398

Cocoa: Aztec, 3:122; England (Victorian era), 5:238; introduction to Europe, 3:222; Latin America (20th Century), 6:314. *See also* Chocolate

Cocom, 3:46

Coconut milk, 5:252

Coconuts: Hindu religious offering of, 6:589; Polynesia, 2:211

Cod, 2:202–3

Code of Hammurabi. *See* Laws of Hammurabi

Codex Borbonicus, 3:217

Codex Borgia, 3:374

Codex Fejérváry-Mayer, 3:217

Codex Justinianus, 2:340

Codex Mendoza: astronomy, 3:185; child care, 3:48, 84; child labor, 3:184; information contained in, 3:217; punishment, 3:73, 86, 183; Tenochtitlan, 3:123; warrior outfits, 3:233

Cod fishing (17th & 18th Centuries), 4:131–32

Codices: Aztec, 3:217; Maya, 3:214

Codpieces, 3:225–26

Cody, William, 5:87

Coemptio marriage in Roman Empire, 1:48–49

Coffee: Civil War soldiers, 5:221, 248, 249–50; England (17th & 18th Centuries), 4:260; England (Victorian era), 5:238; Germany (1914–18), 6:304; India (19th Century), 5:248–49, 251–52; India (20th Century), 6:301, 316; Islamic World (Middle Ages), 2:219; Latin America (19th Century), 5:19, 97, 132–33, 245, 246, 325; Latin America (20th Century), 6:314; Ottoman Empire, 3:244–45, 261; United States (Civil War era), 5:220, 221, 222; United States (1920–39), 6:307; United States (Western Frontier), 5:230, 232, 248, 251

Coffeehouses, 4:143

Coffee wagons in Civil War, 5:250

Coffin Texts, 1:512

Cognatic lineage systems, 4:368

Cognomen, 1:27

Cohabitation and Australian convicts, 4:32–33

Cohn, Roy, 6:377

Coif, 2:239

Coins. *See* Gold coins; Money

Coke, Edward, 3:252

Colbert, Jean-Louis Baptiste, 4:356

Colden, Cadwallader, 4:435

"Cold Food Festival," 2:455

Cold Harbor, Battle of, 5:42, 44

Cold War, 6:40; education and, 6:204; film and, 6:514; historical overview, 6:454, 456, 469; Olympic Games during, 6:499; space race and, 6:187; United States (1940–59), 6:376–77; United States (1945–90), 6:469–70

Colegio Nacional, 5:179

Colhuacan urban life, 3:124

Colitis, 6:271

Collars: Spain (15th & 16th Centuries), 3:227–28; United States (Civil War era), 5:270–71, 275

Collasuyu, 3:300

Collecting as Victorian England activity, 5:439

Colleges. *See* Universities

Collegia, 1:118, 129

Colleone, Bartolomeo, 3:40

Colloquial literature of China, 5:193–94

Collins, Wilkie, 5:191

Collinson, Frank, 5:88

Colombia: coffee, 5:97; gold, 5:132. *See also* Latin America *entries*

Colonial America. *See* British colonies in North America; New England, colonial; North American colonial frontier

Colonial Australia. *See* Australia, colonial

Colonial rule: Arab world, 6:230, 483; Britain, 5:349–52; 6:9, 25, 155, 230; France, 6:25, 230; Inuit, 6:402; Islamic World (19th Century), 5:16–17, 352–53, 455; Italy, 6:230; Latin America (19th Century), 5:340; Roman Empire, 1:98; Spain, 6:230; United States (Civil War era), 5:345; women under, 6:85. *See also* British colonies in North America; New France (17th & 18th Centuries)

Colonial rule of Africa: division of ethnic groups, 6:25; drink, 6:331–32; economic life, 6:86, 124; education, 6:86, 212–13; health and medicine, 6:294; historical overview, 6:25–26; law and crime, 6:431–33; religion, 6:601–2; science and technology, 6:193; sports, 6:509–10; taxes, 6:331–32; urban and rural life, 6:177; women, 6:86

Colonial rule of India: cities, 6:344; communication methods, 6:254; government, 6:388; historical overview, 6:9; medicine, 6:286; military, 6:9; 19th Century, 5:14; revolts against, 6:9

Colonization of New France, 4:9–10

Colors: Australian Aboriginals, 1:314, 315; Byzantium, 2:248; China (Tang Dynasty), 2:254, 262; Europe (Middle Ages), 2:250; Greece (ancient), 1:309, 311; Mesopotamia, 1:232, 234, 271, 303–4; Middle Ages, 2:248; United States (Civil War era), 5:272. *See also* Purple color

Colosseum, 1:107

Colt, Miriam Davis, 5:62, 105, 206, 279

Columbaria, 1:522

Columbia disaster, 6:189–90

Columbus, Christopher, 3:1, 10; 5:122

Combs: China (Tang Dynasty), 2:263; Europe (Middle Ages), 2:260

Comintern, 6:257

Comitia centuriata, 1:351

Comitia tributa, 1:351

Commerce. *See* Merchants; Retail sales; Trade

Committee of Union and Progress, 5:391–92

Common Book of Prayer, 3:367

Commoners: Aztec, 3:280–81; England (15th & 16th Centuries), 3:271–72; England (Victorian era), 5:109; Maya, 3:279; Spain (15th & 16th Centuries), 3:274–75

Common law: England (17th & 18th Centuries), 4:391–94; England (Victorian era), 5:335; Italy (15th & 16th Centuries), 3:306

Common law marriages in Latin America, 6:43–44

Common Sense Teachings for the Japanese Children (Ekken), 4:512–15

Communal property in Spain (15th & 16th Centuries), 3:95

Communes, 2:320

Communication: India (20th Century), 6:253–55; Japan (20th Century), 6:258–59; Mongols' system, 2:363, 385; signals, naval, 4:218; smoke signals (Australian Aboriginals), 1:181; Soviet Union, 6:255–58; 20th Century, 6:241–59; United States (1920–39), 6:242–46; United States (1940–59), 6:246–49; United States (1960–90), 6:242, 249–53. *See also specific methods (e.g., telephones)*

Communism: demise of, 6:371; Soviet Union, 6:392–99. *See also* Cold War

Communist Party, Soviet: membership of, 6:396; structure of, 6:395–96, 398

Community Action program, 6:381

Community colleges, 6:204, 205–6

Compadrazgo, 6:44

Company of One Hundred Associates, 4:10, 351, 372

Compasses: China (19th Century), 5:156; China (Tang Dynasty), 2:281; ocean navigation (17th & 18th Centuries), 4:180–81

Competition: Europe (Middle Ages), 2:97; Vikings, 2:398

Complete Book of Running (Fixx), 6:497, 505

Compurgation (Middle Ages), 2:326, 327, 330

Computers: India (20th Century), 6:254; United States (1940–59), 6:119; United States (1960–90), 6:250–51. *See also* Personal computers (PCs)

Computer virus, 6:253

Comte, Auguste, 5:179

Conan Doyle, Arthur, 5:191

Concentration camps. *See* Holocaust

Concilia plebis, 1:351

Concrete, 1:227

Concubines: China (Tang Dynasty), 2:46, 60; Islamic World (Middle Ages), 2:48; Mesopotamia, 1:65, 110; Middle Ages, 2:40; Ottoman Empire, 3:260, 267. *See also* Polygamy

Conestoga wagons, 4:318

Confederate Army (U.S. Civil War), 5:42–44, 71–72. *See also* Civil War (United States)

Confederate Bible Society, 5:189

Confederate Conscription Act, 5:99–101

Confederate Constitution, 5:490–92

Confederate Subsistence Department, 5:222

Confession: Catholicism (Spain, Italy, England), 3:380, 382; Europe (Middle Ages), 2:459; Maya, 3:419–20

Confessions (Rousseau), 4:210

Confirmation: Catholicism (Spain, Italy, England), 3:380–81; Christianity (England, Spain, Italy), 3:31; England (Victorian era), 5:463; Spain (15th & 16th Centuries), 3:34

Conflict of the Orders, 1:337

Confucianism: China (19th Century), 5:322, 447, 451–52, 463, 464; China (Tang Dynasty),

Centuries), **3**:241; United States (Western Frontier), **5**:234

Deus ex machina, **1**:427

Devi, Phoolan, **6**:79–80

Devil in Catholicism, **3**:363

DeVoto, Bernard, **5**:46–48, 231

Devshirme, **2**:318; **3**:349

Dewey, John, **5**:177, 452; **6**:199, 200, 204

Dharma, **1**:206, 352–53, 466; **5**:466

Dhotis, **5**:286

Dial-a-prayer, **6**:573

Dialects: Europe (Middle Ages), **2**:168; Greece (ancient), **1**:176, 334; India (ancient), **1**:431; Italy (15th & 16th Centuries), **3**:163; Japan (17th & 18th Centuries), **4**:212; Rome (ancient), **1**:189; Spain (15th & 16th Centuries), **3**:161–62; Sumerian, **1**:194. *See also* Language

Diamonds in Latin America, **5**:132

Diapers: life at sea (17th & 18th Centuries), **4**:79; United States (1960–90), **6**:361

Diarrhea, **5**:199, 204

Díaz, Porfirio, **5**:159, 179

Dice: England (15th & 16th Centuries), **3**:318; Europe (Middle Ages), **2**:367, 369, 372; India (ancient), **1**:449; Italy (15th & 16th Centuries), **3**:323; Mesopotamia, **1**:406; Rome (ancient), **1**:415–16; Spain (15th & 16th Centuries), **3**:315, 321; United States (Civil War era), **5**:429; Vikings, **2**:375

Dickens, Charles: Christmas, writings on, **5**:406; Lao She, influence on, **5**:195; magazines, stories published in, **5**:189–90; popularity in U.S., **5**:181, 184–85; white collar workers, writings on, **5**:83, 110

Dickstein, Morris, **6**:222

Dictators of ancient Rome, **1**:351

Diderot, Denis, **4**:210

Diet: Africa (17th & 18th Centuries), **4**:240–42, 430; Australia, colonial, **4**:49, 51, 242–43; Australian Aboriginals, **1**:260, 261; Aztec, **3**:248; Byzantium, **2**:190, 197, 208–10; changes after European conquest of Americas, **3**:221–22, 236; China (19th Century), **5**:248; China (Tang Dynasty), **2**:128, 187, 197, 204–6, 455; Civil War soldiers, **5**:219–27; as cure (Middle Ages), **2**:179; England (15th & 16th Centuries), **3**:238–39; England (1914–18), **6**:303; England (17th & 18th Centuries), **4**:140, 245–48; England (Victorian era), **5**:218, 237–42; Europe (Middle Ages), **2**:124, 197, 198–201, 277; France (1914–18), **6**:303; Germany (1914–18), **6**:303, 304; Greece (ancient), **1**:256; Inca, **3**:105, 106; India (19th Century), **5**:219, 242–44; India (20th Century), **6**:315–17; Inuit, **6**:320–21; Islamic World (Middle Ages), **2**:282; Islamic World (19th Century), **5**:247, 468–69; Italy (15th & 16th Centuries), **3**:242; Japan (17th & 18th Centuries), **4**:114, 146, 229, 248–50; Japan (20th Century), **6**:319–20; Latin America (19th Century), **5**:219, 244–47; Latin America (20th Century), **6**:314–15; Maya, **3**:246–47; Mesopotamia, **1**:246, 263; Native Americans (colonial New England), **4**:250–51; Native Americans (New England, colonial), **4**:61–62; New England, colonial, **4**:117–18, 250–53; 19th Century, **5**:218–48;

North American colonial frontier, **4**:244–45; Nubia, **1**:259; Ottoman, **3**:244–45; Polynesia, **2**:210–12; Rome (ancient), **1**:256; seamen, **4**:253–55; 17th & 18th Centuries, **4**:238–55; United States (1920–39), **6**:306–9; United States (Western Frontier), **5**:218, 227–37; Vikings, **2**:202–3. *See also* Food; *specific types of food and drink*

Diet (Japan governmental body), **6**:399–400

Diet plans, **6**:280, 302, 310

Digest of Roman Law, **1**:365

Dillinger, John, **6**:416

Dining rooms in Victorian England, **5**:263

Dinner: England (15th & 16th Centuries), **3**:237; England (17th & 18th Centuries), **4**:247; England (Victorian era), **5**:219, 238, 240–42; Europe (Middle Ages), **2**:201; Latin America (20th Century), **6**:315; life at sea (17th & 18th Centuries), **4**:254; New England, colonial, **4**:252; North American colonial frontier, **4**:244; Ottoman Empire, **3**:244; 17th & 18th Centuries, **4**:239; United States (Western Frontier), **5**:234. *See also* Meals

Dinner parties. *See* Banquets

Diocletian, **1**:389

Dionysius, **1**:480, 492

Dioscorides, **2**:181, 188

Diphtheria: England (Victorian era), **5**:209; Spain (15th & 16th Centuries), **3**:194

Diplomats (Mesopotamia), **1**:139, 155, 343

"Dirty wars" (Latin America 20th Century): deaths in, **6**:8, 33, 44; historical overview of, **6**:480–81; Honduras, **6**:370; women's role in protests, **6**:61, 77

Disciples of Christ, **5**:458

Disco, **6**:547

Discovery, **6**:189

Discovery and Conquest of Mexico, The (Castillo), **3**:421–22

Discrimination: Africa (20th Century), **6**:193; Catholic Church condemnation of, **6**:577; China (Tang Dynasty), **2**:324; England (17th & 18th Centuries), **4**:492–93; India (20th Century), **6**:110, 140, 154–56; Iran, **6**:161; Japan (20th Century), **6**:140, 159–61; Jews (17th & 18th Centuries), **4**:483; Latin America (20th Century), **6**:134; Title IX of Education Amendments of 1972, **6**:618–19; 20th Century, **6**:139–61; United States (1920–39), **6**:145–49, 516; United States (1940–59), **6**:16, 150–51, 375–76; United States (1960–90), **6**:110, 129, 151–54. *See also* Anti-Semitism; Civil rights movement

Diseases: Africa (17th & 18th Centuries), **4**:220–21; Africa (20th Century), **6**:293–95; China (Tang Dynasty), **2**:185–86; England (17th & 18th Centuries), **4**:224; England (Victorian era), **5**:451; Europe (Middle Ages), **2**:181; 15th & 16th Centuries, **3**:188–90, 194, 196, 199; Greece (ancient), **1**:294–98; India (ancient), **1**:301–2; Inuit, **6**:295–96; Japan (20th Century), **6**:291; Mesopotamia, **1**:284–88; Native Americans (colonial New England), **4**:88, 231; 19th Century working-class people, **5**:217; North American colonial frontier, **4**:223; Paris (Middle Ages), **2**:114–15; Puritans, religious doctrine, **4**:233; Rome (ancient), **1**:298–301; Soviet Union, **6**:288; Spain (15th & 16th Centuries), **3**:194; United States (Civil War era), **5**:137; United States (1960–90), **6**:278; Vikings, **2**:164. *See also specific diseases*

Disney, Walt, **6**:98, 521

Disneyland, **6**:98–99

Dispensaries, **4**:225

Disraeli, Benjamin, **5**:10

Dissection: Greece (ancient), **1**:296; Mesopotamia, **1**:287; Rome (ancient), **1**:301

Dissenters, **4**:471–73, 491–92

Distilleries in colonial New England, **4**:265–66

Ditches, **4**:333

Divination: Inca, **3**:392–93; Japan (17th & 18th Centuries), **4**:423

Divine Comedy (Dante), **2**:461; **3**:396

Divine right of kings, **3**:284

Divine River judgments in Mesopotamia, **1**:359, 362, 526

Diviners: Greece (ancient), **1**:379; Mesopotamia, **1**:370, 527; Rome (ancient), **1**:495, 496. *See also* Entrails, reading of

Divorce: ancient world, **1**:39–40; Byzantium, **2**:63; Catholic Church views on (1960–90), **6**:577; China (Tang Dynasty), **2**:41, 46–47; England (17th & 18th Centuries), **4**:37–38; Europe (Middle Ages), **2**:41, 42; Greece (ancient), **1**:45, 47, 68; India (19th Century), **5**:41; Islamic World (Middle Ages), **2**:40, 49; Islamic World (19th Century), **5**:38; Japan (17th & 18th Centuries), **4**:40; Jesus Christ on, **3**:381; Maya, **3**:46; Mesopotamia, **1**:39, 41, 42; New England, colonial, **4**:42; Polynesia, **2**:68; Rome (ancient), **1**:37, 50; 17th & 18th Centuries, **4**:29; Spain (15th & 16th Centuries), **3**:35, 59; 20th Century, **6**:33; United States (1920–39), **6**:35–36; United States (1940–59), **6**:38; United States (1960–90), **6**:42; United States (Western Frontier), **5**:60; Vikings, **2**:44–45, 57

Diwali, **5**:396, 406, 414–15

Dix, Dorothea, **5**:199

Dixie Primer for Little Folks, **5**:160, 167

Dixie Speller, **5**:160, 167

Dixon, James, **4**:487

Dixon, Thomas, **6**:140, 146

Dobiwallas, **5**:52

Doblado, Leucadio, **3**:227

Dockers (China), **5**:94, 115

Doctorow, E.L., **6**:379

Doctors. *See* Healers and healing; Physicians

Doctors' Plot (Soviet Union), **6**:158

Doctor Zhivago (Pasternak), **6**:614–16

Dodge, Richard I., **5**:280, 369

Doenitz, Karl, **6**:412

Doges: Italy (15th & 16th Centuries), **3**:276; Venice, **3**:277

Dogfighting: 15th & 16th Centuries, **3**:313; Middle Ages, **2**:369

Dogs: England (Victorian era), **5**:440; Mesopotamia, **1**:78, 93; Paris (Middle Ages), **2**:114; Polynesia, **2**:212; United States (Western Frontier), **5**:229; Vikings, **2**:462. *See also* Hunting dogs

Dog shooting, **4**:424

Dog tents, **5**:254, 258

Dokia Makrembolitissa, **2**:63

Dolabra, **1**:386

Dom Casmurro (Machado de Assis), **5**:197

Domestic life: ancient world, **1**:19–72; defined, **1**:19; **2**:29; **6**:31; 15th & 16th Centuries, **3**:29–88; Middle Ages, **2**:29–92; 19th Century, **5**:25–79; 17th & 18th Centuries, **4**:27–100; 20th Century, **6**:31–108. *See also* Children; Family life; Marriage; Sexuality

Domestic Revolutions (Mintz & Kellogg), **6**:39

Domestic violence: Africa (17th & 18th Centuries), **4**:47; China (Tang Dynasty), **2**:333; Europe (Middle Ages), **2**:43; Islamic World (Middle Ages), **2**:48; Latin America (20th Century),

India (19th Century), **5:**244; Islamic World (Middle Ages), **2:**273; Japan (17th & 18th Centuries), **4:**146; life at sea, **4:**255; New England, colonial, **4:**252; Rome (ancient), **1:**256; United States (Western Frontier), **5:**234

Ebla, **1:**140

Ecclesiastical courts in England, **3:**303

Eclipses: Greece (ancient), **1:**225; India (ancient), **1:**216

Eco, Umberto, **6:**227

Economic life: Africa (20th Century), **6:**86, 124–25; ancient cities, **1:**101–8; ancient world, **1:**73–167; 15th & 16th Centuries, **3:**89–154; India (20th Century), **6:**9, 388; Japan (20th Century), **6:**24; Latin America (20th Century), **6:**387; meaning of "economy," **1:**74; Middle Ages, **2:**93–144; 19th Century, **5:**81–148; 17th & 18th Centuries, **4:**101–66; 20th Century, **6:**109–79, 434; United States (1960–90), **6:**40. *See also* Accounting; Money; Rural life and agriculture; Trade; Travel and transportation; Urban life; Work; *specific city and civilization*

Ecuador: language, **3:**168; Peru, border wars with, **6:**479. *See also* Latin America *entries*

Ecumenism (20th Century), **6:**568, 575–78

Eddic poems, **2:**172

Edelin, Kenneth C., **6:**74

Edema, **3:**194

Edict of Nantes (1598), **4:**355, 474

Edict of Toleration, **2:**410

Edicts. *See* Royal decrees and edicts

Edirne, **3:**118, 349

Edison, Thomas Alva, **5:**142; **6:**183–84, 360, 513

Edo (17th & 18th Centuries), **4:**328, 336–37, 358; **6:**160

Education: Africa (17th & 18th Centuries), **4:**181, 183–86; Africa (20th Century), **6:**124, 194, 196, 212–14; ancient world, **1:**182–92; Australian Aboriginals, **1:**28–29, 191–93; Aztec, **3:**47–48, 84–85, 182–86; China (19th Century), **5:**176–78; China (Tang Dynasty), **2:**84, 147, 153–55; England (15th & 16th Centuries), **3:**32–33, 171–74; England (17th & 18th Centuries), **4:**71, 188–90; England (Victorian era), **5:**50, 111, 114, 171–76, 373, 480–81; Europe (Middle Ages), **2:**148–52, 159; Europe (1914–18), **6:**89–90; Florence, **3:**178; France (17th & 18th Centuries), **4:**72, 73, 182, 190–93; Greece (ancient), **1:**187–89, 424; Inca, **3:**186–87; India (19th Century), **5:**67, 77–78; India (20th Century), **6:**104, 105; integration in United States, **6:**17, 153, 154, 195, 206–8; Inuit, **6:**196, 214–15; Islamic World (Middle Ages), **2:**85, 147, 155–57; Islamic World (19th Century), **5:**181; Italy (15th & 16th Centuries), **3:**81, 177–80; Japan (17th & 18th Centuries), **4:**193–95, 512–15; Japan (20th Century), **6:**106, 192, 196, 210–12, 400; Jews in Europe pre-World War II, **6:**143, 144; Latin America (19th Century), **5:**69–70, 178–80; Latin America (20th Century), **6:**88, 101–2; life at sea (17th & 18th Centuries), **4:**79–80, 198–200; Maya, **3:**82–83; Mesopotamia, **1:**54, 183–86; Middle Ages, **2:**146–57; Native Americans (colonial frontier of North

America), **4:**187–88; Native Americans (colonial New England), **4:**195–96; New England, colonial, **4:**182, 195–98, 380; 19th Century, **5:**160–81; North American colonial frontier, **4:**155–56, 182, 186–88; Ottoman Empire, **3:**118, 180–82; Polynesia, **2:**177; Rome (ancient), **1:**189–91; separation of religion and education in U.S., **6:**200, 208, 578, 587; 17th & 18th Centuries, **4:**181–200; Soviet Union, **6:**195, 196, 208–10; Spain (15th & 16th Centuries), **3:**35, 77, 174–77; 20th Century, **6:**195–215; United States (Civil War era), **5:**161–68; United States (1920–39), **6:**195, 196–99; United States (1940–59), **6:**18, 88, 199–205; United States (1960–90), **6:**205–8, 381, 382; United States (Western Frontier), **5:**168–71; Vikings, **2:**152–53. *See also* Curriculum; Schools; *specific subject of teaching*

Education Act of 1870 (England), **5:**10

Educational reforms in Europe, **2:**148

Education Amendments of 1972, Title IX, **6:**618–19

Education of priests: Europe (Middle Ages), **2:**149, 150; Latin America (19th Century), **5:**471; Polynesia, **2:**431

Education of women: Africa (20th Century), **6:**86; Australian Aboriginals, **1:**191–92; England (Victorian era), **5:**485; Europe (Middle Ages), **2:**149; France (17th & 18th Centuries), **4:**58; Greece (ancient), **1:**188; India (20th Century), **6:**78; Islamic World (Middle Ages), **2:**157; Mesopotamia, **1:**184; Rome (ancient), **1:**36; Title IX of Education Amendments of 1972, **6:**618–19; United States (1920–39), **6:**195; United States (1940–59), **6:**202–5; United States (1960–90), **6:**205; Vikings, **2:**153

Edward, Duke of York, **2:**483–85

Edward III (king of England), **3:**12

Edward IV (king of England), **3:**13

Edward VII (king of England), **5:**11

Edward VI (king of England), **3:**16, 409

Edward V (king of England), **3:**13

Edward the Confessor, **2:**109

Edwin Smith Surgical Papyrus, **1:**290–92

Edzna, **3:**102

Eels: Australian Aboriginals, **1:**419; Greece (ancient), **1:**255; Rome (ancient), **1:**256–57

Eggs: Byzantium, **2:**209; England (15th & 16th Centuries), **3:**57; England (1914–18), **6:**303; England (Victorian era), **5:**219, 238, 240; Italy (15th & 16th Centuries), **3:**243; Spain (15th & 16th Centuries), **3:**96; Vikings, **2:**202

Egil's Saga (Skallagrimsson), **2:**89, 398

Egypt, **3:**20, 165; British control of, **6:**11, 230; Byzantine Empire, **2:**19; European control, free from, **6:**483; food variety (Middle Ages), **2:**207; French invasion of, **6:**230; legal system of, **6:**423; Muslim conquest of, **2:**15; Napoleonic invasion, **5:**353–54. *See also* Islamic World *entries*

Egypt (ancient): accounting, **1:**186–87, 197; alimony, **1:**40; alphabet, **1:**175; amulets, **1:**124, 319–21, 514, 524, 531–32, 533; anatomy, **1:**292; animal games, **1:**409–10; appearance, **1:**56, 235, 319–24; apprenticeships, **1:**123; archers, **1:**375, 376, 391, 393–94; architecture, **1:**274; art, **1:**232–37; astronomy, **1:**211; autopsies, **1:**292; axes, **1:**394; bad breath, **1:**289; banks and banking, **1:**135; banquets, **1:**252–53, 423; bas-reliefs, **1:**234, 236; battering rams, **1:**375; battle

casualties, **1:**292, 374; beards, **1:**322; bedrooms, **1:**274; beds, **1:**276; beer, **1:**249, 264; bees, **1:**252; birds, **1:**82, 236, 250; block statues, **1:**234; board games, **1:**408, 409; bows and arrows, **1:**376; brains, **1:**513; bread, **1:**249; breath mints, **1:**289; bricks, **1:**275; bronze, **1:**234–35, 310; bullfighting, **1:**410; cabinetry, **1:**232; calendar and time, **1:**209–11; captives as slaves, **1:**110, 111, 491; carpentry, **1:**125, 395; carvings, **1:**364, 503, 516–17; cataloguing and classifying, **1:**222; cattle, **1:**81; cellars, **1:**275; chariots, **1:**391, 395–96; checkers, **1:**409; cheese, **1:**264; childbirth, **1:**24, 293, 457; childless couples, **1:**24; children, **1:**24, 55–56; circumcisions, **1:**291; clothing, **1:**235, 305–8; clothing manufacturing, **1:**305; colors, **1:**236, 276, 305, 322, 516; combs, **1:**324; cooking methods, **1:**249; cooking utensils, **1:**249; copper used as currency, **1:**134; corpses, care of, **1:**506; cosmetics, **1:**322–23; courts and judges, **1:**362–63; craftsmen, **1:**122–26; creation stories, **1:**475–76; crowns, **1:**308; curses, **1:**533; dance, **1:**253, 422–24; day of rest, **1:**210, 437; death, burial, and the afterlife, **1:**23, 33, 233–34, 249–52, 265, 422, 457, 459, 477, 511–17; debt slavery, **1:**111; deities, **1:**457–58, 474–77; dental care and problems, **1:**253, 289, 293; diet, **1:**250–51; diplomats and ambassadors, **1:**347; diseases, **1:**288–93; divorce, **1:**24, 40, 43–44; dogs, **1:**251, 410; donkeys, **1:**160; doors, **1:**275; dreams and dream interpretation, **1:**293, 491–92; drink, **1:**264–66; drinking methods, **1:**264; drinking water, **1:**375; eating habits, **1:**249, 252–53; education, **1:**56, 186–87; elixers of life, **1:**291; entertainment, **1:**253, 347; epidemics, **1:**291; exile, **1:**363; family life, **1:**23–24; fictional literature, **1:**198; fireplaces, **1:**276; fish, **1:**250; fishing, **1:**82, 409; floods, **1:**3, 75, 80; floorplans, **1:**274, 275; floors and floor coverings, **1:**276; food, **1:**249–53; footwear, **1:**308; fortifications, **1:**375; fowl, **1:**250; fruit, **1:**250; furniture, **1:**125, 276; games, **1:**408–10; gilding, **1:**236; glass, **1:**124–25; gold jewelry, **1:**319–20; gold works of art, **1:**123; government, **1:**344–48; government workers, **1:**122, 143, 345, 347; grains, **1:**250; gymnastics, **1:**408; hair removal, **1:**323; hairstyles, **1:**321; harems, **1:**347; health and medicine, **1:**222, 288–94; hearts, **1:**513; henna, **1:**323; herbs and spices, **1:**249, 251; hieroglyphics, **1:**175, 186, 223, 235, 250, 292, 293; history of, **1:**3–6; holidays, festivals, and spectacles, **1:**210, 437–38; honey, **1:**252; horses, **1:**160, 396; hospitals, **1:**292; houses, multistoried, **1:**275; housing, **1:**274–76; housing materials, **1:**275; hunting, **1:**251–52, 408–10; incense, **1:**323; infant mortality, **1:**56; jewelry, **1:**319; juggling, **1:**408; lamps, **1:**274, 276; landowners, **1:**331, 345; language and writing, **1:**175–76, 186–87, 197; latrines, **1:**274; law, **1:**128, 362–63; leather, **1:**305–6; linen, **1:**305–6; literature, **1:**197–200; litters, **1:**160; love poetry, **1:**199; mace, **1:**394; magic and superstition, **1:**289–300, 531–32; malaria, **1:**289; mansions, **1:**275; map of, **1:**5; marriage, **1:**23–24, 43–44; marriage of slaves, **1:**111; mathematics, **1:**222–24; meat, **1:**249, 251; men's clothing, **1:**305–8, 310; metal artwork, **1:**234; military games, **1:**408; milk and dairy products, **1:**249, 264; mining, **1:**123; mirrors, **1:**323; moat, **1:**375; money,

Heating

6:316; hospitals, 6:287; housing, 6:300, 334, 343–45; humors of the body, 6:286; hygiene, 6:589; independence, 6:371; infant mortality, 6:45–46; language, 6:388–89; literature, 6:228–30; malaria, 6:287; marriage, 6:32, 33, 46, 78, 104, 156, 590; meat, 6:316; men, 6:57–59; menstruation, 6:104; mosques, 6:343; mythology, 6:79, 228; old age, 6:47, 58; patriarchy, 6:57–59, 78; patrilineages, 6:46–47; political life, 6:10, 78; poultry, 6:316; poverty, 6:388; railroads, 6:255, 389; rape, 6:79; religious beliefs, 6:568, 588–91; religious purification, 6:316; religious rituals, 6:46–47, 58, 104, 316; rice, 6:301, 315–16; riots, 6:389; rural life and agriculture, 6:334; schools, 6:344; shrines, 6:345; slums, 6:344; social structure, 6:135–37; sons, 6:45, 47, 58, 103–4; sports, 6:509; tea, 6:301, 316; technology, 6:254–55; temples, 6:343, 589; urban life, 6:334, 344–45; vegetarianism, 6:316; wells, 6:344; wheat, 6:301, 316; widows, 6:79, 156; women, 6:78–80, 156, 611–12

Indigo, 5:132

Indra, 1:352

Industrial Revolution in England, 5:8

Industry: Africa (17th & 18th Centuries), 4:120–21; China (19th Century), 5:115, 156; England (17th & 18th Centuries), 4:2, 123–26, 124; England (Victorian era), 5:92–93, 109, 300; Great Depression, 6:164; India (19th Century), 5:77, 291, 301; Japan (17th & 18th Centuries), 4:126–28; Latin America (20th Century), 6:170–71; life at sea (17th & 18th Centuries), 4:130–32; New England, colonial, 4:13, 128–30; North American colonial frontier, 4:121–23; 17th & 18th Centuries, 4:118–32; United States (Civil War era), 5:2–3; United States (20th Century), 6:110, 114–16

Indus Valley civilization. *See* India (ancient)

Infant care: England (Victorian era), 5:239–40; Europe (Middle Ages), 2:80; Middle Ages, 2:78. *See also* Child care; Wet nurses

Infanticide: Egypt (ancient), 1:56; Greek and Roman, 1:57, 58; 6:141; Japan (17th & 18th Centuries), 4:74–75; Mesopotamia, 2:64; Polynesia, 2:68; Vikings, 2:81–82

Infant mortality: England (15th & 16th Centuries), 3:33, 75; Europe (Middle Ages), 2:79; Greece (ancient), 1:46, 59, 295; India (19th Century), 5:77; India (20th Century), 6:45–46; Islamic World (Middle Ages), 2:85, 318; Latin America (20th Century), 6:314; Mesopotamia, 1:52; Spain (15th & 16th Centuries), 3:77; 20th Century, 6:88; United States (Civil War era), 5:29; United States (1920–39), 6:67; Vikings, 2:34, 81

Infections. *See* Diseases

Infertility. *See* Childless couples

Infidels in Islamic World (19th Century), 5:447

Infirmaries, 5:390. *See also* Hospitals

Inflation: England (15th & 16th Centuries), 3:93, 111, 271; United States (1920–39), 6:436; United States (Western Frontier), 5:61

Influenza: England (15th & 16th Centuries), 3:189; England (Victorian era), 5:209; Europe (20th Century), 6:62–63; Spain (15th & 16th

Centuries), 3:194; United States (1920–39), 6:272

Inheritance. *See* Estates and inheritances

In-line skates, 6:505

Inns: Greece (ancient), 1:162; Rome (ancient), 1:164

Inoculation. *See* Vaccination

Inquisition, 2:326, 411. *See also* Spanish Inquisition

Insanity. *See* Mental illness and treatment

Insecticides, 6:260, 275

Insects: China (Tang Dynasty), 2:205, 206; United States (Western Frontier), 5:105, 254. *See also specific insects*

Insider trading (Japan), 6:400–401

Institutes of the Christian Religion (Calvin), 3:366

Insulae, 1:280

Insurance: England (Victorian era), 5:350–51; long-term care insurance (Japan), 6:292. *See also* Health insurance

Integration. *See* Civil rights movement; School desegregation

Intellectual life: ancient world, 1:169–241; China (Tang Dynasty), 2:11; 15th & 16th Centuries, 3:155–220; France (17th & 18th Centuries), 4:56–58; Middle Ages, 2:4, 145–94; 19th Century, 5:149–216; 17th & 18th Centuries, 4:167–236; 20th Century, 6:181–298. *See also* Art; Literature

Intercalary month: India (ancient), 1:216; Mesopotamia, 1:209; Rome (ancient), 1:214

Intercourse. *See* Sexuality

Internal Security Act of 1950, 6:376

International Workers of the World, preamble, 6:619–20

Internet, 3:155; Japan (20th Century), 6:259

Interstate Highway Act of 1956, 6:362

Inti, 3:53, 376–77, 391–92

Intifada, 6:483

Inti Raymi, 3:391

Inuit: breast feeding, 6:321, 322; cancer, 6:322; childbirth, 6:296; children, 6:50–51, 107; Christianity, 6:603; colonial rule, 6:402; cooking methods, 6:367; discrimination, 6:161; diseases, 6:295–96; education, 6:196, 214–15; environment, 6:296, 321–22; family life, 6:33, 50–51; food, 6:302, 320–22; fur trade, 6:347; government, 6:401–4; health and medicine, 6:261, 295–96, 295–98; historical overview, 6:26–27; housing, 6:51, 346–48; hunting, 6:321; kinship, 6:402; language, 6:214–15; life expectancy, 6:296; literature, 6:239–41; mercury and, 6:302; missionaries, 6:603; music, 6:557–58; names, 6:50; newspapers, 6:240; Nunavut land claims agreement (1993), 6:620–22; old age, 6:51; patrilineages, 6:50; poetry, 6:239; pollution, 6:296, 321–22; religion, 6:603–4; shaman, 6:295; social activism, 6:604; technology, 6:349, 367–68; tuberculosis, 6:296; writing, 6:239–40

Inuit Circumpolar Conference, 6:403

Inuktitut language, 6:214–15, 239, 240–41, 403

Inupiat Ilitquisiat, 6:604

Inventions: England (17th & 18th Centuries), 4:176–77. *See also* Science; Technology

Investiture Controversy, 2:328

Invisible Man (Ellison), 6:441

Invitation to an Inquest: A New Look at the Rosenberg and Sobell Case (Schneir), 6:380

Ionian Rationalism, 1:225

Ionians, 1:225, 333; vs. Dorians, 1:333. *See also* Greece (ancient)

Ionic architecture, 1:504–5

Iormungand, 2:412

Iowa cattle drives, 5:106

Iqbal, Muhammad, 6:229

Iran, 3:20; European colonialism in, 5:353; government, 6:390–91; language, 6:390; revolution, 6:11; war with Iraq, 6:11; women's roles, 5:37

Iran hostage crisis, 6:392

Iraq, 3:20, 164; European control, free from, 6:483; invasion of Kuwait, 6:478; war with Iran, 6:11. *See also* Islamic World (Middle Ages)

Ireland, 3:235, 340; Dublin, founded by Vikings, 2:99; towns founded by Vikings, 2:99

Iron: China (Tang Dynasty), 2:275, 280; England (17th & 18th Centuries), 4:176; England (Victorian era), 5:300; Europe (Middle Ages), 2:124, 275, 276; Islamic World (Middle Ages), 2:275; Italy (15th & 16th Centuries), 3:99; Maya, 3:351; New England, colonial, 4:129; Vikings, 2:100, 126

Iron Age, 1:122, 371. *See also* Mesopotamia

Irons, electric, 6:335

Ironworkers (Japan), 4:409

Iroquois: confederation of tribes, 4:348; New France, 4:10; religious beliefs, 4:469; social structure, 4:372; tribal government, 4:349; villages, 4:332

Irrigation: Byzantium, 2:130, 284; China (Tang Dynasty), 2:127, 197; India (19th Century), 5:14, 302; Islamic World (Middle Ages), 2:282–83; Maya, 3:102; Mesopotamia, 1:75, 78, 79; Nubia, 1:87

Irving, Washington, 5:348

Isaac, Jorge, 5:196

Isabel de Valois, 3:211

Isabella, 3:10, 176, 287, 288, 345

Isadore of Seville, 2:169

Isherwood, Christopher, 6:219

Ishmael, 2:418, 424

Ishtar, 1:471, 488, 510

Isidore of Seville, 2:180–81

Isidoros of Miletus, 2:285, 447

Isis, 1:289, 430, 475, 476, 477

Isla Cerritos, 3:7

Islam: Africa (20th Century), 6:433, 601, 602; alcoholic beverages and, 3:237, 245; 5:252; charity, 6:595; Christianity, relationship with, 6:11; death, burial, and the afterlife, 3:43; ethical behavior as part of, 2:409; fasting, 6:595; founding of, 2:12, 417–25; 5:16, 467–68; 6:10; guilds, 3:119; Hindu vs. Muslim feud in India, 6:9, 10; India, Muslim conquest of, 6:8–9; India (19th Century), 5:466; Jews, relationship with, 2:421; 6:11; life cycles, 3:30–31; Mongols and, 2:429; monotheism, 3:361; Ottoman Empire, 3:65; pork and food restrictions, 2:207–8; 3:241, 245; 6:316; prayers, 5:454, 456, 468, 469; 6:595; prophets and prophecy, 6:594; rituals, exclusion from, 3:30–31; Soviet Union, 6:23, 597; views on women, religion, slaves, and war, 5:494–96; women's dress, 5:287. *See also* Five Pillars of Islam; *Hajj*; Muhammad; Qur'an (Koran); Sharia; Shi'ites

Islamic World (Middle Ages): abandonment of spouse, 2:49–50; age of marriage, 2:85–86; alcoholic beverages, 2:283; archers, 2:358; astronomy, 2:147, 166; banks and banking, 2:143–44; banquets, 2:85; bathhouses, 2:232; beds, 2:273; board games, 2:401; bride-price, 2:47, 62; bubonic plague, 2:85; camels, 2:129, 142; carpentry, 2:273; chairs, 2:267, 273; chess, 2:369; childbirth, 2:423; children, 2:84–86; circumcision, 2:85; civil wars, 2:357; clothing, 2:243–45; coffee, 2:219;

(Middle Ages), 2:122–24, 223, 290–91, 302, 312–13; Italy (15th & 16th Centuries), 3:97–98, 134, 163, 242, 259, 285, 290; Latin America (19th Century), 5:69, 96–98, 117; Maya, 3:279, 341; Middle Ages, 2:121, 310; Ottoman Empire, 3:118; Russian Empire, 6:172–73; Spain (15th & 16th Centuries), 3:34, 36, 77, 94–97, 176, 241, 256, 273, 275. *See also* Serfs

Peasants of Japan (17th & 18th Centuries): children, 4:75, 423; cottage industries, 4:126–27; crimes, 4:395–96; drink, 4:263–64; food, 4:248–49; gambling, 4:422; government, 4:359; hairstyles, 4:295, 311; holidays, 4:437–38; housing, 4:277; men's clothing, 4:294–95; punishment, 4:395–96; religious practices, 4:494; social structure, 4:377–78; uprising, account of, 4:510–12; women, work of, 4:60; women's clothing, 4:311

Peascod bellies, 3:226

Peculium, 1:115

Peddlers (China), 2:103

Pedro I (Brazil), 5:17, 325, 342, 471

Pedro II (Brazil), 5:326, 342, 471

Peers in England, 4:374

Pei Du, 2:252

Pei Min, 2:391

Pelham, Camden, 5:183

Pelham, Charles, 5:181

Pellagra, 6:307

Peloponnesian War: economic effect of, 1:143, 145; food, 1:255; mercenaries, use of, 1:380; moral standards, 1:381; ships, 1:398; start of, 1:84, 333; writings on, 1:202

Peloponnesian War, The (Thucydides), 1:550–52

Pelops, 1:505

Penal colonies of England, 5:336–37

Penal servitude in China, 2:335

Penicillin, 6:260, 274

Peninsulares, 5:116

Pennsylvania government (17th & 18th Centuries), 4:350–51

Penny prick, 3:316

Pentarchs, 2:426

Pentecost: Catholicism (Spain, Italy, England), 3:363; Italy (15th & 16th Centuries), 3:135; Spain (15th & 16th Centuries), 3:134–35

Pentecostalists, 6:581

Pepin the Short, 2:2, 133

Peple, William L., 6:263

Peppers, 5:245

Pepy II, 1:150

Pequot warfare (17th & 18th Centuries), 4:411

Peralta, Angela, 5:427

Percussion: Africa (17th & 18th Centuries), 4:446; Europe (Middle Ages), 2:388; Polynesia, 2:394. *See also* Drums

Perfume: Greece (ancient), 1:324; Mesopotamia, 1:319; Rome (ancient), 1:326

Pericles: Acropolis renovation project, 1:104; death of, 1:533; economic life, 1:144; family of, 1:25, 47; Odeion of Pericles, 1:105; on Peloponnesian War, 1:379; on social structure, 1:335; speeches given by, 1:34, 380; on women's roles, 1:67

Perjury (Mesopotamia), 1:359

Perkins, Arizona, 5:254

Perkins, William, 5:59–60, 102, 204, 437

Péron, Juan, 6:7, 371, 385

Perry, 2:215

Perry, Matthew C., 6:492

Persephone, 1:480; 3:361

Pershing, John, 6:66

Persia as part of Ottoman Empire, 3:20

Persian Empire, 1:3; Greek conquering of, 1:8; invasion of Greece, 1:7–8, 335

Persian language: Islamic World (Middle Ages), 2:402; Islamic World (20th Century), 6:390; Ottoman Empire, 3:157, 164–65

Personal appearance: ancient world, 1:316–26; China (Tang Dynasty), 2:258, 262–64; Egypt (ancient), 1:56, 235, 319–24; Europe (Middle Ages), 2:258–60; 15th & 16th Centuries, 3:222–35; Greece (ancient), 1:324–25; Mesopotamia, 1:317–19; Middle Ages, 2:257–67; Mongols, 2:257, 264–67; Nubia, 1:326; Rome (ancient), 1:325–26; Vikings, 2:257, 260–62. *See also* Beards; Clothing; Hair; Mustaches

Personal computers (PCs), 6:251, 252–53, 496

Personal Politics: The Roots of Women's Liberation in the Civil Rights Movement and the New Left (Evans), 6:68

Peru: Ecuador, border wars with, 6:479; government in 20th Century, 6:387; guano, 5:97; immigrants, 5:98; language of, 3:169; nitrates, 5:97; silver, 5:132; Spanish conquest of, 3:22–24. *See also* Inca; Latin America *entries*

Peruzzi family, 3:8

Pétain, Philippe, 6:5

Peterson, Lou, 6:223

Petrarch (Francesco Petrarca), 3:8, 209, 212–13

Petronius, 1:205

Petry, Ann, 6:224

Pets: England (Victorian era), 5:440; Japan (17th & 18th Centuries), 4:423

Petticoats: England (15th & 16th Centuries), 3:224; England (17th & 18th Centuries), 4:306; England (Victorian era), 5:283

Petty officers in British Royal Navy, 4:365

Peverara, Laura, 3:347

Peyote, 3:281

Peyton Place (Metalious), 6:38

Phalanx, 1:397

Phalerae, 1:399

Phallus sheaths, 1:312

Phantascopes, 5:430

Pharaohs: authority of, 1:340, 344–47; historical overview, 1:4, 6; marriages of, 1:24, 33. *See also* Egypt (ancient)

Pharmacists (Japan), 4:230

Pheidias, 1:479

Philadelphia: immigration, 5:135; population, 5:136–37

Philanthropy: England (Victorian era), 5:449; United States (Civil War era), 5:381, 385. *See also* Charity

Philip I (king of Spain), 3:10, 15

Philip II (king of France), 2:344

Philip II (king of Greece), 1:8

Philip II (king of Spain), 3:17–18, 194, 210–11, 223, 226, 236

Philip III (king of Spain), 3:18, 275, 320

Philip IV (king of Spain), 3:227

Philip of Macedon, 2:119

Philippines as part of Spanish Empire, 3:283, 287

Phillip (governor of Australia), 4:386

Phillip, Arthur, 4:21

Phillip Augustus (king of France), 2:113

Phillips, Wendell, 5:344, 345, 431

Philosophes, 4:190

Philosophy: China (Tang Dynasty), 2:164; Europe (Middle Ages), 2:159–60; France (17th & 18th Centuries), 4:474–75; Greece (ancient), 1:411, 424; India (ancient), 1:206–7; Islamic World (Middle Ages), 2:165, 166; Japan (17th & 18th Centuries), 4:194–95

Phlebotomy. *See* Bloodletting

Phlogiston theory, 4:175

Phoebus Apollo. *See* Apollo

Phoenician alphabet, 1:177

Phoenicians, 1:336, 370

Phooley, Jyothirao, 5:68

Phosgene gas, 6:267

Photography: cameras, invention of, 6:512–13; England (Victorian era), 5:439; United States (Civil War era), 5:430

Phrateres, 1:25

Physical education, 4:73

Physical fitness: Greece (ancient), 1:410, 411, 413; Rome (ancient), 1:414; United States (1960–90), 6:505, 507

Physical perfection in Greek art, 1:237, 410

Physicians: Aztec, 3:424–25; Byzantium, 2:188–89; China (Tang Dynasty), 2:187; England (15th & 16th Centuries), 3:271; England (17th & 18th Centuries), 4:158, 224; England (Victorian era), 5:111, 262; Europe (Middle Ages), 2:182; France (17th & 18th Centuries), 4:226–28; Greece (ancient), 1:294–96; Italy (15th & 16th Centuries), 3:115; Japan (17th & 18th Centuries), 4:230; Mesopotamia, 1:283–84; Mongols, 2:190–91; New England, colonial, 4:232; Rome (ancient), 1:299–300; Soviet Union, 6:288–89; Spain (15th & 16th Centuries), 3:192–93; United States (1960–90), 6:278, 284–85; Vikings, 2:185; World War I, 6:262–66. *See also specific types*

Physicians, eye, 1:283

Physicians, women as. *See* Women as physicians

Physics: England (17th & 18th Centuries), 4:175; Europe (Middle Ages), 2:159, 161

Piankhy, 1:150, 388

Pianos, 5:422

Picasarri, José Antonio, 5:426

Pickett, George, 5:185

Pickpockets, 5:334

Pictographs: Aztec, 3:168; China (Tang Dynasty), 2:173; Mesopotamia, 1:1, 172, 174

Picture carvers (Mesopotamia), 1:231

Piece work, 5:75–76

Piedras Negras, 3:167, 279, 351

Pierce, Benjamin, 5:152, 153

Piercings: Aztec, 3:184; Inca, 3:53, 88; Latin America (19th Century), 5:289; Maya, 3:230

Pigs: Byzantium, 2:209; China (Tang Dynasty), 2:187; Inca, 3:249; introduction to Americas, 3:236; North American colonial frontier, 4:109–10; Paris (Middle Ages), 2:114; Polynesia, 2:212; Spain (15th & 16th Centuries), 3:112; United States (1920–39), 6:436–37; Vikings, 2:125

Pilgrimages: Christian, 2:409; Japan (17th & 18th Centuries), 4:494–95; Muslim, 2:457–58. *See also* Hajj

Pillows: China (Tang Dynasty), 2:272; Islamic World (Middle Ages), 2:273; Japanese (Middle Ages), 2:267; Vikings, 2:270

Pinafores (Victorian England), 5:282

Pineapples as symbols of hospitality, 4:282

Pinky (film), 6:445

Pinochet, Augusto, 6:77, 481

Pioneers, 5:6

Pioneers, The (Cooper), 5:186

Sake, **6:**330; Japan (17th & 18th Centuries),
 4:263–64
Sakharov, Andrei, **6:**190–91
Sakutarou, Hagiwara, **6:**238
Sak Xib Chac, **3:**372
Sala, **3:**257–58
Saladin, **2:**4
Salads, **5:**245
Salah, **6:**11
Salamanca, **3:**112, 156, 175–76
Salat, **5:**16, 454, 456, 468; **6:**595
Salehi, M., **6:**391
Salem witchcraft, **4:**397, 426
Salep, **3:**245
Sales tax, **3:**275
Saletta, **3:**258
Salinger, J.D., **6:**221, 223, 225
"Salivation" treatment of disease, **4:**225
Salmon: United States (Western Frontier), **5:**228,
 229; Vikings, **2:**381
Salonika, capture by Ottoman Empire, **3:**12
Salons, **4:**58
Saloons in Western Frontier, **5:**437
Salt: China (Tang Dynasty), **2:**101; Civil War
 soldiers, **5:**226–27; Japan (20th Century),
 6:320; United States (Western Frontier),
 5:232; Vikings, **2:**202. *See also* Herbs and
 spices
Saltarello, **3:**347
Salt pork: Civil War soldiers, **5:**224; United States
 (Western Frontier), **5:**234
Salutatio, **1:**337
Salviksgropen, **2:**99
Salwar kameez, **5:**287
Sammura-mat, **1:**371
Samoa. *See* Polynesia
Samosas, **5:**243
Samsarra, building of, **2:**317
Samurai (17th & 18th Centuries): crimes and
 punishment, **4:**394–96; education, **4:**193–95;
 games, **4:**424; government, **4:**359; hairstyle,
 4:296; marriage, **4:**39; men's clothing, **4:**294–
 96; sexuality, **4:**92; social structure, **4:**377–
 78; swords, **4:**408–9; women's clothing, **4:**310–11
Sanctuaries: Greece (ancient), **1:**481; Japan (17th
 & 18th Centuries), **4:**493–94; Nubia, **1:**467
Sandals: Aztec, **3:**233; Greece (ancient), **1:**310,
 312; Inca, **3:**234; India (19th Century),
 5:287; Maya, **3:**231; Mesopotamia, **1:**304;
 Nubia, **1:**313. *See also* Footwear
Sand art (Australian Aboriginals), **1:**240–41
Sand Creek Massacre, **5:**6, 370, 386
Sanders, Linda, **6:**549
Sandoz, Mari, **5:**31–32; **6:**221
Sanford, Mollie, **5:**62, 74, 206, 279
San Francisco miners, **5:**90
Sanga, **1:**340
Sanitary napkins, **6:**274
Sankin-kotai, **4:**322–23
San Lorenzo, **3:**3
San Martín, José de, **5:**325, 378
Sannyasa, **6:**58
Sannyasins, **1:**338
San (17th & 18th Centuries), **4:**240–41
Sanskrit, **1:**179–80, 206, 207, 258, 431; **6:**228
Santa Anna, Antonio López de, **5:**325, 378
Santa Hermandad, **3:**303–4
Santayana, George, **6:**564

Santería, **6:**593
Santillana, **3:**162
Saracens, **3:**214
Sarah Lawrence College, **6:**203
Sarapes, **5:**288–89
Saraswati, **5:**78
Sargon: empire of, **1:**1, 30, 140; hairstyle of, **1:**317;
 military of, **1:**371; on social structure, **1:**330
Sargon II, **1:**156, 272, 370, 371
Sari, **5:**40, 286
Sarmiento, Domingo, **5:**19, 179
Sarnoff, David, **6:**242, 244
Sarpedon, **1:**518
Sartre, Jean-Paul, **6:**379
Sashes, **5:**273
Sassoon, Siegfried, **6:**269
Satellites, **6:**187–88
Sathya Shodak Samaj, **5:**68
Sati, **1:**38; **5:**27, 55, 66–67; **6:**79, 156
Sati Prohibition Act, **5:**67
Satire. *See* Humor and satire
Satires, The (Juvenal), **1:**205, 557–59
Saturday Night Fever (film), **6:**547
Saturnalia, **1:**441; **3:**135
Satyricon (Petronius), **1:**205
Sauces, **3:**240–41
Sauckel, Fritz, **6:**412
Saudi Arabia: historical overview, **6:**11; women's
 roles, **6:**37. *See also* Islamic World *entries*
Saunas: Rome (ancient), **1:**414; Vikings, **2:**261
Sausage, **5:**241
Savage, William A., Jr., **5:**87
Savonarola, Michele de, **3:**80
Sawm, **5:**16, 454, 468; **6:**11, 595
Sayre, Francis B., **6:**477
Sayri Tupac, **3:**23
Scaligeri family, **3:**8
Scalp Hunters, The (Reid), **5:**186
Scandinavians. *See* Vikings
Scarab beetle, **1:**474, 532
Scarlet fever, **5:**209
Scarlet Letter, The (Hawthorne), **4:**459; **5:**186
Schacht, Hjalmar, **6:**413
Schine, G. David, **6:**377, 378
Schirra, Walter, **6:**187
Schizophrenia, **6:**281
Schlafly, Phyllis, **6:**73
Schneir, Miriam and Walter, **6:**380
Scholars, **4:**157–58
Scholasticism, **2:**160
School buildings in Middle Ages, **2:**151
School busing, **6:**197, 207
School desegregation: United States (1940–59),
 6:17, 443–44; United States (1960–90),
 6:153, 154, 206–8, 446, 447
School discipline: China (Tang Dynasty), **2:**153;
 England (17th & 18th Centuries), **4:**189;
 Mesopotamia, **1:**185; Rome (ancient), **1:**189–
 90; Vikings, **2:**152
School District of Abington Township v. Schemp
 (1963), **6:**578
School enrollment: China (Tang Dynasty), **2:**153;
 Vikings, **2:**153
Schools: Australian Aboriginals, **1:**191–92; Europe
 (Middle Ages), **2:**148; gladiator school in
 Rome (ancient), **1:**443–44; government-
 subsidized meals for students (United States
 1960–90), **6:**313; grading systems in Tang
 China, **2:**154; grammar schools in colonial
 New England, **4:**197; Greece (ancient),
 1:187–88; India (20th Century), **6:**344;
 Islamic World (Middle Ages), **2:**156, 165;

Mesopotamia, **1:**183–84; Rome (ancient),
 1:189–91. *See also* Curriculum; Education;
 Home schooling; Universities; *headings above
 and below starting with "School"; specific types
 of schools*
School tablets: Islamic World of Middle Ages,
 2:156; Mesopotamia, **1:**184
School term: Europe (Middle Ages), **2:**151; Vikings,
 2:153
Schouten, Williamson Cornelison, **4:**519–21
Schröder, Gustav, **6:**562–63
Schulberg, Budd, **6:**527
Science: Africa (20th Century), **6:**193–94; ancient
 world, **1:**217–29; Australia, colonial, **4:**170–
 71; Australian Aboriginals, **1:**228–30; China
 (19th Century), **5:**156–57; China (Tang
 Dynasty), **2:**158, 163–65; England (17th &
 18th Centuries), **4:**174–77; England
 (Victorian era), **5:**154–55; Europe (Middle
 Ages), **2:**159–61, 182; France (17th & 18th
 Centuries), **4:**57–58, 474–75; Greece
 (ancient), **1:**224–27; Islamic World (Middle
 Ages), **2:**165–67, 188; Japan (20th Century),
 6:191–93; Latin America (19th Century),
 5:158–60; Mesopotamia, **1:**218–22; Middle
 Ages, **2:**145, 157–67; New England, colonial,
 4:169, 178–79; 19th Century, **5:**150–60;
 North American colonial frontier, **4:**172–73;
 Rome (ancient), **1:**227–28; 17th & 18th
 Centuries, **4:**168–81; Soviet Union, **6:**183,
 190–91; 20th Century, **6:**182–94; United
 States (19th Century), **5:**151–53; United
 States (1900–45), **6:**183–85; United States
 (1945–90), **6:**185–90; Vikings, **2:**162–63. *See
 also* Technology
Science fiction, **6:**224, 241, 528
Scientific revolution in Europe, **2:**161
Scopes trial on teaching evolution, **6:**404, 571
Scotch-Irish colonists, **4:**373, 469–70
Scotch whiskey, **6:**330
Scotland marriage act exemption, **4:**37
Scotland Yard, **5:**338
Scott, Paul, **6:**229
Scott, Walter, **5:**185–86
Scottsboro boys, **6:**149, 327
Screens, Chinese, **2:**271–72
Scribes in Mesopotamia, **1:**30, 172–74, 183–85,
 193–94, 248, 487
Scrimshaw, **4:**459–60
Scriptures: India (ancient), **1:**206; Muslims, **2:**409.
 See also Bible; Qur'an (Koran)
Scrofula, **5:**208
Sculpture: Aztec, **3:**339, 355; 15th & 16th
 Centuries, **3:**339; Greece (ancient), **1:**237–
 38; Maya, **3:**350–51; Mesopotamia, **1:**231,
 232, 271, 530; Rome (ancient), **1:**239; Spain
 (15th & 16th Centuries), **3:**344. *See also*
 Statues; Temple statues
Scurvy: Civil War soldiers, **5:**222; England (15th &
 16th Centuries), **3:**189; Europe (Middle
 Ages), **2:**181; life at sea (17th & 18th
 Centuries), **4:**233–35; United States
 (Western Frontier), **5:**203; Vikings, **2:**184
Scutum, **1:**399
Scythian archers, **1:**363
Sea and the States, The (Bryant), **4:**382
Sea Around Us, The (Carson), **6:**17
Sea biscuits, **4:**253–54
Seacliff (DeForest), **5:**188
Seafood. *See* Fish
Sea-lanes, **4:**323
Seals: Greece (ancient), **1:**266, 324; Mesopotamia,
 1:174
Seals as food, **2:**202, 381

Seamen. *See* Life at sea *entries*; Sailors
Seamen's wives, **4**:43–45, 63–65
Seamstress, or The White Slaves of England, The (Reynolds), **5**:190
Sea Peoples, **1**:376
Seaports (17th & 18th Centuries), **4**:338–41; Dutch Republic, **4**:340; France, **4**:340; housing, **4**:282; New England, **4**:339; Seville, **4**:340; social structure, **4**:383–84; Spanish ports in New World, **4**:339; taverns, **4**:427; whaling ports, **4**:443; wharves and docks, **4**:339, 340
Searchers, The (film), **6**:445
Seasonings. *See* Herbs and spices
Seasons: Greece (ancient), **1**:212; Mesopotamia, **1**:209
Seaweed, **2**:205
Sebiumeker, **1**:468
Secession from United States (Civil War), **5**:313–18
Secondhand smoke, **6**:279
Second mates on merchant vessels, **4**:363
Second Opium War, **5**:13, 323
Second Shepherd's Play, The, **3**:206
Second Vatican Council, **6**:577, 581, 592
Secret police (Soviet Union), **6**:424–25
Secular humanism, **6**:582
Sedan chairs, **4**:319
Sedition in colonial Australia, **4**:388
Seers. *See* Diviners
Segregation of sexes. *See* Women's quarters
Seibal, **3**:167
Seine, **2**:112
Seishi, Yamaguchi, **6**:238
Sekhmet, **1**:476
Selamik, **3**:260
Self-help, **5**:449
Self-Help (Smiles), **5**:449
Self-immolation, **1**:38
"Self-made men," **6**:52, 53–54
Self-sufficiency, **5**:450
Selim I, **3**:19–20, 292
Selim II, **3**:26
Selimye Mosque, **3**:349
Semana Santa, **5**:417
Semashko, Nikolai, **6**:288
Semele, **1**:480
Semites. *See* Mesopotamia
Semitic alphabet, **3**:165
Senate. *See* Legislature
Seneca, **1**:100, 204, 414
Senegambia slave trade, **4**:347
Sennacherib, **1**:92, 131, 156, 341–42, 371, 530
Septennial Act (1716), **4**:354
Serbia, **3**:12; **6**:2
Serfs: emancipation in Russia, **6**:173; Europe (Middle Ages), **2**:289, 292, 310, 311–13, 321
Serial films, **6**:522
Sermons in colonial New England, **4**:216
Servants: Aztec, **3**:401; England (15th & 16th Centuries), **3**:56, 110, 252, 260, 272, 342; England (17th & 18th Centuries), **4**:153, 157; England (Victorian era), **5**:36, 92–93, 109, 241–42, 263, 284, 476–77, 479; Europe (Middle Ages), **2**:323, 346; Inca, **3**:71, 144; Islamic World (19th Century), **5**:37; Italy (15th & 16th Centuries), **3**:115–17; Japan (17th & 18th Centuries), **4**:153; Latin America (19th Century), **5**:246, 326; Latin America (20th Century), **6**:103; Maya, **3**:66; New England, colonial, **4**:117, 148–49, 153, 281, 380–81, 397, 426; Ottoman Empire, **3**:64–65, 180; Vikings, **2**:305
Servet, Miguel, **3**:193
Service, John Stuart, **6**:376

Servicemen's Readjustment Act. *See* GI Bill
Set, **1**:471, 475, 476, 477
Seth, Vikram, **6**:229
Settlers of United States (Western Frontier), **5**:99, 104–5
Seven Wonders of the World: Ephesus temple of Artemis, **1**:480; Hanging Gardens of Babylon, **1**:101; as tourist destinations in ancient world, **1**:165; Zeus's statue, **1**:479
Seville: Cervantes in, **3**:212; economic life in 15th & 16th Centuries, **3**:112, 114; gambling in 15th & 16th Centuries, **3**:321; municipal charters, **3**:287; music in 15th & 16th Centuries, **3**:345; as seaport (17th & 18th Centuries), **4**:340; shipping in 15th & 16th Centuries, **3**:108; universities in 15th & 16th Centuries, **3**:176. *See also* Spain *entries*
Sewage: England (Victorian era), **5**:10, 141, 209. *See also* Waste disposal
Sewall, Samuel, **4**:82–83, 156, 266, 297–98
Seward, William, **4**:420; **5**:312
Sewing: England (Victorian era), **5**:110, 283–84; United States (Western Frontier), **5**:62, 123. *See also* Clothing materials
Sewing machines, **6**:335
Sex discrimination: Japan (20th Century), **6**:84; United States (1940–59), **6**:67, 69; United States (1960–90), **6**:71, 74–75
Sex Pistols, **6**:547
Sexual abuse: children, United States (1960–90), **6**:419. *See also* Rape
Sexual harassment: Japan (20th Century), **6**:453; United States (1960–90), **6**:55
Sexuality: ancient world, **1**:62–72; Aztec, **3**:69, 260; China (Tang Dynasty), **2**:83; England (17th & 18th Centuries), **4**:55, 93–95; England (Victorian era), **5**:64–65, 110, 446, 449; 15th & 16th Centuries, **3**:56, 223–24; France (17th & 18th Centuries), **4**:58; Greece (ancient), **1**:66–68; Italy (15th & 16th Centuries), **3**:39, 61, 62; Japan (17th & 18th Centuries), **4**:92, 95–97; life at sea (17th & 18th Centuries), **4**:99–100; Mesopotamia, **1**:62, 63–66, 286; New England, colonial, **4**:97–99, 397; Rome (ancient), **1**:68–72; 17th & 18th Centuries, **4**:28, 92–100; Spain (15th & 16th Centuries), **3**:59; United States, **6**:53–55; United States (1920–39), **6**:34–35, 273, 512, 517–18; United States (1940–59), **6**:37–38; United States (1960–90), **6**:542, 549; United States (Western Frontier), **5**:32. *See also* Virginity
Seymour, Jane, **3**:14–15
Seyss-Inquart, Arthur, **6**:412
Sforza family, **3**:8
Shacks (United States [Western Frontier]), **5**:260
Shadoof, **1**:81
Shafi'i, **3**:65
Shahadah: beliefs, **2**:420; **5**:16; **6**:11; proclamations, **2**:422; **6**:595
Shakespeare, William: death of, **3**:212; *Henry V*, **3**:11; influence of, **3**:15; language, use of, **3**:159; life of, **3**:208–9; performances of, **3**:108, 314; *Romeo and Juliet*, **3**:33, 81; social mobility of, **3**:273; sonnets, **3**:213; start of career, **3**:342; *Titus Andronicus*, **3**:206
Shakti, **1**:466
Shaktism, **6**:588
Shalmaneser III, **1**:371
Shamans: Inuit, **6**:295; Japan (17th & 18th Centuries), **4**:478, 494; Maya, **3**:199, 383–84; Mongols, **2**:190–91, 427–28; Native Americans (colonial New England), **4**:489
Shamash, **1**:361, 510–11

Shamela (Fielding), **4**:208
Shame (Latin America), **5**:68–69
Shangdi, **5**:452
Shanghai: urban life, **5**:145; work, **5**:94. *See also* China (19th Century)
Sharia: Africa (20th Century), **6**:433–34; on hunting, **2**:383; Islamic law, **2**:338–40; Islamic World (20th Century), **6**:422–24; Ottoman Empire, **3**:309
Sharpshooting: United States (Civil War era), **5**:293; United States (19th Century), **5**:397; United States (Western Frontier), **5**:395
Shastri, Lal Bahadur, **6**:10
Shavan Purnima, **5**:415
Shaw, George Bernard, **5**:10
Shawls: China (Tang Dynasty), **2**:243; Latin America (19th Century), **5**:288; Maya, **3**:231; Spain (15th & 16th Centuries), **3**:224; Vikings, **2**:241
Shawms, **3**:343
Shawnee adoption ceremony, **4**:435
Sheen, Fulton, **6**:565, 566, 573
Sheep and goats: Byzantium, **2**:131, 197, 209; England (15th & 16th Centuries), **3**:93; Europe (Middle Ages), **2**:247; Latin America (19th Century), **5**:246; Mesopotamia, **1**:77; Mongols, **2**:66; Nubia, **1**:87; Rome (ancient), **1**:85; Spain (15th & 16th Centuries), **3**:96, 112; Vikings, **2**:125, 223
Shehnai, **5**:424
Sheik, The (film), **6**:512, 517
Shellfish: Byzantium, **2**:197, 209; China (Tang Dynasty), **2**:205; Europe (Middle Ages), **2**:200; Maya, **3**:247
Shell shock (World War I), **6**:268–69
Shepard, Alan, **6**:186
Sheppard-Towner Maternity- and Infancy-Protection Act of 1921, **6**:67, 371
Sherbets, **2**:192
Sherdens, **1**:376
Sherman, William Tecumseh, **5**:366, 369, 370
Shi, **6**:238
Shias in Soviet Union, **6**:597
Shields: Australian Aboriginals, **1**:400; Aztec, **3**:124, 233, 341, 356; Byzantium, **2**:285, 360; Europe (Middle Ages), **2**:349; Greece (ancient), **1**:396; Maya, **3**:341, 371; Mongols, **2**:362; Rome (ancient), **1**:399; Spain (15th & 16th Centuries), **3**:320; Vikings, **2**:352, 353
Shigi-Qutuqu, **2**:342
Shi'ites, **6**:595; development of, **2**:15, 298, 446; **6**:390; holidays, **2**:457; Islamic World (19th Century), **5**:468; leaders, **6**:391; Sufism (Ottoman Empire), **3**:367
Shiki, Masaoka, **6**:238
Shiloh, Battle of, **5**:44, 71–72
Shintō, **4**:95, 229, 422–24, 464–65, 476–77; **6**:599
Shipbuilding: Mesopotamia, **1**:157; New England, colonial, **4**:129
Ship burials by Vikings, **2**:464
Shipmasters, **4**:362
Shipping: Byzantium, **2**:285; China (Tang Dynasty), **2**:101; England (Victorian era), **5**:350, 351; Europe (Middle Ages), **2**:135; Greece (ancient), **1**:161–62; Italy (15th & 16th Centuries), **3**:8; Mesopotamia, **1**:157; Middle Ages, **2**:94; Vikings, **2**:279. *See also* Trade
Ships and vessels: "by and large" able to sail, **4**:326; Byzantium, **2**:285; carvel-built hulls (17th & 18th Centuries), **4**:324; China (Tang Dynasty), **2**:139, 281; construction (17th & 18th Centuries), **4**:324; decks (17th & 18th Centuries), **4**:324–25; East India Company,

Swahili (17th & 18th Centuries)

United States (1850–65)

ABOUT THE CONTRIBUTORS

General Editor

Joyce E. Salisbury is Frankenthal Professor of History at University of Wisconsin–Green Bay. She has a doctorate in medieval history from Rutgers University. Professor Salisbury is an award-winning teacher: she was named CASE (Council for Advancement and Support of Education) Professor of the Year for Wisconsin in 1991 and has brought her concern for pedagogy to this encyclopedia. Professor Salisbury has written or edited more than 10 books, including the award-winning *Perpetua's Passion: Death and Memory of a Young Roman Woman*, *The Beast Within: Animals in the Middle Ages*, and *The West in the World*, a textbook on western civilization.

Volume Editor

Gregory S. Aldrete is an associate professor of history and humanistic studies at the University of Wisconsin–Green Bay. He received his undergraduate degree from Princeton University and his doctorate in ancient history from the University of Michigan. His publications include *Gestures and Acclamations in Ancient Rome* (1999), as well as book chapters on ancient Rome's food supply system and on daily life in Pompeii. Currently, he is writing a book about floods in ancient Rome.

Additional Contributors

David Horton, independent scholar
Robert S. Bianchi, independent scholar
Matthew Bingley, University of Iowa
Eric Rothgery, University of Iowa
Paula Rentmeester, University of Wisconsin–Green Bay

About the Contributors

We also acknowledge the following authors of Greenwood Publishing's "Daily Life through History" series, whose books contributed much to entries in the current volume:

Robert S. Bianchi, *Daily Life in Nubia*, forthcoming
Bob Brier and Hoyt Hobbs, *Daily Life of the Ancient Egyptians*, 1999
Robert Garland, *Daily Life of the Ancient Greeks*, 1998
Karen Rhea Nemet-Nejat, *Daily Life in Ancient Mesopotamia*, 1998